# UNQUIET SOUL

# UNQUIET SOUL

## SOUL

*A Biography of Charlotte Brontë*

MARGOT PETERS

**HODDER AND STOUGHTON**
LONDON SYDNEY AUCKLAND TORONTO

For *Marc* and *Claire*

# Contents

From *Haworth Churchyard*
by Matthew Arnold

April showers
Rush o'er the Yorkshire moors.
Stormy, through driving mist,
Loom the blurr'd hills; the rain
Lashes the newly-made grave.

Unquiet souls!
—In the dark fermentation of earth,
In the never idle workshop of nature,
In the eternal movement,
Ye shall find yourselves again!

# *Haworth Today*

The village of Haworth in Yorkshire, England, is currently the mecca for a strange modern pilgrimage. Yearly, thousands upon thousands of curious visitors crowd to this small, bleak village clinging to the edge of the rolling Yorkshire moors. On Sundays tour busses and private cars choke the steep, narrow main street, often backing up traffic five miles and sending up such a stench of exhaust as they idle bumper to bumper on the tortuous incline that not a few residents feel driven to leave the town.

They come to look at the home of the Brontës. Many have read *Wuthering Heights* or *Jane Eyre* or *The Tenant of Wildfell Hall.* Many only know something of the lives of Charlotte, Emily, and Anne and their brother Branwell. Some of the visitors are overflow from the railroad museum, another attraction the village offers. And some are those indefatigable tourists who visit everything simply because it is there to be seen.

What do these modern pilgrims find? Crowning the steep hill is the Black Bull Hotel, famous as the scene of Branwell Brontë's drinking bouts, and now featuring a "Brontë Room" in his memory. A few steps away stands the old White Lion Hotel where Branwell boxed with local lads in the upper rooms: the eighteenth-century hostelry advertises itself today as "a Brontë Guest House Ltd." A Brontë Tea Room and a Brontë Book Shop front the narrow main street. A brass plaque on the post office announces (erroneously) that from this spot the three sisters posted the manuscripts of their famous novels to London. And, like the booths that clustered at the bases of the great medieval cathedrals offering relics to the credulous, small shops cluster at the threshold of this shrine peddling "Brontë" wares: Brontë dolls, Brontë woolens, Brontë men's wear, Brontë apple liqueur, Brontë gloves, Brontë pottery.

A few steps from the hub of the village and one enters Brontë territory proper. Here stands Haworth parish church, rebuilt since Patrick Brontë, father of the famous family, preached his sermons from its pulpit, yet retaining its original tower and, inside, the communion table and baptismal font the Brontës knew. Its most recent addition is a Brontë memorial chapel occupying the southeast corner, a gift of Sir Tresham Lever, dedicated in 1964. A machine on the wall dispenses slides of the chapel. The "American window," another gift, is inscribed "To the glory of God in pleasant memory of Charlotte Brontë by an American citizen." Under the floor in the family vault all the Brontës except Anne lie buried. A tablet marks the toll: Maria, wife of Patrick Brontë; Maria, Elizabeth, Patrick Branwell, Emily Jane, Charlotte; Patrick Brontë.

A churchyard surrounds St. Michael and All Angels on three sides. More than 40,000 villagers are buried there under pitching, moss-green sarcophagi or ranks of thin, high-shouldered slabs. It was a cold, windy, bare yard when the Brontë children played there among the tombstones. Mr. Wade, Mr. Brontë's successor, planted trees, and now the churchyard is shrouded in a green, leafy gloom. Rooks rise from the branches yawking loudly when visitors intrude, and an occasional black feather drifts down to rest lightly on a worn stone slab. A caretaker, a red-faced man, can be observed scrubbing at a sunken stone with brush and soapy water. He replies cheerfully, "Ah, certainly, a Brontë grave," and makes out for you with his finger the faint inscription "Tabitha Ackroyd." He is cleaning the stone, he explains, so visitors can find the grave site of the Brontës' faithful servant in the crowded churchyard.

The parsonage where the Brontës lived stands adjacent to the churchyard and can be reached down a short cobbled lane. The house is now a museum. The many personal effects of the Brontës preserved there are undoubtedly the main attraction—Charlotte's dresses and bonnets and rings, Emily's writing desk, the huge brass collar of her favorite dog, Keeper, a lock of Charlotte's hair, the minutely stitched samplers worked by all the girls, Mr. Brontë's spectacles, pipe, and Bible—but the museum also houses the fine Bonnell collection of manuscripts, editions, and scholarly works. The north and west wings of the present building were added by the indefatigable Mr. Wade, but much of the parsonage remains as the Brontës knew it: the dining room to the left of the entrance hall where the sisters gathered in the evenings to write or to pace the floor arm in arm in deep discussion; the parlor opposite where Mr. Brontë took his solitary meals, read, and composed his Sunday sermons. Upstairs, the servant Tabby's humble quarters remain, and Emily's room, formerly the nursery where the small Brontës acted out their imaginary adventures. Their tiny childish drawings are still visible on the nursery walls.

If the pilgrim is a real enthusiast, he can leave the village and, equipped with a guidebook, pursue the "Brontë walks"—five routes rich in Brontë associations among the Haworth and Stanbury moors. Here, however, disillusionment lurks. The moors are not the wild, vast, uninhabited stretches of heather and rolling hill and dale that many readers of *Wuthering Heights* imagine them. Farms, houses, neighboring villages, smoking industrial chimneys crowd in upon them. A wrong turn out of Haworth brings you to a well-worked quarry, the sign "Haworth Moor—No Dumping," and strewn about the ground, the ugly violations of that warning. The old footpath to the Brontë waterfalls, a spot well loved by the young Brontës and the destination of Charlotte's last walk before her death, has been paved so that the sluggish modern tourist need not follow the Brontë trail on foot but can drive to within a mile of the falls. If the pilgrim journeys to Top Withins, the house and site most frequently associated with *Wuthering Heights*, he will find—not the grim, imposing front of Heathcliff's dwelling—but a small sheep farm like many others that dot the moors, now quite in ruins. It is perhaps a comfort to know that the quarry and the smoking chimneys down the valley are not twentieth-century corruptions but formed a part of the landscape in the Brontës' time.

Why do so many people—153,000 in one year, according to the museum staff—seek out this village where the Brontës lived and died? Only Shakespeare's birthplace, Stratford-on-Avon, draws more tourists, and Stratford has the very tangible attraction of the Shakespeare Memorial Theatre besides its accessibility by tour bus from London.

One cynic suggests that there is simply nothing else to do in Yorkshire on a dull rainy Sunday—and there is probably more than one grain of truth to this suggestion. But the gigantic wave of tourists that surges across the Atlantic every summer and breaks on England's shores accounts for much of the crowd: even the humblest tourist attraction receives some of the overflow. Many of these wanderers are in search of a better world—in the poet Shelley's words, "something apart from the sphere of our sorrow," and England, a country that still preserves the past, seems to offer it. As much as the effigies in Westminster Abbey, the gray, notched towers of Windsor, or the absurdly elaborate ritual of the changing of the guard, England's writers are linked with this past, for they have preserved it permanently in the written word. No wonder then that the Dickens museum in London does a brisk business, that the doorbell of Carlyle's house in

Chelsea peals regularly, or that even in the remote green village of Somersby, Lincolnshire, the visitors' book in the old gray church records eight or ten summer visitors a day to this birthplace of Alfred, Lord Tennyson.

But a literary shrine does not automatically draw numbers: the caretaker of Milton's cottage, for example, reports that business is poor, while even in the pre-tourist year of 1895 Haworth recorded 85,000 visitors. The solution to the Haworth mystery must lie in the Brontës themselves. For, unlike the author of *Paradise Lost* and unlike many of their Victorian contemporaries, the Brontës are still widely read. *Jane Eyre* and *Wuthering Heights* exude a glamor that captivates readers even in our non-reading audiovisual age. And the lives of the Brontës are surrounded with a similar glamor. Strange word: one imagines love affairs, intrigue, brilliant salons, beauty, wealth. Nothing could be further from the truth. The Brontë glamor is the glamor of fame deified by suffering. They are canonized, these sisters, by the tragedy of their lives.

The tragedy itself has all the appeal of the romantic past. What twentieth-century city dweller would not like to undergo the torments of solitude in a moorland village? In an age where sexual gratification has become as casual as picking one's teeth, does not the frustration of unrequited love possess a peculiar charm? And what antisepticized, tube-drawn patient dying in the sterile whiteness of a modern hospital would not rather expire quickly at home on a couch of a picturesque, wracking, consumptive cough? Sentimentality—the luxury of thinking about emotion without feeling it—draws people to the Brontës as flowers draw bees.

The suffering, of course, was real enough. Mrs. Gaskell's classic 1857 biography of Charlotte is at times almost too painful to read yet, according to Charlotte's lifelong friend Mary Taylor, still minimizes the tragedy of her life. "The book is a perfect success, in giving a true picture of a melancholy life," she wrote Mrs. Gaskell. "Though not so gloomy as the truth, it is perhaps as much as people will accept without calling it exaggerated, and feeling the desire to doubt and contradict it."

Most biographers of the Brontës emphasize only the external tragedy of their lives: the privation, the illness, the solitude, the early deaths. But Emily, Anne, and Mr. Brontë lived comparatively serene lives even in the face of these hardships. Charlotte's unhappiness must then have stemmed largely from internal conflicts, ambivalent drives that warred within her, never allowing her rest. Some of these conflicts were personal. Many were created by her position as a woman in a society which oppressed women and as a writer in a society that thought "female authors" neither legitimate artists nor ornaments of their sex. "Hunger, rage, and rebellion"—this in the opinion of Victorian essayist and poet Matthew Arnold was the whole contents of Charlotte Brontë's mind. It was a repellent mind to Arnold, for the Victorian woman was supposed to feel only complacency, love, and subservience. Arnold was of course only half right; he did not know or perhaps did not care that Charlotte struggled all her life to subdue the rage and suppress the rebellion.

Mrs. Gaskell and the Victorians admired the suppression, canonizing Charlotte for her submission to duty and necessity. Today we are more apt to sympathize with Charlotte's rage. She was, of course, not officially a feminist: she did not directly engage in the legal struggle for women's rights. In fact the "cant" preached on the woman question, as the Victorians called it, often irritated her. But then most of the outstanding women of the period—Harriet Martineau, Elizabeth Barrett Browning, Florence Nightingale, Jane Carlyle, Mrs. Gaskell, George Eliot, Queen Victoria—were not officially feminists either. Their apparent indifference to the women's rights issue seems surprising, but can be explained by the fact that they achieved the success and power their less fortunate sisters still cry for. They won the game. Charlotte Brontë had little motivation to fight for legal equality because as Currer Bell she found artistic and professional fulfillment. Unfortunately, but perhaps understandably, successful women often cannot believe that what they have done other women cannot do.

Clearly, however, the definition of a feminist needs to be expanded. Too often the word is limited to women involved exclusively in rights issues. Less happily, it is also limited to women who merely mouth the jargon of liberation (the "cant" Brontë hated), who exploit the movement for personal gain, or who hate men. The concept of "feminist" should include all women who have broken the mold to fulfill their creative, intellectual impetus. Feminism can learn from Marx, who recognized that Spartacus the slave or the leaders of the German Peasant Revolt were truly revolutionary although they were ignorant of socialist ideology. Eleanor Roosevelt, Madame Curie, Abigail Adams, Mrs. Gaskell, Jane Austen, George Eliot, and Charlotte Brontë did not preach feminist doctrine but were feministic in the deepest sense.

Charlotte Brontë's life and art were both an eloquent protest against the cruel and frustrating limitations imposed upon women and a triumph over them. Seen from this angle, the facts of her life fall into a new pattern, and it is this pattern that these pages propose to explore.

# UNQUIET SOUL

# 1

## Early Sorrow

In April of 1820 those natives of Haworth who chanced to be at their windows or toiling up the narrow stone street of the village would have been entertained by the sight of a canvas-covered wagon followed by seven carts heavily laden with household goods plodding up the steep incline. Patrick Brontë, the new incumbent of Haworth church, had arrived with his family and all his worldly possessions to take up residence in the gray stone parsonage on top of the hill behind the church.

The children in the wagon were young and rather frail. The eldest, Maria, was only seven; the youngest, Anne, an infant in arms. And there were four others huddled together in the swaying wagon: Elizabeth, Charlotte, Branwell, the only boy, and Emily. Maria Branwell Brontë, the wife of the new pastor, was even more frail than her children. Diminutive and delicate of constitution, she was already thirty when she married Patrick Brontë. In true nineteenth-century style, she had rapidly borne him six children in seven years. Now, much weakened, she unprotestingly came to face the rigors of the bleak and raw climate of this Yorkshire village, so different from the sunny warmth of her native Penzance on England's mild southwest coast.[1]

We know Maria Brontë because nine love letters written to Patrick during their courtship have survived. Addressed with increasing warmth to "My Dear Friend," "My Dearest Friend," and "My Dear Saucy Pat," the letters are a touching blend of formality and frankness. The formality is expected in a woman of her time; it is the unusual frankness that plainly reveals a fine, delicate mind. Her protestation that her love is stronger than his might be taken for coy angling in another, but the sincerity radiating from every line of the letters makes this in Maria's case a simple statement of truth. She writes in

October 1812 from her uncle's home, Woodhouse Grove, near Leeds, where she is visiting:

> With the sincerest pleasure do I retire from company to converse with him whom I love beyond all others. Could my beloved friend see my heart he would then be convinced that the affection I bear him is not at all inferior to that which he feels for me—indeed I sometimes think that in truth and constancy it excels. But do not think from this that I entertain any suspicions of your sincerity—no, I firmly believe you to be sincere and generous, and doubt not in the least that you feel all you express. In return, I entreat that you will do me the justice to believe that you have not only a *very large portion* of my *affection* and *esteem*, but *all* that I am capable of feeling, and henceforth measure my feelings by your own. Unless my love for you were very great how could I so contentedly give up my home and all my friends—a home I loved so much that I have often thought nothing could bribe me to renounce it for any great length of time together, and friends with whom I have been so long accustomed to share all the vicissitudes of joy and sorrow? Yet these have lost their weight, and though I cannot always think of them without a sigh, yet the anticipation of sharing with you all the pleasures and pains, the cares and anxieties of life, of contributing to your comfort and becoming the companion of your pilgrimage, is more delightful to me than any other prospect which this world can possibly present. I expected to have heard from you on Saturday last, and can scarcely refrain from thinking you unkind to keep me in suspense two whole days longer than was necessary, but it is well that my patience should be sometimes tried, or I might entirely lose it, and this would be a loss indeed! Lately I have experienced a considerable increase of hopes and fears, which tend to destroy the calm uniformity of my life. These are not unwelcome, as they enable me to discover more of the evils and errors of my heart, and discovering them I hope through grace to be enabled to correct and amend them. . . .
>
> . . . In general, I feel a calm confidence in the providential care and continued mercy of God, and when I consider His past deliverances and past favours I am led to wonder and adore. A sense of my small returns of love and gratitude to Him often abases me and makes me think I am little better than those who profess no religion. Pray for me, my dear friend, and rest assured that you possess a very, very large portion of the prayers, thoughts, and heart of yours truly,
>
> M. Branwell.[2]

Besides love, another theme runs through the nine letters like a troubled whisper: a persistent, morbid self-doubt. Maria Branwell was from all accounts an extremely pious woman. Long years of maidenhood during which her emotions were channeled almost solely into religious feeling intensified the ardent piety of an already religious mind. Yet hers seems to have been the piety that breeds as much apprehension as confidence. It is sad to find such an obviously good person feeling abased and unworthy, or brooding on the evils and errors of her heart. This self-doubt enters into her relationship with her fiancé: she is uneasy when expected letters do not arrive punctually; she fancies a coolness in his tone; she asks, "Do you think you have any cause to complain of me? If you do, let me know it." Patrick Brontë, decisive and self-assured, had the upper hand in this marriage.

Maria Brontë passed on her highly developed piety to her eldest daughter, her namesake Maria, and its mystical aspect to Emily; Charlotte inherited almost nothing of it. But she felt strongly drawn to her mother's memory, and it is curious that, without knowledge of her mother's letters, she put words into the mouth of her heroine, Jane Eyre, that so closely coincide with Maria Brontë's sentiments. In a letter written a few months before their marriage, Maria begs Patrick to pray for her because she fears that he is replacing God as the first object of her love: "I feel that my heart is more ready to attach itself to earth than heaven," she confesses.[3] Says Jane Eyre, with more eloquence, "My future husband was becoming to me my whole world; and more than the world: almost my hope of heaven. He stood between me and every thought of religion, as an eclipse intervenes between man and the broad sun. I could not, in those days, see God for his creature: of whom I had made an idol."[4]

Twenty-nine years after his wife's death, Mr. Brontë put these letters into Charlotte's hands. Reading the words of the mother she had known so briefly, Charlotte was deeply moved. "A few days since," she wrote a friend, "a little incident happened which curiously touched me. Papa put into my hands a little packet of letters and papers, telling me that they were mamma's, and that I might read them. I did read them, in a frame of mind I cannot describe. The papers were yellow with time, all having been written before I was born: it was strange now to peruse, for the first time, the records of a mind whence my own sprang; and most strange, and at once sad and sweet, to find that mind of a truly fine, pure, and elevated order. They were written to papa before they were married. There is a rectitude, a refinement, a constancy, a modesty, a sense, a gentleness about them indescribable. I wish she had lived, and that I had known her."[5]

But Maria Brontë did not live long to share in her husband's pilgrimage, as she so humbly phrased her fondest wish. A few months after the family arrived in Haworth she was driven to her bed, stricken with cancer. A pall fell on the household. The six quiet children became even more subdued and dependent on themselves, for their suffering mother did not often want to see them. Quietly, they would leave the house, Maria and Elizabeth shepherding the littler ones, and walk out hand in hand on the moors that rose in barren brown swells behind the parsonage. An old woman came to help nurse Mrs. Brontë. For Mr. Brontë, faced with clerical duties, the responsibility for six children, and a dying wife, the period of Maria's illness was a nightmare.

". . . all the prudence and skill I could exercise would have availed me nothing had it not been for help *from above*," he later wrote to his former vicar. ". . . one day, I remember it well; it was a gloomy day, a day of clouds and darkness, three of my little children were taken ill of a scarlet fever; and, the day after, the remaining three were all in the same condition. Just at that time death seemed to have laid his hand on my dear wife . . . She was cold and silent and seemed hardly to notice what was passing around her. This awful season however was not of long duration. My little children had a favourable turn, and at length got well; and the force of my wife's disease somewhat abated."[6]

The improvement in Maria's health did not last long, however. She began to sink rapidly. Although in great pain, she was cheerful and uncomplaining in front of her children and the servants; one day, feeling a little better, she begged to be raised up in bed so that she could watch the nurse clean the grate because "she did it like it was done in Cornwall." But there were countless long dark hours when bitter thoughts of her seemingly unfulfilled life, of her health ruined by childbearing, and of her children left motherless shook her religious faith to its foundations. "During many years she had walked with God, but the great enemy, envying her life of holiness, often disturbed her mind in the last conflict," admitted her husband, and he wrestled with her doubt and depression for hours in the darkened sickroom, fighting to help her preserve her faith in God.

More doctors were called in, but they could offer no hope. On the twenty-second of September 1821, Maria Brontë was carried through the low gate of the parsonage wall to be laid under the stone floor of her husband's church. Her last words still echoed in the quiet house: "Oh, God, my poor children—oh, God, my poor children!"

How indeed to raise six small children? The most obvious solution to the problem was a new wife. Two months after his wife's death Patrick Brontë wrote a proposal of marriage to Elizabeth Firth, a friend of the family from Thornton, the Brontës' residence prior to Haworth and the birthplace of Charlotte, Branwell, Emily, and Anne. In a friendly but decisive way, she rejected his proposal. His thoughts then turned to his twenty-ninth year, his first curacy in Wethersfield,

Essex, and a young parishioner named Mary Burder. A lodger in her aunt's home, the tall, good-looking Irish curate with high cheekbones, thick red hair, and aquiline nose had met and won the affections of the girl. Mysteriously, the courtship had not ended in marriage; evidently Mr. Brontë thought the match not quite good enough for him. Now, however, he took up his pen to write, first to her mother and then to Mary Burder herself:

Dear Madam,—
The circumstance of Mrs Burder not answering my letter for so long a time gave me considerable uneasiness; however, I am much obliged to her for answering it at last. . . . I experienced a very agreeable sensation in my heart, at this moment, on reflecting that you are *still* single, and am so selfish as to wish you to remain so, even if you would never allow me to see you. *You* were the *first* whose hand I solicited, and no doubt I was the *first* to whom *you promised to give that hand*.

However much you may dislike me now, I am sure you once loved me with an unaffected innocent love, and I feel confident that after all which you have seen and heard, you cannot doubt my love for you. It is now almost fifteen years since I last saw you. This is a long interval of time and may have effected many changes. It has made me look something older. But, I trust I have gained more than I have lost, I hope I may venture to say I am *wiser* and better. . . . I have a *small* but *sweet* little family that often soothe my heart, and afford me pleasure by their endearing little ways, and I have what I consider a competency of the good things of this life. . . . I want but *one* addition to my comforts, and then I think I should wish for no more on this side eternity. I want to see a dearly Beloved Friend, kind as I *once* saw her, and as *much* disposed to promote my happiness. . . . My dear Madam, all that I have to request at present is that you will be so good as to answer this letter as soon as convenient, and tell me candidly whether you and Mrs Burder would have any objection to seeing me at Finchingfield Park, as an *Old Friend*. . . . I cannot tell how *you* may feel on reading this, but I must say *my* ancient love is rekindled, and I have a *longing* desire to see you. . . .

Most Sincerely,
P. Brontë.[7]

It is hard to imagine a worse beginning than a reminder to the lady that she is *still* single. It is difficult to conceive a more egotistical and patronizing tone. And could the connection between the sudden revival of Mr. Brontë's "ancient love" and the "*small* but *sweet* little family" be made any clearer? Miss Burder retaliated with such scathing hostility that clearly she not only found Mr. Brontë's proposal insulting but had been nursing a grievance against her jilter all fifteen years. "My present condition upon which you are pleased to remark has hitherto been the state of my choice and to me a state of much happiness and comfort," she sneers. Warming to her theme, she goes on to list her blessings: she has, she tells him, the kindest and most indulgent of parents, sisters, and brothers; no domestic cares and anxieties; no husband to control or oppose her; and—unkindest cut of all —a handsome income. In short, she feels "no willingness to risk in a change so many enjoyments in possession." Remarking that she truly sympathizes with him and "the poor little innocents" in their bereavement, she cannot, however, resist a final stab. "The Lord," she suggests pointedly, "can supply all your and their need"![8]

Mr. Brontë was stung by the letter and wrote a bitter reply; and he made no more proposals for a while. But the most pressing problem of the children's supervision was solved temporarily, for his sister-in-law, Miss Branwell, who had come from Cornwall after Maria's death, agreed to stay on at the parsonage for the time being. Moving into the best bedroom, where she promptly shut all the windows and ordered the servant to get up a roasting fire against the Yorkshire damp and chill, Miss Branwell undertook the management of the household with a strict, fussy, but not unkindly hand.

The death of their mother was a deeply traumatic experience for the six young Brontë children. It created in the eight-year-old Maria a sense of responsibility which made her preternaturally old and sober. It created in all the children an insecurity so severe that it can be said without exaggeration that all their lives not one of them was able to cope successfully with the world outside the parsonage walls. At the same time, it drove them together; they clung to each other like tender vines, deriving all their comfort and strength from their intense emotional and physical unity.

Left to themselves (for Mr. Brontë was not a companionable kind of father and Miss Branwell not a kindred spirit), the children were, however, far from unhappy. They had no hoops, or rocking horses, or children's books because they were poor and because Mr. Brontë did not believe in indulgences. They had no playmates, for the Brontës had always kept to themselves, fulfilling parish duties but never associating with the villagers on social terms. They did not miss toys or friends, however, because their precocious imaginations forged into the adult world where real heroes and villains like the Duke of Wellington and Napoleon waged military and political battles that made childish games pale by comparison. Political events in London had for them the excitement other children find in fairy tales or dolls, and they awaited the arrival of the three periodicals to which Mr. Brontë subscribed with passionate eagerness. The small, delicate, gifted Maria would take a newspaper into the study, shut herself up, and devour the fine columns of print; emerging, she could report with minute accuracy the complex details of parliamentary debate. At the same time the atmosphere of austerity, soberness, and rectitude which pervaded the spotless, sparely furnished parsonage created—in the girls, at least —a moral precocity as well. Mr. Brontë, in a letter to Charlotte's first biographer, Mrs. Gaskell, gives us a glimpse of his strange and gifted children:

When mere children, as soon as they could read and write, Charlotte and her brother and sisters used to invent and act little plays of their own, in which the Duke of Wellington, my daughter Charlotte's hero, was sure to come off conqueror; when a dispute would not infrequently arise amongst them regarding the comparative merits of him, Buonaparte, Hannibal, and Caesar. When the argument got warm, and rose to its height, as their mother was then dead, I had sometimes to come in as arbitrator, and settle the dispute according to the best of my judgment. Generally, in the management of these concerns, I frequently thought that I discovered signs of rising talent, which I had seldom or never before seen in any of their age. . . . A circumstance now occurs to my mind which I may as well mention. When my children were very young, when, as far as I can remember, the oldest was about ten years of age, and the youngest about four, thinking that they knew more than I had yet discovered, in order to make them speak with less timidity, I deemed that if they were put under a sort of cover I might gain my end; and happening to have a mask in the house, I told them all to stand and speak boldly from under the cover of the mask.

I began with the youngest (Anne, afterwards Acton Bell), and asked her what a child like her most wanted, she answered, "Age and experience." I asked the next (Emily, afterwards Ellis Bell), what I had best do with her brother Branwell, who was sometimes a naughty boy; she answered, "Reason with him, and when he won't listen to reason, whip him." I asked Branwell what was the best way of knowing the difference between the intellects of man and woman; he answered, "By considering the difference between them as to their bodies." I then asked Charlotte what was the best book in the world; she answered, "The Bible." And what was the next best; she answered, "The Book of Nature." I then asked the next [Elizabeth] what was the best mode of education for a woman; she answered, "That which would make her rule her house well." Lastly, I asked the eldest [Maria] what was the best mode of spending time; she answered, "By laying it out in preparation for a happy eternity." I may not have given precisely their words, but I have nearly done so, as they made a deep and lasting impression on my memory. The substance, however, was exactly what I have stated.[9]

As a clergyman and parent, Mr. Brontë must indeed have been pleased, for the precocity of his children's answers lies not so much in their originality as in their unerring correctness: the little drama gives us in microcosm a handbook of nineteenth-century maxims for good children. Perhaps his children did not feel as safe behind the mask as Mr. Brontë supposed.

How different the course of Charlotte's life—and all their lives— might have been had Mr. Brontë kept the girls at home, tutored by Miss Branwell in needlework and housekeeping, and by their own reading. The Cambridge-educated clergyman had decided to instruct Branwell in Latin and Greek himself. Understandably, perhaps, he felt at a loss to cope with five girls. Maria, the eldest, patiently taught Elizabeth, Charlotte, Emily, and Anne how to read and count. Yet they needed some kind of formal education. Casting about for an in-expensive school, he found what seemed to be a godsend for a parson trying to raise a family on £200 a year: Cowan Bridge, a school for daughters of the clergy, newly founded by a Rev. William Carus Wilson, vicar of Tunstall.

A Cowan Bridge prospectus sheds some interesting light on the ed-ucation of young ladies in 1825. For £14 per year students were clothed, lodged, boarded, and—last—educated.

The system of education [we are told] comprehends History, Ge-ography, the Use of the Globes [mysterious talent!], Grammar, Writ-ing and Arithmetic; all kinds of Needlework, and the nicer kinds of household-work, such as getting up fine linen, etc. If Accomplish-ments are required, an additional charge is made, for French, Music, or Drawing, of £3 a year each. . . . Each pupil must bring with her, a Bible and Prayer Book, a Workbag, with necessary Sewing Imple-ments, etc., Combs, Brushes, Pair of Pattens, Gloves, and the follow-ing Articles of Clothing, etc.

  4 Day Shifts
  3 Night do.
  3 Night Caps
  2 Pair of Stays
  2 Flannel Petticoats
  3 White Upper Petticoats
  1 Grey Stuff do.
  2 Pair of Pockets
  4 Pair of White Cotton Stockings
  3 Pair of Black Worsted do.
  1 Nankeen Spencer
  4 Brown Holland Pinafores
  2 White do.
  1 Short Coloured Dressing Gown

2 Pair of Shoes

The pupils all appear in the same dress [the announcement proceeds]. They wear plain straw cottage bonnets; in summer, white frocks on Sundays, and nankeen on other days. In winter, purple stuff frocks and purple cloth pelisses. . . . There are five weeks holiday at Midsummer . . . All letters and parcels will be inspected by the Governess.[10]

Maria and Elizabeth were enrolled at the Clergy Daughters' School in July 1824. They were examined and the results entered in the school register: Maria "reads tolerably, writes pretty well, ciphers a little, works [i.e., sews] very badly, knows a little grammar, geography and history"; Elizabeth "reads little, writes pretty well, works very badly, knows nothing else."[11] This estimation of the girls' abilities certainly does not tally with other reports of their cleverness. Perhaps Maria's and Elizabeth's shyness prevented their doing well when examined; perhaps the things they did know were not asked—or perhaps the school authorities were unable to recognize ability when they saw it.

In the next weeks, having heard nothing adverse about the school from his two eldest daughters, Mr. Brontë decided that Charlotte should follow. He himself accompanied his eight-year-old daughter in a coach the fifty miles from Haworth to Cowan Bridge in Lancashire. Upon arrival, Charlotte too was examined and the following judgment succinctly penned in the register: "Entered school August 10, 1824. Reads tolerably—Writes indifferently—Ciphers a little and works neatly—Knows nothing of Grammar, Geography, History or Accomplishments—Altogether clever of her age but knows nothing systematically." Despite her distress at having to leave home and her extreme timidity in the new surroundings, Charlotte was overjoyed to be reunited with Maria and Elizabeth. Mr. Brontë himself spent the night at the school and was so satisfied that he left next day determined to send Emily to join her sisters.

Cowan Bridge, however, proved a disaster for the Brontës, and one of the bitterest episodes in Charlotte's often bitter life. Years later, still lacerated by the memory, she wrote her experiences into her novel, *Jane Eyre*. The Rev. William Carus Wilson became Mr. Brocklehurst —"A black pillar! such, at least, appeared to me, at first sight, the straight, narrow, sable-clad shape standing erect on the rug: the grim face at the top was like a carved mask, placed above the shaft by way of capital." The name Cowan Bridge she altered to Lowood, and painted a grim picture of an inhuman institution seen through the eyes of the child, Jane Eyre:

The refectory was a great, low-ceiled, gloomy room; on two long tables smoked basins of something hot, which, however, to my dismay, sent forth an odour far from inviting. I saw a universal manifestation of discontent when the fumes of the repast met the nostrils of those destined to swallow it; from the van of the procession, the tall girls of the first class, rose the whispered words:—

"Disgusting! The porridge is burnt again!"

"Silence!" ejaculated a voice . . . A long grace was said and a hymn sung; then a servant brought in some tea for the teachers, and the meal began.

Ravenous, and now very faint, I devoured a spoonful or two of my portion without thinking of its taste; but the first edge of hunger blunted, I perceived I had got in hand a nauseous mess: burnt porridge is almost as bad as rotten potatoes; famine itself soon sickens over it. The spoons were moved slowly: I saw each girl taste her food and try to swallow it; but in most cases the effort was soon relinquished. Breakfast was over, and none had breakfasted. . . .

The next day commenced as before, getting up and dressing by rushlight: but this morning we were obliged to dispense with the ceremony of washing: the water in the pitchers was frozen. A change had taken place in the weather the preceding evening, and a keen northeast wind, whistling through the crevices of our bed-room windows all night long, had made us shiver in our beds, and turned the contents of the ewers to ice. . . .

During January, February, and part of March, the deep snows, and, after their melting, the almost impassable roads, prevented our stirring beyond the garden walls, except to go to church; but within these limits we had to pass an hour every day in the open air. Our clothing was insufficient to protect us from the severe cold: we had no boots, the snow got into our shoes and melted there; our ungloved hands became numbed and covered with chilblains, as were our feet: I remember well the distracting irritation I endured from this cause every evening, when my feet inflamed; and the torture of thrusting the swelled, raw, and stiff toes into my shoes in the morning.

Sundays were dreary days in that wintry season. We had to walk two miles to Brocklebridge Church, where our patron officiated. We set out cold, we arrived at church colder: during the morning service we became almost paralysed. It was too far to return to dinner, and an allowance of cold meat and bread, in the same penurious proportion observed in our ordinary meals, was served round between the services.

At the close of the afternoon service we returned by an exposed and hilly road, where the bitter winter wind, blowing over a range of snowy summits to the north, almost flayed the skin from our faces. . . .

How we longed for the light and heat of a blazing fire when we got back! But, to the little ones at least, this was denied: each hearth in the school-room was immediately surrounded by a double row of great girls, and behind them the younger children crouched in groups, wrapping their starved arms in their pinafores.[12]

Charlotte raged not only against her own physical and mental suffering at Cowan Bridge. Her charge against the institution was far more severe, for quite literally she blamed Mr. Wilson's school for the deaths of Elizabeth and Maria. Maria's persecution, illness, and death are also recounted in *Jane Eyre* in the story of Helen Burns, but the truth is even more pathetic. A gentle, dreamy, untidy creature, Maria did not fit well into the rigid routine of the boarding school, despite her great abilities as a student. She could not be punctual; she could not keep her possessions in order. Her tardiness, her absent-mindedness, her constant cough—and, not least, her obvious mental superiority—drew down the wrath of a particular mistress, Miss Andrews, on her head. If Maria had rebelled perhaps the tyrant would have been checked, but she accepted the humility of constant punishment with silent dignity. Her passivity only drove the frustrated and sadistic Miss Andrews to new cruelties. In *Jane Eyre* there is a scene in which Miss Scatcherd orders Helen Burns to fetch a bundle of twigs, and then, commanding the girl to loosen her pinafore, delivers a dozen stinging strokes on her bare neck. This incident may well have happened; if not, there were other real punishments just as brutal. Mrs. Gaskell, without revealing Miss Andrews' name, gives this testimony of a fellow pupil of Charlotte and Maria:

"The dormitory in which Maria slept was a long room, holding a row of narrow little beds on each side, occupied by the pupils; and at the end of this dormitory there was a small bed-chamber opening out of it, appropriated to the use of Miss Scatcherd. Maria's bed stood nearest to the door of this room. One morning, after she had become so seriously unwell as to have had a blister applied to her side (the sore from which was not perfectly healed), when the getting-up bell was heard, poor Maria moaned out that she was so ill, so very ill, she wished she might stop in bed; and some of the girls urged her to do so, and said they would explain it all to Miss Temple, the superintendent. But Miss Scatcherd was close at hand, and her anger would have to be faced before Miss Temple's kind thoughtfulness could interfere; so the sick child began to dress, shivering with cold, as, without leaving her bed, she slowly put on her black worsted stockings over her thin white legs (my informant spoke as if she saw it yet, and her whole face flashed out undying indignation). Just then Miss Scatcherd issued from her room, and, without asking for a word of explanation from the sick and frightened girl, she took her by the arm, on the side to which the blister had been applied, and by one vigorous movement whirled her out into the middle of the floor, abusing her all the time for dirty and untidy habits. There she left her. My informant says, Maria hardly spoke, except to beg some of the more indignant girls to be calm; but, in slow, trembling movements, with many a pause, she went downstairs at last—and was punished for being late."¹³

Charlotte, the smallest girl—helpless—witnessed this scene and never forgot.

Reading the account, we are as indignant as Maria's schoolmates in the bare dormitory that cold morning. Oddly enough, however, the fictional Helen Burns is unsatisfactory as a character and leaves many readers not only unmoved but critical. Charlotte insisted again and again that Helen Burns was *exactly* like Maria, but she failed to capture the human quality of her adored sister. Helen Burns is too good; we cannot sympathize with such superhuman patience and resignation. After a public whipping, for example, Helen proclaims, "It is far better to endure patiently a smart which nobody feels but yourself, than to commit a hasty action whose evil consequences will extend to all connected with you; and besides, the Bible bids us return good for evil." This is irreproachable theoretically, but Jane Eyre's reaction impresses us as sounder, even though the thought of a child striking back at an adult is rather disquieting: "When we are struck at without a reason, we should strike back again very hard; I am sure we should—so hard as to teach the person who struck us never to do it again."¹⁴

Even less comprehensible to a modern reader is Helen's willingness to die because, had she lived, she would only have sinned. "By dying young," says Helen, "I shall escape great suffering. I had not qualities or talents to make my way very well in the world; I should have been continually at fault." This is unhealthy, and unhealthiness is unfortunately the chief impression Charlotte's fictional account of her sister conveys, particularly when we learn that Helen was actually the favorite of "Miss Scatcherd." Charlotte revered Maria almost as a saint, but one is relieved that Charlotte herself was a faulty, healthier sinner.

Charlotte evidently did not realize how closely Maria's philosophy corresponded with the teachings of the man she hated so violently, Mr. William Carus Wilson. The director of Cowan Bridge was also a pamphleteer of mean but widely admired abilities. The chief product of his pen was a series of revolting little stories about "good" children and the contented and even eager way they embraced early death. He was a man who could clasp his hands in enthusiastic approval over this inscription on a child's tomb:

> When the archangel's trump shall sound,
> And souls to bodies join;
> Thousands will wish their stay on earth
> Had been as short as mine.

In *The Children's Friend* for December 1826, one of his periodicals, he tells with relish of the death of young Sarah Bicker at Cowan Bridge from inflammation of the bowels:

> I had heard from the teachers that she had expressed a desire to depart and to be with Christ and I was anxious to assure myself that her hopes were well founded. The following conversation took place:
> "Sarah, are you happy?"
> "Yes, very happy, Sir."
> "And what is it makes you happy?"
> "Because Jesus Christ died to save me and he will take me to heaven."
> "And he will save all men?"
> "No, Sir, only those that trust in him. . . ."
> On the Sunday evening she was taken ill, she was asked by a schoolmistress, "If she should like to die?"
> She answered, "Not yet."
> "Why?"
> "I should wish to have time to repent, and be a better child."

Mr. Wilson draws the moral clearly. *"I bless God that he has taken from us the child of whose salvation we have the best hope and may her death be the means of rousing many of her school-fellows to seek the Lord while he may be found."*[15]

It is disturbing to reflect that a man who actually believed, as his many writings bear witness, that little George, or Jane, or Kitty was better off dead because sinless was the director of a children's school. But Mr. Wilson was not an exception. His *Children's Friend* was just one of dozens of Sunday school publications that preached the same philosophy, and most of his contemporaries found him a highly moral, sincere, and intelligent man. The small Charlotte Brontë judged him immoral, hypocritical, and benighted.

In the late winter and early spring of 1825 the grim subject Mr. Wilson enjoyed idealizing became a tragic reality. Maria's cough had grown more wracking, her small frame more wasted. In February, Mr. Brontë journeyed to Lancashire to fetch home his eldest daughter "in ill health," according to the testimony of the school register. Then in April a low fever broke out among the girls. Charlotte recorded the experience in *Jane Eyre*:

> That forest-dell, where Lowood lay, was the cradle of fog and fog-bred pestilence; which, quickening with the quickening spring, crept into the Orphan Asylum, breathed typhus through its crowded school-room and dormitory, and, ere May arrived, transformed the seminary into a hospital. Semi-starvation and neglected colds had predisposed most of the pupils to receive infection . . . The teachers

were fully occupied with packing up and making other necessary preparations for the departure of those girls who were fortunate enough to have friends and relations able and willing to remove them from the seat of contagion. Many, already smitten, went home only to die; some died at the school, and were buried quietly and quickly, the nature of the malady forbidding delay.[16]

Charlotte, Elizabeth, and Emily, who had joined her sisters the previous November, all escaped the infection. Paradoxically, this period of death, sickness, and sorrow was one of liberation for Charlotte and her sisters. Lessons were suspended, the regime relaxed.

. . . they let us ramble in the wood, like gipsies, from morning till night; we did what we liked, went where we liked: we lived better too. . . . our breakfast-basins were better filled: when there was no time to prepare a regular dinner, which often happened, [the housekeeper] would give us a large piece of cold pie, or a thick slice of bread and cheese, and this we carried away with us to the wood, where we each chose the spot we liked best, and dined sumptuously. My favourite seat was a smooth and broad stone, rising white and dry from the very middle of the beck, and only to be got at by wading through the water; a feat I accomplished barefoot.[17]

Then came news from Haworth. Maria was dead. Charlotte, Elizabeth, and Emily could not return home for the funeral. On Branwell, who observed day by day her suffering and slow decline, his sister's death was engraved for life. Years later, in his poem *Caroline*, he recorded with nightmarelike clarity the morbid details of her death and burial:

. . . She lay with flowers about her head—
   Though formal grave-clothes hid her hair!
Still did her lips the smile retain
   Which parted them when hope was high,
Still seemed her brow as smoothed from pain
   As when all thought she could not die. . . .

They came—they pressed the coffin lid
   Above my Caroline,
And then, I felt, for ever hid
   My sister's face from mine![18]

Then Elizabeth, less brilliant than Maria, but almost as stoically good, fell into a decline. By the end of May her condition was grave enough to warrant her being sent home to Haworth in the care of a trusted servant. Thoroughly alarmed, the school authorities were willing to take no more chances with the vulnerable Brontës. Charlotte and Emily were dispatched immediately to William Carus Wilson's own home, and Mr. Brontë was summoned to come to fetch them back to Haworth. Despite their great relief to be home at the parsonage again, they found no escape from sorrow: Elizabeth drooped and sickened, and in a few weeks she too was borne through the low lychgate to be laid beside her mother and sister.

When *Jane Eyre* was published, Lowood was immediately identified as Cowan Bridge—much to Charlotte's consternation—and a great cry of indignation went up from Mr. Wilson's friends and the many distinguished patrons of the school. And the Cowan Bridge Controversy, as it came to be known, is hardly settled today. Did Charlotte tell the truth or didn't she? Evidence suggests she did—or nearly. And one suspects that, besides harshness, bad and scanty food, cold, and neglect, another charge could be leveled against the Clergy Daughters' School —an inadequate curriculum and staff. If the inclusion of *ventriloquy* in the course list does not inspire doubt, then Mr. Wilson's description of his nepotistic staff must. "I have already engaged professional teachers of more than ordinary talent to assist me in superintending the Education of the Students," he announces in a prospectus. "Their abilities need no comment from me; they have already distinguished themselves by their accomplishments. I could afford instances of such, but seeing they are members for the most part of my own family, I refrain from motives of delicacy."[19] When first-class education for girls was so desperately needed, when so many women faced poverty from lack of skill and training, it is discouraging to think that Cowan Bridge was probably just one of dozens of schools that fell severely short of its goal.

Unlike Maria, Charlotte did not collide with the rigid disciplinarians of the school. The headmistress, indeed, did not remember her, stating in a letter to Mrs. Gaskell, "Of the two younger ones (if two there were) I have very slight recollections, save that one, a darling child, was quite the pet nursling of the school." "The pet nursling" is, of course, not Charlotte but Emily. Charlotte did impress some of her schoolmates as a bright, clever little child, but many years later, in a letter to her publisher, she herself said of those ten months at Cowan Bridge, "My career was a very quiet one. I was plodding and industrious, perhaps I was very grave, for I suffered to see my sisters perishing, but I think I was remarkable for nothing."[20]

Outwardly obedient, hard-working, and quiet, Charlotte seethed inside, and the Cowan Bridge affair is interesting not so much for what it tells us about the school as for what it tells us about Charlotte Brontë. So many facets of the child that were to characterize the woman emerge.

We see, for example, Charlotte's capacity for intense resentment and hatred and, at the same time, her compulsion to suppress her feelings under a mask of conformity and submission. "I am a hearty hater," she once wrote her good friend Ellen Nussey in a moment of frank revelation; but few people were ever to see this side of her personality—until, perhaps, they found themselves pilloried in the pages of one of her novels. Reading *Jane Eyre*, one is struck too at how deep the resentment runs against Mr. Brocklehurst, both as an authority figure and, if one takes into account the obvious phallic symbolism with which he is so antagonistically described, as a male. This hostility too was to play a key role in her art and life.

Again, we are struck by the child's independence of mind—her immunity against cant and hypocrisy, her strongly developed critical faculty. Yet Cowan Bridge also shows us that Charlotte's emotions could sometimes distort her critical judgment and bias her irrevocably, even against fact.

At the same time, Cowan Bridge changed Charlotte. It robbed her of childish spirits and confidence and taught her to distrust life. The world, Charlotte concluded, was likely to offer you a cup of happiness and then snatch it from your outstretched hand. The child formulated a new but permanent philosophy: Be slow to reach out—and expect the worst.

# 2

*Chief Genius—*
*and Schoolgirl*

Apart from the tragic circumstances surrounding their return from Cowan Bridge, Charlotte and Emily were overjoyed to be home again, reunited with Branwell and Anne. In their absence Mr. Brontë had made a third proposal of marriage and had a third time been refused. Apparently then he resigned himself to the life of a widower. It was not an unsuitable role for a person of his solitary and austere temperament. We cannot believe that his wife ever received the devoted attention he gave to his writing, his sermons, or his quiet hours of contemplation in his study—or that a successor would have fared any better. Miss Branwell was now permanently established in the best bedroom, unhappy at having left behind the sociable and warm climate of her native Cornwall, but determined to do her duty by her sister's family.

Charlotte's friend Ellen Nussey has left us a lively portrait of Miss Branwell. She was "a very small, antiquated little lady. She wore caps large enough for half a dozen of the present fashion, and a front of light auburn curls over her forehead. She always dressed in silk. She had a horror of the climate so far north, and of the stone floors of the parsonage. She amused us by clicking about in pattens whenever she had to go into the kitchen or look after household operations.

"She talked a great deal of her younger days; the gayeties of her dear native town, Penzance, in Cornwall; the soft, warm climate, etc. The social life of her younger days she used to recall with regret; she gave one the idea that she had been a belle among her own home acquaintances. She took snuff out of a very pretty gold snuff-box, which she sometimes presented to you with a little laugh, as if she enjoyed the slight shock and astonishment visible in your countenance. In summer she spent part of the afternoon in reading aloud to Mr Brontë. In the winter evenings she must have enjoyed this; for she and Mr Brontë had often to finish their discussions on what she had read when we all met for tea. She would be very lively and intelligent, and tilt arguments against Mr Brontë without fear."[1]

It is an attractive portrait: a woman whom financial independence and a consciousness of good works has rendered self-confident; a woman unawed enough by the world to keep the fashion of her youth; a woman sophisticated enough to chuckle inwardly over the fluster her snuffbox produced—a Cornwall exotic, transplanted, but obliging enough to flourish in barren soil.

Ellen Nussey does not mention Miss Branwell's repressive brand of Calvinistic Methodism, which pervaded the atmosphere of the parsonage as thoroughly as Mr. Brontë's more tolerant Anglicanism. Anne absorbed a good deal of it, and Charlotte herself was not immune. Nor does Miss Nussey give an idea of Miss Branwell's asperity, undoubtedly because she never felt its sting like Nancy Garrs, the children's nurse, who claimed that Miss Branwell was "so crosslike an' fault findin' and so close, she ga'e us, my sister Sarah an' me, but a gill o' beer a day, an' she gi'e it hersel', did Miss Branwell, to our dinner, she wouldn't let us go draw it oursel' in t' cellar. A pint a day, she gi'e us, that were half a pint for me an' a half a pint for Sarah." In short, said Nancy Garrs glumly, she was "a bit of a tyke." This must have been the opinion too of Tabitha Ackroyd, the Brontës' faithful servant, who came to supervise the parsonage kitchen that year and remained until her death in 1855.

The strictness of their aunt and the austerity of their father did not wholly dampen the spirits of the four children, however. Much of the time Miss Branwell closeted herself in her stuffy bedroom, sewing or reading, and for hours together their father remained invisible behind his study door. Free from adult interference, the children readily picked up where they had left off before Cowan Bridge interrupted their lives. The old heroes were marshaled, the trumpet of battle sounded, and the children once more threw themselves into the world of make-believe adventure. Now, however, the web of fantasy they wove was more intricate and entangling. A complex saga evolved slowly, inspired, curiously enough, by a set of wooden soldiers. Charlotte chronicled the beginning of this new adventure in an early bit of writing she called "History of the Year 1829." Even though the new plays were of overwhelming interest to her, it is worth noting that she is equally conscious of the factual, ordinary details of parsonage life and takes an obvious pleasure in setting them down.

Once Papa lent my sister Maria a book. It was an old geography book; she wrote on its blank leaf, "Papa lent me this book." This book is a hundred and twenty years old; it is at this moment lying before me. While I write this I am in the kitchen of the Parsonage, Haworth; Tabby, the servant, is washing up the breakfast-things, and Anne, my youngest sister (Maria was my eldest), is kneeling on a chair, looking at some cakes which Tabby had been baking for us. Emily is in the parlour, brushing the carpet. Papa and Branwell are gone to Keighley. Aunt is up-stairs in her room, and I am sitting by the table writing this in the kitchen. Keighley is a small town four miles from here. Papa and Branwell are gone for the newspaper, the *Leeds Intelligencer*, a most excellent Tory newspaper, edited by Mr Wood, and the proprietor, Mr Henneman. We take two and see three newspapers a week. We take the *Leeds Intelligencer*, Tory, and the *Leeds Mercury*, Whig, edited by Mr Baines, and his brother, son-in-law, and his two sons, Edward and Talbot. We see the *John Bull;* it is a high Tory, very violent. Mr Driver lends us it, as likewise *Blackwood's Magazine*, the most able periodical there is. The Editor is Mr Christopher North, an old man seventy-four years of age; the 1st of April is his birth-day; his company are Timothy Tickler, Morgan O'Doherty, Macrabin Mordecai, Mullion, Warnell, and James Hogg, a man of most extraordinary genius, a Scottish shepherd. Our plays were established; *Young Men*, June, 1826; *Our Fellows*, July, 1827; *Islanders*, December, 1827. These are our three great plays, that are not kept secret. Emily's and my bed [Mrs. Gaskell altered this to "best"] plays were established the 1st of December, 1827; the others March, 1828. Bed plays mean secret plays; they are very nice ones. All our plays are very strange ones. Their nature I need not write on paper, for I think I shall always remember them. The *Young Men's* play took its rise from some wooden soldiers Branwell had; *Our Fellows* from *Aesop's Fables;* and the *Islanders* from several events which happened. I will sketch out the origin of our plays more explicitly if I can. First, *Young Men*. Papa bought Branwell some wooden soldiers at Leeds; when Papa came home it was night, and we were in bed, so next morning Branwell came to our door with a box of soldiers. Emily and I jumped out of bed, and I snatched up one and exclaimed, "This is the Duke of Wellington! This shall be the Duke!" When I had said this Emily likewise took one up and said it should be hers; when Anne came down, she said one should be hers. Mine was the prettiest of the whole, and the tallest, and the most perfect in every part. Emily's was a grave-looking fellow, and we called him "Gravey." Anne's was a queer little thing, much like herself, and we called him "Waiting-boy." Branwell chose his, and called him "Buonaparte."[2]

"All our plays are very strange ones." The *Young Men* waged in fantasy the battles and campaigns of Napoleon and Wellington, still vivid in every Englishman's memory. Cracky, Monkey, Goody, Naughty, and Rogue—rank-and-file wooden soldiers—attacked and retreated under the brilliant military tactics of the French and English generals controlled by Branwell and Charlotte. Then, wearying of war, the children concocted a new fantasy inspired by *Aesop's Fables:* each child had an island of her own inhabited by people ten miles tall, (Emily's, however, were only four miles tall), and this drama was called *Our Fellows. Our Fellows* was succeeded by *The Islanders*, and again Charlotte records the "establishment" of this play. The date is June 31, 1829; she is thirteen years old.

> The play of the *Islanders* was formed in December, 1827, in the following manner. One night, about the time when the cold sleet and stormy fogs of November are succeeded by the snow-storms and high piercing night-winds of confirmed winter, we were all sitting round the warm blazing kitchen fire, having just concluded a quarrel with Tabby concerning the propriety of lighting a candle, from which she came off victorious, no candle having been produced. A long pause succeeded, which was at last broken by Branwell, saying, in a lazy manner, "I don't know what to do." This was echoed by Emily and Anne.
>
> TABBY   Wha ya may go t' bed.
> BRANWELL   I'd rather do anything than that.
> CHARLOTTE   Why are you so glum to-night, Tabby? Oh! suppose we had each an island of our own.
> BRANWELL   If we had I would choose the Island of Man.
> CHARLOTTE   And I would choose the Isle of Wight.
> EMILY   The Isle of Arran for me.
> ANNE   And mine should be Guernsey.

The children then chose rulers for their islands. Branwell chose a noted surgeon, a poet, and the mythic symbol, John Bull; Emily chose Sir Walter Scott, his biographer Lockhart, and Lockhart's son; Anne chose two political reformers and a famous physician; and Charlotte chose, inevitably, her hero the Duke of Wellington and his two sons, Christopher North, editor of *Blackwood's Magazine*, and a surgeon, Mr. Abernathy. The choice of so many physicians was a purely practical one: they were needed to take care of the hundreds wounded in Branwell's battles.

"Here our conversation was interrupted," continues Charlotte, "by the, to us, dismal sound of the clock striking seven, and we were summoned off to bed. The next day we added many others to our list of men, till we got almost all the chief men of the kingdom."[3]

Even Branwell got bored with battles, however, and the children devised other occupations for their heroes. The Marquis of Douro, one of Charlotte's favorite creations, is not only a soldier and an author, for example, but member of the Society of Antiquarians, president for 1830 of the Literary Club, honorary member of the Academy of Artists and treasurer to the Society for the Spread of Classical Knowledge, and chief secretary of the Confederate Hundred for Promoting Gymnastic Exercises.

But the soldiers served the imaginative talents of the Brontës best as authors. In 1829, Branwell conceived the idea of bringing out a *Young Men's Magazine,* modeled after *Blackwood's,* a periodical much admired by the children for its literary excellence. The publication was to be written, published, and sold by the soldiers themselves. Painstakingly, Branwell printed his journal on four tiny leaves measuring about 2½ by 1¼ inches—small enough to be held in a soldier's hand and small enough to discourage any adult eyes from attempting to decipher its contents. In these minute books, the chronicles of Glass Town were recorded, for, inspired by a geography book, the children had moved their drama to Africa, wiping out the natives with true imperialistic spirit and establishing the Glass Town Confederacy. And now the children figure directly in the annals, for, influenced by *The Arabian Nights* (every book that came into their hands was grist for their mill), they borrowed the device of the genii and wove themselves into the stories as all-powerful arbiters of their heroes' destinies. Branwell delighted in describing their whirlwind descents upon the terrified residents of Glass Town: ". . . the air suddenly darkened, the hall shook and streams of fire continually flashed through the room, followed by long and loud peals of thunder. While all were standing pale and affrighted at the unusual phenomenon, a dreadful Monster . . . entered the room . . . and said in a loud voice 'I am the chief Genius Brannii, with me there are 3 others; she, Wellesly, who protects you is named Tallii; she who protects Parry is named Emmii; she who protects Ross is called Annii. Those lesser ones whom ye saw are Genii and Fairies, our slaves and minions . . . we are the guardians of you all.'"[4]

Charlotte soon began to cast an envious eye at Branwell's literary project. She who had recorded so lovingly in her "History" their acquaintance with *Blackwood's,* even to the date of the editor's birthday, ought to be in charge. Besides, she could write so much better than Branwell. For months she coaxed and argued and finally persuaded her brother to try his hand at issuing a newspaper instead. "*Blackwood's Young Men's Magazine* Edited by the Genius C.B." soon appeared. Decidedly it was an improvement over Branwell's efforts, for already Charlotte possessed a grasp of character, a flair for vivid description and realistic dialogue, and a strong satirical streak that her brother could not match. Poor Branwell's prose was always to be sober, ponderous, and rather stuffy, and Charlotte had the gracelessness to make fun of his laborious style in the usurped periodical. Glass Town politics, feuds, scandals, literary disputes, love affairs—all became more real to the young author than Tabby baking bread in the kitchen or the rain-soaked village streets outside the parsonage walls. Only London politics offered as much excitement, and we find Charlotte interrupting her editing to write:

> I remember the day when the *Intelligence Extraordinary* came with Mr Peel's speech in it, containing the terms on which the Catholics were to be let in! With what eagerness Papa tore off the cover, and how we all gathered round him, and with what breathless anxiety we listened, as one by one they were disclosed, and explained, and argued upon so ably, and so well; and then when it was all out, how aunt said that she thought it was excellent, and that the Catholics could do no harm with such good security. . . . But this is a digression.[5]

Thus did Charlotte thrive in the masculine world of the *Young Men, Our Fellows,* and the *Islanders*—and dominate it. It was she who initiated the plays by seizing the largest and handsomest soldier, crying, "This shall be the Duke!" Her hero was the man of the hour, the most admired figure in Europe. We have Mr. Brontë's evidence that in the plays "the Duke of Wellington, my daughter Charlotte's hero, was sure to come off conqueror," so that Mr. Brontë himself was obliged to step in and settle the heated disputes. Charlotte aggressively took over the *Young Men's Magazine,* and then, aware of her superior abilities, mocked Branwell's cruder efforts. In writing the Glass Town chronicles, she dealt not with domesticity but with war, politics, coffeehouse intrigues, exploration, and murder. As a genie, she wielded the power of life and death over her subjects. The earth trembled where she walked, oceans groaned, firm mountains shook, and rivers in terror forsook their channels. It was a heady existence.

And then she was rudely shaken from this turbulent dream world. Mr. Brontë fell seriously ill with congestion of the lungs, and although he recovered in time, the precariousness of his daughters' situation was brought sharply home to him. Branwell as a male could make his way somehow in society, but unless Charlotte, Emily, and Anne had some kind of formal education his death would leave them destitute. He communicated his fears in a letter to Elizabeth Firth, now Mrs. Franks, who remained friendly even though she had rejected him as a husband. She, in turn, consulted the Atkinsons, a childless couple, friends of the Brontës from Thornton days, and Charlotte's godparents. A proposal soon arrived that Charlotte should be sent with the financial help of the Atkinsons to a school personally known to them: Roe Head, the Misses Wooler's institution, some twenty miles from Haworth.

Chief Genius Tallii must have been stricken at the news, much as she recognized the necessity of the plan, and the other genii dismayed at the possible destruction of their fantasy world without its leader. Branwell, her closest collaborator, would miss her most keenly, yet he felt a glow of satisfaction at the thought of taking command again.

Having handed over the management of Glass Town to Branwell, Charlotte set out for Roe Head in a covered cart. It was a bleak January day and her heart was heavy as a stone. To the girls who observed her arrival from the schoolroom window, she hardly appeared a shaker of thrones or a wielder of lightning. "I first saw her," wrote one of them, "coming out of a covered cart, in very old-fashioned clothes, and looking very cold and miserable. She was coming to school at Miss Wooler's. When she appeared in the schoolroom her dress was changed, but just as old. She looked a little, old woman, so shortsighted that she always appeared to be seeking something, and moving her head from side to side to catch a sight of it. She was very shy and nervous, and spoke with a strong Irish accent. When a book was given her she dropped her head over it till her nose nearly touched it, and when she was told to hold her head up, up went the book after it, still close to her nose, so that it was not possible to help laughing."[6]

New impressions numbed Charlotte at first. Roe Head itself was an old and spacious building set behind gates facing the Bradford and Huddersfield turnpike. From the easy slope of Mirfield Moor it overlooked the deep valley of the Calder and the old oak woods of Kirklees, mysterious with ruins of an ancient Cistercian nunnery and nuns' graves and legends of Robin Hood. These tales lingered despite the blue smoke from the cloth mills of Huddersfield that now rose in the distance. But the fairies that used to dance in the valley on moonlit nights had disappeared and any old Yorkshire woman could tell how "it wur the factories as had driven 'em away."

Inside the school, the mellow oak paneling, bow windows, deep window seats, and curiously winding passages were at once comfortable and intriguing. Margaret Wooler, the eldest of the four sisters and head of the establishment, was an imposing woman, short and stout, but graceful. Her fluent, sweet voice, embroidered white woolen dresses, and long hair, plaited and wound into a coronet, gave her the air of a lady abbess, and she treated her ten pupils with a dignified kindness. By the end of the week, however, the misery of homesick-

24 UNQUIET SOUL

ness gnawed at Charlotte unbearably, and hiding herself in an empty
schoolroom while the other girls shouted at a rough-and-tumble game
of "French and English" outside on the lawn, she gave way to bitter
tears. Here she was found by a new girl just come that morning.

> Arriving at school about a week after the general assembling of the
> pupils, I was not expected to accompany them when the time came
> for their daily exercise, but while they were out, I was led into the
> schoolroom, and quietly left to make my observations. . . . turning
> to the window to observe the look-out I became aware for the first
> time that I was not alone; there was a silent, weeping, dark little figure
> in the large bay-window; she must, I thought, have risen from the
> floor. . . . A crimson cloth covered the long table down the centre
> of the room, which helped, no doubt, to hide the shrinking little fig-
> ure from my view. I was touched and troubled at once to see her so
> sad and so tearful.
>
> I said *shrinking*, because her attitude, when I saw her, was that of
> one who wished to hide both herself and her grief. She did not shrink,
> however, when spoken to, but in very few words confessed, she was
> "home-sick." After a little of such comfort as could be offered, it was
> suggested to her that there was a possibility of her too having to com-
> fort the speaker by and by for the same cause. A faint quivering smile
> then lighted her face; the tear-drops fell; we silently took each other's
> hands, and at once we felt that genuine sympathy which always con-
> soles, even though it be unexpressed.[7]

Mary Taylor and Ellen Nussey, the two girls who much later recorded their first impressions of the fourteen-year-old Charlotte, were
to become her best friends. But friendship came slowly to her. She
was an oddity at Roe Head, a misfit in almost every respect. She was
poor, and lacking in important connections. She was unattractive—
thin, stunted, meager; sallow of complexion with dry, frizzy-looking
hair screwed up in tight ugly curls. Her dresses were old, rusty, and
dark, and mended. Extreme nearsightedness and her refusal to wear
glasses imprisoned her in a narrow world from which she peered
anxiously and shyly. She loathed games, and always stood apart at
recreation time, or sat under the trees, preferably with a book. She
was physically feeble in everything. Her appetite was small and finick-
ing. She could eat no meat and had to have special portions fixed for
her lunches.

While the others took the business of learning casually, Charlotte
was always conscious of the heavy obligations laid upon her by this
opportunity at Roe Head. She felt that as the eldest child she must
succeed. She denied herself all pleasure and relaxation. When twilight
fell and the other girls had left their books and gathered around the
fireplace to laugh and tell stories, Charlotte still crouched in the bay

window, straining to make out the pages of a French or grammar book, until she was jokingly accused of being able to see in the dark. She took double lessons upon herself and was intensely disturbed if her partner in studies was unprepared, for this wasted the precious hours she had set aside after regular lessons to work on her own. When a fellow pupil fell ill and the other girls took turns at sitting with the invalid, Charlotte would not, for this seemed like idleness to her and she would not allow herself that luxury.

Many of the students thought her ignorant at first because she did not have a grasp of the conventional facts of geography or grammar. To her intense shame, she had been placed in the lowest class upon her arrival at Roe Head. Goaded by this humiliation as well as her determination to train herself for governess work, she quickly outstripped her schoolfellows until she stood at the head of the class—a position she never afterward relinquished. At the end of the first half year Charlotte bore off the silver medal awarded by Miss Wooler for fulfillment of duties and also won three scholastic prizes, tangible proofs of the countless hours she had bent earnestly over her schoolbooks.

But there were not many bright moments for Charlotte during the first months at Roe Head. Despite the slowly flowering friendship of Mary Taylor and Ellen Nussey, she was devastatingly lonely. At Cowan Bridge she had had at least the companionship of Elizabeth, Maria, and Emily; here, at this humane and honest institution, she was essentially alone. Removed from the close, approving circle of brother and sisters, she lost confidence, not in her scholastic abilities, but in herself as a person. She brooded much on her dead sisters, on their perfections and their goodness. Often when she and her new friend Ellen Nussey were quite alone, she would talk of these sisters, her voice intense with adoration. "She described Maria as a little mother among the rest," said Ellen, "superhuman in goodness and cleverness. But the most touching of all were the revelations of [Maria's] sufferings—how she suffered with the sensibility of a grown-up person, and endured with a patience and fortitude that were Christ-like."[8] And Charlotte would sob, suffering herself under the vivid memory of her sisters' deaths and the burden of her own loneliness.

In moments of extreme anguish she imagined herself rejected not only by her schoolmates but by these same beloved sisters. To Mary Taylor, her other companion, Charlotte confided a disturbing dream: "She told me, early one morning, that she had just been dreaming: she had been told that she was wanted in the drawing-room, and it was Maria and Elizabeth. I was eager for her to go on, and when she said there was no more, I said, 'But go on! *Make it out!* I know you can.' She said she would not; she wished she had not dreamed, for it did not go on nicely; they were changed; they had forgotten what they used to care for. They were very fashionably dressed, and began criticizing the room, etc."[9]

The dream disturbed Charlotte so very deeply that she never forgot it. Almost twenty-five years later she used it in *Villette* to climax her heroine's nervous collapse from the combined effects of loneliness and emotional and sexual starvation. Alone in the vast dormitory of a school closed for vacation, Lucy Snowe wakes from the same dream. Trembling in terror, she rises on her knees in bed. "Some fearful hours went over me: indescribably was I torn, racked and oppressed in mind. Amidst the horrors of that dream I think the worst lay here. Methought the well-loved dead, who had loved *me* well in life, met me elsewhere, alienated. . . ."[10]

Gradually, however, scholastic achievement and the steadily growing respect and affection of the small group at Roe Head reassured Charlotte. Her single-minded drive to excel might have alienated her schoolmates, but it did not. They soon came to understand that she was not motivated by personal pride or competitiveness—even though she never *would* whisper a correct answer to a floundering schoolmate —but that she was haunted by a keen sense of duty. She *must* succeed: her education was a gift; loved ones at home relied on her; the necessity of earning her own bread stared her coldly in the face. The near-sighted creature in the dark, rusty dresses was still an oddity, but an oddity to be respected and perhaps pitied a little. Her fierce integrity won them all. Those few who came to know her well found, of course, that she was not the benighted creature they had thought her, but a traveler in undreamed-of lands. She amazed them by her knowledge of painting, drawing, politics, Scripture, literary criticism, and poetry. "List of painters whose works I wish to see," she had written at thirteen. "Guido Reni, Julio Romano, Titian, Raphael, Michael Angelo, Correggio, Annibal Carracci, Leonardo da Vinci, Fra Bartolomeo, Carlo Cignani, Vandyke, Rubens, Bartolomeo Ramerghi." "What do you see in it?" curious schoolmates would ask, as Charlotte bent long over a painting or a drawing, her eyes close to the paper. "She could always see plenty, and explained it very well," said Mary Taylor. "She made poetry and drawing at least exceedingly interesting to me; and then I got the habit, which I have yet, of referring mentally to her opinion on all matters of that kind . . ."[11]

Only rarely did her schoolmates see the other side of Charlotte's character—the powerful, imaginative, creative side. To Mary Taylor she had confided the secret of the *Young Men's Magazine,* had told her one of the tales from it, and promised to show her some of the tiny manuscripts. But later she retracted the promise and Mary could never persuade her to bring any of the tiny journals to school. She also confessed their habit of "making out"—of inventing histories and plays—although she probably did not admit how strongly this fantasy world gripped their lives. The pragmatic Mary was interested but skeptical: could such an inward existence be healthy? "You are like growing potatoes in a cellar," she told Charlotte. To which Charlotte replied sadly, "Yes! I know we are!"

But Charlotte's violent imagination could not be totally suppressed. One evening, shortly after the illness of the fellow pupil mentioned above, when the girls were gathered together without supervision, Charlotte submitted to the temptation to "make out" for the girls. She began to weave a tale, a chilling account of the wanderings of a somnambulist. Ellen Nussey remembered the event very vividly: "She brought together all the horrors her imagination could create, from surging seas, raging breakers, towering castle walls, high precipices, invisible chasms and dangers. Having wrought these materials to the highest pitch of effect, she brought out, in almost cloud-height, her somnambulist, walking on shaking turrets,—all told in a voice that conveyed more than words alone can express. A shivering terror seized the recovered invalid; a pause ensued; then a subdued cry of pain came from Charlotte herself, with a terrified command to others to call for help."[12]

The spellbinder had hypnotized herself. Was it only the somnambulist Charlotte saw? Or herself, precariously skirting chasms, the solid ground of reality crumbling away, always in peril of losing her footing and plunging headlong into the dangerous realm of fantasy? The experience sobered her. She never told another horror story and, for weeks after, could not be persuaded to tell any stories at all. Finally Miss Woller's threat to punish anyone guilty of "late talking" silenced Charlotte altogether.

She was called upon once more to use her eloquence, however. The girls hit upon the idea of having a sort of coronation program during a rare half holiday. Charlotte, an expert at devising ceremonial pomp for the imaginary royalty of Glass Town, drew up the program, issued the invitations, and chose titles for the participants. Miss Wooler's younger sister consented to be crowned as the queen, and Charlotte wrote a graceful little presentation speech for the girl chosen to bestow the crown:

> Powerful Queen! accept this Crown, the symbol of dominion, from the hands of your faithful and affectionate subjects! And if their earnest and united wishes have any efficacy, you will long be permitted to reign over this peaceful, though circumscribed empire.
>
> [Signed, etc., etc.],<br>Your loyal subjects.[13]

The ceremony was climaxed by a quadrille and Scottish reels and a special supper presided over by an imperious servant—Mary Taylor's younger sister Martha, the liveliest girl at Roe Head, disguised as a magnificent mulatto. Charlotte could not eat heartily and did not dance, but in her quiet way she reveled in the make-believe. Slaves, queens, and coronations were quite in her line.

Charlotte was painfully slow to believe in protestations of friendship. Branded by the loss of her mother and sisters, deeply insecure, she shrank from giving her affection. *Should* it be ventured; *could* it be returned? Mary and Ellen persevered, and Charlotte's almost pathological reserve thawed. And once declared, her affection never wavered.

Mary Taylor and Ellen Nussey were very different personalities, having little in common except family homes a mile apart and a strong attraction to Charlotte. Social background, politics, and religion decisively divided the two families: the Taylors were cloth manufacturers, Radicals, and Dissenters; the Nusseys "country," Tory, and Church of England. Both families were experiencing financial difficulties, but rich relatives had come to the Nusseys' rescue, whereas Mary Taylor wore remade dresses. Mary was intelligent, keen, and outspoken, with passionate convictions and an independent mind. She was, in her own words, "of the furious Radical party," and argued politics vehemently with Charlotte in that crucial year of 1832. Mary rejoiced in the passing of the first Reform Bill, a measure granting the franchise to the male lower middle class and breaking up the Tory monopoly by revising the electoral system so that large industrial cities were represented in Parliament as well as landowners. Charlotte opposed the bill. In 1831 she had written to Branwell, "Lately I had begun to think that I had lost all the interest which I used formerly to take in politics, but the extreme pleasure I felt at the news of the Reform Bill's being thrown out by the House of Lords, and the expulsion or resignation of Earl Grey, etc., etc., convinced me that I have not as yet lost *all* my penchant for politics." Although she took most of her political opinions from her father, Charlotte differed from him on this issue: Mr. Brontë, "a warm and true friend to Church and State," favored the bill, understanding that its measures were moderate and a prudent safeguard against more radical reform.[14]

Charlotte exulted too soon; events were reversed; the bill passed, and her hero, the Duke of Wellington, was ousted. He was succeeded by the more liberal Robert Peel, a man Charlotte detested because, she was convinced, he acted not from principle like the Iron Duke but from expediency. "How could any of them trust one another? they are all of them rascals," retorted Mary, showing much wisdom, since the "reformers" were scarcely less conservative than the high Tory ministry they replaced. But Charlotte judged the situation subjectively, swayed by admiration for her hero. And Mary lost the argument, going down before Charlotte's eloquence, violent partisanship, and minute acquaintance with every movement of the great Duke.

When Charlotte visited Mary's home near Roe Head, the Red House in Gomersal, she did not win many verbal battles, however. Instead she found herself in the midst of a large, noisy, outspoken family—all either feminists, non-conformists, or political radicals. To her surprise, she found the Taylors intolerant of her beloved poetry, dismissing it scornfully as impractical and unrealistic. To her astonishment, she found that the children—Joshua, John, Joseph, Waring, Mary, and Martha—spoke out freely in front of their parents, disagreeing without fear. No masks in this house. Charlotte listened quietly but was not overwhelmed. People who possess strong convictions seldom fear them in others—and Charlotte had plenty of unshakable convictions of her own. Rather she was stimulated by the intellectual electricity generated in this lively family and years later wrote, "The society of the Taylors is one of the most rousing pleasures I have known."

Besides, she found the Taylors as cultured as her own family despite their scorn of poetry, and much more cosmopolitan. She observed the father, Joshua Taylor, closely, fascinated by the contradictions of his character. Here was a rough Yorkshireman who spoke fluent French and Italian; a cloth manufacturer who labored over dull ledgers yet traveled abroad to collect works of art; a rustic and a man of the world. Her heart expanded: so people from their remote part of England *could* know that fine world of painting, music, and sculpture she so hungered after. And she drank in the visual beauties of the Red House: the warm red brick from which it took its name, the trellised vines shadowing the walls, the black and white Dutch tiles flagging the entrance hall, the purple and amber stained glass windows in the back parlor "glittering around a grave-tinted medallion in the center of each, representing the suave head of William Shakespeare, and the serene head of John Milton."[15] The Taylors were a rich, colorful episode in Charlotte's life. One wishes she could have known more people like them.

Ellen Nussey was the other side of the coin. Portraits of Ellen and Mary Taylor as older women exist and reveal their very different characters. Mary is all strong nose and determined mouth and serious, forthright eyes; Ellen is gently rounded with soft, silver hair and a soft, refined, rather vacuous face. The keen Charlotte was perfectly conscious of Ellen's intellectual limitations, and also of her strengths. "When I first saw Ellen I did not care for her," she wrote (compare

Ellen's account of their meeting and the instant sympathy between them); "—we were schoolfellows—in course of time we learnt each others faults and good points—we were contrasts—still we suited —affection was first a germ, then a sapling—then a strong tree: now —no new friend, however lofty or profound in intellect . . . could be to me what Ellen is, yet she is no more than a conscientious, observant, calm well-bred Yorkshire girl. She is without romance—if she attempts to read poetry—or poetic prose aloud—I am irritated and deprive her of her book—if she talks of it I stop my ears—but she is good—she is true—she is faithful and I love her."[16]

Thus Charlotte gravitated toward two girls who in their separate characters embodied two aspects of her own very ambivalent character. Ellen was a gentlewoman, conservative, Tory, a girl with a pious regard for the traditional. She was loyal, she was dutiful—and Charlotte was all of these. Above all she was loving, and Charlotte craved love and gave love as only a person who is uncertain of winning it can. Mary Taylor was aggressive, independent, unyielding, intellectual, strong-willed, and energetic—and Charlotte was all of these as well. She quickly learned to expect only blunt honesty from Mary: "I think you are very ugly," Mary told her about this time. This was rough treatment, but Charlotte preferred roughness to hypocrisy. "You did me a great deal of good, Polly, so don't repent of it," she told Mary, who apologized, years later, for her impertinence.[17] In neither girl did she find a spark of her creative genius, but she did not need sympathy from that source: at home were Branwell, Emily, and Anne.

Fortified with the friendship of Mary and Ellen, the approval of Miss Wooler, and the satisfaction of solid achievement, Charlotte thus passed a year and a half at Roe Head. She was far from unhappy. Yet the best moment, the only really joyous occasion, had been the day that Miss Wooler announced she had a visitor in the parlor. It was Branwell, her dear brother, wrapped in the glamorous mantle of Glass Town adventure that she had so reluctantly put off the day she left for Roe Head. He had walked the twenty miles from Haworth just to see her. Pacing the grounds with him arm in arm, talking eagerly, she realized that her whole sojourn at Roe Head had been, after all, an exile.

But now at last it was time to leave. She had learned all the Misses Wooler had to teach of grammar, geography, and the use of the globes. She could sew an exquisitely fine seam, speak a smattering of French, and sketch a rustic scene—ladylike attainments that future employers would demand of the governess. She had accomplished the task she had set for herself. She said her good-bys.

"The last day Charlotte was at school," wrote Ellen Nussey, "she seemed to realize what a sedate, hard-working season it had been to her. She said, 'I should for once like to feel *out and out* a school-girl; I wish something would happen! Let us run around the fruit garden [running was what she never did]; perhaps we shall meet some one, or we may have a fine for trespass.' She evidently was longing for some never-to-be-forgotten incident. Nothing, however, arose from her little enterprise. She had to leave school as calmly and quietly as she had there lived."[18]

# 3

## The Secret Life

At home in the quiet, scrupulously neat parsonage, the grandfather clock on the stair landing ticking away methodically, Papa in the parlor, and Tabby peeling potatoes in the kitchen, Charlotte revived. To Emily and Anne she had a new luster: she took her place as the undisputed leader, older, wiser, and experienced. They pressed her eagerly to share her books and her learning with them. The four were no longer hand in glove, however. During Charlotte's absence, Emily and Anne had broken away from the old play world of Glass Town or Verdopolis, as they had rechristened it. Tiring of always following Charlotte's and Branwell's lead, weary of Branwell's eternal wars, blood baths, and revolutions, they were now deep in a saga of their own invention played out in the new kingdom of Gondal. This dark world of persecution, murder, illegitimacy, adultery, suicide, and passion—unlike Charlotte and Branwell's kingdom—was a feminine world, dominated by a woman called variously Rosina, Alcona, or Augusta. Their imaginative lives had thus drifted beyond Charlotte's reach, and though the three sisters were bound by ties strong as iron, Charlotte had no share in the intense, twinlike attachment that now united Emily and Anne. Although Branwell had always been her closest companion, this locked door must have grieved her.

Branwell had changed. From a childish commander of imaginary soldiers he had become a youthful creator of villains, Byronic heroes, and swashbuckling rogues. Nor did he confine this taste for large posturing to the imaginary world of Verdopolis. He was not Brontë —in Greek, thunder—for nothing. Unknown to the always incurious Mr. Brontë, Branwell, imitating Lord Byron's taste for sporting life, had taken up with the village toughs and spent many afternoons just a few steps from his father's church in rooms above the White Lion or the Black Bull, feinting, dodging, jabbing, and reveling in what he fondly imagined to be the life of the ring. In time he transferred his activities downstairs to the taproom and passed an increasing number of hours downing pints of bitters with drinking friends. So successfully did he enliven the dull village hours with his swaggering talk that he was dubbed court jester to the Black Bull. When strangers passed through Haworth, Branwell was discreetly summoned down to the inn to cheer the hour and loosen a tight Yorkshire purse. The minister's son is often the wildest boy in town, and Branwell did his best to live up to tradition, and surpass it.

Beyond a visiting acquaintance with the Heatons of Ponden House, the best family in the neighborhood, and a professional acquaintance with Mr. Theodore Dury, the rector of Keighley, Mr. Brontë, however, kept strictly to himself. "I have not tried to make any friends, nor have I met with any whose mind is congenial to my own," he told Mrs. Franks. The girls had no friends either among the Haworth people—the Feathers, Greenwoods, Pickles, Sugdens, and Townsends, worsted-manufacturing families; or the Cravens and the Murgatroyds, corn millers; or the Eccleses, Sutcliffs, Wrights, and Newsomes, wool staplers and cotton spinners.[1] They did not "visit" the poor cottage dwellers on the moors. On the other hand, they were snubbed by the small landed proprietors of the district, those families that Mrs. Gaskell described as "dwelling on one spot since Q. Eliz.—and lately adding marvelously to their incomes by using the water power of the becks in the woollen manufacture . . . sprung up during the last 50 years"; arrogant, uneducated, unrestrained families who "build grand houses, and live in the kitchens, own hundreds of thousands of pounds and yet bring up their sons with only just enough learning to qualify them for over-lookers during their father's lifetime and greedy grasping money-hunters after his death."[2] The girls thus remained shy and withdrawn, and so timid that when they went for an afternoon to Keighley or Leeds in their heavy boots and colored stockings and old-fashioned dresses they clung together, shrinking up against the shop buildings out of people's way, speaking to no one. Branwell, who rubbed shoulders, drank, and caroused in the village, seemed to them marked out for a glorious career.

Glimpses of his reckless life of adventure fascinated Charlotte but also amused her, for she could not quite take her brother's heroics seriously. "His form was that of a lad of sixteen, his face that of a man of twenty-five, his hair red, his features not bad, for he had a Roman nose, small mouth, and well-turned chin; his figure, too, though diminutive, was perfectly symmetrical, and of this he seemed not unconscious. . . ." But Patrick Benjamin Wiggins, the portrait of her brother she created half mockingly, half good-naturedly during these years, falls something short of the dashing tough he imagines himself: "A pair of spectacles garnished his nose, and through these he was constantly gazing at Flanagan [a boxer], whose breadth of shoulder appeared to attract his sincere admiration, as every now and then he touched his own with the tip of his fore-finger, and pushed out his small contracted chest to make it appear broader."[3]

At the same time, Branwell's new sophistication quite accorded with her own changing imaginative life. No immediate prospect of employment offering, the quiet of Haworth closed over her head. The spell of Verdopolis reasserted itself stronger than ever, for now the simple adventurousness of the child was replaced by the romantic, sexual yearnings of the sixteen-year-old girl. The old wars and political intrigues no longer satisfied. Gradually her old idol, the white-haired, fatherly Duke of Wellington, faded from her imagination to be replaced by his magnificent son, Arthur Augustus Wellesley, Marquis of Douro. Douro in turn gradually lost his filial aspect, evolving into the Duke of Zamorna, dark, cruel, sexually magnetic, and sinning. Unconsciously she turned from her father to his son to a stranger. The new branches shot from the old tree, however: her male idol continued to be masterful, domineering: she could not separate sexuality from domination since she could not free herself from the powerful authority of her father.

Charlotte returned to close literary collaboration with Branwell but, feeling an adolescent's need for privacy, withdrew from Verdopolis into a kingdom of her own. She called it Angria and created Zamorna and his wife Mary Percy king and queen of the new domain. She wrote often during these years as Lord Charles Albert Florian Wellesley, Douro's virtuous younger brother: through his disapproving eyes she could voice her own objections to Douro-Zamorna's sinful career even while inventing it. Although she still brought out her productions under the auspices of Captain Tree, publisher, her writings gradually assumed the form of long tales rather than the miscellanies of the *Young Men's Magazine*. Leaving Branwell to plot wars against her kingdom and chronicle the misadventures of Zamorna's father-in-law and foe, the devilish Percy, she turned more and more to the theme of love.

She was sixteen. Long ago she had applied to her mirror and with her usual unflinching honesty taken to herself the truth. At twelve she had decided she would never marry; the intervening years had not given her more confidence. "I am not grown a bit, but as short and dumpy as ever," she cried to Ellen. She blamed her tiny frame on the physical privations she had suffered at Cowan Bridge; she felt ashamed that she still wore children's underwear. In truth, she was like a small sparrow. Her feet were tiny and narrow, her boots mere slips of leather. Her hands were tiny, her fingers delicate and tapered, with smooth, shining, perfectly oval nails. Her hair, naturally smooth, brown, and glossy, was still frizzed into unbecoming curls. Her face was plain, almost ill-featured: the forehead prominent, the nose large, the wide mouth uneven. Her nearsighted eyes, hidden behind wire-rimmed spectacles, were beautiful—large, reddish brown, serious, and glowing. The total effect of her neat little person was far from displeasing, but Charlotte believed it was, and shrank when a stranger's eyes turned toward her.

In Angria, lack of beauty, power, and success did not matter. "How few would believe that from sources purely imaginary such happiness could be derived!" she confided to her diary. "Pen cannot portray the deep interest of the scenes, of the continued train of events, I have witnessed in my little room with the low, narrow bed and bare, white-washed walls . . . There I have sat on the low bedstead, my eyes fixed on the window, through which appeared no other landscape than a monotonous stretch of moorland, a grey church tower rising from the center of a churchyard so filled with graves that the rank weeds and coarse grass scarce had room to shoot up between the monuments. . . . Such was the picture that threw its reflections upon my eye but communicated no impression to my heart."[4]

Angria dominated but could not completely drive out the world. "On Tuesday next," she wrote Ellen Nussey, "we shall have all the female teachers of the Sunday-school to tea." The girl who created the drinking, cursing Zamorna, lover of dozens of women, was also the parson's daughter. Yet while she poured tea with her tiny hands and engaged the stiff and earnest ladies in Sunday school chat, her mind might have strayed to more entertaining realms . . .

"Beautiful hypocrite," said he, and paused again, while his finely cut lip quivered with the strongest emotion.

"What is the matter?" asked Lady Emily faintly. "Have I been too forward, too ardent in my expressions of pleasure at seeing you again after so long an absence?"

"Cease this unworthy acting," said her lover sternly. . . . "Another, and doubtless in your opinion a higher prize, has been ensnared by your false though incomparable loveliness. . . . But," he continued in a voice of thunder, while all the lightnings of jealousy gleamed in his fierce dark eyes, "I will not tamely give you up to the scoundrel who has dared to supplant me. No! He shall have an even struggle. He shall wade through blood to obtain his stolen reward."[5]

Ties formed at Roe Head also bound her to the world: her friendships with Ellen Nussey and Mary Taylor continued to flourish. Schoolboy friendships were notorious in early nineteenth-century

England for their emotional intensity. If the sight of two boys walking together locked arm in arm raised any doubts, these could be silenced by referring to the great male friends of antiquity: David and Jonathan, Damon and Pythias, Achilles and Patroclus. Since girls were not considered capable of such exalted feeling, and were seldom sent to school, their school friendships went unsung. Charlotte felt for Ellen, however, some of that fervent and uncritical affection that marked adolescent relationships in that golden, pre-Freudian age. "Farewell my *dear dear dear* Ellen," she gushes, ending a letter. Yet slender finances rather cramped their style. Ellen writes, regretting that high postage rates prevent her sending Charlotte a lock of her hair; Charlotte replies, confessing in turn that for the same reason she is unable to oblige darling Ellen with a lock of hers.

In 1832, Charlotte thus began two correspondences that were to last her lifetime. Her letters to Ellen reveal only a fragment of her personality since she tuned them to her friend's intellectual and emotional range. To Mary she poured out her rebellion and anger, her intellectual hunger, her adoration for the world of books, art, poetry, history, and politics. Ellen Nussey kept most of Charlotte's letters; Mary Taylor destroyed almost all because she believed they were too revealing. And undoubtedly Charlotte's letters to Mary *would* have confirmed the Victorian opinion that Charlotte Brontë was eccentric, crude, and not really a lady.[6]

Gradually Ellen became aware that Charlotte's letters to Mary did not resemble Charlotte's letters to her. She pouted, charging her friend with discrimination. Charlotte answered lightly but never denied the charge. "Now Ellen," she writes after an uncharacteristic outburst on politics, "laugh heartily at all this rodomontade, but you have brought it on yourself; don't you remember telling me to write such letters to you as I write to Mary Taylor? Here's a specimen; hereafter should follow a long disquisition on books, but I'll spare you that."[7]

Once, in the midst of an emotional crisis, she did write to Ellen as she wrote to Mary. "Roe Head, 1836: Last Saturday afternoon being in one of my sentimental humours I sat down and wrote to you such a note as I ought to have written to none but M. Taylor who is nearly as mad as myself; to-day when I glanced it over it occurred to me that Ellen's calm eye would look at this with scorn, so I determined to concoct some production more fit for the inspection of common sense."[8] And Charlotte tore up the letter.

Occasionally she did write to Ellen about books, not to discuss them with an equal, but to recommend from her loftier experience works that might widen the mind of her friend. "If you like poetry let it be first rate," she lectures, "Milton, Shakespeare, Thomson, Goldsmith,

Pope (if you will though I don't admire him) Scott, Byron, Campbell, Wordsworth and Southey. Now Ellen don't be startled at the names of Shakespeare and Byron. Both these were great men and their works are like themselves, you will know how to choose the good and avoid the evil, the finest passages are always the purest, the bad are invariably revolting you will never wish to read them over twice. Omit the Comedies of Shakespeare and the Don Juan, perhaps the Cain of Byron though the later is a magnificent Poem, and read the rest fearlessly. That must indeed be a depraved mind which can gather evil from Henry the 8th, Richard 3d from Macbeth and Hamlet and Julius Cesar, Scott's sweet, wild, romantic Poetry can do you no harm nor can Wordsworth nor Campbell's nor Southey's, the greater part at least of his, some is certainly exceptionable."[9]

Must this patronizing censorship be considered hypocrisy from the creator of amoral Angria? Not so. Charlotte had taken the measure of Ellen Nussey and accurately gauged the limits of her sophistication. Moreover, she knew Ellen's conventional home was not her home: whatever Mr. Brontë's limitations as a parent, he did not restrict his children's reading; they did not have to devour "adult" books guiltily behind closed bedroom doors. Most children did, for England, recoiling from the excesses of romanticism, was fast approaching the Victorian age. Family reading lists excluded novels and plays, heavily endorsed the Bible, *Mrs. Trimmer's Family Magazine*, Hanway's *Virtu in Humble Life*, and Barbauld's *Hymns*. Byron was bad, and James Plumptre, a more assiduous expurgator than Bowdler, took exception to Shakespeare's indecencies, substituting "cardamine" for "ladysmocks," "turtles' coo" for "turtles' tread," and altering "Under the greenwood tree/Who loves to lie with me" to the more uplifting "Who loves to *work* with me."[10]

She did not share her dream world of Angria even with Mary Taylor, although she confessed its existence to this friend who was "almost as mad as herself." She knew that Mary was too pragmatic and unimaginative to condone such escapism. Ellen, on the other hand, would have been shocked, offended, and seriously concerned for her friend's soul. Charlotte wanted neither reaction. Of the visions that swam before her eyes as she gazed from her bedroom window over the bleak churchyard—of the flashing-eyed, cynical heroes, the brandy and champagne they tossed off, the oaths they swore, the swords they drew, the women they embraced—she therefore breathed not a word. Her life, she told Ellen, was strictly commonplace. "Haworth, July 21st, 1832: You ask me to give you a description of the manner in which I have passed every day since I left School: this is soon done, as an account of one day is an account of all. In the morning from nine o'clock to half-past twelve, I instruct my Sisters and draw, then we walk till dinner, after dinner I sew till tea time, and after tea I either read, write, do a little fancy work or draw, as I please. Thus in one delightful, though somewhat monotonous course my life is passed. I have only been out to tea twice since I came home."[11]

Ellen, instantly sympathizing with what she considered a dreary existence, invited Charlotte to Rydings that September. It was the first of a steady stream of invitations over the years, most of which Charlotte for one reason or another had to refuse. This invitation, however, she accepted eagerly. "When I consulted Papa and Aunt about it, they both said they could not possibly have any objection . . . I think, dearest Ellen, our friendship is destined to form an exception to the general rule regarding school friendships."[12]

Branwell escorted Charlotte to Ellen's home in a two-wheeled, one-horse gig, the only conveyance for hire in Haworth besides the covered cart that had carried her to Roe Head. The sight of the Nussey mansion rising imposingly in the midst of green acres—its battlements, its rookery, its fruit gardens and plantations—drove the impressionable fifteen-year-old Branwell into a joyous frenzy. He walked about staring at everything and exclaiming enthusiastically over the fine old chestnut trees, the turret-roofed manor house, the velvet-green lawns, the great rookery. These were friends worth having. "I'm leaving you in Paradise!" he told Charlotte; "if you're not intensely happy here you never will be!" While Branwell stared and exclaimed, Ellen took note of the strong sympathy between Charlotte and her small, gawky, redheaded brother. Even though Charlotte was much quieter than the flamboyant Branwell, they seemed to think, speak, and feel as one. Obviously Charlotte was excessively proud of her brother, imagining for him a bright future of genius although only the drudgery of governessing lay ahead for her.

The visit was as happy for Charlotte as any absence from Haworth could be. That is to say, she suffered acutely except for the time she was alone with Ellen. Ellen was one of the youngest of thirteen children—four sisters, nine brothers; her father was dead; her mother and the older daughters and sons—Ann, Mercy, Sarah, Richard, Henry, and George—were probably at home during Charlotte's visit. To the family she grew somewhat accustomed, although privately finding them a dull lot; but when visitors drove up the well-rolled carriage road, she fled with Ellen to the fruit garden or the plantations. She shrank in a room full of strangers, in pain when anyone's eyes turned toward her, terrified when a stranger leaned across and put a question to her. "One day," relates Ellen, "on being led in to dinner by a stranger, she trembled and nearly burst into tears."

The next summer (visitors were warned away from Haworth in

winter), Ellen returned the visit. To the civilized, elegant, and sheltered Miss Nussey of Rydings the journey appeared wild and hazard-
ous. She rode in an open gig through rough, dipping moorlands
scarred by straggling stone fences and dotted with sheep. As the gig
neared Haworth the descent became so steep that Ellen was forced to
dismount and the manservant to lead the horse carefully down. No
sooner were they down than the rough, stone-paved road began to
climb steeply into the village; the horse took it slowly, hoofs catching
at the cobbles. At the top of the village they were directed left into
an entry so narrow it just admitted the gig. There was the gray-towered church, the churchyard, the short cobbled lane, the parsonage
gateway—and Charlotte herself, small and bespectacled, come to meet
her friend at the sound of rattling wheels in the lane. Inside the parsonage Miss Branwell in black silk and mob-cap waited to welcome
the visitor. There was Emily, tall, graceful, and so reserved that she
hardly looked up at Charlotte's friend with her dark gray eyes. Anne,
slighter and prettier than Emily with graceful brown curls and porcelain skin, was friendlier. Even Mr. Brontë bestirred himself and
emerged from the parlor to welcome the guest and see to the comfort
of the servant and horse. In the kitchen Ellen met the garrulous
Tabby, who took her immediately under her protective wing as just
another of her "childer" or "bairns." Ellen discreetly noted her surroundings: the bare sandstone floors, meticulously scrubbed; the dove-
colored walls and curtainless windows (Mr. Brontë had a terror of
fire); the sparse furnishings—mahogany tables, horsehair-covered
chairs, bookshelves in the parlor. Placid and well bred, Ellen accepted
the Brontës on their own terms. She had Rydings—comforting thought
—but the Brontës had talent and intellect, and she bowed to the fact.

The visit passed pleasantly, although the Brontës could offer their
guest nothing in the way of tea parties, dinners, or visiting. Meals were
simple but nourishing: Ellen observed that Emily and Anne chose
to eat the old north-country breakfast of oatmeal porridge, and insisted
on sharing it with their dog. On fine days there were rambles over the
moors. Ellen was shown the girls' favorite spots: the sudden ravines
and waterfalls that broke the monotony of the rolling moors, the surprising caches of primroses, bluebells, and heath blossoms. Stripping
off boots and stockings, Branwell, Emily, and Anne unhesitatingly
forded the streams. Charlotte, always physically timid, and the ladylike Ellen waited on the bank until the three bolder ones placed step-
pingstones for them to cross. Every flower, every moss, every linnet
fluttering above the heath delighted the Brontës. Ellen discovered that
it was only out on the moors that Emily lost her reserve; only nature
could spring the catch that held her in check.

"One long ramble made in these early days was far away over the moors to a spot familiar to Emily and Anne, which they called 'The Meeting of the Waters,'" Ellen reminisced. "It was a small oasis of emerald green turf, broken here and there by small clear springs; a few large stones served as resting-places; seated here, we were hidden from all the world, nothing appearing in view but miles and miles of heather, a glorious blue sky, and brightening sun. A fresh breeze wafted on us its exhilarating influence; we laughed and made mirth of each other, and settled we would call ourselves the quartette. Emily, half reclining on a slab of stone, played like a young child with the tadpoles in the water, making them swim about, and then fell to moralizing on the strong and the weak, the brave and the cowardly, as she chased them with her hand. No serious care or sorrow had so far cast its gloom on nature's youth and buoyancy, and nature's simplest offerings were fountains of pleasure and enjoyment."[13]

Every evening Mr. Brontë assembled the household at eight o'clock for family worship. Ellen found him awesome with his courteous yet reserved manner, his simple, rigid routine, his snow-white hair and white silk cravat that muffled his neck up to his chin. The cravat was his one extravagance: it had begun as a modest affair, but year after year, as Mr. Brontë cut up more and more yards of silk, always adding to the original while not subtracting an inch, the cravat wound higher and higher until eventually it enveloped half his head. The monstrous cocoonlike affair became his trade mark, adding to the solemnity of his tall, spare figure and his stern face with the large nose, pale blue eyes, and glinting steel-rimmed glasses. He was prone to bronchial attacks, and no doubt thus rationalized this reckless expenditure in silk. At nine o'clock he locked and barred the parsonage door, paused at the sitting-room door to advise the "children" not to sit up late, and took his way upstairs, halting on the landing to wind the clock, an evening ritual.

The girls were then free to pursue their own pleasure—to write, draw, sew, read, or talk. Doubtless Emily and Anne stole away to the kitchen or upstairs where they conspired in setting down the continuing adventures of the Gondals. Ellen noted how Emily and Anne ate together, walked together, and read and sewed together with twinlike inseparability, but she found Anne much more approachable than Emily. Anne was gentle and patient, with graceful curls clustering at her neck, violet-blue eyes, delicately penciled eyebrows, and a translucent complexion. She was the least lively sister, but her aunt's favorite, and she still sewed and studied under Miss Branwell's supervision. Emily, two years older, had been granted leave to pursue her own course. Branwell continued to study the classics with his father. Despite Charlotte's seniority and superior abilities, Branwell was clearly the center of attention and the hope of the family.

All the Brontës painted and drew, and the girls spent a great deal of time drawing and copying engravings. Charlotte particularly labored for hours a day copying mezzotints, wearing out her eyes with the close scrutiny and meticulous duplicating of thousands and thousands of tiny strokes—a process not unlike the printing of the tiny manuscripts. Later she admitted ruefully that it had been useless labor; at the time, however, she evidently believed that copying was the way to learn a craft—or perhaps she lacked the confidence to paint freely. Branwell took to oils, and Mr. Brontë hired an art teacher, William Robinson, to give all his children instruction at two shillings a lesson. The whole family believed that Branwell had talent and began to imagine a career as a portrait painter for him, a field in which Robinson himself had scored successfully. He painted his sisters, capturing a crude likeness. Today the portrait hangs in the National Portrait Gallery in London by virtue of his sisters' fame; then, however, Branwell's future seemed brightest, if only because he was a male. Unable to see, or perhaps ignoring the amateurish quality of his son's work, Mr. Brontë began to indulge visions of Branwell at the Royal Academy School in London.

Branwell himself volleyed from one passion to another, imagining himself successively a great poet, an applauded artist, a professional *bon vivant*, or, as he swayed at the keyboard of the organ, sending peals of mournful music shuddering through the cold dim church, a musical genius. Parodying her brother again as Patrick Benjamin Wiggins in a fragment of writing called "Angria and My Angrians," Charlotte mocked his lofty aspirations. "'My mind was always looking above my station,' says the haughty Wiggins. 'I was not satisfied with being a sign-painter at Howard [Haworth], as Charlotte and them things were with being sempstresses.'" With her critical mind that could pierce through pretention, Charlotte understood Branwell's egotism even while she admired and believed in him. She understood very well the place that Branwell's and Papa's masculine conventionality assigned the sisters, and her portrait of Wiggins, while humorous, is also acid:

". . . I've some people who call themselves akin to me in the shape of three girls," says Wiggins fatuously to his imaginary interlocutor, Lord Charles Albert Florian Wellesley. "They are honoured by possessing me as a brother, but I deny that they are my sisters. . . ."
"What are your sisters' names?"
"Charlotte Wiggins, [Emily] Jane Wiggins, and Anne Wiggins."
"Are they as queer as you?"
"Oh, they are miserable silly creatures not worth talking about. Charlotte's eighteen years old, a broad dumpy thing, whose head does not come higher than my elbow. Emily's sixteen, lean and scant, with

a face about the size of a penny, and Anne is nothing, absolutely nothing."

"What! Is she an idiot?"

"Next door to it."

"Humph! You're a pretty set. . . ."[14]

Not sharing the family's myopic view of his genius, Ellen was more
impressed with the Brontës' confidence in Branwell than with Branwell himself.

On Sunday Ellen went with Charlotte to hear Mr. Brontë sermonize
the congregation of St. Michael's from the same three-decker pulpit
the famous preacher William Grimshaw had won souls to Evangelicalism ninety years before. The rough appearance of the parishioners
surprised her, and she noted critically the apathy with which they listened to the prayers.

> There they sat, or leaned, in their pews; some few, perhaps, were
> resting, after a long walk over the moors. The children, many of them
> in clogs (or sabots), pattered in from the school after service had
> commenced, and pattered out again before the sermon. The sexton,
> with a long staff, continually walked round in the aisles, "knobbing"
> sleepers when he dare, shaking his head at and threatening unruly chil-
> dren; but when the sermon began there was a change. Attitudes took
> the listening forms, eyes were turned on the preacher. It was curious,
> now, to note the expression. A rustic, untaught intelligence, gleamed
> in their faces; in some, a daring, doubting, questioning look, as if they
> would like to offer some defiant objection. Mr. Brontë always ad-
> dressed his hearers in extempore style. Very often he selected a para-
> ble from one of the Gospels, which he explained in the simplest man-
> ner—sometimes going over his own words and explaining them also,
> so as to be perfectly intelligible to the lowest comprehension.[15]

Clearly, Ellen set the Brontës far apart and above the local folk
whom she evidently judged little better than savages. She little
guessed how strong a strain of strong-minded, daring, doubting Yorkshire "crudity" ran in her own Charlotte, outwardly so reserved and
ladylike. Mr. Brontë, it is true, delighted in telling strange stories
handed down to him by some of the oldest inhabitants of the neighborhood—grim, fanatical stories of cruel hatreds and deep passions that
made Ellen shiver and shrink; but the keen enthusiasm the father and
his children had for these gnarled tales Ellen put down to a kind of
objective interest in Yorkshire primitives as a human type. She was
able to report upon arriving home at Rydings that the Brontë family
was what she had expected from her acquaintance with Charlotte:
talented, educated, regrettably poor, but thoroughly well bred. Charlotte in turn wrote Ellen a glowing report of the impression she had

made at Haworth: Papa and Aunt now urged her seriously to model her actions and behavior after Miss Nussey's, both Emily and Anne declared "they never saw any one they liked so well," and Tabby talked "a great deal more nonsense" about her than Charlotte cared to repeat.

The years fled by. Charlotte wrote feverishly, producing more words in her seventeenth year than she would write during the rest of her life, filling tiny, hand-stitched paper books with her nervous, spidery-fine script. ("The wildest and most incoherent things," Mrs. Gaskell cried in amazement when she held the miniature books in her hands years later. "They give one the idea of creative power carried to the verge of insanity."[16]) She was eighteen, then nineteen—years of hope and promise when Love, as she later wrote, if "he comes wandering like a lost angel to our door, is at once admitted, welcomed, embraced: his quiver is not seen; if his arrows penetrate, their wound is like a thrill of new life. . . ." But Love did not come: nothing seemed to offer.

Many girls of eighteen were married and mothers. If a woman was not a wife, then she must be an old maid and take her place along with the village schoolmaster and the preacher as objects of secret scorn. There were no eligible men in Haworth, none at least that the reserved, inbred Brontës came in contact with, and Charlotte herself, having neither looks nor a dowry, was a bad match. The only men in her life were Papa and Branwell. She was *not* content to become a sempstress. Passionate, frustrated, balked, she lived more and more in Angria. The figure of Zamorna loomed gigantic over her life: "there he stood with the red firelight flashing over him, one foot advanced, his head proudly raised, his kindled eyes fixed on the opposite wall and filled with a most inspired glory," wrote Charlotte feverishly. He was all she longed to be—rich, despotic, adored, sinning, and masculine. From this deep well of imagination she thus slaked her sexual and creative thirst. Her pen flew; volume after volume was "published." While Branwell was preparing for a brilliant entry into the world, the girls were forced to retreat from it into Angria and Gondal, seeing no chance either in a career or marriage to take a solid place in society.

And then a door—a low, narrow door—opened. Miss Wooler wrote, offering Charlotte a post as assistant teacher with free schooling for another sister as part payment. Charlotte had trained herself for this opportunity, yet dreaded it. Again, however, her duty was clear. Papa was already wondering where money for Branwell's expenses in London was to come from, for he and Aunt had determined that in the fall Branwell should make a start in the painting profession at the

Academy School. Teaching at Roe Head was, after all, preferable to governessing in a strange family. She could not hide away at Haworth all her life. For independence, self-esteem, and Branwell, then.

Dear Ellen,—I had hoped to have the extreme pleasure of seeing you at Haworth this summer, but human affairs are mutable, and human resolutions must bend to the course of events—We are about to divide, break up, separate, Emily is going to school, Branwell is going to London, and I am going to be a Governess. This last determination I formed myself, knowing that I should have to take the step sometime, and "better sune as syne" to use the Scotch proverb and knowing also that Papa would have enough to do with his limited income should Branwell be placed at the Royal Academy, and Emily at Roe-Head. Where am I going to reside? you will ask—within four miles of yourself dearest at a place neither of us are wholly unacquainted with, being no other than the identical Roe-Head mentioned above. Yes I am going to teach in the very school where I was myself taught—Miss Wooler made me the offer and I preferred it to one or two proposals of Private Governess-ship which I had before received —I am sad, very sad at the thoughts of leaving home but Duty—Necessity—these are stern mistresses who will not be disobeyed. Did I not once say Ellen you ought to be thankful for your independence? I felt what I said at the time, and I repeat it now with double earnestness: if anything would cheer me, it is this idea of being so near you— surely you and Polly [Mary Taylor] will come and see me it would be wrong in me to doubt it you were never unkind yet. Emily, and I leave home on the 29th of this month, the idea of being together consoles us both somewhat, and in truth since I must enter a situation "My lines have fallen in pleasant places"—I both love, and respect Miss Wooler. . . .[17]

# 4

~~~~~~~~~~~~~~~~~~~~~~~~

# Crisis

The day before Emily's seventeenth birthday Charlotte and her sister left for Roe Head. For Charlotte the situation should have had the comfort of familiarity, and no doubt she felt, if not happy, at least not utterly strange as she dismounted from the gig with Emily and passed through the school gates again. But there is a mighty difference between a scholar and a teacher: the scholar, despite her humble status, is indirectly an employer; the teacher is a wage slave who occupies an inferior social and economic position to those she teaches. This was humiliating enough to a proud young woman, but Charlotte soon found that she had to work long, long hours for a pittance. The hope of economic self-sufficiency faded like a dream. Charlotte also discovered rapidly that she had no love for young girls, particularly stupid young girls. She had gladly learned; she found she could not gladly teach.

But the greatest difficulty proved to be Emily. Charlotte had counted on her companionship to make the stint at Roe Head bearable. Week by week, however, as summer turned to autumn, she saw depression fall across Emily like a long shadow. She grew pale and sallow. She drooped and toyed with her food. Her steps, once buoyant as she strode the moors with Anne, dragged. She would not, apparently *could* not, adjust to a life away from Haworth. Charlotte remembered Maria and Elizabeth, and the conviction that Emily too would die seized her. Yet how to explain the inexplicable to Miss Wooler? Emily wanted to learn, the routine was easy, the discipline of the laxest, and Emily's own sister there for companionship. What ailed Emily?

Many years later in a preface to the 1850 edition of Emily's poems, Charlotte offered public explanation of her sister's flight from Roe Head. "Liberty was the breath of Emily's nostrils," she wrote. "The change from her own home to a school, from her own noiseless, very

secluded, but unrestricted and inartificial mode of life, to one of disciplined routine . . . was what she failed in enduring. Her nature
proved too strong for her fortitude. . . . Nobody knew what ailed her
but me—I knew only too well. . . ."[1]

Charlotte's public statement accounts for a fraction of the truth.
She could not very well admit that it was her dream life that Emily
was longing for. Enduring her own agony at the wrench from Angria,
Charlotte could guess the depths of her sister's wretchedness. Emily
was a monolithic personality, as she knew. There were no facets to her
nature, no ambivalences or conflicts. She had given herself totally to
Gondal; now, like a fish out of water, she lay gasping for air. Reading
in Emily's pale cheeks and dull eyes the outcome of an enforced sojourn at Roe Head, Charlotte took action. Urgent letters arrived at
Haworth; Miss Wooler in turn was persuaded that Emily must go
home. In mid-October Emily thus returned to the parsonage, the
moors, and Gondal where she rapidly regained plump cheeks, sparkling eyes, and an elastic step. Anne was sent to Roe Head in her
place.

In no sense did fifteen-year-old Anne compensate Charlotte for the
loss of Emily. Anne's mild, pious nature did not appeal to Charlotte
like Emily's silent ferocity, which she admired and almost understood.
Anne herself yearned for Emily and so, instead of comforting each
other, the two sisters suffered separately. Charlotte would gladly sacrifice for Emily; now, however, she became acutely conscious that
Anne's small needs drained away most of her meager salary. Mary
Taylor drove over to Roe Head from Gomersal five miles away and
found Charlotte gloomy, overworked, nervous, and ill. "I heard that
she had gone as a teacher to Miss Wooler's. I went to see her, and
asked how she could give so much for so little money, when she could
live without it. She owned that, after clothing herself and Anne, there
was nothing left, though she had hoped to be able to save something.
She confessed it was not brilliant, but what could she do? I had nothing to answer. She seemed to have no interest or pleasure beyond the
feeling of duty . . ."[2]

Finding she could not give up Angria, Charlotte managed again to
lead a double life. Now, however, escape was much more difficult.
Onerous duties pressed her: the whole day was occupied with teaching, surveillance, and lesson preparation. There was endless bustle and
confusion about her: the students constantly clamored for help with
their lessons. At night she was not automatically released: she was
vulnerable to requests from pupils for help with lessons or sewing;
there were exercise books to correct; Miss Wooler expected her company in the parlor; Anne was there; her own small affairs must be at-

tended to. Moreover, communication with Branwell was difficult. Angria was still very much a joint effort, and the thought of Branwell back home in the quiet parsonage working away at the saga without interruption drove her frantic: "About a week since I got a letter from Branwell containing a most exquisitely characteristic epistle from Northangerland to his daughter. . . . I lived on its contents for days. In every pause of employment it came chiming in like some sweet bar of music, bringing with it agreeable thoughts such as I had for many weeks been a stranger to. . . ." or again: "I wonder if Branwell has really killed the Duchess. Is she dead? Is she buried? Is she alone in the cold earth on this dreary night? . . ."[3]

Existence divided itself into day and night. Day meant drudgery, noise, and the irritation of struggling with lethargic, giddy, or stupid girls she had no interest in teaching. Night meant escape. As soon as she could extricate herself from pupils and teachers, she took up her bedroom candle and fled up the stairs to her room. There, collapsing on the bed, she gave herself up to visions:

> I am alone: it is the dead of night.
> I am not gone to rest because my mind
> Is too much raised for sleep. The silent light
> Of the dim taper streams in unseen wind;
> And quite as voiceless on the hearth burns bright
> The ruddy ember. Now no ear could find
> A sound, however faint, to break the lull
> Of which the shadowy realm of dreams is full.[4]

War in Angria . . . Zamorna fled, captured, imprisoned . . . his cast-off wife dying of grief . . . Zamorna in exile, his mistress in the hands of enemies, his son tortured and murdered . . . fire, flames, tossing seas . . . "Mina . . . weep no more; I love you as a hawk loves a lark" . . . Zamorna . . . Zamorna . . . Bright visions swam over her, releasing her, until she dropped off into a fitful sleep only to be roused by the morning bell and the prospect of another nerve-wracking day.

The depression that had struck her down at Roe Head four years ago returned with doubled force. Nervous irritation and exhaustion brought on ill-health which in turn cast her down into a prolonged mental crisis. Deeply disturbed over her failure to cheerfully tolerate governess work and renounce her dream world, she became assailed with guilt over Angria. She had penned Zamorna's life of gaudy sin without, apparently, any qualms. Now she became stricken at the immorality of her creations. Was she wicked? A hopeless sinner? No one knows what other "sins" preyed on her mind—sexual frustration,

masturbatory fantasies, a half-conscious awareness of a more than sis-
terly affection for Branwell? In any age these natural but misunderstood drives can be shattering for the adolescent; in the repressive
climate of nineteenth-century England they were unspeakable mon-
strosities: it was a rare child who escaped a crushing sense of guilt
about the most normal experiences.

Charlotte had no religious morbidity when in sound health and
spirits. Aunt Branwell's severe Methodism and the grim prophecies of
the Calvinist tracts she imported into the parsonage had left her unmoved. She had known doubt and was tolerant of it in others; she was
a spirited critic of religious institutions and their employees. Now,
however, the darkest of Calvinistic doctrines threw its shadow over
her spirits. A conviction of eternal damnation swept over her. Desperate for comfort, she turned to Ellen Nussey in a flood of emotion.
Without being able to admit the source of her torment, she felt an
urgent need to confess her guilt to this pious and affectionate friend.

> Roe Head, May 10th, −36: I was struck with the note you sent me
> with the umbrella. It shewed a degree of interest about my concerns
> which I have no right to expect from any earthly creature. I won't
> play the hypocrite I won't answer your kind gentle friendly ques-
> tions in the way you wish me to. Don't deceive yourself by imagining
> that I have a bit of real goodness about me. My darling if I were like
> you I should have my face Zionward though prejudice and error
> might occasionally fling a mist over the glorious vision before me for
> with all your single-hearted sincerity you have your faults. but I am
> *not like you.* If you knew my thoughts; the dreams that absorb me;
> and the fiery imagination that at times eats me up and makes me feel
> Society as it is, wretchedly insipid, you would pity and I dare say de-
> spise me. But Ellen I know the treasures of the Bible I love and adore
> them I can *see* the Well of Life in all its clearness and brightness; but
> when I stoop down to drink of the pure waters they fly from my lips
> as if I were Tantalus. I have written like a *fool.* remember me to your
> Mother and Sister. Good-bye. Charlotte. . . . Come and see me soon;
> don't think me mad, this is a silly letter.[5]

Ellen cannot be blamed if she pounced on this letter like an evangel-
ist on a convert. She had always accepted Charlotte's superior strength
of intellect and character, yet even her placid nature must have been
galled occasionally when Charlotte treated her like a not very bright
child. Now, however, the stronger citadel was under siege and crying
out for help. It was a heady moment. Ellen immediately seized a quill
and poured forth a mixture of encouragement, admonishment, and
cant, at the same time assuring her erring friend of her undying affection. Charlotte trembled with excitement as she read the reply, over-

whelmed by a warmth and sympathy no one had ever given her before. She in turn replied immediately.

> Roe Head: My *DEAR, DEAR* Ellen . . . Religion has indeed elevated your character. I thank you with energy for this kindness. I will no longer shrink from your questions. I *do* wish to be better than I am. I pray fervently sometimes to be made so. I have stings of conscience—visitings of remorse—glimpses of Holy, inexpressible things, which formerly I used to be a stranger to. . . . Do not mistake me, Ellen, do not think I am good, I only wish to be so, I only hate my former flippancy and forwardness. O! I am no better than I ever was. I am in that state of horrid, gloomy uncertainty, that at this moment I would submit to be old, grey-haired, to have passed all my youthful days of enjoyment and be tottering on the verge of the grave, if I could only thereby ensure the prospect of reconcilement to God . . . You have cheered me, my darling; for one moment, for an atom of time, I thought I might call you my own sister, in the spirit, but the excitement is past, and I am now as wretched and hopeless as ever. This very night I will pray as you wish me. May the Almighty hear me compassionately! and I humbly trust He will—for you will strengthen my polluted petition with your own pure requests. . . . If you love me, *do, do, do* come on Friday; I shall watch and wait for you, and if you disappoint me, I shall weep. . . . I dare write no more, I am neglecting my duty. . . . Thank you again a thousand times for your kindness—farewell, my blessed Ellen,
>
> Charlotte.[6]

Ironically, this correspondence irritated rather than healed Charlotte's wounds. Ellen's advice, welcome at first, eventually only reminded Charlotte that she could not follow it. Every exchange of letters between Rydings and Roe Head confirmed Charlotte's unregenerate sinfulness, yet convinced her that she needed Ellen for salvation.

> What am I compared to you? I feel my own utter worthlessness when I make the comparison. I am a very coarse, commonplace wretch, Ellen. I have some qualities which make me very miserable, some feelings that you can have no participation in, that few, very few people in the world can at all understand. I don't pride myself on these peculiarities, I strive to conceal and suppress them as much as I can, but they burst out sometimes, and then those who see the explosion despise me, and I hate myself for days afterwards. . . .[7]
>
> Roe Head, 1836 . . . Ellen I wish I could live with you always, I begin to cling to you more fondly than ever I did. If we had but a cottage and a competency of our own I do think we might live and love on till Death without being dependent on any third person for happiness. —Farewell my own dear Ellen.[8]

Goaded by Ellen to visions of a purer, godlier existence, Charlotte could not, however, give up her creative, erotic, "infernal world." Although she tantalized her friend with confessions of unworthiness, she was too honest to pretend conversion. Angria was her religion; Zamorna her god. She thus continued to write her stories when she could and dream when she could, although at great hazard to her peace of mind. The almost unbearable tensions of this double existence are revealed in an autobiographical fragment Charlotte scrawled in her tense, ragged handwriting on a page of an Angrian story dated from Roe Head on August 11, 1836:

All this day I have been in a dream, half miserable, half ecstatic,—miserable because I could not follow it out uninterruptedly, ecstatic because it showed almost in the vivid light of reality the ongoings of the infernal world. I had been toiling for nearly an hour with Miss Lister, Miss Marriott, and Ellen Cook, striving to teach them the distinction between an article and a substantive. The parsing lesson was completed; a dead silence had succeeded in the schoolroom, and I sat sinking from irritation and weariness into a kind of lethargy. The thought came over me: Am I forced to spend all the best part of my life in this wretched bondage, forcibly suppressing my rage at the idleness, the apathy, and the hyperbolical and most asinine stupidity of these fat-headed oafs, and of compulsion assuming an air of kindness, patience, and assiduity? Must I from day to day sit chained to this chair, prisoned within these four bare walls, while these glorious summer suns are burning in heaven and the year is revolving in its richest glow, and declaring, at the close of every summer day, the time I am losing will never come again? Stung to the heart with this reflection, I started up and mechanically walked to the window. A sweet August morning was smiling without. The dew was not yet dried off the field, the early shadows were stretching cool and dim from the haystacks and the roots of the grand old oaks and thorns scattered along the sunk fence. All was still except the murmur of the scribes about me over their tasks. I flung up the sash. An uncertain sound of inexpressible sweetness came on a dying gale from the south. I looked in that direction. Huddersfield and the hills beyond it were all veiled in blue mist, the woods of Hopton and Heaton Lodge were clouding the water's edge, the Calder, silent but bright, was shooting among them like a silver arrow. I listened—the sound sailed full and liquid down the descent: it was the bells of Huddersfield Parish Church. I shut the window and went back to my seat. Then came on me, rushing impetuously, all the mighty phantasm that this had conjured from nothing,—from nothing to a system strange as some religious creed. I felt I could have written gloriously. The spirit of all Verdopolis—of all the mountainous North—of all the woodland West —of all the river-watered East, came crowding into my mind. If I had

had time to indulge it I felt that the vague suggestions of that moment would have settled down into some narrative better at least than
anything I ever produced before. But just then a dolt came up with a
lesson. I thought I should have vomited. . . .[9]

"Am I forced to spend all the best part of my life in this wretched
bondage?" The cry was wrung from an impatient, proud but, above
all, creative spirit. Society had a clear answer to her question: "Of
course. Apart from marriage you have this choice—governess, seam-
stress, dependent in your father's house. Choose your servitude." She
had chosen, and now she raged against her lot. She despised pounding
knowledge into the heads of "dolts," but she despaired more because
her creative life was thwarted. Yet she could not return home to
dream away her life in Haworth. Only one solution to her dilemma
presented itself: she must write, and be paid for writing. Urged into
action by her misery, Charlotte began to cast exploratory lines from
Yorkshire out into the world.

She was not the first of the family to do so. In October of 1835, a
few months after Charlotte and Emily left for Roe Head, Branwell
had set out for London, "plenty of letters of introduction in his
pocket," to enroll as an art student in the Royal Academy. He was
eighteen with the emotional stability of a thirteen-year-old. Petted,
indulged, and admired at home, he had no real solidity of either character or talent. His personality had all the dazzle of a skyrocket, and
all its durability. To be fair, he knew it himself. Secretly doubting his
talent and his ability to make something of the slender gifts he did
possess, Branwell began to lose enthusiasm for the adventure even as
the coach rolled him toward London. Mile by mile Branwell Brontë,
artist, shrank smaller and smaller, and London—the world—loomed
larger and larger. By the time he had dismounted from the coach and
found his way to lodgings at the Chapter Coffee House in Paternoster
Row, the confusion of the city and his self-doubt had already beaten
him.

He never went to the Academy and never attempted to enroll. Instead he wandered the thronging streets of London, dazed by the giant
he had thought to slay. "He threaded the dense and bustling crowds
and walked for hours, never staying to eat or drink, never calling a
coach or attending to personal appearance, but with a wildish dejected
look of poverty-stricken abstraction. His mind was too restless to stop
and examine anything." His wanderings brought him to the Embank-
ment. Here he paused and, leaning dejectedly against the parapet,
stared into the swirling black waters. He thought of the clear, tumbling moor streams at home in their far-off loneliness, and the contrast
between the solitude he had always known and the filth and dazzle of

seething London made his head whirl. He stayed long, staring helplessly at the great river, "and then he turned, passing through many
noble streets without hardly turning his eyes to look on them. He entered his hotel, stretched himself on a sofa, and listlessly dreamed
away his time till dark."[10]

He spent seven days in London wandering like a lost soul, the letters of introduction in his pocket. At the end of a week he climbed into
the northbound coach, turning his back on London with more realism
than the family that had sent him there. Back at Haworth, he glibly
informed his father and aunt that he had been robbed on the way to
London, and that in any case his real gift was for literature, not art.

His career in art nipped in the bud, he still aspired to fame. Several
months after the defeat in London he gathered his forces to attack
the literary world from the extremely disadvantageous position of
Haworth, Yorks. This he did in a series of increasingly hysterical letters to the editor of *Blackwood's Magazine*. His first two volleys were
greeted with silence. Then, penning the words "Sir,—Read what I
write" in large letters across the top of the page, Branwell launched
into his third assault:

> And would to Heaven you could believe it true, for then you would
> attend to and act upon it. I have addressed you twice before, and
> now I do it again." The letter continues with an overwrought descrip-
> tion of the influence *Blackwood's* wielded over him as a child. He
> quivers at the thought of the death of James Hogg, the magazine's
> most distinguished contributor. Surely *Blackwood's* will decay with-
> out such writers, unless others equally gifted—like Branwell Brontë—
> take their place. . . .
>
> Now, sir, to you I appear writing with conceited assurance: but *I
> am not;* for I know myself so far as to believe in my own originality,
> and on that ground I desire of you admittance into your ranks. And
> do not wonder that I apply so determinedly: for the remembrances I
> spoke of have fixed you and your Magazine in such a manner upon
> my mind that the idea of striving to aid another periodical is *horri-
> bly repulsive.* My resolution is to devote my ability to you, and for
> God's sake, till you see whether or not I can serve you, do not so
> coldly refuse my aid. All, sir, that I desire of you is—*that you would
> in answer to this letter request a specimen or specimens of my writ-
> ing, and I even wish that you would name the subject on which you
> wish me to write.* In letters previous to this I have perhaps spoken
> too openly respecting the extent of my powers. But I did so because
> I determined to say what I believed. I *know* that I am not one of the
> wretched writers of the day. I know that I possess strength to assist
> you beyond some of your own contributors; but I wish to make you
> the judge in this case and give you the benefit of its decision.

Now, sir, do not act like a commonplace person, but like a man willing to examine for himself. Do not turn from the naked truth of my letters, but *prove me*—and if I do not stand the proof, I will not farther press myself on you. If I do stand it—why—You have lost an able writer in James Hogg, and God grant you you may get one in

Patrick Branwell Brontë.[11]

Was ever editor in this humor wooed? Was ever editor in this humor won? It is not difficult to imagine Mr. Robert Blackwood's sensations as he read and hastily thrust aside this letter—if he read it at all. The writer sounds eccentric in the highest degree, even mad. Poor Branwell: he was still only eighteen and too ignorant and fantastic to judge how to approach an editor, believing somehow that the eloquence, bluster, and audacity practiced by his fictional heroes could conquer the literary world as they had conquered Verdopolis. Receiving no answer, he hurled another letter into the void four months later, headed again by a command printed in large letters, "Sir, Read now at least," and accompanied by some pages of poetry sent "because it is soonest read and comes from the heart. If it goes *to* yours," Branwell continues urgently, "print it, and write to me on the subject of *contribution*. Then I will send prose. But if what I now send is worthless, what I have said has only been conceit and folly, yet CONDEMN NOT UNHEARD."[12]

Silence. Still not deterred, but very bitter, Branwell wrote again in January 1837, requesting a personal interview. Throwing courtesy to the winds, he slashes out in anger. "Do you think your Magazine so perfect that no addition to its power would be either possible or desirable?" he cries. "Is it pride which actuates you—or custom—or prejudice? Be a man, sir! and think no more of these things. *Write* to me . . ."[13]

Silence. Discouraged, but not completely daunted, Branwell retrained his guns, daring to address himself this time to William Wordsworth, the most prestigious literary figure in England. Again he sent a sample of his work, explaining that his aim is "to push out into the open world." Again he pleaded for a word of encouragement: "But read it, sir; and, as you would hold a light to one in utter darkness—as you value your own kind-heartedness—*return* me an *answer*, if but one word, telling me whether I should write on, or write no more."[14]

Silence.

Did Charlotte know of her brother's attempts to catch the attention of the literary world? If she did, Branwell's efforts may have stimulated her to try her luck, for as the episode of the *Young Men's Magazine* proves, she was conscious and confident of her superior literary ability. If she did not know, then her identical impulse to write to

Robert Southey, currently poet laureate of England, testifies further
to Charlotte's and Branwell's affinity. Having escaped from Roe Head
during the Christmas holidays, she dared to dream of a more permanent escape. She aimed high. Her letter to Southey has disappeared,
but his answer is preserved.

Keswick, March 1837: Madam,—You will probably ere this, have
given up all expectation of receiving an answer to your letter of December 29. . . . What you are I can only infer from your letter,
which appears to be written in sincerity, though I may suspect that
you have used a fictitious signature. . . .

It is not my advice that you have asked as to the direction of your
talents, but my opinion of them; and yet the opinion may be worth
little and the advice much. You evidently possess, and in no inconsiderable degree, what Wordsworth calls the "faculty of verse." . . .

But it is not with a view to distinction that you should cultivate this
talent, if you consult your own happiness. I, who have made literature my profession, and devoted my life to it, and have never for a
moment repented of the deliberate choice, think myself, nevertheless,
bound in duty to caution every young man who applies as an aspirant
to me for encouragement and advice against taking so perilous a
course. You will say that a woman has no need of such a caution;
there can be no peril in it for her. In a certain sense this is true; but
there is a danger of which I would, with all kindness and all earnestness, warn you. The day dreams in which you habitually indulge
are likely to induce a distempered state of mind; and, in proportion
as all the ordinary uses of the world seem to you flat and unprofita-
ble, you will be unfitted for them without becoming fitted for anything else. Literature cannot be the business of a woman's life, and it
ought not to be. The more she is engaged in her proper duties, the less
leisure will she have for it, even as an accomplishment and a recreation. To those duties you have not yet been called, and when you are
you will be less eager for celebrity. . . .

But do not suppose I disparage the gift which you possess, nor that
I would discourage you from exercising it. I only exhort you so to
think of it, and so to use it, as to render it conducive to your own
permanent good. Write poetry for its own sake; not in a spirit of emu-
lation, and not with a view to celebrity . . . So written, it is wholesome both for the heart and soul . . .

Farewell, madam. It is not because I have forgotten that I was once
young myself, that I write to you in this strain; but because I remember it. You will neither doubt my sincerity, nor my good-will; and,
however ill what has here been said may accord with your present
views and temper, the longer you live the more reasonable it will appear to you. Though I may be an ungracious advisor, you will allow
me, therefore, to subscribe myself, with the best wishes for your happiness here and hereafter, your true friend,

Robert Southey.[15]

A remarkable letter. Charlotte knew better than Branwell how to address the illustrious, evidently writing with tact, humility, and rev-erence—famous men must be soothed, not threatened with Branwel-lian bluster. And Southey must have been impressed with Charlotte's poetry to have bothered writing such a long and courteous reply. His response is therefore the more benighted. Her gifts are acknowledged, then dismissed immediately because—she is a woman. All Southey's eloquence is poured forth to convince her that "literature cannot be the business of a woman's life, and it ought not to be." The most he can allow—the very most—is that she be permitted to scribble a few lines between nursing the baby, getting up the linen, and turning her husband's collars because poetry is, after all, wholesome for a woman's heart and soul. And yet she possesses, "in no inconsiderable degree, what Wordsworth calls the 'faculty of verse.' "

But what could Charlotte have expected from Robert Southey? The man was an archconservative, a reactionary who felt so threatened by the restless and rising lower classes that he seriously advocated a re-turn to the feudal system of serf and master. Nor did he possess enough talent himself to be generous with the gifts of others. Sou-they's reaction was thus predictable. But not one man in ten thousand would have contested in the year 1836 the belief that a woman's "proper duties" did not extend to the sphere of creative effort. Not one man in ten thousand would have written the words Charlotte craved to hear: "Write. You have talent, promise. Let nothing stand in the way of its development!"

Charlotte was understandably overwhelmed that a man of Southey's eminence should answer at all. She wrote back a grateful but spirited reply conceding that she would give up notions of celebrity although she could not stop writing, and chiding him gently for insinuating that she neglected her duties for dreams.

> Roe Head, March 16th, 1837 . . . You do not forbid me to write; you do not say that what I write is utterly destitute of merit. You only warn me against the folly of neglecting real duties for the sake of imaginative pleasure; of writing for the love of fame; for the selfish excitement of emulation. . . .
>
> My father is a clergyman of limited though competent income, and I am the eldest of his children. He expended quite as much on my education as he could afford in justice to the rest. I thought it there-fore my duty, when I left school, to become a governess. In that ca-pacity I find enough to occupy my thoughts all day long, and my head and hands too, without having a moment's time for one dream of the imagination. In the evenings, I confess, I do think, but I never trouble any one else with my thoughts. I carefully avoid any appear-ance of preoccupation and eccentricity, which might lead those I live

amongst to suspect the nature of my pursuits. Following my father's advice—who from my childhood has counselled me, just in the wise and friendly tone of your letter—I have endeavoured not only attentively to observe all the duties a woman ought to fulfil, but to feel deeply interested in them. I don't always succeed, for sometimes when I'm teaching or sewing I would rather be reading or writing; but I try to deny myself; and my father's approbation amply rewarded me for the privation. Once more allow me to thank you with sincere gratitude. I trust I shall never more feel ambitious to see my name in print; if the wish should rise, I'll look at Southey's letter, and suppress it. It is honour enough for me that I have written to him, and received an answer. That letter is consecrated; no one shall ever see it but papa and my brother and sisters. Again I thank you. This incident, I suppose, will be renewed no more; if I live to be an old woman, I shall remember it thirty years hence as a bright dream. The signature which you suspected of being fictitious is my real name. Again, therefore, I must sign myself

C. Brontë.

P. S.—Pray, sir, excuse me for writing to you a second time; I could not help writing, partly to tell you how thankful I am for your kindness, and partly to let you know that your advice shall not be wasted, however sorrowfully and reluctantly it may at first be followed. C.B.[16]

There must be few clearer statements of the conflict the Victorian woman of talent faced. Discouraged on all sides from pursuing a career, persuaded by family, friends, and society to limit herself strictly to those duties a woman *ought* to fulfill, Charlotte could persist with her writing only under great mental and emotional strain. But persist she did. The crumb Southey threw her was enough: she possessed in no inconsiderable degree the faculty of verse.

Robert Southey himself felt that he had dealt with the parson's daughter rather neatly. "I sent a dose of cooling admonition to the poor girl whose flighty letter reached me at Buckland," he wrote Caroline Bowles. "It seems she is the eldest daughter of a clergyman, has been expensively educated, and is laudably employed as governess in some private family. About the same time that she wrote to me her brother wrote to Wordsworth, who was disgusted with the letter, for it contained gross flattery and plenty of abuse of other poets, including me. I think well of the sister from her second letter, and probably she will think kindly of me as long as she lives."[17]

Southey's letter reached Charlotte at Roe Head. She put it carefully by, taking it out again on her birthday to reread and inscribe on its cover, "Southey's advice to be kept forever. My twenty-first birthday. Roe Head, April 21, 1837." Her intentions were good, but her desire to win recognition proved too strong. She kept the letter but not the advice, soon forgetting her promises. Today, by one of fate's delightful twists, Robert Southey is all but forgotten and the young woman he attempted to discourage has won enduring fame.

# 5

## Teach, Teach, Teach

Meantime there was no release from a galling existence. "Stupidity the atmosphere, school-books the employment, asses the society," Charlotte scribbled in her journal, writing with eyes screwed shut in a futile attempt to block out the detested surroundings, while the "asses"—Miss Wooler and two pupils—stared in amazement, "all wondering why I write with my eyes shut—staring, gaping long in their astonishment." Evidently, whatever she told Southey, she did not always manage to avoid any appearance of eccentricity. The compulsion to escape tedium by "setting things down," if only for a moment, was too strong.

Miss Wooler was experiencing upheavals in her family that spring, and in the summer of 1837 moved her school from Roe Head into a smaller establishment, Heald's House, on Dewsbury Moor, fifteen miles southeast of Haworth. The illness and finally the death of her father caused her to be absent a good deal from the school, and the disturbance in routine placed even heavier burdens on Charlotte. "Ever since last Friday I have been busy as I could be in finishing up the half-year's lessons, which concluded with a terrible fag in Geographical Problems (think of explaining that to Misses M[arriott] and L[ister], and subsequently, in mending Miss E. L.'s clothes. . . . Miss Wooler is calling for me—something about my protégé's nightcaps. Good-bye." Or, "Miss Wooler is from home or she would send her love I am sure—little Edward Carter and his baby Sister are staying with [us] so that between nursing and teaching I have my time pretty well occupied."[1]

Adding to Charlotte's misery were thoughts of Emily. Believing that she did not contribute enough to the family welfare, even though she did much of the housework and baking, Emily had answered an advertisement at Miss Patchett's school at Law Hill near Halifax.

Charlotte knew how her sister would suffer in such a situation and a letter from Emily soon confirmed her fears: large school, nearly forty pupils, hard labor from six in the morning till eleven at night, only a half hour of exercise during the day. "This is slavery," Charlotte cried to Ellen; "I fear she will never stand it."[2] Emily had borne the mild routine at Roe Head scarcely three months. How could she endure Law Hill under such oppressive duties?

Ellen continued to send Charlotte spiritual guidance and Charlotte continued to be both lashed and healed by Ellen's pious instructions. She dutifully tried to pray, meditate, and read the Bible, only once replying to her counselor with some asperity that she could not quite understand the spiritual benefit of reciting a psalm out loud every day. Ellen became a kind of idol at whose tranquil shrine Charlotte hoped to find mental rest. Weary after a long day's work, her mind exhausted and dispirited, she now struggled to turn her thoughts from the violently colored landscapes of Angria to Ellen. "It is a stormy evening, and the wind is uttering a continual moaning sound that makes me feel very melancholy. At such times, in such moods as these, Ellen, it is my nature to seek repose in some calm, tranquil idea, and I have now summoned up your image to give me rest. There you sit upright and still in your black dress and white scarf, your pale, marble-like face looking so serene and kind—just like reality. I wish you would speak to me. . . ."[3] Ellen enjoyed the idolatry. Mary Taylor had told Charlotte flatly that her depression was not mental but physical in origin, caused by too much sedentary work and not enough exercise. Ellen, however, unconsciously preyed upon Charlotte's depression, constantly sounding the theme of sin and possible salvation through Ellen Nussey. It drove Charlotte frantic:

> . . . If I could always live with you and daily read the bible with you, if your lips and mine could at the same time drink the same draught from the same pure fountain of mercy, I hope, I trust, I might one day become better, far better than my evil wandering thoughts, my corrupt heart, cold to the spirit and warm to the flesh will now permit me to be. I often plan the pleasant life which we might lead together . . . My eyes fill with tears when I contrast the bliss of such a state brightened by hopes of the future with the melancholy state I now live in, uncertain that I have ever felt true contrition, wandering in thought and deed, longing for holiness which I shall *never, never* attain—smitten at times to the heart with the conviction that ——'s ghastly Calvinistic doctrines are true—darkened in short by the very shadows of Spiritual Death! If Christian perfections be necessary to Salvation I shall never be saved, my heart is a real hot bed for sinful thoughts and as to practice, when I decide on an action, I scarcely remember to look to my Redeemer for direction.

> I know not how to pray, I cannot bind my life to the grand end of
> doing good. I go on constantly seeking my own pleasure, pursuing the
> gratification of my own desires, I forget God and will not God forget
> me? . . . I adore the purity of the Christian faith, my theory is right,
> my practice horribly wrong.—Good-bye, Ellen. . . .[4]

In short, Charlotte Brontë was like everyone else, Ellen Nussey included. A reaction against Ellen's preaching was inevitable: humility
was not Charlotte's forte. Besides, she became aware that she was violating a basic sense of spiritual privacy in confessing to Ellen. Religion for Charlotte, Emily, and Anne was always to remain a private
affair, a communication between God and individual. Mary Taylor
had the privilege of hearing the only words Emily ever uttered on
the subject to an outsider: Mary told Charlotte that when an acquaintance had asked her what religion she belonged to she had answered, "That's between God and me"; Emily, lying on the hearthrug,
overheard and exclaimed, "That's right." Charlotte said of Anne, "It
was not her custom to talk much about religion but she was very
good." Charlotte began to loathe this washing of her dirty spiritual
linen in public; the end of the crisis was drawing near. "I have . . . a
dread lest, if I made the slightest profession, I should sink at once into
Phariseeism, merge wholly into the rank of the self-righteous."

> In writing at this moment I feel an irksome disgust at the idea of us-
> ing a single phrase that sounds like religious cant—I abhor myself—I
> despise myself—if the Doctrine of Calvin be true I am already an out-
> cast—you cannot imagine how hard rebellious and intractable all my
> feelings are—When I begin to study on the subject I almost grow
> blasphemous, atheistical in my sentiments, don't desert me—don't be
> horrified at me, you know what I am—I wish I could see you my
> darling, I have lavished the warmest affections of a very hot, tenacious
> heart upon you—if you grow cold—it's over. . . .[5]

Adding to Charlotte's agitation came the repetition of a pattern that
was already too familiar. Anne, like Maria and Elizabeth, had stoically
accepted a life away from home that could not have been any more
congenial for her than it was for Charlotte. What this quiet, uncomplaining girl suffered away from Emily, Gondal, and home can only
be imagined. After almost two years at Miss Wooler's Anne's spirits
broke. In the winter of 1837 she came down with a cold; she neglected
it. Mental depression followed; like Charlotte she became obsessed
with a fear of damnation. The Rev. James la Trobe was called to Roe
Head to comfort the distraught girl and persuade her to faith in divine
mercy. He succeeded, but the illness, perhaps gastro-enteritis, persisted.

Trying to steal time from teaching to care for and comfort her sister, Charlotte observed with alarm Anne's shortness of breath, her painful cough, her feverish cheeks—the dreaded signs, she believed, of consumption. All perspective gone, she flew to Miss Wooler and insisted Anne be sent home: she was dying. Miss Wooler flatly told her she was acting like a fool, refused to send Anne home, and treated Charlotte with marked coldness for the next few days. This was more than flesh could bear. Charlotte confronted Miss Wooler one night, lost her temper, and lashed out heatedly, accusing her of hardhearted-ness and indifference. Miss Wooler was appalled and fell to crying at this shocking outburst from her dutiful protégée. She wrote to Mr. Brontë, tremulously informing him that Charlotte had taken her se-verely to task. Mr. Brontë, sensing a crisis, sent for his two daughters immediately. As she packed their trunks, Charlotte vowed she would never come back, but just before their departure Miss Wooler called her into her room and, confessing her deep regard for Charlotte, ad-mitted how sorry she would be to part with her. "If anyone likes me I can't help liking them," Charlotte confessed to Ellen. She gave in, and after seeing Anne established comfortably at home and improving, though needing rest and care, she returned to Dewsbury Moor.

She had almost escaped; her sense of duty drove her back. "We have entered on a new Year," she wrote Ellen gloomily on the fourth of January 1838; "—will it be stained as darkly as the last with all our sins, follies, secret vanities, and uncontrolled passions and propensi-ties? I trust not—but I feel in nothing better—neither humbler nor purer."[6] January, February, March crawled by. Her mental depres-sion deepened; Dewsbury Moor had become a poisoned place for her. Anne had escaped. Emily too was at home, driven back after six months of hard labor at Law Hill. She alone was in exile. Insufferable moments, heavy gloom, long hours, preternatural horrors which seemed to clothe existence and nature and made life a continual wak-ing nightmare—this, she wrote, was her life. Clearly she could not stand much more. Finally physical illness, which solves problems as of-ten as it creates them, released her. Her health failed; the doctor con-sulted told her that if she valued her life she must go home. These were the magic words she had waited for, the only words that could persuade her to put duty aside. May had come, warm winds were be-ginning to stir over the Haworth moors. She packed her few belong-ings, accepted from Miss Wooler a leather-bound copy of Scott's poem *The Vision of Don Roderick* inscribed with "the love and best wishes of a Sincere Friend May 23rd 1838," and fled Dewsbury Moor like an animal sprung from a trap.

Not surprisingly, she recovered health and spirits rapidly once back at the parsonage. "A calm and even mind like yours, Ellen," she told her friend, "can not conceive the feelings of the shattered wretch who is now writing to you, when after weeks of mental and bodily anguish not to be described, something like tranquility and ease began to dawn again."[7] Thereupon Charlotte Brontë settled down at the parsonage, took up Angria where she had left it, and lived happily ever after.

She did not. She was twenty-two, going on twenty-three. Angria, once potent enough to vault her immediately into violently colored dreams, was losing its strength like a medicine swallowed too frequently and too long. Still she wrote, producing in the next year, among shorter works, the long narrative "Caroline Vernon" in which Zamorna and the notorious Percy, "coarse voluptuary, filthier than that filthy Jordan," are still going strong. Given a new freedom, she could hardly resist immediately taking up the pen again; yet some of the old rapture with the old subject was missing. Allowed to retreat from the world, she paradoxically felt a need to return to it. Talented, desirous of recognition, and basically aggressive beneath a retiring exterior, she subconsciously missed even the deplorably meager rewards of governessing: usefulness, recognition, authority, and a salary—pitifully small—but one's own. The parsonage was indeed a sanctuary, but at times, to a restless young woman eager somehow to make a mark on the world, the door barred at nine o'clock each night seemed to shut with a terrible finality, and the graveslabs crowding toward the house mutely spoke of oblivion and defeat.

Then late in February 1839 a letter came, addressed to Miss Brontë in a strange hand. Opening it, Charlotte found it to contain no less—and no more—than a proposal of marriage. Her suitor, to her great surprise, was Ellen Nussey's brother Henry.

Henry Nussey, five years Ellen's senior, had undoubtedly met Charlotte during her visits at Rydings or later at Brookroyd nearby where the Nusseys moved in 1836, but in no sense did he know her. He had graduated from Cambridge, had obtained a post as curate in far-off Sussex on the east coast, was living alone in a large rectory, and needed a wife. Charlotte was not his first choice. A diary kept by this conscientious young man reveals that he had first written for the daughter of his former vicar in Yorkshire; unfortunately: "On Tuesday last received a decisive reply from M.A.L.'s papa; a loss, but I trust a providential one. Believe not her will, but her father's. All right, but God knows best what is good for us, for His church, and for His own glory." To this trenchant philosophizing he added the reminder, "Write to a Yorkshire friend, C.B."

The proposal Charlotte held in her hand was unflattering, unimaginative, devoid of sentiment, but honest. The young curate stated that he was comfortably settled near Donnington, that his health had improved (illness had driven him from his last curacy), that he intended to take pupils at the rectory after Easter, and that he needed a wife to take care of the pupils. Would Charlotte Brontë be that wife?

Did the creator of Zamorna laugh or cry as she read the dry, matter-of-fact offer? Henry's proposal was a passport to respectability, and indeed to womanhood, for to the Victorian mind an unmarried female was an incomplete and unnatural being—a blight on the creation. It was a passport to financial security that the daughter of a poor clergyman could hardly afford to reject. Papa and Aunt would firmly approve the alliance. The marriage would unite her in sisterhood with Ellen, who obviously had encouraged Henry to make Charlotte an offer—perhaps Ellen would even live with them. She was almost twenty-three. It was a chance that might never come again.

She could not accept him. She had been writing about idyllic, searing love since she was sixteen. She was not mad enough to believe that a Zamorna would come clattering down the cobbled lane to the parsonage, sweep her into the saddle, and ride off with her across the moors into the swirling mists. Her realism told her there were no Zamornas; her mirror told her that if one existed, he would ride past. Yet she did believe in love, and she did not love Henry Nussey. More than this, she knew herself. What could a woman possessed by "evil wandering thoughts" and a "hot, tenacious heart," "cold to the spirit and warm to the flesh," want with a sober young clergyman? Having just emerged from a scathing mental crisis that left her convinced that she was both erring and unrepentant, she could hardly relish marriage with a man of conventional views. More than this: what nourishment could her vigorous mind derive from a Nussey? She knew him; he did not know her. Without hesitating, she wrote:

Haworth, March 5th, 1839: My Dear Sir,—Before answering your letter I might have spent a long time in consideration of its subject; but as from the first moment of its reception and perusal I determined on what course to pursue, it seemed to me that delay was wholly unnecessary. You are aware that I have many reasons to feel grateful to your family, that I have peculiar reasons for affection towards one at least of your sisters, and also that I highly esteem yourself—do not therefore accuse me of wrong motives when I say that my answer to your proposal must be a *decided negative*. In forming this decision, I trust I have listened to the dictates of conscience more than to those of inclination. I have no personal repugnance to the idea of a union with you, but I feel convinced that mine is not the sort of disposition calculated to form the happiness of a man like you. It has always been my habit to study the characters of those amongst whom I chance to be thrown, and I think I know yours and can imagine what description of woman would suit you for a wife. The character should not be too marked, ardent, and original, her temper should be mild, her piety undoubted, her spirits even and cheerful, and her *personal attractions* sufficient to please your eyes and gratify your just pride. As for me, you do not know me; I am not the serious, grave, cool-headed individual you suppose; you would think me romantic and eccentric; you would say I was satirical and severe. However, I scorn deceit, and I will never, for the sake of attaining the distinction of matrimony and escaping the stigma of an old maid, take a worthy man whom I am conscious I cannot render happy. . . . Let me say also that I admire the good sense and absence of flattery and cant which your letter displayed. Farewell I shall always be glad to hear from you as a *friend*.—Believe me, yours truly,

C. Brontë.[8]

An unflinchingly honest self-portrait: a strong, ardent, original, romantic character; temperamental, eccentric, irreverent, and satirical; personal attractions not sufficient to please the male eye. Henry Nussey, Victorian clergyman, was well saved. Three days later in far-off Sussex, Henry opened the letter, sighed, and made another diary entry: "Received an unfavourable reply from C.B. The Will of the Lord be done."

Ellen *had* been active in promoting the union and, hearing nothing from either her friend or her brother, finally sent off a letter to Haworth asking Charlotte point-blank whether she had heard from Henry. Charlotte replied frankly, but as usual held back the deepest truth.

I feel that though I esteemed, though I had a kindly leaning towards him . . . yet I had not, and could not have, that intense attachment which would make me willing to die for him; and, if I ever marry, it must be in that light of adoration that I will regard my husband. Ten to one I shall never have the chance again, but *n'importe*. Moreover, I was aware that Henry knew so little of me he could hardly be conscious to whom he was writing. Why, it would startle him to see me in my natural home character; he would think I was a wild, romantic enthusiast indeed. I could not sit all day long making a grave face before my husband. I would laugh, and satirise, and say whatever came into my head first. And if he were a clever man, and loved me, the whole world weighed in the balance against his smallest wish should be light as air. Could I, knowing my mind to be such as that, conscientiously say that I would take a grave, quiet, young man like Henry? No, it would have been deceiving him, and deception of that sort is beneath me. . . . Write to me soon and say whether you are angry with me or not.[9]

A momentary prospect gone, Charlotte turned from thoughts of marriage to thoughts of employment. She could live on at home at her father's expense, but the thought of dependence was irksome. Still, no teaching position offered. ". . . I am as yet wanting a situation—like a housemaid out of place," she tells Ellen wryly. (Was Ellen herself content—stitching lace cuffs, working beaded purses, putting up jellies, and reading novels at Brookroyd while her life slipped away?) "—by the bye Ellen I've lately discovered that I've quite a talent for cleaning—sweeping up hearths dusting rooms—making beds &c. so if everything else fails—I can turn my hand to that—if anybody will give me good wages, for a little labour. I won't be a cook—I hate cooking—I won't be a nursery-maid—nor a lady's-maid far less a lady's companion—or a mantua-maker—or a straw-bonnet maker or a taker-in of plain-work—I will be nothing but a house-maid." And more seriously: "Papa wishes me to remain at home a little longer, but I begin to be anxious to set to work again; and yet it will be *hard work* after the indulgence of so many weeks, to return to that dreary 'gin-horse' round."[10]

Other factors besides a deep-rooted desire for independence urged her to leave the quiet, orderly parsonage for a strange roof and the "dreary 'gin-horse' round." Anne, now nineteen and only recently recovered from the lung congestion that had driven her from Roe Head, had quietly determined to find work. Of the three sisters she seemed most unfit for the demanding task of governessing because physically the weakest, as well as the shyest. Emily was robust compared to Anne and Charlotte worldly. Charlotte especially worried that Anne would not do as a governess: she stuttered, for example, in the presence of strangers, she was painfully reserved, and she was inexperienced. But Anne was firm. Like her dead sisters Maria and Elizabeth, she could endure quietly under affliction. Charlotte raged, Emily turned self-destructive, but Anne bore hard work, long hours, and homesickness patiently. Besides, unlike Charlotte and Emily, she liked children.

A position was found for Anne through the Rev. Edward Nicholl Carter, curate of Mirfield, Susanna Wooler's husband, Miss Wooler's brother-in-law, and father of the small children Charlotte had cared for occasionally at Roe Head. On April 8, Anne left for Blake Hall, Mirfield, a few miles from unhappy Dewsbury Moor, and the task of supervising the children of Mr. and Mrs. Ingham. She firmly refused to let any of the family accompany her; she felt that she could summon up more courage to face her new surroundings alone. Emily and Charlotte helped her pack her few belongings in the small bedroom upstairs: chemises, cuffs, a plain dark dress, her books, her work-

basket, her Bible. The next morning she rose, washed her face, made a
hasty breakfast, embraced Aunt, Papa, Charlotte, and Emily, kissed
Black Tom the cat, stepped into the gig, drew her veil over her face,
and burst into a flood of tears. The April morning was dark and cold.
The gig rolled away down the cobbled lane, lurched down the steep
hill to the bottom of the village, crossed the valley, and began to climb
again. "As we were toiling up, I looked back again: there was the village spire, and the old grey parsonage beyond it, basking in a slanting
beam of sunshine—it was but a sickly ray, but the village and surrounding hills were all in sombre shade, and I hailed the wandering
beam as a propitious omen to my home. With clasped hands I fer-
vently implored a blessing on its inhabitants, and hastily turned away
for I saw the sunshine was departing; and I carefully avoided another
glance, lest I should see it in gloomy shadow like the rest of the landscape."[11]

They anxiously waited for a letter; when it came it brought relief:
Anne was doing well. "She expresses herself very well satisfied,"
Charlotte told Ellen, "and says that Mrs Ingham is extremely kind; the
two eldest children alone are under her care, the rest are confined to
the nursery—with which and its occupants she has nothing to do.
Both her pupils are desperate little dunces—neither of them can read
and sometimes they profess a profound ignorance of their alphabet,
the worst of it is the little monkies are excessively indulged and she is
not empowered to inflict any punishment—she is requested when they
misbehave themselves to inform their Mamma—which she says is utterly out of the question as in that case she might be making complaints from morning till night—'So she alternately scolds, coaxes and
threatens—sticks always to her first word and gets on as well as she
can'—I hope she'll do, you would be astonished to see what a sensible,
clever letter she writes . . ."[12] Charlotte rather underestimated Anne,
mistaking her patience and piety for weakness.

Anne gone, another Brontë unfortunately returned to take her
place—the brother who might have been making all their fortunes out
in the big world. Branwell had gone over to Leeds to take further lessons in oils from his former teacher, William Robinson; then, with his
usual impetuosity, had prematurely set up as a portrait painter in a
studio of his own at Bradford. Bradford was a town of 40,000, center
of the woolen trade, prosperous enough to support a small coterie of
provincial artists, and so close to Haworth that Branwell could walk
home over the moors on weekends. The venture began with high
hopes and the financial encouragement of Papa and Aunt. Branwell
was not good, but somehow he got several commissions and painted a
few passable portraits, among them, studies of Mr. and Mrs. Kirby, his

landlords. Charlotte, visiting his lodgings at No. 3 Fountain Street, was impressed and encouraged. But painters with a better knack than his dominated the business, and the new popularity of the daguerreo-type was beginning to edge out the traditional art of the portrait painter. Customers fell off, then stopped coming altogether, and Bran-well, fleeing from an empty studio and bare canvases, spent more and more time with artistic cronies in the warm, dark, obliviating Bradford pubs. He had always been a lively talker and a good drinker. At the George, the Bull's Head, and the Talbot talking and drinking now be-came his main business. The heady liquor animated him and the intri-cate fabric of words he wove protected him against the cold reality of failure. He could not last indefinitely without funds, however; and in May he packed his palette and oils and returned to quiet Haworth, de-feated again. He was twenty-one.

Charlotte, taught by her culture to excuse masculine weakness, still welcomed him happily. But she had been brooding more than usual over the problem of loving and respecting a brother whose weak, er-ratic character deeply challenged her loyalty. Inevitably, she turned her conflict into prose. In a long narrative, "Captain Henry Hastings," written late that winter, she had dwelt on the brother-sister relation-ship, curiously forecasting Branwell's coming defeat. Henry's sister knew he was an unredeemed villain, a Cain-like wanderer, she wrote, and knew he had suffered public disgrace, yet—human nature is so in-consistent—she did not think "a pin the worse of him for all his dis-honour. . . . Natural affection is a thing never rooted out," Charlotte concluded, "where it has once existed."[13] Perhaps not; but it can be rapidly transmuted into disgust and hate.

Taught equally that a sister must sacrifice for a brother, Charlotte became more urgently convinced that she must find work. Perhaps, too, Branwell's failure challenged her to succeed. Shortly after his re-turn a situation offered. Edward Nicholl Carter, Miss Wooler's brother-in-law, had left Mirfield for the church at Lothersdale. Mr. John Benson Sidgwick, owner of a fine estate near Lothersdale, was patron and warden of Carter's new church. Carter had known Char-lotte since her student days at Roe Head; clearly he was responsible for the post of governess to the Sidgwick children being offered to her. Leaving behind Papa in the parlor, Aunt sewing in her room, Emily sturdily working away at the Gondals, and Branwell already re-established in the local pubs, Charlotte set out for Lothersdale.

What *was* a governess? Victorian novels are full of them; pale, oppressed creatures hovering unhappily in drawing-room corners; spir-ited minxes who marry their masters; frustrated neurotics who corrupt their innocent charges. Reality was somewhat less exotic. A governess was the unmarried daughter of a "good" middle-class family fallen upon bad times, or, as in Charlotte's case, the daughter of a respectable educated man in a poorly paid profession. Governessing was almost the only work a lady could commit herself to without losing caste; yet her departure to a stranger's house announced a family in financial straits, and to a culture dedicated feverishly to getting ahead nothing could be more shameful. The young lady, having submitted to destiny and hung up her bonnet in the house of a prosperous gentleman, found herself in a difficult position. She was not a servant, yet she was not her employer's equal: thus she had to keep the servants at heel yet humble herself before the master and mistress. If she was too humble she was exploited; if proud, she was disliked. She could not take her meals belowstairs in the kitchen with the housemaid and the butler; neither was she admitted to the family table except by gracious dispensation. She could not pass her evening gossiping in the servants' quarters, yet she found herself ignored or patronized in the master's drawing room. She must teach the master's children to respect her while treated as an inferior dependent by the master. She must control spoiled children while denied the authority to punish them for misbehavior. If she was ugly, the master and his children disliked her; if she was handsome, the mistress of the house was her enemy. In short, she was isolated, powerless, and exploited. *Punch*, always ready to champion a safe cause, finally sympathized in 1890 in a set of verses:

> Poor Miss HARKER went to Stockton, to
>     Stockton on the Tees,
> But not to make her fortune, or to loll at home at
>     ease;
> She went to be a governess, and hoped, it would
>     appear,
> To board and lodge and dress herself on £15
>     a-year.
>
> So all day long with urchins three Miss HARKER
>     toiled in chains,
> And she poured the oil of learning well upon
>     their rusty brains,
> And she practised them in music, and she
>     polished up their sense
> With the adverbs and the adjectives, and verbs
>     in mood and tense.

And they said, "She's doing nicely, we will give
    her something more
(Not of money, but of labour) ere we show her
    to the door,
Why, we've got two baby children, it is really
    only fair
That Miss HARKER should look after them,
    and wash and dress the
    pair.

"And, Miss HARKER, it will save us such a lot
    of trouble too,
If when our servants leave us, they can leave
    their work to you
So you'll please to cook our dinner, let your
    motto be *Ich Dien*,
(No, no, you needn't thank us) and you'll keep
    our dishes clean.

"And, of course, you'll do it daily—what was
    that you dared to say?
You would like to rest a week or so, and want
    a holiday?
Who ever heard such nonsense? Well, there's
    one thing we can show,
Not politeness, but the door to you—Miss H.
    you'd better go."

To master and mistress, the quiet, genteel, black-clad creature in the background was the *pièce de résistance* of the establishment—a gentlewoman whom they could still patronize as a servant. Still she was valued much less than the cook, the groom, or the butler since her services were less tangible. Children are second-class citizens; by association their teachers are second-class citizens too—no matter that their education and talents may far surpass those of the master and lady of the house. The English are notorious in any case for their aloofness to children, usually committing them to nurseries, nannies, tutors, governesses, or prep schools until they come of age. No wonder then that the groom who leads out a prize bay from the stables or the butler who discreetly pours the vintage port is respected, while the governess is regarded as ornamental but a nuisance. Given this anomalous position, a successful governess must possess large quantities of patience, adaptability, cheerfulness, and calm. She would be fortunate, in addition, if she were thick-skinned, conventional, and not excessively intelligent.

Behold Charlotte Brontë as governess to the Sidgwicks: short-tempered, nervous, intolerant, shy, eccentric, excessively intelligent, and proud as the devil.

Her first impressions as the gig carried her up the sloping hill toward the Sidgwick estate were deceptively pleasant. The May sky was blue, and Stonegappe, an eighteenth-century house overlooking a valley threaded by a little stream, beautifully situated. Groves of oak and beech sheltered the grounds and the lawns rolled emerald green, laced with winding white paths. Twenty-four hours in her new position effaced all pleasant first impressions. Charlotte had thought herself exploited at Miss Wooler's. Roe Head now took on a rosy glow as Charlotte found herself the dependent of a woman who evidently had no intention of acknowledging her as an equal or even as an individual. Had she found the adolescent girls at Miss Wooler's difficult to manage? The Sidgwick children were a hundred times worse. Furious at Mrs. Sidgwick's patronizing officiousness and duties that kept her running from early morning till late at night, uncharmed by Matilda and John Benson, the six- and four-year-old in her charge, sick for home, and already sinking into morbid depression, she poured forth her grievances in a letter to Emily.

> Stonegappe, June 8th, 1839: Dearest Lavinia. . . . I have striven hard to be pleased with my new situation. . . . The children are constantly with me, and more riotous, perverse, unmanageable cubs never grew. As for correcting them, I soon quickly found that was entirely out of the question: they are to do as they like. A complaint to Mrs Sidgwick brings only black looks upon oneself, and unjust, partial excuses to screen the children. I have tried that plan once. It succeeded so notably that I shall try it no more. I said in my last letter that Mrs Sidgwick did not know me. I now begin to find that she does not intend to know me, that she cares nothing in the world about me except to contrive how the greatest possible quantity of labour may be squeezed out of me, and to that end she overwhelms me with oceans of needlework, yards of cambric to hem, muslin nightcaps to make, and, above all things, dolls to dress. I do not think she likes me at all, because I can't help being shy in such an entirely novel scene, surrounded as I have hitherto been by strange and constantly changing faces. I used to think I should like to be in the stir of grand folks' society but I have had enough of it—it is dreary work to look on and listen. I see now more clearly than I have ever done before that a private governess has no existence, is not considered as a living and rational being except as connected with the wearisome duties she has to fulfil.

While she is teaching the children, working for them, amusing them, it is all right. If she steals a moment for herself she is a nuisance. . . .

Don't show this letter to papa or aunt, only to Branwell. They will think I am never satisfied, wherever I am. I complain to you because it is a relief, and really I have had some unexpected mortifications to put up with. However, things may mend, but Mrs Sidgwick expects me to do things that I cannot do—to love her children and be entirely devoted to them. I am really very well. I am so sleepy that I can write no more. . . .[14]

Charlotte was incapable of humbling herself to play the role of an obedient, faceless dependent. Her nerves on edge, her sense of humor in strict abeyance, she viewed her existence in the Sidgwick household as high tragedy. She grew hypersensitive and imagined slights that perhaps were never intended. A biography of Archbishop Edward White Benson, a cousin of Mr. Sidgwick, gives us a glimpse of Charlotte Brontë as governess from the Sidgwick point of view, naturally a very different one. Charlotte, says A. C. Benson, the archbishop's son and biographer, was impossibly touchy. If the family desired her to accompany them to church—"Oh, Miss Brontë, do run up and put on your things, we want to start"—Charlotte was plunged into dudgeon because she was being treated like a hireling; if, on the next Sunday, she was not invited, she was infinitely depressed because she was treated like an outcast and a friendless dependent. Furthermore, she had no talent for managing children and was in morbid condition all during her stay. On the other hand, says Benson, "Both Mr. and Mrs. John Sidgwick were extraordinarily benevolent people, much beloved, and would not wittingly have given pain to anyone connected with them."

Much beloved by whom? Charlotte herself admitted to Ellen that Mrs. Sidgwick was generally considered an agreeable woman, and that in society she was undoubtedly cheerful. With a subordinate, Mrs. Sidgwick was not obliged to be either charming or sensitive; undoubtedly, therefore, she unwittingly did mortify the hypersensitive Charlotte in many ways. And yet she treated her with more consideration than she showed the housemaid or the cook!

The biography of Archbishop Benson does mention that one Sidgwick boy, John Benson, once threw a Bible at Miss Brontë. Since she could not complain to his mother, she bore this and all other affronts with silence. Paradoxically her stoicism eventually won the regard of the Sidgwick children. One day, finding John and William playing in the stable yard where they had expressly been forbidden to trespass, Charlotte protested, knowing that, while she was not allowed to punish, she would be blamed by Mrs. Sidgwick if the boys were caught.

John and William retaliated for this interference by pelting her with stones, cutting her forehead and further shattering her nerves. Charlotte kept silent, resigned to the fact that Mrs. Sidgwick would consider the cut forehead *her* fault, not the children's. The boys appreciated this sportsmanship, and one day when the family was gathered John, the youngest boy, sidled up to her, took her hand, and lisped winningly, "I love 'ou Miss Brontë." Whereupon Mrs. Sidgwick, overhearing, raised her eyebrows and rebuked her son in front of all the children: "Love the *governess*, my dear!"

A month after Charlotte came to Stonegappe, the family moved to a summer home of Mrs. Sidgwick's father—Swarcliffe, near Harrogate and Ripon, "a beautiful place in a beautiful country—rich and agricultural," Charlotte wrote Ellen. But she carried her misery along with her.

> I must not bother you too much with my sorrows, Ellen, of which I fear you have heard an exaggerated account; if you were near me, perhaps I might be tempted to tell you all—to grow egotistical and pour out the long history of a Private Governess' trials and crosses in her first situation. As it is, I will only ask you to imagine the miseries of a reserved wretch like me, thrown at once into the midst of a large family—proud as peacocks and wealthy as Jews—at a time when they were particularly gay, when the house was full of company—all strangers, people whose faces I had never seen before—in this state of things having the charge given me of a set of pampered, spoilt, and turbulent children, whom I was expected constantly to amuse as well as instruct. I soon found that the constant demand on my stock of animal spirits reduced them to the lowest state of exhaustion; at times I felt and I suppose seemed depressed. To my astonishment I was taken to task on the subject by Mrs Sidgwick with a stress of manner and a harshness of language scarcely credible. Like a fool, I cried most bitterly; I could not help it—my spirits quite failed me at first. I thought I had done my best—strained every nerve to please her—and to be treated in that way merely because I was shy and sometimes melancholy was too bad.[15]

Charlotte served out her sentence with gritted teeth. "I could like to be at home," she wrote Emily. "I could like to work in a mill. I could like to feel mental liberty. I could like this weight of restraint to be taken off."[16] A mill? We smile, mentally comparing the Sidgwick estate with the notorious Victorian factories: hours six in the morning to ten at night, damp cold dark buildings, shrieking machinery, fifteen minutes to eat a cold mouthful of dinner, machine dust in the lungs, backs bent—and all for starvation wages. Yet government blue books offer evidence that in Victorian England the female house servant worked the hardest and longest for the poorest wages, without, in addition, the freedom of the factory worker. Charlotte was no house-maid, yet often worked housemaid's hours for only slightly higher wages, and without the housemaid's consolation of companionship: Charlotte had no kitchen mates to share her troubles with. A de-pendent, but not of the servant class, she felt her loss of dignity keenly, and did not entirely joke when she talked of working in a mill.

One of the few pleasant afternoons of the entire summer was spent in the company of Mr. Sidgwick, who took a stroll with his children and ordered Charlotte to follow behind. Since he asked her kindly and relieved her of the children's wearisome company, she did not feel this command as a slight. As she preferred Branwell to her sisters, she preferred the master of the house to the mistress. He was a hun-dred times better, she told Emily: "less profession, less bustling con-decension, but a far kinder heart. It is very seldom that he speaks to me, but when he does I always feel happier and more settled for some minutes after. He never asks me to wipe the children's smutty noses or tie their shoes or fetch their pinafores or set them a chair."

Of course not. Since Mr. Sidgwick was spared the immediate super-vision of his children, he was also spared the duty of nagging their governess, thus winning Charlotte's preference. And clearly, since she did not like children, or housework, or domesticity in general, she had little sympathy with most women whose lives ran in this narrow channel. Nor could she appreciate the alternate feminine role of so-ciety matron, since society terrified and repulsed her. Convinced that women played inferior roles, she therefore rather despised them, at the same time despising herself, perhaps, for her failure to be conven-tionally feminine. A man's mind seemed to her broader, stronger, less censorious, more generous—and she felt at ease with these qualities. As she followed the little group along the white paths, under the oaks and beeches, and through the fields, she appraised the figure that strolled before her, a huge Newfoundland dog trotting at his side. "He looked very like what a frank, wealthy, Conservative gentleman ought to be. He spoke freely and unaffectedly to the people he met, and though he indulged his children and allowed them to tease himself far too much, he would not suffer them grossly to insult others."[17] Unlike, she mentally added, his wife.

By the third week of July her duties as nursery governess were over, for the Sidgwicks had not intended to retain her past the sum-mer. The relief was intense on both sides.

# 6

*Young Men*

Three months with the Sidgwick family taught her that private governessing was not her calling, yet Charlotte felt obliged to begin advertising immediately for another position. "I intend to force myself to take another situation when I can get one," she told Ellen, "though I *hate* and *abhor* the very thought of governessship— But I must do it and therefore I heartily wish I could hear of a Family where they want such a Commodity as a Governess."[1]

While she waited for a summoning letter with mingled dread and anticipation, chance once again offered an alternative. Mr. Hodgson, Patrick Brontë's former curate, now a vicar, came to spend the day at Haworth with his old friend, bringing with him *his* curate, a young Irishman fresh from Dublin University. Mr. David Bryce soon made himself at home with a combination of brashness and charm, and the quiet parsonage rang with the unaccustomed sound of male laughter. Charlotte judged him critically at first, put off by his lack of dignity. Yet the young man soon broke down her reserve with his jests and enthusiasm. Charlotte was never shy in her own home, and Mr. Bryce awoke the satirical, clever, fun-loving part of her personality, her "natural home character" that would have shocked Henry Nussey. Animated, witty, the spectacles laid aside and her large eyes glowing with good humor, Charlotte was by no means unattractive to the young curate, especially when laughing at his jests. Encouraged, Mr. Bryce grew warmer toward evening, gazed at her more eloquently, and sugared his remarks liberally with flattery. Charlotte drew back, cooling as he warmed, displeased with his too easy familiarity: by the end of the evening she was anxious to have him go. The two men finally took their leave and no more was thought about them, until three days later, opening a letter addressed in an unfamiliar hand,

Charlotte found it to contain an ardent proposal of marriage from her Irish visitor. She could not take this impetuous offer seriously for a minute. Writing to Ellen, she laughs, ". . . well thought I—I've heard of love at first sight but this beats all. I leave you to guess what my answer would be—convinced that you will not do me the injustice of guessing wrong. . . . I hope you are laughing heartily. This is not like one of my adventures is it?"[2]

Under the laughter was bitterness. The marriage offers of Henry Nussey and Mr. Bryce were hollow mockery; she had already closed the door on any marriage not founded on a tested affinity of mind and heart. Was *this* all she was to be offered? Evidently—and it would not do. "I am certainly doomed to be an old maid," the letter to Ellen concludes.

Meanwhile Ellen had proposed an excursion to the seaside as a reward for Charlotte's unhappy stint with the Sidgwicks. Unused to holidays, Charlotte seized upon the idea eagerly—"your proposal has almost driven me clean daft." Papa and Aunt reluctantly consented, then threw up one objection after another. Of course, Victorian young ladies did not often travel about the countryside unescorted, so objections were perhaps to be expected. But Charlotte was always to have difficulty getting away from Haworth. Branwell could come and go, but the conscientious and dutiful daughter was strictly reined in. Her frustrated letters to Ellen about the postponements and restrictions laid down by Papa and Aunt over the seaside excursion begin a theme that runs through her letters all her life.

July 26th: I should indeed like to go—but I can't get leave of absence for longer than a week. . . .

August 4th: I have got leave to accompany you for a week, at the utmost stretch a fortnight, but no more—

August 9th: I am very sorry to throw you back in your arrangements, but I really cannot go to-morrow—I could not get my baggage and myself to Leeds by 10 o'clock to-morrow morning if I was to be hanged for it.

August 14th: I have in vain packed my box, and prepared everything for our anticipated journey. It so happens that I can get no conveyance this week or the next. The only gig let out on hire here in Haworth is at Harrogate, and likely to remain there, for aught I can hear. Papa decidedly objects to my going by the coach, and walking to Birstall, though I am sure I could manage it. Aunt exclaims against the weather, and the roads, and the four winds of heaven. . . . I grieve that I should have so inconvenienced you; but I need not talk of either Friday or Saturday now, for I rather imagine there is small chance of my ever going at all. The elders of the house have never cordially acquiesced in the measure; and now that impediments seem to start up at every step opposition grows more open. . . . Reckon on me no more; leave me out in your calculations: perhaps I ought, in the beginning, to have had prudence sufficient to shut my eyes against such a prospect of pleasure, so as to deny myself the hope of it.[3]

Ellen heard Charlotte's cry of despair. Seizing matters in her own hands, she coaxed an affluent Nussey relative into lending her a carriage and descended upon remote Haworth, *fait accompli*. Charlotte, drooping, revived. Papa and Aunt, taken by surprise, were forced to surrender. Emily and Anne helped whisk Charlotte's belongings together, and the pair climbed into the carriage before the horses had rested and clattered off down the cobblestone lane cheered on by Branwell, who declared it was "a brave defeat, a victory over the doubters." You only have to *will* a thing to *get* it, decided Ellen, well rewarded by Charlotte's happy face.

Their destination was Bridlington, a watering place a hundred miles across Yorkshire on the eastern coast. It was the first railway journey for either of them, and the lurching cars, rattling wheels, and black soot sifting through their veils must have had all the charm of novelty. Halfway, at York, the railroad stopped, and since the regular stage-coach was too crowded to accommodate them, Charlotte and Ellen made the rest of the journey in an open "fly." The sun shone on the green and gold September landscape; the air was mild. As they neared the coast Ellen caught a glimpse of the sea and cried out in enthusiasm, but Charlotte was without her glasses and blind as a mole. Ellen obligingly began to describe the sight, but Charlotte, always impatient with Ellen's feeble imagination, soon cried out, "Don't tell me any more. Let me wait!"

They intended to make immediately for the seaside, but when the fly stopped at the Black Lion in Bridlington they found a post chaise waiting with orders to convey them to a friend's house at Easton, two or three miles from the sea. Here was frustration. The whole adventure lay in their being absolutely independent and right on the shore, yet they could not reject the hospitality of Mr. and Mrs. John Hudson, alerted to their coming by Ellen's brother Henry. The day after their arrival they could bear their captivity no longer and, breaking away from their protective hosts, set out to walk to the sea.

From adolescence Charlotte had devoured Byron's poetry, absorbing his passion for the grandeurs of nature. Wordsworth might celebrate the violet and the stream, but Charlotte shared with Byron a taste for heaving oceans, towering mountains, deep chasms, and crashing waterfalls, none of which she had ever seen. "The soul can flee,/ And with the sky, the peak, the heaving plain of ocean, or the stars, mingle," wrote Byron, and certainly Charlotte's soul fled as the crash of the breakers met her ears and the tossing blue sea met her eyes. She stood on the sands, a small creature in shawl and straw bonnet, quite overcome. She was speechless with pain and joy; tears filled her eyes; she cried bitterly. She turned her head away from Ellen and signaled her to leave her, and Ellen withdrew, respecting her friend's passion although not sharing it. When she returned after a tactful interval, she found Charlotte still trembling like a poplar leaf, her eyes red and swollen. The calm Ellen led her away to a spot where the view was less overwhelming, and Charlotte consented to be led. She was pale, subdued, and exhausted for the rest of the day.

From then on Charlotte longed for the sea and whenever the roar of the surf reached her ears in her captivity at Easton she was wild to be off. The Hudsons finally relented and permitted the young women to take lodgings at Bridlington Quay, and for a week—until their money ran out—they rambled the shore and the high chalk cliffs in sunlight and moonlight, exhilarated with their hard-won freedom.

Yet they were hardly isolated. Was Charlotte disappointed to find the seaside crowded with stolid Britons come to take the sea air or the mineral waters, or to exchange the tedium of tea, whist, and gossip at home for the novelty of tea, whist, and gossip at the shore? Here were the great Victorian middle classes on holiday: *paterfamilias* with his whiskers, checked waistcoat, and top hat; his wife, swathed in bonnet, shawl, cloak, veil, skirts, petticoats, and high boots, leaning on his arm; his children in sailor suits, black stockings, and straw hats swarming behind. In the evenings the crowds surged to the small pier to solemnize a ritual known as the Evening Parade. Crushed shoulder to shoulder, Britons on vacation promenaded slowly round and round in regular file, nodding here, bowing there, or cutting dead with a glance. Charlotte and Ellen joined the march once, then fled, appalled. The parson's daughter had no ties with the fertile, burgeoning, materialistic bourgeoisie. Alien and amused, she watched the spectacle and pronounced judgment upon it: stupid and conventional. But she never forgot the sea, and sometimes, years afterward, would break off in the middle of a conversation to exclaim, "I wonder how it looks, just now!"

Back home again after a whole month of holiday, she waited for news of a position, an uneasy state, for she could hardly enjoy such freedom when the certainty of losing it haunted her. After nine months of wrestling with little Inghams who threw food at meals, spit in her handbag, emptied its contents out the window, and refused to attend at lesson time, Anne came home in December, dismissed by Mrs. Ingham who one day found her darlings tied to the nursery table legs and Anne correcting their lessons in peace. Her return made it all the more urgent that Charlotte find a situation. Life was wasting. Henry Nussey, still a friend, wrote to ask her advice: he had proposed to a fortuneless young lady; had he been foolish? Charlotte replied pedantically, tuning her style to his mind. A wealthy wife, she suggested soothingly, might bring riches to a marriage, but also might bring an unwelcome idea of her own importance. "On the other hand," lectures Charlotte, "it must be considered that when two persons marry without money, there ought to be moral courage and physical exertion to atone for the deficiency—there should be spirit to scorn dependence, patience to endure privation, and energy enough to labour for a livelihood. . . . The bread earned by honourable toil is sweeter than the bread of idleness; and mutual love and domestic calm are treasures far preferable to the possessions rust can corrupt and moths consume away."[4]

Was she fated always to advise about love and never to know it herself? So it seemed. Nothing offered, not even governessing. "I am still at home, as I have not yet heard of any situation which meets with the approbation of my friends. I begin, however, to grow exceedingly impatient of a prolonged period of inaction. I feel I ought to be doing something for myself, for my health is now so perfectly re-established by this long rest that it affords me no further pretext for indolence. . . ."[5]

She was not really indolent, however, for the family had lost the services of Tabby. Two years before, descending the steep village street on an errand, Tabby had slipped on the icy cobblestones and fallen, shattering and dislocating her leg. Lameness finally drove her from the parsonage kitchen, and now she lived nearby, constantly visited by Charlotte and Emily. Little Martha Brown, one of the sexton's six daughters, came to help, but the girl, barely eleven, only ran errands. Loyal to Tabby and disliking new faces, Charlotte and Emily took on all the housework—radical move, for genteel parsons' daughters might sew or brush the carpet, but they did not—as Charlotte now did—iron, sweep, dust, make beds, and black-lead the stove, or—like Emily—manage the kitchen and the baking. Charlotte burned the clothes the first time she ironed, much to the anger of Aunt Branwell, but for a time she was happy enough wielding a mop and broom. Always, however, dependence and the consciousness of talents unused gnawed at her heart. Was life doomed to pass away in this even, quiet flow?

Still, the parsonage was livelier than it had ever been: Mr. Brontë had a new curate. Charlotte generally cast a bleak eye upon her father's clerical assistants, finding them narrow, pompous, and thoroughly dull. William Weightman was a bird of different feather: a

pretty fellow, eloquent, educated, and flirtatious—a young Greek god
among the Haworth primitives. Gentle Anne gazed at him shyly with
her violet eyes, stern Emily thawed, and Charlotte alternately laughed
at his nonsense and shook her head over his vanities, finding herself
nevertheless drawn by his intelligent and amiable ways. Because of his
auburn curls and frequent blushes the girls immediately christened
him "Miss Celia Amelia." It was a way of dealing with a man they
found both charming and—because of his wide female following—
annoying. Clearly he did not intend to limit his attentions to the parsonage. Yet his very presence in the bleak village was like April sunshine and Anne and Charlotte at least basked in the uncertain but welcome warmth.

Ellen visited Haworth in February of the new year 1840, and there
was a good deal of fun and nonsense. "Miss Celia Amelia," discovering that none of the girls had ever received valentines, sat down and
composed eloquent verses under the titles "Fair Ellen, Fair Ellen,"
"Away fond love," and "Soul Divine." He then walked ten miles to
Bradford to post them anonymously, fearful that Mr. Brontë and Miss
Branwell would frown on such lighthearted trivialities under the sober
parsonage roof. For Weightman the valentines were a spontaneous and
quickly forgotten act of amiability; Charlotte, Ellen, and Anne cherished them like rubies. He was welcome at their fireside and on their
walks. He flirted with Ellen, apparently unencumbered by thoughts of
his fiancée back home in Westmoreland. When he tried to lure her
away from the others to walk over the moors, Emily insisted upon accompanying them, perhaps to tease him, perhaps to actually protect
Ellen from the advances of an engaged man. Tall and lank, she sternly
followed in their wake. Celia Amelia dubbed her "The Major."

He sat to Charlotte for his portrait in his master's silk and velvet
cap and gown, and the sittings grew alarming for their frequency and
length. Clearly he attracted her. But he attracted everyone. Mr. Brontë
appreciated his high-church views and his classical scholarship. Branwell found him a lively and unaffected companion and perhaps more—
crediting the curate in a poem with "lips that even me beguile." Aunt
Branwell was won by his good manners, amiable conversation, and
his harmlessness as an engaged man. Frowning nearsightedly over her
drawing board, Charlotte listened to his banter as she limned the graceful head, the auburn curls, the dancing eyes, and found him handsome,
clean, prepossessing, and good-humored. He talked to her frankly,
ignoring her shyness, and her reserve melted. A pity his conversation
dwelt so often on his love difficulties with other young ladies.

He was asked to give a lecture on the classics at the Mechanics Institute in Keighley, and he decided that the Brontë girls must be pres-

ent to admire. This apparently simple invitation caused a world of trouble. Weightman could not apply directly to the formidable Mr. Brontë, but had to write to the rector of Keighley, a friend and a married man, and ask him to petition for the favor. Mr. Dury did write, inviting the girls for tea and assuring them of an escort to and from the lecture. It would be a cold, windy walk of four miles each way. Papa and Aunt frowned and grumbled, loath to grant the pleasure; the daughters waited in suspense. Mr. Brontë finally gave his permission and the girls set off in winter bonnets and heavy cloaks down the long dark road to Keighley, escorted by Weightman. He must have pleased his audience, particularly the Haworth contingent, for he was an attractive and fluent speaker. Walking home in the keen February night, the party of five laughed and chattered in high spirits; it was midnight before they had climbed the steep village street and reached the parsonage door. The two clergymen rushed in with their charges and found Miss Branwell waiting up. She had prepared hot coffee for the girls, but not enough for their escorts. Always opposed to the excursion, she now lost her temper at this final inconvenience to her sense of propriety. Charlotte was deeply embarrassed, but the amiable Weightman could not be ruffled and, countering the woman's anger with light words, he managed to salvage some of the pleasure of the evening before he and Mr. Dury bid the parsonage good night.

Weightman gave another lecture at Keighley and Mr. Brontë was also invited to speak there: "both are spoken of very highly in the Newspaper," Charlotte told Ellen, "and it is mentioned as a matter of wonder that such displays of intellect should emanate from the village of Haworth 'situated amongst the bogs and mountains and until very lately supposed to be in a state of semi-barbarism' such are the words of the newspaper."[6] Weightman was also called upon to use his eloquence in Haworth itself, for a row was brewing among the Dissenters over increased church rates. Charlotte went one Sunday afternoon to hear Weightman and a colleague sermonize on the evils of dissent. The Dissenters closed their chapel in the West Lane behind the parsonage and came in a body: St. Michael's was tightly packed with curious and hostile villagers. Weightman gave them a high-church, Apostolic Succession harangue, and "banged the dissenters most fearlessly and unflinchingly." Charlotte, who loathed all interference in private belief, found his views "bigoted, intolerant and wholly unjustifiable on the ground of common sense"; yet she admired his courage in the teeth of the enemy. However: "if I were a dissenter I would have taken the first opportunity of kicking or horse-whipping both the gentlemen for their stern bitter attack on my religion and its teachers."[7]

Ellen recognized her friend's partiality for Weightman, but Charlotte, convinced day by day of Celia Amelia's fickleness, sternly forbade herself to be fond of him. "Let me have no more of your humbug about Cupid &c. you know as well as I do it is all groundless trash."[8] In turn, she teased Ellen: "I know Mrs Ellen is burning with eagerness to hear something about Wm Weightman, whom she adores in her heart, and whose image she cannot efface from her memory."[9] But as Weightman spread his net, catching the hearts of girls for miles around, Charlotte cooled toward him. Was he not, after all, callously using her companionship only when nothing better offered? She wrote Ellen in a new mood, coldly censoring the charming curate: male flirt, scattering his impressions far and wide, Sarah Sugden smitten, likewise Caroline Dury, perfectly conscious he's irresistible, vain as a peacock, troops of victims. "I have seen little of him lately and talked precious little to him—when he was lonely and rather melancholy I had a great pleasure in cheering and amusing him—now that he has got his spirits up and found plenty of acquaintances I don't care and he does not care either."[10]

Yet he had many redeeming qualities. He went home to Westmoreland and overwhelmed the parsonage with presents of game while he was away: braces of wild ducks, black grouse, partridges, snipe, curlews, and a large salmon. And he had a sympathetic heart. One Saturday night as he sat talking with Mr. Brontë in the parlor he could not conceal his gloom, and when he took his leave at the door, Mr. Brontë challenged him:

"What is the matter with you? You seem in very low spirits tonight?"

"Oh, I don't know. I've been to see a poor young girl, who, I'm afraid, is dying."

"Indeed, what is her name?"

"Susan Bland, the daughter of John Bland, the superintendent." And Weightman dispiritedly bid his rector good night.[11]

Charlotte overheard the conversation from the dining room and hurried to the Bland house the next day, for Susan was her oldest and best Sunday school scholar. She found the girl very ill and weak. Asking the mother whether she could send Susan a little wine to strengthen her, she was told that Mr. Weightman had already sent over a bottle of port and a jar of preserves. He was very good to poor folks, said Mrs. Bland warmly; he had a great deal of feeling and kindheartedness. Charlotte melted. "God bless him!" she wrote Ellen. "I wonder who, with his advantages, would be without his faults . . . where I am, he shall always find rather a defender than an accuser."[12] She still could not bring herself to resume her once friendly relations with the handsome curate. His candor had persuaded her to be cheer-

ful and open with him; as a result he had become "almost contemptuously familiar." Was this Charlotte's Victorian way of saying that
Weightman had tried to hold her hand or even kiss her? Perhaps. He
had once lectured her on the subject of young ladies who said "no"
when they meant "yes," and then to Charlotte's angry retort assured
her that he meant nothing personal. A more insulting familiarity, however, was the fact that Weightman poured out his lovesickness for
other girls in her ear, tacitly ignoring the possibility that she could feel
something for him herself. Some plain women are satisfied with
counseling young men like mothers. Charlotte was too proud to accept this role with Weightman. He could keep his love affairs to himself. She grew cold and reserved, and they seldom spoke except on
church matters or the weather. Writing to Ellen a year after that first
merry Valentine's Day, she summed up her still ambivalent feelings
for her father's frustrating curate:

"I dare say you have received a valentine this year from our bonny-
faced friend the curate of Haworth. I got a precious specimen . . . but
I knew better how to treat it than I did those we received a year ago.
I am up to the dodges and artifices of his lordship's character. He
knows I know him, and you cannot conceive how quiet and respectful
he has long been. Mind I am not writing against him—I never *will* do
that. I like him very much. I honour and admire his generous, open
disposition, and sweet temper—but for all the tricks, wiles, and insin-
cerities of love, the gentleman has not his match for twenty miles
round. He would fain persuade every woman under thirty whom he
sees that he is desperately in love with her."[13]

Charlotte sent the valentine on to Ellen. "Make much of it. Remember the writer's blue eyes, auburn hair, and rosy cheeks. You may
consider the concern addressed to yourself, for I have no doubt he intended it to suit anybody."[14] And, weeks later: "Have you lit your
pipe with Mr. Weightman's valentine?" He was the first appealing
man she had known. Meanwhile Anne, unprotected by Charlotte's
quickly donned armor, was deeply smitten and loved Weightman in
silence. Doubtless he never knew it.

Thus, for several years, Charlotte's and Ellen's correspondence was
full of the curate of Haworth. Ellen might have fallen in love with
him, but her attention was distracted by a real suitor. Over this man,
a Mr. Vincent, she dithered endlessly. Should she marry without being
madly in love? Naturally she turned to her friend for advice, and
Charlotte, sober and sage at twenty-four (at least where others were
concerned), wrote an energetic reply. Do not marry a man you cannot respect, she warns. If there is respect, love will come later. Intense passion is madness: it is hardly ever requited; if requited, it can-

not outlast the honeymoon; once exhausted, disgust and indifference speedily take its place. Of the two, indifference is the worse—and God help the woman if she is left to love passionately and alone.

"My good girl, 'une grande passion' is *'une* grande *folie.'* . . . No young lady should fall in love till the offer has been made, accepted—the marriage ceremony performed and the first half year of wedded life has passed away—a woman may then begin to love, but with great precaution—very coolly—very moderately—very rationally—if she ever loves so much that a harsh word or a cold look from her husband cuts her to the heart—she is a fool—if she ever loves so much that her husband's will is her law—and that she has got into a habit of watching his looks in order that she may anticipate his wishes she will soon be a neglected fool. . . . Ellen, Helen, Eleonora, Helena, Nell, Nelly—Mrs. Vincent. Does it sound well, Nell? I think it does. I'll never come to see you after you are married."[15]

This from the girl who wrote that one of Zamorna's smiles could compensate his mistress for a year of neglect. Who told Ellen she could not marry her brother because she was not willing to die for him. What had changed Charlotte Brontë?

Nothing. Her heart was as passionate as ever, but her reason taught her that a woman in love was painfully vulnerable and must arm herself against this defenselessness. She had learned that a woman's position in society, and therefore in love and marriage, was one of utmost disadvantage. She had observed that a woman was subject to the whim and the rule of the male. Without money, she decided, a woman possesses only one slender thread of power—her self-esteem. Once prostrate herself before husband or lover, confessing herself his slave, and she snaps the thread in her hand. Man is a tyrant; only a rational and spirited sense of independence in the woman can hope to check his rule.

Part of this lesson was learned long ago at Cowan Bridge where she found herself opposed to an oppressive masculine authority. Much of it was learned from Papa, quiet tyrant of her life. Still more was taught to her by William Weightman as she listened to his callous chatter about his many conquests. Her impulse was to love deeply and completely; her reason told her that to do so was madness.

In addition, she had the example of Mary Taylor and her own brother to meditate upon. Charlotte had continued to visit Gomersal, one time walking to Keighley, coaching as far as Bradford, and walking the rest of the distance to the Red House in the cool of the evening. Mary and Martha in return enlivened the parsonage from time to time with their visits. "They are making such a noise about me I cannot write any more," Charlotte scribbled to Ellen on one of these occasions. "Mary is playing on the piano; Martha is chattering as fast as her little tongue can run; and Branwell is standing before her, laughing at her vivacity."[16] Mary had grown from the blooming, open-faced girl at Roe Head ("Too pretty to live!" said Miss Wooler) into a gray-eyed young woman whose quiet demeanor was often shattered by flashes of quick intelligence and deep feeling. Branwell admired her; she, in turn, was drawn to the extravagant redheaded brother of her friend. Without the guile to say no when she meant yes, Mary frankly responded to Branwell's overtures. Branwell was terrified. Nourished on romance and neurotically insecure, he recoiled at her open avowal of affection; his admiration perversely turned to contempt. Charlotte watched the little drama, wretched, for she admired Mary as the noblest and most intelligent person she knew: her price, she told Ellen, was above rubies. The incident forced her to admit that Ellen's cool, cautious, and tranquil nature was the best protection a woman could have in the game of love. She predicted that Mary would never marry: she was too exceptional to tolerate the conventional role of wife and mother. She "has more energy and power in her nature than any ten men you can pick out in the united parishes of Birstall and Gomersal," she wrote Ellen later, speculating on Mary's future at the death of her father, that fascinating, contradictory man she had observed with such interest on her visits to the Red House. "It is vain to limit a character like hers within ordinary boundaries—she will overstep them."[17] Weak, dissipated, and evidently conventional where a woman was concerned, Branwell cowered before the honest strength of Mary Taylor.

Although Charlotte had not essentially changed, the years had robbed her imaginative life of much of its gorgeous color. Henry Nussey wrote, offering to send her some poetry and requesting some verses from her. She answered wearily. "Once indeed I was very poetical, when I was sixteen, seventeen, eighteen and nineteen years old—but I am now twenty-four approaching twenty-five. . . . At this age it is time that the imagination should be pruned and trimmed—that judgment should be cultivated—and a *few* at least, of the countless illusions of early youth should be cleared away. I have not written poetry for a long while."[18]

Charlotte had in fact been pruning and trimming her imagination. The result was a decision to abandon Angria. The violent fortunes of Zamorna, Mary Percy, and Mina Laury had occupied her too long; she was satiated and exhausted with lurid dreams. In the cold light of earning a living, of growing older without prospect of love, her dream world had faded although her creative impulse was just as strong. Late in 1839, therefore, she took up her pen and formally bid farewell to the world which had absorbed her for ten years:

I have now written a great many books and for a long time have dwelt on the same characters and scenes and subjects. I have shown my landscapes in every variety of shade and light which morning, noon, and evening—the rising, the meridian and the setting sun can bestow upon them. Sometimes I have filled the air with the whitened tempest of winter: snow has embossed the dark arms of the beech and oak and filled with drifts the parks of the lowlands or the mountain-pass of wilder districts. Again, the same mansion with its woods, the same moor with its glens, has been softly coloured with the tints of moonlight in summer, and in the warmest June night the trees have clustered their full-plumed heads over the glades flushed with flowers. So it is with persons. My readers have been habituated to one set of features, which they have seen now in profile, now in full face, now in outline, and again in finished painting—varied but by the change of feeling or temper or age; lit with love, flushed with passion, shaded with grief, kindled with ecstasy; in meditation and mirth, in sorrow and scorn and rapture; with the round outline of childhood, the beauty and fullness of youth, the strength of manhood, and the furrows of thoughtful decline; but we must change, for the eye is tired of the picture so oft recurring and now so familiar.

Yet do not urge me too fast, reader: it is no easy theme to dismiss from my imagination the images which have filled it so long; they were my friends and my intimate acquaintances, and I could with little labour describe to you the faces, the voices, the actions, of those who peopled my thoughts by day, and not seldom stole strangely even into my dreams by night. When I depart from these I feel almost as if I stood on the threshold of a home, and were bidding farewell to its inmates. When I strive to conjure up new inmates I feel as if I had got into a distant county where every face was unknown and the character of all the population an enigma which it would take much study to comprehend and much talent to expound. Still, I long to quit for awhile that burning clime where we have sojourned too long—its skies flame—the glow of sunset is always upon it—the mind would cease from excitement and turn now to a cooler region where the dawn breaks grey and sober, and the coming day for a time at least is subdued by clouds.[19]

A poignant farewell, but a necessary one if Charlotte was ever to address real rather than imaginary readers. The Victorian public enjoyed melodrama—witness the success of Dickens—but melodrama within a recognizable social context, enacted by innocent heroines, pure young heroes, and heartless villains. Angria was not recognizable, nor could Charlotte reveal her amoral fantasies to an age which turned up its eyes at the mere suggestion of sex. Her swearing, drinking, amorous men belonged to a bygone era of Byronic heroes and Regency bucks. Her Zamorna's adulterous passions were now taboo in print, the curses of her Captain Henry Hastings—"G-d d--n blast such folly! cursed conceited Humbug! infernal——petticoat perverseness! fated foppery!"—must shock a new and decorous age. And Charlotte craved a public: Southey's advice had been laid aside with his letter. About this time, therefore, she ventured to appeal to a famous writer again. This time she wisely decided not to admit she was a woman. Disguising her sex with the signature "C.T.," she sent off an Angrian prose fragment to the distinguished poet William Wordsworth. Would he acknowledge her although he had ignored Branwell?

In 1840, Wordsworth, the greatest if not the most flamboyant of the Romantic poets, was living with the burden of his burned-out genius at Rydal Mount, Westmoreland. Long ago he had renounced his mission "to teach the young and the gracious of every age to see, to think, and feel." An old man, white-haired, Roman-nosed, he now lived on his laurels, collecting homage from visitors and honorary degrees from universities, and functioning as the Stamp Distributor of Westmoreland, the kind of office awarded to public figures who have prudently renounced their youthful radicalism. Byron had dismissed Wordsworth in *Don Juan* as incomprehensible and crazed beyond all hope, but Charlotte did not share her hero's puerile judgment, revering Wordsworth because his poetry best captured the spiritual magic of nature. Yet the conservative and now uninspired old man was not the ideal critic for Charlotte's vigorous, romantic prose. Nor was he a man to deal justly with a writer he immediately suspected to be feminine because of handwriting and certain ladylike touches in style and imagery.

Wordsworth's answer is lost, but its contents can be deduced from Charlotte's letter thanking him for noticing her bit of prose. Speculating unkindly that she must be either an attorney's clerk or a novel-reading dressmaker, he advises her to abandon the novelette, remarking that her characters might have found a public fifty years ago but are too unrealistic for current taste. Charlotte swallowed the medicine bravely and returned a gracious but spirited reply.

> Authors are generally very tenacious of their productions, but I am not so much attached to this production but that I can give it up without much distress. . . . Of course it is with considerable regret I relinquish any scheme so charming as the one I have sketched. . . . I am pleased that you cannot quite decide whether I am an attorney's clerk or a novel-reading dressmaker. I will not help you at all in the

discovery . . . Seriously, sir, I am very much obliged to you for your
kind and candid letter, and on the whole I wonder you took the trouble to read and notice the demi-serious novelette of an anonymous
scribe, who had not even the manners to tell you whether he was a
man or a woman, or whether his "C. T." meant Charles Timms or
Charlotte Tomkins.[20]

Branwell too had not given up hope of public recognition, although
he looked more and more to opium to solve the agonies of an uncertain talent wedded to an indecisive disposition. For his working model
in elegant drug addiction he had Thomas de Quincey's *Confessions of
an English Opium Eater;* for his rationalization of the habit, De
Quincey's belief that opium arrested the consumption Branwell dreaded,
that it enlivened rather than deadened the mind, and that it opened a
rosy world of soothed nerves and warm pleasures. That summer of
1839, stinging from the defeat at Bradford, Branwell had taken to
opium, finding that he could get it cheaply and easily from the
Haworth chemist, who sold it as a pain reliever. A sublime solution.
He did not have to press his father for undue sums of money, he was
not on display at the local pubs as a conspicuous drinker, and he did
not have to disguise a reeking breath and tottering steps from the sharp
nose and eyes of Aunt Branwell. Charlotte was away at the Sidgwicks',
Anne with the Inghams at Mirfield, his father eternally preoccupied
with church affairs and private study. Emily was shrewd but would
not pry. Branwell continued to fraternize with the local men, sharing
a pint with Thomas Sugden, the landlord of the Black Bull, and,
sponsored by John Brown, the sexton, joining the Three Graces, a
Masonic lodge whose rituals appealed to his love of the arcane and his
desperate need of acceptance. He retained his reputation as the village
rake, but now he undoubtedly felt superior in his opium-invigorated
mind to the crude imbibers of Haworth.

A wonder that he ever gathered energy to leave his village again.
Perhaps the example of the successful and energetic William Weightman—always before him—roused Branwell to a sense of shame. Perhaps he confided his despair to Weightman on a stroll over the summer
moors and was encouraged to take a new stand by that amiable young
curate. A position turned up, Branwell accepted it, and in December
prepared to journey into Lancashire as tutor to the two sons of the
Postlethwaite family. Writing to Ellen, Charlotte adopted a tone of
cautious optimism: "Branwell, who used to enliven us, is to leave us
in a few days to enter the situation of a private tutor in the neighborhood of Ulverston. How he will like or settle remains yet to be seen;
at present he is full of hope and resolution. I, who know his variable
nature, and his strong turn for active life, dare not be too sanguine.

We are as busy as possible preparing for his departure, and shirt-making and collar-stitching fully occupy our time. . . ."[21]

The sisters stitched and hemmed in vain. Before he reached Brough-ton House, the Postlethwaite home in Lancashire, Branwell lapsed into the kind of behavior that forecast a short term as tutor. "I took a half-year's farewell of old friend whiskey at Kendal on the night after I left. There was a party of gentlemen at the Royal Hotel, and I joined them. We ordered in supper and whiskey-toddy as 'hot as hell!' They thought I was a physician, and put me in the chair. I gave sundry toasts, that were washed down at the same time, till the room spun round and the candles danced in our eyes." The party grew wilder. A "respectable old gentleman with powdered head, rosy cheeks, fat paunch, and ringed fingers" had to be helped to bed by the waiter. An Irishman and a Jew began to quarrel, and "discharged their glasses, each at his neighbour's throat instead of his own." Flinging his tumbler to the floor, Branwell joined battle for Ireland. "A regular rumpus en-sued, but we were tamed at last. I found myself in bed next morning, with a bottle of porter, a glass, and a corkscrew beside me."[22]

Charlotte had not underestimated Branwell's strong turn for an active life. Branwell, however, pulled himself together before knock-ing at his employer's door the next day, and even managed to feign an air of virtue during the first months of his stay.

If you saw me now [he confides in the same letter to John Brown, sexton, gravedigger, Worshipful Master of the Three Graces, and friend] you would not know me, and you would laugh to hear the character the people give me. Oh, the falsehood and hypocrisy of this world! I am fixed in a little retired town by the sea-shore, among wild, woody hills that rise round me—huge, rocky, and capped with clouds. My employer is a retired County magistrate, a large landowner, and of a right hearty and generous disposition. His wife is a quiet, silent, and amiable woman, and his sons are two fine, spirited lads. My landlord is a respectable surgeon, two days out of seven is as drunk as a lord! His wife is a bustling, chattering, kind-hearted soul; and his daughter! oh! death and damnation! Well, what am I? That is, what do they think I am? A most calm, sedate, sober, abstemious, patient, mild-hearted, virtuous, gentlemanly philosopher,—the picture of good works, and the treasure-house of righteous thoughts. Cards are shuf-fled under the table-cloth, glasses are thrust into the cupboard if I en-ter the room. I take neither spirits, wine, nor malt liquors. I dress in black, and smile like a saint or martyr. Everybody says, "what a good young gentleman is Mr Postlethwaite's tutor!" . . . I am getting as fat as Prince William at Springhead, and as godly as his friend, Parson Winterbotham. My hand shakes no longer. I ride to the bank-er's at Ulverston with Mr Postlethwaite, and sit drinking tea and talk-

0

ing scandal with old ladies. As to the young ones! I have one sitting by me just now—fair-faced, blue-eyed, dark-haired, sweet eighteen— she little thinks the devil is so near her!

Unlike Charlotte and Anne, Branwell was not confined to his employer's house, but boarded with a Dr. Gibson in the market town of Broughton. His lot was fifty times easier. A tutor was not expected to wipe children's smutty noses, patrol his pupils' leisure hours, dress them, or set their chairs at table. Nor was he buried under the mountains of sewing and fancy work forced upon Charlotte by Mrs. Sidgwick. He evidently was not obliged to attend gatherings in the Postlethwaite drawing room; nor was he patronized by the mistress of the house. His tutorial duties over, he closed the door of Broughton House and walked out into the village, a free man. He had the use of a riding horse and was free to patronize the Sun Hotel, the King's Arms, or the Rose—which he did. His wages for less work were better than his sisters'. Lacking Charlotte's talent, he nevertheless found himself with plenty of leisure to write. He was enraptured with the wild mountainous country of the Furness peninsula and had the freedom to explore it. Small wonder he decided that on the whole he was content with his lot.

Branwell had been tutored in Greek and Latin in long sessions with his father behind the parlor door. In his spare time he now turned to translation, and settled down to recast Horace's odes into English. Discovering that he had rather a flair for this sort of literary work, he sent off some sample passages, this time to Hartley Coleridge, son of the famous poet and friend of Wordsworth, Samuel Taylor Coleridge. Hartley lived at Nab Cottage on the shores of Rydal Water near Wordsworth's home at Rydal Mount, a dark-eyed, childlike, dreamy little man, floating quite out of touch with reality on the wings of dissipation and opium. Conscious of wearing his father's literary mantle, he read the odes sympathetically, and—lo—invited Branwell to visit him at Nab Cottage. There Branwell came on May 1, intoxicated with this sudden, magic entry into the fabled Lake District of Wordsworth, Coleridge, De Quincey, and romanticism. Did they converse under the beech trees bordering the lake? Or in Hartley's darkened cottage piled high with dusty newspapers? Little matter. That day Branwell fed on honeydew and drank the milk of paradise.

Hartley's encouragement immediately ruined Branwell for tutoring. He arrived back at Broughton elated and drunk—the Devil's cleft hoof showing for the first time beneath the saint's robe. Convinced he was made for greater things, unable to forget Coleridge's praise, he grew derelict in duty. Instead of coaching John and William Postlethwaite in mathematics and Greek, he spent the lesson hours idly sketching

and weaving fanciful stories for the boys about his drawings. One day
he disappeared without warning in the company of a poet friend;
night came and he did not return. Mr. Postlethwaite's brother rode
out in search of him. Branwell was discovered drunk, and Mr. Postlethwaite dismissed him on the spot.[23]

What concoction of lies did Branwell invent to get his father to send
a letter to Broughton requesting that his son be sent home immediately? No doubt he wrote dramatically of long hours, harsh exploita-
tion, breaking health, and mental anguish. Or perhaps that he was on
the threshold of a brilliant literary career. In June, Branwell arrived
back in Haworth to be greeted as a martyr by Mr. Brontë, always
willing to have the wool pulled over his eyes where Branwell was concerned. Conscious of their own sufferings under strange roofs, his
sisters could only outwardly sympathize. Charlotte at least must have
guessed, however, that he had been sent away in disgrace.

The translation affair came to nothing. Hartley Coleridge, as mud-
dled as he was sympathetic, probably forgot the odes the minute their
translator walked away from his door.

# 7

*Plotting Escape*

Branwell was not at home long, however. That fall the family summoned up their shaken faith once more and bid him good speed.
Charlotte to Ellen, September 29, 1840: "A distant relation of mine,
one Patrick Boanerges, has set off to seek his fortune in the wild,
wandering, adventurous, romantic, knight-errant-like capacity of
clerk on the Leeds and Manchester Railroad. Leeds and Manchester,
where are they? Cities in a wilderness—like Tadmor, alias Palmyra—
are they not?"[1] Here are detachment and irony. Charlotte had
already called Branwell "a distant relation of mine" when writing to
Ellen of his unfortunate coldness toward Mary Taylor. Clearly, she
was regarding Branwell more and more objectively: once he might
have been Boanerges—"son of thunder"; now the title mocked him.

Yet the railroad was the marvel of the age. To some poor-spirited
souls out of tune with the great Victorian hymn to progress, the sight
of the tranquil green English countryside hacked and scarred to make
way for a shrieking monster belching smoke, scattering cinders, and
stampeding horses was, of course, distressing. But for most Victorians
the railroad crowned the achievements of their industrial age. Branwell's new post as "Assistant Clerk in Charge" at Sowerby Bridge
Station two miles southwest of Halifax was not, therefore, entirely a
comedown. Even the unworldly Brontës eventually invested in Man-
chester-Leeds railway stock, and Emily took a particular pleasure in
managing this small business. The investments brewed one of the few
quarrels between Charlotte and Emily: Charlotte, cautious, wanted to
sell when the "railroad mania" threatened to bankrupt many small
investors, but Emily held firm. Mysticism formed only one aspect of
Emily's character. At her soul she was shrewd, calm, and aggressive.
Buried in Haworth, she nevertheless believed that to invest in the

future of a railroad serving the two great industrial centers of England was to invest in a certainty.[2]

As for Charlotte, liberty in this autumn of 1840 was growing wearisome. The urgent voice of duty whispered to her of Aesop's grasshopper who sang all summer and starved all winter. She exchanged letters with a Mrs. Brooke who advertised for a governess. "If you want a showy, elegant, fashionable personage, I am not the man for you," she wrote candidly. Mrs. Brooke replied, requesting music and singing. Charlotte, too nearsighted to play the piano and innocent of a singing voice, relinquished another situation.

Winter swept down on Haworth. William Weightman took ill, then mended, and went about preparing for his ordination. Mary Taylor came in January and played chess with "his lordship," each game terminating in mock hostility. Weightman continued to sigh prettily over half a dozen young ladies, Ellen Nussey included. Ellen herself still hesitated over Mr. Vincent while Charlotte dispatched warnings to Brookroyd advising her to forget the rosy-cheeked curate of Haworth. Then in March 1841, after almost two years of advertising, correspondence, and interviews that came to nothing, Charlotte packed her trunk, said her good-bys, and set out for a new position as governess to the White family at Rawdon, six miles from Bradford. Several weeks later Anne too left to be a governess at Thorp Green Hall, seventy miles from home near the great minster city of York, and only Emily was left to sew with Aunt Branwell in her stuffy bedroom or wander the spring-awakening moors.

The Whites had offered Charlotte a very low salary: nominally £20 a year, but after deductions for laundry, £16—the wages of a rather well paid housemaid. She accepted it in expectation that the Whites had "minds and hearts not dug out of a lead mine, or cut from a marble quarry"; evidently she did not stop to consider that the best proof of a good master lies in his financial generosity. She approached Rawdon with nerves on edge and the dread of new faces like a cold stone in her stomach; yet at first Upperwood House and the White family appeared almost as human as she could wish. The house was not as grand as the Sidgwicks' Stonegappe, but it was comfortable and well regulated, and the spacious grounds promised great beauty in the coming spring. The Whites seemed good people, she was treated with consideration, and her pupils, a girl of eight and a boy of six, although wild and unbroken, were not, apparently, vicious.

She vowed earnestly to please them—and yet ". . . no one but myself is aware how utterly averse my whole mind and nature are to the employment. Do not think that I fail to blame myself for this . . . I find it so hard to repel the rude familiarity of children. I find it so difficult to ask either servants or mistress for anything I want, however much I want it. It is less pain to me to endure the greatest inconvenience than to request its removal. I am a fool. Heaven knows I cannot help it!"[3]

Pride was again her downfall. Superior in character and intelligence, she had to endure patronage from the *nouveau riche*—the showy, loud, thick-rinded, materialistic merchant class. She retaliated with the only defense of the genteel poor—snobbery. The Whites' nurse, she wrote vindictively to Ellen, when dressed up has much more the air of a lady than her mistress. Well she could believe that Mrs. White had been an exciseman's daughter; she was convinced that Mr. White's origins were low. Mrs. White could not fool her by bragging about her fine family connections and sneering at what she called the low race of tradesfolk. She *had* begun to think Mrs. White a good sort of body in spite of her bouncing and boasting, her bad grammar and worse orthography, but one trait condemned her a long way: after treating her governess familiarly as an equal for a long time, she could still fly into a coarse, unladylike passion if the slightest thing went wrong. Passion, after all, was the true test of vulgarity or refinement.

Admitting that Upperwood House was far better than Stonegappe and the children not "such little devils incarnate as the Sidgwicks'," she nevertheless found her day exhaustingly full. Mrs. White piled mountains of sewing upon her. Since the children occupied almost every minute of the day, she had to tackle this task in the evenings. Often it was nearly midnight before she could take up her candle and wearily mount the shadowy stairs to her room: these were housemaid's wages for more than housemaid's hours. Taking out her portable writing desk, she would scratch a few lines to Emily or Ellen; *then* the ache of homesickness throbbed. She found that under such an oppressive routine simply to mail a letter was difficult: she seldom could be spared the forty or fifty minutes to walk a mile to the post and a mile back. If this heavy duty was not enough, there were the mandatory sessions in the drawing room: the ex-tradesman must have a governess on display. A visitor to Upperwood House remembered much later a tiny, silent figure "sitting apart from the rest of the family in a corner of the room, poring, in her shortsighted way, over a book . . . a shy nervous girl, ill at ease, who desired to escape notice and to avoid taking part in the general conversation."[4]

Brookroyd was a tantalizing nine miles away. Uncertain whether a governess was allowed visitors and too shy to ask, Charlotte nevertheless encouraged Ellen to visit her in captivity—"if it be a breach of etiquette, never mind." Then she seized joyously on Ellen's counter-invitation to Brookroyd:

> —as soon as I had read your shabby little note—I gathered up my spirits directly—walked on the impulse of the moment into Mrs White's presence—popped the question—and for two minutes received no answer—will she refuse me when I work so hard for her? thought I
> Ye-es-es, drawled Madam—in a reluctant cold tone—
> thank you Madam said I with extreme cordiality, and was marching from the room when she recalled me with—
> "You'd better go on Saturday afternoon then—when the children have holiday—and if you return in time for them to have all their lessons on Monday morning—I don't see that much will be lost"
> you *are* a genuine Turk thought I but again I assented. . . .
> I'll come—God knows with a thankful and joyful heart—glad of a day's reprieve from labour—if you don't send the gig I'll walk. . . .
> God bless you—I want to see you again. Huzza for Saturday afternoon after next!⁵

Mrs. White's insecurity in her new role as merchant's lady was again in evidence when Charlotte returned. Ellen's brother George drove her back in the gig, helped her to descend at the door, and bowled off down the drive. Charlotte stepped in to find Mrs. White very red in the face and ready to tear into her governess at what she imagined to be a slight from the Nusseys of Brookroyd. The little incident convinced Charlotte further of the vulnerability of the Whites under their thin veneer of good breeding; she was conscious that her stock rose considerably with them because of her Nussey connection. Ellen would have quite a fuss made over her if she chose to visit, Charlotte knew. The grounds were exquisite now in May, green as emerald, and Mrs. White would be pleased as punch to show off her beautiful establishment. Mr. White even wrote Mr. Brontë, urging him to come for a week's visit, but Charlotte shuddered at the thought of his patronizing her father, even though she liked Mr. White a great deal better than his wife.

Despite hard work and Mrs. White's bursts of temper, Upperwood House did prove more congenial to Charlotte than Stonegappe. More experienced and self-confident, she won control over the children by a combination of courage, firmness, and sincerity. Like *Punch's* Miss Harker, she was rewarded for her success with the additional burden of caring for the Whites' youngest child, but even then she did not flag: ". . . by dint of nursing the fat baby it has got to know me and be fond of me—I occasionally suspect myself of growing rather fond of it." Her health held. The rest of the family seemed to be managing equally well. Anne wrote from Thorp Green Hall that she was in good

Maria Branwell, aged sixteen—by Tonkin, 1799. BY COURTESY OF THE
BRONTE SOCIETY

Haworth Parsonage, Churchyard and Church—drawn by Mrs. Gaskell in 1855. PHOTO-
GRAPH FROM THE BRONTE PARSONAGE MUSEUM

The "gun" portrait of Branwell and his sisters—painted by Branwell. Charlotte is second
from left. Emily is probably to the right and Anne left, although the reverse has been
argued. PHOTOGRAPH FROM THE BRONTE PARSONAGE MUSEUM

Branwell Brontë's painting of his sisters—c. 1835. The column dividing Charlotte from Anne (far left) and Emily is a painted-out figure of Branwell himself; presumably he was dissatisfied with his self-portrait. BY COURTESY OF NATIONAL PORTRAIT GALLERY, LONDON

Ellen Nussey as a schoolgirl. PHOTOGRAPH FROM THE
BRONTE PARSONAGE MUSEUM

Tiny "editions" of *The Young Men's Magazine* written by Charlotte. The pages, compared here with a ten-pence piece, measure about 2 to 3 inches by 1½ inches, and are
stitched neatly together and bound in sugar-bag or store paper. PHOTOGRAPH FROM THE
BRONTE PARSONAGE MUSEUM

The Duke of Zamorna, flambouyant hero of Charlotte's Angrian tales—drawn by Branwell. BY COURTESY OF THE BRONTE SOCIETY

Medallion of Branwell Brontë—by his friend, Joseph Bentley Leyland. BY COURTESY
OF THE BRONTE SOCIETY

Anne Brontë—watercolor by Charlotte. BY COURTESY OF THE BRONTE
SOCIETY

Emily Brontë—by Branwell, c. 1835. This portrait was originally part of a group.
Mr. Nicholls supposedly destroyed the figures of Charlotte and Anne because they
were poor likenesses. BY COURTESY OF NATIONAL PORTRAIT GALLERY, LONDON

health, although Charlotte, without seeing for herself, suspected that Anne was simply being stoical. Branwell did not write, but Emily informed her that he had been transferred from Sowerby Bridge Station to the post of "Clerk in Charge" at Luddenden Foot. His salary was £130 a year—more than six times Charlotte's wages for far less work. "It looks like getting on at any rate," wrote Emily with her devastating candor.

She might have been content, yet the tensions generated by subservience, loneliness, and an acute sense of wasting talents never slackened. Sitting alone in the empty schoolroom on a still Sunday evening, the fragrance of a May twilight stealing through the open windows from the gardens, she dreamed of freedom from servitude. Must she always win her bread among strangers in the "land of Egypt and the house of Bondage"? Yes, forever, unless—and the idea, once conceived, seized her with irresistible force—unless, somehow, they could establish themselves in a school of their own.

Summer came. Charlotte asked for a vacation, flatly rejected Mrs. White's offer of ten days, and returned to Haworth on the evening of the last day in June triumphantly possessed of three weeks' leave. She just missed Anne, already returned from her vacation to Thorp Green Hall, and found that little Black Tom the cat was dead, but nothing could make her sad for long—it felt like paradise to be home again. The school project immediately became the main topic of debate at the parsonage. Charlotte was on fire with the plan. Emily, content at home, was not eager, but willing. Papa and Aunt murmured cautiously. And then Aunt, to Charlotte's utter amazement, announced that she was willing to advance them a loan *if* an eligible place for the school could be found and *if* pupils could be guaranteed in advance before any money was risked. Totally uninitiated into the mysteries of schoolmistressing, Charlotte found herself feverishly making plans. She appealed to Ellen. Did she think that £150 would be sufficient to establish a respectable, though by no means *showy* school? Would she please ask her sister Ann? They would not hear of getting in debt. She was considering Burlington as a location, although it was far from home and they had no acquaintance there; she fancied, however, that there were fewer schools in the East Riding than in the West. Did Ellen know any school near Burlington besides the establishment of Miss J——?

Back at Upperwood House, Charlotte wrote, planned, rejected plans, and worried. Emily remained serene through this storm of uncertainty. Her tranquillity illuminates a rare scrap of her writing, a diary fragment written July 30, 1841, her twenty-third birthday. Anne wrote a similar statement the same day: the girls had a secret agreement that every four years they would write an assessment of their lives to be opened four years later on Emily's birthday or Anne's. Emily's scrap begins, "A PAPER to be opened when Anne is 25 years old, or my next birthday after if all be well":

It is Friday evening, near 9 o'clock—wild rainy weather. I am seated in the dining-room alone, having just concluded tidying our desk boxes, writing this document. Papa is in the parlour—aunt upstairs in her room. She has been reading *Blackwood's Magazine* to papa. Victoria and Adelaide [pet geese] are ensconced in the peat-house. Keeper is in the kitchen—Hero in his cage. We are all stout and hearty, as I hope is the case with Charlotte, Branwell, and Anne, of whom the first is at John White, Esq., Upperwood House, Rawdon; the second is at Luddenden Foot; and the third is, I believe, at Scarborough, inditing perhaps a paper corresponding to this.

A scheme is at present in agitation for setting us up in a school of our own; as yet nothing is determined, but I hope and trust it may go on and prosper and answer our highest expectations. This day four years I wonder whether we shall still be dragging on in our present condition or established to our heart's content. Time will show.

I guess that at the time appointed for the opening of this paper we *i.e.* Charlotte, Anne, and I, shall be all merrily seated in our own sitting-room in some pleasant and flourishing seminary, having just gathered in for the midsummer holy day. Our debts will be paid off, and we shall have cash in hand to a considerable amount. Papa, aunt, and Branwell will either have been or be coming to visit us. It will be a fine warm summer evening, very different from this bleak look-out, and Anne and I will perchance slip out into the garden for a few minutes to peruse our papers. I hope either this or something better will be the case.

The *Gondalians* are at present in a threatening state, but there is no open rupture as yet. All the princes and the princesses of the Royalty are at the Palace of Instruction. I have a good many books on hand, but I am sorry to say that as usual I make small progress with any. However, I have just made a new regularity paper! and I mean *verb sap* to do great things. And now I must close, sending from far an exhortation, "Courage, courage," to exiled and harassed Anne, wishing she was here.[6]

Anne needed encouragement, for she suffered much in her quiet way. "She has so much to endure," Charlotte once wrote to Ellen. "When my thoughts turn to her, they always see her as a patient, persecuted stranger. I know what concealed susceptibility is in her nature, when her feelings are wounded. . . . She is more lonely, less gifted with the power of making friends, even than I am."[7] On Emily's birthday, Anne was at the seaside resort of Scarborough with the Robinsons. Sometime that day she managed to steal a few moments to write her paper:

July the 30th, A.D. 1841: This is Emily's birthday. She has now completed her 23rd year, and is, I believe, at home. Charlotte is a governess in the family of Mr White. Branwell is a clerk in the railroad station at Luddenden Foot, and I am a governess in the family of Mr Robinson. I dislike the situation and wish to change it for another. I am now at Scarborough. My pupils are gone to bed and I am hastening to finish this before I follow them.

We are thinking of setting up a school of our own, but nothing definite is settled about it yet, and we do not know whether we shall be able to or not. I hope we shall. And I wonder what will be our condition and how or where we shall all be on this day four years hence; at which time, if all be well, I shall be 25 years and 6 months old, Emily will be 27 years old, Branwell 28 years and 1 month, and Charlotte 29 years and a quarter. We are now all separate and not likely to meet again for many a weary week, but we are none of us ill that I know of, and all are doing something for our own livelihood except Emily, who, however, is as busy as any of us, and in reality earns her food and raiment as much as we do.

> How little know we what we are
> How less what we may be!

Four years ago I was at school. Since then I have been a governess at Blake Hall, left it, come to Thorp Green, and seen the sea and York Minster. Emily has been a teacher at Miss Patchett's school, and left it. Charlotte has left Miss Wooler's, been a governess at Mrs. Sidgwick's, left her, and gone to Mrs. White's. Branwell has given up painting, been a tutor in Cumberland, left it, and become a clerk on the railroad. Tabby has left us, Martha Brown has come in her place. We have got Keeper, got a sweet little cat and lost it, and also got a hawk. Got a wild goose which has flown away, and three tame ones, one of which has been killed. All these diversities, with many others, are things we did not expect or foresee in the July of 1837. What will the next four years bring forth? Providence only knows. But we ourselves have sustained very little alteration since that time. I have the same faults that I had then, only I have more wisdom and experience, and a little more self-possession than I then enjoyed. How will it be when we open this paper and the one Emily has written? I wonder whether the *Gondalians* will still be flourishing, and what will be their condition. I am now engaged in writing the fourth volume of *Solala Vernon's Life*.

For some time I have looked upon 25 as a sort of era in my existence. It may prove a true presentiment, or it may be only a superstitious fancy; the latter seems most likely, but time will show.

Anne Brontë.[8]

At Rawdon Charlotte grew more urgent for release as letters arrived from the Taylors abroad. Martha had entered a smart boarding school in Brussels, while Mary, traveling in France with her brother John, wrote enthusiastically of the fine sights and sent Charlotte an elegant gift—a handsome black silk scarf and a pair of kid gloves. The letters added fuel to Charlotte's fire. She poured out her frustration to Ellen:

> Mary's letters spoke of some of the pictures and cathedrals she had seen—pictures the most exquisite—and cathedrals the most venerable—I hardly know what swelled to my throat as I read her letter: such a vehement impatience of restraint and steady work. Such a strong wish for wings—wings such as wealth can furnish—such an urgent thirst to see—to know—to learn—something internal seemed to expand boldly for a minute—I was tantalised with the consciousness of faculties unexercised—then all collapsed and I despaired. . . . I know my place is a favourable one for a Governess—what dismays and haunts me sometimes is a conviction that I have no natural knack for my vocation—if teaching only were requisite it would be smooth and easy—but it is the living in other people's houses—the estrangement from one's real character—the adoption of a cold frigid apathetic exterior that is painful. . . .[9]

In the same letter Charlotte alluded to the school project as "our polar star," but told Ellen that no further steps had been taken in the matter. This was not true. In the past Charlotte had often appealed to Margaret Wooler when seeking a situation; now she appealed to her again for advice, and Miss Wooler responded by offering her the chance of reviving the school at Dewsbury Moor. The establishment would be turned over to Charlotte; the furniture would stay as a loan until she was financially solvent. This was kind, and Charlotte seized on the offer despite grim memories of Dewsbury, mentally forgiving Peg Wooler all the foibles that had irritated her in the past. Then a still better plan was proposed. She had confided her hopes for the school project to the Whites. They were sympathetic but realistic: with so many flourishing academies in Yorkshire, could the sisters hope to attract enough pupils to their obscure village to make the venture a success? It seemed doubtful. Why not postpone the project and contrive immediately to further their education on the Continent for half a year? Then, with a prospectus announcing French, German, and perhaps Italian lessons by the continentally educated Miss Brontës, *then* they might succeed.

The Whites could not have uttered words Charlotte more longed to hear. Tantalized by Mary's letters and sick to death of governessing, she immediately felt the truth of the Whites' suggestion. To return to

Dewsbury Moor was a step backward into the dreary past; success surely lay in broadening her experience and knowledge by travel and study abroad.

Aunt Branwell was the only person who might finance such an adventure. She had agreed to a loan if the school project seemed absolutely secure. Would she agree to finance Charlotte and Emily—Emily *must* go—for half a year at a foreign school? Charlotte sat down to compose the most tactful letter of her life. She appealed, wisely, to Aunt's lively concern for the safety of her investment. Mr. and Mrs. White had assured them, Charlotte urged, that without continental experience they might easily fail and her capital be lost. Half of Aunt's money at least should therefore be laid out to send them abroad, thereby assuring success and a speedy return both of interest and principal.

> I feel certain [she continued persuasively], . . . that you will see the propriety of what I say; you always like to use your money to the best advantage; you are not fond of making shabby purchases; when you do confer a favour, it is often done in style; and depend upon it £50, or £100, thus laid out, would be well employed. Of course, I know no other friend in the world to whom I could apply on this subject except yourself. I feel an absolute conviction that, if this advantage were allowed us, it would be the making of us for life. Papa will perhaps think it a wild and ambitious scheme; but who ever rose in the world without ambition? When he left Ireland to go to Cambridge University, he was as ambitious as I am now. I want us *all* to go on. I know we have talents, and I want them to be turned to account. I look to you, aunt, to help us. I think you will not refuse. I know, if you consent, it shall not be my fault if you ever repent your kindness.[10]

Her fingers must have trembled as she blotted and folded the paper; she posted it in a state of extreme excitement, and returned to spend the intervening days in a state of acute suspense. A reply, opened with pounding heart. Consent. Her letter had carried the day.

But a hundred obstacles still lay in her way. Her first duty was to appease Ellen, who had ferreted out her plans and, always insecure wherever Mary Taylor figured in Charlotte's life, now wrote in hurt anger, accusing Charlotte of plotting behind her back. She answered soothingly, explaining that she had not wanted to raise the alarm until plans were more firmly fixed. "Believe me my dear Ellen," she ended kindly, "though I was born in April the month of cloud and sunshine I am not changeful . . . if you will let the cloud and shower only pass by without upbraiding—be sure the sun is always behind obscured but still existing. Write to say all is forgiven. I'm fit to cry."[11] The next duty was to appease Anne, who might feel hurt at being excluded, for

Charlotte, always partial to Emily, had set her heart on having Emily's company. Emily had had only a few months' formal schooling; Anne had been almost two years at Miss Wooler's. Anne had a paying job; Emily earned nothing at home. Anne's turn would come later. So Charlotte argued, rashly ignoring the lesson of Roe Head and Law Hill which should have taught that Emily could not flourish away from Haworth.

A suitable school must be found. Aunt's money in no way could accommodate them at Martha Taylor's school in Brussels, the fashionable Château de Koekleberg. Letters must be sent to the British consul in Brussels, asking him to recommend a modest establishment; the name of a Mr. Evan Jenkins was given Mr. Brontë. Mr. Jenkins turned out to be the Episcopalian minister and chaplain to the embassy rather than the British consul. Inquiries flagged. Charlotte fidgeted at the unbearable suspense: people were so "hard to spur up to the proper speed." Then Mr. Brontë received a letter from Mrs. Jenkins declaring that she could not recommend any of the inexpensive French schools in Brussels and suggesting an inexpensive institution in Lille in the north of France instead. Mr. Brontë thought it wise to heed her advice; but Charlotte felt the change of plans like a blow, for she deeply regretted losing the company of the Taylors in Brussels. Still, she yielded to the inevitable.

She gave notice to the Whites. Even though they had made much of her the last six months, she was touched by the sincere regard they displayed as she stood at their door for the last time, trunk packed, winter bonnet tied under her chin, and extended her tiny gloved hand in farewell. Their good wishes did much to erase the frustration and loneliness of the long months at Upperwood House. Outside, the horses stamped and steamed in the keen winter air, and then the carriage was off, rattling over the frozen rutted roads. She reached the parsonage on Christmas Eve.

Christmas in Yorkshire meant a great spice cake, cheese, and mulled ale; a hearty and tuneful chorus of "Christians Awake" from a band of roving singers stamping in the cold outside the window and accompanied by flute, violin, and hautbois; church bells from the gray tower of St. Michael and All Angels. Did a festive band find its way down the dark lane to carol at the parsonage door? Or did Charlotte, after thawing her frozen fingers at the fire, hurry off with Emily to hear her father preach the Christmas Eve sermon in the dim and drafty church? Whatever the celebration, excited talk about going abroad must have dominated the conversation that Christmas Eve.

Ellen begged Charlotte to visit Brookroyd before leaving England. Charlotte countered with an invitation to Haworth. Neither visit materialized, however: Ellen's family refused to let her hazard a winter journey after a recent illness and Charlotte pleaded preparations for the momentous step ahead.

> January 20, 1842: I have had letters to write lately to Brussels to Lille and to London—I have lots of chemises—night-gowns—pocket handkerchiefs and pockets to make besides clothes to repair—and I have been every week since I came home expecting to see Branwell and he has never been able to get over yet—we fully expect him however next Saturday. Under these circumstances how can I go a-visiting? . . . you bother and tantalise one to death with talking of conversations by the fireside or between the blankets—depend upon it we are not to have any such for many a long month to come—I get an interesting impression of old-age upon my face and when you see me next I shall certainly wear caps and spectacles.

The topic of William Weightman is still green and Charlotte closes her last letter from England with news of the charming curate.

> Your darling "his young reverence" as you tenderly call him—is looking delicate and pale—poor thing don't you pity him? I do from my heart—when he is well and fat and jovial I never think of him—but when anything ails him I am always sorry—He sits opposite to Anne at Church sighing softly and looking out of the corners of his eyes to win her attention—and Anne is so quiet, her looks so down-cast—they are a picture—He would be the better of a comfortable wife like you to settle him, you would settle him I believe—nobody else would.—
> Yours affectionately,
>
> C.B.[12]

They were due to leave in less than three weeks for Lille. Then at the last minute another letter arrived from Mrs. Jenkins in Brussels. She could, it seemed, recommend a French school in Brussels after all: the Pensionnat Heger, *"Maison d'Education Pour les Jeunes Demoiselles sous la direction de Madame Heger-Parent, Rue d'Isabelle à Bruxelles."* Charlotte fired off a letter of inquiry to Madame Heger; reading it, the woman and her husband were so struck by its simple, urgent tone that they immediately returned an accommodating reply. Reprieve. Lille was abandoned. On to Brussels!

# 8

## Rue d'Isabelle

London, 1842. Yellow fog, gaslight, narrow streets, reeking court-yards, foghorns moaning on the Thames. Broad thoroughfares, carriages bowling through Hyde Park, umbrellas and top hats in Oxford Street. Pickpockets, beggars, whores. Sir Robert Peel in the House of Lords. Gin palaces, gutters oozing filth, dark putrid flights of stairs. Gilt carriages drawn up before Swan and Edgar's silk shop in Regent Street. Sherry, claret, roast beef, and the discreet gleam of heavy silver in clubs in Pall Mall. Mud, hackneys, horse-drawn omnibuses, flaring gas jets, fog. Costermongers bawling the price of herrings, gloves, and onions; women street-sellers in rags; haunches of veal, mutton, and beef in Butcher Row. Circuses, theater, pantomime, and opera in Drury Lane. Newgate Prison, a dirty hulk. Paupers. Work-houses. Chimney sweeps, crossing sweeps, peddling Jews, sewer-hunt-ers. Clerks scuttling to keep the countinghouses of numberless Scrooges. Smart boots, cigars, lemon-colored gloves, fluttering veils in Rotten Row. At Buckingham Palace a twenty-three-year-old queen, small, plump, energetic; stubborn, humorless, conventional; fertile and adoring of her husband—symbol of an age.

Alighting from the Leeds train in Euston Square, north London, on a February evening, a provincial-looking clergyman in high, white silk cravat and two soberly clad young women, one of whom at least was trembling with confusion, fatigue, and the excitement of a first visit to London. The high-vaulted Doric arches of the fog-filled, echo-ing station, the foreign Cockney patter of the cabmen, the powdered footmen guarding gilt carriages, and the thronging crowds were at once delightful and bewildering. Mr. Brontë got his daughters to the only hostelry he knew in London, the Chapter Coffee House in Pater-noster Row, the same quiet inn Branwell had sought out on his in-auspicious journey to London. The Ostend packet sailed too early the next morning for convenience. They determined to spend three days in London and sail on Saturday, February 12. They had extinguished their candle and were settling down to sleep when the silence of the dark room was shattered: "a deep, low, mighty tone swung through the night." One, two, three—by the twelfth "colossal hum and trembling knell" they knew the great voice that now told London it was midnight. They lay "in the shadow of St. Paul's."

The next morning clamorous London lay waiting to be explored. "Prodigious was the amount of life I lived that morning. Finding myself before St. Paul's, I went in; I mounted to the dome; I saw thence London, with its river, and its bridges, and its churches; I saw antique Westminster, and the green Temple Gardens with the sun upon them, and a glad blue sky of early spring above; and in between them and it, not too dense a cloud of haze. Descending, I went wandering whither chance might lead, in a still ecstasy of freedom and enjoyment; and I got—I know not how—I got into the heart of city life. I saw and felt London at last: I got into the Strand; I went up Cornhill; I mixed with the life passing along; I dared the perils of crossings."[1]

Most Victorians were entranced with the fine shops, the parks, and the squares of the West End. Charlotte loved the City proper—its rush and roar as it went about its business. But chiefly London was a mecca of art for Charlotte and Emily, a city of fine buildings, statues, galleries, and museums. Mary Taylor, returning to Brussels accompanied by her brother Joe, had considerately offered their escort as experienced travelers; she remembered with amusement Charlotte's determination to do the rounds of all the museums and galleries in London. "She seemed to think our business was and ought to be, to see all the pictures and statues we could. She knew the artists and knew where other productions of theirs were to be found. I don't remember what we saw except St. Paul's. Emily was like her in these habits of mind, but certainly never took her opinion, but always had one to offer." Tolerant and amused, Mary followed in Charlotte's wake, smiling as her enthusiastic friend paused with reverently clasped hands to gaze at the paintings and buildings she had imagined so vividly back in Haworth. For Charlotte, London was like having a whole loaf in her hand instead of a crust, and she gorged on it.

The packet sailed Saturday morning from the wharf at London Bridge; a Channel crossing took at least fourteen hours. Charlotte stayed on deck after the others deserted to revel in the sea breeze, the spray-soaked deck, the heaving Channel waves with sea birds on their ridges, the low-hanging cloudy sky; then, unfortunately, "Becoming excessively sick, I faltered down into the cabin!" At Ostend the five travelers found rooms at a hotel, rested a day, then set out the forty miles to Brussels in a diligence, the French equivalent of the English stagecoach, and like its counterpart, fast disappearing from the travel scene. Was Emily already homesick, looking out at the flat, treeless Belgian countryside, the canals that "crept, like half-torpid green snakes," the rows of pollarded willows edging the flat wet fields, the gray monotonous sky? All in Belgium was tilled, planted, squared, and clipped. If Emily already craved her rough heathery hills, Charlotte did not. "I gazed often, and always with delight, from the window of the diligence . . . not a beautiful, scarcely a picturesque object met my eye along the whole route; yet to me all was beautiful, all more than picturesque . . . as it grew dark . . . the rain recommenced, and it was through streaming and starless darkness my eye caught the first gleam of the lights of Brussels."[2]

Another hotel for the weary travelers, then a parting from Mary and Joe Taylor the next morning, for Mary must return to the Château de Koekleberg and Charlotte and Emily report at the Pensionnat Heger. Mr. and Mrs. Jenkins came to fetch them and escort them the short distance through strange streets to the Rue d'Isabelle. The sisters found themselves in a narrow sunken street, overhung by buildings and shadowed by the great Gothic towers of a church. A larger house, "loftier by a storey than those around it," a brass plate bearing the legend "Pensionnat des Demoiselles," a pull at the bell, and they found themselves inside a cold square hall. There they were greeted by a smooth, plump Frenchwoman with dark eyes under dark curves of brow and abundant dark hair, still fresh though in her late thirties, and eight months pregnant: Madame Heger. Clearly this was no English schoolmistress, straight of spine, steely of eye, and large of foot. Madame greeted them with suave composure, no doubt smiling inwardly at these eccentric-looking *anglaises*, particularly at the taller daughter, who stood silently, her eyes downcast, dressed in the narrow skirts and gigot sleeves of twenty years before. Did Emily manage to raise her eyes or mutter more than a monosyllable? Mr. Brontë summoned up his gallantry, pronounced himself well satisfied, bade his daughters good-by, and left with the Jenkinses, at whose home he planned to put up for a few days while seeing the sights of Brussels and visiting the battlefield of Waterloo. Mrs. Jenkins issued the girls a standing invitation to visit on Sundays and half holidays. Then the Pensionnat door closed on England.

Madame Heger had acquired the school property in 1830 after the Belgian revolution. The house dated from the turn of the century; the Rue d'Isabelle, however, named for the Infanta Isabella when Brussels headquartered the Spanish governors of the Netherlands, had been a thoroughfare since the sixteenth century. The Pensionnat was a spacious establishment: its high-walled façade, flush with the street, enclosed a quadrangle of buildings, playgrounds, and gardens so large that it bordered the Rue Terarken on the south and the Rue des Douze Apôtres on the west. Inside, a *carré*—the large square hall Charlotte and Emily stepped into from the street—divided the living quarters from the schoolrooms. Off the *carré*, a portress sat in her tiny *cabinet*, trimming a cap as she waited to answer a pull at the bell or run with a message to Madame. Great double doors on the right opened into three schoolrooms, all large, airy, and well lit, a refectory, a greater and a lesser drawing room, and a small dark oratory where a lamp burned before an image of the Virgin and pupils met for singing and prayer. Opposite the street door and across the *carré* another glass door gave onto a large garden and the playgrounds, a quiet refuge undisturbed by the noise of the great city lying outside the walls. There on summer days the students came to stroll along the white paths among orange trees and huge old rosebushes, or to say their lessons to Madame, who set sewing in a vine-draped arbor shaded by the towering branches of an old acacia tree.[3]

Along the back of the premises ran a wall of blank stone marked only by small loopholes of windows high up: the rear buildings of the most prestigious boys' school in Brussels, the Athénée Royale. Between the high walls of the Pensionnat and the stone wall of the Athénée lay a narrow alley, accessible through a small door in the Pensionnat wall. Into this *allée défendue* the students of both schools were forbidden to set foot under the strictest penalties, and many, indeed, did not care to venture there, for the alley was narrow and dark, overgrown with shrubbery that climbed the walls and wove a tangled roof of vines overhead through which the sun seldom penetrated. The grounds were ordinary enough at midday when they were flooded with sunlight and filled with trampling, shrieking girls, but at sunset, when the *externes* were gone home and the boarders quiet at their studies, then the garden, heavily scented with orange and rose and darkening in the blue twilight, became a place of tranquil beauty.

Travel, said Bernard Shaw wisely, is narrowing. All one's vague prejudices against foreigners solidify the instant foot is set on foreign soil. To rootless Americans Shaw's aphorism perhaps does not apply, but Shaw knew the nineteenth-century Britisher who took four o'clock tea in a steaming jungle and boasted he could travel the world speaking nothing but the Queen's (and God's) English. When the Britisher was a stubborn and provincial young lady, raised in the austerities of a Protestant parsonage, shot through with deep partialities and prejudices, and timid and insecure in the bargain, contact with a foreign country was bound to dig the trenches of her prejudices even deeper.

Thus, even while excited by new impressions and freedom, Charlotte paradoxically recoiled from the French and Belgians around her rather than sought to appreciate or understand them. She and Emily, who is not known to have spoken a word to anyone during her whole stay in Brussels, clung together, alienated and alienating, two free-born English girls among an infidel host. Emily never accepted Brussels for a minute, although she did not complain. For Charlotte alienation came more gradually. It grew with her recognition that the great bells of Ste. Gudule's gray tower rising above the Pensionnat walls tolled for Catholic services; that the bell ringing through the school-rooms summoned pupils for the Catholic *prière du soir;* that the hastily muttered prayers in the oratory were sent up to an alien God. The students, Belgian and French, further antagonized her. As at Roe Head, Charlotte found herself among financially secure, marriage-destined girls to whom learning was an indifferent affair. In contrast, Charlotte and Emily had thrown themselves into their studies, conscious that they must use Aunt's money to the fullest advantage. The placid Belgians, sublimely indifferent to their own ignorance, infuriated Charlotte: she scornfully wrote them off as vain, lazy, and stupid. From a combined sense of diffidence and superiority she cut them, and perhaps was a little startled to find herself in turn almost totally ignored. To complete their isolation, Charlotte and Emily were going on twenty-six and twenty-four; they were by far the oldest pupils—hardly schoolgirls any more. In recognition of this fact they were mercifully assigned two beds at the end of the long dormitory room, curtained off from the stares, whispers, and laughter of the other twelve boarders.

Both Charlotte and Emily settled immediately to hard work and at first Charlotte scarcely had time to be homesick. Besides a brief note scribbled to Ellen on Mary Taylor's stationery during a rare visit to the Taylor sisters at the Château de Koekleberg, Charlotte did not find time to write to Ellen until May:

Brussels, May, 1842: Dear Ellen . . . I· was twenty-six years old a week or two since, and at this ripe time of life I am a schoolgirl, a complete schoolgirl, and, on the whole, very happy in that capacity. It felt very strange at first to submit to authority instead of exercising it—to obey orders instead of giving them; but I like that state of things. I returned to it with the same avidity that a cow, that has long been kept on dry hay, returns to fresh grass. Don't laugh at my simile. It is natural to me to submit, and very unnatural to command.

This is a large school, in which there are about forty *externes* or day-pupils, and twelve *pensionnaires* or boarders. Madame Heger, the head, is a lady of precisely the same cast of mind, degree of cultivation, and quality of intellect as Miss Catherine Wooler [Charlotte had found Miss Wooler's sister highly intelligent and excessively unamiable]. I think the severe points are a little softened, because she has not been disappointed, and consequently soured. In a word, she is a married instead of a maiden lady. There are three teachers in the school—Mademoiselle Blanche, Mademoiselle Sophie, and Mademoiselle Marie. The first two have no particular character. One is an old maid, and the other will be one. Mademoiselle Marie is talented and original, but of repulsive and arbitrary manners, which have made the whole school, except myself and Emily, her bitter enemies. No less than seven masters attend to teach the different branches of education—French, Drawing, Music, Singing, Writing, Arithmetic, and German. All in the house are Catholics except ourselves, one other girl, and the *gouvernante* of Madame's children, an English-woman, in rank something between a lady's-maid and a nursery governess. The difference in country and religion makes a broad line of demarcation between us and all the rest. We are completely isolated in the midst of numbers. Yet I think I am never unhappy; my present life is so delightful, so congenial to my own nature, compared with that of a governess. My time, constantly occupied, passes too rapidly. Hitherto both Emily and I have had good health, and therefore we have been able to work well. . . . Brussels is a beautiful city. The Belgians hate the English. Their external morality is more rigid than ours. . . .[4]

Of the disturbing differences between English and French schools, the fact that the Pensionnat's directress was a married woman rather than a maiden lady like Miss Wooler seems to have particularly unsettled Charlotte. Although five years older than her husband Constantin, Madame Heger was still ripely attractive and fertile: she gave birth to a son, Prospère, six weeks after the Brontës arrived, and already had three small daughters, Marie, Louise, and Claire. The school was not run, therefore, from the parlor of a spinstress, but as a family establishment, and Madame's husband and children were very much a part of the scene. The maternal atmosphere of the school sharpened Charlotte's awareness of her own wasting womanhood. So did conversations with the three unmarried teachers Madame employed. One of them, Mademoiselle Sophie, a lady of thirty-six, harped incessantly on the theme of marriage, bewailing the fact that she was getting so old; she got her father or her brother to carry letters to various men who might be willing to marry her; she spoke with dread of having to become a Sister of Charity, her only resource if marriage failed. Charlotte listened, curious and almost frightened. Could she be driven to such monomania in ten years? A subtle and unconscious resentment of Madame crept into her heart.

Besides, Madame was French—or at least a French-speaking Belgian of French parentage—and every good Englishman knew what that meant. As a girl, Charlotte had devoured dozens of French novels sent over by the Taylors from the abundant library of the Red House. While she admired George Sand's passionate simplicity, no doubt many of the novels confirmed her impressions of the moral laxity of the French. Madame was also a Catholic. The essence of Catholicism as Charlotte interpreted it was also a kind of moral laxity. It was a religion of indulgence that softly granted forgiveness for a few muttered words of contrition; a religion of rich gold idols, scarlet robes, and pungent incense; a religion of smooth, Jesuitical sophistries that veiled the face of truth. If Protestantism was the virgin of religion, Catholicism was its whore.

The sensuality of Madame and the indulgences of Catholicism thus merged in Charlotte's mind and her antipathy to both deepened. Madame's method of running the school further disgusted her, although when she compared the Pensionnat with the Clergy Daughters' School, she was forced to admit the superiority of the French regime. In this school all was indulgence and ease. "Nothing could be better than all her arrangements for the physical well-being of her scholars," Charlotte granted in *Villette*. "No minds were overtasked; the lessons were well-distributed and made incomparably easy to the learner; there was a liberty of amusement, and a provision for exercise which kept the girls healthy; the food was abundant and good: neither pale nor puny faces were anywhere to be seen in the Rue Fossette. She never grudged a holiday; she allowed plenty of time for sleeping, dressing, washing, eating; her method in all these matters was easy, liberal, salutary, and rational: many an austere English school-mistress would do vastly well to imitate her—and I believe many of them would be glad to do so, if exacting English parents would let them."[5]

Admirable indeed. Only in knowing Charlotte's intellectual energy and self-discipline, her capacity for hard work, and her scorn of physical indulgence can one gauge the contempt with which she wrote, "No minds were overtasked; the lessons were well-distributed and made incomparably easy to the learner." More reprehensible to Charlotte—although again she had to admit it worked—was Madame's method of regulating the complex machinery of the school. This she accomplished by a discreet system of *surveillance*—in Charlotte's vocabulary, spying. There were no visible discipline, no harsh words, no punishments; merely Madame, "shod with the shoes of silence," her eye to every keyhole, her hand in every drawer. By this thorough, unflagging invasion of privacy Madame subdued her pupils and her teachers. No master was ever fired at the Pensionnat Heger. Madame listened, watched, and one day a teacher would disappear forever and another quietly take his place. Not a ripple disturbed the smooth-flowing current of Madame's establishment.

Such *surveillance* was the rule in continental schools rather than the exception; nevertheless, Madame's plotting and counterplotting shocked Charlotte to the depths of her English soul. This kind of espionage was part and parcel of moral laxity and Catholicism. How could girls be taught honest behavior with Madame's example before them? Obviously they could not. Charlotte and Emily, taking cold stock of the rows of dark, glossy-haired girls in the large classroom, rejected the lot. Back in the long dormitory, Charlotte wrote a scathing denunciation of her fellow students to Ellen in which her hatred of Catholicism, mental laxity, and sensuality is all interwoven with her contempt for the Belgians:

> If the national character of the Belgians is to be measured by the character of most of the girls in the school, it is a character singularly cold, selfish, animal and inferior—They are besides very mutinous and difficult for the teachers to manage—and their principles are rotten to the core—we avoid them—which is not difficult to do—as we have the brand of Protestantism and Anglicism upon us.
>
> People talk of the danger which protestants expose themselves to in going to reside in Catholic countries—and thereby running the chance of changing their faith—my advice to all protestants who are tempted to anything so besotted as turn Catholic—is to walk over the sea on to the continent—to attend mass regularly for a time to note well the mummeries thereof also the idiotic, mercenary, aspect of *all* the priests, and *then* if they are still disposed to consider Papistry in any other light than a most feeble childish piece of humbug let them turn papists at once that's all—I consider Methodism, Dissenterism, Quakerism, and the extremes of high and low Churchism foolish but Roman Catholicism beats them all.
>
> At the same time allow me to tell you that there are some Catholics who are as good as Christians can be to whom the bible is a sealed book and much better than scores of Protestants. . . .[6]

There was, indeed, one Catholic who seemed to Charlotte better than many Protestants, and this was the husband of Madame Heger. Constantin Heger was a professor of French and mathematics at the Athénée Royale, the boys' school that bordered the *allée défendue;* he also gave lessons in literature to the pupils at his wife's school, where, of course, he also lived. Zoë Parent Heger was his second wife; nine years before he had lost his first wife and child in a cholera epidemic that swept through Brussels like a fire. He was possessed by two enthusiasms—teaching and religion—and he drove so hard at the former task that his fame as a teacher spread throughout Brussels. A genius for teaching and a kind heart balanced a temper by turns explosive, harsh, and moody: evidently a second marriage could not alter a sensitive disposition already made irritable by tragedy. At heart he was a generous man, and his explosions of rage were invariably followed by a smile, an apology, or a kind word of encouragement.

Seated at her desk in the large *salle de classe*, Charlotte watched with lively interest this whirlwind of energy and imperiousness that swept through the door and mounted the *estrade* to give the daily lesson in French literature. Hypocrisy, affectation, and indolence revolted her, but a harsh temper—when combined with honesty, wit, and a kind heart—set an electric current of excitement vibrating within her. Many pupils dissolved into tears when Monsieur turned his flashing black eyes upon them and snarled at their stupidity. Charlotte cried too (noting that tears flattered his ego), but enjoyed her emotion intensely, finding herself perversely stimulated to achievement by his harshness. Here was challenge. One word from Monsieur began to mean more than a thousand from a less exacting teacher. Who can resist the flattery of anger?

There is one individual of whom I have not yet spoken, [she writes to Ellen]—M. Heger, the husband of Madame. He is a professor of rhetoric, a man of power as to mind, but very choleric and irritable as to temperament; a little black ugly being, with a face that varies in expression. Sometimes he borrows the lineaments of an insane tom-cat, sometimes those of a delirious hyena; occasionally, but very seldom, he discards these perilous attractions and assumes an air not above 100 degrees removed from mild and gentlemanlike. He is very angry with me just at present, because I have written a translation which he chose to stigmatise as *peu correcte*. He did not tell me so, but wrote the accusation on the margin of my book, and asked in brief, stern phrase, how it happened that my compositions were always better than my translations? adding that the thing seemed to him inexplicable. The fact is, some weeks ago, in a high-flown humour, he forbade me to use either dictionary or grammar in translating the most difficult English compositions into French. This makes the task rather arduous, and compels me now and then to introduce an English word, which nearly plucks the eyes out of his head when he sees it. Emily and he don't draw well together at all. When he is very ferocious with me I cry; that sets all things straight. Emily works like a horse, and she has had great difficulties to contend with, far greater than I have had. . . . The few private lessons M. Heger has vouchsafed to give us are, I suppose, to be considered a great favour, and I can perceive they have already excited much spite and jealousy in the school.[7]

Indeed, Monsieur's personality did offer perilous attractions for Charlotte. Sexually repressed, yearning for intellectual communion, Charlotte was as vulnerable to Heger's attentions as dry straw to a match. On the other hand, it is not surprising that Emily and Heger did not "draw well together at all." Emily's cool, self-sufficient mind was unmoved by Heger's pyrotechnics. She did not need masculine approval to confirm her self-esteem; she was therefore immune to Heger's bullying, which was, after all, an exercise in male power. Charlotte herself could laugh at Heger's antics, but was powerfully drawn by them at the same time. His tantrums probably disgusted Emily.

Emily was beyond Monsieur's comprehension, but he recognized an original spirit when he saw one. That such a powerful personality should be so limited by her sex and poverty struck him as near tragic. "She should have been a man," he exclaimed once in admiration: "—a great navigator. Her powerful reason would have deduced new spheres of discovery from the knowledge of the old; and her strong, imperious will would never have been daunted by opposition or difficulty; never have given away but with life."[8] Yet he found Emily egotistical and exacting compared with Charlotte who appeared always unselfish, and noted that Emily's discontent subtly tyrannized the older sister, since she felt responsible for Emily's well being. In Charlotte he also recognized exceptional talent and an aggressive desire to excel. A superb teacher, he exploited both these qualities to the hilt by at once encouraging her power and originality of expression and at the same time forcing her to take a logical, disciplined approach to her subject matter.

Monsieur Heger talked about his teaching methods to Mrs. Gaskell, who sought him out while she was writing her *Life*. As Charlotte complained to Ellen, he forced the sisters to give up both dictionaries and grammars, preferring that they learn the French language through the ear and the heart rather than by rote. To this purpose he would frequently read aloud to them from works of the great French writers. On one occasion he chose Victor Hugo's portrait of Mirabeau. The reading was followed by a close analysis of Hugo's technique—his point of view, tone, organization, and language. He pointed out that Hugo's fault was an "exaggeration in conception"; that, however, they must notice the "extreme beauty of his nuances of expression." Then he assigned Charlotte and Emily a similar portrait of a subject of their own choosing: "I cannot tell on what subject your heart and mind have been excited. I must leave that to you." Emily chose to depict Harold, King of England, on the eve of the Battle of Hastings where he was to fall before William the Conqueror. Charlotte, who frequently chose subjects from the Old Testament—*"elle était nourrie de la Bible,"* said Monsieur—chose this time for her *devoir* a portrait of Pierre the Hermit, preacher of the First Crusade. It is not surprising that she should be interested in a small man of scarcely agreeable appearance, yet with stormy passions, courage, constancy, and enthusiasm "that overwhelmed all opposition, making the will of one man the law of a whole nation." Monsieur's comments score the margins of this composition. Pierre the Hermit, writes Charlotte, was a gentleman of Picardy, in France. "Unnecessary," writes Monsieur, underlining *en France,* "when you are writing in French." A few lines later Charlotte brings in the biblical hero Samson. "You have commenced speaking of Pierre," Monsieur Heger scolds: "you have begun the subject: see it through to the end." And pouncing on a redundancy, he remarks, "It is unnecessary to say 'an illusion to which he could never attain' when you have said 'illusion.' "

Monsieur also confided his method of "synthetic" teaching to Mrs. Gaskell. He would read to the sisters several different works on the same subject, then ask them to analyze the different viewpoints—for example, Bossuet's, Guizot's, and Carlyle's descriptions of Oliver Cromwell. Where the writers differed he made them search into the character and thought of each author to seek out the reason for his bias. Then Heger would demand that they sift out and collect the particles of truth in each portrait and try to unite them into an impartial whole. Charlotte responded enthusiastically to these analytical exercises. With characteristic ambivalence, she was at once subjective to the point of bigotry and capable of cool and critical analysis.

Charlotte was happy at first, therefore, in Brussels, and Emily, although never ceasing to mourn privately for home, felt that they were both making good progress toward their ultimate goal of independence. "I am happier submitting to authority than exercising it," Charlotte had written to Ellen. Like many creative people, she preferred to do rather than teach others how to do; the frustrated artist in her reveled at this chance to write and receive approbation from a superior male mind: this was literary success in microcosm. Such submission to authority comforted her. Thus the first months in Brussels passed pleasantly enough. The sisters seldom spoke to anyone except the Hegers. Alone together, thin and sallow among the blooming Belgians, they paced the garden walks under the old pear trees, Emily, although taller, leaning for support on Charlotte. To the Belgians they were incomprehensible foreigners, eccentric *anglaises.* One could perhaps sympathize with the tiny birdlike person with the large, grave eyes, but that tall grim creature in lank petticoats—*ah, ciel!*

In England Charlotte had dreamed that the Continent would open for her the world of art and cultivated people, slaking her thirst to see, to know, and to learn. Brussels widened her experience, of course, but did not fulfill her dreams. She was as prisoned inside the school walls as she had been in Yorkshire. From time to time they did escape the schoolgirl routine, not to mingle with artists and authors, but to pay a visit to Mary and Martha at the Château de Koekleberg. Charlotte yearned for these visits—such happy times, "for one's blood requires a little warming, it gets cold with living amongst strangers."

At Koekleberg, Charlotte and Emily found their friends half exasperated, half amused at the strict regime and eternal studies. "Before breakfast I draw," Mary complained, "after breakfast I practise, say German lessons and *draw*, after dinner walk out, learn German and *draw*. [I] go to bed sometimes at nine o'clock heartily tired and without a word to throw at anyone." A strange menagerie of teachers put them through their paces. "Madame Ferdinand the music-mistress is [a] little thin, black talkative French woman. Monsieur her husband is a tall broad shouldered man with a tremendous mouth who [is] constantly telling his pupils that the voice has but a very little hole to get out at. . . . Mons. Sciéré . . . a dancing master . . . has the faults of a french puppy, and they make it advisable never to exchange more words with him than the overlasting 'Oui Monsieur—Non, Monsieur.' . . . There is also a Mons. Hisard, who makes strange noises in the back school room teaching gymnastics to some of the girls and I had nearly forgotten a grinning, dirty, gesticulating, belgian who teaches cosmography and says so often 'Ansi donc! c'est bien compris! n'est-ce pas?' that he has earned himself the names of Ainsi donc and Mr Globes."[9]

There was opportunity to learn, Mary admitted—if one chose to learn; and she and Martha *were* learning, even though they were both tired of "cracking their heads over the everlasting German." Only the dancing lessons confounded Mary: she did not put out her feet enough despite Monsieur Sciéré's cries of *"Allongez—plus long!* more!" But she lacked Charlotte's and Emily's motivation and approached her studies far less reverently. She did not intend to make a career of teaching; she studied because she had a good mind and could find nothing useful to do with her energies. Charlotte was happier in Brussels than her undirected friend.

On Sundays Charlotte and Emily deserted the Catholic premises and went to hear Mr. Jenkins preach the Anglican service at the Chapel Royal, a little sanctuary tucked away in the Place de Musée, a portion of the formerly splendid palace of Charles of Lorraine. No official Protestant church existed in Catholic Brussels, but the growing numbers of the English colony in the city demanded some sort of permanent place of worship, and Napoleon had officially granted them the Chapel Royal in 1803. After Mrs. Jenkins' pressing invitations, Charlotte and Emily felt obliged to visit the chaplain's home, although nothing was further from their inclination. The Jenkinses had two sons who were sent to escort the sisters from church to their parents' house after the two o'clock service and back to the Rue d'Isabelle. On these merry occasions not a single word was ever exchanged. The brothers met downcast eyes and miserable embarrassment. The scene over the teacups was scarcely more lively, and after several sessions of Charlotte's trembling nervousness and Emily's silent abstraction, Mrs. Jenkins gave up her attempts to make the Rev. Mr. Brontë's daughters at home in Brussels.

But where were the great works of art, the concerts, the brilliant throngs, the cultivated minds that Charlotte had dreamed of? For two poor, hard-working, socially inept young women they did not exist. The great world (it appeared great, at least) lay outside the walls of the Pensionnat, inaccessible.[10] Like Tantalus, Charlotte saw all its pleasures just out of reach and suffered more than if she had never seen them at all. Emily was untouched by this craving to escape obscurity, so Charlotte poured out her frustration in Mary Taylor's ears. "Of course artists and authors stood high with Charlotte," Mary wrote, recalling her friend's grievances, "and the best thing after their works would have been their company. She used very inconsistently to rail at money and money-getting, and then wish she was able to visit all the large towns in Europe, see all the sights, and know all the celebrities. This was her notion of literary fame—a passport to the society of clever people."

Charlotte held no passport. "My youth is leaving me; I can never do better than I have done, and I have done nothing yet," she cried. Paradoxically, in the midst of new experience she felt herself going dead; she was losing the ability to feel. Was this the fate of all human nature—to gradually lose sight, sound, taste, touch until one fell into the grave, insensate? "I hope I shall be put in my grave as soon as I'm dead," she wailed; "I don't want to walk about so." Mary, nurtured on radical rather than Tory sociology, understood Charlotte's predicament. Apathy and insensibility were not innate human qualities— they were the product of poverty and toil without hope. Millions in England slaving in mines and starving on the land suffered such degradation. Compared to the wretchedness of England's poor, Charlotte's condition seemed almost luxurious, yet her genteel poverty tortured an aspiring and aggressive spirit. Mary advised her to give her attention to earning money. On this point too Charlotte was divided. She admitted that money alone would free her from slavery. On the other hand, to concentrate one's whole energies on getting it was in itself enslaving, if not hopeless. Mary admitted this: "Indeed, in her position, nothing less than entire constant absorption in petty money matters could have scraped together a provision."[11] By stitching trousers seventeen hours a day a woman in 1842 could earn a shilling—fourteen cents—a day. By turning her collars, darning stockings already mended, and stuffing paper in her boots, Charlotte might scrape together nine or ten pounds a year. It hardly bore thinking about.

If cultural adventure failed them, scholastically Charlotte and Emily were taking giant strides. "I consider it doubtful whether I shall come home in September or not," Charlotte wrote Ellen. "—Madame Heger has made a proposal for both me and Emily to stay another half year—offering to dismiss her English master and take me as an English teacher—also to employ Emily some part of each day as in teaching music to a certain number of the pupils—for these services we are to be allowed to continue our studies in French and German—and have board without paying for it—no salaries however are offered—the proposal is kind and in a great selfish city like Brussels and a great selfish school containing nearly ninety pupils (boarders and day-pupils included) implies a degree of interest which demands gratitude in return—I am inclined to accept it—what think you?" Writing of Madame's "kindness" in *Villette* years later, Charlotte viewed her benevolence with a colder eye. True, she had dismissed the English master to make way for Charlotte, "but she got thrice the work out of me she had extracted from Mr. Wilson, at half the expense."

Now, however, the proposal was tempting. "I don't deny that I sometimes wish to be in England," Charlotte continues, "or that I have brief attacks of home-sickness but on the whole I have borne a very valiant heart so far—and I have been happy in Brussels because I have always been fully occupied with the employments that I like— Emily is making rapid progress in French, German, Music and Drawing—Monsieur and Madame Heger begin to recognize the valuable points of her character under her singularities."[12]

To Emily's piano students, three young English girls, this happy perception was denied. In July an English doctor fallen upon ill health and reduced circumstances crossed the Channel with his wife and children to take up residence in Brussels. Dr. Thomas Wheelwright had five daughters whom he promptly enrolled at the Heger school: Laetitia, Emily, Frances, Sarah, and Julia. Although there was one other English girl at the Pensionnat, the Brontës had dismissed Maria Miller as vain and foolish; the appearance of five more English girls, however, considerably boosted their numbers among the enemy Catholic host: they were as welcome to the two sisters as heather and good English tea. Charlotte was irrevocably drawn to the fourteen-year-old Laetitia when she first saw her stand up in the schoolroom and glance contemptuously around her at her Belgian classmates. "It was so very English," laughed Charlotte, her deeply nationalistic heart won. The young Wheelwrights liked Charlotte but hated Emily.

"I simply disliked her from the first," Laetitia wrote in 1896, "her tallish, ungainly, ill-dressed figure contrasting so strongly with Charlotte's small, neat, trim person, although their dresses were alike; always answering our jokes with 'I wish to be as God made me.'" The Wheelwrights' obvious antipathy to Emily cramped Charlotte's association with them, as did their fondness for the wealthy Maria Miller which impressed her as a piece of uncritical folly. Maria Miller played up to Laetitia and Emily, the eldest Wheelwright girls, giving them lavish presents, although a lock of her hair pressed into a ring and presented sentimentally to Laetitia turned out to be not a personal keepsake at all but a piece of the hearth rug! At least one Wheelwright saw through the calculating friendliness of Miss Miller. Frances noticed that Maria's interest did not extend to the three youngest girls, whom she contemptuously ignored because they were of no social value to her. Frances remembered that Charlotte, on the other hand, treated the little girls very kindly.

Emily was not kind. Unwilling to give up an hour or a minute of precious study time, she insisted on giving Frances, Sarah, and Julia lessons during recreation time. While the other children ran and shrieked on the sunny playground, the Wheelwrights were condemned to lessons at the piano with a grim wolf in the oratory. Impervious to excuses, laziness, and tears, Emily was a stern taskmistress. She worked like a horse; why couldn't others? The undisciplined and unmotivated little girls did not share her severe enthusiasm, and hated the lessons and their teacher.

Summer waned, the pears ripened in the garden, and a September moon rose over the walls of the Pensionnat. Charlotte and Emily had been in Brussels eight months. Madame, domesticity itself with a husband and four young children to look after, still oiled the intricate machinery of the school with a discreet and capable hand. When Charlotte and Emily met her face to face she was affable and appreciative. More often she was a figure seen at a distance, sewing under the arbor surrounded by the lower classes, gliding down a hallway on her "shoes of silence," chatting amiably with a visiting parent, listening with head cocked outside a classroom door. Monsieur whirled in and out of the Pensionnat, descending upon Charlotte to rail, inspire, encourage, and threaten. If he became too vehement and Charlotte burst into tears, the scene abruptly altered: out came a handkerchief from one pocket and bonbons from another—he offered both in a fit of sentimental contrition. After Charlotte wiped her reddened eyes and accepted a sweet the tiger became a lamb, and the lesson continued under calmer conditions. Torn between dismay and delight at this fiery little man with the black mustaches, Charlotte braced herself for the lessons, reveled in them, and throve under his tutelage. "Charlotte and Emily are well," Mary Taylor wrote Ellen September 24; "not only in health but in mind and hope. They are content with their present position and even gay and I think they do quite right not to return to England though one of them at least could earn more in the beautiful town of Bradford than she is now doing. . . ."[13]

Then suddenly, in less than eight weeks, death swept three persons out of Charlotte's small world. Late in August William Weightman fell ill with cholera. Branwell, home from Luddenden Foot, tended the sickbed and watched him die as he had watched Maria seventeen years ago. Weightman had become his close friend—the only friend in Haworth tolerant, intellectual, and socially his equal. Many times they had tramped the moors, guns slung under their arms, looking for grouse; they had shared many a bottle in Weightman's rooms. After two weeks of vomiting, dysentery, fever, and finally delirium, Weightman died on September 6; he was twenty-eight. On October 2, Mr. Brontë preached his funeral sermon in gray-towered Haworth church, his voice vibrating with emotion. The young curate had been like a son to him—an ideal son, temperate, benevolent, respected, and successful. The un-ideal son sat in the family pew, his red head bent, his sobs audible throughout the church, probably drugged or drunk against the ordeal. His father's words of praise for Weightman flew like arrows: "His character wore well, the surest proof of real worth. He had, it is true, some peculiar advantages. Agreeable in person and manners, and constitutionally cheerful, his first introduction was prepossessing. But what he gained at first, he did not lose afterwards. . . ."[14] How many times Branwell had lost.

In August schools in Brussels closed for the "long vacation." Charlotte and Emily could not afford to go home, but Mary and Martha returned to Yorkshire to open a house at Hunsworth Mills in the Spen Valley. Although the widowed mother still lived on at the Red House, her gloomy and bitter disposition had thoroughly alienated her children, "preparing for her," as Charlotte told Ellen, "a most desolate old age." Martha sent off a characteristically buoyant note to Ellen Nussey: ". . . we will have the house warmed next Wednesday, and my cousins, my uncle, and my Aunt Sarah are coming over. . . . My brothers and I shall be exceedingly gratified if you, your sister Mercy, and your brothers will come to tea on that day to meet them. Now, will you come? or you will be stupid as you were about going to Brier Hall, and if you refuse you will make me seriously angry with you, and you had better not, or I will tell all kinds of things of you to Miss Brontë."[15] The house properly warmed, Mary and Martha returned to Brussels, Martha perhaps already infected with cholera.[16] On September 24 she fell ill with dysentery. Vomiting and chills followed, then ebbing strength. Charlotte did not find out she was ill until October 12. The next day being a half holiday, she hastened through the streets to the Château de Koekleberg and found that Martha had died in the night.

The Taylors were Dissenters; Martha was buried in the Protestant cemetery on the outskirts of Brussels. On Sunday, October 30, Charlotte and Emily set out to walk with Mary the six miles to the cemetery. Charlotte wondered at Mary's self-control. "She is in no ways crushed by the event; but while Martha was ill she was to her more than a mother—more than a sister: watching, nursing, cherishing her so tenderly, so unweariedly. She appears calm and serious now: no bursts of violent emotion, no exaggeration of distress."[17] For Charlotte the occasion was oppressive. A livid and thunderous-looking sky threatened rain; the cemetery seemed a strange and sinister spot with its pale parapets, its thick groves of cypress and yew that crowded around a hulking cross of black marble, its heavy gates that swung back groaning on rusty hinges, its thick crowding of slabs, monuments, and crosses. After trudging back the six miles, the three spent the evening with Mary's cousins, the Dixons, who could not have been impressed with the liveliness of the sisters if Charlotte's fictional account is true: ". . . a howling, rainy autumn evening . . . when certain who had that day performed a pilgrimage to a grave new-made in a heretic cemetery, sat near a woodfire on the hearth of a foreign dwelling . . . they knew that heavy falling rain was soaking into the wet earth which covered their lost darling: and that the sad, sighing gale was mourning above her buried head. . . ."[18] Mary, no novelist, wrote to Ellen of the same day with irony: "There is nothing to regret, nothing to recall—not even Martha. . . . We have walked about six miles to see the cemetery and the country round it. We then spent a pleasant evening with my cousins, and in presence of my uncle and Emily, one not speaking at all, the other once or twice."[19]

Branwell had sat alone in the family pew at Weightman's funeral service, for Aunt Branwell, fond as she was of the young curate, was too ill to leave her bed. Branwell buried one friend and turned to attend another. Two pathetic notes to Francis Grundy, a friend who had

written reproaching him for his silence, testify to the misery Branwell
was undergoing that autumn.

> October 25th, 1842: My Dear Sir,—There is no misunderstanding.
> I have had a long attendance at the death-bed of the Rev. Mr Weight-
> man, one of my dearest friends, and now I am attending at the death-
> bed of my aunt, who has been for twenty years as my mother. I ex-
> pect her to die in a few hours. . . .
>
> 29th October 1842: My Dear Sir. . . . Death only has made me neg-
> lectful of your kindness, and I have lately had so much experience
> with him, that your sister would not *now* blame me for indulging in
> gloomy visions either of this world or another. I am incoherent, I fear,
> but I have been waking two nights witnessing such agonizing suffer-
> ing as I would not wish my worst enemy to endure; and I have now
> lost the guide and director of all the happy days connected with my
> childhood. . . .[20]

The rustle of black silk and the clicking of pattens on the cold stone
parsonage floor were stilled. Two days after the pilgrimage to Martha's
grave, Charlotte and Emily opened a letter containing news of Aunt's
illness. Anne was at Thorp Green Hall, Mr. Brontë sixty-five and
totally unable to cope with a woman's illness, Branwell as likely to be
drugged or drunk as not. There was no alternative but to start for
England immediately, and accordingly they hurried with explanations
to the Hegers and began to pack. The next post informed them that
Aunt Branwell had died October 29, six days before. Reeling from
this third and heaviest blow, they pursued their plans for departure
even though they were too late, sailing from Antwerp on Sunday,
November 6. Emily wiped the dust of the Pensionnat from her feet
with profound relief. For Charlotte, tied by strange threads of emotion
to one member of the Heger household, the parting was difficult.
Yet she carried with her a letter from Monsieur to her father which
might have the power to bring her back again.

# 9

*Monsieur*

On December 28, 1842, Elizabeth Branwell's will was proved in the prerogative court of York:

Depending on the Father, Son, and Holy Ghost for peace here, and glory and bliss forever hereafter, I leave this my last Will and Testament: Should I die at Haworth, I request that my remains may be deposited in the church in that place as near as convenient to the remains of my dear sister; I moreover will that all my just debts and funeral expenses be paid out of my property, and that my funeral shall be conducted in a moderate and decent manner. My Indian workbox I leave to my niece, Charlotte Brontë; my workbox with a china top I leave to my niece, Emily Jane Brontë, together with my ivory fan; my Japan dressing-box I leave to my nephew, Patrick Branwell Brontë; to my niece Anne Brontë, I leave my watch with all that belongs to it; as also my eye-glass and its chain, my rings, silver-spoons, books, clothes, etc., etc., I leave to be divided between my above-named three nieces, Charlotte Brontë, Emily Jane Brontë, and Anne Brontë, according as their father shall think proper. And I will that all the money that shall remain, including twenty-five pounds sterling, being the part of the proceeds of the sale of my goods which belong to me in consequence of my having advanced to my sister Kingston the sum of twenty-five pounds in lieu of her share of the proceeds of my goods aforesaid, and deposited in the bank of Bolitho Sons and Co., Esqrs., of Chiandower, near Penzance, after the aforesaid sums and articles shall have been paid and deducted, shall be put into some safe bank or lent on good landed security, and there left to accumulate for the sole benefit of my four nieces, Charlotte Brontë, Emily Jane Brontë, Anne Brontë, and Elizabeth Jane Kingston; and this sum or sums, and whatever other property I may have, shall be equally divided between them when the youngest of them then living shall have arrived at the age of twenty-one years. . . . I appoint my brother-in-law, the Rev. P. Brontë, A.B., now Incumbent of Haworth,

Yorkshire; the Rev. John Fennell, now Incumbent of Cross Stone, near Halifax; the Rev. Theodore Dury, Rector of Keighley, Yorkshire; and Mr George Taylor of Stanbury, in the chapelry of Haworth aforesaid, my executors. Written by me, ELIZABETH BRANWELL, and signed, sealed, and delivered on the 30th of April, in the year of our Lord, one thousand eight hundred and thirty-three, ELIZABETH BRANWELL. Witnesses present, William Brown, John Tootill, William Brown, Junr.[1]

Aunt Branwell's death thus left Charlotte, Emily, and Anne in possession of a small income of about £300 each at a time when, because of the school project, they particularly needed funds. Branwell was excluded except for the sentimental remembrance of the case of toilet articles: presumably his aunt believed he would be well established in a career by the time of her death. Nothing could have been further from the truth, for on March 31, 1842, Branwell had been fired from his post as clerk of the railroad at Luddenden Foot.

His year at Luddenden Foot had equaled Charlotte's stint at Roe Head in misery. Like his sister, he suffered acutely from uncongenial employment and the consciousness that his creative talents were stifled and wasted. Like his sister, he plunged into a mental crisis. He had forsaken everything of religion except its horrors; now sin and damnation came to haunt him with lurid vengeance. His health was failing, his literary ambitions were stalled. In her crisis, Charlotte had clung to the gods of Conscience and Duty, serving out her sentence with gritted teeth until her health collapsed. Branwell sought escape, and solved his distaste for keeping railroad ledgers in dissipation. Francis Grundy, an engineer on the Leeds–Bradford line, watched his new friend's dizzying downward course with awe, recognizing it was no common mortal who fell—"Poor, brilliant, gay, moody, moping, wildly excitable, miserable Brontë!"

The line had just been opened; the station was a crude wooden hut; there was only the porter to talk to and only hills rising in the distance to contemplate out the window. Branwell could not bear to be alone. At first he waited for the last train to rumble off down the line before snatching up his coat and hat and repairing to the Lord Nelson Inn atop the steep, winding main street of the nearby village of Luddenden. More and more frequently, however, Branwell's post at the ticket office was vacant during working hours. Soon hours of hard afternoon drinking with a local set of mill owners turned into days of drunken half-consciousness in dark cheerless rooms and a return to full consciousness accompanied by the tortures of the damned. "I would rather give my hand," Branwell shuddered, looking back on that nightmare year, "than undergo again the grovelling carelessness, the malignant yet cold debauchery, the determination to find how far mind could carry body without both being chucked into hell, which too often marked my conduct when there, lost as I was to all I really liked. . . ."[2]

Left increasingly to mind the ticket office in his superior's absence, Walton the porter saw how the land lay and began to help himself to cash from the till, confident its loss would be blamed on Branwell. At the end of the year the company auditor came round, went over the clerk's accounts, found them short £11 1s. 7d. Branwell could not account for the missing money. The auditor examined his ledgers; he discovered indifferent bookkeeping and margins embellished with drawings, verse fragments, and caricatures. Much to the porter's chagrin, Branwell was not accused of stealing company funds, but he was convicted of gross carelessness. Extract, Meeting of Directors of the Manchester and Leeds Railway, Hunts Bank, Manchester, April 4, 1842:

> Report from Messrs Robinson and Greenish on certain irregularities of the Clerk in Charge at the Luddenden Foot Station, Mr. Bronte, who had been found deficient £11 1. 7. He had been discharged in consequence and the amount deducted from his quarter's salary.

Branwell appealed the decision, but the Board rejected his plea. His quarter's salary after the deduction (more than Charlotte's yearly salary at the Whites') barely paid the debts he had run up that fatal year. His flight from the Academy and London, his failure as a portrait painter at Bradford, his dismissal as tutor to the Postlethwaites— all might have been written off as the youthful scrapes of a gifted, searching young man. Luddenden Foot, however, was no private, youthful escapade. Branwell was twenty-five, had botched an easy, respectable job, lost his reputation around the area, and forfeited a salary of £130 a year.

Aunt Branwell had frequently come to her nephew's aid in the past, financing art lessons and standing surety for him with the railroad company. The friend of his childhood was gone. What woman would rescue him now? The honor fell to Anne. Always tender and full of pity for dumb, weak creatures, Anne pitied her miserable brother after his disgrace at Luddenden Foot. She hated her position with the shallow, materialistic Robinsons; she had wanted to leave them, although they valued her highly and paid her a reasonable salary of £50. The family, however, were looking about for a tutor for their only son, Edmund. On her recommendation they would undoubtedly accept Branwell for the post without prying into his past. It was a woman's duty to sacrifice and it was Anne's nature to salvage sinners. She petitioned the Robinsons and obtained the post for her brother.

Charlotte, Emily, and Anne spent a quiet Chrsitmas at home with Papa and Branwell, subdued but not heartbroken at their aunt's death, for although they had all respected her, only Branwell had loved her. Then in January 1843, the holidays over, Anne and Branwell set out for Thorp Green Hall, the brother rather elated at the thought of joining a rich family whose immediate connections included a member of Parliament and a marquis, the sister resigned to another year of drudgery, and, since she no longer had the tutoring of Edmund, to a reduction in wages of £10.

Charlotte passed the months at Haworth in a state of supreme restlessness. Arriving home from Brussels, she had handed Monsieur Heger's letter to her father. Monsieur had written with glowing respect of Charlotte's and Emily's accomplishments: Mr. Brontë's children had made remarkable progress in all branches of study, progress due entirely to their zeal, good will, and perseverance. Miss Emily had studied piano with the best music professor in Brussels and already taught her own pupils; Miss Charlotte had begun to teach French and acquire that skill and poise so necessary for a teacher. It would be near-tragedy for his daughters to abandon such promising careers; accordingly Madame and he offered both or one of his daughters a teaching position for the coming year, not from personal interest but from affection, for Mr. Brontë must know that Mlles Charlotte and Emily had become "partie de notre famille."[3]

Monsieur's persuasiveness, allied to Charlotte's new authority in the household as eldest female and legatee, and her own urgent desire to return to Brussels convinced Mr. Brontë to give up his daughter again. He could not, however, be left alone: his eyesight was deteriorating rapidly, and rumors flitting through the village whispered that the incumbent of Haworth tipped a pint too many. As president of the Haworth Temperance Society, Mr. Brontë denied this charge vigorously, claiming that slanderers had mistaken the smell of his eye lotion for "a smell of a more exceptionable character." Still, his daughters would not leave him to the servants. As it turned out, Emily had every intention of staying at home. Ambition did not goad her: she preferred the freedom of housekeeping at the Parsonage to foreign exile.

Charlotte decided as early as November, therefore, that she *must* return to Brussels, although her conscience warned her against this self-indulgence. For once she ignored its persistent voice: another voice was more compelling. She spent the months at Haworth marking time, exchanging visits and brief, trivial letters with Ellen, currently involved in a social and romantic whirl with Mary Taylor's brothers Joe and John: "I admire exceedingly the costume you have chosen to appear in at the Birstall rout. I think you say pink petticoat, black jacket, and a wreath of roses—beautiful! For a change I would advise a black coat—velvet stock and waistcoat—white pantaloons and smart boots!"4 But her mind was far from Ellen's romances and ball gowns across the Channel in a sunny spacious schoolroom dominated by a fierce, black-mustached little man.

On Friday, January 27, Charlotte left for Brussels alone. The journey was not propitious. She had intended to make for the familiar Chapter Coffee House upon arriving in London, but the train from Leeds, delayed, did not pull into Euston Station until ten o'clock at night. At home in Yorkshire Papa barred the front door at nine. How could she know that London never sleeps? Too fearful to ask for admittance at such a late hour, she asked a cabman to drive her directly to London Bridge Wharf, hoping that she might be able to board the Ostend packet that rode at anchor on the river.

> It was a dark night. The coachman instantly drove off as soon as he had got his fare; the watermen commenced a struggle for me and my trunk. Their oaths I hear at this moment . . . One laid hands on my trunk. I looked on and waited quietly; but when another laid hands on me, I spoke up, shook off his touch, stepped at once into a boat, desired austerely that the trunk should be placed beside me—"just there" —which was instantly done; for the owner of the boat I had chosen became now an ally: I was rowed off.
>
> Black was the river as a torrent of ink; lights glanced on it from the piles of building round, ships rocked on its bosom. They rowed me up to several vessels; I read by lantern light their names printed in great white letters on a dark ground: the *Ocean*, the *Phoenix*, the *Consort*, the *Dolphin*, were passed in turns; but the *Vivid* was my ship, and it seemed she lay further down.
>
> Down the sable flood we glided; I thought of the Styx, of Charon rowing some solitary soul to the Land of the Shades. Amidst the strange scene, with a chilly wind blowing in my face and midnight-clouds dropping rain above my head; with two rude rowers for companions, whose insane oaths still tortured my ears, I asked myself if I was wretched or terrified. I was neither. . . . I could not tell how it was.5

At last the name of her ship leaped out of the blackness, but Charlotte's troubles were not over: she was told in a tone of sneering dismissal that no passengers were allowed to sleep on board. She stood in the rocking boat in the cold winter night; she looked back at the lights of London gleaming like so many hostile eyes out of the darkness; she begged to be allowed to speak to someone in charge. The captain came, and in quiet, urgent, heartfelt tones she pleaded her case. Her eloquent simplicity convinced him, and overpaying the watermen in crowns instead of shillings (her third mistake that day), she clambered aboard. The packet sailed the next morning. On Sunday evening she pulled the bell of the Pensionnat Heger in the Rue d'Isabelle and was received with great kindness by Madame.

Charlotte returned as a teacher rather than a pupil, although she continued German lessons, paying the ten francs a month she and Emily had paid together, although the Hegers considered her *partie de notre famille*. They welcomed her as a peer. By Monsieur's orders she was called Mademoiselle Charlotte and told that she must consider the Heger sitting room her sitting room. She was given command of the First Class in a new schoolroom; there she taught English lessons and, when not teaching, ruled as *surveillante* over the class. Knowing her extreme shyness and the unruliness of the Belgian pupils, Monsieur and Madame offered to be present to maintain order while she gave the English lesson. Charlotte politely but firmly declined this offer, scorning the thought of owing obedience to the presence of a policeman in the classroom. She was fearful, but she must win the pupils' respect by her own methods or not at all.

She mounted the *estrade* the first day flushed and nervous. The pupils were notorious for rude insubordination. Her disadvantages were many: she was scarcely larger than a ten-year-old child, she was very nearsighted and very gauche, her spoken French was far from perfect, she was mistrusted as an *anglaise*, she was decidedly outnumbered. Moreover, Madame inevitably yielded to the students in these matters. If a teacher proved unpopular, she quickly and silently disappeared. If Charlotte's account of that first day in *Villette* is true in fact (it is true in spirit), her worst fears were confirmed. Three girls in the front row opened the campaign against the intruder. Titterings and whispers swelled to murmurs and laughter which the girls in the back rows echoed more loudly: soon the class would be rioting out of control. Charlotte took desperate action. Snatching up a composition from a desk, she read it aloud above the disturbance, pronounced it "very stupid," and tore it in two before astonished eyes. The noise was checked. However:

One girl alone, quite in the background, persevered in the riot with undiminished energy. I looked at her attentively. She had a pale face, hair like night, broad strong eyebrows, decided features, and a dark, mutinous, sinister eye. I noted that she sat close by a little door, which door, I was well aware, opened into a small closet where books were kept. She was standing up for the purpose of conducting her clamour with freer energies. I measured her stature and calculated her strength. She seemed both tall and wiry; but if the conflict were brief and the attack unexpected, I thought I might manage her.

Advancing up the room, looking as cool and careless as I possibly could, in short, *ayant l'air de rien;* I slightly pushed the door and found it was ajar. In an instant, and with sharpness, I had turned on her. In another instant she occupied the closet, the door was shut, and the key in my pocket. . . .

"C'est bien," said Madame . . . when I came out of the class, hot and a little exhausted. "Ça ira."

She had been listening and peeping through a spy-hole the whole time.[6]

Eventually Charlotte's stoical dignity and uncompromising character won the respect of the First Class. Teaching was not governessing: there were no noses to wipe, no chairs to be set at table. No mother asked her to adore her child or hem her linen. The exercise of authority was not unpleasant. So, although she sometimes went quite red-faced and tight-lipped at her pupils' infuriating stupidity, she succeeded as a teacher where she had been unhappy as a governess.

But what of Monsieur? She had come back for Monsieur. At first, because he had decided to learn English, she was drawn closer to him than before: "I now regularly give English lessons to M. Heger and his brother-in-law, M. Chapelle. M. Heger's first wife was sister of M. Chapelle's present wife. They get on with wonderful rapidity, especially the first. He already begins to speak English very decently. If you could see and hear the efforts I make to teach them to pronounce like Englishmen, and their unavailing attempts to imitate, you would laugh to all eternity." And there were other kindnesses to report to Ellen. "The Carnival is just over, and we have entered upon the gloom and abstinence of Lent. The first day of Lent we had coffee without milk for breakfast; vinegar and vegetables, with a very little salt fish, for dinner; and bread for supper. The Carnival was nothing but masking and mummery. M. Heger took me and one of the pupils into the town to see the masks. It was animating to see the immense crowds, and the general gaiety, but the masks were nothing. . . . I have had two letters from Mary. She does not tell me she has been ill, and she does not complain; but her letters are not the letters of a person in the enjoyment of great happiness. She has nobody to be as good to her as M. Heger is to me; to lend her books, to converse with her sometimes, etc."[7]

At the same time she was furious at rumors that she had returned to Brussels because of a romance, unreasonably upset because the rumor was bitterly half true. To Ellen: " 'Three or four people' it seems 'have the idea that the future époux of Mademoiselle Brontë is on the

Continent.' These people are wiser than I am—they could not believe
that I crossed the sea merely to return as teacher to Mde Heger. . . .
I must forsooth have some remote hope of entrapping a husband
somehow—or somewhere—if these charitable people knew the total
seclusion of the life I lead—that I never exchange a word with any
other man than Monsieur Heger and seldom indeed with him—they
would perhaps cease to suppose that any such chimerical and groundless notion influenced my proceedings— Have I said enough to clear
myself of so silly an imputation? Not that it is a crime to marry—or a
crime to wish to be married—but it is an imbecility which I reject with
contempt for women who have neither fortune nor beauty to make
marriage the principal object of their wishes and hopes and the aim
of all their actions—not to be able to convince themselves that they
are unattractive—and that they had better be quiet and think of other
things than wedlock."[8] She was quiet, she could not think of wedlock, but she loved Monsieur.

For a time Charlotte was happy. It was enough that in the midst of
indifferent faces, hostile Catholic customs, and long hours in the
classroom *one* face smiled and *one* voice was kind. The fact of Monsieur's learning English seemed to forge an unbreakable bond between them of his own making, and his flattering concern for the
progress and welfare of his little English friend seemed proof of a
unique, enduring friendship. Although she missed Emily's company
sorely she did not have her homesickness weighing on her conscience,
and, several English houses in Brussels welcomed her now that their
invitations did not have to include the aloof, uncommunicative sister.
Charlotte thus renewed her friendship with the Wheelwrights, especially Laetitia, accepted once more the Jenkinses' invitations to
tea after the Sunday Anglican service, and grew to like Mary Taylor's
cousins: "I have been twice to the Dixons. They are very kind to me.
. . . Miss Dixon is certainly an elegant and accomplished person."
She was independent, she was learning, and a few minutes of Monsieur's company could recompense her for hours of solitude in the
long dormitory, the empty classrooms, or the silent *allée défendue*.

Exactly when Madame Heger realized that the English teacher she
had encouraged to return to Brussels was in love with her husband is
uncertain. Charlotte was incapable of forwardness or display. Nor had
she acknowledged what she felt for Monsieur even to herself. With
a woman's quick grasp of such matters, Madame read the message in
the glowing eyes Charlotte lifted to her husband's face, in her restless abstraction as she paced the garden paths, in the quick lifting
of her head at the sound of his rapid footsteps crossing the *carré*. She
watched with vigilance, stealing down corridors, bending to keyholes.

Her husband, she concluded, was unaware of the English teacher's adoration. Good. He must remain so.

Calm, shrewd, and competent, Madame set about discreetly but ruthlessly to separate Charlotte and her husband. There must be no scandal, no dismissal; the school must run on as smoothly as ever. Subtly but with great efficiency, she began to discourage Constantin Heger's interest in the English teacher. Small disparagements, vague hints about propriety, a little frown at the mention of "Mees's" name, little errands to take him out of her way—who can guess her methods? They succeeded marvelously well.

At first Charlotte scarcely realized what was happening. She had sometimes found Monsieur in the garden at twilight where he strolled out with his cigar to tend some favorite roses; he came there no longer. Sometimes he had sought her out in the First Class where she sat as *surveillante* when not teaching; her classroom door now never opened. She trembled at the sound of footsteps striding across the *carré*, and despaired as they receded. When she did meet him, heart pounding, he was cordial; but these meetings were few. Finally he became too busy to continue giving her lessons in French literature, and—heaviest blow of all—too busy to take English lessons himself.

Baffled and sick at heart, Charlotte permitted herself to reveal a little of her sorrow to Branwell, who, with unconscious cruelty, neglected to write his lonely sister from Thorp Green:

> Brussels, May 1st, 1843 . . . As for me, I am very well and wag on as usual. I perceive, however, that I grow exceedingly misanthropic and sour. You will say that this is no news, and that you never knew me possessed of the contrary qualities—philanthropy and sugariness. *Das ist wahr* (which being translated means, that is true); but the fact is, the people here are no go whatsoever. Amongst 120 persons which compose the daily population of this house, I can discern only one or two who deserve anything like regard. This is not owing to foolish fastidiousness on my part, but to the absence of decent qualities on theirs. They have not intellect or politeness or good-nature or good-feeling. They are nothing. I don't hate them—hatred would be too warm a feeling. They have no sensations themselves and they excite none. But one wearies from day to day of caring nothing, fearing nothing, liking nothing, hating nothing, being nothing, doing nothing . . . They are very false in their relations with each other, but they rarely quarrel, and friendship is a folly they are unacquainted with. The black Swan, M. Heger, is the only sole veritable exception to this rule (for Madame, always cool and always reasoning, is not quite an exception). But I rarely speak to Monsieur now, for not being a pupil I have little or nothing to do with him. From time to time he shows his kind-heartedness by loading me with books, so that I am

still indebted to him for all the pleasure or amusement I have. Except for the total want of companionship I have nothing to complain of. I have not too much to do, sufficient liberty, and I am rarely interfered with. I lead an easeful, stagnant, silent life, for which, when I think of Mrs Sidgwick, I ought to be very thankful. Be sure you write to me soon, and beg of Anne to enclose a small billet in the same letter; it will be a real charity to do me this kindness. Tell me everything you can think of.

It is a curious metaphysical fact that always in the evening when I am in the great dormitory alone, having no other company than a number of beds with white curtains, I always recur as fanatically as ever to the old ideas, the old faces, and the old scenes in the world below. Give my love to Anne, and believe me

YOURN!

Dear Anne,—Write to me,—Your affectionate Schwester,

C.B.

Mr Heger has just been in and given me a little German Testament as a present. I was surprised, for since a good many days he has hardly spoken to me.[9]

*"Herr Heger hat mir dieses Buch gegeben, Brüssel, Mai 1843. C.B.,"* wrote Charlotte on the flyleaf in Gothic script, and took what comfort in the little book she could. But it was not enough to satisfy her craving. She was utterly deserted. She and Madame had never been close, but Madame had always been affable and appreciative of her work. Now even Madame had begun to cool toward her. Her manner became distant and unenthusiastic. Charlotte's heart sank, for now there was no one to give her a kind word. She had little liking for the three Frenchwomen who taught and boarded at the school; she judged them vicious, narrow, and materialistic. Now she became convinced that one of them at least spied on her actions for Madame. The little world of the Pensionnat, so golden, so longed-for at Haworth, had become a dark, chilly, alien place.

Charlotte to Emily, May 29, 1843:

. . . Things wag on much as usual here. Only Mdlle Blanche and Mdlle Haussé are at present on a system of war without quarter. They hate each other like two cats. Mdlle Blanche frightens Mdlle Haussé by her white passions (for they quarrel venomously). Mdlle Haussé complains that when Mdlle Blanche is in fury, *"elle n'a pas de lèvres."* I find also that Mdlle Sophie dislikes Mdlle Blanche extremely. She says she is heartless, insincere, and vindictive, which epithets, I assure you, are richly deserved. Also I find she is the regular spy of Mme Heger, to whom she reports everything. Also she invents—which I should not have thought. . . . Of late days, M. and Mde Heger rarely speak to me, and I really don't pretend to care a fig for any body else in the establishment. You are not to suppose by that expression that I am under the influence of *warm* affection for Mde Heger. I am convinced that she does not like me—why, I can't tell, nor do I think she herself has any definite reason for the aversion; but for one thing, she cannot comprehend why I do not make intimate friends of Mesdames Blanche, Sophie, and Haussé. M Heger is wondrously influenced by Madame, and I should not wonder if he disapproves very much of my unamiable want of sociability. He has already given me a brief lecture on universal *bienveillance*, and, perceiving that I don't improve in consequence, I fancy he has taken to considering me as a person to be let alone—left to the error of her ways; and consequently he has in a great measure withdrawn the light of his countenance, and I get on from day to day in a Robinson Crusoe-like condition—very lonely. That does not signify. In other respects I have nothing substantial to complain of, nor is even this a cause for complaint. Except the loss of M. Heger's goodwill (if I have lost it) I care for none of 'em.[10]

Still believing that all she wished from Monsieur was an occasional friendly word, Charlotte searched her heart to discover the reason for the Hegers' sudden coldness. It was bitterly ironical that they should punish her lack of sociability by withdrawing their own friendship from her. Yet how else had she offended? Baffled and heartsick, she hung on, trusting that the breach would somehow be healed. The end of the term drew near. Madame watched her misery and waited quietly for her resignation. She could not demand it since there were no grounds for dismissal. Moreover, her system of knowing all but admitting nothing precluded direct action. On August 15 the Catholic schools in Brussels would break up for the "long vacation." Charlotte watched its approach with dread, wondering how she could bear the five long weeks with no teaching duties, no lessons, no glimpse of Monsieur—no human companionship at all. Near despair, she confided her distress to Ellen:

Brussels, August 6th, 1843: Dear Ellen,—You never answered my last letter; but, however, forgiveness is a part of the Christian Creed, and so having an opportunity to send a letter to England, I forgive you and write to you again. If I complain in this letter, have mercy and don't blame me, for, I forewarn you, I am in low spirits, and that earth and heaven are dreary and empty to me at this moment. In a few days our vacation will begin; everybody is joyous and animated at the prospect, because everybody is to go home. I know that I am to stay here during the five weeks that the holidays last, and that I shall be much alone during that time, and consequently get downcast, and find both days and nights of a weary length. It is the first time in my life that I have really dreaded the vacation. . . .

Alas! I can hardly write, I have such a dreary weight at my heart;

and I do so wish to go home. Is not this childish? Pardon me, for I
cannot help it. However, though I am not strong enough to bear up
cheerfully, I can still bear up; and I will continue to stay (D.V.) some
months longer, till I have acquired German; and then I hope to see all
your faces again. Would that the vacation were well over! it will pass
so slowly. Do have the Christian charity to write me a long, long letter; fill it with the minutest details; nothing will be uninteresting. Do
not think it is because people are unkind to me that I wish to leave
Belgium; nothing of the sort. Everybody is abundantly civil, but
homesickness keeps creeping over me. I cannot shake it off. You may
scold me or say what you like about this being a scanty, shabby letter;
if you had answered my last I might perhaps have had courage to
write more. As it is I am incapable. Remember me to your mother
and Mercy, and believe me, very merrily, vivaciously, gaily yours,

C.B.[11]

The dreaded August 15 arrived and paradoxically brought a brief
burst of happiness. Monsieur, his heart touched perhaps by some dim
recognition of the loneliness that lay ahead for Mademoiselle Charlotte, sought her out and presented her with a little gift of books. He
had chosen well: the exotic romanticism of Bernardin de St. Pierre
was, as he knew, congenial to Charlotte's mind. She took the volumes
as the starving take food; they were sustenance for the empty days
ahead. Again she consecrated the gift with an inscription, "The Gift
of Monsieur Heger, Brussels, August 15th, 1843." On that day also
Monsieur had the honor of delivering the annual Speech Day Address
at his school, the Athénée Royale. His address, "*Discours prononcé
à la distribution de prix le août 1843*," he presented to Charlotte as a
personal token of his regard. The day climaxed at ten o'clock in the
evening with a concert in the park, marking the holiday of the Assumption of the Virgin. Charlotte must have been among the group
of teachers who attended with Monsieur and Madame, since she described such a concert so vividly in *Villette*—the warm summer night
aglow with jewels of light, the thick groves of dark feathery trees,
the brilliant throngs surrounding a kiosk in the center of the illumi-
nated park, the wild notes of a German hunting song that filled the
evening air. If she did not have the supreme pleasure of a seat beside
Monsieur—and Madame would see that she did not—at least he was
near and she was not forgotten, nor yet alone.

After this crescendo of events, activity abruptly ceased. The next
day the school began to empty. Sitting alone in the First Class, a book
lying idly open on her lap, Charlotte heard the incessant peal of the
bell as groups of friends and relatives descended upon the Pensionnat
to whisk away the local students to their homes or to the seaside. The
*carré* rang with chatter and laughing good-bys. Foreign students went

happily off with Belgian friends. Mademoiselle Sophie and Mademoiselle Haussé went home. Mademoiselle Blanche, a Parisienne, left for
France. The Hegers packed their belongings, Madame serene and
pregnant with their fifth child, and set out with their children for
Blankenberghe, the watering place where they were accustomed to
spend their holidays. The schoolrooms were dismantled, swept out
with damp coffee grounds, and shut up. The portress and the maids
disappeared. Charlotte was left alone in the silent buildings with the
cook.

A thick silence descended over the empty Pensionnat. During the
day she paced the garden walks, her skirts whispering as they stirred
the gray dust. Sometimes she withdrew with a book to the cooler
gloom of the somber *allée défendue*, but while this secret spot had
been a refuge when the garden rang with the shouts of girls, the thick
vines and dark branches now seemed oppressive and sinister. At night
in the great silent dormitory the long rows of white-curtained beds
glimmered like pale tombstones in the moonlight. The great bell from
the tower of Ste. Gudule tolled away the long hours. Her heart died
within her.

Mary Dixon was out of town. The Wheelwrights had her once or
twice to tea but, preoccupied with their own affairs, did not wonder
how she passed the hours before she came or after she left them. At
the end of August they too left Brussels. The days crept by like pain-
stricken invalids. Quite desperate for the sight and sound of human
beings, she was often driven from the Pensionnat, "crushing as the
slab of a tomb," out into the city where she walked for hours, mingling
with the crowds, until fatigue drove her back to the vast, deserted
premises of the school. There she paced the garden paths once more
or tried to read. How little comfort to take up the books Monsieur had
given her, how meaningless the inscription, "Gift of Monsieur Heger."
And in despair she would flee the silent garden to roam the streets of
the city once more until nightfall.

> Yesterday I went on a pilgrimage to the cemetery, and far beyond
> it on to a hill where there was nothing but fields as far as the horizon
> [she confided to Emily]. When I came back it was evening; but I had
> such a repugnance to return to the house, which contained nothing
> that I cared for, I still kept threading the streets in the neighbourhood
> of the Rue d'Isabelle and avoiding it. I found myself opposite to Ste
> Gudule, and the bell, whose voice you know, began to toll for eve-
> ning *salut*. I went in, quite alone (which procedure you will say is not
> much like me), wandered about the aisles where a few old women
> were saying their prayers, till vespers begun. I stayed till they were
> over. Still I could not leave the church or force myself to go home

—to school I mean. An odd whim came into my head. In a solitary part of the Cathedral six or seven people still remained kneeling by the confessionals. In two confessionals I saw a priest. I felt as if I did not care what I did, provided it was not absolutely wrong, and that it served to vary my life and yield a moment's interest. I took a fancy to change myself into a Catholic and go and make a real confession to see what it was like. Knowing me as you do, you will think this odd, but when people are by themselves they have singular fancies. A penitent was occupied in confessing. They do not go into the sort of pew or cloister which the priest occupies, but kneel down on the steps and confess through a grating. Both the confessor and the penitent whisper very low, you can hardly hear their voices. After I had watched two or three penitents go and return, I approached at last and knelt down in a niche which was just vacated. I had to kneel there ten minutes waiting, for on the other side was another penitent invisible to me. At last that went away and a little wooden door inside the grating opened, and I saw the priest leaning his ear towards me. I was obliged to begin, and yet I did not know a word of the formula with which they always commence their confessions. It was a funny position. I felt precisely as I did when alone on the Thames at midnight. I commenced with saying I was a foreigner and had been brought up a Protestant. The priest asked if I was a Protestant then. I somehow could not tell a lie, and said "yes." He replied that in that case I could not "*jouir du bonheur de la confesse*"; but I was determined to confess, and at last he said he would allow me because it might be the first step towards returning to the true church. I actually did confess—a real confession. When I had done he told me his address, and said that every morning I was to go to the rue du Parc—to his house—and he would reason with me and try to convince me of the error and enormity of being a Protestant!!! I promised faithfully to go. Of course, however, the adventure stops there, and I hope I shall never see the priest again. I think you had better not tell papa of this. He will not understand that it was only a freak, and will perhaps think I am going to turn Catholic.[12]

To Charlotte's whispered confession that she loved a married man of the Catholic faith the priest could have made but one reply. But Charlotte could not yet tear herself away from Brussels.

More than half the vacation was over. Mademoiselle Blanche returned from Paris. Charlotte took meals with her but hardly spoke, so much did she detest this false confidant and spy of Madame Heger. Perceiving her intense dislike, Mademoiselle Blanche soon learned to avoid her, and Charlotte was as solitary as ever.

Welcoming anything that would "yield a moment's interest," she noted the bills posted all over the city announcing the fact that "H.M. the Queen of England will visit the capital of Belgium where she will make her entry by the Porte de Cologne on Monday at 1 P.M. and will drive to the Palace by the Boulevard du Jardin Botanique and the Rue Royale." Accordingly, she stationed herself among the crowds on September 18 and managed to glimpse her sovereign "flashing through the Rue Royale in a carriage and six, surrounded by soldiers. She was laughing and talking very gaily. She looked a little stout, vivacious lady, very plainly dressed, not much dignity or pretension about her. The Belgians liked her very well on the whole," she concluded her report to Emily. "They said she enlivened the sombre Court of King Leopold, which is usually as gloomy as a conventicle. . . ."[13] In happier days of outings with the Hegers or English friends, Charlotte herself had scrutinized Victoria's uncle and his queen as they sat dejectedly in the royal box at a concert, and judged the king a victim of acute melancholia. But the chief sufferer was the queen. "Let us not joke, please, madame!" he had rebuked his wife when in the early days of their marriage she had attempted a feeble witticism; and poor Queen Louisa had scarcely smiled since.

The great Victoria come and gone, Brussels prepared to celebrate the thirteenth anniversary of the revolution with speeches, parades, races, balloon ascensions, concerts, and illuminations in the park. There was little comfort for Charlotte in mingling with crowds in festival mood. For the most part she remained inside the walls of the Pensionnat, reminded of the festivities outside, as she wrote in *Villette*, only by the sounds of a city in celebration drifting through her window:

> In summer it was never quite dark, and then I went up stairs to my own quarter of the long dormitory, opened my own casement (that chamber was lit by five casements large as great doors), and leaning out, looked forth upon the city beyond the garden, and listened to band-music from the park or the palace-square, thinking meantime my own thoughts, living my own life in my own still, shadow-world. . . .[14]

September drew to a close. Pupils, teachers, and domestics began to reassemble. Footsteps sounded in the corridors, voices filled the garden. The long vacation was over. Who can doubt that Charlotte had passed long hours imagining her reunion with Monsieur? Would he seek her out? Would he speak kindly as before? Would he ask how she had spent the long weeks? Could she confess, and might he sympathize with "Mees Charlotte" in her solitude?

The Hegers returned. She waited for some sign. But the gulf between them was as deep as before. After so many weeks of despair and hope, this was hard. On a Sunday morning shortly after the school had swung once more into motion, she sat alone at a long table in the empty refectory. At no time did she feel more estranged from Monsieur than when he was conspicuously a Catholic—taking his family to mass at St. Jacques sur Coudenberg, closeting himself in the little oratory before the candle-lit image of the Virgin, conducting the evening *lecture pieuse*, a little exercise in Catholic doctrine that had so enraged Charlotte that her attendance was speedily excused. Her recent flirtation with the confessional, far from comforting her, had only emphasized Monsieur's consecrated unapproachability. Home on this foreign Sunday seemed more desirable than ever; still, as she wrote Emily, she could not yet leave Brussels:

> Dear E.J.,—This is Sunday morning. They are at their idolatrous "messe," and I am here—that is, in the *réfectoire*. I should like uncommonly to be in the dining-room at home, or in the kitchen, or in the back kitchen. I should like even to be cutting up the hash, with the clerk and some register people at the other table, and you standing by, watching that I put enough flour, and not too much pepper, and, above all, that I save the best pieces of the leg of mutton for Tiger and Keeper, the first of which personages would be jumping about the dish and carving-knife, and the latter standing like a devouring flame on the kitchen floor. To complete the picture, Tabby blowing the fire, in order to boil the potatoes to a sort of vegetable glue! How divine are these recollections to me at this moment! Yet I have no thought of coming home just now. I lack a real pretext for doing so; it is true this place is dismal to me, but I cannot go home without a fixed prospect when I get there; and this prospect must not be a situation; that would be jumping out of the frying-pan into the fire. *You* call yourself idle! absurd, absurd! . . . Is papa well? Are you well? and Tabby? . . . Tell me whether papa really wants me very much to come home, and whether you do likewise. I have an idea that I should be of no use there—a sort of aged person upon the parish. I pray, with heart and soul, that all may continue well at Haworth; above all in our grey, half-inhabited house. God bless the walls thereof! Safety, health, happiness, and prosperity to you, papa and Tabby. Amen.[15]

Uncertain which way to turn, Charlotte stayed on, unable to leave Monsieur, rationalizing her conduct with the excuse that she must learn sufficient German before quitting Brussels. Mary Taylor had left the city for Hagen, Germany, where she continued to study and began to give English lessons to German boys. Aware of her friend's suffering, she wrote Charlotte, urging her to come to Germany. Pupils were plentiful: she herself was giving forty-two lessons a week and would soon have more boys than she could teach. But Charlotte refused, explaining to Ellen that she could not be so imprudent as "to

leave a certainty for a complete uncertainty." Reading letters filled
with woe, neither Emily nor Ellen could understand why Charlotte
did not come home. "Charlotte has never mentioned a word about
coming home," Emily wrote Ellen, "if you would go over for half a
year perhaps you might be able to bring her back with you, otherwise
she may vegetate there till the age of Methuselah for mere lack of
courage to face the voyage."[16]

Then, less than two weeks after she had declared firmly to Emily
that she would not come home without a "fixed prospect," Charlotte
flung into Madame's sitting room and gave notice. For Madame it was
a moment of triumph: the fly was in the web at last. Coolly eying her
agitated opponent, she accepted Charlotte's resignation on the spot.
Her triumph was short-lived, however. Informed of Charlotte's insurrection, Monsieur Heger immediately opposed the notion of her
leaving them. What could his wife say? Having never admitted that a
campaign against the English teacher existed, she could utter no word
of protest against her staying. The next day Monsieur sent for Charlotte and in a fine rage insisted vehemently that she must not leave
Brussels. His anger warmed Charlotte like the sun breaking forth after
months of heavy cloud. Monsieur still cared whether she lived or died.
She agreed to stay.

The episode confirmed absolutely that Madame Heger no longer
wanted her in Brussels; had it been otherwise, she would have protested Charlotte's resignation. At the same time, it convinced her that
Monsieur Heger had not initiated the estrangement between them.
"Madame Heger is a polite—plausible and interested person," she
wrote Ellen on October 13; "—I no longer trust her."[17] It was the
most she could say against her, for Madame's discretion had never permitted hard words, accusations, or open confrontations between them.
Merely Charlotte had felt herself helplessly enmeshed in the subtle
restraining strands woven by Madame's capable hand.

October passed, November wore on. In mid-month Madame gave
birth to her fifth child, a girl, christened Victorine. The event, drawing Monsieur still deeper into the vortex of family life, did not cheer
Charlotte. She wrote the same day, November 15, to Ellen, sounding
again the incessant theme of loneliness, but hinting for the first time
at the existence of a deeper distress than solitude:

> To-day the weather is gloomy, and I am stupefied with a bad cold
> and a headache. I have nothing to tell you, my dear Ellen. One day is
> like another in this place. I know you, living in the country, can
> hardly believe it possible life can be monotonous in the centre of a
> brilliant capital like Brussels; but so it is. I feel it most on the holidays,
> when all the girls and teachers go out to visit, and it sometimes hap-

pens that I am left, during several hours, quite alone, with four great desolate schoolrooms at my disposition. I try to read, I try to write; but in vain. I then wander about from room to room, but the silence and loneliness of all the house weighs down one's spirits like lead. You will hardly believe that Madame Heger (good and kind as I have described her) never comes near me on these occasions. She is a reasonable and calm woman, but, Nelly, as to warm-heartedness she has as much of that article as Mrs Taylor. I own, I was astonished the first time I was left alone thus; when everybody else was enjoying the pleasures of a fête-day with their friends, and she knew I was quite by myself, and never took the least notice of me. Yet, I understand, she praises me very much to everybody, and says what excellent lessons I give. She is not colder to me than she is to the other teachers; but they are less dependent on her than I am. They have relations and acquaintances in Brussels. You remember the letter she wrote me, when I was in England? How kind and affectionate that was? Is it not odd? I fancy I begin to perceive the reason of this mighty distance and reserve; it sometimes makes me laugh, and at other times nearly cry. When I am sure of it I will tell it you. In the meantime, the complaints I make at present are for your ear only—a sort of relief which I permit myself. In all other respects I am well satisfied with my position, and you may say so to people who inquire after me (if any one does). Write to me, dear Nell, whenever you can. You do a good deed when you send me a letter, for you comfort a very desolate heart. . . .[18]

Incredibly, Charlotte was just beginning to understand the reason for Madame's coldness—so little did she admit to herself the case that was plainly evident to Monsieur's wife. While she only hinted to Ellen, it is probable that she wrote Mary Taylor openly. At least Mary urged Charlotte more emphatically than ever to leave Brussels immediately while her health and sanity were still sound. Mary's good sense proved the impetus Charlotte needed to extricate herself from a hopeless situation. By the seventeenth of December it was general news in the Pensionnat that the English teacher was leaving Brussels.

She did not leave in defeat. However unhappy her days, however much she despised the Belgians, their country, and their religion, however keen her disappointment in the Hegers, she had learned and taught superbly. She had always suffered—at Roe Head, the Sidgwicks', and the Whites'—but she had always triumphed professionally. Paradoxically, the moment her departure was announced, many teachers and pupils came forward with expressions of good will. Much of the aloofness she had criticized in the Belgians had been of her own creating; now she found she had friends and admirers among staff and students. "I was surprised," she told Ellen later, ". . . at the degree of

regret expressed by my Belgian pupils, when they knew I was going
to leave. I did not think it had been in their phlegmatic nature. . . ."[19]
Mademoiselle Blanche would remain an enemy, but Mademoiselle Sophie surprised and touched her with a little parting gift and note to
*"Ma Chère Charlotte"*:

> Please do me the pleasure of accepting this little box as a keepsake. I
> have far too good an opinion of your heart to suppose that it needs
> the sight of any object to recall me to your indulgent memory. No, I
> am convinced that the friendship you have always shown me has its
> source in the finest feelings. All the same, you would grieve me if you
> refused me this mark of your affection. Goodbye, my good kind
> Charlotte; I like to think that I shall not be losing you for ever in a
> couple of weeks' time and that you will deign from time to time,
> when you have seen your homeland again to turn your thoughts
> towards dreary Belgium, where more than one person will be think-
> ing of you. Devotedly,
>
> > Your Friend Sophie.
> > Brussels, 17th December 1843.[20]

In former days Madame Heger had been one of Charlotte's most
vocal admirers, waxing enthusiastic over her talents, her industry,
and her success with the First Class. Now that the English teacher was
leaving, she became amiable again, and Charlotte, her weary heart
glad of any kindness, welcomed her friendship. Evidently she also permitted her husband to express some of his old kindly interest in Mademoiselle, or perhaps he undertook to express it without his wife's consent. So that she might boast a tangible record of her accomplishments
in German and French, Monsieur presented her with a diploma crested
with the official seal of the Athénée Royale. In those last days Charlotte felt him again as a friend.

The day of her departure drew near. *Villette*, the story of her love
for Monsieur and her hatred of his wife, contains much truth and much
invention. Monsieur Paul's farewell to the English teacher Lucy Snowe
is not fact, but it is emotional truth, and as such admissible evidence of
the ordeal Charlotte suffered in leaving the Pensionnat. In the novel,
it is Paul Emanuel who is leaving Brussels:

> M. Emanuel wore the dress in which he probably purposed to
> travel—a surtout, guarded with velvet . . . He looked well, and
> cheerful. He looked kind and benign: he came in with eagerness; he
> was close to me in one second; he was all amity. . . . I could not
> meet his sunshine with cloud. If this were my last moment with him, I
> would not waste it in forced, unnatural distance. I loved him well—
> too well not to smite out of my path even Jealousy herself, when she
> would have obstructed a kind farewell. A cordial word from his lips,

or a gentle look from his eyes, would do me good, for all the span of life that remained to me; it would be comfort in the last strait of loneliness; I would take it—I would taste the elixir, and pride should not spill the cup.

The interview would be short, of course: he would say to me just what he had said to each of the assembled pupils; he would take and hold my hand two minutes; he would touch my cheek with his lips for the first, last, only time—and then—no more. Then, indeed, the final parting, then the wide separation, the great gulf I could not pass to go to him—across which, haply, he would not glance, to remember me.

He took my hand in one of his, with the other he put back my bonnet; he looked into my face, his luminous smile went out, his lips expressed something almost like the wordless language of a mother who finds a child greatly and unexpectedly changed, broken with illness, or worn-out by want. A check supervened.

"Paul, Paul!" said a woman's hurried voice behind, "Paul, come into the salon; I have yet a great many things to say to you—conversation for the whole day—and so has Victor; and Josef is here. Come, Paul, come to your friends."

Madame Beck, brought to the spot by vigilance or an inscrutable instinct, pressed so near, she almost thrust herself between me and M. Emanuel. "Come, Paul!" she reiterated, her eye grazing me with its hard ray like a steel stylet. . . . Pierced deeper than I could endure, made now to feel what defied supression, I cried—

"My heart will break!"

Happy fiction that can create what life denies. Monsieur, clasping the weeping, trembling Lucy Snowe in his arms, turns fiercely upon the woman who is seeking so desperately to part them.

"Laissez-moi!" he cries deeply, harshly, and briefly. "Laissez-moi!"[21]

In reality, Charlotte suppressed her pain, admitting to Ellen only afterward, "I suffered much before I left Brussels. I think, however long I live, I shall not forget what the parting with M. Heger cost me; it grieved me so much to grieve him, who has been so true, kind, and disinterested a friend. . . ."[22] On the day of her departure she was summoned into the Hegers' sitting room and handed a parting gift, a book of French poetry which she inscribed after reaching home, "Given to me by Monsieur Heger on the 1st of January, the morning I left Brussels." They parted in seeming friendship, the Hegers even offering to send Charlotte one of their little girls as a pupil when she should establish her own school. She was assured again of Monsieur's interest in her success; she was invited to correspond.

Madame Heger escorted her in person from Brussels to the boat at

Ostend, a gesture of amiability—and a determination that under no circumstances should her husband be allowed a parting scene with Miss Charlotte of the plain face and glowing eyes. The packet would sail with the next morning's tide. Her sigh of relief as she bid the English teacher good-by must have been profound.

# 10

*Punished*

Often when an object is removed from view the imagination fills the void with an image a hundred times more vivid. Thus, as Charlotte receded from Monsieur's world mile by mile—across the Channel by packet, from London to Leeds by train, from Leeds to Keighley by coach, from Keighley to winter-locked Haworth by open gig—the vision of her beloved friend expanded, filling her heart and dominating her thoughts. She arrived at the parsonage bursting with plans for establishing the school. Monsieur had encouraged such an undertaking; she would write to him for advice; he would send her his daughters as pupils; perhaps he would cross the Channel to bring them to her—surely he would.

A day at home sufficed to check three years of hopes, dreams, and struggle. Charlotte found Papa in the parlor, dejected and morose, half blinded with cataracts, increasingly dependent on Emily to read him the papers and write his letters. Tabby, now back in her rocking chair before the kitchen fire, was so lamed that even hobbling to the front door to answer the postman's knock was a painful task. Another family would have dismissed her, but the Brontës, always delicate with animals and dependents, gallantly pretended that she was as indispensable to them as before. Martha Brown was young and strong, but unable to care for the heavy cleaning and washing and Mr. Brontë's needs. Charlotte had suffered qualms at leaving Papa to return to Brussels; now, face to face with the stricken white-haired old man, she decided she could not in conscience abandon him again. Anne and Branwell were home for the holidays from Thorp Green Hall; a council was held, and the "Misses Brontë's Establishment" was for the time being abandoned, reluctantly by Anne, who longed to leave the uncongenial Robinsons, and with anguish by Charlotte. Emily was not unduly disappointed: she hated teaching, had no love for young girls, preferred to iron, bake, and sew and, those tasks done, escape to Gondal again.

Charlotte's case was far different. The impetus that had driven her since that May evening in the Whites' deserted schoolroom was balked. Primed with French, German, literature, composition, and teaching experience, she now found no outlet for her skills. Haworth deadened her energies as wool muffles a shot. The montonous ticking of the clock, the silent graveyard, the moors blockaded with snow smothered her hopes. Restless, frustrated, she wrote to convey the bad news to Ellen, who, perversely enough, was away visiting Henry at Chichester just when she wanted most to see her:

Haworth, January 23rd, 1844: My Dear Ellen,—It was a great disappointment to me to hear that you were in the south of England. I had counted on seeing *you soon*, as one of the great pleasures of my return; now, I fear, our meeting will be postponed for an indefinite time.

Every one asks me what I am going to do, now that I am returned home; and every one seems to expect that I should immediately commence a school. In truth, it is what I should wish to do. I desire it above all things. I have sufficient money for the undertaking, and I hope now sufficient qualifications to give me a fair chance of success; I cannot yet permit myself to enter upon life—to touch the object which seems now within my reach, and which I have been so long straining to attain. You will ask me why. It is on Papa's account; he is now, as you know, getting old, and it grieves me to tell you that he is losing his sight. I have felt for some months that I ought not to be away from him; and I feel now that it would be too selfish to leave him (at least as long as Branwell and Anne are absent) in order to pursue selfish interests of my own. With the help of God I will try to deny myself in this matter, and to wait. . . . I do not know whether you feel as I do, but there are times now when it appears to me as if all my ideas and feelings, except a few friendships and affections, are changed from what they used to be; something in me, which used to be enthusiasm, is tamed down and broken. I have fewer illusions; what I wish for now is active exertion—a stake in life. Haworth seems such a lonely, quiet spot, buried away from the world. I no longer regard myself as young—indeed, I shall soon be twenty-eight; and it seems as if I ought to be working and braving the rough realities of the world, as other people do. It is, however, my duty to restrain this feeling at present, and I will endeavour to do so. Write to me soon, my dear Ellen, and believe as far as regards yourself, your *unchanged* friend,

C. Brontë.

Remember me with kindness to your brother Henry. Anne and Branwell have just left us to return to York. They are both wondrously valued in their situations.[1]

Ellen returned to Brookroyd and Charlotte visited her in March. There on cold spring evenings as they sat doing up their hair in curl papers, their feet on the fender, the firelight dancing on the walls, Charlotte could confide to Ellen the sufferings she dared not commit to paper, the long heartache of her second sojourn in Brussels. And Ellen herself could confess that, despite Birstall routs and pink petticoats and wreaths of roses, she had not had a very gay time of it in Charlotte's absence. Her placid nature could not quite insulate her against the uninspiring tedium of life at Brookroyd. She longed to venture out into the world but, not in need of a governess' wages, could find no pretense to do so. As a result, she was forced to rationalize her existence by pretending that her mother needed her at home, or by pleading a delicate constitution—so many young ladies of her acquaintance cultivated delicate constitutions for lack of anything better to do. Illness and death had also plagued the Nussey household: her sister Sarah had died the preceding summer; her brother George was beginning to show those symptoms of nervous melancholy that would end in insanity. And despite Charlotte's raillery over Mr. Vincent and the Taylor brothers ("I know it will soon be Mrs. J. Taylor —I can't for the life of me tell whether the initial J. stands for John or Joe"), none of Ellen's romances had come to anything.

Charlotte stayed three weeks, returning home in better spirits and in rather better health, bearing a small gift for Emily, for Ellen never let her leave empty-handed, although the gifts—jars of preserves, apples, a cheese—must be as modest as the Brontës were proud: "Emily is much obliged to you for the flower seeds. She wishes to know if the Sicilian pea and crimson corn-flower are hardy flowers, or if they are delicate, and should be sown in warm and sheltered situations? . . . Our poor little cat has been ill two days, and is just dead. It is piteous to see even an animal lying lifeless. Emily *is* sorry."[2]

Winter gales softened into fresh spring winds. Unable to throw off completely her sense of emptiness and frustration, Charlotte could now at least escape out of doors. She and Emily walked out together on the moors morning and afternoon, to the great damage of their shoes, as she told Ellen, but to the probable benefit of their health.

Then in April Mary Taylor returned suddenly from Germany and plans were made for a reunion at the house at Hunsworth Mills, for Mary still avoided the Red House and her sour-tempered mother. In May Charlotte journeyed to Hunsworth in the Spen Valley. Ellen joined them a few days later, arriving with her brother George at nine in the evening. She was able to make out figures walking and talking "with all their might" in the garden, but dark had fallen and she was uncertain whether it was Charlotte and Mary. All three drew close, "cautiously peered into each other's faces," then burst out with "Bless you!" as they warmly embraced. However happy the reunion, however, none of them could claim satisfaction with their lives in the confidential talks that followed: Mary found no real challenge tutoring boys in English, Ellen languished at Brookroyd, and Charlotte longed for her master and a school.

In June Charlotte was asking Ellen to come to Haworth: "Anne and Branwell are now at home—and they and Emily add their request to mine that you will join us in the beginning of next week—write and let us know what day you will come and how—if by coach we will meet you at Keighley—do not let your visit be later than the beginning of next week or  you will see little of A. and B. as their holidays are very short. They will soon have to join the family at Scarborough."[3]

Ellen came—by virtue of her quiet manners and good nature perhaps the only outsider as welcome to Emily, Anne, and Branwell as she was to Charlotte. On this summer visit, her good nature also appealed to Mr. Brontë's curate, the Rev. James William Smith: he paid her a good deal of attention. Charlotte did not like the fellow—a tall, strongly built Irishman with a proud, petrified face and arrogant manners. Her dislike went beyond her usual antagonism toward "the Holyes," as she called her father's curates, for it was the hard-drinking Smith who had enticed Mr. Brontë into long sessions with bottles of Irish whiskey to while away the bleak Yorkshire hours and set the rumors flying in the village. Smith was also a lively glutton. Was it during Ellen's visit that he dined so voraciously and arrogantly at the parsonage table, downing quantities of beef and bread, Yorkshire pudding, vegetables, cheese, and spice cake, and washing down the whole with great draughts of "flat beer"? Still, he claimed to be a gentleman, he could be amusing in a boisterous way, and he paid Ellen so much attention during her visit that Charlotte began to entertain lively visions of her friend installed in Haworth village as a curate's wife.

Ellen left, bearing one of Flossie's pups as a parting gift, and Charlotte met Mr. Smith expectantly for days after, waiting for eager inquiries after Miss Nussey. None, as she was forced to admit to Ellen in a letter of July 16, were forthcoming:

> Dear Nell,—We were all very glad to get your letter this morning. *We*, I say, as both Papa and Emily were anxious to hear of the safe arrival of yourself and the little *varmint*.
>
> As you conjecture, Emily and I set to shirt-making the very day after you left, and we have stuck to it pretty closely ever since. We miss your society at least as much as you miss ours, depend upon it. Would that you were within calling distance, that you could as you say burst in upon us in an afternoon, and, being despoiled of your

bonnet and shawl, be fixed in the rocking-chair for the evening once or twice every week. I certainly cherished a dream during your stay that such might one day be the case, but the dream is somewhat dissipating. I allude of course to Mr Smith, to whom you do not allude in your letter, and I think you foolish for the omission. I say the dream is dissipating, because Mr Smith has not mentioned your name since you left, except once when papa said you were a nice girl, he said, "Yes, she is a nice girl—rather quiet. I suppose she has money," and that is all. I think the words speak volumes; they do not prejudice one in favour of Mr Smith. I can well believe what papa has often affirmed, and continues to affirm, *i.e.*, that Mr Smith is a very fickle man, that if he marries he will soon get tired of his wife, and consider her as a burden, also that money will be a principal consideration with him in marrying. . . .

Mr Smith be hanged! I never thought very well of him, and I am much disposed to think very ill of him at this blessed minute. I have discussed the subject fully, for where is the use of being mysterious and constrained?—it is not worth while.[4]

Even Mr. Brontë abandoned his aloofness to trivialities of the heart and intervened, begging Charlotte to dissuade Ellen from thoughts of the curate; obviously he distrusted the man who had lured him into intemperance. "I never saw papa make himself so uneasy about a thing of the kind before," Charlotte confided to Ellen; "he is usually very sarcastic on such subjects." She herself grew daily more sarcastic as Smith showed no revival of his interest in her friend. "I have nothing new to tell you about the Revd Mr Lothario-Lovelace Smith—I think I like him a little bit less every day—I am glad now he did not ask you to marry him—you are far too good for him—Mr Weightman was worth 200 Mr Smiths tied in a bunch." Finally Mr. Smith left Haworth for a curacy at Keighley, and Charlotte shut the book on that highly unsatisfactory young man in a letter to Ellen on September 16: "He has left neither a bad nor a good character behind him. Nobody regrets him, because nobody could attach themselves to one who could attach himself to nobody. I thought once he had a regard for you, but I do not think so now. He has never asked after you since you left, nor even mentioned you in my hearing, except to say once when I purposely alluded to you, that you were 'not very locomotive.' The meaning of the observation I leave you to divine."[5]

Ellen Nussey was perhaps spared an unsympathetic husband in failing to attract Mr. Smith, yet why was a young woman possessed of all the wifely virtues—passivity, good looks, piety, common sense, money —still not married at twenty-eight? Charlotte judged that Ellen would make as good a wife as she herself would make a bad one, to most men. ". . . the perfect serenity with which you endured the disaster," she replied with only slight irony to Ellen's report that Flossie junior, "that infamous little *bitch*," had chewed up a muslin dress and a lace bertha, "—proves most fully to me that you would make the best wife, mother, and mistress of a family in the world—you and Anne are a pair, for marvelous philosophical powers of endurance—no spoilt dinner—scorched linen, dirtied carpets—torn sofa-covers, squealing brats, cross husbands would ever discompose either of you—You ought never to marry a good-tempered man such a union would be mingling honey with sugar. . . ."⁶ Perhaps Ellen's extraordinary tranquillity prevented her bestirring herself enough to fall in love. There is Mr. Smith's testimony that she "was not very locomotive."

Mr. Smith's place was taken by the Rev. Joseph Brett Grant, who also served as head of the Haworth Grammar School, and by the Rev. Arthur Bell Nicholls. Charlotte found the first as conceited, insipid, and commonplace as he seemed to find the natives of Yorkshire dull, benighted, and brutish. As for Nicholls: "I cannot for my life see those interesting germs of goodness in him you discovered," she told Ellen; "his narrowness of mind always strikes me chiefly. I fear he is indebted to your imagination for his hidden treasure." So much for curates.

During Ellen's visit Charlotte had again lamented the lost school and, with it, her lost career and independence. But was all really lost? A new plan evolved: Charlotte could not leave home, but pupils could come to her; the parsonage could be transformed into a boarding school. The plan, daring at first, seemed more possible after Papa's surprising consent. Emily refused to teach but agreed to take on the heavy ironing, cleaning, and baking that would inevitably accompany five or six boarders. The parsonage was not large, but narrow cots in Aunt Branwell's old bedroom, the dining room turned into a school-room, a small parlor made out of the back kitchen—the house might stretch. Nothing could be done about the isolated situation, however; and Charlotte doubted in her heart that any parent could be persuaded to believe that a civilized school existed in a rough little village on the edge of the moors. Nevertheless she wrote Mrs. White, not to ask for her daughter (although she wanted to), but to inform her of her plans. An answer from Mr. White was both disappointing and encouraging: his own daughter and the daughter of his neighbor, Colonel Stott, were already promised to Miss Corkhill, a friend of both Ellen and Mary Taylor; had Charlotte written sooner, he would have been delighted to send her both girls. Such a near miss was disappointing but, pleased because the Smiths did not seem to be put off by Haworth, Charlotte wrote again to a Mrs. Busfeild of Keighley, enclosing the diploma given her by Monsieur Heger and asking for her patronage.

By the end of July, however, nothing had yet come of the school plan. "I am driving on with my small matter as well as I can," she wrote Ellen in frustration.

> I have written to all the friends on whom I have the slightest claim, and to some on whom I have no claim—Mrs Busfeild, for example. On her, also, I have actually made bold to call. She was exceedingly polite; regretted that her children were already at school in Liverpool; thought the undertaking a most praiseworthy one, but feared I should have some difficulty in making it succeed on account of the *situation*. Such is the answer I receive from almost every one. I tell them the *retired situation* is, in some points of view, an advantage; that were it in the midst of a large town I could not pretend to take pupils on terms so moderate—Mrs Busfeild remarked that she thought the terms very moderate—but that, as it is, not having house-rent to pay, we can offer the same privileges of education that are to be had in expensive seminaries, at little more than half their price; and, as our number must be limited, we can devote a large share of time and pains to each pupil. Thank you for the very pretty little purse you have sent me. I make you a curious return in the shape of half a dozen cards of terms. Make such use of them as your judgment shall dictate. You will see that I have fixed the sum at £35, which I think is the just medium, considering advantages and disadvantages. What does your wisdom think about it?[7]

Charlotte had composed and had printed an advertisement modeled after the prospectus of the Pensionnat des Demoiselles in Brussels:

THE MISSES BRONTË'S ESTABLISHMENT

FOR

## THE BOARD AND EDUCATION

OF A LIMITED NUMBER OF

YOUNG LADIES,

## THE PARSONAGE, HAWORTH

NEAR BRADFORD.

---

## TERMS

|  | £ | s. | d. |
|---|---|---|---|
| Board and Education, including Writing, Arithmetic, History, Grammar, Geography, and Needle Work, per annum | 35 | 0 | 0 |
| French ⎫ German ⎬ each per Quarter Latin ⎭ | 1 | 1 | 0 |
| Music ⎫ Drawing ⎬ each per Quarter | 1 | 1 | 0 |
| Use of Piano Forte, per Quarter | 0 | 5 | 0 |
| Washing, per Quarter | 0 | 15 | 0 |

Each Young Lady to be provided with One Pair of Sheets, Pillow Cases, Four Towels, a Dessert and Tea-Spoon.

A Quarter's Notice, or a Quarter's Board, is required previous to the Removal of a Pupil.

Having placed the announcements in the hands of every friend and nodding acquaintance she could muster, she awaited a response, but July, August, and September passed and not the ghost of a pupil materialized. In the interim she had been offered a post as governess in a large school in Manchester at the impressive salary of £100 a year; she turned it down; she could not leave Papa. By October she was ready to admit defeat:

> Dear Ellen,—I, Emily, and Anne are truly obliged to you for the efforts you have made on our behalf, and if you have not been successful you are only like ourselves. Every one wishes us well, but there are no pupils to be had. We have no present intention, however, of breaking our hearts on the subject, still less of feeling mortified at defeat. The effort must be beneficial whatever the result may be, because it teaches us experience and an additional knowledge of the world.[8]

Had the school ever been real to her? Had she clearly imagined three or four well-bred young ladies arriving with their sheets and teaspoons to enjoy their stay in a buried moorland village whipped by winds, in a bleak parsonage crowded round by a dank churchyard, in the company of a severe, half-blind old man, a hobbling servant, an uncommunicative mystic guarded by a tall, black-jawed bull mastiff, and a dipsomaniac son liable to descend upon the household at any moment in disgrace? No. ". . . depend upon it Ellen," she wrote, "if you were to persuade a mamma to bring her child to Haworth—the aspect of the place would frighten her and she would probably take the dear thing back with her instanter."[9] Not all of Charlotte's hard-won teaching experience or Anne's gentle patience could have assured the success of the "Misses Brontë's Establishment."

At Roe Head, at the Sidgwicks' and the Whites', Charlotte had lamented that she could not steal an hour in the day to write. Now, with nothing but time, she still did not return to the occupation that had been her passion and her solace since childhood. Since returning from Brussels her eyesight had deteriorated. She did not know why, she was not afflicted with cataracts like Papa, but by evening she often could not see to put pen to paper. Her eyes ached; some days she could barely see to scratch out a brief note to Ellen; fine sewing and reading had to be abandoned. Had her eyesight been sound, however, she still imagined herself under a prohibition. On her return to Brussels, she had taken back a few Angrian stories written in her eighteenth and nineteenth years to show to her good and sympathetic master of literature. Monsieur read, frowned over the vivid and eccentric little melodramas, and, like Southey and Wordsworth, delivered his advice: You have talent, mademoiselle, but a talent you must suppress rather than cultivate. Abandon vain dreams of authorship; teaching is the proper sphere for a young woman. Charlotte prized Monsieur's words as gold. His advice was disappointing and difficult, very difficult, to accept, but she determined to abide by it, and she had, throwing herself wholeheartedly into the school plan because Monsieur approved it. The school had failed, and there was little now to fill the days except thoughts of Monsieur.

Separation had only intensified her craving for his affection. Each day was haunted by memories of her master. Every morning brought the chance of a letter from Brussels. All her efforts she stamped with the imaginary seal of his approval. A correspondence had been authorized by Madame herself; she took advantage of the invitation to write to Monsieur soon after her return; he answered with letters like himself—warm, sympathetic, magnetic. Deceived, she imagined she could open her heart a little to him; she wrote him a letter which, considering the intensity of her feelings, she believed to be innocent enough. It did not seem so to Monsieur, or to his wife, who read it and saw with deep chagrin that she was not rid of "Mees Charlotte" after all. Was Monsieur wondrously influenced by Madame, as Charlotte believed, or genuinely appalled at the flood of emotion he had unwittingly released in his former pupil? He replied; the letter with the foreign stamp arrived at the parsonage, was torn open with trembling fingers, and read with a sinking heart. It contained a rebuke and a command: in the future she must write infrequently and with restraint. He was interested in her studies, her teaching, her family, the development of her character. He would be pleased to hear from time to time about these matters, but beyond these bounds she must not go.[10]

This was a cruel privation, difficult indeed to bear. She could not, in fact, bear it. Knowing full well that she should not write to Brussels again for many months, she nevertheless wrote immediately, undoubtedly to beg pardon with a passionate eloquence as unacceptable as the immoderate emotion of her previous letter. To this indiscretion she received no reply.

Romance feeds on denial: Charlotte was romantic. Had the little professor answered her letters with moderate friendliness and some frequency, she might have forced herself to live quietly on plain fare. But he denied himself to her, leaving her imagination free to rush in and fill the void. Monsieur Heger became an obsession.

In July, although she had had no letter from Brussels for many months, Charlotte wrote to Monsieur again. She had two excuses: the plans for taking pupils at the parsonage were at their height and he would wish to hear of them, and Mrs. Wheelwright, visiting in England, was now returning to her family in Brussels and would carry a letter to the Pensionnat Heger.

July 24th, 1844: Monsieur,—I am well aware that it is not my turn to write to you, but as Mrs Wheelwright is going to Brussels and is kind enough to take charge of a letter—it seems to me that I ought not to neglect so favourable an opportunity of writing to you.

I am very pleased that the school-year is nearly over and that the holidays are approaching.—I am pleased on your account, Monsieur— for I am told that you are working too hard and that your health has suffered somewhat in consequence. For that reason I refrain from uttering a single complaint for your long silence—I would rather remain six months without receiving news from you than add one grain to the weight, already too heavy, which overwhelms you. I know well that it is now the period of compositions, that it will soon be that of examinations, and later on of prizes—and during all that time you are condemned to breathe the stifling atmosphere of the class-rooms— to wear yourself out—to explain, to question, to talk all day, and then in the evening you have all those wretched compositions to read, to correct, almost to re-write—Ah, Monsieur! I once wrote you a letter that was less than reasonable, because sorrow was at my heart; but I shall do so no more.—I shall try to be selfish no longer; and even while I look upon your letters as one of the greatest felicities known to me, I shall await the receipt of them in patience until it pleases you and suits you to send me any. Meanwhile, I may well send you a little letter from time to time:—you have authorised me to do so.

I greatly fear that I shall forget French, for I am firmly convinced that I shall see you again some day—I know not how or when—but it must be, for I wish it so much, and then I should not wish to remain dumb before you—it would be too sad to see you and not be able to speak to you. To avoid such a misfortune I learn every day by heart half a page of French from a book written in a familiar style: and I take pleasure in learning this lesson, Monsieur; as I pronounce the French words it seems to me as if I were chatting with you.

I have just been offered a situation as first governess in a large school in Manchester, with a salary of £100 (i.e. 2,500 francs) per annum. I cannot accept it, for in accepting it I should have to leave my father, and that I cannot do. Nevertheless I have a plan—(when one lives retired the brain goes on working; there is the desire of occupation, the wish to embark on an active career). Our parsonage is rather a large house—with a few alterations there will be room for five or six boarders. If I could find this number of children of good family, I should devote myself to their education. Emily does not care much for teaching, but she would look after the housekeeping, and, although something of a recluse, she is too good-hearted not to do all she could for the well-being of the children. Moreover, she is very generous, and as for order, economy, strictness—and diligent work— all of them things very essential in a school—I willingly take that upon myself.

That, Monsieur, is my plan, which I have already explained to my father and which he approves. It only remains to find the pupils— rather a difficult thing—for we live rather far from towns, and people do not greatly care about crossing the hills which form as it were a barrier around us. But the task that is without difficulty is almost without merit; there is great interest in triumphing over obstacles. I do not say I shall succeed, but I shall *try* to succeed—the effort alone will do me good. There is nothing I fear so much as idleness, the want of occupation, inactivity, the lethargy of the faculties: when the body is idle, the spirit suffers painfully.

I should not know this lethargy if I could write. Formerly I passed whole days and weeks and months in writing, not wholly without re- sult, for Southey and Coleridge—two of our best authors, to whom I sent certain manuscripts—were good enough to express their approval; but now my sight is too weak to write.—Were I to write much I should become blind. This weakness of sight is a terrible hindrance to me. Otherwise do you know what I should do, Monsieur?—I should write a book, and I should dedicate it to my literature-master—to the only master I ever had—to you, Monsieur. I have often told you in French how much I respect you—how much I am indebted to your goodness, to your advice; I should like to say it once in English. But that cannot be—it is not to be thought of. The career of letters is closed to me—only that of teaching is open. It does not offer the same attractions; never mind, I shall enter it, and if I do not go far it will not be from want of industry. You too, Monsieur—you wished to be a barrister—destiny or Providence made you a professor; you are happy in spite of it.

Please convey to Madame the assurance of my esteem. I fear that Maria, Louise, Claire have already forgotten me. Prospère and Vic- torine never knew me well; I remember well all five of them, espe- cially Louise. She had so much character—so much naïveté in her little face.—Good-bye, Monsieur,—Your grateful pupil,

C. Brontë.

I have not begged you to write to me soon as I fear to importune you—but you are too kind to forget that I wish it all the same—yes, I wish it greatly. Enough; after all, do as you wish, Monsieur. If, then, I

received a letter, and if I thought that you had written it *out of pity*
—I should feel deeply wounded.

It seems that Mrs Wheelwright is going to Paris before going to
Brussels—but she will post my letter at Boulogne. Once more good-
bye, Monsieur; it hurts to say good-bye even in a letter. Oh, it is certain that I shall see you again one day—it must be so—for as soon as I
shall have earned enough money to go to Brussels I shall go there—
and I shall see you again if only for a moment.[11]

Monsieur Heger found this letter as unacceptable as the others and
did not answer it. Fully conscious that she was breaking promises,
Charlotte could not resist sending three months later a brief note with
Joe Taylor, who was returning to the Continent to escort his sister
back to England:

October 24, 1844: Monsieur,—I am in high glee this morning—and
that has rarely happened to me these last two years. It is because a
gentleman of my acquaintance is going to Brussels, and has offered to
take charge of a letter for you—which letter he will deliver to you
himself, or else his sister, so that I shall be certain you have received
it.

I am not going to write a long letter; in the first place, I have not
the time—it must leave at once; and then, I am afraid of worrying
you. I would only ask of you if you heard from me at the beginning
of May and again in the month of August? For six months I have
been awaiting a letter from Monsieur—six months' waiting is very
long, you know. However, I do not complain, and I shall be richly
rewarded for a little sorrow if you will now write a letter and give it
to this gentleman—or to his sister—who will hand it to me without fail.

I shall be satisfied with the letter however brief it be—only do not
forget to tell me of your health, Monsieur, and how Madame and the
children are, and the governesses and pupils.

My father and my sister send you their respects. My father's infirmity increases little by little. Nevertheless he is not yet entirely
blind. My sisters are well, but my poor brother is always ill.

Farewell, Monsieur; I am depending on soon having your news.
The idea delights me, for the remembrance of your kindnesses will
never fade from my memory, and as long as that remembrance en-
dures the respect with which it has inspired me will endure likewise.—

Your very devoted pupil,
C. Brontë.

I have just had bound all the books you gave me when I was at
Brussels. I take delight in contemplating them; they make quite a little library. To begin with, there are the complete works of Bernardin
de St Pierre—the Pensées de Pascal—a book of poetry, two German
books—and (worth all the rest) two discourses of Monsieur le Pro-

fesseur Heger, delivered at the distribution of prizes of the Athénée Royal.[12]

Reading over the books he had given her, studying his language so that she might not "remain dumb" when she saw him again, seeing in her mind the autumn moon hanging above the garden of the Pensionnat where he might be strolling now in the dusk among the pear trees, recalling the fragrance of his cigar mingling with the cool scent of jasmine—these were at once the comforts and the torments of her days. Mary had written momentous news: she was leaving Brussels and England: she had decided to abandon civilization and emigrate to New Zealand. Charlotte fretted for her return from Brussels, anxious, of course, to see her friend in England before she sailed, but more anxious for the letter from Monsieur she was confident he would send with her friends. He was good, he was charitable. He would write his suffering pupil a kind word, since she needed it so much.

The Christmas holidays arrived and with them Branwell and Anne. The long year of her separation from Monsieur dragged to a close. For eight months, since April, she had had no letter. Then news came that the Taylors were back in England. Charlotte immediately invited Mary to Haworth, where she came in January. But she brought no letter from Monsieur, nor even a word of greeting.

This was more than flesh could bear. She must protest this cruelty. She sat down to write to Brussels on January 8, unable to conceal her anguish any longer:

> Mr. Taylor has returned. I asked him if he had a letter for me. "No, nothing." "Patience," said I—"his sister will be here soon." Miss Taylor has returned. "I have nothing for you from Monsieur Heger," says she; "neither letter nor message."
>
> Having realised the meaning of these words, I said to myself what I should say to another similarly placed: "You must be resigned, and above all do not grieve at a misfortune which you have not deserved." I strove to restrain my tears, to utter no complaint.
>
> But when one does not complain, when one seeks to dominate oneself with a tyrant's grip, the faculties start into rebellion, and one pays for external calm with an internal struggle that is almost unbearable.
>
> Day and night I find neither rest nor peace. If I sleep I am disturbed by tormenting dreams in which I see you, always severe, always grave, always incensed against me.
>
> Forgive me then, Monsieur, if I adopt the course of writing to you again. How can I endure life if I make no effort to ease its sufferings?
>
> I know that you will be irritated when you read this letter. You will say once more that I am hysterical [or neurotic]—that I have black

thoughts, &c. So be it, Monsieur; I do not seek to justify myself; I submit to every sort of reproach. All I know is that I cannot, that I will not, resign myself to lose wholly the friendship of my master. I would rather suffer the greatest physical pain than always have my heart lacerated by smarting regrets.

If my master withdraws his friendship from me entirely I shall be altogether without hope; if he gives me a little—just a little—I shall be satisfied—happy; I shall have reason for living on, for working.

Monsieur, the poor have not need of much to sustain them—they ask only for the crumbs that fall from the rich men's table. But if they are refused the crumbs they die of hunger. Nor do I, either, need much affection from those I love. I should not know what to do with a friendship entire and complete—I am not used to it. But you showed me of yore a *little* interest, when I was your pupil in Brussels, and I hold on to the maintenance of that *little* interest—I hold on to it as I would hold on to life.

You will tell me perhaps—"I take not the slightest interest in you, Mademoiselle Charlotte. You are no longer an inmate of my House; I have forgotten you."

Well, Monsieur, tell me so frankly. It will be a shock to me. It matters not. It would be less dreadful than uncertainty.

I shall not re-read this letter. I send it as I have written it. Nevertheless, I have a hidden consciousness that some people, cold and common-sense, in reading it would say—"She is talking nonsense." I would avenge myself on such persons in no other way than by wishing them one single day of the torments which I have suffered for eight months. We should then see if they would not talk nonsense too.

One suffers in silence so long as one has the strength so to do, and when that strength gives out one speaks without too carefully measuring one's words.

I wish Monsieur happiness and prosperity.

C.B.[13]

Casting about for some explanation of Monsieur's silence, Charlotte found it readily enough in the "cold, common-sense" woman who had so inexplicably influenced her husband in the matter of their friendship. But there was little comfort in fixing blame. The task was now to live from day to day; in her own words (for she had begun to write again), to crush the heart, to curb its life and "with outward calm mask inward strife." She could tell no one of her anguish—not Mary, not Ellen, not Anne, not Emily.

Crushed under the double burden of anguish for Monsieur and sorrow at Mary's leaving, she went to Hunsworth in February for a last visit and found the house bursting with Taylors and Taylor connections whose liveliness only threw her own depression into stronger relief. Mary seized upon this last opportunity to propagandize her friend. She had encouraged her in the past to go out as a governess, to travel, to stretch her wings. Charlotte was educated and experienced; she might teach in Brussels, Paris, Germany, or New Zealand. Haworth was a living death. In the past Mary's bold enthusiasm had always roused Charlotte's own zest for action. Now Mary found her strangely unresilient and broken. She admitted she did not want to stay at home—her health was weak, her days blank—but she could not leave. Brussels had taught her the vanity of seeking happiness in mere change of scene. She had been as lonely and fettered there as at Haworth. Some people were destined to live lives full of variety and human contact; fate had cast a different lot for her. Alarmed at this passivity, Mary argued warmly: year after year of solitude, ill-health, and inactivity at Haworth—it would ruin her. "Think of what you'll be five years hence!" At these words such a dark shadow fell across her friend's face that Mary broke off instantly, saying, "Don't cry, Charlotte!" "She did not cry," Mary told Mrs. Gaskell many years later, "but went on walking up and down the room, and said in a little while, 'But I intend to stay, Polly.' "[14]

Mary left England convinced that Charlotte wronged herself deeply by staying home; she remained convinced of it the rest of her life. She cast Mr. Brontë as the villain of the tragedy: "I can never think without gloomy anger of Charlotte's sacrifices to the selfish old man," she wrote Ellen from New Zealand after Charlotte's death. "—how well we know that, had she left him entirely and succeeded in gaining wealth and name and influence she would have had all the world lauding her to the skies for any trivial act of generosity that wd cost her nothing! . . . No one ever gave up more than she did and with full consciousness of what she sacrificed. I don't think myself that women are justified in sacrificing themselves for others, but since the world generally expects it of them they should at least acknowledge it. But where much is given we are all wonderfully given to gra[sp] at more. If Charlotte had left home and made a favour of returning she wd have got thanks instead of tyranny. . . ."[15]

Charlotte herself struggled through the days at Hunsworth tormented by thoughts of Monsieur's silence and frequently wondering that she seemed the only person there saddened by Polly's leaving. "I spent a week at Hunsworth not very pleasantly," she wrote Ellen on her return to Haworth; "headache, sickliness, and flatness of spirits made me a poor companion, a sad drag on the vivacious and locquacious gaiety of all the other inmates of the house. I was never fortunate enough to be able to rally, for so much as a single hour, while I was there. I am sure all, with the exception perhaps of Mary, were very glad when I took my departure. I begin to perceive that I have too little life in me, nowadays, to be fit company for any except very quiet people. Is it age, or what else, that changes one so?"[16] She knew the bitter answer to her own question too well.

# 11

## A Burial

On March 21, 1845, when the gale winds of the spring equinox hurled themselves across the moors, Mary Taylor sailed from Plymouth on the *Louisa Campbell* for New Zealand with her youngest brother Waring, an event for Charlotte "as if a great planet fell out of the sky." Mary's bold act of rebellion alarmed and fascinated her. "Have you heard any particulars of Mary Taylor's departure," she asked Ellen, "—what day she sailed—what passengers were in the ship—in what sort of spirits and health she set off—&c. glean what intelligence you can and transmit it to me."[1] Mary's decision to leave England was a long-contemplated revolt against the limits forced upon an intelligent and unconventional young woman by Victorian society. She had met no man her equal, nor a man unequal but willing to put up with a vigorous female mind. *Had* she met one, she might not have married him. The alternative for a lady—governess to a few well-bred pupils—she had tried and found herself dissatisfied. She would not be a dressmaker, a milliner, or a housemaid. Living unemployed at home like Ellen Nussey was unthinkable for this energetic, independent woman. Uncertain what hazards New Zealand might offer, she was still quite willing to risk refined boredom for hardship, loneliness, or poverty. In leaving England, she took a step that many anti-feminists sarcastically offered the dissatisfied Victorian woman. The Age of Reform had not yet extended a helping hand to the female sex. Did women want better wages, shorter hours, suffrage, legal control of their own children? Let them emigrate and see how hard life could be away from dear old England. Many women did. By 1851, 26,707 British emigrants had landed in New Zealand alone to settle the new cities of Wellington, Wanganui, New Plymouth, Nelson, and Christchurch.[2] Not a few of the settlers were women like Mary Taylor.

Dubious when Mary first confided her plan in Brussels, Charlotte was now convinced that Polly had found her element. "Mary Taylor finds herself free—and on that path for adventure and exertion to which she has so long been seeking admission," she wrote Ellen wistfully on April 2, 1845. "Sickness—Hardship—Danger are her fellow-travellers—her inseparable companions. She may have been out of the reach of these S.W. N.W. gales before they began to blow—or they may have spent their fury on land and not ruffled the sea much —if it has been otherwise she has been sorely tossed while we have been sleeping in our beds or lying awake thinking about her.

"Yet these real—material dangers when once past, leave in the mind the satisfaction of having struggled with a difficulty and overcome it —Strength—Courage—experience are their invariable results—whereas I doubt whether suffering purely mental [h]as any good result unless it be to make us by comparison less sensitive to physical suffering."[3]

How gladly, she believed, would she exchange her chained existence and private anguish for seasickness, storms, fatigue, hunger, and burning suns. Instead: "I can hardly tell you how time gets on here at Haworth— There is no event whatever to mark its progress—one day resembles another—and all have heavy, lifeless physiognomies— Sunday—baking-day and Saturday are the only ones that bear the slightest distinctive mark—meantime life wears away—I shall soon be 30—and I have done nothing yet— Sometimes I get melancholy—at the prospect before and behind me—yet it is wrong and foolish to repine—and undoubtedly my duty directs me to stay at home for the present— There was a time when Haworth was a very pleasant place to me, it is not so now— I feel as if we were all buried here—I long to travel—to work to live a life of action. . . ."[4]

Instead, trapped in what she once described as a "windowed grave," she mended collars, read to Papa sitting dull and solitary in his parlor, walked out on the spring-wakening moors with Emily, the dogs bounding at their heels, and read with a sense of holy communion the French newspapers Joe Taylor obligingly sent her, for they spoke in Monsieur's tongue. She lived for the letter from Brussels that someday must come:

> My hour of torment was the post-hour. Unfortunately I knew it too well, and tried as vainly as assiduously to cheat myself of that knowledge; dreading the rack of expectation, and the sick collapse of disappointment which daily preceded and followed upon that well-recognised ring.
>
> I suppose animals kept in cages, and so scantily fed as to be always upon the verge of famine, await their food as I awaited a letter. Oh!—to

speak truth, and drop that tone of false calm which long to sustain, out-wears nature's endurance—I underwent . . . bitter fears and pains, strange inward trials, miserable defections of hope, intolerable en-croachments of despair. This last came so near me sometimes that her breath went right through me. I used to feel it, like a baleful air or sigh, penetrate deep, and make motion pause at my heart, or proceed only under unspeakable oppression. The letter—the well-beloved letter—would not come; and it was all of sweetness in life I had to look for.[5]

She confided in no one, permitting herself only occasional, oblique references to her plight. Ellen wrote of her embarrassment at dis-covering that a man with whom she had dared to be natural and friendly was not married, as she thought, but single. Charlotte an-swered with bitterness:

Ten years ago I should have laughed heartily at your account of the blunder you made in mistaking the bachelor doctor of Burlington for a Married Man . . . Now however I can perceive that your scruples are founded on common-sense. I know that if women wish to escape the stigma of husband-seeking they must act and look like marble or clay—cold—expressionless, bloodless—for every appearance of feeling of joy—sorrow—friendliness, antipathy, admiration—disgust are alike con-strued by the world into an attempt to hook in a husband." So, she felt keenly, had Madame Heger miscontrued her innocent joy in Monsieur's company. "Never mind Nell," she continues, "—well meaning women have their own consciences to comfort them after all—do not therefore be too much afraid of shewing yourself as you are—affectionate and good-hearted—do not too harshly repress sentiments and feelings ex-cellent in themselves because you fear that some puppy may fancy that you are letting them come out to fascinate him—do not condemn your-self to live only by halves because if you shewed too much animation some pragmatical thing in breeches (excuse the expression) might take it into its pate to imagine that you designed to dedicate your precious life to its inanity. . . . Write again soon—for I feel rather fierce and want stroking down.[6]

She herself was incapable of repressing "sentiments and feelings excellent in themselves"; had she done so, the longed-for letters might from time to time have arrived at the parsonage door. Often now she took up her pen, not to break her vow of silence by writing to Brus-sels, but to ease her mind of some of its torment in writing verse. Since Monsieur was indifferent to her fate, she need no longer obey his strictures against "setting things down." While Emily sat apart bent over her small writing box, and Keeper and Flossie stretched before the fire, and cold, rain-filled winds beat and screamed around the

house, Charlotte wrote again, filling page after page with anguish that
could find no other outlet:

> Unloved I love, unwept I weep,
>     Grief I restrain, hope I repress;
> Vain is this anguish, fixed and deep,
>     Vainer desires or dreams of bliss.
>
> My life is cold, love's fire being dead;
>     That fire self-kindled, self-consumed;
> What living warmth erewhile it shed,
>     Now to how drear extinction doomed!
>
>             . . .
>
> Alas! there are those who should not love;
>     I to this dreary band belong;
> This knowing let me henceforth prove
>     Too wise to list delusion's song.
>
> No, Syren! Beauty is not mine;
>     Affection's joy I ne'er shall know;
> Lonely will be my life's decline,
>     Even as my youth is lonely now.
>
>             . . .
>
> Soft may the breeze of summer blow,
>     Sweetly its sun in valleys shine;
> All earth around with love may glow,—
>     No warmth shall reach this heart of mine.
>
> Vain boast and false! Even now the fire
>     Though smothered, slacked, repelled, is burning
> At my life's source; and stronger, higher,
>     Waxes the spirit's trampled yearning.
>
> It wakes but to be crushed again:
>     Faint I will not, nor yield to sorrow;
> Conflict and force will quell the brain;
>     Doubt not I shall be strong to-morrow.
>
> Have I not fled that I may conquer?
>     Crost the dark sea in firmest faith
> That I at last might plant my anchor
>     Where love cannot prevail to death?[7]

On April 21 she awoke to her thirtieth birthday. Assessing her life, she had cause to be discouraged: the school unrealized, her skills rusting, a literary career abandoned, her love unrequited—and not one hint that the future held anything kinder in store. On the contrary, chances for escape were narrowing rapidly: week by week Papa's sight diminished; he could scarcely read or write now. She felt increasingly reluctant to leave him for a single day.

In June Anne and Branwell returned from Thorp Green Hall. Branwell had only a week, since he was to take a longer vacation when the Robinsons went to Scarborough in July. He was restless, uncommunicative, irritable, and often drunk. Anne herself seemed more oppressed than five months of governessing the spoiled Robinson children would warrant. She announced, as quietly as she did everything, that she had voluntarily quit her post with the Robinsons; she gave as her reason the fact that two of her three pupils were now beyond governessing age. This seemed reasonable, and the family accepted her resignation without surprise. Emily was overjoyed to have her partner in fantasy close to her after four years of separation. Charlotte was relieved, for Anne's presence at home would give her more freedom. Emily refused all duties that took her out of the parsonage and into contact with strangers; and no one dared challenge her demand for seclusion. A passer-by could see her on warm summer days through the open kitchen window kneading dough with capable hands, intently studying from a German book propped open before her, serene, busy, remote. It devolved upon Charlotte to teach the Sunday school classes (she was strict, a pupil recalled, and stuck to business), to carry bone soup to the sick in the parish, to negotiate household needs in the village, to give visiting clerics their tea.

Quickly taking advantage of Anne's willingness in these matters, Charlotte set off on June 26 to visit Ellen at Hathersage in Derbyshire where she was serving as chatelaine of Henry's vicarage in his absence. At last that sober and uninspired clergyman had been able to make a cheering entry in his diary: on May 22 he had made a financially sound marriage with Miss Emily Prescott of Hampshire; they were now on their honeymoon. Charlotte found Ellen fretting over the business of having everything in perfect readiness for the return of Henry and his bride, a type of feminine fussing she herself was immune to. Nevertheless, she enjoyed her liberty and, with Anne at home, even dared to get Ellen to write begging for an extension. It was granted by a letter from Emily in her usual trenchant style:

Dear Miss Nussey,—If you have set your heart on Charlotte staying another week, she has our united consent. I, for one, will take everything easy on Sunday. I am glad she is enjoying herself; let her make the most of the next seven days to return stout and hearty. Love to her and you from Anne and myself—and tell her all are well at home.[8]

Despite Emily's assurance that all was well at home, Charlotte left Ellen "strongly impressed with the feeling that she was going back to sorrow." She was subject to such "presentiments," as she called them: her high-strung, impressionable nature vibrated to psychic atmosphere like a weather vane to wind. In the railroad coach her forebodings were temporarily forgotten, however, in her interest in a fellow passenger. The foreign features of the man seated next to her set her heart racing. She was sure he was a Frenchman; she dared to address him: "*Monsieur est français, n'est-ce pas?*" To her delight he answered her in French, and was even more astonished when she guessed from his impure accent that he had spent most of his life in Germany. The incident was precious because it reminded her of Monsieur. To such crumbs had she been reduced.

Traveling the four miles uphill from Keighley, her anxiety returned. It was ten o'clock at night when she alighted at the parsonage gate. Lights gleamed in several windows; the household was still up. In the front hall she caught the sounds of incoherent raving from upstairs. Branwell was drunk again. Since Luddenden Foot, he had alternated between maudlin bouts of drunken self-pity and weeks of agonized repentance. She was not, therefore, unduly surprised or shocked as she removed her traveling bonnet and shawl, until Anne came with a troubled face and took her aside to confide the reason for the present crisis.

The story, as it gradually emerged, was sordid and pitiful. On Thursday, July 21, Branwell had received a cold letter from Mr. Robinson dismissing him from his post as tutor to Edmund. Robinson intimated that he had discovered Branwell's "vile proceedings," and charged him on pain of exposure to instantly break off all communication with his family, forever. The "vile proceedings," it turned out, was the tutor's love affair with Robinson's wife Lydia. Anne now confessed that Branwell's conduct had driven her from Thorp Green Hall. If Mr. Robinson had been blind, the children and servants had interpreted clearly enough the looks, sighs, and signals that flashed between the small red-haired tutor and his buxom mistress. Her position had become too embarrassing to endure. Branwell was less delicate: the moaning and thrashing going on now upstairs was due not to shame at his dismissal but to agony at being separated from the woman he loved to distraction.

The portrait of their brother and son as the seducer of a married woman was not a pleasing one, and the family soon took the view that

Branwell was less sinning than sinned against. Mrs. Robinson was forty-five, seventeen years older than Branwell. Anne had never liked her worldliness, her cold, grudging charity toward dependents, her lack of culture. They began to recast the roles of the tragedy in their minds: an attractive, bored, calculating woman; a young tutor too ardent to suspect his emotions were being played with; genuine love on his part, cold seduction on hers. "My brilliant and unhappy son," cried Mr. Brontë; "his diabolical seducer!" The older woman as seducer was a conventional villainess, and despite Branwell's proven lack of stability, veracity, and temperance, the Brontës immediately assigned Mrs. Robinson the role.

In her youth Charlotte had recorded the adulterous passions of the Duke of Zamorna with passionate absorption. The wronged wife, the faithful mistress, the hero whose dark magnetism drew women to him as to the edge of an abyss—these were the essence of romance. She had not forgotten the dreams that ruled her adolescence; nor could she forget that she herself loved a married man. She was no hypocrite. She did not, therefore, blame Branwell for his adulterous passion, yet from that day on she began to cool toward her brother until finally she washed her hands of him altogether. She understood his tempestuous emotions but deplored his inability to master them. She could not help but contrast the stoicism with which she endured her anguish for Monsieur with her brother's self-indulgent ravings. No one knew that for more than a year her life had been a daily torment; the whole household was made to suffer along with Branwell. *She* forbade personal sorrow to interfere with duty; *he* galloped headlong to the devil. He was weak and depraved and hopeless. Because she had loved him best she now revolted furthest from him. Papa indulgently forgave him, gentle Anne prayed seriously for his soul, Emily calmly dragged him upstairs in her strong arms when he staggered home drunk from the Bull, but Charlotte recoiled in scorn and fury. In doing so, she of course sent him down faster to destruction.

She spoke of him now to Ellen with cold detachment. "We have had sad work with Branwell since," she wrote, describing the aftermath of that inauspicious homecoming. "He thought of nothing but stunning or drowning his distress of mind. No one in the house could have rest. At last we have been obliged to send him from home for a week, with someone to look after him; he has written to me this morning, and expresses some sense of contrition for his frantic folly, he promises amendment on his return, but so long as he remains at home I scarce dare hope for peace in the house. We must all, I fear, prepare for a season of distress and disquietude."[9]

Ellen could sympathize: her favorite brother George had suffered a severe nervous breakdown in January. "Poor Mr George!" Charlotte had written, "I am very sorry for him, very sorry; he did not deserve this suffering."[10] But although Ellen had experienced the horror of watching a personality disintegrate, Charlotte would not let her set foot in the parsonage while Branwell shattered its quiet: ". . . while *he* is here—*you* shall not come. I am more confirmed in that resolution the more I see of him. I wish I could say one word to you in his favour, but I cannot, therefore I will hold my tongue."[11]

While Branwell and Charlotte were thus suffering acutely, Emily and Anne remained comparatively serene. Both still played the creative, timeless drama of Gondal. When they went off together on a little summer holiday to York, they enjoyed pretending to be characters from that saga. On Emily's birthday they crept away in secret to open the diary papers written four years before, only to discover that Emily's birthday had slipped by unnoticed and that the day was actually July 31. "I guess that at the time appointed for the opening of this paper," Emily had written and they now read, "we *i.e.* Charlotte, Anne, and I, shall be all merrily seated in our own sitting-room in some pleasant and flourishing seminary, having just gathered in for the midsummer holy day. Our debts will be paid off, and we shall have cash in hand to a considerable amount. Papa, aunt, and Branwell will either have been or be coming to visit us." Less robust than Emily, Anne had not speculated but only wondered: "What will the next four years bring forth? Providence only knows." Well, Emily had certainly been wrong about 1845. The flourishing seminary had not materialized, Aunt was dead, Papa's sight sadly afflicted, Charlotte pale and frustrated with some deep sorrow, Branwell disgraced and depraved. Nevertheless, they sat down separately to write new papers:

Haworth, Thursday, July 30th, 1845: My birthday—showery, breezy, cool. I am twenty-seven years old to-day. This morning Anne and I opened the papers we wrote four years since, on my twenty-third birthday. This paper we intend, if all be well, to open on my thirtieth—three years hence, in 1848. Since the 1841 paper the following events have taken place. Our school scheme has been abandoned, and instead Charlotte and I went to Brussels on the 8th of February 1842.

Branwell left his place at Luddenden Foot. C. and I returned from Brussels, November 8th, 1842, in consequence of aunt's death.

Charlotte returned to Brussels the same month, and after staying a year, came back again on New Year's Day 1844.

Branwell went to Thorp Green as a tutor, where Anne still continued, January 1843.

Anne left her situation at Thorp Green of her own accord, June 1845.

Anne and I went on our first long journey by ourselves together, leaving home on the 30th of June, Monday, sleeping at York, returning to Keighley Tuesday evening, sleeping there and walking home on Wednesday morning. Though the weather was broken we enjoyed ourselves very much, except during a few hours at Bradford. And during our excursion we were, Ronald Macalgin, Henry Angora, Juliet Angusteena, Rosabella Esmaldan, Ella and Julian Egremont, Catherine Navarre, and Cordelia Fitzaphnold, escaping from the palaces of instruction to join the Royalists who are hard driven at present by the victorious Republicans. The Gondals still flourish bright as ever. I am at present writing a work on the First Wars. Anne has been writing some articles on this, and a book by Henry Sophona. We intend sticking firm by the rascals as long as they delight us, which I am glad to say they do at present. I should have mentioned that last summer the school scheme was revived in full vigour. We had prospectuses printed, despatched letters to all acquaintances imparting our plans, and did our little all; but it was found no go. Now I don't desire a school at all, and none of us have any great longing for it. We have cash enough for our present wants, with a prospect of accumulation. We are all in decent health, only that papa has a complaint in his eyes, and with the exception of B., who, I hope, will be better and do better hereafter. I am quite contented for myself: not as idle as formerly, altogether as hearty, and having learnt to make the most of the present and long for the future with the fidgetiness that I cannot do all I wish; seldom or ever troubled with nothing to do, and merely desiring that everybody could be as comfortable as myself and as undesponding, and then we should have a very tolerable world of it.

By mistake I find we have opened the paper on the 31st instead of the 30th. Yesterday was much such a day as this, but the morning was divine.

Tabby, who was gone in our last paper, is come back, and has lived with us two years and a half, and is in good health. Martha, who also departed, is here too. We have got Flossy; got and lost Tiger; lost the hawk Hero, which, with the geese, was given away, and is doubtless dead, for when I came back from Brussels, I inquired on all hands and could hear nothing of him. Tiger died early last year. Keeper and Flossy are well, also the canary acquired four years since. We are now all at home, and likely to be there some time. Branwell went to Liverpool on Tuesday to stay a week. Tabby has just been teasing me to turn as formerly to "Pilloputate." Anne and I should have picked the black currants if it had been fine and sunshiny. I must hurry off now to my turning and ironing. I have plenty of work on hands, and writing, and am altogether full of business. With best wishes for the whole house till 1848, July 30th, and as much longer as may be,—I conclude.

E. J. Brontë.[12]

Composing her own paper, Anne could not match Emily's buoyant spirits. Four years at Thorp Green Hall had subdued her already
pessimistic nature. Gondal, still so green and flourishing for Emily,
seemed tattered and faded when examined in the cool gray light of
reality—although she would not admit it to her sister. How uncertain, really, life was. What would the future bring? She could only
hope and wonder:

Thursday, July the 31st, 1845. Yesterday was Emily's birthday, and
the time when we should have opened our 1841 paper, but by mistake
we opened it today instead. How many things have happened since it
was written—some pleasant, some far otherwise. Yet I was then at
Thorp Green, and now I am only just escaped from it. I was wishing to
leave it then, and if I had known that I had four years longer to stay
how wretched I should have been; but during my stay I have had some
very unpleasant and undreamt-of experience of human nature. Others
have seen more changes. Charlotte has left Mr White's, and been twice
to Brussels, where she stayed each time nearly a year. Emily has been
there too, and stayed nearly a year. Branwell has left Luddenden Foot,
and been a tutor at Thorp Green, and had much tribulation and ill
health. He was very ill on Thursday, but he went with John Brown
to Liverpool, where he now is, I suppose; and we hope he will be better and do better in future. This is a dismal, cloudy, wet evening. We
have had so far a very cold, wet summer. Charlotte has lately been to
Hathersage, in Derbyshire, on a visit of three weeks to Ellen Nussey.
She is now sitting sewing in the dining-room. Emily is ironing upstairs.
I am sitting in the dining-room in the rocking-chair before the fire
with my feet on the fender. Papa is in the parlour. Tabby and Martha
are, I think, in the kitchen. Keeper and Flossy are, I do not know
where. Little Dick is hopping in his cage. When the last paper was written we were thinking of setting up a school. The scheme has been
dropt and long after taken up again, and dropt again, because we
could not get pupils. Charlotte is thinking about getting another
situation. She wishes to go to Paris. Will she go? She has let Flossy in,
by-the-by, and he is now lying on the sofa. Emily is engaged in writing
the Emperor Julius's Life. She has read some of it, and I want very
much to hear the rest. She is writing some poetry, too. I wonder what
it is about? I have begun the third volume of *Passages in the Life of an
Individual*. I wish I had finished it. This afternoon I began to set about
making my grey figured silk frock that was dyed at Keighley. What
sort of hand shall I make of it? E. and I have a great deal of work to
do. When shall we sensibly diminish it? I want to get a habit of early
rising. Shall I succeed? We have not yet finished our *Gondal Chronicles* that we began three and a half years ago. When will they be
done? The Gondals are at present in a sad state. The Republicans are
uppermost, but the Royalists are not quite overcome. The young

sovereigns, with their brothers and sisters, are still at the Palace of Instruction. The Unique Society, about half a year ago, were wrecked on a desert island as they were returning from Gaul. They are still there, but we have not played at them much yet. The Gondals in general are not in first-rate playing condition. Will they improve? I wonder how we shall all be, and where and how situated, on the thirtieth of July 1848, when, if we are all alive, Emily will be just 30. I shall be in my 29th year, Charlotte in her 33rd, and Branwell in his 32nd; and what changes shall we have seen and known; and shall we be much changed ourselves? I hope not, for the worst at least. I for my part cannot well be flatter or older in mind than I am now. Hoping for the best, I conclude.

Anne Brontë.[13]

Occupied and twinlike, Emily and Anne thus moved tranquilly together through the summer days, picking the black currants in the sunshine, sewing together quietly on gray, rainy evenings, playing the piano when Papa was out of his parlor, reading aloud the latest pages of Gondal adventure. For her companions Charlotte had the pale specters of a lost brother and a lost friend. Branwell returned from his "cure"—a week in Liverpool and Wales with that tolerant and original villager, John Brown. Although he had written Charlotte in deep contrition during his absence, he did not mend his ways back in Haworth except when lack of money prevented excursions to the druggist and the Bull. "The late blow to his prospects and feelings has quite made him reckless," Charlotte wrote Ellen in August. "It is only absolute want of means that acts as any check to him— One ought indeed to hope to the very last and I try to do so—but occasionally hope—in his case, seems a fallacy."[14]

Summer waned, the heather bloomed and faded, autumn storms screamed across the moors, the year withered to a close. In November Charlotte could write Monsieur again, for six months had passed since her last letter—six months of blank silence. Without a crumb from the rich man's table, her hopes were all but dead. She marked off the days to the very date; then, all but numb with misery, allowed herself to address her master once again:

Monsieur,—The six months of silence have run their course. It is now the 18th of Novr.; my last letter was dated (I think) the 18th of May. I may therefore write to you without failing in my promise.

The summer and autumn seemed very long to me; truth to tell, it has needed painful efforts on my part to bear hitherto the self-denial which I have imposed on myself. You, Monsieur, you cannot conceive what it means; but suppose for a moment that one of your children was separated from you, 160 leagues away, and that you had to remain six months without writing to him, without receiving news of him, without hearing him spoken of, without knowing ought of his health, then you would understand easily all the harshness of such an obligation. I tell you frankly that I have tried meanwhile to forget you, for the remembrance of a person whom one thinks never to see again, and whom, nevertheless, one greatly esteems, frets too much the mind; and when one has suffered that kind of anxiety for a year or two, one is ready to do anything to find peace once more. I have done everything; I have sought occupations; I have denied myself absolutely the pleasure of speaking about you—even to Emily; but I have been able to conquer neither my regrets nor my impatience. That, indeed, is humiliating—to be unable to control one's own thoughts, to be the slave of a regret, of a memory, the slave of a fixed and dominant idea which lords it over the mind. Why cannot I have just as much friendship for you, as you for me—neither more nor less? Then should I be so tranquil, so free—I could keep silence then for ten years without an effort.

My father is well but his sight is almost gone. He can neither read nor write. Yet the doctors advise waiting a few months more before attempting an operation. The winter will be a long night for him. He rarely complains; I admire his patience. If Providence wills the same calamity for me, may He at least vouchsafe me as much patience with which to bear it! It seems to me, Monsieur, that there is nothing more galling in great physical misfortunes than to be compelled to make all those about us share in our sufferings. The ills of the soul one can hide, but those which attack the body and destroy the faculties cannot be concealed. My father allows me now to read to him and write for him; he shows me, too, more confidence than he has ever shown before, and that is a great consolation.

Monsieur, I have a favour to ask of you: when you reply to this letter, speak to me a little of yourself, not of me; for I know that if you speak of me it will be to scold me, and this time I would see your kindly side. Speak to me therefore of your children. Never was your brow severe when Louise and Claire and Prosper were by your side. Tell me also something of the School, of the pupils, of the Governesses. Are Mesdemoiselles Blanche, Sophie, and Justine still at Brussels? Tell me where you travelled during the holidays—did you go to the Rhine? Did you not visit Cologne or Coblentz? Tell me, in short, my master, what you will, but tell me something. To write to an ex-assistant-governess (No! I refuse to remember my employment as assistant-governess—I repudiate it)—anyhow, to write to an old pupil cannot be a very interesting occupation for you, I know; but for me it is life. Your last letter was stay and prop to me—nourishment to me for half a year. Now I need another and you will give it me; not because you bear me friendship—you cannot have much—but because you are compassionate of soul and you would condemn no one to prolonged suffering to save yourself a few moments' trouble. To forbid me to write to you, to refuse to answer me would be to tear from me my only joy on earth, to deprive me of my last privilege—a privilege I shall never consent willingly to surrender. Believe me, my master, in writing to me it is a good deed that you will, do. So long as I believe you are pleased with me, so long as I have hope of receiving news from you, I can be at rest and not too sad. But when a prolonged and gloomy silence seems to threaten me with estrangement of my master—when day by day I await a letter, and when day by day disappointment comes to fling me back into overwhelming sorrow, and the sweet delight of seeing your handwriting and reading your counsel escapes me as a vision that is vain, then fever claims me—I lose appetite and sleep—I pine away.

May I write to you again next May? I would rather wait a year, but it is impossible—it is too long.

C. Brontë.

I must say a word to you in English—I wish I could write to you more cheerful letters, for when I read this over, I find it to be somewhat gloomy—but forgive me my dear master—do not be irritated at my sadness—according to the words of the Bible: "Out of the fulness of the heart, the mouth speaketh" and truly I find it difficult to be cheerful so long as I think I shall never see you more. You will perceive by the defects in this letter that I am forgetting the French language—yet I read all the French books I can get, and learn daily a portion by heart—but I have never heard French spoken but once since I left Brussels—and then it sounded like music in my ears—every word was most precious to me because it reminded me of you—I love French for your sake with all my heart and soul.

Farewell my dear Master—may God protect you with special care and crown you with peculiar blessings. C. B.[15]

Across the Channel in Brussels within the walls of the Pensionnat, Monsieur Heger, "compassionate of soul," read this eloquent, heart-rending letter, put it aside, eventually jotted some commonplace notes in the margins, among them the name and address of a shoemaker, and finally, as he had its counterparts, tore it into pieces and threw it into his wastebasket. There Madame, shod in the shoes of silence and acting on the highest principles of *la surveillance,* found it, reassembled it, read it, pasted and stitched it carefully together, and hid it among her possessions with three others she had managed to salvage. To do so was prudence, since Mademoiselle's letters were proof that her husband had committed no indiscretion in this abominable *affaire anglaise.*

Monsieur himself maintained his silence. Charlotte never heard from him again. Madame's behavior is comprehensible if not commendable; he, on the other hand, seemed the one person capable of appreciating that the young English teacher was no ordinary mortal but a woman of extraordinary intelligence, will, talent, and feeling. He *had* understood it, for his enthusiastic letter to her father had

brought her back to Brussels. If anyone merited his friendship, surely
it was she. Why then did he so cruelly refuse to send her even the
yearly letter that she craved? She had pleaded again and again that
she needed only a *little* affection, only a *little* of his interest to sustain her.

Monsieur Heger had been kind to Charlotte as he was kind to
many. His was a naturally magnetic, benevolent, and perhaps flirtatious personality; it was his way to praise deserving pupils, to rage, to
atone with bonbons and little gifts of books, to encourage and exhort. Cursed with an indifferent father, innocent of lovers, Charlotte
had responded to this male attention with the vehemence of long-
thwarted love. Monsieur was startled at the intensity of the emotion
he had unleashed; his wife soon made him appalled. Gradually he
came to believe that her feeling for him was unbalanced, unreasonable. "*Pauvre coeur blessé*," he said of Charlotte, replying to a letter
Ellen Nussey wrote him ten years after Charlotte's death; then struck
out the word "*blessé*" and substituted "*malade*." She seemed to ask
little of him—a letter, a word of counsel. In reality she demanded
that he accept the fact that she adored him. She could not be silenced; she could not be controlled. This was a burden that he—a de-
vout Catholic, a family man, a public figure—could not bear.

Paul Emanuel in *Villette* comes to understand that Lucy Snowe's
quiet, dutiful demeanor conceals a fiery and craving spirit, at one
point in the novel edging up to her where she stands passive and silent in the midst of gaiety and hissing in her ear: "*Petite chatte,
doucerette, coquette! vous avez l'air bien triste, soumise, rêveuse,
mais vous ne l'êtes pas: c'est moi qui vous le dis: Sauvage! la flamme
à l'âme, l'éclair aux yeux*—[You little cat! flirt! you have a sad, submissive, pensive manner; but that is not your true character, I tell
you: You savage! with heart aflame and lightnings hidden in your
eyes]!"[16] Monsieur had won a similar knowledge of Charlotte. Now
he felt it his duty to quench the flame and lightning, to cure her of
her obsession. Her dark, painful letters must trouble him no more.

If Charlotte wrote again, the letters have not survived.[17] The
small, imperious black-browed professor dominated her whole life,
but she buried her love and all her hopes of him. It was a slow, weary
task. Two years later her agony was still fresh enough to inspire these
lines:

> He saw my heart's woe, discerned my soul's anguish,
>   How in fever, in thirst, in atrophy it pined;
> Knew he could heal, yet looked and let it languish,—
>   To its moans spirit-deaf, to its pangs spirit-blind.

But once a year he heard a whisper low and dreary
   Appealing for aid, entreating some reply;
Only when sick, soul-worn and torture-weary,
   Breathed I that prayer, heaved I that sigh.

He was mute as is the grave, he stood stirless as a tower;
   At last I looked up, and saw I prayed to stone;
I asked help of that which to help had no power,
   I sought love where love was utterly unknown.

Idolator I kneeled to an idol cut in rock!
   I might have slashed my flesh and drawn my heart's best blood:
The Granite God had felt no tenderness, no shock;
   My Baal had not seen nor heard nor understood. . . .[18]

# 12

## Currer, Ellis, and Acton Bell

Although Charlotte believed her brother totally abandoned to destruction, Branwell in fact made several attempts to right himself. Hearing that Francis Grundy, his old friend from Luddenden Foot days, had advanced to the position of resident engineer on the Skipton Railway, he applied to him in August. When Grundy did not reply, he wrote more urgently in October:

> I fear you will burn my present letter on recognizing the handwriting; but if you will read it through, you will perhaps rather pity than spurn the distress of mind which could prompt my communication . . .
>
> Since I last shook hands with you in Halifax, two summers ago, my life till lately has been one of apparent happiness and indulgence. You will ask, "Why does he complain then?" I can only reply by showing the under-current of distress which bore my bark to a whirlpool, despite the surface waves of life that seemed floating me to peace. In a letter begun in the spring of 1844 and never finished, owing to incessant attacks of illness, I tried to tell you that I was tutor to the son of [Mr Edmund Robinson, Thorp Green Hall], a wealthy gentleman whose wife is sister to the wife of ——, M.P., for the county of ——, and the cousin of Lord ——. This lady (though her husband detested me) showed me a degree of kindness which, when I was deeply grieved one day at her husband's conduct, ripened into declarations of more than ordinary feeling. My admiration of her mental and personal attractions, my knowledge of her unselfish sincerity, her sweet temper, and unwearied care for others, with but unrequited return where most should have been given . . . although she is seventeen years my senior, all combined to an attachment on my

part, and led to reciprocations which I had little looked for. During nearly three years I had daily "troubled pleasure soon chastised by fear." Three months since, I received a furious letter from my employer, threatening to shoot me if I returned from my vacation, which I was passing at home; and letters from her lady's-maid and physician informed me of the outbreak, only checked by her firm courage and resolution that whatever harm came to her, none should come to me . . . I have lain during nine long weeks utterly shattered in body and broken down in mind. The probability of her becoming free to give me herself and estate never rose to drive away the prospect of her decline under her present grief. I dreaded, too, the wreck of mind and body, which, God knows during a short life have been severely tried. Eleven continuous nights of sleepless horror reduced me to almost blindness, and being taken into Wales to recover, the sweet scenery, the sea, the sound of music caused me fits of unspeakable distress. . . . Of course, you will despise the writer of all this. I can only answer that the writer does the same, and would not wish to live if he did not hope that work and change may yet restore him.

Apologising sincerely for what seems like whining egotism, and hardly daring to hint about days when in your company I could sometimes sink the thoughts which "remind me of departed days," I fear departed never to return, I remain, etc.

P. B. Brontë.[1]

In the same month he applied for the post of secretary to the Manchester and Hebden Bridge Railway Company; he was refused. He composed poetry sporadically "to wile away his torment." In an effort to write something salable, he began a three-volume novel; he called it *And the Weary Are at Rest*. A continuation of Angrian adventure, the narrative soon metamorphized into a thinly disguised tale of his love for Lydia Robinson. His hero, Percy, Earl of Northangerland, had possessed from time immemorial raven hair and whiskers, curling lips, and a disdainful brow. These were now replaced by the curly auburn hair, sad face, and quivering lips of his tormented creator. Scenes were straight from the exquisitely dangerous days at Thorp Green Hall: seeking out Maria Thurston in the sitting room where she is bent over her embroidery, Percy declares himself in bold, peremptory fashion: "You know you are a lady, and that a man, if worthy of the name, can neither dislike or even feel indifferent to you. You know you are a *neglected* lady, and that I know you are so." In loving a neglected woman, Branwell assured himself, Percy had done the only manly thing.

Between unsteady attempts to chronicle his passion, he roused himself enough to supervise a subscription for a memorial tablet to William Weightman, dead these three years. It was a project after his own heart: coffins, flowers, clasped waxen hands, black mourning—the trappings of death had fascinated him since childhood. He arranged that his friend Joseph Leyland should design and execute the tablet; it was the mournful gesture of a damned soul to a young man he had admired but failed to imitate. By now, however, his eroded health, his addiction to laudanum and drink, and his reputation for instability made all literary or business efforts empty gestures. Perhaps he did not make them seriously, for he lived on the wild hope of eventually winning his beloved and, with her, her fortune.

He believed that Lydia Robinson was only biding time until her ailing husband should die, when they would be speedily married. Whether she actually promised marriage during one of their clandestine meetings in the shrubbery, or whether he only imagined she did, the fact that she continued to send him letters by her lady's maid, Ann Marshall, and her physician, Dr. Crosby, fed his expectations. Many of his letters to her mingled pleas for money with protestations of undying love. She sent him the money via her accomplices. Branwell took it as a token of her love and of her suffering. He chose to see himself in heroic guise as the rescuer of wronged womanhood. They were noble lovers persecuted by the machinations of a cruel, bilious-faced, tyrannical husband.

At Thorp Green Hall, however, Lydia Robinson was finding Branwell a decided pest. The small, dissipated tutor *had* fascinated her for a time. His sensitivity charmed her; his eloquence enchanted her into believing herself the deeply wronged beauty of his dreams. But he was hardly a fatally attractive man, and now that he was gone she was forced to reflect upon the realities of the situation. Her lover was an unemployed tutor; her husband a wealthy and powerful gentleman, master of her body and soul, if not her heart. She could not bring herself to sacrifice her reputation or her easy life. Thus while Branwell tossed feverishly on his bed and brandished Papa's pistols at his temples, Lydia prudently went off to enjoy herself on holiday at Scarborough where she and her husband made several shopping excursions together, as his account book testifies: "Lydia's chain £4. 0. 0—Lydia's shawl £1. 17. 6—Lydia's brooch £1. 8. 0—Lydia's scarf," etc.[2] Husbands seldom reward infidelity with gifts. The dark probability arises that Lydia herself ended the precarious affair, betraying Branwell and thus checking Edmund Robinson's suspicions about her own role in the matter. But she had not cleared her life of danger and intrigue. Branwell's requests for money were a modest but annoying form of blackmail.

The new year thus found Branwell unredeemed and Charlotte as bitterly critical of him as ever. She did not know of his attempts to find work because he no longer confided in his sisters, blaming them, of course, for the estrangement between them. "You ask about Branwell," Charlotte wrote Miss Wooler, January 30, 1846; "he never thinks of seeking employment and I begin to fear he has rendered himself incapable of filling any respectable station in life, besides, if money were at his disposal he would use it only to his own injury—the faculty of self-government is, I fear almost destroyed in him— You ask me if I do not think men are strange beings—I do indeed, I have often thought so—and I think too that the mode of bringing them up is strange, they are not half sufficiently guarded from temptations— girls are protected as if they were something very frail and silly indeed while boys are turned loose on the world as if they—of all beings in existence, were the wisest and least likely to be led astray."[3]

The injustice of such discrimination must have been the subject of indignant discussion that winter, for two years later Anne introduced the topic in *The Tenant of Wildfell Hall* with unusual vehemence and almost in Charlotte's words. Her narrator, Gilbert Markham, holds forth on the rearing of children: *boys* must be armed and strengthened against temptation by exposure to vice—an oak sapling raised in a hothouse cannot grow into a hardy tree; *girls,* however, must be sheltered at all costs from sordid reality. Helen Graham turns on Markham indignantly to challenge his prejudice. Why must a girl be protected? "It *must* be, either, that you think she is essentially so vicious, or so feeble-minded that she *cannot* withstand temptation,—and though she may be pure and innocent as long as she is kept in ignorance and restraint, yet, being destitute of *real* virtue, to teach her how to sin, is at once to make her a sinner, and the greater her knowledge, the wider her liberty, the deeper will be her depravity,—whereas, in the nobler sex, there is a natural tendency to goodness, guarded by a superior fortitude. . . ." With the example of Branwell before them that season, Charlotte, Emily, and Anne cast a cold eye upon the privileges and superiorities of the nobler sex.

Nor could they forget how Branwell had been spoiled. Even in that austere household the son had been petted, indulged, and financed while the girls were strictly bent to duty. Now, instead of administering the thrashing he deserved, Mr. Brontë studied remedies for intoxication and nursed the boy through the nights, bemoaning the fate of his "brilliant" and "unhappy" son. Again, Anne remembered this injustice keenly, lashing out at male privilege in the same novel. Gilbert Markham strides into the house; he is late; the tea things have long been put away; he demands, however, his tea. His sister Rose responds with a tirade that Anne must often have mentally rehearsed:

"Well!—if it had been *me* now, I should have had no tea at all . . . but *you*—we can't do too much for you—It's always so—if there's anything particularly nice at table, Mamma winks and nods at me, to abstain from it, and if I don't attend to that, she whispers, 'Don't eat so much of that, Rose, Gilbert will like it for his supper'— *I'm* nothing at all—in the parlour it's, 'Come, Rose, put away your things, and let's have the room nice and tidy against they come in; and keep up a good fire; Gilbert likes a cheerful fire.' In the kitchen— 'Make that pie a large one, Rose, I dare say the boys'll be hungry;— and don't put so much pepper in, they'll not like it I'm sure'—or, 'Rose, don't put so many spices in the pudding, Gilbert likes it plain'—or 'Mind you put plenty of currants in the cake, Fergus likes plenty.' If I say, 'Well, Mamma, *I* don't,' I'm told I ought not to think of myself— 'You know, Rose, in all household matters, we have only two things to consider, first, what's proper to be done, and secondly, what's most agreeable to the gentlemen of the house—anything will do for the ladies.' "[4]

But Charlotte, Emily, and Anne had other business on their minds that winter besides Branwell's tragedy and its causes. In spite of—or perhaps because of—her brother's self-destructive course, Charlotte had roused Emily and Anne to make a bid for literary success for all three of them. On January 28 she had sent the following letter to Aylott & Jones, booksellers and publishers, 8 Paternoster Row, London:

Gentlemen,—May I request to be informed whether you would undertake the publication of a Collection of short poems in one vol. oct.

If you object to publishing the work at your own risk—would you undertake it on the Author's account?—I am gentlemen, Your obdt. hmble. Servt.

C. Brontë.

Address
Revd. P. Brontë,
Haworth—Bradford—Yorkshire.[5]

The catalyst of this long-dreamed-of venture was Charlotte's discovery that Emily was an extremely fine poet. "One day, in the autumn of 1845, I accidentally lighted on a MS. volume of verse in my sister Emily's handwriting," she explained years after. "Of course, I was not surprised, knowing that she could and did write verse: I looked it over, and something more than surprise seized me,—a deep conviction that these were not common effusions, nor at all like the poetry women generally write. I thought them condensed and terse, vigorous and genuine. To my ear, they had also a peculiar music—wild, melancholy, and elevating. My sister Emily was not a person of demonstrative character, nor one, on the recesses of whose mind and feelings, even those nearest and dearest to her could, with impunity, intrude unlicensed; it took hours to reconcile her to the discovery I had made, and days to persuade her that such poems merited publication. . . . Meantime, my younger sister quietly produced some of her own compositions, intimating that since Emily's had given me pleasure, I might like to look at hers. I could not but be a partial judge, yet I thought that these verses too had a sweet sincere pathos of their own. We had very early cherished the dream of one day becoming authors. . . . We agreed to arrange a small selection of our poems, and, if possible, get them printed. . . ."[6]

In November and December, therefore, days of weary torment for Mr. Brontë and his wretched son, Charlotte, Emily, and Anne conferred, revised, and dared to dream of success as they restlessly paced the dining room on long winter nights after the rest of the household had gone to bed. Like Aurore Dudevant before them and Mary Ann Evans after, they decided to mask their feminine identity behind pseudonyms. With irreverent glee, they chose the middle name of Papa's young curate Arthur Bell Nicholls for their *nom de plume* —a grand joke, since that stolid, unimaginative person would be the last to suspect the parson's daughters of being more than they seemed. Charlotte later explained their decision in a preface to the 1850 edition of Emily's and Anne's novels:

> . . . we veiled our own names under those of Currer, Ellis, and Acton Bell; the ambiguous choice being dictated by a sort of conscientious scruple at assuming Christian names positively masculine, while we did not like to declare ourselves women, because—without at that time suspecting that our mode of writing and thinking was not what is called "feminine"—we had a vague impression that authoresses are liable to be looked on with prejudice; we noticed how critics sometimes use for their chastisement the weapon of personality, and for their reward, a flattery, which is not true praise.[7]

Charlotte's public account was not quite candid, however. She had recognized immediately that Emily's poetry was not traditionally feminine, and that Anne's verses too rose far above the sentimental or pious effusions of many "lady poets." Furthermore, her experiences with Southey, Wordsworth, and Monsieur Heger had left her with more than a "vague impression" of the strong liability women suffered under when they chose to make writing a career rather than a pastime.

Yet it was an age in which women writers prospered. The new and voracious public appetite for fiction encouraged women to take to the pen in the privacy of their homes, since they were not free to leave them for other pursuits. Maria Edgeworth, Mrs. Gore, Mrs. Trollope, Mrs. Marsh, Mrs. Oliphant, Jeraldine Jewsbury, Lady Bulwer Lytton, Eliza Lynn, Dinah Mulock, Charlotte Yonge, Harriet Martineau, Julia Kavanagh, Anne Manning—all had been or would be widely read. But the Brontës had little access to current fiction.[8] Literature for them was very much the golden age, recently passed, of Scott, Byron, Campbell, Southey, Coleridge, and Wordsworth. *Had* they read "the lady novelists," as literary women were then called, they might still have chosen masculine pen names to disassociate themselves from the too frequent mediocrity of the domestic novel and its practitioners.

Armed then with the shield of masculine identity, they still faced the novice's difficulty in finding a publisher. Many firms simply did not answer Charlotte's letters of inquiry: "neither we nor our poems were at all wanted," Charlotte recalled. Finally she wrote for advice to Messrs. Chambers of Edinburgh; the firm replied and, evidently assuming from the cover address that the author was a clergyman, recommended the small firm of Aylott & Jones, publishers and sellers of religious works. Messrs. Chambers also intimated that C. Brontë himself would have to pay for the printing.

The advice was good. Aylott & Jones replied immediately: they would gladly undertake to print the volume—at the author's expense. This disappointment could not check the excitement in the parsonage that day, excitement suppressed behind the dining-room door, for the enterprise was to be kept secret from everybody—Papa, Tabby, Martha, Ellen, and, sadly enough, their childhood partner in literary adventure, Branwell Brontë. Aunt's legacy would pay the publishing costs. The very same day the news arrived, Charlotte sat down to launch an extensive correspondence with the firm, the crisp, business-like tone of her letters not concealing her profound delight in every detail of the publishing process:

> Jany. 31st, '46: Gentlemen,—Since you agree to undertake the publication of the work respecting which I applied to you—I should wish now to know as soon as possible the cost of paper and printing. I will then send the necessary remittance together with the manuscript. I should like it to be printed in one octavo volume of the same quality of paper and size of type as Moxon's last edition of Wordsworth. The poems will occupy—I should think from 200 to 250 pages. They are not the production of a Clergyman nor are they exclusively of a religious character—but I presume these circumstances will be immaterial. . . .

Feby. 6th, '46: Gentlemen,—I send you the MS. as you desired. You will perceive that the Poems are the work of three persons—relatives—their separate pieces are distinguished by their respective signatures.—

Feby. 16th, '46: Gentlemen . . . The MS. will certainly form a thinner vol. than I had anticipated—I cannot name another model which I should like it precisely to resemble—yet I think a duodecimo form and a somewhat reduced—though still *clear* type would be preferable. . . . I only stipulate for *clear* type—not too small—and good paper.

March 3rd, '46: Gentlemen,—I send a draft for £31, 10s. being the amount of your Estimate.

I suppose there is nothing now to prevent your immediately commencing the printing of the work. . . .[9]

Meanwhile, life for the rest of the household was less auspicious. Poor old Tabby suffered "a sort of fit"; Martha Brown fell ill with a swelling in her knee and had to go home. The white-haired master sat with Branwell or in his parlor all day, sorrowful and nearly sightless. He roused himself when breakfast was brought in to him, or when Charlotte came to read the papers, or when Grant and Nicholls came on church matters. He bore his darkness stoically, but his thoughts as he sat in the quiet house listening to the bell tolling from the church tower, the whisper of voices from the room across the hall, the heavy moans from the bedroom overhead—his thoughts were as heavy as stone. He was a man of few pleasures; his few pleasures were now denied him. Blind, he must fail in his duties and become a dependent on the parish and a burden to his daughters. His only son rushed headlong to destruction. And although he knew his eldest daughter to be dutiful, he suspected that she longed for a life away from home.

Charlotte visited Ellen in February, said not a word about the volume of poems. In her absence Branwell took advantage of a reduced guard. Full of indignation at his latest escapade, Emily and Anne walked down to Keighley to meet Charlotte on her return and air their grievances, but Charlotte walked home by the old road and they missed her. She entered the house; she went up reluctantly to speak to her once loved brother. The room was darkened and reeked of whiskey. She spoke to him but he was too stupefied to notice her presence. Emily and Anne arrived breathless and drenched from a heavy afternoon shower that had caught them on the way home. Usually calm and tolerant, Emily burned with indignation at Branwell's latest maneuver. The sisters had agreed to deny him money no matter how he begged and whined for it. Branwell had nevertheless connived to wring a sovereign out of his still credulous father by convincing him that he had a pressing debt to pay. The debt was paid promptly over the counter of the nearest public house; eight or nine drams of cheap whiskey wrought the usual havoc. Large of soul and sympathy, Emily had been lenient with her brother's conduct thus far, hoping mildly in her diary that he would "be better and do better in the future." Now her tolerance was exhausted. "He is a hopeless being," she told Charlotte in cold scorn.

By mid-March they were worrying instead over proof sheets. "If there is any doubt at all about the printer's competency to correct errors," Charlotte wrote anxiously, "I would prefer submitting each sheet to the inspection of the Authors—because such a mistake, for instance as *tumbling* stars instead of *trembling* would suffice to throw an air of absurdity over a whole poem . . ."[10] In April Charlotte was urging Aylott & Jones to send copies and advertisements *as early as possible* to *Colburn's New Monthly Magazine, Bentley's Magazine, Hood's Magazine, Jerrold's Shilling Magazine, Blackwood's Magazine,* the *Edinburgh Review, Tait's Edinburgh,* the *Dublin University Magazine,* and also to the *Daily News* and the *Britannia* newspapers.

*The Poems of Currer, Ellis, and Acton Bell* appeared the third week in May, a slender volume bound in dark green cloth with gilt lettering. It contained, in alternating order, nineteen poems by Currer and twenty-one poems each by Ellis and Acton. Of the Bells, however, only one was truly a poet, but she the finest woman poet in English literature: Ellis Bell.

Charlotte knew better than anyone that poetry was not her forte, writing later of her share of the volume, "Of that portion I am by no means proud. Much of it was written in early youth; I feel it now to be crude and rhapsodical." She lacked the alchemy that transmutes powerful but diffuse emotion into the succinct vigor of verse. Searching for this transmuting power, she often substituted exclamatory rhetoric for terse precision, and melodramatic images for simple, fresh language. A born storyteller, she chose the narrative rather than the lyric mode; the interest of her poems remains in their subject matter rather than their poetic form. *Frances* and *Gilbert* are thinly veiled accounts of the festering resentment that had eaten its way into her love for Monsieur Heger. The narrator of *Gilbert* is a callous trifler, a man who finds a woman's adoration soothing to his ego as long as he is not obliged to return it:

> There was a sort of quiet bliss
> To be so deeply loved,
> To gaze on trembling eagerness
> And sit myself unmoved;

And when it pleased my pride to grant
    At last some rare caress,
To feel the fever of that hand
    My fingers deigned to press.
'Twas sweet to see her strive to hide
    What every glance revealed;
Endowed, the while, with despot-might
    Her destiny to wield.
I knew myself no perfect man,
    Nor, as she deemed, divine;
I knew that I was glorious—but
    By her reflected shine. . . .[11]

Charlotte, however, has revenge upon this unfeeling monster. Contented, surrounded by his wife and children, Gilbert suddenly starts from his chair one day at a vision of the woman he scorned drowning before his eyes. This vision proves the precursor to others: the specter pursues him relentlessly until, finding her even at his door when he returns home, he rushes upstairs in terror and guilt, seizes a knife, and slashes his throat. "And thus died by shameful death," Charlotte wrote with gusto, "a wise and worldly man,/Who never drew but selfish breath/Since first his life began"!

More typical than melodramatic revenge, however, is the theme of woman's equality, a theme that came to dominate Charlotte's fiction. Since they find themselves a man's equal in courage, passion, and daring, the female narrators of *The Wife's Will*, *The Wood*, and *Apostasy*, for example, refuse to accept the traditional woman's role of resigned inaction. "Passive, at home, I will not pine," Charlotte declares in *The Wife's Will*; "Thy toils, thy perils shall be mine." The same theme is developed at length in *The Wood*, a narrative in which two lovers flee persecution. For the woman, the danger is a joy—"For now I have my natural part of action with adventure blent . . . And all my once waste energy/To weighty purpose bent":

I am resolved that thou shalt learn
    To trust my strength as I trust thine;
I am resolved our souls shall burn
    With equal, steady, mingling shine . . .
Our lives in the same channel flow,
    Along the self-same line . . .[12]

Thus Charlotte wrote urgently of a woman's yearning for adventure, action, challenge, and a man whose heart and mind could equal hers in courage and passion. She called this yearning "natural"—unaware of the deep radicalism of her desire. She lacked Emily's sure cadences, her precise diction, her objective, broad spirit. She lacked Anne's unforced tranquillity and gentle pathos. Her poetry is often crude, often melo-dramatic. Yet it is as far removed from the commonplace as her own proud, vigorous, restless, indomitable self.

While his sisters triumphed in secret over the green and gilt volume that was the culmination of long dreams of authorship, Branwell too was shaken by a brief moment of triumph. Early in June, opening the *Leeds Mercury* to casually scan its pages, his eye was arrested by a particular notice in the obituary column:

> On Tuesday last [May 26] at Thorp Green near Boroughbridge, aged 46, the Rev. Edmund Robinson. He died as he had lived, in firm and humble trust in his Saviour.

The moment he had almost destroyed himself waiting for had come. The husband was dead. Lydia Robinson was his. Flinging down the paper, he burst out of the house and ran leaping through the crowded graveyard to carry the good news to his cronies at the Black Bull. Anne the barmaid watched his progress in astonishment, remember-ing years after how "he fair danced down the churchyard as if he were out of his mind." Drinks all round—Thorp Green Hall, a handsome income, and above all—for Branwell was after all more a romantic than a materialist—the blooming widow he had adored for three years—all, all were his. Flushed with celebratory whiskey, he hastened back to the parsonage to pack his belongings, preparing to set out immediately to claim his Lydia. In the midst of triumph, a knock at the front door, a message that the young master was wanted down at the inn. At the Bull waiting for him, a familiar figure that set Branwell's nerves racing—his lady's coachman, George Gooch, surely come with summons to Thorp Green. Calling gaily for a bottle of wine, Branwell hurried the coachman into the back parlor where they would conduct the momentous business of his succession in private.

Anne the barmaid, drawing pints of bitters and laughing with the customers, was too busy to notice that the coachman soon emerged from the parlor alone, called for his horse, paid his account, and rode away. Much later, alarmed by a strange noise from the back parlor— a noise that sounded for all the world like the bleating of a young calf —she wiped her hands and hastened to the back room. There she found Branwell Brontë writhing and foaming on the floor in a fit.

George Gooch had not been the bearer of good news. The story he unfolded to Branwell over the wine was calculated to dash his hopes forever. Edmund Robinson, diabolically vindictive, had attached a codicil to his will. Unless his wife wished to forfeit her entire estate and the custody of her four children, the codicil stated, she must abandon all communication with Branwell Brontë, tutor, forever. Mrs. Robinson, the coachman assured Branwell soberly, was a woman in despair, a woman half dead with grief and guilt. If Mr. Brontë had the slightest concern for Lydia Robinson's health and sanity, he would never seek to communicate with her or see her again.

Dear as her money and position were to him, Branwell would instantly have sacrificed both for the sake of marrying the woman he loved. As a gentleman, however, he could not ask *her* to do so. Neither, as a gentleman, could he tread upon the sacred ground of a woman's moral conscience. Faced with the insurmountable barrier of a lady's fortune and feeling, Branwell was forced to bow to Lydia Robinson's wishes. George Gooch rode away bearing Branwell's promise to quit the field. At Thorp Green Hall, Mrs. Robinson received her coachman's account of his journey to Haworth with satisfaction, as did her advisers, the trustees appointed by her husband's will. They congratulated each other. There was no codicil: their invention for silencing the romantic and persistent little tutor had succeeded brilliantly.

If Branwell had inflicted torment upon the household before, he inflicted it doubly now. Charlotte would not confide literary matters to Ellen, but she was not reticent about the family disgrace. "We, I am sorry to say, have been somewhat more harassed than usual lately," she wrote unsympathetically on June 17.

> The death of Mr Robinson, which took place about three weeks or a month ago, served Branwell for a pretext to throw all about him into hubbub and confusion with his emotions, etc., etc. Shortly after, came news from all hands that Mr Robinson had altered his will before he died and effectually prevented all chance of a marriage between his widow and Branwell, by stipulating that she should not have a shilling if she ever ventured to reopen any communication with him. Of course, he then became intolerable. To papa he allows rest neither day nor night, and he is continually screwing money out of him, sometimes threatening that he will kill himself if it is withheld from him. He says Mrs Robinson is now insane; that her mind is a complete wreck owing to remorse for her conduct towards Mr Robinson (whose end it appears was hastened by distress of mind) and grief for having lost him. I do not know how much to believe of what he says, but I fear she is very ill. Branwell declares that he neither can nor will do anything for himself; good situations have been offered him more than once, for which, by a fortnight's work, he might have qualified himself, but he will do nothing, except drink and make us all wretched.[13]

Fearful lest Branwell should still make trouble, Mrs. Robinson and her advisers thought it prudent to remind him again that all communi-

cation with his "lady of grief," as he called her, was impossible. Her
physician, Dr. Crosby, was delegated the task. He performed it successfully, as Branwell's account of his letter to his friend Leyland testifies:

> Well, my dear Sir, I have got my finishing stroke at last—and I feel
> stunned into marble by the blow.
> I have this morning received a long, kind and faithful letter from
> the medical gentleman who attended Mr R. in his last illness and who
> has since had an interview with one whom I can never forget. . . .
> When he mentioned my name—she stared at him and fainted. When
> she recovered she in turns dwelt on her inextinguishable love for me—
> her horror at having been the first to delude me into wretchedness,
> and her agony at having been the cause of the death of her husband,
> who, in his last hours, bitterly repented of his treatment of her.
> Her sensitive mind was totally wrecked. She wandered into talking
> of entering a nunnery; and the Doctor fairly debars me from hope in
> the future. . . .
> I never cared one bit about the property. I cared about herself—and
> always shall do.
> May God bless her, but I wish I had never known her![14]

Madness, guilt, fainting fits, deathbed repentances, nunneries—all
could have come right out of Angrian fantasy. Lydia Robinson understood the workings of Branwell's mind extremely well. He would suffer
in noble silence for such a glamorous cause.

Inevitably Branwell became dangerous to the rest of the household
as well as to himself. His sleepless nights lapsed into daytime stupors
followed in turn by more sleepless nights through which he tried to
lull his tortured mind with laudanum, whiskey, or occasionally the
books so precious to him in happier years. Lighting a candle with
unsteady hands, he would attempt to read, then fall into a heavy
stupor, the candle guttering in its stick forgotten. With strange
prescience, Anne knocked at his door one evening; receiving no answer,
she entered the room. She found the bed curtains blazing and Branwell,
drunk, lying unconscious across the bed in the middle of the flames.
She flew to him but could not drag his emaciated but heavily inert body
out of danger; nor did he respond to her cries. Frantic, she ran down
for Emily below in the kitchen, who heard the news calmly, seized
a bucket, filled it with water, flew up the stairs and through the door,
seized Branwell in her strong arms, flung him onto the floor in an
unconscious heap, ripped down the blazing curtains, dashed them with
water, and threw open the windows. The fire well out, the charred,
watery ruin cleared away, Emily said only, "Don't tell Papa."

Papa found out, however, and from that night added to his burden
of failing sight the task of watching the long night hours with his son.

He insisted Branwell's bed be moved into his room, and his son's tormented ravings, threats of suicide, pleas for money, and tears of remorse became his nightly fare. He listened, and wrestled for his son's soul as he had wrestled with Maria's doubts as she lay dying twenty-five years ago. "The old man and I have had a terrible night of it," Branwell would report on the rare mornings he came downstairs for breakfast.

Falling into exhausted sleep only when the morning light crept into the room, Branwell and Mr. Brontë were thus oblivious to the extreme interest aroused that spring by the postman's ring, to the rustling of proof sheets, to the whispers and consultations. Even before the success of the poems was known, the sisters were preparing to launch another literary venture. In April, in fact, more than a month before the poems had appeared, Charlotte had written a momentous letter of query to Aylott & Jones:

> Gentlemen,—C. E. & A. Bell are now preparing for the Press a work of fiction, consisting of three distinct and unconnected tales which may be published either together as a work of 3 vols. of the ordinary novel size, or separately as single vols. as shall be deemed most advisable.
>
> It is not their intention to publish these tales on their own account.
>
> They direct me to ask you whether you would be disposed to undertake—after having of course by due inspection of the MS. ascertained that its contents are such as to warrant an expectation of success.
>
> An early answer will oblige as in case of your negativing the proposal—inquiry must be made of other Publishers—I am, Gentlemen Yrs. truly
>
> C. Brontë.[15]

Aylott & Jones replied courteously, refusing the tales on the grounds that they specialized in religious works, but encouraging the Bells to find another publisher. Still puzzled how to proceed, Charlotte queried again: "What publishers would be most likely to receive favourably a proposal of this nature? Would it suffice to *write* to a publisher on the subject or would it be necessary to have recourse to a personal interview?"[16] Assured that no personal interviews were necessary, and armed with the names of several firms, Charlotte, Emily, and Anne bent all their energies toward completing the tales: *The Professor, Wuthering Heights*, and *Agnes Grey*.

In *The Professor*, Charlotte told the story of Brussels, but reshaped, recast, and muted incidents and characters in a deliberate effort at restraint. She did not trust herself to tell the story in her own words —the pain was still too fresh. The narrator is thus a man, a professor of English, William Crimsworth. The story recounts his discovery of a shy, impoverished pupil, Frances Henri, in a *pensionnat* in Brussels, their slow-flowering love, its frustration, their eventual courtship and marriage, and—Charlotte's favorite dream—the successful establishing of their own school. The master-pupil relationship of Crimsworth and Frances is a fulfillment of dreams of Monsieur Heger, but Crimsworth is not the fiery little Belgian professor. He is English, he travels to Brussels, he is hired to teach English at both the Athénée Royale and a neighboring *pensionnat des demoiselles* run by Zoraïde Reuter, a cold, calculating, perverse woman faithfully modeled on Charlotte's hatred of Madame Heger. Crimsworth loathes the vain and stupid Belgians but triumphs in the classroom over their insolence. Thus the hero is very much Charlotte herself. For this reason he fails in credibility, for she failed to mask her feminine sensibilities and prejudices under a waistcoat and cravat, although she narrated the story in what she believed to be cool, manly tones. But Crimsworth emerges as an uneasy grafting of two sexes, at once too emotional to convince a reader of his masculinity, and too wooden to be human.

Frances Henri, the insignificant pupil, is also Charlotte, of course. She is pensive, timid, and reserved, but her quiet exterior conceals a burning desire both to excel intellectually and to be loved as an equal by the master who has guided her toward excelling. At one point in the narrative Crimsworth overhears Frances reading aloud a poem of her own composition in which her love for him and her zest for academic triumph are curiously mingled:

> Low at my master's knee I bent,
>   The offered crown to meet;
> Its green leaves through my temples sent
>   A thrill as wild as sweet.
>
> The strong pulse of Ambition struck
>   In every vein I owned;
> At the same instant, bleeding broke
>   A secret, inward wound.
>
> The hour of triumph was to me
>   The hour of sorrow sore;
> A day hence I must cross the sea,
>   Ne'er to cross it more. . . .

Yet Frances Henri is not really content to remain bent at her master's knee, a dramatic pose but quickly conducive to physical and spiritual cramp. She has knelt there only to be crowned. Crimsworth proposes after overhearing these declarations of love, but if he expected a timid, submissive wife, his illusions are quickly dispelled. Sitting demurely on his knee just after she has consented to be his wife, Frances introduces with indecent haste the subject closest to her heart—closer, obviously, than her worship for her master:

> "Monsieur est raisonnable, n'est-ce pas? . . . Well, Monsieur, I wished merely to say, that I should like, of course, to retain my employment of teaching. You will teach still, I suppose, Monsieur?"
> "Oh, yes! It is all I have to depend on."
> "Bon!—I mean good. Thus we shall have both the same profession. I like that; and my efforts to get on will be as unrestrained as yours—will they not, Monsieur?"
> "You are laying plans to be independent of me," said I.
> "Yes, Monsieur. . . ."[17]

This is highly subversive doctrine, the respectful "Monsieur" notwithstanding. Frances insists not merely on working but on pursuing a career with "unrestrained effort"—the difference between a wife taking in a little sewing for pocket money and establishing herself in a profession like teaching, medicine, or law. Equally subversive is Frances' discontent with the working woman's economic inequality: "'How rich you are, Monsieur! . . . Three thousand frances . . . while I get only twelve hundred!'" Although this dialogue seemed unexceptional to Charlotte, such a conversation had not been recorded in a novel before.

This then was the manuscript Charlotte finished in May or June of 1846. The novel was in no way comparable to Emily's masterpiece of tormented love and hellish despair. Nor did it possess the fine simplicity and sustained tone of Anne's *Agnes Grey*, a quiet story of her trials as a governess and her love for William Weightman, idealized as the sensitive, plain-spoken curate, Edward Weston. Artistically *The Professor* was uneven, veering erratically in tone between the abrupt and the overwrought, undoubtedly because Charlotte labored so strenuously to be cool about the wracking Brussels experience, and succeeded only some of the time. The qualities that would distinguish her later novels—vital, eccentric characters, vivid language, eloquent feeling conveyed in powerful prose—were only promised in *The Professor*. On July 4 the three manuscripts were wrapped and posted to Henry Colburn, publisher, to make their way in the great world.

Days later two journals forwarded by Aylott & Jones arrived at the parsonage: the *Athenaeum* and the *Critic* had noticed the volume of poems. Charlotte, Emily, and Anne read with elation the kind words of the *Athenaeum* critic who had recognized the originality of Ellis Bell:

> A Fine, quaint spirit has the latter . . . and an evident power of wing that may reach heights not here attempted. . . . How musical he can be, and how lightly and eagerly the music falls from his heart and pen. . . . He is no copyist. There is not enough in this volume to judge him by, but to our mind, an impression of originality is conveyed beyond what his contribution to these pages embody.[18]

Overjoyed by the notice (and no doubt by the success of the pseudonym, for an authoress was apt to be congratulated merely on having surpassed the limitations of her sex), Charlotte wrote to Aylott & Jones, advising them to lay out a further sum of £10 for advertising, and requesting that this extract from the *Critic* be appended to each advertisement: "They in whose hearts are chords strung by Nature to sympathise with the beautiful and true, will recognise in these compositions the presence of more genius than it was supposed this utilitarian age had devoted to the loftier exercise of the intellect."[19] They then impatiently awaited some response. Hearing nothing, Charlotte wrote again on July 15 to ask, "Whether *any*, or how many copies have yet been sold. . . ."

Bad news travels fast. By return mail Aylott & Jones replied: two copies had been disposed of. Always businesslike, Charlotte replied gravely on July 18 with no trace of regret for the £31. 10s the venture had cost them: "The Messrs Bell . . . are obliged to you for the information respecting the number of copies sold." Of their two readers, one was impressed enough to request their autographs from Aylott & Jones. The Bells obliged him, writing their names on a single sheet of paper which Charlotte then forwarded to their publisher with the request that he send it to Mr. F. Enoch of Leamington under cover of a London postmark since "the Messrs Bell are desirous for the present of remaining unknown." Although the failure of the poems made such obscurity a distinct possibility, the sisters were not discouraged. "Ill-success failed to crush us," Charlotte wrote later, recalling those heady days of unfolding powers and limitless horizons; "the mere effort to succeed had given a wonderful zest to existence; it must be pursued. . . ."[20] The poems were in print, the novels with a publisher, and all three sisters eager to set their hands to a new literary task.

# 13

*Triumph*

By midsummer, after months of professional and unprofessional advice about his eyes, Mr. Brontë reluctantly agreed with Charlotte that he must have the opinion of a specialist. Accordingly, Charlotte and Emily journeyed to Manchester to seek out an eye surgeon for consultation. Luckily they found a reputable man, a Mr. William James Wilson, but he could not tell from Charlotte's description whether Mr. Brontë's eyes were ready to be operated on: Mr. Brontë must come to Manchester himself. As the daughter most capable of dealing with the world, Charlotte accompanied him there in August.

Manchester in 1846 was not a congenial milieu for a Tory Anglican clergyman. The soot-clogged air, the shrieking mill machinery, the dyehouses spewing their filth into the ink-black Irwell, the festering slums whose residents, worn with long mill hours and a starvation diet of oatmeal, potatoes, and tea often brewed with stinking sewer water, boasted an average life expectancy of twenty-five years, the new breed of capitalists who fattened on it all—such was the city hailed by many Victorians as a modern miracle of industrial progress and deplored by others as an abyss of human misery.[1] Manchester could also present a more respectable though hardly less depressing face: solid blocks of blackened red brick, chimney pots, brass door knockers, heavy lace curtains dripping with ball fringe, drooping aspidistra in sooty windows. This face it turned to Charlotte as she sought out rooms, clean but modest, for the two of them. Established in lodgings in a quiet street off Oxford Road, she quickly wrote Ellen her whereabouts in anticipation of a long, lonely ordeal:

83 Mount Pleasant, Boundary Street, Oxford Road, Manchester, Augst 21, '46: Dear Ellen,—I just scribble a line to you to let you know where I am—in order that you may write to me here for it

seems to me that a letter from you would relieve me from the feeling of strangeness I have in this big town.

Papa and I came here on Wednesday, and saw Mr Wilson the Oculist the same day; he pronounced papa's eyes quite ready for an operation and has fixed next Monday for the performance of it.— Think of us on that day dear Nell.

We got into our lodgings yesterday—I think we shall be comfortable, at least our rooms are very good, but there is no Mistress of the house (she is very ill and gone out into the counry) and I am somewhat puzzled in managing about provisions—we board ourselves— I find myself excessively ignorant—I can't tell what the deuce to order in the way of meat—&c. . . . For ourselves I could contrive—papa's diet is so very simple—but there will be a nurse coming in a day or two—and I am afraid of not having things good enough for her— Papa requires nothing you know but plain beef and mutton, tea and bread and butter but a nurse will probably expect to live much better—give me some hints if you can—

Mr Wilson says we shall have to stay here for a month at least—it will be dreary—I wonder how poor Emily and Anne will get on at home with Branwell—they too will have their troubles—What I would not give to have you here. One is forced step by step to get experience in the world Ellen—but the learning is so disagreeable—One cheerful feature in the business is that Mr Wilson thinks most favourably of the case—[2]

On August 25 the operation to remove the cataract was performed by Mr. Wilson and two assisting surgeons. At Papa's request, Charlotte remained in the surgery during the ordeal. She waited, poised on her chair, neither moving nor speaking, scarcely breathing, while the fifteen-minute extraction proceeded. Mr. Brontë bore the operation as firmly and stoically as he bore all troubles sent by the Lord; his patience surprised the doctors. Back at Boundary Street, he was confined to his bed in a dark room, forbidden to stir for four days, and prohibited all unnecessary speech. The nurse arrived, much to Charlotte's discomfort, for she hated strangers. Unlike Sairey Gamp, this nurse did not tipple gin; still, Charlotte found her "somewhat too obsequious" and "not much to be trusted." The long days of suspense dragged on; the nights were made longer for Charlotte by a recurrence of the throbbing toothache that had plagued her severely that summer. On August 31, Mr. Wilson visited the depressed and weary patient; bandages were removed, the curtains drawn back: for the first time Mr. Brontë was allowed to try his sight. He could make out objects dimly. Mr. Wilson pronounced himself perfectly satisfied and took his leave. Charlotte herself was uneasy: Papa complained of extreme weakness and soreness in the eye. He was now allowed to sit up, however, and have a fire in the room, although he was carefully screened from the blaze. A month passed. Papa "is still a prisoner in his darkened room—into which however a little more light is admitted than formerly," Charlotte wrote Ellen on September 22. "The nurse goes to day—her departure will certainly be a relief though she is I dare say not the worst of her class. . . ."³

Added to her fears for her father, a keen disappointment: the manuscript of *The Professor* came back to her door, rejected. There was nothing to do but send it out again, and she did so, crossing out the old address and printing in a new one—too naïve to realize that a secondhand wrapper would prejudice the next firm against the book. Yet the blow of rejection was not as sharp as it might have been if she were not deeply absorbed in writing another novel.

Sitting alone in the still rooms, her father silent in the darkened chamber beyond, the occasional rattle of a horse-drawn carriage sounding down Boundary Street, she wrote swiftly in her small, nervous, slanted hand.

> There was no possibility of taking a walk that day [her narrative began]. We had been wandering, indeed, in the leafless shrubbery an hour in the morning; but since dinner (Mrs. Reed, when there was no company, dined early) the cold winter wind had brought with it clouds so sombre, and a rain so penetrating, that further out-door exercise was now out of the question.
> I was glad of it: I never liked long walks, especially on chilly afternoons: dreadful to me was the coming home in the raw twilight, with nipped fingers and toes, and a heart saddened by the chidings of Bessie, the nurse, and humbled by the consciousness of my physical inferiority to Eliza, John, and Georgiana Reed. . . .

*The Professor* had been an uncertain performance, torn as she was between her urge to tell the Brussels story and her determination to subdue the telling. Released now from factual truth, she was free to write with imaginative truth: she was in her element. In Brussels in 1843 she had written an exercise for Monsieur Heger in which she described the impact when genius and a dominant passion meet: "I believe that genius, thus awakened, has no need to seek out details, that it scarcely pauses to reflect, that it never thinks of unity: I believe that the details come naturally without search by the poet, that inspiration takes the place of reflection and as for unity, I think there is no unity so perfect as that which results from a heart filled with a single idea; it would be as impossible for the torrent, swollen by rains, hurried forward by the storm, to turn from its impetuous course, as for the man, moved by passion, broken by grief, to quit voluntarily his sorrow or his joy and speak of matters which are foreign to them."⁴ "Excellent," Monsieur had written in the margin, little dreaming that the odd, shy English pupil had such a genius which would one day be so awakened.

She wrote swiftly, sure of her style, her idea, her purpose. Steadily, eloquently, the wonderfully compelling story unfolded—the story of an orphan, Jane Eyre, honest, fierce, and proud; her struggles against the mean hypocrisies of caste, custom, and religion; her triumph as a scholar and a governess; her love affair with her master, Edward Rochester; their thwarted marriage; their chastened reunion. The story was a strange, magical blending of the dominant passions of her life. The mad wife, the sinning hero, the fiery destruction of Thornfield Hall surfaced from the turbid depths of the Angrian past she had never quite abandoned. In the love affair between a master and a governess who is nevertheless his moral, intellectual, and emotional equal, she re-created her love for Monsieur Heger. Her heroine's craving for independence and selfhood, her hatred of hypocrisy, her loneliness, her pride, her sexual hunger, her puritanism were Charlotte's own cravings and hatreds. But the disparate elements were fused in the white heat of a single theme—a woman's triumph in love.

As usual, no trace of her literary activity surfaced in her account of herself to Ellen, except in oblique references to the subject of woman's equality, a theme central to *Jane Eyre*. On August 9 she wrote in warning, "There is a defect in your reasoning about the feelings a wife ought to experience in paying money for her husband. Who holds the purse will wish to be Master, Ellen; depend on it whether man or woman. . . . I do not wish for you a *very* rich husband—I should not like you to be regarded by any man even as '*a sweet object of charity*.' "⁵ It was clear to her, as it was not to many more ardent feminists, that money created mastery. To preserve her heroine from the indignities of dependence on the man she loved, Charlotte prudently provided her with a legacy. She also waxed indignant over Ellen's account of Joe Taylor's casual but endless female conquests: "This is an unfair state of things, the match is not equal I only wish I had the power to infuse into the soul of the persecuted a little of the quiet strength of pride—of the supporting consciousness of superiority (for they are superior to him because purer) of the fortifying resolve of firmness to bear the present and wait. Could all the virgin population of Birstall and Gomersall receive and retain these sentiments," she concluded with pre-Freudian innocence, "—Joe Taylor would eventually have to vail his crest before them."⁶ She could not infuse the quiet strength of pride into Joe Taylor's victims, but she infused a great deal of it into her heroine, Jane Eyre.

Back at Haworth, she expressed only frustration with a wasting life, although she was in the full throes of creative excitement, and although, in her own words, "the mere effort to succeed had given a wonderful zest to existence":

> Octr. 14th, '46: Dear Ellen,—I read your letter with attention—not on my own account—for any project which infers the necessity of my leaving home is impracticable to me—but on yours. . . . If I *could* leave home Ellen—I should not be at Haworth now—I know life is passing away and I am doing nothing—earning nothing a very bitter knowledge it is at moments—but I see no way out of the mist—More than one very favourable opportunity has now offered which I have been obliged to put aside—probably when I am free to leave home I shall neither be able to find place nor employment—perhaps too I shall be quite past the prime of life—my faculties will be rusted— and my few acquirements in a great measure forgotten—These ideas sting me keenly sometimes—but whenever I consult my Conscience it affirms that I am doing right in staying at home—and bitter are its upbraidings when I yield to an eager desire for release.

In an unusual burst of confidence, she went on:

> I returned to Brussels after Aunt's death against my conscience— prompted by what then seemed an irresistible impulse—I was punished for my selfish folly by a total withdrawal for more than two years of happiness and peace of mind—I could hardly expect success if I were to err again in the same way.[7]

The trap of conscience, baited with traditions of duty, subservience, sacrifice, and dependence—sugar-sweet on the surface, bitter inside—sprang shut with cruel vengeance on its female victims. Deeply resenting both Papa's and Branwell's imposition on her freedom, Charlotte could only comfort herself with the belief that duty was a sacred necessity and blame herself when she resented the weight of its yoke. Thus she was sternly unyielding when Ellen applied to her for advice that summer. Ellen was discontent at Brookroyd. Knowing full well that governessing was drudgery, she nevertheless longed for a source of income and a change of scene. Yet her mother was old and claimed her at home. What path would Charlotte advise her to take? Charlotte was quite clear on the matter: "The right path is that which necessitates the greatest sacrifice of self-interest . . . Your mother is both old and infirm; old and infirm people have few sources of happiness, fewer almost than the comparatively young and healthy can conceive; to deprive them of one of these is cruel. . . . I recommend you to do what I am trying to do myself."[8]

Outwardly resigned, she cried out against this tyranny in her novel —the tyranny of doors barred at nine, a father who thought only of his son while his daughter stayed to serve him, the rusting of her skills, the monotony of the blue encircling hills, the want of contact with cultured minds. "Anybody may blame me who likes," cries Jane Eyre, chafing at the monotony of Thornfield,

> when I add further, that, now and then, when I took a walk by myself in the grounds; when I went down to the gates and looked through them along the road; or when, while Adèle played with her nurse, and Mrs. Fairfax made jellies in the storeroom, I climbed the three staircases, raised the trap-door of the attic, and having reached the leads, looked out afar over sequestered field and hill, and long dim sky-line—that then I longed for a power of vision which might overpass that limit; which might reach the busy world, towns, regions full of life I had heard of but never seen; that then I desired more of practical experience than I possessed; more of intercourse with my kind, of acquaintance with variety of character, than was here within my reach. . . .
>
> It is vain to say human beings ought to be satisfied with tranquillity: they must have action; and they will make it if they cannot find it. Millions are condemned to a stiller doom than mine, and millions are in silent revolt against their lot. Nobody knows how many rebellions besides political rebellions ferment in the masses of life which people earth. Women are supposed to be very calm generally: but women feel just as men feel; they need exercise for their faculties, and a field for their efforts as much as their brothers do; they suffer from too rigid a constraint, too absolute a stagnation, precisely as men would suffer; and it is narrow-minded in their more privileged fellow-creatures to say that they ought to confine themselves to making puddings and knitting stockings, to playing on the piano and embroidering bags. It is thoughtless to condemn them, or laugh at them, if they seek to do more or learn more than custom has pronounced necessary for their sex.[9]

As Mr. Brontë's sight improved, the burden of frequent attendance to his wants was lifted from Charlotte's shoulders. By November he was able to resume his place behind the three-decker pulpit in the cold damp church, first only to read the prayers, but then, when his curate Mr. Nicholls left to visit cousins in Ireland, to preach all three Sunday sermons. He had come back to life from darkness. The daughters rejoiced to see him erect and independent after more than a year of groping helplessness; rejoiced to see him grasp his walking stick and stride out alone through the gate and down the lane; rejoiced to know he no longer sat idly behind the parlor door, his white head bent, his hands lifeless on his knees, but passed the hours reading and writing as before. His vision was not perfect; he continued to see spots before the afflicted eye; but since Mr. Wilson showed no alarm at this symptom, Charlotte attempted to quiet her uneasiness on the point.

Apart from Papa's recovery and the hours alone in the dining room during which her pencil covered page after page, the winter was bleak enough that year. "I hope you are not frozen up in North-amptonshire," Charlotte wrote Ellen, "—the cold here is dreadful I do not remember such a series of North-Pole-Days—England might really have taken a slide up into the Arctic Zone—the sky looks like ice—the earth is frozen, the wind is as keen as a two-edge blade—I cannot keep myself warm."[10] How Aunt Branwell, with her horror of icy-cold stone floors, would have suffered and complained that winter and taken to her bed with closed windows, bright peat fires in the grate, and quilts. As it was, the whole family came down with severe coughs and colds, and Mr. Brontë, just recovered from blindness, was driven to bed with influenza. Anne was particularly afflicted: through bitter cold, wind-torn nights Charlotte and Emily listened to her deep, barking cough and her gasping struggles to breathe. Again Charlotte was forced to marvel at Anne's extraordinary power to endure suffering. She uttered no complaint, only sighing now and again when worn out by prolonged bouts of coughing. Charlotte admired her resignation without wholly understanding or even approving the passivity that such stoicism seemed to imply. She felt herself incapable of imitating Anne's silent suffering.

Nor was it particularly cheering that bitter winter to answer the postman's knock and find that another publisher had rejected *The Professor* or *Wuthering Heights* and *Agnes Grey*. She continued to send the manuscript out in its increasingly battered wrapper, only crossing out one address to write in a new one. Another knock at the door one day in December brought an even more unpleasant surprise, however. On the doorstep stood a sheriff's officer from Halifax with an invitation for one Branwell Brontë either to immediately pay up debts incurred to Thomas Nicholson, landlord of the Old Cock, Halifax, or step along with him to York prison on the spot.

In their quiet, winter-locked existence, this event, as Charlotte put it, stung them into life. Laudanum and whiskey were ruinous habits, but private ones: as long as Branwell pursued them, he injured chiefly himself. Debt, however, was an injury to others, a public disgrace; the presence of an officer of the law on one's doorstep a shameful stain on family honor. Obviously the debt had to be paid. Conditioned by now to shield the men of the family from harsh truths, the sisters quickly and quietly paid over the money—enough at least to settle the immediate bills at the Old Cock. For other debts

Branwell counted on—and still received—cash gifts from "the Lady": often £20 at a time. Had Branwell's behavior been at all frank, had he confessed openly to running up debts he could not meet, Charlotte could have felt a twinge of sympathy for his plight. ᴜt he whined, evaded, hurled counteraccusations, and lied. Coldly ᵥ sessing his opium-wasted body, the coarsened lines about the sensual mouth, the shifty glance of the small blue eyes, she found nothing to remind her of the brother she had loved.

Branwell, however, continued to see himself as a doomed hero, a victim caught in the web of destiny. This was his tragedy, for the vision excused him from struggling to extricate himself. "I have been in truth too much petted through life," he wrote Leyland with rare frankness in January 1847, "and in my last situation I was so much master, and gave myself so much up to enjoyment, that now when the cloud of ill-health and adversity has come upon me it will be a disheartening job to work myself up again through a new life's battle, from the position of five years ago to which I have been compelled to retreat with heavy loss and no gain." Life was still very much the Verdopolis battlefield for Branwell. "My army stands now where it did then, but mourning the slaughter of Youth, Health, Hope, and both mental and physical elasticity. . . ."

> *I* know only that it is time for me to be something when I am nothing. That my father cannot have long to live, and that when he dies, my evening, which is already twilight, will become night— That I shall then have a constitution still so strong that it will keep me years in torture and despair when I should every hour pray that I might die. . . .
>
> For four years . . . a lady intensely loved me as I did her . . . she loved me even better than I did her. . . . I have received to-day, since I began my scrawl, a note from her maid Miss Ann Marshall, and I *know* from it that she has been terrified by vows which she was forced to swear to, on her husband's deathbed, (with every addition of terror which the ghastly dying eye could inflict upon a keenly sensitive and almost *worried* woman's mind) a complete severance from him in whom lay her whole heart's feelings. When that husband was scarce cold in his grave her relations, who controlled the whole property overwhelmed her with their tongues, and I am *quite conscious* that she has succumbed in terror to what they have said. . . .[11]

The bitter winter lagged toward spring. "I shall scribble you a short note about nothing," Charlotte wrote Ellen on February 14, "just to have a pretext for screwing a letter out of you in return. . . . I hope this excessively cold weather has not harmed you or *yours* much— It has nipped me severely—taken away my appetite for a while and given me a toothache. . . . I look almost old enough to be your Mother—grey sunk and withered. . . ." March 24: "I owe you a grudge for giving [Miss Wooler] some very exaggerated account about my not being well—and setting her on to urge my leaving home as quite a duty—I'll take care not to tell you next time when I think I am looking specially old and ugly—as if people could not have that privilege without being supposed to be at the last gasp!

"I shall be 31 next birthday—My youth is gone like a dream—and very little use have I ever made of it—What have I done these last thirty years?—Precious little."[12] On March 16, however, she had begun the fair copy of *Jane Eyre, An Autobiography*, edited by Currer Bell.

That spring another secret was added to the ever growing hoard at the parsonage: Elizabeth and Mary Robinson, Anne's former pupils, began a correspondence, proving themselves emancipated from their mother's snobbery. Lydia, the eldest Robinson girl, had indeed become very emancipated. Eloping to Gretna Green with Henry Roxby, a play actor from Scarborough, she had been cut off from both her father's and her mother's fortunes without a shilling; nor was she any longer received at Thorp Green Hall. The respect Anne had won from these spoiled and willful but evidently goodhearted girls now surfaced. They had teased her, snubbed her, flung down their books, wept over the exercises she assigned, ignored her as she walked quietly but indignantly behind them to church. But nothing had disturbed their governess' innate dignity; Anne had impressed them in spite of themselves. ". . . for a fortnight they sent her a letter almost every day," Charlotte told Ellen, "—crammed with warm protestations of endless esteem and gratitude—they speak with great affection too of their Mother—and never make any allusion intimating acquaintance with her errors. . . . We take special care that Branwell does not know of their writing to Anne."

As for Branwell, his conduct worsened as spring drew on. "I expect from the extravagance of his behaviour," Charlotte continued in the same letter, "and from mysterious hints he drops—(for he never will speak out plainly) that we shall be hearing news of fresh debts contracted by him soon."[13] Nevertheless, she retracted her vow that Ellen should never step foot inside the door while Branwell was at home, writing her on April 4 to ask whether Whitsuntide would suit her for a visit. Ellen's reply stung Charlotte a little. A visit to Haworth would depend on Miss Ringrose's movements—Amelia Ringrose, a close friend of Ellen's whose name had figured more and more prominently in her letters the past few years. She hoped Charlotte would not be jealous? Undoubtedly Ellen was not as blind to the literary mysteries at the parsonage as Charlotte believed, and was rather hurt that her friend did not confide in her. She would have her little revenge, the only kind her good nature was capable of. On April 21, her thirty-first birthday, Charlotte rebuked her old friend for such a notion: "I was rather amused at your fearing I should be jealous. I never thought of it, Nell. She and I could not be rivals in your affections. You allot her, I know, a different set of feelings to what you allot me. . . . In short, I should as soon think of being jealous of Emily and Anne in these days as of you."[14]

In May, Ellen's long-awaited visit was imminent and Charlotte wrote joyfully: "You must direct [your luggage] to Mr Brontë's, Haworth, and we will tell the carrier to inquire for it. The railroad has been open some time, but it only comes as far as Keighley. The remaining distance you will have to walk. . . . If you can arrive at Keighley by about four o'clock in the afternoon, Emily, Anne, and I will all three meet you at the station. We can take tea jovially together at the Devonshire Arms, and walk home in the cool of the evening. This, with fine weather, will, I think, be a much better arrangement than fagging through four miles in the heat of the noon."[15] She always preferred Ellen to arrive in the late afternoon after the bustle and business of the day, when twilight was falling and a fire danced in the hearth and tea was brought steaming in the flowered porcelain pot from the kitchen by Martha. A few days later, however, a letter of regret came from Brookroyd. Ellen was sorry, but as her sisters wished to visit from home, she must stay. Would Charlotte come to Brookroyd? Seldom angry with her gentle friend, Charlotte was angry now, and wrote a strong retort, concluding, ". . . this is bitter, but I feel bitter—As to going to Brookroyd it is absurd—I will not go near the place till you have been to Haworth."[16] Peace was eventually made, however, and the much-postponed visit took place finally in July.

That same month, perhaps even during Ellen's visit, for the sisters were adept at juggling two lives, the moment they had been waiting for arrived one morning with a letter from Thomas Cautley Newby, head of a small publishing firm in Mortimer Street, Cavendish Square, and the fifth publisher to read the three manuscripts. He announced himself prepared to consider *Wuthering Heights* and *Agnes Grey* but *not* willing to accept *The Professor*. Newby drove a hard bargain with Messrs Ellis and Acton Bell: to offset the risk of publishing unknown authors, they were to stand £50 of the production costs, a sum he would refund if the 350 copies printed were sold and the work went into a second edition. If Emily and Anne accepted Newby's offer, *The Professor* was almost certainly unsalable on its own since it fell far short of the standard three-volume length. Here was a dilemma—or at least Charlotte believed it to be, for she argued seriously the pros and cons of Newby's offer with her sisters, at last gallantly urging them to accept it and let her novel fend for itself. She underestimated Emily's and Anne's desire for success, however. It was as keen as her own; they had no intention of refusing Newby's offer; they swiftly closed with him and by August were reading proofs.

Almost hopeless, Charlotte sent out *The Professor* again on July 15 to the firm of Smith, Elder and Company along with the usual letter: "Gentlemen,—I beg to submit to your consideration the accompanying manuscript. I should be glad to learn whether it be such as you approve, and would undertake to publish at as early a period as possible. Address, Mr Currer Bell, under cover to Miss Brontë, Haworth, Bradford, Yorkshire."[17] So doing, she settled down for the usual long, disheartening silence. To her great surprise, a reply came back in August, addressed to the confusion of the postman to Mr. Currer Bell. She did not allow herself to hope: she opened the envelope in "the dreary anticipation of finding two hard, hopeless lines." Instead she drew out a letter of two pages. Trembling violently, she read. Smith, Elder indeed declined to publish *The Professor* for business reasons, but the editor discussed the merits and demerits of her manuscript so intelligently, so courteously, with such an enlightened and rational discrimination that Charlotte, long inured to disappointment, found this kind of refusal as good as—and better than—a casual acceptance. Most important: the letter added that a novel in three volumes by Currer Bell would meet with careful attention.

She had such a novel almost ready.

> To Mssrs. Smith, Elder and Co., August 24th, 1847: I now send you per rail a MS. entitled "Jane Eyre," a novel in three volumes, by Currer Bell. I find I cannot prepay the carriage of the parcel, as money for that purpose is not received at the small stationhouse where it is left. If, when you acknowledge the receipt of the MS., you would have the goodness to mention the amount charged on delivery, I will immediately transmit it in postage-stamps. It is better in future to address Mr Currer Bell, under cover to Miss Brontë, Haworth, Bradford, Yorkshire, as there is a risk of letters otherwise directed not reaching me at present. To save trouble, I enclose an envelope.
> Currer Bell.[18]

In London the manuscript was received at Smith, Elder and Company with a smile at Currer Bell's "suspicion as to the excessive parsimony of London publishers in regard to postage stamps," and handed over to the firm's reader, William Smith Williams, the man who had read and written to Currer Bell regarding *The Professor.* "The MS. of 'Jane Eyre' was read by Mr. Williams in due course," George Murray Smith, owner of the firm, reminisced in a memoir of 1901. "He brought it to me on a Saturday, and said that he would like me to read it. There were no Saturday half-holidays in those days, and, as was usual, I did not reach home until late. I had made an appointment with a friend for Sunday morning; I was to meet him about twelve o'clock, at a place some two or three miles from our house, and ride with him into the country.

"After breakfast on Sunday morning I took the MS. of 'Jane Eyre' to my little study, and began to read it. The story quickly took me captive. Before twelve o'clock my horse came to the door, but I could not put the book down. I scribbled two or three lines to my friend, saying I was very sorry that circumstances had arisen to prevent my meeting him, sent the note off by my groom, and went on reading the MS. Presently the servant came to tell me that luncheon was ready; I asked him to bring me a sandwich and a glass of wine, and still went on with 'Jane Eyre.' Dinner came; for me the meal was a very hasty one, and before I went to bed that night I had finished reading the manuscript.

"The next day we wrote to 'Currer Bell' accepting the book for publication. . . ."[19]

Moving swiftly, Smith, Elder had proofs in Charlotte's hands that September. The book appeared October 16—an operation of six weeks between acceptance and publication. On October 19, Charlotte wrote the firm acknowledging the complimentary copies that had arrived at the parsonage and been quickly whisked out of Papa's and Branwell's sight:

> Gentleman,—The six copies of "Jane Eyre" reached me this morning. You have given the work every advantage which good paper, clear type, and a seemly outside can supply; if it fails the fault will lie with the author; you are exempt.
>
> I now await the judgment of the press and public.—I am gentlemen, yours respectfully,
>
> C. Bell.[20]

In London *Jane Eyre* began its progress through the ranks of that novel-devouring age. The reaction came, fitfully at first and scattered:

". . . a remarkable production," enthused *The Times.* "Freshness and originality, truth and passion, singular felicity in the description of natural scenery, and in the analysis of human thought, enable this tale to stand out boldly from the rest."

"Decidedly the best novel of the year," trumpeted the *Westminster Review*.

"After laughing over the *Bachelor of the Albany*, we wept over *Jane Eyre*," wrote that lively and intelligent critic G. H. Lewes in *Fraser's Magazine* for December 1847. "This indeed is a book after our own heart . . . no such book has gladdened our eyes for a long while. . . . The story is not only of singular interest, naturally evolved, unflagging to the last, but fastens itself upon your attention, and will not leave you. The book closed, the enchantment continues. . . ."

At 13 Young Street, Kensington, William Makepeace Thackeray picked up *Jane Eyre* with a professional's curiosity and sat down to look it through. Hours passed: he read on with delight and wonder, forgetting the demands of his own work pressing upon him, weeping over the love passages to the great astonishment of his butler, John, who came in with a bucket of coals, unable to stop until he had turned the last page, putting the book down reluctantly, still under the spell of its fascination.[21]

Exclamations swelled to a chorus that surged to a roar. Currer Bell's *Jane Eyre* had taken Victorian England by storm.

# 14

❧❧❧❧❧❧❧❧❧

# *Fame*

Although Thomas Cautley Newby had in hand Ellis Bell's *Wuthering Heights*, a greater though less appealing work than *Jane Eyre*, he did not play fair with his unknown authors. While *Jane Eyre* was on everyone's lips, Emily and Anne still waited anxiously for their novels to appear. Charlotte had fortunately met with a publisher who, although a shrewd man of business, took a keen delight in authors and their works. Newby was only a businessman—and an unscrupulous one at that. He delayed publishing *Wuthering Heights* and *Agnes Grey* until *Jane Eyre* went into a second edition in December 1847; then he acted, hoping to capitalize on Currer Bell's success and even to mislead the public into thinking all three novels were written by Currer.

His scheme was on the whole successful. While the great and immediate success of *Jane Eyre* woke attention to the name Bell and paved the way for Anne's and Emily's novels, *Wuthering Heights* and *Agnes Grey* were attributed by many to Currer or, if not attributed to him, compared to his novel and found wanting. Charlotte's success at once helped and hindered Emily and Anne. In 1850 the *Palladium* would still be asking, "Who is Currer Bell?" and refusing to believe that the hand that shaped *Jane Eyre* and *Shirley* did not "cut out the rougher earlier statues."

The cries of outrage that greeted *Wuthering Heights* and the refusal of many critics to believe in "the brothers Bell" caused Charlotte great anguish in the midst of triumph. She could hardly bear to watch Emily's pale, set face or Anne's troubled one as they read the reviews, although neither of them said much. They did not need to. Charlotte could gauge the depths of Emily's scorn for the fools of the world and Anne's quiet hurt as they were told in the *Athenaeum* for December 25 that the three Bell novels might be the work of one hand, although the first issued remained the best. Several critics, of course, found *Wuthering Heights* clever and powerful, but this praise was often canceled by the reviewer's disgust at the novel's bestiality. Thus the *Athenaeum:* "The Bells seem to affect painful and exceptional subjects:—the misdeeds and oppressions of tyranny—the eccentricities of 'woman's fantasy.' They do not turn away from dwelling on those physical acts of cruelty which we know to have their warrant in the real annals of crime and suffering,—but the contemplation of which true taste rejects. . . . Enough of what is mean and bitterly painful and degrading gathers round every one of us during the course of his pilgrimate through this vale of tears to absolve the Artist from choosing his incidents and characters out of such a dismal catalogue; and if the Bells, singly or collectively, are contemplating future or frequent utterances in Fiction, let us hope that they will spare us further interiors so gloomy as the one here elaborated with such dismal minuteness. . . ." The gloomy interior objected to is, of course, Heathcliff's dwelling; if Charlotte's success detracted from Emily's novel, conversely *Wuthering Heights* convinced the critics that all the Bells dwelt in realms of brutality, insurrection, and torment.

The *Athenaeum*'s disgust with the "tastelessness" of Ellis' novel was echoed by most reviewers. Powerful, claimed most of the journals, but also—revolting, coarse, loathesome, and savage. The *Examiner* found Heathcliff "an incarnation of evil qualities; implacable hate, ingratitude, cruelty, falsehood, selfishness, and revenge." Douglas Jerrold's *Weekly Newspaper* took up the refrain in a January review, dismayed at the novel's "brutal cruelty, and semi-savage love." The reader must be "shocked, disgusted, almost sickened by details of cruelty, inhumanity, and the most diabolical hate and vengeance." However, the critic bowed to Ellis Bell's uniqueness: "We strongly recommend all our readers who love novelty to get this story, for we can promise them that they never have read anything like it before."[1]

Often criticism reveals more about the prejudices of an age than about the merits of a work of art: the Victorian reaction to the novels of the Bells was no exception. The novel as a genre had just gained respectability: earlier in the century evangelicals and moralists had condemned it as a frivolous pastime and a temptation to sin. More than anyone else, Sir Walter Scott had put the novel on a respectable footing, not only because he was a first-rate writer but because he became an upstanding influential country squire. Charles Dickens, tickling the Victorian conscience with social issues but not wounding it, firmly established the three-decker novel as a respectable institution.

But earlier prejudices were slow to wear off. Prince Albert declared that art should uplift the soul and purify the body, evidently assigning it to a vague limbo between religion and hygiene. Many critics got no further than the good Prince. Literature should provide a stout moral staff to help the reader through "this vale of tears"; it should also shed a little sunshine on the path. It should guide him swiftly past mud and ruts and bleak views. Above all, it must never lead him into that field where Squire Western fondled a farm girl in the haystacks or through that copse where Tom Jones fornicated happily with Molly Seagrim. Thackeray lamented that the writer was no longer free to paint a real man like Fielding's hero, yet even he praised Dickens' "unsullied page" and found George Sand and Balzac obscene. Nor must the reader meet on the path a heroine who was not pure and passive, a hero not a Christian gentleman, or a villain dyed any color but midnight black. The novel had no business to confuse conventional morality; it must confirm it.

The Bells could not please critics who judged by these criteria. Even Anne's mild *Agnes Grey* boasted a governess heroine who, in her quiet way, knows herself distinctly superior to the rich family she serves, and who frankly admits her love for the local curate long before she knows he returns it. As long as critics and readers believed the Bells to be men, however, they were largely excused their crudities, which reviewers interpreted as the undisciplined *masculine* vigor of novice writers. "We confess that we like an author who throws himself into the front of the battle, as the champion of the weaker party," announced the *Examiner* of Currer Bell in a November 27, 1847, review; "and when this is followed up by bold and skillful soldiership, we are compelled to yield him our respect." Ellis found himself granted great powers and originality, but warned that in the future he must curb his forces and direct them to a higher end than that of displaying sullen rage and brutal passion. And there was much in the novels that seemed conventionally male: vigorous language sprinkled freely with curses, frank passion, bold insurrection, rough, eccentric characters, a notable lack of interest in domestic concerns.

From the beginning, however, there were scores of readers and some critics who suspected that the notorious Bells were women. Dickens, Harriet Martineau, Thackeray, and G. H. Lewes all detected an unusual feminine mentality in the novels, and admired it. Lesser minds revolted at the thought of women producing such fiction. Frankness, rebellion, roughness, strong passions, brutality, vigor—all admirable in an author—became crimes in an authoress. Charlotte sickened over a review in the *Christian Remembrancer* that ridiculed the belief that Currer Bell was a man, proposing instead a virago: ". . . a book more unfeminine, both in its excellences and its defects, it would be hard to find in the annals of female authorship. Throughout there is a masculine power, breadth and shrewdness, combined with masculine hardness, coarseness, and freedom of expression. Slang is not rare. The humour is frequently produced by the use of Scripture, at which one is rather sorry to have smiled. The love-scenes glow with a fire as fierce as that of Sappho, and somewhat more fulginous. . . . If the authoress has not been like her heroine, an oppressed orphan, a starved and bullied charity-school girl, and a despised and slighted governess (and the intensity of feeling which she shows in speaking of the wrongs of this last class seems to prove that they have been her own), at all events we fear she is one to whom the world has not been kind. And assuredly, never was unkindness more cordially repaid. Never was there a better hater. . . ."[2]

Some critics, obviously baffled, could only conclude that the novels were written by a man *and* a woman. Edwin Percy Whipple, writing in the *North American Review*, October 1848, declared that the elaborate descriptions of dress in *Jane Eyre*, the various niceties of female thought and emotion, and the minutiae of the sickroom could only be a woman's work. Often little subtleties like these escape women writers unawares, giving their works authenticity, Whipple concedes— but the "noblest and best representations of female character have been produced by men." Therefore, the novel's clear, distinctive style, its firm grasp of character, and its charm Whipple attributes to the male partner. He *hopes* he can attribute its violence to the same source: "when the admirable Mr. Rochester appears, and the profanity, brutality, and slang of the misanthropic profligate give their torpedo shocks to the nervous system . . . we are gallant enough to detect the hand of a gentleman in the composition. There are also scenes of passion, so hot, so emphatic, and condensed in expression, and so sternly masculine in feeling, that we are almost sure we observe the mind of the author of Wuthering Heights at work in the text."

Mrs. Sara Ellis, author of those standard Victorian manuals of feminine behavior *Daughters of England, Wives of England,* and *Women of England,* also suspected joint authorship "because the work contains passages, of which the reader is disposed to say, that no man could have written them if he would; and others, of which the reader is still more disposed to say, that no woman *would* have written them if she could."[3] If Currer Bell *were* a woman, she violated Mrs. Ellis' sense of what was proper in a good daughter, wife, or woman of England.

The game "Who are the Bells?" thus became a favorite literary pastime that season, and speculation about the identity and sex of the authors created as much publicity for the novels as their strange excellence. The sisters had hoped to enter the literary world via a forged passport; this plan had succeeded. Now, however, their credentials were suspect and a storm of controversy rose around them. They had anticipated this prejudice against their sex; they were aware their novels challenged conventional beliefs about women. Anticipation and awareness did not dull the outrage Charlotte, Emily, and Anne experienced, however, as these derogatory reviews found their way to far-off Yorkshire.

But in the months immediately following the publication of *Jane Eyre,* most of these angry clouds were not yet lowering on Charlotte's horizon. Despite acute unhappiness over the critical injustices to *Wuthering Heights*, she could not help basking a little in the warmth of success. Her whole notion of fame, she had told Mary in Brussels, was as a passport to the company of intellectual minds. Now, in a limited way, intellectual minds were available to her. Had she admitted her identity and gone up to London, she would have reigned as the literary lion of the season—wined, dined, and fought for. As it was, the business communications from 65 Cornhill, the boxes of complimentary books that began arriving at the parsonage, the reviews, the friendly, stimulating letters from W. S. Williams—these to a person of Charlotte's retiring nature seemed like overwhelming fame. The postman must have been a dull dog indeed if he did not guess that some great event was transpiring for the shy, bespectacled parson's daughter, but apparently he remained innocent. So did Papa. To her horror, Charlotte saw the postman stop her father one day as he was stepping out the door to start on his parish rounds and heard him ask whether the parson knew of a Mr. Currer Bell in the neighborhood. "Never heard of the fellow," replied Mr. Brontë and swung off down the lane, but Charlotte was thoroughly alarmed. "Allow me to intimate that it would be better in future not to put the name of Currer Bell on the outside of communications," she hurriedly wrote Williams; "if directed simply to Miss Brontë they will be more likely to reach their destination safely. Currer Bell is not known in the district, and I have no wish that he should become known."[4]

One of her first admirers was George Henry Lewes, critic, novelist, biographer of Goethe and lover of George Eliot.[5] He read *Jane Eyre* with enthusiasm and went down to the offices of *Fraser's* to ask the editor to let him review it. He then wrote to Currer Bell expressing his delight in the book, but at the same time admonishing him to exercise a stronger control over his imagination in the future. Stubborn as the devil where she believed herself right, Charlotte sat down to refute

Lewes's criticism. She had not humbled herself before Southey or Wordsworth; she would not humble herself before an unknown critic:

> November 6th, 1847: Dear Sir,— . . . You warn me to beware of melodrama, and you exhort me to adhere to the real. When I first began to write, so impressed was I with the truth of the principles you advocate, that I determined to take Nature and Truth as my sole guides, and to follow to their very footprints; I restrained imagination, eschewed romance, repressed excitement; over-bright colouring, too, I avoided, and sought to produce something which should be soft, grave, and true.
>
> My work (a tale in one volume) being completed I offered it to a publisher. He said it was original, faithful to nature, but he did not feel warranted in accepting it; such a work would not sell. I tried six publishers in succession; they all told me it was deficient in "startling incident" and "thrilling excitement," that it would never suit the circulating libraries . . .
>
> "Jane Eyre" was rather objected to at first, on the same grounds, but finally found acceptance. . . .
>
> You advise me, too, not to stray far from the ground of experience, as I become weak when I enter the region of fiction; and you say "real experience is perennially interesting, and to all men."
>
> I feel that this also is true; but, dear sir, is not the real experience of each individual very limited? And, if a writer dwells upon that solely or principally, is he not in danger of repeating himself, and also of becoming an egotist? Then, too, imagination is a strong, restless faculty, which claims to be heard and exercised: are we to be quite deaf to her cry, and insensate to her struggles? When she shows us bright pictures, are we never to look at them, and try to reproduce them? And when she is eloquent, and speaks rapidly and urgently in our ear, are we not to write to her dictation?
>
> I shall anxiously search the next number of "Fraser" for your opinions on these points.—Believe me, dear sir, yours gratefully,
>
> C. Bell.[6]

The vehemence of Currer's defense surprised Lewes, who thought he had written a flattering letter. Meanwhile, Charlotte asked Williams about Lewes. Told he was a clever and sincere critic and the author of a new novel, *Ranthorpe,* she got hold of the novel, read it, liked it, and wrote Lewes again in a friendlier but hardly less dramatic spirit:

> I await your criticism on "Jane Eyre" now with other sentiments than I entertained before the perusal of "Ranthorpe."
>
> You were a stranger to me. I did not particularly respect you. I did not feel that your praise or blame would have any special weight. I knew little of your right to condemn or approve. *Now* I am informed on these points.

You will be severe; your last letter taught me as much. Well! I shall try to extract good out of your severity; and besides, though I am now sure you are a just, discriminating man, yet being mortal, you must be fallible; and if any part of your censure galls me too keenly to the quick—gives me deadly pain—I shall for the present disbelieve it, and put it quite aside, till such time as I feel able to receive it without torture.—I am, dear sir, yours very respectfully,

C. Bell.[7]

What a prickly and passionate fellow, this Currer Bell! But Lewes had no intention of torturing him—or *her*. Briefly critical of the mad wife in the upper story of Thornfield (little dreaming that Currer had a near model upstairs in Papa's bedroom), Lewes praised the personal magnetism of *Jane Eyre* in his *Fraser's* review: ". . . it is soul speaking to soul; it is an utterance from the depths of a struggling, suffering, much-enduring spirit: *suspiria de profundis!*"

Fame also brought Charlotte indirect contact with the contemporary author she most admired, William Makepeace Thackeray. Nothing delighted her more—not even a bank bill from Smith, Elder—than a letter from Williams relaying Thackeray's praise: he had been exceedingly moved and pleased by *Jane Eyre* and asked Williams to give his respects and thanks to the author for the first English novel he had been able to read for many a day.[8] She replied to Williams enthusiastically, delighted to be able to speak her mind about literature at last, to be heard with respect, to be considered an authority on literary matters. She praised Thackeray to Williams as above all a great moralist: "Mr. Thackeray is a keen, ruthless satirist. I had never perused his writings but with blended feelings of admiration and indignation. Critics, it appears to me, do not know what an intellectual boa-constrictor he is. They call him 'humourous,' 'brilliant'—his is a most scalping humour, a most deadly brilliancy: he does not play with his prey, he coils round it and crushes it in his rings. He seems terribly in earnest in his war against the falsehood and follies of 'the world.' "[9]

Elated by Thackeray's praise, she screwed up her courage to dedicate the second edition of *Jane Eyre* to him, combining in a preface a defense of her novel's morality and praise of Thackeray as a moralist. *Jane Eyre* had been attacked as unchristian, but a protest against bigotry is *not* an insult to piety or to God, she declared vigorously. "Conventionality is not morality. Self-righteousness is not religion. To attack the first is not to assail the last. To pluck the mask from the face of the Pharisee, is not to lift an impious hand to the Crown of Thorns." In prose that rose higher and higher in strenuous eloquence, she cited Thackeray as the modern champion of truth, hurling "the Greek fire of his sarcasm" and "the levin-brand of his denunciation" at the vanities of the world. "They say he is like Fielding," she concluded: "they talk of his wit, humour, comic powers. He resembles Fielding as an eagle does a vulture: Fielding could stoop on carrion, but Thackeray never does. His wit is bright, his humour attractive, but both bear the same relation to his serious genius, that the mere lambent sheet-lightning playing under the edge of the summer-cloud, does to the electric death-spark hid in its womb. . . . I have alluded to Mr. Thackeray, because to him—if he will accept the tribute of a total stranger—I have dedicated this second edition of *Jane Eyre*. Currer Bell, Dec. 21st, 1847."

The dedication, so eloquent and well meant, misfired painfully. Unfortunately Thackeray had among his household both a mad wife and a governess. In a flash, London drew scandalous connections: Thackeray was Rochester, Mrs. Thackeray the mad wife, Currer Bell his governess; and, of course, Currer Bell and Thackeray must be conducting a violent love affair à la Rochester and Jane Eyre. The embarrassment caused Thackeray by this scandal was only exceeded by Charlotte's agony when she opened the great author's letter of thanks and read of the unfortunate coincidence between her fiction and his private life.

"Well may it be said that fact is often stranger than fiction!" she wrote Williams, January 28, 1848, severely dismayed at the unhappy turn her well-meant gesture had taken. "The coincidence struck me as equally unfortunate and extraordinary. Of course, I knew nothing whatever of Mr Thackeray's domestic concerns, he existed for me only as an author. . . .

"The very fact of his not complaining at all and addressing me with such kindness, notwithstanding the pain and annoyance I must have caused him, increases my chagrin. . . .

"Can you tell me anything more on this subject? or can you guess in what degree the unlucky coincidence would affect him—whether it would pain him too much and deeply: for he says so little himself on the topic, I am at a loss to divine the exact truth—but I fear . . ."[10]

In March she still brooded over the preface, confessing to Williams that to read it over caused her pain. She had written it in hot enthusiasm, fired over the revolutionary events transpiring in France, eager to plead the cause of truth and justice, ardent to raise Thackeray's standard as a champion of truth. She saw now that one could be enthusiastic about a writer dead a hundred years, but that to praise a living writer was a fault and a bore. "*Still*," she concluded with that stubborn self-conviction Cornhill had only begun to know, "I will *think* as I please."

Williams soothed and encouraged her. Of all the literary friends *Jane Eyre* made for her, W. S. Williams was the most satisfying. Her letters to him—more than a hundred over the years—illuminate a Charlotte Brontë that Ellen Nussey never knew. She was grateful to him with that unique gratitude one feels toward the discoverer of one's genius; she was delighted with his prompt, kindly, intelligent mind: "I cannot thank you sufficiently for your letters, and I can give you but a faint idea of the pleasure they afford me; they seem to introduce such life and light into the torpid retirement where we live like dormice."

As Smith, Elder's chief reader, Williams held a prominent position in the literary world of London. His enthusiasm for writers and literature dated from a boyish reverence for Coleridge, a reverence quickly extinguished when he met that tarnished angel of the dark glowing eyes, weak mouth, and ponderous bulk. He had seen Keats off on his ill-fated journey to Rome. He was on terms of friendship with Hazlitt, Leigh Hunt, and Ruskin. When Charlotte made his acquaintance by letter that winter of her success, he was forty-seven, a diffident intellectual, a firm liberal, and a family man. His official business with Charlotte was to urge and guide her toward producing more money-making novels for his firm. He did this, but his attentions went far beyond a commercial relationship.

He revived her when reviewers attacked *Jane Eyre* ("Your letter made me ashamed of myself that I should have uttered a murmur or expressed by any sign that I was sensible of pain from the unfavourable opinions of some misjudging but well-meaning people"); he described literary London for her ("You have raised the veil from a corner of your great world—your London—and have shown me a glimpse of what I might call loathsome, but which I prefer to call *strange*"); he argued the politics of the 1848 French Revolution (". . . every struggle any nation makes in the cause of Freedom and Truth has something noble in it . . . but I cannot believe that France—or at least Paris—will ever be the battle-ground of true Liberty"); he debated the question of his daughters' education ("If I might plead with you in behalf of your daughters, I should say, 'Do not let them waste their young lives in trying to attain manifold accomplishment. Let them try rather to possess thoroughly, fully, one or two talents'"). Most satisfying, he discussed with her the subject nearest her heart, literature. Charlotte answered his letters firmly, eloquently, perceptively. She possessed an almost uncanny ability to adapt her letters to her correspondent's mind. Writing to Henry Nussey, she had been a rather dull Christian moralist; to Miss Wooler, a respectful pupil; to Ellen, a feminine friend; to Mary Taylor, an ardent, intelligent, and discontented fellow sufferer. To Williams she wrote as an artist and intellectual. In these months his letters were the most tangible reward of fame.

His curiosity aroused by the mysterious correspondent he suspected to be a woman, Williams tried to lure Currer and his brothers
to London. Charlotte refused, reluctantly: "I should much—very
much—like to take that quiet view of the 'great world' you allude to,
but I have as yet won no right to give myself such a treat: it must
be for some future day—when, I don't know. Ellis, I imagine, would
soon turn aside from the spectacle in disgust. I do not think he admits
it as his creed that 'the proper study of mankind is man'—at least
not the artificial man of cities." This, then, was a point of disagreement
between Charlotte and Emily: "In some points I consider Ellis somewhat of a theorist," she continued: "now and then he broaches ideas
which strike my sense as much more daring and original than practical;
his reason may be in advance of mine, but certainly it often travels
a different road. I should say Ellis will not be seen in his full strength
till he is seen as an essayist."[11]

In all this novelty Ellen was not forgotten, although, not surprisingly, the correspondence from Haworth to Brookroyd subsided
that winter. Writing to thank Ellen for Christmas gifts—three watch-
guards, hand-worked out of glittering steel beads—Anne maintained
admirably the Brontë code of secrecy: "You do not tell us how *you*
bear the present unfavourable weather. We are all cut up by this cruel
east wind, most of us, *i.e.* Charlotte, Emily, and I have had the influenza, or a bad cold instead, twice over within the space of a few
weeks. Papa has had it once. Tabby has escaped it altogether. I have
no news to tell you, for we have been nowhere, seen no one, and done
nothing (to speak of) since you were here—and yet we contrive to be
busy from morning to night. Flossy is fatter than ever, but still active
enough to relish a sheep hunt. . . ."[12]

Branwell's behavior continued to be regulated by the supply of
money sent him by Lydia Robinson. When his cash was exhausted,
he lapsed into melancholy, irritation, and contrition, and the house
knew some quiet. When he could screw a sovereign out of his father
under false pretenses, or when an envelope filled with pound notes came
from Lydia Robinson's physician or lady's maid, he would immediately
take himself down to the Bull or over to Halifax to drink punch at
the Talbot with Leyland and other cronies. Returning home drunk,
lurching against the gate, stumbling up the stairs, he would proceed
to turn the quiet parsonage into bedlam. The red-brown drops of
laudanum he drank as a substitute route to oblivion quieted and nerved
him for a time, but brought fearful dreams, dreams echoing with vast
hollow sounds that menaced him as he climbed endless shifting stair-
ways and fell slowly headlong into bottomless abysses watched by
millions of gleaming winking eyes.[13] From these visions he would

wake sweating and in terror, and in need of a drink to steady his nerves. Frequently now, when drunk, he fell down in fits.

During one of these sessions Charlotte wrote Williams, defending her portrayal of Rochester's mad wife against critics who found the creature luridly overdrawn: "I agree with them that the character is shocking, but I know that it is but too natural. There is a phase of insanity which may be called moral madness, in which all that is good or even human seems to disappear from the mind and a fiend-nature replaces it. The sole aim and desire of the being thus possessed is to exasperate, to molest, to destroy, and preternatural ingenuity and energy are often exercised to that dreadful end. The aspect, in such cases, assimilates with the disposition; all seems demonised."[14] It was Branwell she described.

To make matters worse, the sisters now believed they had indisputable proof that Branwell was destroying himself for a worthless woman. Elizabeth and Mary Robinson wrote constantly to Anne, now condemning their mother for her weakness, perverseness, and deceit, for her heartlessness in breaking up the household and pawning them off on uncles or a grandmother. The mother herself had gone to live with a distant relative, Sir Edward Dolman Scott. Sir Edward's wife was dying. Her eye fixed firmly on Sir Edward, Lydia Robinson waited for the event. Obviously there was no truth to the story that her husband's will bound her to remain single on pain of disinheritance. Anne found herself in the painful position of counseling and comforting the two Robinson girls while keeping their confidences secret from Branwell when they might have arrested his suicidal course. But no: he would have believed no word against "his lady of grief." Besides, he found destroying himself for love easier than facing his deficiencies as a writer, painter, and human being.

Branwell, however, could not dominate Charlotte's life that season: she was much too preoccupied with the joys and pains of authorship. She felt a shock of pleasure one day when she came upon an elderly clergyman carrying in his hand a copy of *Jane Eyre*, and overheard him exclaim to a companion, "Why, they have got the Clergy Daughters' School, and Mr. Carus-Wilson here, I declare! and Miss Evans!" (the originals of Lowood, Mr. Brocklehurst, and Miss Temple). "I know them all; the portaits are faithful and just." She hid a smile as she heard him wonder aloud who this mysterious Currer Bell could be. She felt a shock of pain to read in a March issue of the *Christian Remembrancer* that Currer Bell seldom evokes religion in *Jane Eyre* "but for the purpose of showing that all Christian profession is bigotry and all Christian practice is hypocrisy." She comforted herself by defending her position spiritedly to Williams: she loved the Church of England—

the profane Athanasian creed excluded—but Currer Bell would not stint in criticizing its administration or administrators if the spirit moved him. More portraits like Brocklehurst's might very well appear: "if their brethren in general dislike the resemblance and abuse the artist—*tant pis!*"

A few corrosive reviews could not offset the fact that her novel was a triumphant success. *Jane Eyre* had even invaded Buckingham Palace. Queen Victoria, author of *Leaves from the Journal of Our Life in the Highlands* ("*We* authors, Ma'am," the politic Disraeli used to murmur in her ear), did not like or read much fiction, but read and liked Charlotte's novel. "Finished Jane Eyre," she recorded, "which is really a wonderful book, very peculiar in parts, but so powerfully and admirably written, such a fine tone it is, such fine religious feeling, and such beautiful writings. The description of the mysterious maniac's nightly appearances awfully thrilling, Mr. Rochester's character a very remarkable one, and Jane Eyre's herself a beautiful one. . . ." Jane's independence and rebelliousness evidently did not disturb Victoria. Or perhaps, since the Queen was that paradox —a powerful, autocratic woman who filled a man's role but nevertheless violently opposed women's emancipation ("Lady —— ought to get a *good whipping*," she raged in 1870 over a supporter of woman's suffrage. "It is a subject which makes the Queen so furious she cannot contain herself")—perhaps she was drawn to Charlotte's heroine, sensing danger only in that the book was "very peculiar in parts."[15]

And indeed, Charlotte did not fret over the reviews as much as she fretted over the problem of a worthy successor. One book just off the press, she could not rest on her laurels: she felt keenly the pressure a best seller levels on its author. Smith, Elder obviously expected great things of Currer Bell: Williams had written almost immediately proposing a serial. Charlotte vetoed this emphatically. She was no Dickens who could pour forth episode after episode under a deadline, working always with attention to sales, expanding one character if it proved popular, dropping another if it didn't take the public fancy, not knowing when he began, perhaps, where a story would end. Of her writing ability she had no doubts. But she lacked the vast experience and physical stamina of a Dickens. She must work slowly, at her own pace, not the public's. Her next novel must grow to maturity "as the grass grows or the corn ripens."

Chiefly she worried that her quiet life would not provide enough material for many novels. Lewes had already chided her for resorting to imagined rather than factual life in *Jane Eyre*. If she was not free to *imagine*, certainly her subject matter was circumscribed. Nor would she write a line that she did not personally *believe* to be truth, whether actual or invented. She could not explain to Williams, of course, how her sex kept her caged like an animal; she assured him instead that she would try to live up to the world's expectations: "Yet though I must limit my sympathies; though my observation cannot penetrate where the very deepest political and social truths are to be learnt; though many doors of knowledge which are open for you are for ever shut to me; though I must guess and calculate and grope my way in the dark . . . yet with every disadvantage, I mean still, in my own con-tracted way, to do my best. Imperfect my best will be, and poor, and compared with the works of the true masters—of that greatest modern master Thackeray in especial (for it is him I at heart reverence with all my strength)—it will be trifling, but I trust not affected or counter-feit."[16]

She had begun a new novel almost immediately after *Jane Eyre* appeared, making three starts, each of which displeased her. As an alternative to a new book, she looked over *The Professor* again; found the beginning weak and the narrative lacking in exciting incident. On the other hand, she judged the Belgian portions of the novel more real than much of *Jane Eyre*, the writing in those chapters her best, and the treatment of the teaching profession—an occupation seldom dealt with in fiction—fresh and original. But Smith, Elder would have none of *The Professor*, revised or unrevised, so she took up her new narrative again.

She had chosen a story based on the Luddite riots of 1811–13, events that had captured her imagination when as a child she had listened to her father's talk of the rough and desperate mill workers, their daring attack on Rawfold's mill at Liversedge, their futile attempts to storm the building and break the machinery, the wounded insurgents welter-ing in their own blood, the arrival of a scarlet-clad detachment of the Queen's Bays. Into this scheme she planned to work the story of an amazing young heiress, Shirley Keeldar—a woman bursting with health, confidence, and high spirits; a woman free equally to dream away an afternoon in luxurious indolence in the grass, or to swagger about in boots, directing the business of a large estate. The portrait was to be a loving re-creation of Emily, or what Charlotte believed Emily might be, given the blessings of prosperity and health. In Shirley Keeldar she would try to capture Emily's courage and lofty mind, her dreamy abstraction and energy, the insouciance that allowed her to refer to herself as "a gay young fellow."

In telling this story she abandoned one of her great strengths, first-person narrative, for an omniscient point of view. Scorning the type of woman novelist who writes blithely about experiences com-pletely alien to her (Mrs. Trollope and her *Factory Boy*, she felt, was a prime example), Charlotte searched the *Leeds Mercury* files for accounts of the Yorkshire riots. The subject, however, did not come naturally to her: on February 15, 1848, she wrote Williams that she was making slow progress thus far. In any event, she was not a writer who sat down to her desk at a regular hour every day. Sometimes days or weeks would pass during which she could not write a word; then inspiration would seize her, and she would write vigorously until the creative spurt was exhausted. She had written the whole Thornfield portion of *Jane Eyre* in this kind of inspired transport, never stopping until Jane left Rochester, finding herself exhausted and feverish for days afterward. So far her new novel had not gripped her imagination in the same way.

No matter. She must wait patiently for inspiration, trusting her genius, confident her narrative must grow like the green grass or the ripening corn.

# 15

〜〜〜〜〜〜〜〜

# *Revelations*

In April *Jane Eyre* went into a third edition with a prefatory note from Currer Bell "to explain that my claim to the title of novelist rests on this one work alone." *Wuthering Heights,* now selling very well, and *Agnes Grey,* selling well, were still attributed to Currer Bell by many critics and readers, although Charlotte had been startled and amused to find the tables turned in a January review in the *Athenaeum* and *Jane Eyre* given to Ellis Bell. Despite the confusion, the sisters still clung to their anonymity. " 'Currer Bell' only I am and will be to the Public," Charlotte wrote Williams in April, "if accident or design should deprive me of that name, I should deem it a misfortune—a very great one. Mental tranquility would then be gone; it would be a task to write, a task which I doubt whether I should continue. If I were known, I should ever be conscious in writing that my book must be read by ordinary acquaintances, and that idea would fetter me intolerably."[1]

In London the mystery of the Bells was as deep as ever, and the rumors as rife. Almost every writer found at one time or another *Jane Eyre, Wuthering Heights,* or *Agnes Grey* laid suggestively on his doorstep. At the same time, Currer Bell was relentlessly being tracked to his lair by curious Yorkshire locals who believed they had recognized the regional dialect, the originals of Thornfield Hall and Ferndean Manor in Norton Conyers and Wycoller Hall, or the Clergy Daughters' School and its directors. Ellen Nussey heard rumors that the famous Currer Bell was none other than a Haworth parson's daughter. Long suspicious, she intimated as much in a letter, at the same time expressing deep hurt at Charlotte's lack of confidence. Charlotte replied to this disturbing letter curtly, lying, of course, through her teeth:

April 28th, '48: Dear Ellen,—Write another letter and explain that last note of yours distinctly. If your allusions are to myself, which I suppose they are—understand this—I have given no one a right to gossip about me and am not to be judged by frivolous conjectures emanating from any quarter whatever. Let me know what you heard and from who you heard it.

You do wrong to feel any pain from any circumstance or to suppose yourself slighted. You can only chagrin me and yourself by such an idea—and not do any good or make any difference in any way.

C. Brontë.[2]

Charlotte's vehemence rose chiefly from her own conflict over the question of secrecy. Disguised as a man, she could speak her mind as a parson's daughter might tremble to do, and she treasured this freedom. But from childhood she had yearned for fame. Currer Bell's triumph was only half a victory since Charlotte Brontë could not claim it. At least she would have liked to tell Ellen, but Emily was adamant: the Bells must remain unknown. Two people, however, were let in on the secret. Mr. Brontë claimed afterward that he had known about the novel writing all along, had overheard his daughters reading their manuscripts aloud behind the dining-room door, but had never interfered, lest his adult cynicism dampen their youthful hopes. He did not suspect, however, that his eldest daughter was a published author until Charlotte informed him herself. The success of *Jane Eyre* established beyond a doubt, Emily and Anne, whose novels had not yet appeared, urged her to tell Papa the great news. Persuaded, she gathered together several reviews, including an adverse one, and took them with a copy of *Jane Eyre* into the parlor.

"Papa, I've been writing a book."

"Have you, my dear?"

"Yes, and I want you to read it."

"I am afraid it will try my eyes too much."

"But it is not in manuscript; it is printed."

"My dear! you've never thought of the expense it will be! It will be almost sure to be a loss, for how can you get a book sold? No one knows you or your name."

"But, papa, I don't think it will be a loss; no more will you, if you will just let me read you a review or two, and tell you more about it."

"So she sate down," wrote Mrs. Gaskell to whom Charlotte had later reported the incident, "and read some of the reviews to her father; and then, giving him the copy of *Jane Eyre* that she intended for him, she left him to read it. When he came in to tea, he said, 'Girls, do you know Charlotte has been writing a book, and it is much better than likely?' "[3]

Thus was the old man accustomed to credit the brilliance of his son at the expense of his daughters.

Another person was permitted to know the identity of Currer, Ellis, and Acton Bell:

Wellington, New Zealand, June to 24 July 1848: Dear Charlotte,—About a month since I received and read *Jane Eyre*. It seemed to me incredible that you had actually written a book. Such events did not happen while I was in England. I begin to believe in your existence much as I do in Mr Rochester's. In a believing mood I don't doubt either of them. After I had read [it] I went on to the top of Mt. Victoria and looked for a ship to carry a letter to you. There was a little thing with one mast, and also H.M.S. *Fly*, and nothing else. If a cattle vessel came from Sydney she would probably return in a few days and would take a mail, but we have had east wind for a month and nothing can come in.—[July 1.] The Harlequin has just come in from Otago and is to sail for Singapore *when the wind changes* and by that route (which I hope to take myself some time) I send you this. Much good may it do you.

Your novel surprised me by being so perfect as a work of art. I expected something more changeable and unfinished. You have polished to some purpose. If I were to do so I should get tired and weary every one else in about two pages. No sign of this weariness is in your book—you must have had abundance, having kept it all to yourself!

You are very different from me in having no doctrine to preach. It is impossible to squeeze a moral out of your production. Has the world gone so well with you that you have no protest to make against its absurdities? Did you never sneer or declaim in your first sketches? I will scold you well when I see you—I don't believe in Mr Rivers. There are no *good* men of the Brocklehurst species. A missionary either goes into his office for a piece of bread, or he goes from enthusiasm, and that is both too good and too bad a quality for St. John. It's a bit of your absurd charity to believe in such a man. You have done wisely in choosing to imagine a high class of readers. You never stop to explain or defend anything and never seem bothered with the idea—If Mrs Fairfax or any other well intentioned fool gets hold of this what will she think? And yet you know the world is made up of such, and worse. Once more, how have you written through 3 vols. without declaring war to the knife against a few dozen absurd do[ct]rines each of which is supported by "a large and respectable class of readers"? Emily seems to have had such a class in her eye when she wrote that strange thing Wuthering Heights. Ann too stops repeatedly to preach commonplace truths. She has had still a lower class in her mind's eye. Emily seems to have followed th[e b]ook seller's advice. As to the price you got it [was] certainly Jewish. But what could the people do? If they had asked you to fix it, do you know yourself how many cyphers your sum would have had? And how should they know better? And if they did, that's the knowledge they get their living by. If I were in your place the idea of being bound in the sale of 2! more would prevent from ever writing again. Yet you are probably now busy with another. . . .

I mention the book to no one and hear no opinions. I lend it a good deal because it's a novel and it's *as good as another!* They say "it makes them cry." They are not literary enough to give an opinion. If ever I hear one I'll embalm it for you.

As to my own affair I have written 100 pages and lately 50 more. It's no use writing faster. I get so disgusted I can do nothing. . . .

I have now told you everything I can think of except that the cat's on the table and that I'm going to borrow a new book to read. No less than an account of all the systems of philosophy of modern Europe. I have lately met with a wonder a man who thinks Jane Eyre would have done better [to] marry Mr Rivers! he gives no reasons—such people never do.

Mary Taylor.[4]

Feminist and political radical, Mary thus criticized Charlotte for shirking social issues in *Jane Eyre*. If she expected a didactic novel, a narrative constantly interrupted by opinionizing and moral-pointing, certainly she was disappointed. Charlotte herself admitted that her concern was with private rather than social rebellion. *Jane Eyre* is not a social tract; it is, as Mary recognized, a work of art. Curious, however, that she should have missed the radicalism inherent in a story of a plain, obscure, impoverished woman who by dint of will, energy, and a highly developed sense of selfhood triumphs over caste, wealth, and custom. Or that she did not applaud Jane's aggressiveness, which is so strong that she often plays roles that are traditionally male. Fictional love affairs do not usually begin with the heroine rescuing the hero, for example, but Charlotte's novel does as Jane helps the limping Rochester to remount his horse, which has stumbled and thrown him. He has hardly recovered from this mishap when Jane saves him again, this time from dying in a fire set by his mad wife. Her physical resourcefulness encourages Rochester to make her his moral counselor and soon she is reforming his philosophy and behavior. She is so much in control of their relationship, in fact, that her aggressive announcement of their union comes as a fitting climax: "Reader, I married him!" The great appeal of Jane's love affair with Rochester derives not from the often improbable romance enveloping it but from the fact that it unites a woman and man equal in mind, heart, and will. Every meeting between them scintillates, because they meet on common ground. Rochester has not been accustomed to thinking of women as equals, however. It is Jane's triumph that her courage, wisdom, and passion force the admission from him:

"Do you think, because I am poor, obscure, plain, and little, I am soulless and heartless? You think wrong!—I have as much soul as you,—

and full as much heart! And if God had gifted me with some beauty, and much wealth, I should have made it as hard for you to leave me, as it is now for me to leave you. I am not talking to you now through the medium of custom, conventionalities or even of mortal flesh:—it is my spirit that addresses your spirit; just as if both had passed through the grave, and we stood at God's feet, equal,—as we are!"

"As we are!" repeated Mr. Rochester. . . .[5]

Once Jane has consented to be his wife, however, Rochester slips back quickly into a dominating role. There is a debate whether the child, Adèle, will accompany them to Millcote; Rochester grows peremptory, Jane uneasy: "I half lost my sense of power over him." In the silk warehouse and the jeweler's shop in Millcote, Rochester turns sultanic, insisting that Jane allow him to heap her with rich pink and amethyst silks and costly jewels, until her cheeks burn "with a sense of annoyance and degradation," and she longs for a small income: "I never can bear being dressed like a doll by Mr. Rochester." At Thornfield, still in the interim before their marriage, Rochester insists that Jane give up governessing Adèle and spend all her hours with him; she refuses. He insists that she share his moods and passions; she puts him off. He plays her a ballad that ends, "My love has sworn with sealing kiss,/ With me to live—to die"; Jane informs him crisply that *she* has no intention of dying with him. Her decision to leave Thornfield upon discovering that Rochester has a wife is no sudden whim, therefore, but the culmination of a long struggle to preserve the self Rochester always threatens to obliterate with his own aggressive personality. Jane cannot live with him until he understands fully that her person and her rights are as important as his. Charlotte could not imagine any man learning this except by cataclysm. Only after fire, blinding, and mutilation is Rochester's male vanity humbled and Jane able to report that their married felicity is founded securely upon equality: "I am my husband's life as fully as he is mine."

Anne meanwhile had completed her second novel, a narrative written unhappily under a grim sense of duty to warn the world of the evils of drink. More than Charlotte and Emily, Anne had taken Branwell's dissolution to heart. His debauchery had cast a deep dark shadow across her already sensitive and morbid mind; she saw his disgrace not as a wreck of promise and character, like Charlotte, but as a mortal sin. In June *The Tenant of Wildfell Hall* was published by Newby. The novel scored an immediate success and notoriety: the unpleasant tale of a dipsomaniac and the miserable woman he persecutes did nothing to dispel the criticism that the Bells insisted on describing human nature at its dregs. One more novel by a Bell compounded the confusion over the authors' identity, a confusion the unscrupulous

Newby hastened to take advantage of. Advertising the new novel, he mingled blurbs from reviews of *Jane Eyre, Wuthering Heights,* and *Agnes Grey,* deliberately implying that all four novels proceeded from the same pen—an impossibly prolific one. He went further: negotiating with Harper Brothers in New York, a firm that had rejected *Agnes Grey* but accepted *Wuthering Heights,* he claimed that to the best of his knowledge *The Tenant of Wildfell Hall* was the work of Currer Bell, author of the famous best seller *Jane Eyre.*

This time Newby had gone too far. Dazzled by the American success of *Jane Eyre,* Harper Brothers had already negotiated with Smith, Elder for Currer's next novel. Was, Harpers asked, *The Tenant of Wildfell Hall* by Currer? If so, he had violated his contract with Smith, Elder by giving it to Newby. If the new novel was really Acton's, then Newby was caught in a lie. Smith, Elder immediately wrote to Currer, informing him that Newby announced himself the publisher of the new novel of Currer Bell under his other nom de plume of Acton. Smith, Elder stated tactfully that they would be glad to be in a position to contradict Newby, adding at the same time that they were quite sure his claim was false.

Charlotte received Smith's letter on Friday, July 7. Highly indignant, she immediately called a council with Emily and Anne. She had always mistrusted Newby. Now the professional honor of Currer Bell was in doubt. There was only one way to solve the Bell mystery: they must all go up to London and prove in the flesh that Currer, Ellis, and Acton were three.

Emily promptly and flatly refused to have any part of such an adventure. She hoarded her privacy as a miser hoards gold; she hated society—would have, in fact, none of it. Anne and Charlotte might go if they liked, but they would please keep her out of the picture. Ideally, three Bells were needed to substantiate the dramatic proof, but Charlotte was forced to be content with two. She and Anne packed a few things hurriedly and set out for London that very day, impelled by Charlotte's desire to confound Newby and vindicate Currer Bell, of course, but impelled even more strongly by Charlotte's great—though so far suppressed—desire for public recognition. Aloofness was Emily's forte, not Charlotte's. Anti-social, suspicious, neurotically shy, she paradoxically yearned for the world's approval.

Charlotte related the whole heady adventure to Mary Taylor two months later:

> Haworth, September 4th, 1848: Dear Polly . . . About two months since I had a letter from my publishers—Smith and Elder—saying that "Jane Eyre" had had a great run in America, and that a publisher there

had consequently bid high for the first sheets of a new work by Currer Bell, which they had promised to let him have.

Presently after came another missive from Smith and Elder; their American correspondent had written to them complaining that the first sheets of a new work by Currer Bell had been already received, and not by their house, but by a rival publisher, and asking the meaning of such false play; it enclosed an extract from a letter from Mr Newby . . . affirming that to the best of his belief "Jane Eyre," "Wuthering Heights," and "Agnes Grey," and "The Tenant of Wildfell Hall" (the new work) were all the production of one author.

This was a *lie*, as Newby had been told repeatedly that they were the production of three different authors, but the fact was he wanted to make a dishonest move in the game to make the public and the trade believe that he had got hold of Currer Bell, and thus cheat Smith and Elder by securing the American publisher's bid.

The upshot of it was that on the very day I received Smith and Elder's letter, Anne and I packed up a small box, sent it down to Keighley, set out ourselves after tea, walked through a thunderstorm to the station, got to Leeds, and whirled up by the night train to London with the view of proving our separate identity to Smith and Elder, and confronting Newby with his *lie*.

We arrived at the Chapter Coffee-House (our old place, Polly, we did not well know where else to go) about eight o'clock in the morning. We washed ourselves, had some breakfast, sat a few minutes, and then set off in queer inward excitement to 65 Cornhill. Neither Mr Smith nor Mr Williams knew we were coming—they had never seen us—they did not know whether we were men or women, but had always written to us as men.

We found 65 to be a large bookseller's shop, in a street almost as bustling as the Strand. We went in, walked up to the counter. There were a great many young men and lads here and there; I said to the first I could accost: "May I see Mr Smith?" He hesitated, looked a little surprised. We sat down and waited a while, looking at some books on the counter, publications of theirs well known to us, of many of which they had sent us copies as presents. . . .[6]

Unaware that the author who had overnight made the publishing reputation of Smith, Elder waited at this moment in his outer office, George Smith was bent over his desk that Saturday, rushed with correspondence and editorial work, anxious to finish up and go home for the weekend. He was twenty-four and unmarried, tall and a little stout. His handsome face was open and genial, his dark eyes shrewd. He was intelligent, aggressive, and very able. When only twenty, he had taken over his father's publishing business; almost singlehanded, he had set about making Smith, Elder a flourishing concern. Harassed with business, he was not pleased when his clerk tapped at the door,

George Henry Lewes—drawing by Anne Gliddon, 1840. Comparing this portrait with Branwell's paintings of Emily, it is easy to see why Charlotte was almost moved to tears by Lewes' face because it was "so wonderfully like Emily." BY COURTESY OF NATIONAL PORTRAIT GALLERY, LONDON

The churchyard and parsonage. The figure near the house may be Charlotte. PHOTO-
GRAPH FROM THE BRONTE PARSONAGE MUSEUM

Roe Head, Miss Wooler's school—
drawn by Anne Brontë. BY COUR-
TESY OF THE BRONTE SOCIETY

*The Poor Teacher*—by Richard Redgrave, 1843. A young governess, holding a black-bordered letter, longs for her family. The music on the piano is "Home Sweet Home."

The Heger Family—painting by Ange François, 1847, three years after Charlotte left Brussels. Monsieur Heger, looking as keen and dynamic as Charlotte described him, is to the left. COURTESY PHOTO SELECTION, BABLIN; AND RENE PECHÈRE, BRUSSELS

Pages of Charlotte's letter, in French, to Monsieur Heger, October 24, 1844. Madame Heger pieced together the torn letter: her stitches are clearly visible. BY COURTESY OF TRUSTEES OF THE BRITISH MUSEUM

The Pensionnat Heger, its gardens and walks, from the rear. PHOTOGRAPH FROM THE BRONTE PARSONAGE MUSEUM

Charlotte Brontë—crayon drawing by George Richmond, 1850. The portrait, gift of
George Smith to Mr. Brontë, hung in Charlotte's sitting room, was taken to Ireland by
Mr. Nicholls after Mr. Brontë's death, and was finally bequeathed to the National
Portrait Gallery by Nicholls. BY COURTESY OF NATIONAL PORTRAIT GALLERY, LONDON

Jane Eyre
by Currer Bell
Vol. I.

Chap. 1st

There was no possibility of taking a walk that day.
We had been wandering, indeed, in the leafless shrubbery
an hour in the morning; but since dinner ( Mrs Reed,
when there was no company, dined early) the cold winter
wind had brought with it clouds so sombre, a rain so pen-
etrating that further out-door exercise was now out of the
question.

I was glad of it; I never liked long walks, especially
on chilly afternoons; dreadful to me was the coming
in the raw twilight with nipped fingers and toes, and a
heart saddened by the chidings of Bessie, the nurse, and humbled by the consciousness of my physical inferiority to Eliza
and Georgiana Reed.

The said Eliza, John and Georgiana were now clustered round their mamma in the drawing-room:

First page of the manuscript of *Jane Eyre*. PHOTOGRAPH FROM THE BRONTE PARSONAGE MUSEUM

Interior of Old Haworth Church, built before 1500. The church was rebuilt in 1879; only the tower was retained. PHOTOGRAPH FROM THE BRONTE PARSONAGE MUSEUM

The Reverend Patrick Brontë, about 1860. BY COURTESY OF THE BRONTE SOCIETY

stuck in his head, and announced that two ladies wished to see him. "I was very busy," he recalled later, "and sent out to ask their names. The clerk returned to say that the ladies declined to give their names, but wished to see me on a private matter. After a moment's hesitation I told him to show them in. I was in the midst of my correspondence, and my thoughts were far away from 'Currer Bell' and 'Jane Eyre.' Two rather quaintly dressed little ladies, pale-faced and anxious-looking, walked into my room; one of them came forward and presented me with a letter addressed, in my own handwriting, to 'Currer Bell, Esq.' I noticed that the letter had been opened, and said, with some sharpness, 'Where did you get this from?' 'From the post-office,' was the reply; 'it was addressed to me. We have both come that you might have ocular proof that there are at least two of us.' This then was 'Currer Bell' in person."[7]

Charlotte's account of the meeting to Mary tallied closely with Smith's: " 'Is it Mr Smith?' I said, looking up through my spectacles at a tall young man. 'It is.' I then put his own letter into his hand directed to Currer Bell. He looked at it and then at me again. 'Where did you get this?' he said. I laughed at his perplexity—a recognition took place. I gave my real name: Miss Brontë. We were in a small room—ceiled with a great skylight—and there explanations were rapidly gone into; Mr Newby being anathematized, I fear, with undue vehemence. Mr Smith hurried out and returned quickly with one whom he introduced as Mr Williams, a pale, mild, stooping man of fifty, very much like a faded Tom Dixon. Another recognition and a long, nervous shaking of hands. Then followed talk—talk—talk; Mr Williams being silent, Mr Smith loquacious."

It was a woman's fate, then as now, to be judged by her looks rather than her mind, and George Smith's reaction to Charlotte was no exception: nothing about her struck him so much as the fact that she somehow sinned in not being pretty. "I must confess that my first impression of Charlotte Brontë's personal appearance was that it was interesting rather than attractive," Smith wrote in his memoirs. "She was very small, and had a quaint old-fashioned look. Her head seemed too large for her body. She had fine eyes, but her face was marred by the shape of the mouth and by the complexion. There was but little feminine charm about her; and of this fact she herself was uneasily and perpetually conscious. It may seem strange that the possession of genius did not lift her above the weakness of an excessive anxiety about her personal appearance. But I believe that she would have given all her genius and her fame to have been beautiful. Perhaps few women ever existed more anxious to be pretty than she, or more angrily conscious of the circumstance that she was *not* pretty."

Portraying George Smith later in *Villette* as Dr. John, Charlotte painted him as charming, virile, and shrewd, but egocentric and not very profound. His conclusion that Charlotte would have forfeited genius for beauty seems to bear out her characterization. Certainly she would have given a great deal for an attractive man who could look past her face and form into her mind and heart and love the beauties there. This the hero of *Villette* does, when, in startling metaphor, he opens Lucy Snowe's eyelids wide "with pitiless finger and thumb" and gazes deep through the pupil into her mind and heart to discover whether the ore of her soul is tarnished or true. But in real life Charlotte had long ago concluded that a man who could go beyond superficialities was as rare as Diogenes' honest citizen.

In their low, dark room at the Chapter Coffee House, the thrill of recognition past, Charlotte paid severely for her triumph. Social contact created tension, tension unstrung a delicate nervous system: violent migraine headache and vomiting followed.

> Mr Smith said we must come and stay at his house [Charlotte continued to Mary], but we were not prepared for a long stay and declined this also; as we took our leave he told us he should bring his sisters to call on us that evening. We returned to our inn, and I paid for the excitement of the interview by a thundering headache and harassing sickness. Towards evening as I got no better and expected the Smiths to call, I took a strong dose of sal-volatile. It roused me a little; still, I was in grievous bodily case when they were announced. They came in, two elegant young ladies, in full dress, prepared for the Opera—Mr Smith himself in evening costume, white gloves, etc. We had by no means understood that it was settled we were to go to the Opera, and were not ready. Moreover, we had no fine, elegant dresses with us, or in the world. However, on brief rumination I thought it would be wise to make no objections—I put my headache in my pocket, we attired ourselves in the plain, high-made country garments we possessed, and went with them to their carriage, where we found Mr Williams. They must have thought us queer, quizzical-looking beings, especially me with my spectacles. I smiled inwardly at the contrast, which must have been apparent, between me and Mr Smith as I walked with him up the crimson-carpeted staircase of the Opera House and stood amongst a brilliant throng at the box door, which was not yet open. Fine ladies and gentlemen glanced at us with a slight, graceful superciliousness quite warranted by the circumstances. Still, I felt pleasantly excited in spite of headache and sickness and conscious clownishness, and I saw Anne was calm and gentle, which she always is.

Still insisting upon anonymity, Charlotte and Anne took the name "Brown" for the occasion and met people under that disguise. In high-necked plain gowns and walking boots, she and Anne kept their self-possession among plumes, bare shoulders, opera sticks, and pearl-studded cravats. Only the splendor of the Opera House with its deep soft crimson carpets, crimson curtains, alabaster and gold-fluted ceilings, and its chandelier—"a mass, I thought, of rock-crystal, sparkling with facets, streaming with drops, ablaze with stars, and gorgeously tinted with dews of gems dissolved, or fragments of rainbows shivered"—took her breath away. Smith, escorting her up the majestic crimson stairway to their box, felt a tremor thrill the small figure at his side; his arm was involuntarily pressed as Currer Bell whispered, "You know I am not accustomed to this sort of thing."

The performance was Rossini's opera of the "Barber of Seville" [Charlotte continued], very brilliant, though I fancy there are things I should like better. We got home after one o'clock; we had never been in bed the night before, and had been in constant excitement for twenty-four hours. You may imagine we were tired.

The next day, Sunday, Mr Williams came early and took us to church. He was so quiet, but so sincere in his attentions, one could not but have a most friendly leaning towards him. He has a nervous hesitation in speech, and a difficulty in finding appropriate language in which to express himself, which throws him into the background in conversation; but I had been his correspondent and therefore knew with what intelligence he could write, so that I was not in danger of undervaluing him. In the afternoon Mr Smith came in his carriage with his mother, to take us to his house to dine. Mr Smith's residence is at Bayswater, six miles from Cornhill; the rooms, the drawing-room especially, looked splendid to us. There was no company—only his mother, his two grown-up sisters, and his brother, a lad of twelve or thirteen, and a little sister, the youngest of the family, very like himself. They are all dark-eyed, dark-haired, and have clear, pale faces. The mother is a portly, handsome woman of her age, and all the children more or less well-looking—one of the daughters decidedly pretty. We had a fine dinner, which neither Anne nor I had appetite to eat, and were glad when it was over. I always feel under an awkward constraint at table. Dining out would be hideous to me.

Mr Smith made himself very pleasant. He is a *practical* man. I wish Mr Williams were more so, but he is altogether of the contemplative, theorising order. Mr Williams has too many abstractions.

On Monday we went to the Exhibition of the Royal Academy and the National Gallery, dined again at Mr Smith's, then went home with Mr Williams to tea and saw his comparatively humble but neat residence and his fine family of eight children. A daughter of Leigh Hunt's was there. She sang some little Italian airs which she had picked up among the peasantry in Tuscany, in a manner that charmed me.

On Tuesday morning we left London laden with books which Mr Smith had given us, and got safely home. A more jaded wretch than I looked when I returned it would be difficult to conceive. I was thin when I went, but was meagre indeed when I reurned; my face looked grey and very old, with strange, deep lines ploughed in it; my eyes stared unnaturally. I was weak and yet restless. In a while, however, the bad effects of excitement went off and I regained my normal condition. . . .

Unharassed by Charlotte's love-hate for the world, Emily greeted them serenely, but hung on every detail of the wonderful journey. When Charlotte came to the moment of revelation, however, Emily bounded up in anger. What right had Charlotte to expose her identity! She had not given permission. Her anger was severe enough to prompt Charlotte to warn Williams against indiscretions in a letter written a day after Emily's thirtieth birthday:

> Permit me to caution you not to speak of my sisters when you write to me. I mean, do not use the word in the plural. Ellis Bell will not endure to be alluded to under any other appelation than the *nom de plume*. I committed a grand error in betraying his identity to you and Mr Smith. It was inadvertent—the words "we are three sisters" escaped me before I was aware. I regretted the avowal the moment I had made it; I regret it bitterly now, for I find it is against every feeling and intention of Ellis Bell.

Nor was Ellis Bell ever likely to be persuaded to come up to London to sample the social and literary life of that great metropolis.

> There would be an advantage in it [Charlotte wrote in reply to Williams' urging],—a great advantage; yet it is one that no power on earth could induce Ellis Bell, for instance, to avail himself of. And even for Acton and Currer, the experiment of an introduction to society would be more formidable than you, probably, can well imagine. An existence of absolute seclusion and unvarying monotony, such as we have long—I may say, indeed, ever—been habituated to, tends, I fear, to unfit the mind for lively and exciting scenes, to destroy the capacity for social enjoyment.
>
> The only glimpses of society I have ever had were obtained in my vocation of governess, and some of the most miserable moments I can recall were passed in drawing-rooms full of strange faces. At such times, my animal spirits would ebb gradually till they sank quite away, and when I could endure the sense of exhaustion and solitude no longer, I used to steal off, too glad to find any corner where I could really be alone. Still, I know very well, that though that experiment of seeing the world might give acute pain for the time, it would do good afterwards; and as I have never, that I remember, gained any important good without incurring proportionate suffering, I

mean to try to take your advice some day, in part at least—to put off, if possible, that troublesome egotism which is always judging and blaming itself, and to try, country spinster as I am, to get a view of some sphere where civilised humanity is to be contemplated.[8]

Disturbing as the London experience had proved, Charlotte almost immediately began to contemplate returning someday. Emily was perfectly content with the "unvarying monotony" of Haworth; indeed, she would have taken Charlotte sharply to task over the words. The changing face of the moors, the winds that swept the heights, the stars wheeling slowly past her bedroom window—this was not monotony but the rhythm of life itself. Charlotte too loved moors, wind, and stars; but she could not easily forget 65 Cornhill, a tall, astonished young publisher who gripped her hand with enthusiasm, and his admiring exclamation: "*You* are Currer Bell!"

# 16

## Death

At the height of his sisters' success, Branwell Brontë sank swiftly toward destruction. Had he possessed real literary or artistic talent, writing or painting might have deflected the agony of unrequited love. Had marriage with Lydia Robinson materialized, prosperity and happiness might have dulled the pangs of artistic failure. Had he not been cursed with a keen but morbid imagination, he might cheerfully have damned love and art to hell, and settled down to a less exalted lot in life. But seeds of greatness cankered in his soul. If he could not achieve brilliantly, he could destroy brilliantly. "Branwell is the same in conduct as ever," Charlotte wrote Ellen at the end of July 1848; "his constitution seems shattered. Papa, and sometimes all of us, have sad nights with him, he sleeps most of the day, and consequently will lie awake at night. But has not every house its trial?"[1]

Branwell's despair, had he known that the sisters who continued to bake bread, sweep the carpets, and turn his shirt collars were Currer, Ellis, and Acton Bell, is inestimable. For that reason, they kept all knowledge of their literary activity from him, hoping to spare him, in Charlotte's words, "too deep a pang of remorse for his own time misspent, and talents misapplied." Their silence had a deeper cause, however. Branwell had drifted beyond their respect and confidence: he had become, as Charlotte told Ellen, their phantom, their scourge, their skeleton behind the curtain.

Charlotte's contempt had been forcibly brought home to Branwell one afternoon early in his desperate career, and he complained of her coldness to his friend Searle Phillips, editor of the Leeds *Times*, over a bottle at the Black Bull. A young Sunday school pupil in the parish had fallen ill and seemed in danger of dying. ". . . I went to see the poor little thing, sat with her half an hour and read a psalm to her and a hymn at her request. I felt very much like praying with her too but you see I was not good enough. How dare I pray for another who had almost forgotten how to pray for myself? I came away with a heavy heart, for I felt sure she would die, and went straight home, where I fell into melancholy musings. I often do; but no kind word finds its way to my ears, much less to my heart. Charlotte observed my depression and asked what ailed me. So I told her. She looked at me with a look which I shall never forget, if I live to be a hundred years old—which I never shall. It was not like her at all. It wounded me, as if some one had struck me a blow in the mouth. It involved ever so many things in it. It was a dubious look. It ran over me, questioning and examining, as if I had been a wild beast. It said, 'Did my ears deceive me, or did I hear ought?' And then came the painful, baffled expression which was worse than all. It said, 'I wonder if that's true?' But, as she left the room, she seemed to accuse herself of having wronged me, and smiled kindly upon me and said, 'She is my little scholar and I will go and see her.' I said not a word. I was too much cut up. . . ." If Charlotte's cynicism was not like her, neither was Branwell's conduct like *him*, a point he refused to recognize. "When Charlotte was gone," he concluded, "I came over here to the Black Bull and made a night of it in sheer disgust and desperation. Why could they not give me some credit when I was trying so hard?"[2]

Now his only efforts were bent toward scraping up a few shillings to buy oblivion. Desperation made him preternaturally clever. When he could scrounge enough from Leyland (who would die in 1851 hounded by debts, many of which he assumed for Branwell Brontë), he fled to the Talbot over at Halifax where he drank until disorderly, then fell down jerking in fits. If he lacked the money or energy to get to Halifax, he crept down the dark cobblestone lane past the gravestones to the Bull where Anne the barmaid would serve him cheap gin and listen to his increasingly incoherent ramblings. The name of Lydia Robinson was sure to come up: "He loved that woman so, he would speak of her to a dog," said Anne. When no cash was forthcoming from Leyland, or Dr. Crosby, or Papa, Branwell could try his luck at coaxing a tiny vial of laudanum out of Bessy Hardacre at the chemist's across from the Bull. Or John Brown the sexton might be good for a touch:

> Dear John [Branwell wrote feverishly one Sunday morning, the bells of Haworth church ringing from the gray tower, his sisters bonneting and shawling themselves for church]—I shall feel much obliged to you if [you] can contrive to get me Five pence worth of Gin in a proper measure.

Should it be speedily got I could perhaps take it from you or Billy at
the lane top, or, what would be quite as well, sent out for, to you.

I anxiously ask the favour because I know the good it will do me.

*Punctually* at Half-past Nine in the morning you will be paid the
5d out of a shilling given me then.—

Yours,<br>P. B. B.[3]

If all these sources failed, the terrified man was left to face reality
naked and unarmed.

Meanwhile, the Robinson family were proceeding on their eminently pragmatic but not necessarily happy way. "Anne continues to
hear constantly, almost daily, from her old pupils, the Robinsons,"
Charlotte had written Ellen July 28. "They are both now engaged to
different gentlemen, and if they do not change their minds, which
they have done already two or three times, will probably be married
in a few months. Not one spark of love does either of them profess
for her future husband, one of them openly declares that interest
alone guides her, and the other, poor thing! is acting according to her
mother's wish, and is utterly indifferent herself to the man chosen for
her. . . . Of their mother I have not patience to speak; a worse
woman, I believe, hardly exists; the more I hear of her the more
deeply she revolts me; but I do not like to talk about her in a letter."[4] In August the event Lydia Robinson evidently calculated upon
occurred. "The unhappy Lady Scott is dead," Charlotte reported
August 18, "after long suffering—both mental and physical. I imagine
she expired two or three weeks ago. Mrs. Robinson is anxious to get
her daughters husbands of any kind, that they may be off her hands,
and that she may be free to marry Sir Edward Scott, whose infatu-
ated slave, it would appear, she is."[5] Had Charlotte loathed the lady
less, she might have seen that Lydia Robinson and her daughters
were indeed slaves, but slaves of a class system that bought and sold
women like the pieces of property they were. Her shame and grief
demanded a more tangible villain, however.

Laudanum robbed Branwell of appetite. He grew skeletal. His
clothes sagged from his emaciated frame and John Brown laughed
and asked him whether he was wearing his old man's coat, he looked
so lost in it. Sleeplessness and prolonged bouts of coughing dragged
him down into exhaustion. Francis Grundy had not responded to
Branwell's plea for a job, but came over from Skipton to see his bad,
mad friend. He had been up to the parsonage once before, remembered (inaccurately) three daughters "distant and distrait, large of
nose, small of figure, red of hair, prominent of spectacles; showing
great intellectual development, but with eyes constantly cast down,

very silent, painfully retiring." He had no love for Branwell's tall, stern father, however; and now sent up a note to "the great square, cold-looking Rectory" asking Branwell to come down and join him at the Bull.

"I had ordered a dinner for two," Grundy recalled, "and the room looked cosy and warm, the bright glass and silver pleasantly reflecting the sparkling firelight, deeply toned by the red curtains. Whilst I waited his appearance, his father was shown in. Much of the Rector's cold stiffness of manner was gone. He spoke of Branwell with more affection than I had ever heretofore heard him express, but he also spoke almost hopelessly. He said that when my message came, Branwell was in bed, and had been almost too weak for the last few days to leave it; nevertheless, he had insisted upon coming, and would be there immediately. We parted and I never saw him again.

"Presently the door opened cautiously, and a head appeared. It was a mass of red, unkempt, uncut hair, wildly floating round a great, gaunt forehead; the cheeks yellow and hollow, the mouth fallen, the thin white lips not trembling but shaking, the sunken eyes, once small, now glaring with the light of madness,—all told the sad tale but too surely. I hastened to my friend, greeted him in my gayest manner, as I knew he best liked, drew him quickly into the room, and forced upon him a stiff glass of hot brandy. Under its influence, and that of the bright, cheerful surroundings, he looked frightened—frightened of himself. He glanced at me for a moment, and muttered something of leaving a warm bed to come out into the cold night. Another glass of brandy, and returning warmth gradually brought him back to something like the Brontë of old. He even ate some dinner, a thing which he said he had not done for long; so our last interview was pleasant, though grave. I never knew his intellect clearer. He described himself as waiting anxiously for death—indeed, longing for it, and happy, in these his sane moments, to think that it was so near. He once again declared that that death would be due to the story I knew, and to nothing else. When at last I was compelled to leave, he quietly drew from his sleeve a carving-knife, placed it on the table and holding me by both hands, said that having given up all thoughts of ever seeing me again, he imagined when my message came that it was a call from Satan. Dressing himself, he took the knife, which he had long secreted, and came to the inn, with a full determination to rush into the room and stab the occupant. In the excited state of his mind he did not recognize me when he opened the door, but my voice and manner conquered him and 'brought him home to himself.' I left him standing bareheaded in the road, with bowed form and dropping tears. . . ."[6]

Shortly after the meeting with Grundy, Branwell left his bed again to go down into the village one day. William, John Brown's brother, came across the gaunt, wild-eyed creature in the lane struggling to get home, "quite exhausted, panting for breath, and unable to proceed." Throwing a sturdy arm around the parson's son, William helped him to the house. He would not leave it again alive.

On Friday, September 22, approaching death threw a softening shadow across Branwell's tormented mind. The mocker, blasphemer, and disbeliever who had not entered his father's church since William Weightman's funeral turned toward his father and admitted that, after all, he had faith in religion and its teachings. At the same time, he yielded to his sisters and struggled to tear apart the web of lies, cynicism, and resentment he had woven between them. Mr. Brontë rejoiced at this great change in his prodigal son, but Branwell had not really changed. From youth he had played at satanism, imagining himself as desperate and sinning as his Angrian alter ego, Percy, Earl of Northangerland. Now he doffed the mask of the profligate, and there was the real Branwell Brontë—insecure, craving for affection, and as terrified for his soul as any backsliding Christian. His atheism had not been the logical conclusion of a rational mind but the uneasy jeering of the parson's bad boy; his debauchery an impotent gesture of defiance at a world he was at once too exceptional and too weak to win.

On Sunday, September 24, John Brown went up to sit with his friend while the family prepared to go to church. Branwell was conscious and clear. "I've done nothing—either great or good," he told his tolerant and comfortable old companion. It was a confession he could not have made to his father. Then suddenly the last agony came on. He seized the sexton's hands, crying out, "Oh, John! I'm dying!"

John Brown started up and hastened to call the family. Mr. Brontë came, knelt stiffly by his son's bed, and bending his white head, prayed aloud. Charlotte, hovering near with Emily and Anne, heard with "painful, mournful joy" Branwell's murmured response, and, when his father's petition ceased, his faint "Amen."

Shortly after nine John Brown began to toll the passing bell from the tower of St. Michael's.

"I do not weep from a sense of bereavement—there is no prop withdrawn, no consolation torn away, no dear companion lost—but for the wreck of talent, the ruin of promise, the untimely dreary extinction of what might have been a burning and a shining light. My brother was a year my junior. I had aspirations and ambitions for him once, long ago—they have perished mournfully. Nothing remains of him but a memory of errors and sufferings. There is such a bitterness of pity for his life and death, such a yearning for the emptiness of his whole existence as I cannot describe."[7]

Branwell's wasted limbs had scarcely been composed when headache and nausea attacked Charlotte violently. By Monday she could not eat a morsel. On Tuesday she took to her bed with a bilious fever; she could not get up for a week.

She found quickly that the pain of remembering only Branwell's errors and sufferings was too great to bear: forgiveness must wash away her bitterness, and she did forgive. Gazing on his marble brow noble in death, "I felt as I had never felt before that there was peace and forgiveness for him in Heaven," she wrote Williams. "All his errors—to speak plainly—all his vices seemed nothing to me in that moment; every wrong he had done, every pain he had caused, vanished; his sufferings only were remembered. . . . Had his sins been scarlet in their dye—I believe now they are white as wool—He is at rest—and that comforts us all."[8]

Yet, casting her mind over the last grim years of her brother's debauchery, she could not help reflecting upon the injustice of her father's partiality for his reckless son; to compare his cool judgment on her achievement—"much better than likely"—with his impassioned cry for Branwell's folly—"my brilliant, unhappy son!"—his joy at Branwell's change of heart, his agony as he wept over the pale corpse, brought home forcefully the old man's preference. As the eldest daughter, almost a mother to Emily and Anne, she felt the injustice most since hers was the hardest servitude. She permitted a reference to this private grievance in a letter of October 2 to Williams: "My poor father naturally thought more of his *only* son than of his daughters, and, much and long as he had suffered on his account, he cried out for his loss like David for that of Absalom—my son! my son!—and refused at first to be comforted. And then when I ought to have been able to collect my strength and be at hand to support him, I fell ill. . . ."[9] For once, when Papa needed her, she did not respond.

Her illness lingered, and with it depression and an incapacity to write that tormented her. Currer Bell, as she sadly told Williams, was under a cloud. Although her identity was no longer a secret, she clung to the masculine name and pronoun as to a rock, submerged as she was in a rough sea of domestic distress. "Do not talk about not being on a level with Currer Bell, or regard him as 'an awful person,'" she told the diffident Williams, who continued to address her with great respect; "if you saw him now, sitting muffled at the fireside, shrinking before the east wind (which for some days has been blow-

ing wild and keen over our cold hills), and incapable of lifting a pen
for any more formidable task than that of writing a few lines to an indulgent friend, you would be sorry not to deem yourself greatly his
superior, for you would feel him to be a poor creature."[10] At times
like these she felt the schism between Charlotte Brontë, daughter, sister, and housekeeper, and Currer Bell, author, as wide as the ocean.

But Branwell's death was only the prologue to tragedy. His funeral had taken place on Thursday, September 28, a day of cold east
winds and soaking rain. Emily followed the casket through the graveyard to the church in the cold rain, sat in the damp icy church
through the service conducted by Mr. Brontë's old friend, William
Morgan, walked home again, shivering and wet. That night her fitful
cough sounded through the still house. October was a month of
damp, cold east winds, a month when fires burned low and sickly in
the grates and the stone floors of the parsonage exuded a deadly chill.
By the end of October Charlotte was deeply apprehensive. Emily had
grown thin and pale; her cold hung on obstinately. Whenever she
moved quickly, she gasped for breath and the involuntary movement
of her hand to her heart betrayed a sharp and recurring pain in her
chest.

She was obviously very ill, but the horror of the situation was that
she would not admit or discuss her illness with anyone. To Charlotte's
anxious questions, to her suggestions of remedies, she turned away her
white face and was silent. This inexplicable obstinacy terrified Charlotte more than the illness itself. It emphasized the impassable wall
of Emily's reserve, a wall Charlotte had never quite reached across,
try as she would. "Mine own Bonnie love," she had tenderly called
Emily long ago; but Emily had preferred Anne, a simpler, less demanding sister who could share the childlike part of Emily and leave
her mysteries alone. Now, to Charlotte's knowledge, even Anne was
excluded. Together they watched their beloved, inscrutable sister
drag herself about her daily chores, her face ashen, her breath catching, her hand wearily pushing back her heavy dark hair. Still she
baked fine white bread, carried broken bread and meat in her apron
to the dogs, and in the evenings, too languid to write, sat with her
workbasket before the fire. But her needlework often lay idle in her
thin hands as she stared into the firelight; then Charlotte and Anne
could only exchange secret, fearful glances: Emily's silence forbade
them to speak.

Emily had not needed ties with the world; now, it seemed, she
deliberately cut ties with the sisters who had been all in all to her.
This was cruel: she must know how her silence made *them* suffer.
"I would fain hope that Emily is a little better this evening," Charlotte
wrote Williams November 2, sitting at the dining-room table, her

anxious eyes constantly lifting from the page to Emily's thin, listless figure in the rocking chair, "but it is difficult to ascertain this. She is a real stoic in illness: she neither seeks nor will accept sympathy. To put any questions, to offer any aid, is to annoy; she will not yield a step before pain or sickness till forced; not one of her ordinary avocations will she voluntarily renounce. You must look on and see her do what she is unfit to do, and not dare to say a word—a painful necessity for those to whom her health and existence are as precious as the life in their veins. When she is ill there seems to be no sunshine in the world for me. The tie of sister is near and dear indeed, and I think a certain harshness in her powerful and peculiar character only makes me cling to her more. But this is all family egotism (so to speak)—excuse it, and, above all, never allude to it, or to the name Emily, when you write to me. I do not always show your letters, but I never withhold them when they are inquired after."[11]

November wore on to December. Lying awake at night listening to Emily's hoarse, wracking cough, Charlotte could not help reflecting on Branwell's suicidal destruction, or—a closer model—on the slow suicides of Emily's own Cathy and Heathcliff. Fiction had merged into reality: like her own characters, Emily seemed to have set her eyes on death, toward which she moved in a deep, impenetrable trance. Or was she simply trusting to nature to cure her, confident that the force she had so long worshiped would not betray her? To Charlotte, who wanted to win the world, not lose it, this intractability was terrifying because it was inexplicable.

November 23rd, '48: Dear Ellen,—Whatever my inclination may be to let all correspondence alone for the present, I feel that to *you* at least I ought to write a line. I told you Emily was ill, in my last letter. She has not rallied yet. She is *very* ill. I believe, if you were to see her, your impression would be that there is no hope. A more hollow, wasted, pallid aspect I have not beheld. The deep, tight cough continues; the breathing after the least exertion is a rapid pant; and these symptoms are accompanied by pains in the chest and side. Her pulse, the only time she allowed it to be felt, was found to beat 115 per minute. In this state she resolutely refuses to see a doctor; she will not give an explanation of her feelings, she will scarcely allow her illness to be alluded to. Our position is, and has been for some weeks, exquisitely painful. God only knows how all this is to terminate. More than once, I have been forced boldly to regard the terrible event of her loss as possible and even probable. But nature shrinks from such thoughts, I think Emily seems the nearest thing to my heart in this world. . . .[12]

[Undated] My Dear Ellen,—I mentioned your coming here to Emily as a mere suggestion, with the faint hope that the prospect might cheer her, as she really esteems you perhaps more than any other person out of this house. I found, however, it would not do; any, the slightest excitement or putting out of the way is not to be thought of, and indeed I do not think the journey in this unsettled weather, with the walk from Keighley and walk back at all advisable for yourself. Yet I should have liked to see you, and so would Anne. Emily continues much the same; yesterday I thought her a little better, but to-day she is not so well. I hope still—for I *must* hope—she is dear to me as life—if I let the faintness of despair reach my heart I shall become worthless. The attack was, I believe, in the first place, inflammation of the lungs; it ought to have been met promptly in time, but she would take no care, use no means; she is too intractable. I *do* wish I knew her state and feelings more clearly. The fever is not so high as it was, but the pain in the side, the cough, the emaciation are there still. . . .[13]

[To W. S. Williams] December 7th, 1848: My Dear Sir,—I duly received Dr Curie's work on Homoeopathy. . . . My sister has read it, but as yet she remains unshaken in her former opinion: she will not admit there can be efficacy in such a system. . . .

I can give no favourable report of Emily's state. My father is very despondent about her. Anne and I cherish hope as well as we can, but her appearance and her symptoms tend to crush that feeling. Yet I argue that the present emaciation, cough, weakness, shortness of breath are the results of inflammation, now, I trust, subsided, and that with time these ailments will gradually leave her. . . . I must cling to the expectation of her recovery, I cannot renounce it.

Much would I give to have the opinion of a skilful professional man. . . .[14]

[To W. S. Williams] December 9th, 1848: My Dear Sir,—Your letter seems to relieve me from a difficulty and to open my way. I know it would be useless to consult Drs Elliotson or Forbes: my sister would not see the most skilful physician in England if he were brought to her just now, nor would she follow his prescription. With regard to Homoeopathy, she has at least admitted that it cannot do much harm; perhaps if I get the medicines she may consent to try them; at any rate, the experiment shall be made.

Not knowing Dr Epps's address, I send the enclosed statement of her case through your hands. . . .[15]

December 9th, 1848. The patient, respecting whose case Dr. Epps is consulted, and for whom his opinion and advice are requested is a female in her 31st year. A peculiar reserve of character renders it difficult to draw from her all the symptoms of her malady, but as far as they can be ascertained they are as follows:

Her appetite failed; she evinced a continual thirst, with a craving for acids, and required a constant change of beverage. In appearance she grew rapidly emaciated; her pulse—the only time she allowed it to be felt—was found to be 115 per minute. The patient usually appeared worse in the forenoon, she was then frequently exhausted and drowsy; toward evening she often seemed better.

Expectoration accompanies the cough. The shortness of breath is aggravated by the slightest exertion. The patient's sleep is supposed to be tolerably good at intervals, but disturbed by paroxysms of coughing. Her resolution to contend against illness being very fixed, she has never consented to lie in bed for a single day—she sits up from 7 in the morning till 10 at night. All medical aid she has rejected, insisting that Nature should be left to take her own course. She has taken no medicine, but occasionally a mild aperient and Locock's cough wafers, of which she has used about 3 per diem, and considers their effect rather beneficial. Her diet, which she regulates herself, is very simple and light.

The patient has hitherto enjoyed pretty good health, although she has never looked strong, and the family constitution is not supposed to be robust. Her temperament is highly nervous. She has been accustomed to a sedentary and studious life.

If Dr Epps can, from what has here been stated, give an opinion on the case and prescribe a course of treatment, he will greatly oblige the patient's friends.

Address—Miss Brontë, Parsonage, Haworth, Bradford, Yorks.[16]

December 10th, 1848: My Dear Ellen,—I hardly know what to say to you about the subject which now interests me the most keenly of anything in this world, for, in truth, I hardly know what to think myself. Hope and fear fluctuate daily. The pain in her side and chest is better; the cough, the shortness of breath, the extreme emaciation continue. Diarrhoea commenced nearly a fortnight ago, and continues still. Of course it greatly weakens her, but she thinks herself it tends to good, and I hope so. I have endured, however, such tortures of uncertainty on this subject that at length I could endure it no longer; and as her repugnance to seeing a medical man continues immutable—as she declares "no poisoning doctor" shall come near her, I have written, unknown to her, to an eminent physician in London, giving as minute a statement of her case and symptoms as I could draw up, and requesting an opinion. I expect an answer in a day or two. . . .[17]

On Monday evening, December 18, Emily got up slowly from her chair and took herself painfully to the kitchen to fetch the bread and meat for Keeper's and Flossy's supper. Charlotte and Anne, following her, saw her stagger on the cold stone flags of the passage and fall against the wall. They rushed to her, but she motioned them off and went on. Shaking the scraps out of her apron, she gave the dogs their supper. That night Charlotte took a book of Emerson's essays sent by Cornhill and went up to read to her feverish sister, who had expressed once an interest in the American writer. Drawing a chair close to the bed, Charlotte read by candlelight until, glancing up through her spectacles, she saw Emily was not listening.

On Tuesday morning Charlotte and Anne woke to the sound of Emily moaning low in her sleep. Impelled by a strange urgency, Charlotte left the house to comb the frozen, winter-bare moors above the house for heather, believing that the sight of the well-loved moor heath would cheer and encourage her suffering sister. She could find only a sprig, but she brought it back and laid it on Emily's pillow. But Emily looked at the brown wisp with indifferent eyes.

Finally she rose and crawled weakly about the room, collecting her clothes and dressing herself. Martha had lit a fire in the hearth; she went to sit before it to comb her long brown hair. But the comb slipped from her nerveless fingers and, too weak to bend after it, she sat helplessly and watched it smolder. When Martha came up again, the nauseous stench of burnt bone filled the room. "Martha," said Emily, "my comb's down there; I was too weak to stoop and pick it up."

Eventually she came down the stairs slowly, past the grandfather clock, across the chilly passage, and into the dining room where Anne was dusting and Charlotte writing a letter. She took up her work-basket and tried to sew, but the needle was heavy. Charlotte watched her, sick with dread. Nevertheless she continued her letter to Ellen, her quill scratching in the silent room: "I should have written you before, if I had had one word of hope to say; but I had not. She grows daily weaker. The physician's opinion was expressed too obscurely to be of use. He sent some medicine which she would not take. Moments so dark as these I have never known. I pray for God's support to us all. Hitherto He has granted it—"[18] Fastening her winter cloak about her shoulders, she went down the lane into the village to post the letter.

It was getting on toward noon when she returned. One frightened glance at Emily's face told her she was worse. She writhed with pain she could no longer conceal. They helped her to the black horsehair sofa. Barely able to speak, she gasped out, "If you will send for a doctor, I will see him now!" It was too late. They tried to get her to bed, but she struggled in their hands, crying, "No, no!" She tried to rise of her own accord but fell back. She gasped now for life, "turning her dying eyes reluctantly from the pleasant sun." But by two o'clock she was dead.

Again the low gate swung back and another procession wound through the wintry graveyard to the church, Mr. Brontë walking behind the coffin with black-jowled Keeper at his heels, then Anne and Charlotte clinging together, young Martha and old Tabby following after.

[To W. S. Williams] December 25th, 1848: My Dear Sir,—I will write to you more at length when my heart can find a little rest—now I can only thank you very briefly for your letter, which seemed to me eloquent in its sincerity.

Emily is nowhere here now—her wasted mortal remains are taken out of the house; we have laid her cherished head under the church aisle beside my mother's, my two sisters', dead long ago, and my poor, hapless brother's. But a small remnant of the race is left—so my poor father thinks.

Well—the loss is ours—not hers, and some sad comfort I take, as I hear the wind blow and feel the cutting keenness of the frost, in knowing that the elements bring her no more suffering—their severity cannot reach her grave—her fever is quieted, her restlessness soothed, her deep, hollow cough is hushed for ever; we do not hear it in the night nor listen for it in the morning; we have not the conflict of the strangely strong spirit and the fragile frame before us—relentless conflict—once seen, never to be forgotten. A dreary calm reigns round us, in the midst of which we seek resignation.

My father and my sister Anne are far from well—as to me, God has hitherto most graciously sustained me—so far I have felt adequate to bear my own burden and even to offer a little help to others—I am not ill,—I can get through daily duties—and do something toward keeping hope and energy alive in our mourning household. My father says to me almost hourly, "Charlotte, you must bear up—I shall sink if you fail me." These words—you can conceive are a stimulus to nature. The sight too of my sister Anne's very still but deep sorrow wakens in me such fear for her that I dare not falter. Somebody *must* cheer the rest.

So I will not now ask why Emily was torn from us in the fulness of our attachment, rooted up in the prime of her own days, in the promise of her powers—why her existence now lies like a field of green corn trodden down—like a tree in full bearing—struck at the root; I will only say, sweet is rest after labour and calm after tempest, and repeat again and again that Emily knows that now.—Yours sincerely,

C. Brontë.[19]

The death of Branwell was pitiful; the death of Emily tragic. A rare personality was gone. Even Ellen Nussey, unimaginative and an outsider, had felt Emily's powerful, unearthly charm: "Few people have the gift of looking and smiling as she could look and smile. One of her rare expressive looks was something to remember through life, there was such a depth of soul and feeling, and yet a shyness of revealing herself." More than this, the death of Emily meant the death of Ellis Bell. Charlotte did not fully understand *Wuthering Heights* or the poems, would even apologize publicly for the crudity of Heathcliff, but she recognized the high genius of her sister. It was Emily's great gift to understand that the spiritual mysteries of life are made tangible in simple, daily, natural things— snow, hearth fire, gate, wind, stable, heath blossom, linnet. Her novel is a triumph of realistic art because its clear, homely, concrete detail has the power to evoke mysteries beyond the visible—mysteries of love, hate, suffering, and the yearning of the spirit for immortality. In this the novel and poems are like their creator: at once a homely, simple girl who baked white bread, ironed and starched and sewed, picked the black currants, whistled to the dogs, and lay on her back in the heather to hear the lark's song pouring through the air; and a silent, aloof being whose mind, unfettered from the daily fret and care of ordinary mortals, ranged far into the mysteries of nature to commune with the soul of things—a shy yet strong creature, curiously compounded of love and hate, kindness and indifference, pride and humility.

The fact that the world misunderstood or denied her genius did nothing to persuade Emily to live. She died, Matthew Arnold was to write, "baffled, unknown, self-consumed." Among the five clippings Charlotte found in her desk box was a review of *Wuthering Heights* and *Agnes Grey* from the *Atlas* of January 22, 1848: "One thing is certain," announced the critic; "as in the poems, so in the novels, the signature of 'Currer Bell' is attached to pre-eminently the best performance. . . ."[20] During that crucial November when Emily might have sought medical help to arrest galloping consumption had she a will to, four more reviews arrived at the parsonage praising Currer at the expense of Ellis. "Blind is he as any bat, insensate as any stone, to the merits of Ellis," Charlotte raged against the critic of the *Revue des Deux Mondes* to Williams. "He cannot feel or will not acknowledge that the very finish and *labor limae* which Currer wants, Ellis has; he is not aware that the 'true essence of poetry' pervades his compositions. Because Ellis's poems are short and abstract, the critics think them comparatively insignificant and dull. They are mistaken."[21] Did Emily find Charlotte's own praise a little patronizing, the overflow of Currer Bell's full cup of fame? No genius can be indifferent to the world's verdict. However aloof Emily seemed, the little sheaf of clippings that Charlotte sadly lifted from her dead sister's desk box testified mutely that she was far from indifferent.

In January Charlotte herself was attacked by the most venomous notice of *Jane Eyre* yet to appear. Like her enemy in the *Christian Remembrancer*, the anonymous critic of the *Quarterly* was a woman. John Lockhart, editor of the *Quarterly Review*, had sent Elizabeth

Rigby *Jane Eyre* and *Vanity Fair* to review with high praise for
Currer Bell: in his opinion, "Miss Jane Eyre was worth fifty Trollopes
and Martineaus rolled into one counterpane, with fifty Dickens and
Bulwers to keep them company. But she is rather a brazen minx."[22]
Elizabeth Rigby agreed only that Jane Eyre was a brazen minx.

Comparing Charlotte's novel unfavorably with *Vanity Fair*, Rigby
launched into a tirade against the author or authoress (for the question
of Currer Bell's sex had still not been solved) as a person who, with
great mental powers, combined "a total ignorance of the habits of
society, a great coarseness of taste, and a heathenish doctrine of religion"; a writer whose "animal" characters were "too odiously and
abominably pagan to be palatable even to the most vitiated class of
English readers." Warming to her theme, the reviewer pronounced
*Jane Eyre* pre-eminently anti-Christian: "There is throughout it a
murmuring against the comforts of the rich and against the privations
of the poor, which, as far as each individual is concerned, is a murmuring against God's appointment—there is a proud and perpetual assertion
of the rights of man, for which we find no authority either in God's
word or in God's providence—there is that pervading tone of ungodly
discontent which is at once the most prominent and the most subtle
evil which the law and the pulpit, which all civilized society in fact
has at the present day to contend with . . . which has overthrown
authority and violated every code human and divine abroad, and
fostered Chartism and rebellion at home. . . ." Rigby concluded with
a carefully poisoned barb: ". . . if we ascribe the book to a woman
at all, we have no alternative but to ascribe it to one who has, for some
sufficient reason, long forfeited the society of her own sex."

Had she not been numb with private grief, the *Quarterly Review*,
as Charlotte told Williams, would have sickened her indescribably. She
would find, however, when the pain of bereavement subsided, that her
indignation at the anonymous review rankled deeply. Not all Williams'
tact would be able to persuade her not to lash back.

After Emily's death, Anne moved into her vacant chair before the
fire, and Charlotte noticed with some horror that her youngest sister
was not well. The little cough, the small appetite, the tendency to
take cold—seemingly innocent symptoms—now took on a sinister
familiarity. The two of them now occupied the dining room alone
during long, wintry evenings, but they did not talk eagerly of books,
and reviews, and writing, or even bend their heads together over
French or German books: Anne seemed too listless to write or read
or even to talk. Instead she rocked absently, staring into the fire, griev-
ing quietly for her lost sister.

She admitted she was ill. Unlike Emily, she readily consented to see a doctor. Dr. Teale, a skilled medical man, came over from Leeds, examined her chest with a stethoscope, and pronounced a verdict of advanced consumption. She had not, he told the pretty, delicate young woman, long to live. The news drew Mr. Brontë out of his parlor into the dining room where Anne still sat on the black horsehair sofa where the doctor had examined her. "My *dear* little Anne!" he said, taking her hands in his. There was nothing else to say. Wearily, out of principle rather than conviction, Charlotte refused to give up hope but, lying awake at night listening to Anne's suppressed but relentless cough, she feared. "I must not look forwards, nor must I look backwards," she told Williams, her faithful correspondent through these nightmare months. "Too often I feel like one crossing an abyss on a narrow plank—a glance around might quite unnerve."[23]

Anne submitted quietly to treatment: she was as co-operative as Emily had been stubborn. To Charlotte's inexpressible relief she talked about her illness: "The agony of forced, total neglect, is not now felt, as during Emily's illness," Charlotte told Ellen. The remedies were, of course, useless—blisters, cod-liver oil that smelled and tasted like train oil, carbonate of iron, draftless rooms, a respirator that Ellen procured and sent over to Haworth. The cod-liver oil, far from helping, nauseated Anne so much that she could not eat. Hydropathy was recommended. Appalled at what was happening to the family of Smith, Elder's best-selling writer, Williams again urged homeopathy, the currently popular method of treating a disease with the very drugs that would produce symptoms of the disease in healthy persons. Charlotte thanked him for his advice but declined: so many people were suggesting so many cures; they could not try them all. Anne was now feeling some benefit from Gobold's Vegetable Balsam; if she thought it helped, let her continue it. Most of all, she looked forward to a change of air: she had set her heart on going to Scarborough.

Ellen wrote, kindly offering Brookroyd as a place of convalescence, but Charlotte firmly vetoed this suggestion. Anne was encouraged by Ellen's sympathy, however, and asked her to go along as a companion on the Scarborough journey, since Charlotte could not leave Papa, who was ailing and depressed. Charlotte wrote privately to Ellen, begging her to reject Anne's request; she had no notion of the situation: Anne might die on her hands. Seeing the wisdom of Charlotte's objection, Ellen evaded Anne's proposal, pleading visitors in May. Anne returned a dignified, moving reply:

> And then your going with me before the end of May is apparently out of the question, unless you are disappointed in your visitors; but I should be reluctant to wait till then if the weather would at all

permit an earlier departure. You say May is a trying month, and so say others. The early part is often cold enough, I acknowledge, but according to my experience, we are almost certain of some fine warm days in the latter half, when the laburnums and lilacs are in bloom; whereas June is often cold, and July generally wet. But I have a more serious reason than this for my impatience of delay. The doctors say that change of air or removal to a better climate would hardly ever fail of success in consumptive cases, if the remedy be taken *in time;* but the reason why there are so many disappointments is that it is generally deferred till it is too late. Now I would not commit this error; and, to say the truth, though I suffer much less from pain and fever than I did when you were with us, I am decidedly weaker, and very much thinner. My cough still troubles me a good deal, especially in the night, and, what seems worse than all, I am subject to great shortness of breath on going up stairs or any slight exertion. Under these circumstances, I think there is no time to be lost. I have no horror of death: if I thought it inevitable, I think I could quietly resign myself to the prospect, in the hope that you, dear Miss Nussey, would give as much of your company as you possibly could to Charlotte, and be a sister to her in my stead. But I wish it would please God to spare me not only for papa's and Charlotte's sakes, but because I long to do some good in the world before I leave it. I have many schemes in my head for future practice, humble and limited indeed, but still I should not like them all to come to nothing, and myself to have lived to so little purpose. But God's will be done. . . .[24]

The thought of the Scarborough journey distressed Charlotte unutterably, convinced as she was that her sister could not outrun death. Anne herself could not understand Charlotte's reluctance to let her leave home; did not comprehend that death was written on her sunken cheeks and her wasted arms, no thicker now than a little child's. Charlotte stalled for time: ". . . if she leaves home, it certainly should not be in the capricious month of May which is proverbially trying to the weak," she urged to Ellen. "—June would be a safer month—if we could reach June—I should have good hopes of her getting through the summer. Write such an answer to this note as I can shew Anne. . . ."[25]

The fine spring weather Charlotte had hoped so much from proved more trying to Anne than the cold. The pain in her side became rending, emaciation quickened, and though she went out every day with Charlotte to support her, they crept across the grass plot in front of the house rather than walked. The symptoms that marked Emily in her last days—evening fever, sleepless nights, morning lethargy—now marked Anne. Charlotte gave up arguing about the journey: rooms were engaged at No. 2 Cliff, Scarborough, paid for out of a small legacy Anne had just received from her godmother, Miss Fanny Outhwaite of Bradford. Papa agreed that Charlotte could leave him. Tabby was too old and lame to stir often from her chair by the kitchen fire, but Martha Brown was strong and able, and could care for his needs for a time. Ellen agreed to accompany them. They would leave Haworth May 23, rest a night in York, and proceed to Scarborough the next day.

Amidst this distress, Cornhill could not refrain from reminding Currer Bell that the world and Smith, Elder awaited a new success from the author of *Jane Eyre*. A pity he had so many domestic crises to distract him from business. In lieu of a new work, Smith was considering a cheap edition of *Jane Eyre;* what did Currer think? Although her new manuscript was gradually taking shape even in the midst of personal tragedy, Charlotte could promise nothing under the circumstances. Her inability to work tortured her; she wrote, however, a dignified defense of her position:

I hope Mr Smith will not risk a cheap edition of "Jane Eyre" yet; he had better wait awhile—the public will be sick of the name of that one book. I can make no promise as to when another will be ready—neither my time nor my efforts are my own. That absorption in my employment to which I gave myself up without fear of doing wrong when I wrote "Jane Eyre," would now be alike impossible and blamable; but I do what I can, and have made some little progress. We must all be patient.

Meantime, I should say, let the public forget at their ease, and let us not be nervous about it; and as to the critics, if the Bells possess real merit, I do not fear impartial justice being rendered them one day. I have a very short mental as well as physical sight in some matters, and am far less uneasy at the idea of public impatience, misconstruction, censure, etc., than I am at the thought of the anxiety of those two or three friends in Cornhill to whom I owe much kindess, and whose expectations I would earnestly wish not to disappoint. If *they* can make up their minds to wait tranquilly, and put some confidence in my goodwill, if not my power, to get on as well as may be, I shall not repine; but I verily believe that the "nobler sex" [Charlotte called it "the coarser sex" when writing to Ellen or Miss Wooler] find it more difficult to wait, to plod, to work out their destiny inch by inch, than their sisters do. They are always for walking so fast and taking such long steps, one cannot keep up with them. One should never tell a gentleman that one has commenced a task till it is nearly achieved. Currer Bell, even if he had no let or hindrance, and if his path was quite smooth, could never march with the tread of a Scott, a Bulwer, a Thackeray, or a Dickens. I want you and Mr Smith clearly to understand this. I have always wished to guard you against exaggerated anticipations—calculate low when you calculate on me. An honest man—and woman too—would always rather rise above expectation than fall below it.

Have I lectured enough—and am I understood? . . .[26]

The last week of May, the month of white hawthorn blossom, lilacs, and skylark song, Charlotte and Anne prepared to set out for Scarborough, Anne weak but hopeful, Charlotte beyond hope and fear. They were to meet Ellen at Leeds on Wednesday the twenty-third. "I fear you will be shocked when you see Anne," Charlotte had warned her friend, "but be on your guard, dear Ellen, not to express your feelings. . . ." On Wednesday, however, Anne was too faint to start; consequently Ellen waited for hours at Leeds until, dreading the worst, she set out for Haworth.[27] She arrived on Thursday just as Charlotte, Martha, and the curate Nicholls were helping Anne, wasted and fainting, into a waiting chaise. The carriage moved off, Anne too weak to bid good-by. Nicholls knelt, restraining Flossy, who would have rushed down the lane after his mistress; Tabby and Martha watched the chaise disappear around the corner, knowing they would never see the youngest daughter alive again. The journey was not the horror Charlotte had imagined it, however. Train passengers, catching one glimpse of Anne's death-marked face, gave up their places; strong arms lifted her in and out of railway coaches and carried her across the lines. At York she miraculously revived, and asked to be taken to the Minster, which had awed and excited her religious nature in the past. This time, weakness and emotion choked her as she gazed at the soaring spires and magnificent stained glass windows. "If finite power can do this, what is the . . . ?" she began, but could not finish.

"Our lodgings are pleasant," Charlotte wrote Williams Sunday morning, May 27. "As Anne sits at the window she can look down on the sea, which this morning is calm as glass. She says if she could breathe more freely she would be comfortable at this moment—but she cannot breathe freely."[28] The previous day Anne had driven in a donkey cart on the sands, taking the reins herself in gentle protest because she thought the driver too rough on the little beast. This morning she had begged to go to church, but Charlotte and Ellen had firmly dissuaded her from such exertion. Sunday afternoon she walked a little on the sands. All this might have been flattering, but under the temporary surge of vitality, her strength ebbed inexorably away. Visitors looked askance at the invalid, and solicitously whispered to the poor sister that she must not expect to have her long. On Sunday evening the sun went down in a blaze of gold and red that gilded the castle on the cliff and touched with fire the little boats rocking off shore on the ebbing tide. It glowed on Anne's pale cheeks when her chair was brought up to the window so she might look upon the splendid sunset. She was calm, but with vague premonition wondered whether they should start for home next day, not on her account, but Charlotte's.

The next morning she was no worse. At eleven o'clock, however, she felt a change come over her. Could they start for home immediately?—she knew she was going to die. A physician was summoned; she begged him for the truth; he admitted she was dying. At these words, she became tranquil until the death throes began. Charlotte and Ellen carried her to the sofa. "Are you more comfortable now?" Ellen asked anxiously. Anne gave her a grateful look: "It is not *you* who can give me ease, but soon all will be well, through the merits of our Redeemer." Seeing her sister's grief-twisted face, she whispered, "Take courage, Charlotte; take courage." So saying, she died peacefully without a sigh.

[To W. S. Williams] 2, Cliff, Scarbro', June 4th, 1849: My Dear Sir . . . You have been informed of my dear sister Anne's death. Let me now add that she died without severe struggle, resigned, trusting in God—thankful for release from a suffering life—deeply assured that a better existence lay before her. She believed, she hoped—and declared her belief and hope with her last breath. Her quiet, Christian death did not rend my heart as Emily's stern, simple, undemonstrative end did. I let Anne go to God, and felt He had a right to her. I could hardly let Emily go. I wanted to hold her back then, and I want her back now. Anne, from her childhood, seemed preparing for an early death. Emily's spirit seemed strong enough to bear her to fulness of years. They are both gone, and so is poor Branwell, and Papa has now me only—the weakest, puniest, least promising of his six children. Consumption has taken the whole five.

For the present Anne's ashes rest apart from the others. I have buried her here at Scarbro', to save Papa the anguish of the return and a third funeral. . . .

I have heard from Papa. He and the servants knew when they parted from Anne they would see her no more. All tried to be resigned. I knew it likewise, and I wanted her to die where she would be happiest. She loved Scarbro'. A peaceful sun gilded her evening.[29]

Anne's resignation to illness, her quiet death were harder won, however, than Charlotte knew. "A dreadful darkness closes in/On my bewildered mind," she had written during those death-stricken months; "O let me suffer, and not sin,/Be tortured, yet resigned." Charlotte did rather underestimate young Anne.

Always spared and shielded by Charlotte, Papa now wrote, granting her permission to stay on at Scarborough until her nerves and health were better restored. This she did, sending meanwhile one of her considerate little notes to Martha, begging her not to tire herself too much with the cleaning, signing it "your sincere friend."

On Thursday, June 21, she came home to Papa, Tabby, Martha, and the dogs. She was welcomed like the sole survivor of a shipwreck, but there were dark mutterings in the kitchen against her for not having brought poor Anne home to rest her head next to the others, where she belonged.

> I got home a little before eight o'clock. All was clean and bright waiting for me—Papa and the servants were well—and all received me with an affection which should have consoled. The dogs seemed in strange ecstasy. I am certain they regarded me as the harbinger of others—the dumb creatures thought that as I was returned—those who had been so long absent were not far behind.
>
> I left Papa soon and went into the dining-room—I shut the door—I tried to be glad that I was come home—I have always been glad before—except once—even then I was cheered, but this time joy was not to be the sensation. I felt that the house was all silent—the rooms were all empty—I remembered where the three were laid—in what narrow dark dwellings—never were they to reappear on earth. So the sense of desolation and bitterness took possession of me—the agony that *was to be undergone*—and *was not* to be avoided came on—I underwent it and passed a dreary evening and night and a mournful morrow—to-day I am better.
>
> I do not know how life will pass—but I certainly do feel confidence in Him who has upheld me hitherto. Solitude may be cheered and made endurable beyond what I can believe. The great trial is when evening closes and night approaches—At that hour we used to assemble in the dining-room—we used to talk—Now I sit by myself—necessarily I am silent—I cannot help thinking of their last days—remembering their sufferings and what they said and did, and how they looked in mortal affliction—perhaps all this will be less poignant in time.
>
> Let me thank you once more, dear Ellen, for your kindness to me which I do not mean to forget—How did they think you looking at home? Papa thought me a little stronger—he said my eyes were not so sunken. I am glad to hear a good account of your Mother and a tolerable one of Mercy. . . . Give my love to her and to all. . . .[30]

Thus in eight months, September 24 to May 28, Branwell, Emily, and Anne were all swept away, Branwell only thirty-one, Emily thirty, and Anne twenty-nine. Brief as their lives were, all three had bettered the 25.8 years' average life expectancy of Haworth residents. Harsh climate, poor sanitation, crowded living conditions, and poverty took their toll of the population. Measles, croup, whooping cough, scarlet fever, enteric fever, typhoid fever, bronchitis, diarrhea, diphtheria, rheumatic fever, tuberculosis—all raged though the villages of Yorkshire, all fatal diseases.

The worst evil was contaminated water. Mr. Brontë had sent off letters of complaint to London in the past. Now in August 1849, two months after Anne's death, he collected 222 signatures on a petition to the General Board of Health. The petition brought Superintending Inspector Benjamin Herschel Babbage north to Haworth in 1850. He found 316 houses in Haworth sharing 69 privies (no water closets existed); in one case twenty-four families used the same privy. One privy "perched upon an eminence commanding the whole length of the main street"; underneath festered a cesspool that could and did overflow. He found an open channel running down the steep main street, a sluice for refuse of all descriptions. There were no sewers. He found 50 middensteads, one in the West Lane behind the parsonage heaped with entrails, slaughterhouse refuse, and "green meat." He found 23 manure piles. He found 11 pumps (2 out of order) that gave up impure water. Fastidious villagers walked half a mile to the Head Well to draw their water, which nevertheless was scanty in the summer and occasionally so green and putrid that cattle refused to drink it. The parsonage boasted a pump in the kitchen—the well sunk in ground just yards from the cemetery.[31]

Babbage shook his head over the graveyard that crowded the parsonage, a site that had seen 1,344 burials in the last ten years alone, and drew up a memorandum condemning the use of large, flat stones as grave covers: "This practice is a very bad one as it prevents that access of atmospheric air to the ground, which is necessary for promoting decomposition; and, besides, the stones take the place of those grasses and shrubs which, if planted there, would tend to absorb the gases evolved during decomposition, and render the process less likely to contaminate the atmosphere."[32]

In her grief, Charlotte did not calculate the fatal forces that cut down her brother and sisters: the diseased air and water of Haworth, the weak constitutions, their own self-destructiveness—moral weakness in Branwell's case, stoicism in Emily's, religious melancholy in Anne's. She knew only that "in the very heat and burden of the day, the labourers had failed over their work"; and she was alone.

# 17

## Shirley

The leader, the driving force that had propelled the sisters to success, was now alone. Charlotte had been the first to leave home to earn a wage, the first to dream of a school of their own, the impetus that took them to Brussels, the energy behind the ill-fated "Misses Brontë's Establishment," the instigator of their first publishing venture, the sister whose novel had led them all to fame. During October, November, and December of 1848 while Emily was dying, she had put aside her new work, too sick at heart to write a line. In January she had begun again, not—as the popular notion of female creativity then had it—to escape sorrow in an activity inherently uncongenial to a woman, but because, as she told Williams, she had "an artist's own bent to the course—inborn, decided, resistless." Thus in late winter, when Anne seemed less harassed by cough and fatigue, she had taken up her second novel again, although at times, remembering that Ellis Bell could no longer listen and encourage, she felt the effort hollow. At Scarborough, after Anne's death, she had again returned to her novel.

Smith, Elder, kind but impatient for another triumph, kept up a steady flow of letters and book parcels from London to Haworth, at once cheering and pressuring her. Macaulay's *History*, Emerson's *Essays* ("of mixed gold and clay," thought Charlotte, "—deep and invigorating truth, dreary and depressing fallacy"), Tennyson's *Poems*, Thackeray's *Journey from Cornhill*, Leigh Hunt's *The Town*, George Borrow's *Bible in Spain* ("I felt as if I had actually travelled at his side"), and Mrs. Gaskell's *Mary Barton* ("clever though painful") all found their way to the parsonage door. The last book stung Charlotte to action. She feared that Mrs. Gaskell's labor-management plot anticipated her new novel in subject and incident. Would Mr. Williams read the first volume of her manuscript on the condition that no one else but Mr. Smith see it and that he give her an honest opinion—although she could not promise to be swayed by it?

*Jane Eyre* had been written with swift assurance; *Shirley* caused her doubts. Feeling the burden of fame, she had undertaken a broad socio-historical theme more significant, she believed, than the narrative of a governess' personal trials; she had striven to adopt a loftier, more impersonal moral tone befitting a Victorian oracle. This new subject and stance, merging uneasily with her native vehemence and subjectivity, gave the narrative an uneven, multifocused quality that she felt but could not analyze. The swift stream of personal intensity that had carried *Jane Eyre* to a triumphant close was now slowed, muddied, and diverged into many channels. Shirley herself, based lovingly on Emily imagined as an heiress, was vital and attractive—though not Emily. The three curates and their egotistical, self-righteous squabbling were amusing and vivid: loud cries against Currer Bell's rough handling of the clergy in *Jane Eyre* had deterred Charlotte not one whit. Her treatment of the labor-management struggle was both forceful and liberal. Still, she felt uneasy about the quality of this book. Replying to Williams' suggestion that a third member of the firm, a Mr. James Taylor, also be allowed to look at the manuscript, Charlotte betrayed her anxiety: "I shall be glad of another censor— and if a severe one, so much the better, provided he is also just. I court the keenest criticism. far rather would I never publish more than publish anything inferior to my first effort."[1]

This sounded humble enough, but when the opinions came in, Charlotte, with an intractability that equaled Emily's, accepted only those that conformed to her judgment after all. James Taylor criticized a "want of distinctness and impressiveness in [her] heroes." Charlotte agreed and offered an explanation: "In delineating male character I labour under disadvantages: intuition and theory will not always adequately supply the place of observation and experience. When I write about women I am sure of my ground—in the other case, I am not so sure."[2] Ironically, Robert Moore, the hero of *Shirley*, was far more realistic than Mr. Rochester. Charlotte's complaint to Lewes that publishers wanted romantic drama rather than realism had some foundation.

Cornhill objected to the curates and the anti-clericalism apparent throughout; it also felt that the opening scene with the curates did not bear directly on the novel's theme. Strongly suspecting that Smith, Elder's objections concealed timidity or an anti-feminine bias, Charlotte stood fast: "The curates and their ongoings are merely photographed from the life. I should like you to explain to me more fully the ground of your objections. Is it because you think this chapter will render the work liable to severe handling by the press? Is it because knowing as you now do the identity of 'Currer Bell,' this scene strikes you as unfeminine? Is it because it is intrinsically defective and inferior? I am afraid the two first reasons would not weigh with me— the last would."[3] She was just as unreceptive to Williams' and Taylor's remarks on aesthetics: "You both of you dwell too much on what you regard as the *artistic* treatment of a subject. Say what you will, gentlemen—say it as ably as you will—Truth is better than Art; Burns' songs are better than Bulwer's Epics. Thackeray's rude, careless sketches are preferable to thousands of carefully finished paintings. Ignorant as I am, I dare to hold and maintain that doctrine."[4] Thus she insisted on retaining the episode in which Shirley is bitten by a mad dog, cauterizes the wound with a red-hot iron, and lives in private horror of hydrophobia—it was true, it had happened to Emily—while Cornhill argued fruitlessly that the incident lacked artistic and universal truth.

Perhaps detrimental in the case of *Shirley*, Charlotte's stubborn belief in her own vision saved her much agonizing over the strictures of petty critics who still stung and buzzed over *Jane Eyre*. She could not, however, forget the *Quarterly*. Its arrows had struck when she was numb with grief; now the wounds began to smart. She would not show the review to Papa; she brooded over phrases like "coarseness of language and laxity of tone," "horrid taste," "sheer rudeness," "pendantry, stupidity, gross vulgarity." By April the wound still rankled: she predicted to Williams that her treatment of the clergy in her new novel would stir up the *Christian Remembrancer* and the *Quarterly*—but let them come on: Currer Bell had no fears. By summer, against Williams' advice, she was planning to answer the *Quarterly* (she believed the critic a man) in a preface to *Shirley;* in August 1849 she sent her "Word to *The Quarterly*" to Cornhill. Williams advised her to change it. She answered with her usual compliancy: "My Dear Sir,—I cannot change my preface. . . . Let Mr Smith fearlessly print the preface I have sent—let him depend upon me this once; even if I prove a broken reed, his fall cannot be dangerous: a preface is a short distance, it is not three volumes." Smith, Elder won this battle, however, and the preface did not appear.[5]

The *Quarterly* hurt, partly because the review was trivial and false, more because it was true. Charlotte would have denied with her last breath that *Jane Eyre* was subversive. Wasn't she a clergyman's daughter? A believer in religion? Hadn't she felt almost as much sympathy for the deposed Louis Philippe as for the French revolutionaries of 1848? Yes, yes, and yes. But there *was* in *Jane Eyre* "a proud and perpetual assertion of the rights of man." There *was* pervasive discontent.

Although not ungodly, it was a dangerous discontent because it clearly could not be appeased by reform: by trivial raises in a governess' wages, by shorter hours or pensions. The resentment of a Jane Eyre could only be quieted by her triumph over the upper classes which exploited her: the *Quarterly* rightly felt Charlotte's novel as a threat. Had Charlotte ever been able to consciously sanction the protest she unconsciously poured into her writing, she might have congratulated the reviewer for understanding *Jane Eyre* very well. Instead, she could think only of defending herself.

She was more vulnerable to reviewers now that writing had become her whole life, her reason for existence. ". . . sometimes when I wake in the morning—and know that Solitude, Remembrance—and Longing are to be almost my sole companions all day through—that at night I shall go to bed with them, that they will long keep me sleepless—that next morning I shall wake to them again—Sometimes—Nell—I have a heavy heart of it.

"But crushed I am not—yet: nor robbed of elasticity nor of hope—nor quite of endeavour—Still I have some strength to fight the battle of life."[6] Writing gave her this strength. Without a career, she told Williams, she would be a raven without an ark to fly to in the midst of the deluge.

Now that they were alone, Charlotte and her father might naturally have drawn closer together, but they did not. Mr. Brontë continued to take his meals behind the parlor door; Charlotte read, wrote, sewed, and ate her beef and pudding at one o'clock alone at the dining-room table across the hall. When they did take tea together, Papa was sure to poison the hour with endless queries after her health. She had caught a cold in July; it lingered, turned to a cough and pains between her shoulders. Were these the harbingers of consumption? Was she too marked for early death? She could not sneeze, cough, or hint of pain to her father: he had become fanatic in his worry. His anxiety "harassed her inexpressibly" because it stimulated her own fears, which were morbid enough.

Nor could she talk to him about her writing. He was pleased with her success but indifferent to the means by which she achieved it. She had, in fact, never told him what an overwhelming success *Jane Eyre* had scored. She held back most of the reviews, minimized the critics' praise, did not show him her correspondence: the novel was not mentioned between them once in a month. As he kept aloof from his parishioners' affairs—and they thanked him heartily for minding his own business—he kept aloof from his daughter's, and since she had never had the benefit of his attentions, she did not expect them now.

Neither did she draw closer to Tabby, taking her knitting to the kitchen fire in the evenings, as she might have, to listen to the servant talk about days gone by or tell the tales of the strange, wild moor people she had told to Emily. Charlotte respected the servant and loved her, but she could not communicate with her simply, as Emily had done. So she sat alone in the dining room, listening to the wind rush around the house or, when it died, to the loud ticking of the clock. From drama, life had turned to pantomime: since there is no one to talk to, she had told Ellen grimly—"necessarily I am silent." The £500 Smith, Elder gave for *Jane Eyre* had made little material difference in her life since most of the money was invested. She indulged in small luxuries, sending Ellen £5 to buy her a newly patented shower bath and a fur boa and cuffs; but these little extravagances were rare. Her letters to Ellen, who now knew the identity of Currer Bell, continued to be domestic, affectionate, and usually limited to the concerns of Ellen and her small circle of Birstall friends and relatives. "I suppose you have not yet heard anything more of poor Mr Gorham," she concluded a letter of August 23, 1849. "Does Rosy Ringrose continue to improve? How are Mrs Atkinson and Mrs Charles Carr? I am glad to hear that Miss Heald continues tolerable, but, as you say, it really seems wonderful. I hope Mercy will derive benefit from her excursion."[7]

By the end of August the manuscript that had alternately been called *Hollow's Mill, Fieldhead*, and finally *Shirley* was finished. "I thought I should be able to tell whether it was equal to 'Jane Eyre' or not," she told Williams, "but I find I cannot—it may be better, it may be worse. I shall be curious to hear your opinion, my own is of no value."[8] James Taylor, a third partner at Cornhill, had taken a strong interest in Currer Bell; he now offered to collect the manuscript in person. Charlotte wrote to Williams in some alarm:

> I would with pleasure offer him the homely hospitalities of the Parsonage for a few days, if I could at the same time offer him the company of a brother or if my Father were young enough and strong enough to walk with him on the moors and show him the neighbourhood, or if the peculiar retirement of papa's habits were not such as to render it irksome to him to give much of his society to a stranger even in the house: without being in the least misanthropical or sour-natured—papa habitually prefers solitude to society, and Custom is a tyrant whose fetters it would now be impossible for him to break. Were it not for difficulties of this sort, I believe I should ere this have asked you to come down to Yorkshire. Papa—I know, would receive any friend of Mr Smith's with perfect kindness and goodwill, but I likewise know that, unless greatly put out of his way—he could not give a guest much of his company, and that, consequently, his entertainment would be but dull.

You will see the force of these considerations, and understand why I only ask Mr Taylor to come for a day instead of requesting the pleasure of his company for a longer period; you will believe me also, and so will he, when I say I shall be most happy to see him. He will find Haworth a strange uncivilised little place such as—I dare say—he never saw before. It is twenty miles distant from Leeds; he will have to come by rail to Keighley (there are trains every two hours I believe) he must remember that at a station called Shipley the carriages are changed—otherwise they will take him on to Skipton or Colne, or I know not where; when he reaches Keighley, he will yet have four miles to travel—a conveyance may be hired at the Devonshire Arms, there is no coach or other regular communication.[9]

On Saturday, September 8, having successfully threaded the maze, Mr. Taylor arrived at the parsonage door. Charlotte took an instant dislike to him. George Smith was tall, handsome, and gilded with youthful success; Williams was distinguished, gentlemanly, and diffident. Both had pleased her. The man she now ushered into the parlor to meet her father was small, abrupt, red-haired, and, she decided immediately, no gentleman. He had criticized portions of her manuscript before, particularly the mad dog episode which Charlotte refused to change. In person he was just as blunt and stubborn as his strictures had suggested he might be. Since Charlotte was equally stubborn, he antagonized her immediately: she decided he was "rigid, despotic, and self-willed." Fortunately, considering Mr. Brontë's profound unsociability and Charlotte's instant distaste for him, Mr. Taylor had come only for the day. He left with the manuscript under his arm, and the quiet, momentarily shattered by this invasion from the brusque and hurried business world of London, settled down over the parsonage again like fine dust. Charlotte was left in suspense to await the verdict of Smith, Elder.

The verdict came in, and it was generally favorable. On the whole, *Shirley* was no falling off from *Jane Eyre*. Still, the mad dog episode was unreal and melodramatic, and Cornhill disliked Currer Bell's excessive use of French throughout. Charlotte agreed to cancel out much of the French; the rest must stand: ". . . it cannot now be altered. I can work indefatigably at the correction of a work before it leaves my hands, but when once I have looked on it as completed and submitted to the inspection of others, it becomes next to impossible to alter or amend. With the heavy suspicion on my mind that all may not be right, I yet feel forced to put up with the inevitably wrong."[10] Not quite believing, with Byron, that the artist must strike only once like the tiger, Charlotte still relied heavily on the natural inspiration of native genius, mistrusting the objective, critical polishing of a writer

like Flaubert. "No matter," she had told Williams in reference to a recent condemnation of *Jane Eyre* as a wicked book, "—whether
known or unknown—misjudged or the contrary—I am resolved not
to write otherwise. I shall bend as my powers tend. . . . I must have
my own way in the matter of writing. . . . I am thankful to God, who
gave me this faculty; and it is for me a part of my religion to defend
this gift and to profit by its possession."[11]

Because she had woven the story of *Shirley* from Yorkshire characters and events, Charlotte professed herself extremely anxious to remain invisible behind the mask of Currer Bell. Williams was doubtful:
the secret might be kept in London, but surely down in Yorkshire
people would recognize places and people disguised so thinly? But
Charlotte relied on her fox-in-a-hole existence to preserve her secret:
she had been so few places, knew so few people, so few people knew
her. Clergymen's daughters from Keighley, Ilkley, and Skipton paid
calls and went out to tea, but Charlotte had always discouraged such
invitations, having little taste for the society of parsons' daughters.
Curates came to tea occasionally, she paid calls to Brookroyd, and before Mary's departure, to Gomersal and Hunsworth: that was all. Cot-
tagers who knew the tiny figure wrapped in shawls who walked the
moors in all weathers, who welcomed her into their kitchens with a
friendly "Wha', sit ye down, Miss Brontë," did not read novels. Besides, the characters of *Shirley* were not exact replicas of real people
as Williams supposed. Mr. Helstone, the minister, for instance: "I
never saw him except once—at the consecration of a church—when
I was a child of ten years old. I was then struck with his appearance
and his stern, martial air. At a subsequent period I heard him talked
about in the neighbourhood where he had resided: some mentioned
him with enthusiasm, others with detestation. I listened to various
anecdotes, balanced evidence against evidence, and drew an inference.
The original of Mr Hall I have seen; he knows me slightly; but he
would as soon think I had closely observed him or taken him for a
character—he would as soon, indeed, suspect me of writing a book—
a novel—as he would his dog Prince."[12]

There was a deeper reason for concealing her identity. Carping
critics who believed Currer Bell to be a woman had handled *Jane Eyre*
very roughly. The anti-clericalism, the explicit love scenes (explicit
for 1848), the virility of the hero, the dynamic language, the out-
rageous circumstance of a young, single girl listening calmly to the
history of a man's sexual escapades—all were blamable in a man, but
inexcusable in a woman. "If *Jane Eyre* be the production of a woman,"
proclaimed the *North British Review* in August 1849, the month
Charlotte finished *Shirley*, "she must be a woman unsexed." "To such

critics," Charlotte wrote Williams, "I would say, 'To you I am neither man nor woman—I come before you as an author only. It is the sole standard by which you have a right to judge me—the sole ground on which I accept your judgment."[13] Acutely conscious of anti-feminine prejudice, Charlotte insisted on protecting her new novel by protecting the anonymity of Currer Bell. "Do you think this book will tend to strengthen the idea that *Currer Bell* is a woman—or will it favour a contrary opinion?" she asked Williams anxiously. On the other hand, her pride had been roused by the viciousness of these reviewers. If discovery came, let it: "I am ashamed of nothing I have written—not a line."[14]

Charlotte underestimated the insatiable curiosity of the public, however. She was being run to earth. John Greenwood, the only person in Haworth for whom Charlotte felt any intellectual kindred, had sold the sisters reams of paper over the years. "I had not much acquaintance with the family till 1843, when I began to do a little in the stationery line," he later told Mrs. Gaskell. "Nothing of that kind could be had nearer than Keighley when I began. They used to buy a great deal of writing paper, and I used to wonder whatever they did with so much. When I was out of stock I was always afraid of them coming they seemed always so distressed if I had none. I have walked to Halifax (a distance of 10 miles) many a time for half a ream of paper, for fear of being without when they came. I could not buy more at once for want of capital; I was always short of that. I did so like them to come when I had anything for them; they were so much different to any one else, so gentle, & kind and so very quiet. They never talked much; but Charlotte would sometimes sit, and enquire about my family so feelingly."[15] Greenwood suspected that the sisters "scribbled"—perhaps for the magazines—but in the last year his suspicions had deepened, although he said nothing.

At the end of September, Charlotte caught the close baying of hounds: going over the mail one morning, she discovered that a large envelope from London containing proof sheets of *Shirley* and a letter from Williams had been opened and then resealed. She found it impossible to suspect Samuel Feather at the Haworth post office or his brother James, who carried the mail: they had long set the parson's eldest daughter down as quiet and unexceptional; they never troubled their heads about her; they were too honest, moreover, to open mail, or so she believed. The guilt must lie over at Keighley, a gossipy, inquisitive town that had always speculated unpleasantly about the unsociability of the Incumbent of Haworth's daughters. The stream of letters, packets, and rough brown parcels from London to Haworth by way of Keighley had at last been too much for local curiosity and integrity. But no matter where the guilt: the secret was out, the mischief made.

Proofs read and the business out of her hands at last, Charlotte went off to visit Ellen for a week and discovered that in the Birstall district the identity of Currer Bell was no secret although, under Ellen's coaching, no one dared to charge her with the fact. To her genuine surprise, she found that *everyone* had read *Jane Eyre*. The Nusseys always entertained the respectable, Anglican, Tory circle of Birstall, but there seemed to be more calls than usual on this occasion. Cousins, second cousins, old school friends from Roe Head, clergymen's wives —all met her with an attentiveness mere Charlotte Brontë had never commanded. She also met high indignation from some of the clerical contingent that formed the Nussey acquaintance: "ecclesiastical brows lowered thunder at me." She longed for these "large-made priests" to speak out plainly; she would have relished a good battle; but they contented themselves by glaring silently over their tea cups. A good daughter of the Church, Ellen evidently took the clerical displeasure calmly, perhaps too unimaginative to see the threat of the novel's anti-institutional view of God and man, perhaps blindly loyal to Charlotte, or perhaps rightly convinced that, since her friend's independent, unorthodox religion was founded on the firmest rock of high moral principle, it needed no apology from her.

On the last day of October she returned to find "Papa very well, Tabby better, and Martha quite fat," and letters laid out on the dining-room table: reactions to *Shirley* were beginning to come in. In the past she had faced such moments with Emily and Anne. Strong in their unity, they had laughed off injustices and rejoiced at worthy praise. Now Charlotte must face praise and blame alone. A letter from Williams reassured her: George Smith had high expectations of *Shirley* being a commercial success. A letter from George Henry Lewes pleased and pained her: *Shirley* was powerful, but he did not like the opening "curate chapter." Worst of all, he insisted on believing Currer Bell a woman and judging her performance accordingly. Charlotte answered, at once rebuking him for his bias and proclaiming her aloofness to criticism:

> November 1st, 1849: My Dear Sir,—It is about a year and a half since you wrote to me; but it seems a longer period, because since then it has been my lot to pass some black milestones in the journey of life. Since then there have been intervals when I have ceased to care about literature and critics and fame; when I have lost sight of whatever was prominent in my thoughts at the first publication of "Jane Eyre"; but now I want these things to come back vividly, if possible: consequently it was a pleasure to receive your note. I wish you did not

think me a woman. I wish all reviewers believed "Currer Bell" to be a man; they would be more just to him. You will, I know, keep measuring me by some standard of what you deem becomming to my sex; where I am not what you consider graceful you will condemn me. All mouths will be open against that first chapter, and that first chapter is a true as the Bible, nor is it exceptional. Come what will, I cannot, when I write, think always of myself and of what is elegant and charming in femininity; it is not on those terms, or with such ideas, I ever took pen in hand: and if it is only on such terms my writing will be tolerated, I shall pass away from the public and trouble it no more. Out of obscurity I came, to obscurity I can easily return. Standing afar off, I now watch to see what will become of "Shirley." My expectations are very low, and my anticipation somewhat sad and bitter; still, I earnestly conjure you to say honestly what you think; flattery would be worse than vain; there is no consolation in flattery. As for condemnation, I cannot, on reflection, ẹee why I should much fear it; there is no one but myself to suffer therefrom, and both happiness and suffering in this life soon pass away. Wishing you all success in your Scottish expedition,—I am, dear sir, yours sincerely,

C. Bell.[16]

The same day she wrote Lewes, the first review came in, and her resolution failed. She felt a shock of anger and pain to read that the three curates and their junketing were "vulgar, unnecessary, and disgusting." The same charges of coarseness and crudity were flung at her again; the same assertions that if Currer Bell was a woman she must be a woman singularly depraved. Stunned at first, she quickly took fire: a "thrill of mutiny" went through her.

"Are there no such men as the Helstones and the Yorkes?" she raged to Williams.

"Yes, there are.

"Is the first chapter disgusting or vulgar?

"*It is not, it is real.*

"As for the praise of such a critic, I find it silly and nauseous, and I scorn it.

"Were my sisters now alive they and I would laugh over this notice; but they sleep, they will wake no more for me, and I am a fool to be so moved by what is not worth a sigh. . . .

"You must spare me if I seem hasty, I fear I am really not so firm as I used to be, nor so patient. Whenever any shock comes, I feel that almost all supports have been withdrawn."[17]

Williams wrote back hastily, begging her to weather the critical storms more calmly. Well, she would try. On November 5 the complimentary copies of *Shirley* finally arrived, having laid at the Bradford post office for nearly a week. She was pleased with the book's appearance and sent off copies to Ellen and to their mutual friend, Mary Gorham, immediately. Gradually more notices came in; they did not echo the first review; they applauded, not condemned.

"'Shirley' is an admirable book," praised the *Morning Chronicle*, "totally free from cant, affectation, or conventional tinsel of any kind: genuine English in the independence and uprightness of the tone of thought, in the purity of heart and feeling, which pervades it; genuine English in the masculine vigour or rough originality of its conception of character; and . . . genuine English in style and diction. Like the author's former work, it is a tale of passion and character rather than of incident; and, thus considered, it is a veritable triumph of psychology." "It will unquestionably add to the reputation of the author," said the *Morning Post*, pronouncing the words Charlotte most wished to hear. As opinion after opinion came in, it became clear that, in Charlotte's words, "mere novel-readers" were disappointed at not finding the excitement they had found in *Jane Eyre;* critics of *Jane Eyre*, on the other hand, found *Shirley* more acceptable.

In her Chelsea sitting room, dark, lively, hypochondriacal Jane Welsh Carlyle read *Shirley* and did not like it, although she had been told that Shirley "was so ridiculously like myself that the author must have drawn it from me feature by feature." With a curious lack of critical judgment, she pronounced the book little better than Mrs. Trollope's latest rubbishy novel and advised a friend not to send her a copy since ". . . I have just finished that non-masterly production. Now that this Authoress has left off 'Corsing and schvering' (as my German master used to call it) one finds her neither very lively nor very original. Still I should very much like to know her name—*can* you tell it me?—as if she have not *kept company* with *me* in this life, we must have been much together in some previous state of existence—I perceive in her book so many things I have said myself, printed without alteration of a word."[18]

Charlotte was more complimentary about Mrs. Carlyle's husband. "I like Carlyle better and better," she had written Williams, April 16, 1849, having just read the *Miscellanies*. "His style I do not like, nor do I always concur in his opinions, nor quite fall in with his hero-worship; but there is a manly love of truth, an honest recognition and fearless vindication of intrinsic greatness, of intellectual and moral worth, considered apart from birth, rank, or wealth, which commands my sincere admiration."[19] These were Charlotte's own standards for judging human nature and, like Carlyle, she was herself an eccentric, vehement moralist.

Sara Coleridge, daughter of the poet, who seemed to De Quincey "the most perfect of all pensive, nun-like, intellectual beauties that I have seen in real breathing life," read Currer Bell's new work and liked it. A brilliant figure in literary circles, a novelist, and later her father's editor and apologist, she criticized the novel intelligently, discounting entirely reviewers' objections to coarseness of style and breeding, going immediately to the real weakness of the novel: "The worst fault by far is the development of the story. Mrs. Pryor's reason for putting away her daughter is absurdly far-fetched and unnatural. No wonder the 'Old Cossack' disliked her, and thought her a queer sort of maniac."[20] Mrs. Pryor, whose stout dignity and stouter Toryism Charlotte borrowed from Miss Wooler, *was* a weakness, one of those literary blind spots which Charlotte could not hold at a distance and find absurd. Mrs. Pryor abandons her daughter Caroline in infancy *because* the child is beautiful and because its beauty, like her wicked husband's, must conceal a warped and evil mind. Mrs. Pryor's motive is eccentric, a purely personal prejudice of her creator, who had suffered from being plain, who mortally resented the easy passport to love and success the world provides for beauty.

Swifter than ever rumors flew about London: who *was* Currer Bell? Catherine Winkworth, friend both of Mrs. Gaskell and Harriet Martineau, had by this time stumbled upon half the truth. She found *Shirley* "infinitely more original and full of character than the ordinary run of novels," but, with understandable partiality for her friends, "infinitely below such as Mary Barton and 'Deerbrook.'" Complaining of the book's stiffness, dryness, its utter lack of wit, and the painfully unhappy tone, she explained to her friend Eliza Patterson, "That is not, however, to be wondered at, when one knows that the author is herself threatened with consumption at this time, and has lost her two sisters, Ellis and Acton Bell by it. Their real name is Brontë; they are of the Nelson family."[21] The fact mixed with this fiction warned that Charlotte could not possibly keep her anonymity much longer. Indeed, a Liverpool man, formerly of Haworth, now read *Shirley* and, struck with the familiar dialect and locations, became convinced that it was the work of a Haworth resident. No one in the village was capable of such a feat except the parson's daughter, Miss Brontë. He published his views in a Liverpool paper, and the hounds were on the quarry.

Smith, Elder's enthusiasm, a shower of favorable notices raining upon the parsonage, letters from admirers—all the sweetness of fame —turned Charlotte's thoughts once more south to London. Longing to reap further rewards of success, yet shrinking from the mere thought of social contact, she slowly but inevitably made up her mind to return to "the big Babylon." "I am trying by degrees to inure myself to the thought of someday stepping over to Keighley, taking the train to Leeds—thence to London—and once more venturing to set foot in the strange, busy whirl of the Strand and Cornhill," she wrote Williams, November 15. "I want to talk to you a little and to hear by word of mouth how matters are progressing—Whenever I come I must come quietly and but for a short time—I should be unhappy to leave Papa longer than a fortnight."[22] Williams replied that he would be delighted to talk, particularly since he personally was not completely satisfied with the new book. To this Charlotte replied, as usual, with stubbornness and powerful metaphor: "I shall come to be lectured . . . but I forewarn you, I have my own doctrines, not acquired, but innate, some that I fear cannot be rooted up without tearing away all the soil from which they spring, and leaving only unproductive rock for new seed."[23]

While she debated a departure date, more letters continued to arrive, some from the famous, some from the obscure. One lady, "not quite an old maid, but nearly one," vowed that if Currer Bell were a gentleman and like his heroes she should fall in love with him at once. A pity Smith, Elder would not let her announce herself as a single, mature gentleman, Charlotte laughed to Williams: "a great many elderly spinsters would have been pleased." A letter from a man enthused wildly over *Shirley* and vowed his intention to "institute a search after Currer Bell, and sooner or later to find him out." By far the most precious appreciations came from Elizabeth Cleghorn Gaskell and the famous Harriet Martineau. Mrs. Gaskell's note, claiming that she would keep Currer Bell's works as a treasure for her daughters, brought tears to Charlotte's eyes. ". . . she is a good—she is a great woman," Charlotte effused to Williams, "—proud am I that I can touch a chord of sympathy in souls so noble. In Mrs. Gaskell's nature it mournfully pleases me to fancy a remote affinity to my sister Emily—In Miss Martineau's mind I have always felt the same—though there are wide differences—Both these ladies are above me—certainly far my superiors in attainment and experience—I think I could look up to them if I knew them."[24]

Miss Martineau's letter, addressed to Currer Bell, Esq., but beginning "Dear Madam," thanked the author for a gift copy of *Shirley* sent through Smith, Elder with the following note: "Currer Bell offers a copy of 'Shirley' to Miss Martineau's acceptance, in acknowledgment of the pleasure and profit she he has derived from her works. When C. B. first read 'Deerbrook,' he tasted a new and keen pleasure, and experienced a genuine benefit. In his mind 'Deerbrook' ranks with the writings that have really done him good, added to his stock of ideas, and rectified his views of life."[25] Charlotte's slip of the pen—or perhaps her deliberate use of the feminine pronoun—revealed how deeply she wished personal recognition. She was very lonely; she dared to believe that friendship with women like Gaskell and Martineau might compensate just a little for the loss of Emily and Anne; yet, hidden behind "Currer Bell," she was powerless to further these friendships.

On Thursday, November 29, 1849, having thoroughly warned Williams that she must remain anonymous and quiet, she went up to London for the fourth time in her life, her second as an author. She had intended to stay with her friend Laetitia Wheelwright whom she corresponded with but had not seen since Brussels days; but George Smith must have Currer Bell at his own home in Bayswater—he would be seriously hurt otherwise. Arriving in a dress made especially for the occasion but still Quaker-plain, Charlotte was greeted with great politeness by Mrs. Smith but also with stiffness, "like one who had received the strictest orders to be scrupulously attentive"—as, of course, she had. Maids were in instant attendance, the best wax candles in superabundance, and Mrs. Smith and her daughters Eliza, Sarah, and Isabella hung carefully on each of Currer Bell's words. They were few enough, and although some of the "alarm" and "estrangement" disappeared gradually, Currer Bell's silent gravity made her a rather formidable guest.

Mildly critical of George Smith's eminently shrewd, businesslike manner on their first meeting, Charlotte now observed him in the role of son and brother: "he pleases me much." Mr. Williams came around to Bishop's Road to greet Currer Bell with his quiet, diffident courtesy, and so, unfortunately, did James Taylor. "Mr Taylor—the little man—has again shown his parts," Charlotte wrote Ellen; "in fact, I suspect he is of the Helstone order of men—rigid, despotic, and self-willed. He tries to be very kind and even to express sympathy sometimes, but he does not manage it. He has a determined, dreadful nose in the middle of his face which when poked into my countenance cuts into my soul like iron. Still he is horribly intelligent, quick, searching, sagacious, and with a memory of relentless tenacity. To turn to Williams after him, or to Smith himself, is to turn from granite to easy down or warm fur."[26] James Taylor was, in fact, very like her own harsh, abrupt, temperamental characters. Since she had created men like Helstone, Yorke, Brocklehurst, Rivers, and even Rochester half in protest at their domineering and brutal insensitivity, she shied away from any flesh and blood counterpart. On his part, James Taylor had fallen in love with Currer Bell.

She got away as quickly as she could to visit the Wheelwrights in Kensington, friends she prized for their ineradicable, bitter-sweet association with the Pensionnat. Laetitia was now twenty-one, Frances and Sarah-Anne, Emily's little piano students, eighteen and fifteen. They charged her immediately with the authorship of *Shirley*: Hortense Moore could be no one but Mademoiselle Haussé of the Pensionnat Heger, and no one but Charlotte could have created that living and breathing portrait. Unlike Charlotte's godmother, Mrs. Atkinson, who cut her after reading "that wicked book, *Jane Eyre*," and unlike Miss Wooler, who wrote that *despite* what Charlotte had done nothing would be changed between them, the Wheelwrights were enchanted with the idea that Charlotte Brontë was Currer Bell. Much as Charlotte may have wished to reminisce about Brussels that day, however, she was far too agitated to dwell on the past: a great event was in store: that very evening Thackeray was to dine at the Smiths'.

If Charlotte was nervous at the prospect of meeting the great author at last, George Smith and his mother had their own misgivings. With her quiet but obstinate refusal to be known or to go into company, Charlotte managed to be more difficult than a prima donna. The very quality that made her a great writer—intense self-absorption—made her an impossible guest. She could not escape the burden of her personality; she could not direct her nervous self-preoccupation outward and thus throw off her agonizing shyness and sensitivity. Smith had invited Thackeray and some other literary gentlemen to dinner but had to caution Thackeray not to breathe the words "Currer Bell," *Jane Eyre*, or *Shirley* when speaking to Miss Brontë, as she was incognito in London. "I see," replied Thackeray in his large way. "It will be all right: you are speaking to a man of the world."[27]

The four actors in the little drama thus prepared for the momentous evening: Thackeray with great interest although he was still weak from a recent illness, the Smiths with trepidation (Miss Brontë was often silent—was something offending her?), and Charlotte with growing mental and physical distress. She had breakfasted very lightly that morning and, in the rush of her call on the Wheelwrights, had eaten nothing since. By seven o'clock when the butler announced Mr. Thackeray to the little party assembled in the drawing room, she was trembling from hunger, fatigue, and tension. They were not introduced, since Charlotte huddled for safety in the shadow of Mrs. Smith and her daughters, but when everyone rose to go down to dinner, "the Titan" came up, put out his large hand, and said quietly, "Shake hands." She did shake, gazing up at his towering six-foot six-inch bulk from somewhere in the vicinity of his third waistcoat button. He was not handsome but rather ugly: a great pale babyish face oddly at variance with prematurely white hair, spectacles straddling a wide, flat, short nose, satirically peaked eyebrows that belied the flaccidity of the face.

Quite paralyzed by nervous exhaustion, Charlotte had a bad time of it at dinner, finding herself scarcely able to utter a word, let alone a witty one. George Smith remembered vividly what followed: "When the ladies had left the dining-room I offered Thackeray a cigar. The custom of smoking after dinner was not common then, but I had been told he liked a cigar, and so provided for his tastes. To my dismay, when we rejoined the ladies in the drawing-room, he approached Miss Brontë and quoted a familiar and much criticised passage from Jane Eyre. It was that in which she describes 'the warning fragrance' that told her of the approach of Mr. Rochester:

"'Sweetbriar and southern wood, jasmine, pink and rose, had long been yielding their evening sacrifice of incense. This new scent was neither shrub nor flower. It was—I knew it well—it was the scent of Mr. Rochester's cigar!' "[28]

Already disturbed by a flippant streak in the man she revered as a great moralist, Charlotte became greatly discomposed at this allusion, not knowing whether Thackeray intended to insult either her person or her privacy. She turned off the allusion coolly, at the same time darting an accusing glance across the room at George Smith, who heard Thackeray's betrayal with horror. "Thackeray, however, had no sense of either awkwardness or guilt," Smith continued. "From my house he went to the smoking-room of the Garrick Club and said: 'Boys! I have been dining with "Jane Eyre."' To have her identity expounded in the smoking-room of the Garrick Club was the last experience which the morbidly shy and sensitive little lady would have chosen."

Charlotte reproached herself bitterly for her tongue-tied confusion and considered the encounter with her literary idol a failure. "What he thought of me I cannot tell," she wrote Ellen. Thackeray was not only a satirist and a clubman, however; a worldly exterior hid a soft center full of romantic sympathy for young girls, mothers, and aging belles. He was ready to idealize Charlotte, and did so in a posthumous tribute in 1860: "I first saw her as I rose out of an illness from which I had never thought to recover. I remember the trembling little frame, the little hand, the great honest eyes. An impetuous honesty seemed to me to characterise the woman. . . . I fancied an austere little Joan of Arc marching in upon us, and rebuking our easy lives, our easy morals. She gave me the impression of being a very pure, and lofty, and high-minded person. A great and holy reverence of right and truth seemed to be with her always."[29] These, of course, were the very qualities Charlotte had expected to find in Thackeray: her notion of his character was a projection of her own: she was doomed to disappointment.

The Smiths piloted their guest through a brisk round of sight-seeing, playgoing, and dinners. Charlotte observed everything and everyone silently, minutely, often through the lens of personal prejudice. Nothing, she told Miss Wooler, had charmed her more than the art galleries, particularly one or two private collections of Turner's water colors; his later painting she found strange, however, and baffling description. Mr. Williams escorted her to the new Houses of Parliament (an attack of rheumatic fever had driven Mr. Taylor from the field). She was taken to see Macready act in *Macbeth* and *Othello*, and dismissed his performances as false, artificial, and a travesty of Shakespeare's intention—despite, or perhaps because of, the fact that Macready's acting was all the rage in London. She found both the actor and the London stage system "hollow nonsense," and produced a blank silence and then consternation at a dinner table by plainly saying so. "I was, indeed, obliged to dissent on many occasions, and to offend by dissenting," she wrote Miss Wooler. Revering Emily's austere, powerful verse, she could not agree either with current taste in poetry. "—It seems now very much the custom to admire a certain wordy, intricate, obscure style of poetry—such as Elizabeth Barrett Browning writes—Some pieces were referred to about which Currer Bell was expected to be very rapturous—and failing in this—he disappointed." Elizabeth Barrett Browning in turn did not admire Currer Bell, deploring in a letter to Miss Mitford, the "half savage and half free-thinking" qualities of *Jane Eyre*.[30]

She had been distressingly tongue-tied with Thackeray. Sitting down to dinner with literary critics from the *Times*, *Athenaeum*, *Examiner*, *Spectator*, and *Atlas*—awesome figures in the world of letters—she found herself in good form, even though (or, again, perhaps because) some of them had attacked her vigorously in their columns. She relished a battle and expected one but, surprisingly, these men proved "prodigiously civil face to face." She found them "infinitely grander, more pompous, dashing, showy than the few authors I saw"—an observation of truth and wit. Awed only by true greatness, she talked with great spirit on this occasion; however: "I did not know how much their presence and conversation had excited me till they were gone, and then reaction commenced. When I had retired for the night I wished to sleep; the effort to do so was vain—I could not close my eyes. Night passed, morning came, and I rose without having known a moment's slumber."[31]

In the midst of this exhilarating but exhausting activity, normal

for a Londoner but for Charlotte an ordeal, she had time to observe
with some amusement Mrs. Smith's possessive watchfulness over her
son George. He was a flagrantly eligible man—tall, handsome, cheerful, energetic, financially astute—and his proud mother jealously
screened any female who drifted within his range. Charlotte felt Mrs.
Smith's brown eyes upon her whenever she conversed tête-à-tête
with Smith: was Currer Bell out to capture her George? Charlotte
felt that her scrupulously modest behavior satisfied the mother on
that point. She convinced herself, at any rate, that she looked upon
George Smith only as "a very fine specimen of a young English
man-of-business: so I regard him, and I am proud to be one of his
props."

Smith proposed to introduce her to Charles Dickens and two
women writers then in vogue, Mrs. Trollope and Mrs. Gore, but
Charlotte declined, not liking Dickens' books much and fearing the
notoriety these introductions would bring. Hearing, however, that
Harriet Martineau was staying with her cousin Richard Martineau
just around the corner from the Smiths, she could not resist requesting
a meeting with the famous political economist, even though she must
forfeit her incognito. Accordingly, she sent round a note expressing
her strong desire to pay a call, a request quickly granted by Miss
Martineau, who was twice as curious about that unknown quantity
Currer Bell as Charlotte was about her. Indeed, when Currer Bell's
note had arrived with the copy of *Shirley*, Miss Martineau and her
friends had eagerly passed the paper from hand to hand, trying to
guess whether the "cramped and nervous" writing was a woman's
or a man's. Harriet herself flatly proclaimed that the author of *Jane
Eyre* was either a woman or an upholsterer: no one else could have
written the passage that described Grace Poole sewing rings to new
curtains. Her real reason for "knowing" Currer Bell to be a woman
was less superficial. Parts of the novel, touching her profoundly,
could have come from her own unhappy childhood: *Jane Eyre* was a
woman's experience as only a woman could have told it.

So although Charlotte had replied, "I hope to have the pleasure
of seeing you at six o'clock to-day: and I shall try now to be patient
till six o'clock comes," Harriet Martineau's impatience surpassed
Charlotte's that Sunday in December. "We were in a certain state
of excitement all day," Martineau recalled, "and especially toward
evening. A little before six there was a thundering rap: the drawing-
room door was thrown open, and in stalked a gentleman six feet high."

The party held its breath. Was this the mysterious Currer Bell?

"It was not 'Currer', but a philanthropist who had an errand about
a model lodging-house. Minute by minute I, for one, wished him

away; and he did go before any body else came. Precisely as the time-piece struck six a carriage stopped at the door; and after a minute of suspense, the footman announced, 'Miss Brogden'; whereupon my cousin informed me that it was Miss Bronti [sic]; for we had heard the name before, among others, in the way of conjecture."

A bold, dashing gentleman as the sensationalism of *Jane Eyre* would seem to suggest? A cigar-smoking female in fawn-colored breeches à la George Sand? Neither: a plain little lady in lace mittens, spectacles, and dark Quaker-like dress and shawl, very shy, whose great luminous eyes went around the circle of faces timidly but purposefully.

"I thought her the smallest creature I had ever seen (except at a fair) and her eyes blazed, as it seemed to me. She glanced quickly round; and my [ear] trumpet pointing me out, she held out her hand frankly and pleasantly; and then came a moment which I had not anticipated. When she was seated by me on the sofa, she cast up at me such a look—so loving, so appealing—that, in connexion with her deep mourning dress, and the knowledge that she was the sole survivor of her family, I could with the utmost difficulty return her smile, or keep my composure. I should have been heartily glad to cry. We soon got on very well; and she appeared more at her ease that evening than I ever saw her afterwards, except when we were alone together. My hostess was so considerate as to leave us together after tea, in case of Charlotte Brontë desiring to have private conversation with me. She was glad of the opportunity to consult me about certain strictures of the reviewers which she did not understand, and had every desire to profit by. I did not approve of the spirit of those strictures; but I thought them not entirely groundless."[32]

By December 20, Mrs. Gaskell had heard and was writing about the meeting of December 9.

Have you heard that Harriet Martineau has sworn an eternal friendship with the authoress of Shirley[;] if not I'll tell you [she wrote Anne Shaen]. She sent Shirley to Harriet Martineau. H M. acknowledged it in a note directed to Currer Bell *Esq*—but inside written to a *lady*. Then came an answer requesting a personal interview. This was towards or about last Saturday week, and the time appointed was 6 o'clock on Sunday Eveng; and the place appointed was at Mr Richard Martineau's, (married a Miss Needham,) in Hyde Park Square. So Mr & Mrs R. Martineau and Harriet M. sat with early tea before them, awaiting six o'clock, & their mysterious visitor, when lo! and behold, as the clock struck, in walked a little, very little, bright haired sprite, looking not above 15, very unsophisticated, neat & tidy. She sat down & had tea with them; her name being still unknown; she said to H M,

"What did you really think of Jane Eyre?" H. M. I thought it a first rate book, whereupon the little sprite went red all over with pleasure. After tea Mr & Mrs R M. withdrew and left sprite to a 2 hours tête-a-tête with H M, to whom she revealed her name & the history of her life. Her father a Yorkshire clergymen who has never slept out of his house for 26 years; she has lived a most retired life;—her first visit to London, never been in society, and many other particulars which H M. is not at liberty to divulge any more than her name, which she keeps a profound secret; but Thackeray does *not*. H M. is charmed with her; she is full of life and power &c &c, & H M hopes to be of great use to her. There! that's all I know, but I think it's a pretty good deal, it's something to have seen somebody who has seen nominis umbra.[33]

Charlotte herself commented briefly on her meeting with England's most prestigious woman writer: "This evening I am going to meet Miss Martineau. She has written to me most kindly. She knows me only as Currer Bell. I am going alone in the carriage; how I shall get on I do not know." And later, assessing the whole London experience: "I sometimes fancied myself in a dream—I could scarcely credit the reality of what passed. For instance, when I walked into the room and put my hand into Miss Martineau's, the action of saluting her and the fact of her presence seemed visionary."[34] Charlotte later recounted the experience to Mrs. Gaskell, who then described in her *Life* how Charlotte had singled out Miss Martineau among the group and gone straight to her "with intuitive recognition." Harriet Martineau practiced mesmerism, but evidently had little sympathy for intuition: "Seeing the trumpet," she commented crisply.

A political radical, abolitionist, social reformer, atheist, and feminist, Harriet Martineau had little in common with Charlotte Brontë, as time would show. Now, however, the two women were drawn together by their fame and by their common love of truth and courage; and Charlotte counted the Sunday meeting the highlight of her London visit.

A low point was a lengthy attack on *Shirley* in the *Times* by one of the critics who had been so "prodigiously civil face to face." Charlotte expected the review, and knew immediately when all the Smiths seemed to have mislaid the paper that day that the review was bad. She insisted on seeing it, however, and Mrs. Smith was deeply distressed to watch her read sentences like, " 'Shirley' is at once the most high flown and stalest of fictions," her face hidden behind the newspaper, and to know that tears were racing down her cheeks. She recovered quickly, however, expressing only fears that the bad review would hurt sales; when Thackeray came round to see how she had taken it, she was as controlled and quiet as ever.

The Smiths begged her to stay on for a month, but she firmly declined. They were all so sociable, energetic, and equable; they could never guess how ordinary experiences taxed her energies. Since they always interpreted her silence as displeasure, she had made every effort not to flag. They did not know how comfortable and creative that silence was; how she was far more content to observe and analyze people than to make sociable noises with them. All in all, she felt she had been a disappointment. Everyone had expected something more flamboyant, vivid, and commanding since the novels promised it. How could such a plain, grave, silent little lady have written with such force and passion? So wondering, they touched on the heart of Charlotte Brontë's mystery. Only a few would ever unveil it.

She came home on December 15 to a house that seemed "dumb and vacant," carrying with her memories, ideas, images, sensations to be stored away against her solitude in the coming months as the mouse stores summer grain against the bitter winter.

# 18

## Recognition

Unable to endure the silence after London, Charlotte quickly invited Ellen for a visit. She came, exciting considerable interest among her acquaintance in Birstall who now knew that Ellen's old friend from Roe Head and Currer Bell were one. At least one person still was unsure, however. A letter from William Margetson Heald, canon of Ripon, followed Ellen to Haworth: he could not restrain his curiosity, especially since it was rumored that he or his father appeared as a character in Currer Bell's new novel.

Fame says you are on a visit with the renowned Currer Bell, the "great unknown" of the present day [he wrote]. The celebrated "Shirley" has just found its way hither . . . the story goes that either I or my father . . . are part of "Currer Bell's" stock-in-trade, under the title of Mr Hall, in that Mr Hall is represented as black, bilious, and of dismal aspect, stooping a trifle, and indulging a little now and then in the indigenous dialect . . . though I had no idea that I should be made a means to amuse the public, Currer Bell is perfectly welcome to what she can make of so unpromising a subject. But I think *I have a fair claim in return to be let into the secret of the company I have got into.* Some of them are good enough to tell, and need no OEdipus [sic] to solve the riddle. I can tabulate, for instance, the Yorke family for the Taylors, Mr Moore—Mr Cartright, and Mr Helstone is clearly meant for Mr Roberson, though the authoress has evidently got her idea of his character through an unfavourable medium, and does not understand the full value of one of the most admirable characters I ever knew or expect to know. Mary thinks she descries Cecilia Crowther and Miss Johnstone . . . in two old maids.

Now pray get us a full light on all other names and localities. . . . Mary and Harriet wish also to get at this information; and the latter at all events seems to have her own peculiar claim, as fame says

she is "in the book" too. One had need "walk . . . warily in these
dangerous days," when, as Burns (is it not he?) says—
"A chield's among you taking notes,
And faith he'll prent it."—

Yours sincerely,
W. M. Heald.[1]

This then was the *Shirley* game that whiled away the winter hours
that year in Haworth and environs. To Charlotte's surprise there
seemed to be little resentment over the more acrimonious portraits
and a great deal of local pride in "our authoress." True, Mary Taylor's
mother did not enjoy her portrait as the cross and gloomy Mrs.
Yorke; and wrote her son Waring in New Zealand "abusing Miss
Brontë for writing Shirley."[2] Joseph Brett Grant, once curate at
Haworth, now at Oxenhope, also burned a little to find himself
pilloried as the silly, snobbish Mr. Donne, and took exception to
the chapter "Mr. Donne's Exodus" in which he is turned off the
premises of Fieldhead by a wrathful Shirley who cannot bear his
haughty criticisms of her people and her county: "How dare the
pompous priest abuse his flock? How dare the lisping cockney revile
Yorkshire?" After a few weeks of resentful muttering, however, the
"lisping cockney" gradually took comfort in his fame: "only yesterday I had the pleasure of making him a comfortable cup of tea, and
seeing him sip it with revived complacency," Charlotte reported to
Williams. "It is a curious fact that, since he read 'Shirley,' he has
come to the house oftener than ever, and been remarkably meek,
and assiduous to please. Some people's natures are veritable enigmas:
I quite expected to have had one good scene at least with him; but
as yet nothing of the sort has occurred."[3]

James Smith, the curate whose indifference to Ellen had angered
Charlotte, had left England for Canada and was not on hand to resent
his treatment as the brazen Irishman, Peter Augustus Malone. In 1902
the third curate, James Chesterton Bradley (Mr. Sweeting), came be-
latedly to his defense, praising his colleague in a letter to Smith's
nephew that concluded: ". . . I was anxious to give my testimony
against the false and cruel way in which Charlotte Brontë held him
up in her book."[4] Had Charlotte's anti-clerical bias made her unjust
or even untruthful? Her publisher would not have thought so.
"Charlotte Brontë had much nobility of character," George Smith
stated in his memoirs; "she had an almost exaggerated sense of duty;
she was scrupulously honest and perfectly just. When Sir James
Stephen . . . said to me during a long conversation I had with him
at Cambridge on a very delicate subject, 'I have lived a long and not
unobservant life, and I have never yet met with a perfectly just

woman,' I could not help thinking that he had never met Charlotte Brontë. Miss Brontë was critical of character, but not of action; this she judged favourably and kindly. Generally, I thought, she put too kind an interpretation on the actions of a friend." Mary Taylor would have been quick to agree with Smith's estimate of Charlotte: "I found that I seldom differed from her," she told Mrs. Gaskell, "except that she was far too tolerant of stupid people, if they had a grain of kindness in them."[5]

Arthur Bell Nicholls got hold of *Jane Eyre*, read it, admired it, cried out for "the other book." "He is to have it next week, much good may it do him," said Charlotte tartly. But she had let Nicholls off lightly as Mr. Macarthey. He read the book eagerly in his room at the sexton's house down the lane from the parsonage. "John Brown's wife seriously thought he had gone wrong in the head as she heard him giving vent to roars of laughter as he sat alone, clapping his hands and stamping on the floor. He would read all the scenes about the curates aloud to papa, he triumphed in his own character. What Mr Grant will say is another thing. No matter."[6]

And finally, one day, even the parsonage servants knew:

"Martha came in yesterday, puffing and blowing, and much excited. 'I've heard sich news,' she began.

" 'What about?'

" 'Please ma'am, you've been and written two books, the grandest books that ever was seen. My father has heard it at Halifax, and Mr George Taylor and Mr Greenwood, and Mr Merrall at Bradford; and they are going to have a meeting at the Mechanics' Institute, and to settle about ordering them.'

" 'Hold your tongue Martha, and be off.' I fell into a cold sweat. 'Jane Eyre' will be read by John Brown, by Mrs Taylor, and Betty. God help, keep, and deliver me!"[7]

Now when Tabby limped down into the village, curious villagers arrested her and, rolling their eyes in the direction of the parsonage, whispered, "Are they terribly larn'd?"

As news of her identity spread, strange faces began to appear in the village on the "wise errand" of seeing Currer Bell in the flesh, but, as Charlotte told Williams, "our rude hills and rugged neighbourhood will I doubt not form a sufficient barrier to the frequent repetition of such visits." John Greenwood began to dream of adding a little bookstore to his stationer's shop. He approached Charlotte with the plan, and although she still shuddered a little at the thought of *Jane Eyre* and *Shirley* in the hands of "all the worthy folk of Haworth and Keighley," she petitioned Smith, Elder, who kindly agreed to sell her books to Greenwood on easy terms. Charlotte thanked Smith and Williams for the delight and hope they had given "a good and intelligent though poor man. . . . I wish he could permanently establish a little bookselling business in Haworth; it would benefit the place as well as himself."

In the midst of sweet fame, a bitter dart: a copy of the *Edinburgh Review* containing the long-awaited review of *Shirley* by G. H. Lewes. After joking laboriously for five pages about men's superiority to women and women's "grand function"—*Maternity*—Lewes finally took aim at Charlotte. "It is now scarcely a secret that Currer Bell is the pseudonym of a woman," said Lewes, claiming that he had known it all the time, and went on to assure the public that Currer Bell, far from being a heathenish *author* educated among heathens, was in fact an *authoress* and the daughter of a clergyman. Praising *Jane Eyre* again, Lewes soon lapsed into harping on the old string of the novel's coarse, masculine, unladylike vigor. "This same over-masculine vigour is even more prominent in Shirley," continued Lewes, and went on to specify his complaints. The novel's "texture" was coarse and frequently flippant; the characters disagreeable and intolerably rude; the style was saturated with rude and offensive harshness; vulgarities such as "getting up the steam," or "cash up to the tune of," or "pipe up in most superior style" offended the reader on almost every page.

But Currer Bell's unfeminine nature was responsible for worse crimes than these. Mrs. Pryor, for example, who abandons her child in infancy—no true woman could have drawn such a character or imagined such an act. "Currer Bell! if under your heart had ever stirred a child, if to your bosom a babe had ever been pressed,—that mysterious part of your being, towards which all the rest of it is drawn, in which your whole soul is transported and absorbed,—never could you have imagined such a falsehood as that!" Lewes culminated his attack by quoting Schiller on Madame de Staël: " 'This person wants everything that is graceful in a woman; and nevertheless, the faults of her book are altogether womanly faults. She steps out of her sex—without elevating herself above it.' This brief and pregnant criticism is quite as applicable to Currer Bell," concluded Lewes. ". . . She has extraordinary power—but let her remember that 'on tombe de côté où l'on penche!'"[8]

Outraged, feeling "cold and sick," Charlotte sent Lewes one line: "I can be on guard against my enemies, but God deliver me from my friends!"[9] She might have said more pertinently, "I can be on guard against reactionaries, but God deliver me from liberals"; for it was the sex issue harped on by a man who professed enlightenment that constituted the betrayal. Charlotte's indignation burned white-hot. Why must the quality of Currer Bell's writing always be weighed on the scales of "masculinity," "overmasculinity," "ladylikeness," and "un-womanliness"? Yet the very fact that critics took this line of attack with the Bells suggested that for the first time the male monopoly of all fiction except the domestic novel had been broken.

A few days later she recovered her equanimity enough to write Lewes in calmer tone:

> I will tell you why I was so hurt by that review in the "Edinburgh"—not because its criticism was keen or its blame sometimes severe; not because its praise was stinted (for, indeed, I think you give me quite as much praise as I deserve), but because after I had said earnestly that I wished critics would judge me as an *author*, not as a woman, you so roughly—I even thought so cruelly—handled the question of sex. I dare say you meant no harm, and perhaps you will not now be able to understand why I was so grieved . . . I imagine you are both enthusiastic and implacable, as you are at once sagacious and careless; you know much and discover much, but you are in such a hurry to tell it all you never give yourself time to think how reckless eloquence may affect others; and, what is more, if you knew how it did affect them, you would not much care.
>
> However, I shake hands with you . . . I still feel angry, and think I do well to be angry; but it is the anger one experiences for rough play rather than for foul play.—I am yours, with a certain respect, and more chagrin,
>
> > Currer Bell.[10]

Paradoxically, Charlotte's male pseudonym and the confusion it generated intensified the sex question instead of avoiding it. Critics and public forgot that "Currer Bell" was a device to win recognition, quickly assumed that a masculine pen name belonged to an unfeminine and unnatural female, and then began to search the novels for proof of their assumption.

Another sharp criticism of *Shirley* reached Charlotte that year, a criticism very different from Lewes', first because it came from a woman and second because the critic did not raise trivialities of "womanliness" or "unwomanliness," but went straight to the heart of the feminist issue:

"I have seen some extracts from Shirley in which you talk of women working," wrote Mary Taylor in April 1850. "And this first duty, this great necessity you seem to think that *some* women may indulge in—if they give up marriage and don't make themselves too disagreeable to the other sex. You are a coward and a traitor. A woman who works is by that alone better than one who does not and a woman who does not happen to be rich and who *still* earns no money and does not wish to do so, is guilty of a great fault—almost a crime—A dereliction of duty which leads rapidly and almost certainly to all manner of degradation. It is very wrong of you to *plead* for tolerance for workers on the ground of their being in peculiar circumstances and few in number or singular in disposition. Work or degradation is the lot of all except the very small number born to wealth."[11]

Basing *Shirley* on the Luddite riots, Charlotte had been attracted more and more as she wrote by the idea of contrasting the lives of two young women, Shirley Keeldar and Caroline Helstone. Caroline is Charlotte's only pathetic heroine because her only non-working heroine. She lives a life of tedious tea parties, calls, and charity work, fluttering like a pale ghost in her uncle's silent house.

Helstone, the uncle, is a woman hater and a tyrant, and completely unsympathetic to Caroline's longing for independence and usefulness. "Stick to the needle," he tells her impatiently, "—learn shirt-making and gown-making, and pie-crust making, and you'll be a clever woman some day. Go to bed now; I'm busy with a pamphlet here." When on a different occasion Caroline suggests going out as a governess, he turns on her: " 'Pooh! mere nonsense! I'll not hear of governessing. It is rather too feminine a fancy. I have finished breakfast. Ring the bell. Put all crotchets out of your head, and run away and amuse yourself.'

" 'What with? My doll?' asked Caroline to herself as she quitted the room."

Ellen believed Caroline to be *her* portrait, but Charlotte wrote her own frustrations into the character as well, transcribing in the following conversation between Caroline and Rose Yorke (Mary Taylor) some of Mary's horror at her stagnant life at Haworth and Mary's own determination to escape:

> ". . . I cannot live always in Briarfield" [Rose Yorke insists]. ". . . I am resolved that my life shall be a life: not a black trance like the toad's, buried in marble; nor a long, slow death like yours in Briarfield Rectory."
>
> "Like mine! What can you mean, child?"
>
> "Might you not as well be tediously dying, as for ever shut up in that glebe-house—a place that, when I pass it, always reminds me of a windowed grave? I never see any movement about the door: I never hear a sound from the wall: I believe smoke never issues from the chimneys. What do you do there?"
>
> "I sew, I read, I learn lessons."
>
> "Are you happy?"
>
> "Should I be happier wandering alone in strange countries as you wish to do?"
>
> "Much happier, even if you did nothing but wander. . . ."

Because Caroline has nothing else to occupy her mind or time, her whole life hangs on the balance of Robert Moore's affection. Nowhere else did Charlotte portray the contrast between man's active and woman's passive lives so vividly. Moore, a busy mill owner and man of affairs, strides carelessly in and out of Caroline's small, insipid world. When he deigns to give her a word or a smile, she is touched into life; when he ignores her she falls into depression, illness, and almost dies. Caroline is the quintessential Victorian young lady, languishing amidst a little piano playing, a little sewing for the Jew basket, a little fancy work, a little visiting; waiting for a man to transport her through marriage to the more exhilarating realm of linen presses, pantry shelves, darned stockings, and childbearing.

In violent contrast, Shirley Keeldar manages an estate, closes business deals, patronizes the district. She radiates confidence and vitality. Even her movements are free: she throws herself on the grass, strides about with hands clasped behind her back, swaggers like "a little gentleman," and throws back her head in laughter. Yet, despite her masculine name and pose, she is completely feminine. Feminine, however, does not mean ladylike, and she makes the distinction clear to a conservative uncle who worries whether she is "a young lady": "I am a thousand times better," declares Shirley: "I am an honest woman, and as such I will be treated." *She* is not waiting for marriage; in fact, the idea alarms her: " 'I could never be my own mistress more. A terrible thought!—it suffocates me! Nothing irks me like the idea of being a burden and a bore,—an inevitable burden,—a ceaseless bore! Now, when I feel my company superfluous, I can comfortably fold my independence round me like a mantle, and drop my pride like a veil, and withdraw to solitude. If married, that could not be.' "

The source of Shirley's independence is not genius like Emily's, however, but wealth. Since few women are heiresses, Mary Taylor attacked Charlotte for shirking the real issue of female economic independence. What was her remedy for the Caroline Helstones of the world? "To teach is not my vocation," Charlotte told Ellen; and *Shirley* voices deep frustration but provides no answers. Convinced that all women should have useful work to do, she believed that eight out of ten women would find that work in raising a family. She could not imagine a labor market that would support a vast influx of women workers. At the same time she saw clearly that women's economic dependence upon men kept them subordinate. But she saw no ready political or economic solution to the problem.

I often wish to say something about the "condition of women" question [she had written Williams in the spring of 1848], but it is one respecting which so much "cant" has been talked, that one feels a sort of repugnance to approach it. It is true enough that the present market for female labour is quite overstocked, but where or how could another be opened? Many say that the professions now filled only by men should be open to women also; but are not their present occupants and candidates more than numerous enough to answer every demand? Is there any room for female lawyers, female doctors, female engravers, for more female artists, more authoresses? One can see where the evil lies, but who can point out the remedy? When a woman has a little family to rear and educate and a household to conduct, her hands are full, her vocation is evident; when her destiny isolates her, I suppose she must do what she can, live as she can, complain as little, bear as much, work as well as possible. This is not high theory, but I believe it is sound practice, good to put into execution while philosophers and legislators ponder over the better ordering of the social system. At the same time, I conceive that when patience has done its utmost and industry its best, whether in the case of women or operatives, and when both are baffled, and pain and want triumph, the sufferer is free, is entitled, at last to send up to Heaven any piercing cry for relief, if by that cry he can hope to obtain succour.[12]

This "piercing cry for relief" rings through all Charlotte's fiction, no matter how much she rationalized the "condition of women" case in fact. But in fact, too, she said much that Mary Taylor would have agreed with, and felt a great deal more. "I think you speak excellent sense when you say that girls without fortune should be brought up and accustomed to support themselves," she wrote, again to Williams, who over the years discussed at length with her the education of his daughters Ellen, Fanny, and Louisa; "and that if they marry poor men, it should be with a prospect of being able to help their partners. If all parents thought so, girls would not be reared on speculation with a view to their making mercenary marriages; and, consequently, women would not be so piteously degraded as they now too often are."[13]

Many Victorians believed that a woman should be educated—so she could be a better companion for her husband. This was not Charlotte's view. "I hope she will succeed," she replied to Williams' news that Louisa might be accepted at the newly founded Queen's College in Harley Street, London.[14]

Do not—my dear Sir—be indifferent—be earnest about it. Come what may afterwards, an education secured is an advantage gained—a priceless advantage . . . a step toward independency—and one great curse of a single female life is its dependency . . . encourage her in the wish. Your daughters—no more than your sons—should be a burden on your hands. Your daughters—as much as your sons—should aim at making their way honourably through life. Do not wish to keep them at home. Believe me—teachers may be hard-worked, ill-paid and despised— but the girl who stays at home doing nothing is worse off than the

hardest-wrought and worst-paid drudge of a school. . . . Lonely as I
am—how should I be if Providence had never given me courage to
adopt a career—perseverance to plead through two long, weary years
with publishers till they admitted me? How should I be with youth
past—sisters lost—a resident in a moorland parish where there is not a
single educated family? In that case I should have no world at
all. . . . As it is, something like a hope and motive sustains me
still. I wish all your daughters—I wish every woman in England had
also a hope and a motive: Alas there are many old maids who have
neither.[15]

As a single woman, partly from circumstance, partly from predilec-
tion, Charlotte naturally thought and wrote most about that class.
Only *The Professor* deals with marriage; it does so briefly, and shows
both wife and husband managing a school, much like the enviable
Heger arrangement: Frances Henri's independence is intact. Jane
Eyre is both a governess and a schoolteacher, and the novel ends
abruptly with her marriage before the reader can wonder what this
energetic woman will do without new obstacles to triumph over. In
*Villette*, Charlotte would drown the hero and give Lucy Snowe a
schoolroom for comfort instead.

*Shirley* ends with a double wedding, but in defiance, for the novel
has sounded throughout an anti-marriage theme.[16] There are no good
marriages in *Shirley*. Matthew Helstone, Caroline's woman-hating
uncle, has buried one neglected, downtrodden wife and considers *committing* matrimony a second time, but only if he can find a woman
foolish enough to despise. Mr. and Mrs. Yorke tolerate each other, but
Mrs. Yorke is gloomy and resentful from a heavy sense of martyrdom
to Woman's Duty. Mrs. Pryor and her infant daughter are abandoned
by a drunken, profligate husband. The position of the mill foreman's
wife is revealed indirectly in her husband's pronouncement, "Women
is to take their husband's opinion, both in politics and religion. It's
wholesome for them." The brazen curate Malone and the practical
Mr. Yorke advocate marrying—for money. The keynote is voiced by
Helstone: "Millions of marriages are unhappy. If everybody confessed
the truth, perhaps all are more or less so."

Charlotte was not so naïve that she believed single women lived in
bliss. Hortense Moore keeps house for her brother Robert, compulsively and vacantly tidying drawers already neat and spending endless hours with her workbasket because darning is one of "the first
duties of woman." Miss Mann, Miss Ainley, and Margaret Hall, three
old maids, are neglected, mildly despised, and lonely. But they are not
exploited, and Charlotte found single women pitiable only when they
had no useful work to do. Thus, in 1846, she had written Miss Wooler

rejoicing that her friend was finding happiness and tranquillity apart from family life: ". . . I am glad of that—I speculate much on the existence of unmarried and never-to-be-married women nowadays, and I have already got to the point of considering that there is no more respectable character on this earth than an unmarried woman who makes her own way through life quietly perseveringly [sic]—without support of husband or brother, and who, having attained the age of 45 or upwards—retains in her possession a well-regulated mind—a disposition to enjoy simple pleasures—fortitude to support inevitable pains, sympathy with the sufferings of others, and willingness to relieve want as far as her means extend."[17]

Mary Taylor criticized Charlotte for shirking the work issue in *Shirley*, but in emigrating to New Zealand tacitly admitted that she herself could not solve the problem in England. There, after the initial shock of finding that she had left all the cultural heritage of England behind, she reveled in her new independence. "I think I told you I built a house," she had written Charlotte in the summer of 1848, full of her new business ventures.

> I get 12/- a week for it. Moreover in accordance with a late letter of John's I borrow money from him and Joe and buy cattle with it. I have already spent £100 or so and intend to buy some more as soon as War [i.e., Waring] can pay me the money.—perhaps as much *by degrees* as £400, or £500. As I only pay 5 per Ct. interest I expect [to] profit much by this. viz. about 30 per Ct. a year—perhaps 40 or 50. Thus if I borrow £500 in two years' time (I cannot have it quicker) I shall perhaps make £250 to £300. I am pretty certain of being able to pay principal and interest. If I could command £300 and £50 a year afterwards I would "*hallack*" about N.Z. for a twelve-month then go home by way of India and write my travels which would prepare the way for my novel. . . .
>
> I must now tell you the fate of your cow. The creature gave so little milk that she is doomed to be fatted and killed. In about 2 months she will fetch perhaps £15 with which I shall buy 3 heifers. Thus you will have the chance of getting a calf *sometime*. My own thrive well and possibly I [shall] have a calf myself. Before this reaches England I shall have 3 or 4.
>
> It's a pity you don't live in this world that I might entertain you about the price of meat. Do you know I bought 6 heifers the other day for £23? and now it is turned so cold I expect to hear one half of them are dead. One man bought 20 sheep for £8 and they are all dead but 1. Another bought 150 and has 40 left; and people have begun to drive cattle through a valley into the Wairau plains and thence across the Straits to Wellington. etc etc. This is the only legitimate subject of conversation we have . . ."[18]

In February 1849, despite dead cattle, Maori uprisings, and earth-quakes ("Two fifths if not half the houses in Wellington were shaken down by the earthquake and the town is vastly improved in conse-quence"), Mary was so pleased with life in New Zealand that she wrote Ellen Nussey seriously urging her to come out:

> I hear fm C. Brontë that you are staying in Sussex. What in the world are you doing there? Getting your living in any way? not at all— you are only wishing to do. Wishing for something to turn up that wd enable you to work for yourself instead of for other people and that no one shd know that you were working. Now no such thing exists. There are no means for a woman to live in England but by teaching, sewing or washing. The last is the best. The best paid the least unhealthy and the most free. But it is not paid well enough to live by. Moreover it is impossible for any one not born to this position to take it up after-wards. I don't know why but it is. You might as well ask why one can't move when they have the nightmare, when they know very well— the stupid things! that they need only just move to send the horror away. If you do it at all it will be by making a desperate plunge, and you will come up in another world. The new world will be no Paradise but still much better than the nightmare. Am I not right in all this? and dont you know it very well? Or am I shooting in the dark? . . . What in the world keeps you? Try and persuade some of your twenty brothers to fit you out for N. Zealand. You could get your living here at any of the trades I have mentioned which you wd only d[ie] of in England. As to "society" position in the world you must have found by this time it is all my eye seeking society without the means to enjoy it. Why not come here then? and be happy.[19]

Ellen must have shaken her smooth brown head at this, sighed, and answered, "Home, mother, and duty." Nor did she follow Mary's ad-vice to send the articles she patiently hemmed, beaded, and netted with her plump white hands out to New Zealand for Mary to sell— the elegant little collars, ear warmers, cuffs, wrist warmers, purses, slippers, watch guards, garters, watch chains, bracelets, scissors cases, caps, foot warmers, bags, wrist frills, and collar ribbons. Ellen was dis-content, but not energetically discontent. Afternoon tea, clerical visits, churchgoing, morning calls, heavy Sunday dinners, religious tracts to dutifully read and profit by, gossips, visiting within her little circle of Healds, Carrs, Claphams, and Gorhams: all wove a net too heavy to slip. Had Mary mentioned New Zealand statistics—528 bachelors and 500 redcoats to 248 spinsters in the Wellington settlement—Ellen might have been tempted, but Mary was more interested in cattle prices than in men. Here she differed from many female immigrants. Mary Swainson Marshall, daughter of New Zealand's attorney-gen-eral, claimed she had more offers of marriage in a few years than she would have had in a whole lifetime in England. Nor were youth and beauty requisite: "Fancy, the mother of a woman I had for a month had a wooden leg, a son of 22, and six children, yet has just been married again! No one need despair after that, I think."[20]

Mary's enthusiasm did convince her cousin Ellen Taylor to come out with her brother Henry. Together the two women set up a shop: "We *like* it, and that's the truth." Despite Charlotte's success and fame, Mary still pitied her from afar, for Charlotte's letters contained the eternal plaint of loneliness and frustration.

> Your next letter to me ought to bring me good news; more cheerful than the last [Mary closed her letter of April 1850]. You will some how get drawn out of your hole and find interests among your fellow creatures. Do you know that living among people with whom you have not the slightest interest in common is just like living alone, or worse. Ellen Nussey is the only one you can talk to, that I know of at least. Give my love to her, and to Miss Wooler if you have the opportunity. I am writing this on just such a night as you will likely read it. Rain and storm—coming winter and a glowing fire—Ours is on the ground, wood, no fender or irons—no matter we are very comfortable
>
> Pag.[21]

Congenial or uncongenial, people were beginning to seek Charlotte out, drawn by her success; and with characteristic ambivalence, she compulsively resisted their attention, lonely as she was. In January 1850 a letter came to the parsonage from Sir James Kay-Shuttleworth, physician, philanthropist, and literary patron: he begged to make Charlotte's acquaintance and have the honor of visiting her. Charlotte demurred, but other letters followed: by March Sir James had pressed her into inviting him to Haworth. That same month his fine carriage rattled up to the door, and he leaped out, a vigorous man looking younger than his forty-four years, accompanied by a rather young, dark-haired, dark-eyed wife. For the occasion Mr. Brontë forsook his slippers and wound a fresh silk cravat. He was jealous of his daughter's fame and anxious that she pursue every important connection. Sipping tea before the fire, Sir James and his lady pressed Charlotte to visit Gawthorpe Hall, their estate in East Lancashire. Charlotte replied promptly that her father's poor health must keep her at home, and thought the matter closed. To her surprise, Papa took up the Kay-Shuttleworths' cause: she must go, he would not hear of her refusing. Left without an excuse, Charlotte gave in, promising the baronet that she would come to them soon, refusing absolutely to be bundled into the carriage immediately, as Sir James proposed.

She viewed the visit with apprehension: she hated accepting favors she could not repay; she did not entirely trust the baronet's motives:

"Sir James is very courtly, fine-looking; I wish he may be as sincere as he is polished. He shows his white teeth with too frequent a smile; but I will not prejudge him."[22]

She packed her good black silk, still reluctant, and took the train as far as Burnley where she found Sir James waiting in the carriage, very gallant, very courtly. A drive of three miles took them out of smoke-blackened Burnley through hilly, forested country to the gates of Gawthorpe, then up a long, "somewhat desolate" tree-arched avenue. Gawthorpe Hall hulked at the end of the drive, a huge, gray, castellated pile. The Jacobean estate, two hundred and fifty years old, belonged to Lady Janet Kay-Shuttleworth and not to the baronet, who had taken her name upon marriage. As the arms and crest carved deep in the oak paneling of every room testified, this was no parvenu family like the Smiths, but old county stock that could trace its lineage back to Richard III.

A day of acute observation and obedient attendance upon Sir James's monologues by the fireside in the oak-paneled drawing room, and Charlotte had summed up the Kay-Shuttleworths to her satisfaction: ". . . Lady Shuttleworth is a little woman 32 years old, with a pretty, smooth, lively face. Of pretension to aristocratic airs, she may be entirely acquitted—of frankness, good-humour and activity she has enough—truth obliges me to add that as it seemed to me—grace, dignity, fine feeling were not in the inventory of her qualities. These last are precisely what her husband possesses—in manner he can be gracious and dignified—his tastes and feelings are capable of elevation: frank he is not, but on the contrary—politic—he calls himself a man of the world and knows the world's ways; courtly and affable in some points of view—he is strict and rigourous in others. . . . They get on perfectly together. The children, there are four of them, are all fine children in their way."[23]

Judging her betters with the same cool, critical assurance that had infuriated some readers of *Jane Eyre*, she was characteristically drawn in sympathy to the German governess, "a quiet, well-instructed, interesting girl whom I took to at once—and, in my heart, liked better than anything else in the house. She also instinctively took to me. She is very well treated for a governess—but wore the usual pale, despondent look of her class—She told me she was homesick—and she looked so."[24] Unimpressed by wealth and breeding, Charlotte admitted people to her confidence when they met the standards of her private meritocracy: deep feeling, sincerity, simple manners, kindness.

Her visit passed more pleasantly than she had hoped, chiefly because Sir James's nerves and health were poor so that he did not invite the entire neighborhood to meet her but took her on quiet drives through the ancient woods and hills to visit gray ruins or medieval mansions like Townley Hall, or treated her to his long monologues before the drawing-room fire. Ready to go home, feeling that she had escaped very well, Charlotte was then appalled by the Kay-Shuttleworths' suggestion that she go up to London with them at the height of the season. The idea was "a perfect terror," "a menace hanging over her head." At the same time she was forced to admit that the observation of London society at its crest would provide her with new, bright-colored strands to weave into her gray existence. Reluctantly, she began to turn her thoughts again to London.

Another fame-hunting but far less distinguished guest found out the quiet parsonage one day, much to everyone's mystification.

> Yesterday, just after dinner, I heard a loud bustling voice in the kitchen demanding to see Mr Brontë [Charlotte wrote Ellen], somebody was shown into the parlour; shortly after wine was rung for. "Who is it, Martha?" I asked. "Some mak of a tradesman," said she, "he's not a gentleman, I'm sure." The personage stayed about an hour, talking in a loud vulgar key all the time. At tea-time I asked papa who it was. "Why," said he, "no other than the Rev. ——, vicar of Bierley!" Papa had invited him to take some refreshment, but the creature had ordered his dinner at the Black Bull, and was quite urgent with papa to go down there and join him, offering by way of inducement a bottle, or if papa liked, "two or three bottles of the best wine Haworth could afford!" He said he was come with a Mr C——, I think, from Bradford, just to look at the place, and reckoned to be in raptures with the wild scenery! He warmly pressed papa to come and see him at ——, and to bring his daughter with him!!! Does he know anything about the books, do you think? he made no allusion to them. I did not see him, not so much as the tail of his coat. Martha said he looked no more like a parson than she did. . . . Papa asked him if he were married. . . .[25]

No less than Mrs. Smith, Papa scrutinized the motives of all visitors: were they after his Charlotte? The old man had got it into his head that she was laying plans to be married and leave him. Only Charlotte knew how groundless his suspicions were. The only marriage plans she knew about were Joe Taylor's. Suddenly and strangely, Mary's brother had sought her out as a confidant. He was in love with Amelia Ringrose, George Nussey's fiancée before he went mad, but her father opposed the match. Disliking Joe's materialism and fickleness, Charlotte now suspected he was in love with Amelia's money rather than Amelia. Always willful, Joe Taylor had recently begun to exhibit a recklessness that reminded Charlotte too vividly of Branwell. Mr. Brontë so disliked him that he took to his bed to avoid meeting him in the house. Joe thrust his unwelcome presence upon Charlotte, how-

ever, and she found herself in the unpleasant position of mediating between him and Amelia and listening to him rage against "old Ringrose."

She found him coarse, sensual, and selfish. "—And to think," she
raged to Ellen, "that such men take as wives, as second selves, women
young, modest, sincere, pure in heart and life, with feeling all fresh,
and emotions all unworn, and bind such virtue and vitality to their
own withered existence . . . Nature and Justice forbid the banns of
such wedlock. I write under excitement."[26] The affair triggered some
deep resentment in her, for she did not particularly care for Ellen's
dear friend Amelia Ringrose. Civil to her in letters, she could not resist a few well-aimed stabs when writing to Ellen: "I have just got a
note from Amelia Ringrose enclosing a little ear-cap. I hope she won't
trouble herself to make me these small presents often"; or: "I have
just got another letter from Amelia—she is a good and kind girl—but
when she is married she must take care to be more sparing of her love
to her spouse than she is of epistles to her friends."

With such rather unsatisfactory episodes the winter of 1850 wore
on to spring. Her spirits and health varied with sun, wind, and rain.
Cold damp winds driving across the bald moors from the northeast
played havoc with her delicate constitution: headache, gastric pain,
toothache, facial neuritis, colds, sore throat—all harried her in rapid
succession. Unable yet to begin another book, she depended more
than usual on messages from Cornhill to bind her to the faraway
world of literary affairs. If London kept silent for long, she fretted:
"I cannot help feeling something of the excitement of expectation
till the post hour comes, and when, day after day, it brings nothing, I
get low. This is a stupid, disgraceful, unmeaning state of things. I feel
bitterly enraged at my own dependence and folly . . . If I could
write, I dare say I should be better, but I cannot write a line."[27]
When a letter or a package did come, she was too happy, realized it,
and tried to moderate her reaction. But the packages brought pain as
well, for, untying the cords and lifting out the green- and red-bound
volumes, she felt how quiet the room was, and empty, and remembered that it had not always been so.

The books, loaned unless some author sent her a presentation copy
through Smith, Elder, were her chief companions. She enthused over
*Southey's Life*, admiring the poet because his life was both literary
and domestic: he lived privately, turning his back on London and the
coteries, as she was both forced and inclined to do. Lewes had long
ago recommended that she read Jane Austen. She obeyed his command and was antagonized by the unemotional, objective, and satiric
tone of *Pride and Prejudice*. Now she read *Emma*, "read it with in-

terest and with just the degree of admiration which Miss Austen herself would have thought sensible and suitable," she wrote Williams.
". . . there is a Chinese fidelity, a miniature delicacy in the painting:
she ruffles her reader by nothing vehement, disturbs him by nothing
profound: the Passions are perfectly unknown to her; she rejects even
a speaking acquaintance with that stormy Sisterhood . . . Her business
is not half so much with the human heart as with the human eyes,
mouth, hands and feet . . . Jane Austen was a complete and most
sensible lady, but a very incomplete, and rather insensible (*not sense-
less*) woman, if this is heresy—I cannot help it."[28]

No more could she. Jane Austen was as great in her rational, comic
objectivity as Charlotte in her passional, poetic subjectivity. They
were poles apart in the way they viewed experience, although often
the experience did not differ. The subject of both *Pride and Prejudice*
and *Jane Eyre*, for example, is a woman's efforts to preserve her identity in the face of marriage with a socially and financially superior
man. But, in Austen, Charlotte at least recognized an equal and rejected with contempt the suggestion that current writers like Eliza
Lynn could be ranked with the author of *Pride and Prejudice:* "You
mention the authoress of 'Azeth the Egyptian'; you say you think I
should sympathize 'with her daring imagination and pictorial fancy,'"
she had written Lewes, January 1848. "Permit me to undeceive you:
with infinitely more relish I can sympathize with Miss Austen's clear
common sense and subtle shrewdness. If you find no inspiration in
Miss Austen's page, neither do you find there windy wordiness; to use
your words again, she exquisitely adapts her means to her end: both
are very subdued, a little contracted, but never absurd."[29]

But she could not feed on books forever. She decided to accept the
Kay-Shuttleworths' invitation and go up to London with them—if
Papa was well and could spare her. Arrangements were made: they
would all make a slow progress up to London together, taking a week
along the way to call on Shuttleworth friends and relatives. Rightly
recognizing that she would be exhibited as the main attraction on
these stops, Charlotte declared she would "as lief have walked among
red-hot ploughshares" as meet these friends and relatives. She was
saved this agony by the sudden illness of Sir James, which made traveling with them impossible. She only regretted missing the anniversary
dinner of the Royal Literary Fund Society held in Freemason's Hall.
"Octavian Blewitt, the secretary, offered me a ticket for the Ladies'
Gallery. I should have seen all the great literati and artists gathered in
the hall below, and heard them speak," she sighed to Ellen. "Thackeray and Dickens are aways present among the rest. This cannot now
be. I don't think all London can afford another sight to me so interest-

ing."[30] Natural diffidence and unchallenged custom made Charlotte consider this slight to Currer Bell a privilege. Not till the turn of the century did women writers protest the custom that kept them suspended hungry and unacclaimed above the feast; in 1907 the Society relented and invited them to the table.

She pursued her plans alone; she would leave in May or as soon as Papa's health permitted. Spring softened the winds and she walked out often on fine days, feeling however joy neither in the sunshine nor in the swift-tumbling becks rushing down their narrow, rocky beds nor in the prospect of her journey. In London James Taylor had not forgotten her. Too reticent to tell her that he awaited her coming eagerly, he wrote, complaining obliquely about his restlessness in the fine spring weather. Missing or ignoring the compliment, she answered in tragic tones: "It is a pity to think of you all toiling at your desks in such genial weather as this. For my part, I am free to walk on the moors; but when I go out there alone everything reminds me of the times when others were with me, and then the moors seem a wilderness, featureless, solitary, saddening. My sister Emily had a particular love for them, and there is not a knoll of heather, not a branch of fern, not a young bilberry leaf, not a fluttering lark or linnet, but reminds me of her. The distant prospects were Anne's delight, and when I look round she is in the blue tints, the pale mists, the waves and shadows of the horizon. In the hill-country silence their poetry comes by lines and stanzas into my mind: once I loved it; now I dare not read it, and am driven often to wish I could taste one draught of oblivion, and forget much that, while mind remains, I never shall forget."[31]

By the end of May, Papa pronounced himself well enough for Charlotte to leave him. He was not being co-operative; he wanted her to get the trip over and done with and come back home. Eager for "one draught of oblivion" no matter what the price in frayed nerves, Charlotte went up to London for the fifth time.

# 19

Uncaged

Although the Kay-Shuttleworths plagued her to stay with them in London, Charlotte preferred to be with Mrs. Smith and her handsome, genial son; she therefore excused herself as having business to conduct which could be carried on most conveniently at her publisher's home. George Smith had taken a new house at 76 Gloucester Terrace in Hyde Park Gardens. There Mrs. Smith and her daughters prepared for Currer Bell's arrival on May 30, 1850, with some trepidation. Everything must be done to please her, but there was difficulty in deciding precisely what *would*. Much of the early reserve had thawed between them, yet Mrs. Smith was not quite at ease with Miss Brontë's gravity, her large luminous eyes that gazed with almost mesmerizing intensity, her quivering timidity. She tended to be either overwrought or silent as a stone; she had no easy chat, no sophistication. George Smith was less apprehensive. Charlotte's eccentricities could not easily unnerve his confident disposition. He liked her intelligent and quick responses, her sudden eloquence when something profoundly touched her. He admired her genius and her fierce pride. And his vanity was touched a little by the admiration in her eyes, an admiration she still believed to be quite businesslike.

Accordingly, Smith drew up an itinerary with some confidence: he believed he knew what would please Currer Bell. And she was pleased, less nervous and exhausted than she could have dared to hope. The weather was warm, the sun almost dispersed the perpetual pall of coal smoke that hung over the city. London glittered at the height of the season, crowded and gay with smart carriages and liveried footmen, dandies on horseback, pink and white parasols, brilliant shops, music in the cool green parks. Safe in a carriage or leaning on George Smith's arm, Charlotte was not forced to be clever or talkative, but could lose herself in watching the great tide of life that flowed through the streets.

Smith escorted her to the opera ("a good many Lords and Ladies . . . and, except for their elegant dresses, do not think them either much better or much worse than other people"), to the offices of the *Times,* and to the General Post Office. At the exhibition of the Royal Academy she paused long before two pictures, attracted, as always, by the heroic and the dramatic: ". . . there were some fine paintings, especially a large one by Landseer of the Duke of Wellington on the field of Waterloo, and a grand, wonderful picture of Martin's from Campbell's poem of the 'Last Man,' showing the red sun fading out of the sky, and all the soil of the foreground made up of bones and skulls." She wrote Papa a detailed account of the zoo to entertain him: American birds that made "inexpressible noises," "Ceylon toads not much smaller than Flossy," and most repellantly fascinating of all, a huge cobra that had "the eyes and face of a fiend, and darted out its barbed tongue sharply and incessantly."[1]

Of equal interest was the House of Commons where Smith escorted her to the Ladies' Gallery and left her. "The Ladies' Gallery of those days was behind the Strangers' Gallery," recalled Smith, "and from it one could see the eyes of the ladies above, nothing more. I told Miss Brontë that if she felt tired and wished to go away, she only had to look at me; I should know by the expression of her eyes what she meant and that I would come round for her. After a time I looked and looked. There were many eyes, they all seemed to be flashing signals to me, but much as I admired Miss Brontë's eyes I could not distinguish them from the others. I looked so earnestly from one pair of eyes to another that I am afraid that more than one lady must have regarded me as a rather impudent fellow. At length I went round and took my lady away. I expressed my hope that I did not keep her long waiting, and said something about the difficulty of getting out, after I saw her signal. 'I made no signal,' she said. 'I did not wish to come away. Perhaps there were other signals from the Gallery.' "[2]

Aware of Charlotte's enthusiasm for the Duke of Wellington, Smith took her to the Chapel Royal, St. James, where the Iron Duke often attended Sunday service. To her delight he was there, an old man of eighty-one, only two years from death, white-haired, Roman-nosed, still her ideal of "a real grand old man." They followed him out of the chapel and Smith was obliging enough to map their walk so that their path crossed the Duke's twice before he reached Apsley House.

Driving through Fleet Street and the Strand late at night, Charlotte exclaimed at the lights still glowing in the newspaper offices. She had always liked the City proper with its hum and bustle; the lights winking now like the eyes of the great pulsing city that never slept excited her imagination. Perhaps best of all she liked driving in the snug carriage through the cool nights under the stars with such a cheerful and friendly companion. The throngs of carriages, the velvet sky, the brilliant thoroughfares all had a wonderful charm. How much of the charm lay in "the atmosphere of friendship diffused about her," in her delight in George Smith's lively courtesy, she could not tell.

Relieved at the success of the sight-seeing expeditions, the Smiths were more apprehensive about the social gatherings at Gloucester Terrace. With Charlotte's permission, Smith invited the offending G. H. Lewes for dinner along with other literary people. Charlotte asked Smith not to point Lewes out to her. She wished to test her intuition: after the *Shirley* review, she had formed a mental picture of him as a coarse, clever man with a taste for notoriety. Seeing a vigorous, bold man enter the drawing room, a man with hollow cheeks deeply pitted by smallpox, bright, expressive eyes, and a moist, sensual mouth, she immediately—and correctly—fixed upon him as George Henry Lewes. Lewes, playing the same game, did not succeed so well, probably because he was looking for a coarse, clever, bold-looking woman. In this he was disappointed. Currer Bell was "a little, plain, provincial, sickly-looking old maid," he later confided to George Eliot. "Yet what passion, what fire in her! Quite as much as in George Sand, only the clothing is less voluptuous."

He got a blast of the passion at dinner when he had the indiscretion to lean across the table and murmur with his moist mouth, "There ought to be a bond of sympathy between us, Miss Brontë, for we have both written naughty books." Nerves on edge, thoroughly sick of the word "wicked," still rankled by the *Shirley* review, Charlotte went off like a rocket, and poor George Smith listened with mingled admiration and dismay to the dressing-down she proceeded to give Lewes. But Lewes was only echoing public opinion: Lady Herschel, finding a copy of *Jane Eyre* on Mrs. Smith's drawing-room table one evening, exclaimed, "Do you leave such a book as *this* about at the risk of your daughters reading it?"

Lewes was not intimidated by the outburst at the dinner table, however, and later he sought out Charlotte in the drawing room and sat down beside her. She could not bear a grudge long in his presence. "I have seen Lewes," she wrote Ellen, ". . . he is a man with both weaknesses and sins, but unless I err greatly the foundation of his nature is not bad—and were he almost a fiend in character—I could not feel otherwise to him than half sadly, half tenderly—a queer word the last—but I use it because the aspect of Lewes' face almost moves me to tears—it is so wonderfully like Emily—her eyes, her features—the very nose, the somewhat prominent mouth, the forehead—even at moments the expression: whatever Lewes does or says, I believe I cannot hate him."[3] On parting, she offered her small hand, smiling, and said: "We are friends now, are we not?" Still unconscious how deeply his comments in the *Edinburgh Review* had hurt her, Lewes was surprised. "Were we not always, then?" he asked. "No! not always," Charlotte replied significantly, the only allusion she ever made to the offending article.

It was her fate to be bitterly reminded of the dead even though she had come to London to elude them. She visited Julia Kavanagh, a young writer who had sent her novel *Madeleine* to Charlotte and expressed a longing to meet Currer Bell. Here was a life far more impoverished than her own, yet similar: a grotesque London caricature. ". . . I found a little, almost dwarfish figure to which even I had to look down—not deformed—that is—not hunchbacked but long-armed and with a large head and (at first sight) a strange face. She met me half-frankly, half tremblingly; we sat down together . . . She lives in a poor but clean and neat little lodging—her mother seems a somewhat weak-minded woman who can be no companion to her—her father has quite deserted his wife and child—and this poor little feeble, intelligent, cordial thing wastes her brain to gain a living. She is twenty-five years old."[4] As she talked with the sensitive Miss Kavanagh, the past reasserted itself again: the face lost its strangeness, becoming mournfully familiar—"it was Martha Taylor on every lineament."

At last even her own face haunted her with ghosts from the past. George Smith persuaded her to have her portrait done by the famous George Richmond as a gift for her father. She consented; had several sittings during which Richmond with difficulty tried to make her relax; at last was allowed to view the finished crayon drawing. At the sight she burst into tears. Quickly wiping them away, she explained that the face reminded her so much of her sister Emily.

Thackeray came round to Gloucester Terrace one morning and the "strange scene" that followed proved conclusively that, much as the Titan admired *Jane Eyre* and Currer Bell the Titan, they mixed together not quite as well as oil and water. The fault was Charlotte's. Having put the author of *Vanity Fair* on a pedestal as a great moralist, a great thinker, and an Oracle of Truth, she would settle for no less from the man in person. Here were two errors: one, that a writer must talk always like the greatest passages of his books; the other, that Thackeray *was* indeed a great moralist, thinker, and Oracle of Truth. He wrote fine novels but was no Carlylean sage; he had no mission; earnestness rather appalled him; humorlessness brought out the cynical in him.

Strolling over then for a casual morning call, Thackeray found himself face to face with a grave, intense little lady prepared to worship. Annoyed at this stance, he immediately became sardonical and offhand. His jesting in turn evoked more earnestness from Charlotte: he soon found himself being taken to task for his literary shortcomings. She had been disappointed in his last Christmas book; had complained to Williams that, "whenever he writes, Mephistopheles stands on his right hand and Raphael on his left; the great doubter and sneerer usually guides the pen, the Angel, noble and gentle, interlines letters of light here and there. Alas! Thackeray, I wish your strong wings would lift you oftener above the smoke of cities into the pure region nearer heaven!"[5] Addressed now in this strain, Thackeray could only become irreverent. Charlotte herself described the scene that Smith witnessed with mingled amusement and dismay in his drawing room that June morning: "The giant sat before me— I was moved to speak to him of some of his shortcomings (literary of course) one by one the faults came into my mind and one by one I brought them out and sought some explanation or defense—He did defend himself like a great Turk and heathen—that is to say, the excuses were often worse than the crime itself. The matter ended in decent amity—if all be well I am to dine at his house this evening."[6]

Charlotte prepared for the evening with a great deal of care since it was to be a party in her honor, donning a light silky dress patterned with faint green moss, and pinning a plait of conspicuously false hair across the top of her head, for such plaits were all the rage and her smooth brown hair was not thick enough to make one. Did she, like Lucy Snowe, glance into the mirror "with fear and trembling," and "with more fear and trembling" turn away?

Across Hyde Park at 13 Young Street, Kensington, Thackeray's young daughters, Anne and Harriet, were in ecstasies at the prospect of an evening with "Jane Eyre." Thackeray and Miss Truelock, the governess who had survived the scandal Charlotte unwittingly created by her dedication, had given the girls permission to stay up just this once for an adult affair. Anne Thackeray, later Lady Ritchie, never forgot that warm evening in June:

> One of the most notable persons who ever came into our bow-windowed drawing-room in Young Street is a guest never to be forgotten by me—a tiny, delicate, little person, whose small hand nevertheless grasped a mighty lever which set all the literary world of

that day vibrating. I can still see the scene quite plainly—the hot summer evening, the open windows, the carriage driving to the door as we all sat silent and expectant; my father, who rarely waited, waiting with us; our governess and my sister and I all in a row, and prepared for the great event. We saw the carriage stop, and out of it sprang the active, well-knit figure of Mr. George Smith, who was bringing Miss Brontë to see our father. My father, who had been walking up and down the room, goes out into the hall to meet his guests, and then, after a moment's delay, the door opens wide, and the two gentlemen come in, leading a tiny, delicate, serious, little lady, pale, with fair straight hair, and steady eyes. She may be a little over thirty; she is dressed in a little barège dress, with a pattern of faint green moss. She enters in mittens, in silence, in seriousness; our hearts are beating with wild excitement. This, then, is the authoress, the unknown power whose books have set all London talking, reading, and speculating; some people even say our father wrote the books—the wonderful books. To say that we little girls had been given "Jane Eyre" to read scarcely represents the facts of the case; to say that we had taken it without leave, read bits here and bits there, been carried away by an undreamed of and hitherto unimagined whirlwind into things, times, and places, all utterly absorbing, and at the same time absolutely unintelligible to us, would more accurately describe our state of mind on that summer's evening as we look at Jane Eyre—the great Jane Eyre— the tiny little lady. The moment is so breathless that dinner comes as a relief to the solemnity of the occasion, and we all smile as my father stoops to offer his arm; for, though genius she may be, Miss Brontë can barely reach his elbow. My own personal impressions are that she is somewhat grave and stern, especially to forward little girls who wish to chatter. Mr. George Smith has since told me how she afterwards remarked on my father's wonderful forebearance and gentleness with our uncalled-for incursions into the conversation. She sat gazing at him with kindling eyes of interest, lighting up with a sort of illumination every now and then as she answered him. I can see her bending forward over the table, not eating, but listening to what he said as he carved the dish before him.

I think it must have been on this very occasion that my father invited some of his friends in the evening to meet Miss Brontë—for everyone was interested and anxious to see her. Mrs. Crowe, the reciter of ghost-stories, was there. Mrs. Brookfield, Mrs. Carlyle, Mr. Carlyle himself was present, so I am told, railing at the appearance of cockneys upon Scotch mountain sides; there were also too many Americans for his taste, "but the Americans were as gods compared to the cockneys," says the philosopher. Besides the Carlyles, there were Mrs. Elliott and Miss Perry, Mrs. Procter and her daughter, most of my father's habitual friends and companions. In the recent life of Lord Houghton I was amused to see a note quoted in which Lord Houghton also was convened. Would that he had been present—perhaps the party would have gone off better. It was a gloomy and silent evening. Every one waited for the brilliant conversation which never began at all. Miss Brontë retired to a sofa in the study, and murmured a word now and then to our kind governess, Miss Truelock. The room looked very dark, the lamp began to smoke a little, the conversation grew dimmer and more dim, the ladies sat round still expectant, my father was too much perturbed by the gloom and the silence to be able to cope with it at all. Mrs. Brookfield, who was in the doorway by the study, near the corner in which Miss Brontë was sitting, leant forward with a little commonplace, since brilliance was not to be the order of the evening. "Do you like London, Miss Brontë?" she said; another silence, a pause, then Miss Brontë answers, "Yes and No," very gravely. Mrs. Brookfield has herself reported the conversation. My sister and I were much too young to be bored in those days; alarmed, impressed we might be, but not yet bored. A party was a party, a lioness was a lioness; and—shall I confess it?—at that time an extra dish of biscuits was enough to mark the evening. We felt all the importance of the occasion; tea spread in the dining-room, ladies in the drawing-room. We roamed about inconveniently, no doubt, and excitedly, and in one of my incursions crossing the hall, after Miss Brontë had left, I was surprised to see my father opening the front door with his hat on. He put his fingers to his lips, walked out into the darkness, and shut the door quietly behind him. When I went back into the drawing-room again, the ladies asked me where he was. I vaguely answered that I thought he was coming back. I was puzzled at the time nor was it all made clear to me till long afterwards, when one day Mrs. Procter asked me if I knew what had happened once when my father had invited a party to meet Jane Eyre at his house. It was one of the dullest evenings she had ever spent in her life, she said. And then with a good deal of humour she described the situation—the ladies who had all come expecting so much delightful conversation, and the gloom, and the constraint, and how, finally overwhelmed by the situation, my father had quietly left the room, left the house, and gone off to his club. The ladies waited, wondered, and finally departed also; and as we were going up to bed with our candles after everybody was gone, I remember two pretty Miss L——'s, in shiny silk dresses, arriving full of expectation. . . . We still said we thought our father would soon be back, but the Miss L——'s declined to wait upon the chance, and drove away again almost immediately.[7]

In her own way, Charlotte Brontë could dominate a drawing room. Long afterward, Mrs. Brookfield loved to tell the story of her "conversation" with Charlotte Brontë, mimicking her grave, "Yes, and No." When her audience would ask, "Yes, and then?" she would triumphantly exclaim, "But that's all!" The socialite dismissed Currer Bell as gauche and dull and unable to "fall in with the easy badinage of the well-bred people with whom she found herself surrounded."

Charlotte herself never stinted on severe judgments: she had little use for the Mrs. Brookfields of the world and their fashionable jargon. "Your well-bred people," she had written Ellen four years previously, "appear to me (figuratively speaking) to walk on their heads, to see everything the wrong way up; a lie is with them truth,—truth a lie; eternal and tedious botheration is their notion of happiness, sensible pursuits their *ennui* . . . if I were called upon to 'swap' . . . tastes and ideas and feelings . . . I should prefer walking into a good Yorkshire kitchen fire and conclude the bargain at once by an act of voluntary combustion."[8]

Jane Carlyle found Charlotte "extremely unimpressive to *look* at," but one guest, at least, was impressed with Currer Bell that evening. John Everett Millais, only twenty-two but already a successful painter, was taken up to be introduced by Thackeray and found the eyes lifted to his face "quite remarkable." He immediately offered to paint her, but she refused since she was committed to Richmond. Nevertheless, Millais never forgot those kindling eyes: Currer Bell remained his idea of a woman of genius. Was it common prejudice against "literary ladies" or Charlotte's nervous pallor that led Millais to conclude that "the little lady looked tired with her own brains"?

If Thackeray had paid more heed to the drawing-room scenes in *Jane Eyre*, he might have guessed how little Charlotte could appreciate such entertainment. As a matter of fact, Charlotte had faced the situation more calmly than her host who fled in confusion. Driving back to Gloucester Terrace through the warm London night lit by gaslight, she seemed unaware that her presence had turned a whole gathering to stone. Instead she was pondering the meaning of the admiring glances George Smith had thrown all evening at a very charming young lady, Miss Adelaide Procter.[9] Smith was startled when suddenly the small figure opposite him leaned forward out of the gloom, put her hands on his knees, and said: "She would make you a very nice wife." "Whom do you mean?" Smith answered in some confusion. "Oh! You know whom I mean," said Charlotte, and lapsed into silence. It was the sort of masochistic exercise she loved to break her teeth on, for the good of her soul. In her own metaphor: "You held out your hand for an egg and fate put into it a scorpion. Show no consternation: close your fingers firmly upon the gift; let it sting through your palm. Never mind: in time, after your hand and arm have swelled and quivered long with torture, the squeezed scorpion will die, and you will have learned the great lesson how to endure without a sob."[10] To ride through the summer night with a good and charming man in a carriage, to be plain, puny Currer Bell on the outside and a being of soul and fire within—this was indeed a lesson in how to endure without a sob.

George Smith was not afraid of Charlotte. He did not squirm when her serious eyes seemed to analyze him to the bone; he was not offended when she sometimes confided the analysis. He was, in fact, rather drawn to her. As a result, he climaxed the fortnight in London by inviting her to take a journey with him to Edinburgh. Charlotte received the proposal as a joke, laughed, and turned it off; but Smith was serious. His young brother Alick was at school in Scotland; he and his sister Eliza planned to fetch him home for the vacation. Since Charlotte was going from London to Brookroyd, she could simply extend her holiday, meet them in Argyllshire, travel with them through the Highlands and then to Edinburgh where his brother would join them. Suspicious of Charlotte if not of her son, Mrs. Smith joined in Charlotte's objections to the journey with unflattering eagerness. But Smith was determined. "His mother is master of the house, but he is master of his mother," Charlotte wrote Ellen as her visit in London drew to a close. "This morning she came and entreated me to go. 'George wished it so much'; he had begged her to use her influence, etc., etc. Now I believe that George and I understand each other very well, and respect each other very sincerely," she went on, squeezing the scorpion tighter. "We both know the wide breach time has made between us; we do not embarrass each other, or very rarely, my six or eight years of seniority, to say nothing of lack of all pretension to beauty, etc., are a perfect safeguard. I should not in the least fear to go with him to China. I like to see him pleased, I greatly *dis*like to ruffle and disappoint him, so he shall have his mind, and, if all be well, I mean to join him in Edinburgh after I have spent a few days with you. With his buoyant animal spirits and youthful vigour he will make severe demands on my muscles and nerves, but I dare say I shall get through somehow, and then perhaps come back to rest a few days with you before I go home."[11]

At Brookroyd, a kind of masochistic delight in self-denial (or perhaps a desire to ruffle George Smith after all) inspired her to write Smith canceling the first part of the trip: "It is written that I should not meet you at Tarbet [sic], and at this perversity of the Fates I should be much more concerned than I am if I did not feel very certain that the loss in the matter will be chiefly my own."[12] She took care to announce the change in plans to Mrs. Smith, again on the scorpion principle: ". . . I only hope he will not be at all disappointed—and indeed, as he is now in the full excitement of his tour, the change of plan will probably appear of no consequence."

She ended by allowing herself barely three days in Scotland, meeting Smith in Edinburgh the evening of July 3 to find him decidedly put out at her willfulness. Two happy days followed, however:

"some hours as happy almost as any I ever spent," said Charlotte, not given to careless statement. Compared to London's sober, utilitarian face, she found Edinburgh a stirring, romantic town, a bright lyric instead of "a rambling, heavy epic"; a "vivid page of history compared to a huge dull treatise on political economy." They climbed high, windy Arthur's Seat and looked long at the spacious city below dominated by the castle brooding on its cliff; then turned to the sea and the port town of Leith and the Pentland Hills. The Scottish character pleased her, for it was like the Yorkshire—rough, dour, independent, romantic. From Edinburgh the four proceeded south through the border country beloved of Walter Scott to his home Abbotsford on the banks of the Tweed, and then to Melrose with its fragile, rosy-hued abbey. "Melrose and Abbotsford," said Charlotte, reveling in youthful memories of *Waverley*, *Rob Roy*, and *The Bride of Lammermoor*, "the very names possess music and magic." Yet how much of the journey's delight was due to the high spirits and intelligent company of George Smith she did not know, and hardly dared to know.

They parted at York, the three Smiths returning to London and Charlotte to Ellen for a few days of companionship before facing the stillness of Haworth. At Brookroyd she fell ill, and Ellen tried to persuade her to stay until completely well but, uneasy about her long absence from home, she forced herself to leave after a few days. She was glad she did, for near Haworth, at the foot of Bridge-house hill, she met the tiny, hunched figure of John Greenwood coming along, staff in hand. He hailed down the conveyance and informed her he was on his way to Brookroyd on Mr. Brontë's orders to find out what she was up to and bring her home. She reached the parsonage to find Papa "worked up to a sad pitch of nervous excitement and alarm," to which Martha and Tabby were adding their cries. The old man had it in his head that she was married or sick—both were bad, but the first was worse. Such unwarranted suspicions must have caused her tears of vexation in private, for they made more painful a fact she was too honest to deny—that George Smith's attentions had never slipped across the line of friendship.

The house was topsy-turvy, having undergone a reroofing while she was away; there was enough rearranging to keep her disagreeably busy for days to come; there was the heavy stone of solitude to heave up again and struggle under. Her depression was so severe on these homecomings that she did not dare write to London until the gloom lifted and her feelings were again under control. At these times she seriously considered closing all correspondence with Cornhill, feeling it painful and degrading to be dependent upon such transitory stimulants as letters, which, when withdrawn, made her more wretched than before. To make matters worse, she must disguise every trace of depression or illness from Papa, who tormented her daily with his anxieties over her health and her heart. He had a fixed belief that his daughter's delicate constitution could not survive the marriage or the childbed; he had an equally fixed idea that she was about to be married. His fears, his suspicions, his warnings tyrannized her unbearably. When Ellen joined in from Brookroyd, Charlotte could stand no more. She wrote: would her friend please never broach the subject of health and marriage to her again? "It is the undisguised and most harassing anxiety of others that has fixed in my mind thoughts and expectations which must canker wherever they take root—against which every effort either of religion or philosophy must at times totally fail . . . I have had to entreat Papa's consideration on this point—indeed I have had to command it—my nervous system is soon wrought on. . . ."[13]

She could not give up the London stimulants, of course. A package arrived from Smith containing a portrait of Wellington and her own portrait by Richmond; her life was again touched by a warm southern sun. Mr. Brontë declared the portrait of the Iron Duke to be his very image; and Richmond's crayon drawing elicited equal enthusiasm from "the few people" who saw it. Only old Tabby insisted that the picture was not like her at all, that it was much too old-looking, "but, as she, with equal tenacity, asserts that the Duke of Wellington's picture is a portrait of 'the Master' (meaning papa)," Charlotte told Smith, "I am afraid not much weight is to be ascribed to her opinion; doubtless she confuses her recollections of me as I was in childhood with present impressions."[14] But Papa too thought that the face gazing from the frame with such sad, luminous eyes did not do Charlotte justice: it looked older than his daughter and the features were far from flattered, although the expression was lifelike. When an old man of seventy-four, George Smith confided to Mrs. Humphrey Ward that Charlotte Brontë had no charm or grace of person. Yet the sensitive head of Richmond's drawing with its wide-set eyes, broad, intellectual forehead, wistful, rather crooked smile, and firm chin, the smooth brown hair parted in the middle and drawn back loosely over the ears *en bandeau* is not the portrait of a graceless person.

Within three weeks the oppression of solitude had driven her to leave Haworth again. "I am going on Monday (D. V.) a journey—whereof the prospect cheers me not at all," she wrote Ellen, August 16, 1850, "—to Windermere in Westmoreland to spend a few days with Sir J. K. Shuttleworth who has taken a house there for the

Autumn and Winter—I consented to go with reluctance—chiefly to please Papa whom a refusal on my part would much have annoyed—but I dislike to leave him."[15] Mr. Brontë—the old Tory—loved a baronet. So Charlotte packed her good black silk again and, seeking "something apart from the sphere of her sorrow," fled to Windermere just as though she could leave discontent behind her.

# 20

*Gain*

Arriving at eight o'clock the evening of August 18 after a tedious
journey involving three carriage changes and an hour-and-a-half
wait at Lancaster, Charlotte was greeted by the large, white-toothed
smile of Sir James Kay-Shuttleworth and whisked off to the Briery
on Windermere. The next day through sifting mists and clouds and
sudden bursts of sunshine she caught glimpses of the Langdale Pikes
and Coniston Fell looming in the distance, and below the Briery, the
waters of Windermere—magical scenery Branwell had rejoiced in
long ago on his journey to Hartley Coleridge's cottage farther north
on Derwent Water.

That same day she waited with interest for the arrival of Mrs.
Gaskell, although with no premonition that seven years later this
writer would secure her fame with *The Life of Charlotte Brontë*,
one of the finest biographies in the English language. On her part,
Elizabeth Gaskell had already fallen under the spell of Charlotte's
personality, and, as she wrote Lady Kay-Shuttleworth, strongly wished
to meet her:

> . . . I should like to hear a great deal more about her, as I have
> been so much interested in what she has written. I don't mean merely
> in the story and mode of narration, wonderful as that is, but in
> glimpses one gets of *her*, and her modes of thought, and, all uncon-
> sciously to herself, of the way in wh she has suffered. I wonder if
> she suffers *now*. Soon after I saw you at Capesthorne I heard such a
> nice account of her, from a gentleman who went over to see her
> father, & staid at the inn, where he was told of her doings as well as
> her writings. I should like very much indeed to know her: I was going
> to write to "see" her, but that is not it. I think I told you that I dis-
> liked a good deal of the plot of Shirley, but the expression of her own
> thoughts in it is so true and brave, that I greatly admire her. I am half
> amused to find you think I could do her good. . . .[1]

So Mrs. Gaskell came to Windermere, met Charlotte, and promptly relayed her impressions to her good friend Catherine Winkworth.

> Dark when I got to Windermere station; a drive along the level road to Low-wood, then a regular clamber up a steep lane; then a stoppage at a pretty house, and then a pretty drawing room . . . in which were Sir James and Lady Kay-Shuttleworth, and a little lady in a black silk gown, whom I could not see at first for the dazzle in the room; she came up & shook hands with me at once—I went up to unbonnet, &c, came down to tea, the little lady worked away and hardly spoke; but I had time for a good look at her. She is, (as she calls herself) *undeveloped;* thin and more than ½ head shorter than I, soft brown hair not so dark as mine; eyes (very good and expressive looking straight & open at you) of the same colour, a reddish face; large mouth and many teeth gone; altogether *plain;* the forehead square, broad, and *rather* overhanging. She has a very sweet voice, rather hesitates in choosing her expressions, but when chosen they seem without an effort, *admirable* and *just* befitting the occasion. There is nothing overstrained but perfectly simple.[2]

On her part, Charlotte found a handsome woman of forty, six years older than herself, but with far softer features and far happier face. Mrs. Gaskell's brown hair was looped in shining bands and drawn back into a knot, her eyes were blue and lucid, her nose straight and narrow, her mouth and teeth small. Elizabeth Stevenson had been a beauty in her youth, a social, careless creature. Underneath the flightiness ran a serious strain that emerged when she married William Gaskell in 1832 and became a Unitarian minister's wife in Manchester. She bore him five children, carried soup and mittens to Manchester's poor, dabbled in writing. In 1847 the death of her only son turned her seriously to literature. While Charlotte nursed her father and wrote *Jane Eyre* during those long, grim weeks in lodgings in Manchester, Mrs. Gaskell was writing her first novel, *Mary Barton,* in the same city. Her forte was quiet realism, homely description, simplicity: *Mary Barton* brought her instant fame. No poetry ran in her veins as it ran in Charlotte's, no passion, no anger, little eloquence. But a kind heart and a discerning intellect made her ripe for sympathy with the mysterious and lonely Currer Bell.

Charlotte found her reserve melting under the charm of this famous but unpretentious woman. The day was theirs: Lady Kay-Shuttleworth, pregnant and ailing with a cold, took to her bed after their arrival. Boating on the lake, they found themselves in agreement in liking Father Newman's soul, Ruskin's *Modern Painters,* and the idea of *The Seven Lamps of Architecture.* With this communion established Charlotte was moved to speak of her life—of her never ending bitterness for the Clergy Daughters' School that had cut her sisters' lives short and stunted her own body; of her rude village; of the deaths that had emptied her home; of her solitude with an old, ailing, and eccentric father. A great narrator, she painted her life in tragic, somber tones. Mrs. Gaskell was horrified. "She is more like Miss Fox in character & ways than anyone, if you can fancy Miss Fox to have gone through suffering enough to have taken out every spark of merriment, and shy & silent from the habit of extreme intense solitude. Such a life as Miss B's I never heard of before Lady K S described her home to me as in a village of a few grey stone houses perched up on the north side of a bleak moor—looking over sweeps of bleak moors. . . . The parsonage has never had a touch of paint, or an article of new furniture for 30 years; never since Miss B's mother died. She was a 'pretty young creature' brought from Penzance in Cornwall by the Irish Curate, who got this moorland living. Her friends disowned her at her marriage. She had 6 children as fast as could be; & what with that, & the climate, & the strange half mad husband she had chosen she died at the end of 9 years. . . ."[3] Pity crept into Mrs. Gaskell's heart for this gifted yet unhappy creature. She contrasted her own good fortune—a healthy mind, a charming person, a ready talent, a good husband, lively daughters, an attractive home, a wide acquaintance. Poor, *poor* Miss Brontë.

After agreeing on Newman and Ruskin, they quarreled amicably about everything else, and in truth the two had little in common. Mrs. Gaskell was Dissenting chapel, Charlotte established church; Mrs. Gaskell a liberal, Charlotte a Tory ("She called me a democrat," wrote Mrs. Gaskell to Mrs. Froude); Mrs. Gaskell middle class, Charlotte poor clergy; Mrs. Gaskell social, Charlotte a recluse. On a less crucial level, Charlotte did not like Tennyson and Mrs. Gaskell did, and was extremely put out because the hypercaution of their host prevented her from visiting the poet: "After dinner we went a drive to Coniston to call on the Tennysons who are staying at Mr. Marshall's Hunt Lodge—Sir James on the box, Miss B & I inside very cosy; but alas it began to rain so we had to turn back without our call being paid, which grieved me sorely and made me cross."[4]

Mutual annoyance with their host forged a bond between Charlotte and Mrs. Gaskell, who were forced to be grateful to Sir James for his courteous hospitality and yet could not really warm to him. He was a man of business, of boards, of medicine, sanitation, and education, shot through with the hard iron of pragmatic capitalism. Charlotte found him "worldly" and "formal" and could not relax with him for a moment. "Nine parts out of ten in him are utilitarian," she wrote Williams, "—the tenth is artistic. This tithe of his nature seems to me at war with all the rest—it is just enough to incline him restlessly towards the artist class, and far too little to make him one of them."[5] With Gradgrindian efficiency, Sir James insisted on lecturing his captured authors on practical aesthetics—on "the beauty of expediency" and the advisability of "bringing themselves down to a lower level." Mrs. Gaskell chafed under art lectures from the man who had made the sanitary survey of Manchester; the man, as she told her close friend Tottie Fox, "who has never indulged in the exercise of any talent which could not bring a tangible and speedy return. However, he was very kind; and really took trouble in giving us, Miss Brontë especially, good advice; which she received with calm resignation."[6]

On the whole it was rather a torment to be in the misty fell and lake country of Wordsworth, although that poet no longer walked the district in cloak and Scotch bonnet, but since April lay quietly in the earth by Grasmere church. It was not Charlotte's taste to look out at lake and cloud from a drawing-room window, or from a swaying carriage full of people. "If I could only have dropped unseen out of the carriage and gone away by myself in amongst those grand hills and sweet dales, I should have drank in the full power of this glorious scenery," she lamented to Ellen.[7] "Vagrant artist instincts" tormented her, longings to escape into the mysterious hills that loomed past the carriage window, to feel the spray of the waterfalls that rushed in hidden glens, to fling herself down among fern and wildflower. Something of an old enthusiasm she had believed quite dead rose in her again; but catching sight of Sir James's worldly, civil smile, she struggled to repress any action or word that might seem poetic or emotional, or eccentric. When she could escape her host, she wandered with Mrs. Gaskell above the Briery, perched itself high above the lake, where she amazed the Manchester woman with her lore of cloud, wind, and sky. "I was struck by Miss Brontë's careful examination of the shape of the clouds and the signs of the heavens, in which she read, as from a book, what the coming weather would be. I told her that I saw she must have a view equal in extent at her own home. She said that I was right, but that the character of the prospect from Haworth was very different; that I had no idea what a companion the sky became to anyone living in solitude—more than any inanimate object on earth—more than the moors themselves."[8]

Among the interesting people residing in the Lake District not least were the widow of Dr. Arnold and her family, who extended an invitation to the Kay-Shuttleworth party to drink tea with them one evening at Fox How. Now that Charlotte had finally won the passport to the society of famous people, she trembled to use it. Mrs. Gaskell noted with amazement Charlotte's agitation the day of the tea drinking. It did no good to remind her that Mrs. Arnold had promised to invite no more than twelve people: she was pale, bilious, and suffered from acute headache the entire day. As the carriage approached Fox How nestled at the foot of Loughrigg Gill in the twilight, she was just calm enough to admire this new glimpse of lake scenery: "The house looked like a nest half buried in flowers and creepers, and, dusk as it was, I could feel that the valley and the hills round were beautiful as imagination could dream." The evening was not, of course, the terror she had imagined. Mrs. Arnold was faded, pretty, and amiable; her daughters exceedingly pleasant; and Charlotte found herself regretting that she had not read the recent *Life* of Dr. Arnold so that the people and conversation might mean more to her. "Merry Matt," the careless, debonair son who would eventually emerge as a great poet, was not at home.

Although the Kay-Shuttleworths' German governess had greeted Charlotte like a long-lost friend and, on parting, begged her to come again, Charlotte had found a better friend on this visit. In three days Elizabeth Gaskell had impressed her as a woman "of the most genuine talent, of cheerful, pleasing and cordial manner, and, I believe, of a kind and good heart." Ellen Nussey was soothing, Mary Taylor invigorating; Mrs. Gaskell combined Mary's intelligence and spirit with Ellen's more traditional feminine charm. Mrs. Gaskell in turn both admired and pitied Charlotte, concluding that, in spite of faults of gracelessness and morbid silence, she possessed a "charming union of simplicity and power." "Miss Brontë," she told Charlotte Froude decidedly, "I like." They parted friends. Yet the three-day visit at Windermere could not compare with the three days in Scotland. Sir James could rob even the Lake District of its charm, while George Smith had the power to make the most commonplace event a delight.

Back at Haworth, Charlotte eagerly picked up the thread of friendship spun at the Briery. "Papa and I have just had tea," she wrote in response to a letter from her new friend; "he is sitting quietly in his room, and I in mine; 'storms of rain' are sweeping over the garden and churchyard: as to the moors, they are hidden in thick fog. Though alone I am not unhappy; I have a thousand things to be thankful for, and, amongst the rest, that this morning I received a letter from you, and that this evening I have the privilege of answering it."[9] Charlotte had opened Mrs. Gaskell's first letter to find a little bunch of wildflowers. The pledge of friendship was simple, graceful, and warm—

like the sender. Charlotte lifted them carefully from the envelope, put them in water, and reveled in the perfume of heliotrope for a whole week.

Since the deaths of Emily and Anne, she had craved communication with another woman whose life was centered in literature. Correspondence with Smith, Williams, James Taylor, and, less frequently, Lewes stimulated her, of course; yet she could not look to them for sympathy or awareness of the problems unique to women writers. In one sense, since Elizabeth Gaskell had to juggle five lives at once—wife, mother, clergyman's aid, hostess to a wide circle of friends, and author—her struggle to achieve and maintain a career in letters was more difficult than Charlotte's. The question that must haunt every woman who steps outside her traditional role frequently haunted Mrs. Gaskell: how much of a married woman's life must be devoted to home duties? How much to the development of her individuality? Six months before meeting Charlotte she was debating this question with her closest friend, Eliza (Tottie) Fox:

One thing is pretty clear [she wrote in a letter of February 1850], *Women*, must give up living an artist's life, if home duties are to be paramount. It is different with men whose home duties are so small a part of their lives. However we are talking of women. I am sure it is healthy for them to have the refuge of the hidden world of Art to shelter themselves in when too much pressed upon by daily small Lilliputian arrows of peddling cares; it keeps them from being morbid as you say; and takes them into the land where King Arthur lies hidden, and soothes them with its peace. I have felt this in writing, I see others feel it in music, you in painting, so assuredly a blending of the two is desirable. (Home duties and the development of the Individual I mean), which you will say it takes no Solomon to tell you but the difficulty is where and when to make one set of duties subserve and give place to the other. I have no doubt that the cultivation of each tends to keep the other in a healthy state,—my grammar is all at sixes and sevens I have no doubt but never mind if you can pick out my meaning.

Mrs. Gaskell set this letter aside, thought more about the problem, received another note from Tottie in the interim, and added a firmer postscript: "I've been reading over yr note, and believe I've only been repeating in different language what you said. If Self is to be the end of exertions, those exertions are unholy, there is no doubt of *that*—and that is part of the danger in cultivating the Individual Life; but I do believe we have all some appointed work to do, whh no one else can do so well; Wh. is *our* work; what *we* have to do in advancing the Kingdom of God; and that first we must find out what we are sent into the world to do, and define it and make it clear to ourselves, (that's *the* hard part) and then forget ourselves in our work, and our work in the End we ought to strive to bring about. . . ."[10] Like all people with a will to achieve, Mrs. Gaskell was adept at tailoring theory to fit practice: if authorship was her appointed work to further the kingdom of God on earth, she could pursue it with a clear conscience.

Charlotte had never any problem in defining what work was hers to do: she had "an artist's own bent to the course—inborn, decided, resistless"; her struggle had been to win the world's recognition. Mrs. Gaskell had been deeply impressed at Windermere by Charlotte's strong sense of the genius that ran like a flame through her veins, by her almost religious pledge of responsibility to her gift. They must have discussed "the woman question" at the Briery since Mrs. Gaskell's first letter to Charlotte recommended a French book on the topic. Charlotte replied with her own recommendation, an article on "Woman's Mission" in the *Westminster Review* that appeared to her just and candid.

Reading the article now with its turgid rhetoric extolling women as muses and Delphic Sybils, bestowers of wine and roses, elemental forces and ennoblers of men, it is perhaps difficult to see why "Woman's Mission" would appeal to a Charlotte Brontë. "Women did not invent the steam-engine, nor write Macbeth," states the author; but no matter: her work is superior work. Since she is created spiritually and morally superior to man, it is her calling to build "*his* life of thought and act by her ideal of the right." Woman's mission is to inspire, to diffuse "an atmosphere of light and love, from which her sons shall go forth into the world to act, as from the temple of the living God." If her children fail morally in the world, it is her failure, for *she* taught them; if her husband does not respect her, *she* is responsible, for women give the tone to morals—"nothing which they really dislike,—from their souls disapprove,—can live."[11]

The author thus subscribes to a fundamental Victorian dichotomy: the coarse, brutal male who gouges and hacks his way out in the harsh world; the gentle, spiritual angel who guards the moral decencies and refinements of the home. The dichotomy was part fact, part myth. Charlotte could testify to the fact: she had often enough observed the middle-class Yorkshireman intent only on wresting a fortune out of the new woolen mills whose belching stacks blackened Leeds and Bradford and Halifax—a brutal man, made callous in society by the new capitalism and in his home by unlimited power over wife and children.[12] In defense, the Victorian woman could only grasp the empty weapon of moral and spiritual superiority and try to convince herself and her master that it was loaded. To her

credit, she often succeeded. Fact expanded to myth; myth perpe-
trated fact. It was Charlotte's triumph that in her fiction she tran-
scended this violent, mythic polarity between sainted, passive woman
and active, brutal male—the myth Dickens subscribed to. Her Roch-
esters, Rivers, Brocklehursts, Helstones, Yorkes, Hunsdens, and
Emanuels are tyrannical enough, but her women—Jane Eyre, Miss
Temple, Zoraïde Reuter, Shirley, Madame Beck, Lucy Snowe—match
them, will for will, brains for brains, passion for passion.

Perhaps Charlotte approved most the challenge "Woman's Mission"
offered to women to improve their own lot. They are the chattels
of men—"but does one married woman in a thousand know any
thing about this, much less desire to erase it from the statute-book?
Yet she can only teach man how she shall be served . . ." Does she
wish to work? Men "are willing to yield into her hands whatever
work she can do; so let her choose. Any position truly won they
will guarantee to her; then let her oil be ready." A successful
woman who had triumphed over great obstacles, Charlotte was willing
to believe that men would guarantee women any position truly won,
was willing to share the author's scarcely veiled contempt for women's
passivity to their own lot. *Her* oil had been ready; let other women
prepare theirs.

Charlotte concluded her first letter to Mrs. Gaskell with the old
diffident distrust in her ability to inspire friendship: "I shall be glad
to hear from you whenever you have time to write me, *but you are
never on any account to do this except when inclination prompts and
leisure permits.*" Her keen, analytical eye had read the pity in Mrs.
Gaskell's expressive face.

Once more, the quiet days, the ticking clock. But Charlotte was
not quite as alone as she believed. James Taylor sent copies of the
*Athenaeum* to Haworth in an oblique gesture of courtship, stopping
them at one point because he feared they annoyed her, then, gathering
courage, sending them forth again. Charlotte greeted the reappear-
ance of the weekly with her own abrupt diffidence: "I only fear that
its regular transmission may become a task to you; in that case,
discontinue it at once." She wrote Ellen to comment that "the little
man" had begun sending "his little newspaper" again; yet he was not
so very little that she did not enclose one of his letters, requesting
Ellen to study it and "tell me exactly how it impresses you regarding
the writer's character, etc."[13] The newspaper, since it was the property of Smith, Elder, happily put her under no obligation; yet she
was glad to get it, and found "this little Taylor" not totally lacking
in spirit and sense.

Another tribute found its way to the parsonage that early autumn of 1850, a review by Sydney Dobell in the *Palladium*, "one of those notices over which an author rejoices with trembling." Tribute was paid at last to *Wuthering Heights*—"late justice . . . alas! in one sense too late"—but justice nevertheless. "Not a subordinate place or person in this novel but bears more or less the stamp of high genius," Dobell enthused. "It is the unformed writing of a giant's hand; the 'large utterance' of a baby god. . . . There are few things in modern prose to surpass these pages for native power." Unfortunately, Dobell persisted in believing that one author was responsible for *Wuthering Heights*, *Jane Eyre*, *The Tenant of Wildfell Hall*, and *Shirley*, and persisted in judging Emily's novel the earlier, cruder work. Ellis and Acton were both Currer Bell, the trinity was one. And who was Currer Bell? "A year or two ago, we mentally solved the problem thus: Currer Bell is a woman. Every word she utters is female. Not feminine, but female. . . . It is not merely improbable, but impossible that a man has written 'Jane Eyre.' Only a woman's eye could see man as she sees him. . . . Never since or before the destruction of cities has man looked on man with this romance of latent love." Yet, said Dobell, in this great sensibility lay Currer's greatness: if Currer Bell could continue in her powerful vein, she "with one or two other poets, may have to carry down to posterity the ideal literature of our day."[14]

Here was high praise; and yet how frustrating at the same time to be told that *Shirley* was a falling off from *Jane Eyre*, and that if Currer Bell was to produce again a great novel she must try to capture the simplicity and reality of her first immature novel—*Wuthering Heights*. ". . . you see, even here, 'Shirley' is disparaged in comparison with 'Jane Eyre,'" she complained to James Taylor, "and yet I took great pains with 'Shirley.' I did not hurry; I tried to do my best, and my own impression was that it was not inferior to the former work; indeed I had bestowed on it more time, thought, and anxiety . . ."[15]

The ghosts of Emily and Anne haunted the parsonage with a vengeance that cold, rainy autumn, for in September Charlotte agreed to provide an explanatory preface for Smith, Elder's edition of *Wuthering Heights* and *Agnes Grey* in one volume, a preface that would establish the claims of Ellis and Acton Bell once and for all. More than a preface was involved, however, for Charlotte had also agreed to go over all her dead sisters' papers and decide whether or not they should be made public.

She proved a rigorous censor. Did the icy fingers of Emily and Anne tap in protest against the windowpane as she ruthlessly determined to suppress all but seven of Anne's and eighteen of Emily's poems? When she pruned and reworded Emily's poems to disguise

their origin in Gondal, that secret and now rather shameful land?
When she destroyed—as destroyed she must have—Emily's second,
incomplete novel? When she decided that *The Tenant of Wildfell Hall*
was too repugnant to merit another edition? When she turned from
Anne's poems, shocked at the religious melancholy breathing through
some, disturbed by the pangs of unrequited love too evident in others?
When she tampered with Anne's lines of grief for Emily—

> O thou has taken my delight
> And hope of life away
> And bid me watch the painful night
> And wait the weary day

—changing *my* to *our* and *me* to *us*, unable to admit even now that
she had been excluded from Emily's and Anne's bond of love?[16]
Strange justice. Was she so weakened by critical attack that she
dreaded the volley that might be unleashed against loved sisters unable
to defend themselves? Did the sentiments and style of her two comparatively uncivilized sisters really appear crude to her now more sophisticated mind? Did she believe that she was faithfully preserving
everything that would add to their reputation? Did she seriously believe that she was following the unspoken wishes of Emily and Anne?

So she publicly claimed in a "Memoir" composed for a new edition
of Ellis' and Acton's poems: "It would not have been difficult to com-
pile a volume out of the papers left by my sisters, had I, in making the
selection, dismissed from my consideration the scruples and wishes of
those whose written thoughts these papers held. But this was impossible. An influence stronger than could be exercised by any motive of
expediency, necessarily regulated the selection. I have, then, culled
from the mass only a little poem here and there. The whole makes but
a tiny nosegay, and the colour and perfume of the flowers are not such
as fit them for festal uses."[17] But the elaborate, oblique explanation
left her motives as obscure as before.

Those painful autumnal weeks in which she read, sorted, edited, and
suppressed are shrouded in mystery, for no one knows precisely what
manuscripts Emily and Anne left behind. What happened, for example, to the volumes and volumes of Gondal fiction both Emily and
Anne wrote for almost fifteen years? Did Anne herself destroy the
chronicles before she died, at Emily's request? Charlotte's final statement to Smith, Elder was veiled, but unequivocal: "As to additional
compositions, I think there would be none, as I would not offer a line
to the publication of which my sisters themselves would have objected."[18] All that is clear is that she suffered: ". . . I found the task
at first exquisitely painful and depressing . . . It is work however that

I cannot do in the evening—for if I did, I should have no sleep at night . . . for one or two nights I scarcely knew how to get on till morning—and when morning came I was still haunted with a sense of sickening distress—I tell you these things," she moaned to Ellen, "—because it is absolutely necessary to me to have some relief. . . ."[19]

Her "Biographical Notice of Ellis and Acton Bell" was simple and poignant. She briefly sketched the genus of the novels ("The highest stimulus, as well as the liveliest pleasure we had known from childhood upwards, lay in attempts at literary composition"); she told of her sisters' courage under failure; of the day when their novels were accepted at last; of the critical injustices done to *Wuthering Heights;* of the death of Ellis Bell. The mystery of that death still possessed Charlotte; she could not leave it alone. "My sister Emily first declined," she wrote, reliving those terrible months again. "The details of her illness are deep-branded in my memory, but to dwell on them, either in thought or narrative, is not in my power. Never in all her life had she lingered over any task that lay before her, and she did not linger now. She sank rapidly. She made haste to leave us. Yet, while physically she perished, mentally she grew stronger than we had yet known her. Day by day, when I saw with what a front she met suffering, I looked on her with an anguish of wonder and love. I have seen nothing like it; but, indeed, I have never seen her parallel in anything. Stronger than a man, simpler than a child, her nature stood alone. The awful point was, that, while full of ruth for others, on herself she had no pity; the spirit was inexorable to the flesh; from the trembling hand, the unnerved limbs, the faded eyes, the same service was exacted as they had rendered in health. To stand by and witness this, and not dare to remonstrate, was a pain no words can render."

Even in memorial, Charlotte could not extend her enthusiasm to Anne. So little had she appreciated this sister's quiet strength, or, perhaps, so much she still resented Anne's usurpation of Emily's love. About Anne's second novel she was curt: "*The Tenant of Wildfell Hall* by Acton Bell, had likewise an unfavourable reception. At this I cannot wonder. The choice of subject was an entire mistake." On her death she was ineloquent: ". . . we received distinct intimation that it was necessary to prepare our minds to see the younger sister go after the elder." On Anne's personality she was lukewarm: "Anne's character was milder and more subdued; she wanted the power, the fire, the originality of her sister, but was well-endowed with quiet virtues of her own. Long-suffering, self-denying, reflective, and intelligent, a constitutional reserve and taciturnity placed and kept her in the shade, and covered her mind, and especially her feelings, with a sort of nun-like veil, which was rarely lifted." Comments like these seemed calculated to push Anne much further into much deeper shade until almost invisible to posterity. In reality, Acton Bell's poetry had the merit of simplicity and taste, *The Tenant of Wildfell Hall* was not a failure, and *Agnes Grey* possessed the merits of clarity, feeling, and truth.

That autumn with its drizzle, its gray clouds scudding in low from the northeast, was thus dreary enough, particularly because Charlotte found herself unable to write a line. With pain and humility she recognized her incapacity to bear solitude. Other minds might rouse themselves in isolation to greater productivity; her mental powers languished, stagnated, turned inward and back to memory. Letters and the weekly newspaper from James Taylor were not enough. Correspondence with Smith, Williams, Lewes, Martineau, Gaskell, and Ellen was not enough. Yet even the society of friends could not permanently help, as she confessed to Ellen: "You will recommend me I daresay to go from home—but that does no good—even could I again leave Papa with an easy mind (thank God! he is still better) I cannot describe what a time of it I had after my return from London—Scotland &c. there was a reaction that sunk me to the earth—the deadly silence, solitude, desolation were awful—the craving for companionship—the hopelessness of relief—were what I should dread to feel again."[20]

A visitor to Haworth that autumn of 1850, introduced by Mrs. Gaskell, confirmed the deadly quiet of the parsonage. Arriving in a gig, snugly tucked under a buffalo robe against the chill, Elizabeth Parkes viewed the dreary scene with astonishment: "There was the house before us, a small, oblong stone house, with not a tree to screen it from the cutting wind . . . There was an old man in the churchyard, brooding like a ghoul over the graves, with a sort of grim hilarity on his face." Ushered into a small, bare parlor, they waited until the door opened and an old mastiff crept into the room followed by an old white-haired man who shook their hands with stiff courtesy and then went to call his daughter.

> A long interval, during which we coaxed the old dog, and looked at a picture of Miss Brontë, by Richmond, the solitary ornament of the room, looking strangely out of place on the bare walls, and at the books on the little shelves, most of them evidently the gift of the authors since Miss Brontë's celebrity. Presently she came in, and welcomed us very kindly, and took me upstairs to take off my bonnet, and herself brought me water and towels. The uncarpeted stone stairs and floors, the old drawers propped on wood, were all scrupulously clean and neat. When we went into the parlour again we began talking very comfortably, when the door opened and Mr. Brontë looked in; seeing his daughter there, I suppose he thought it was all

right, and he retreated to his study on the opposite side of the passage, presently emerging again to bring W—— a country newspaper. This was his last appearance until we went.

. . . Miss Brontë put me so in mind of her own "Jane Eyre." She looked smaller than ever, and moved about so quietly, and noiselessly, just like a little bird, as Rochester called her, barring that all birds are joyous, and that joy can never have entered that house since it was first built; and yet, perhaps, when that old man married, and took home his bride, and children's voices and feet were heard about the house, even that desolate crowded graveyard and biting blast could not quench cheerfulness and hope. Now there is something touching in the sight of that little creature entombed in such a place, and moving about herself like a spirit, especially when you think that the slight still frame encloses a force of strong fiery life, which nothing has been able to freeze or extinguish.[21]

By December, Charlotte decided to accept Harriet Martineau's invitation to Westmoreland, pressed upon her for several months: the second anniversary of Emily's death was too intimidating to face alone, especially since she was forced to hide all traces of depression from Papa who, if he saw her unhappy, would begin to scold and fret. On December 16, 1850, she therefore retraced her steps to the Lake District.

When she crossed the threshold of the Knoll, Harriet's ivy-grown Elizabethan-style cottage at Ambleside, Charlotte stepped into a world that at once lifted her spirits and emphasized her own tormented existence. Harriet Martineau was forty-eight and, like Charlotte, single, but she radiated vigor and serenity. She had triumphed over an unhappy childhood, deafness, ill health, and femininity to become one of the most prestigious writers, economists, and radicals of her day. In 1845, convinced that every woman needed domesticity in her life, she had come to the Lake District, designed and supervised the building of her own home, and set up housekeeping at the Knoll. Since then she had amazed, charmed, and terrorized the Lakers, from peasant to poet. Brown, strong, her sleeves rolled back on sturdy arms, she threw herself into running her two-acre estate: she gardened, sewed, churned, put up preserves, turned out fragrant custards and gingerbread, swept and dusted, fed cows, scrupulously trained her hired help —and still poured forth volumes of writing.[22]

The obscure and the famous came to the Knoll. Wordsworth walked over, chose a motto for her sundial—"Come Light, visit me"; planted two sturdy pines "in the most experienced manner," said Harriet, "then washed his hands in the watering pot, took my hands in his, and wished me happy days in my new abode." At the same time he instructed Harriet seriously to deal with guests as he and his sister Dorothy had at Grasmere: "When you have a visitor," said he, "you must do as we did;—you must say, 'If you like to have a cup of tea with us, you are very welcome: but if you want any meat—you must pay for your board.' Now promise you will do this." But Harriet, laughing, said she could promise no such thing.[23] Macready came, was trotted over hill and dale at Harriet's sturdy clip, strained his back planting a couple of oaks. Nieces, nephews, writers, commissioners, politicians, mesmerists, abolitionists, celebrity hunters—all found their way to her door; all were welcomed, walked, harangued, fed, and amazed by, in George Eliot's words, "that tonic in the shape of Harriet Martineau." She smoked cigars, warred with the local parson, meddled kindly in the affairs of the local laborers—her "workies"—scandalized Mrs. Wordsworth by insisting that the miracles of mesmerists were as great as those of Christ and the apostles. Eventually she became too strong a dose for that high-Tory lady, and Mrs. Wordsworth, threatened with a visit from Harriet, stole from the house for days at two o'clock to avoid "the pest." Harriet's servant girls loved her, the peasants welcomed her into their cottages, and she drew young people to her like a magnet. She was eccentric, autocratic, generous, didactic, and fearless.

Such vitality could not help but rouse Charlotte and sweep the cobwebs of melancholy from her "painstruck mind." Her letter of December 18, 1850, to Ellen reveals that the tonic had taken effect:

I can write to you now for I am away from home and relieved, temporarily at least, by change of air and scene from the heavy burden of depression which I confess has for nearly 3 months been sinking me to the earth. I never shall forget last Autumn. Some days and nights have been cruel—but now—having once told you this—I need say no more on the subject. My loathing of solitude grew extreme; my recollection of my Sisters intolerably poignant; I am better now.

I am at Miss Martineau's for a week—her house is very pleasant both within and without—arranged at all points with admirable neatness and comfort—Her visitors enjoy the most perfect liberty; what she claims for herself she allows them. I rise at my own hour, breakfast alone—(she is up at five, takes a cold bath and a walk by starlight and has finished breakfast and got to her work by 7 o'clock) I pass the morning in the drawing-room—she in her study. At 2 o'clock we meet, work, talk, and walk together till 5—her dinner hour—spend the evening together—when she converses fluently, abundantly and with most complete frankness—I go to my own room soon after ten—she sits up writing letters till twelve. She appears exhaustless in strength and spirit, and indefatigable in the faculty of labour. She is a great and a good woman; of course not without peculiarities but I have seen none yet that annoy me. She is both hard and warm-hearted, abrupt and affectionate—liberal and despotic. I believe she is not at all conscious of her own absolutism. When I tell her of it, she denys the charge warmly—then I laugh at her. I believe she almost rules Ambleside. Some of the gentry dislike her, but the lower orders have a great regard for her. . . .[24]

Different in temperament and opinion, the two women in retrospect were great feminine rebels of their day—Harriet in her economic, political, and religious radicalism, Charlotte in her unconscious but almost total alienation from the mores of bourgeois mid-Victorian England. Harriet was a progressive with faith in institutional reform, Charlotte an isolationist with faith only in the private morality and stoicism of the individual. Harriet lived her rebellion fearlessly; Charlotte released hers into the violent energy of her novels. With more differences than similarities, their mutual respect for individualism, energy, and rigorous self-discipline drew them into each other's orbits for a time.

Thus, hour by hour, Charlotte's respect for Harriet Martineau grew. She felt somewhat like a child as she listened to the older, more famous woman's confident dissertations on history, political economy, and scientific farming while they sat before a winter fire or paced the dales together. Like the Wife of Bath, also deaf, Harriet was hard to interrupt. ". . . I admire her and wonder at her more than I can say," Charlotte wrote her father. "Her powers of labour, of exercise, and social cheerfulness are beyond my comprehension. In spite of the unceasing activity of her colossal intellect she enjoys robust health. She is a taller, larger, and more strongly made woman than I had imagined from that first interview with her. She is very kind to me, though she must think I am a very insignificant person compared to herself."[25] This humility was a little disingenuous, for Charlotte was not really intimidated by Harriet Martineau. Long ago, a schoolgirl, she had listened to the noisy debates of the radical Taylor family at Gomersal and, although quiet among them, had been exhilarated rather than oppressed by their lively self-confidence. She liked strong women; she found in Harriet Martineau some of Emily's and Mary Taylor's large strength. "Miss Martineau I relish inexpressibly," she declared to Ellen.

It was Harriet's creed to let no visitor interfere with her writing, and from seven in the morning till two in the afternoon she remained invisible behind her study door, hard at work on her *History of the Thirty Years Peace 1815–1845.* Aware of Charlotte's enthusiasm for Waterloo politics, battles, and the Duke of Wellington, she was kind enough, however, to consult Charlotte's opinion: "One morning I brought her the 1st part of the chapter of the Peninsular War in my Introductory History, and said, 'Tell me if this will do for a beginning, etc.' I read a page or two to her as we stood before the fire, she looked up at me and stole her hand into mind, and to my amazement the tears were running down her cheeks. She said, 'Oh! I do thank you! Oh! we are of one mind! Oh! I thank you for this justice to the man!' I saw at once there was a touch of idolatry in the case, but it was a charming enthusiasm."

While Harriet labored, Charlotte had ample time for carriage rides with the irrepressibly attentive Sir James, who called for her during the morning from Briery Close and bore her off for more sight-seeing from a carriage window. Harriet, a great hiker, despised such soft recreations; Charlotte herself preferred walking, but this time could not deny that the courtly, smiling baronet was sincerely friendly. Yet she consented to the rides chiefly to placate him, for Sir James and Lady Kay-Shuttleworth, now near her confinement, were pressing her to stay with them again on Lake Windermere. This she would not consent to; she wanted to visit Ellen instead. Brookroyd had become a regular stop on the way home from the strenuous excitements of London, Scotland, and the Lake District—a stretch of quiet-flowing water between the rapids and the still, dark pond.

Having read the *Life* of Dr. Arnold between lake visits, Charlotte now looked forward to visiting the family at Fox How with Harriet. She had found the headmaster of Rugby a stern, exacting, almost hard man, but just, pure, and earnest; a giant among men, five of which "might save any country, might victoriously champion any cause." "I was struck, too, by the almost unbroken happiness of his life," she had written Taylor that bitter, lonely autumn. ". . . His wife was what he wished; his children were healthy and promising; his own health was excellent; his undertakings were crowned with success; even Death was kind, for however sharp the pains of his last hours, they were but brief. God's blessing seems to have accompanied him from the cradle to the grave. One feels thankful to know that it has been permitted to any man to live such a life."[26]

Dining with the Arnolds four days before Christmas, she could not, however, wholeheartedly admire. Dr. Arnold's widow impressed her as amiable and good, but "the intellectual is not her forte, and she has no pretensions to power and completeness of character." The daughters struck her as replicas of the mother. On this occasion the eldest son, Matthew, was home for the Christmas holidays, and Charlotte, silent and analytical as always ("as though she alone were not enjoying the party," complained Mrs. Arnold years after), concluded that he too "inherits his mother's defect." "Striking and prepossessing in appearance, his manner displeases, from its seeming foppery. I own it caused me at first to regard him with regretful surprise; the shade of Dr Arnold seemed to me to frown on his young representative. I was told, however, that 'Mr Arnold improved upon acquaintance.' So it was: ere long a real modesty appeared under his assumed conceit, and some genuine intellectual aspirations, as well as high educational acquirements, displaced superficial affectations. I was given to understand that his theological opinions were very vague and unsettled, and indeed he betrayed as much in the course of the conversation. Most unfortunate for him, doubtless, has been the untimely loss of his father."[27] Matthew Arnold had still not stepped out of the long shadow cast by the great headmaster.

As for Dr. Arnold's son, he rushed upstairs after Charlotte's and Harriet's early departure to write to "Flu," his fiancée Frances Lucy Wightman, in sadly flippant strain: "At seven came Miss Martineau and Miss Brontë (Jane Eyre); talked to Miss Martineau (who blasphemes frightfully) about the prospects of the Church of England, and, wretched man that I am, promised to go and see her cow-keeping miracles to-morrow—I, who hardly know a cow from a sheep. I talked to Miss Brontë (past thirty and plain, with expressive grey eyes, though) of her curates, of French novels, and her education in a school in Brussels, and sent the lions roaring to their dens at half-past nine, and came to talk to you."[28]

Had she lived to read his poetry, Charlotte, who disliked Tennyson's lyric, public rehearsal of grief in *In Memoriam*, should have responded to Matthew Arnold's simple, profound, stoical turn of thought. Nor could she have guessed that in a few years Arnold would write of this same winter evening in far different mood:

. . . Four years since, on a mark'd
Evening, a meeting I saw.

Two friends met there, two fam'd
Gifted women. The one,
Brilliant with recent renown,
Young, unpractis'd, had told
With a Master's accent her feigned
Story of passionate life:
The other, maturer in fame,
Earning, she too, her praise
First in Fiction, had since
Widened her sweep, and survey'd
History, Politics, Mind. . . .

I beheld; the obscure
Saw the famous. Alas!
Years in number, it seem'd
Lay before both, and a fame
Heighten'd, and multiplied power.
Behold! The elder, to-day,
Lies expecting from Death
In mortal weakness, a last
Summons: the younger is dead. . . .

How shall we honour the young,
The ardent, the gifted? how mourn?
Console we cannot; her ear
Is deaf. Far northward from here,
In a churchyard high mid the moors
Of Yorkshire, a little earth
Stops it for ever to praise. . . .

Strew with roses the grave
Of the early-dying. Alas!
Early she goes on the path
To the Silent Country, and leaves
Half her laurels unwon,
Dying too soon: yet green
Laurels she had, a course
Short, but redoubled by Fame. . . .[29]

In the same poem, *Haworth Churchyard*, Arnold spoke of Charlotte and her sisters as "passionate souls/ Plung'd in themselves, who
demand/ Only to love and be lov'd." Although Charlotte demanded a
good deal more—that her literary voice be heard, for example—Arnold
had touched upon qualities that separated Charlotte from Harriet Martineau. Curiously enough, Harriet's atheism generated no friction between them on this visit. Harriet spoke frankly about her disbelief during those long, firelit evenings at Ambleside; she was planning a book
on the subject with Henry Atkinson, a friend with similar views. Charlotte of course dissented: her mind and spirit were stained like a
church window with the powerful, somber poetry of the Old Testament; she pessimistically believed humanity too weak to live without
some moral and spiritual creed. She was "very far indeed from sym-
pathising in our doctrine and emphatically said so," Harriet wrote in
her *Autobiography;* "but this did not prevent her doing justice to us."
Nor was Charlotte shocked by Harriet's faith in mesmerism, which,

unlike atheism, was swiftly becoming a fad. On the contrary, she eagerly volunteered to be hypnotized, and responded so quickly to Harriet's amateur passes that Harriet herself abruptly stopped the experiment, afraid that her sensitive visitor might go off into an irrecoverable trance.

As Arnold had recognized, Charlotte was passionately "plunged in herself"; it was this quality that created the chasm between the two women. By an effort of will, Harriet had long ago submerged her personal sorrows beneath an active social concern. Her writings on political economy were inspired by a genuine interest in the welfare of the poor and uneducated; her abolitionism by her moral outrage at slavery; her interference in the lives of her Ambleside "workies" by a humane desire to better lives. She was an old maid—good: social welfare was her master, the poor her children. Thus she lived creatively and usefully at Ambleside, a benevolent if eccentric philanthropist, interested in everything from calving to local elections—plunged not in herself, like Charlotte, but in others. If her indifference to romantic love was unusual and rather hard, it saved her a world of sorrow, for what man would have been courageous enough to marry the redoubtable Harriet Martineau!

Charlotte observed this healthy life and rejected the possibility of imitation with few regrets, being only a fraction less absolute than her hostess. "I trust to have derived benefit from my visit to Miss Martineau," she wrote Williams the first day of the new year, 1851, from Haworth. "A visit more interesting I certainly never paid. If self-sustaining strength can be acquired from example, I ought to have got good. But my nature is not hers; I could not make it so though I were to submit it seventy times seven to the furnace of affliction and discipline it for an age under the hammer and anvil of toil and self-sacrifice. Perhaps if I was like her I should not admire her so much as I do. . . . Her animal spirits are as unflagging as her intellectual powers. . . . I believe neither solitude nor loss of friends would break her down. I saw some faults in her, but somehow I liked them for the sake of her good points. It gave me no pain to feel insignificant, mentally and corporeally, in comparison with her."[30]

Harriet's efficient combination of professionalism and domesticity impressed Charlotte perhaps the most. Her house was orderly, her kitchen fragrant with good cooking, her garden trim, her cows sleek. Despite the cigars, mesmerism, and blaspheming, Harriet was motherly, practical, and kind: ". . . all she does is well done, from the writing of a history down to the quietest female occupation." Harriet was equally generous in her appraisal of Charlotte. Although she saw traces of morbidity in her guest, they were less than might be expected in a woman of her unhappy circumstances. Currer Bell's visit confirmed, she wrote in her *Autobiography*, "my deep impression of her integrity, her noble conscientiousness about her vocation, and her consequent self-reliance in the moral conduct of her life . . . her permanent temper was one of humility, candour, integrity, and conscientiousness. She was not only unspoiled by her sudden and prodigious fame, but obviously unspoilable. . . ."[31]

Braced by "the tonic that was Harriet Martineau," Charlotte returned to Haworth to pick up the strands of narrative she had begun so falteringly that autumn, the novel that would provoke an unreconcilable quarrel with the good woman she had just left.

# 21

## Loss

With a heart sternly disciplined against hope, Charlotte Brontë would not consciously allow herself to fall in love with George Smith. At the same time, she had begun a very personal novel in which her unrequited love for him formed a part of the history of her heroine, Lucy Snowe. In the new year a letter came from Smith that she read with fear and trembling. He proposed, casually enough, a summer trip up the Rhine. Firmly reining in the emotions this proposal aroused, Charlotte nevertheless could not help introducing Smith's name in letters to Ellen, provoking an intense curiosity in her friend which she then quickly rebuked. There were no suggestive "undercurrents" in her frequent allusions to her publisher:

> Dear Nell—your last letter but one made me smile. I think you draw great conclusions from small inferences. I think those "fixed intentions" you fancy—are imaginary—I think the "undercurrent" amounts simply to this—a kind of natural liking and sense of something congenial. Were there no vast barrier of age, fortune, &. there is perhaps enough personal regard to make things possible which are now impossible. If men and women married because they like each others' temper, look, conversation, nature and so on—and if besides, years were more nearly equal—the chance you allude to might be admitted as a chance—but other reasons regulate matrimony—reasons of convenience, of connection, of money. Meantime I am content to have him as a friend—and pray God to continue to me the common-sense to look on one so young, so rising and so hopeful in no other light."[1]

All of which meant that Charlotte cared for George Smith very much indeed. She needed, therefore, all her will power in this matter, for she was very vulnerable to Smith's charm.

> That hint about the Rhine disturbs me [she continued the same letter]; I am not made of stone—and what is mere excitement to him—

is fever to me. However it is a matter for the Future and long to look forward to—As I see it now, the journey is out of the question—for many reasons—I rather wonder he should think of it—I cannot conceive either his mother or his sisters relishing it, and all London would gabble like a countless host of geese—Good-bye, dear Nell, Heaven grant us both some quiet wisdom—and strength not merely to bear the trial of pain—but to resist the lure of pleasure when it comes in such a shape as our better judgment disapproves.

Ellen, however, was not to be subdued by this pious stoicism. Currer Bell, in her mind, was more than an equal match for a mere publisher. She replied, therefore, with hints about marriage and playful allusions to "Jupiter" and "Venus" that of course drew down Charlotte's wrath upon her head: ". . . what do you mean by such heathen trash? The fact is, no fallacy can be wilder and I won't have it hinted at even in jest, because my common sense laughs it to scorn. The idea of the 'little man' shocks me less—it would be a more likely match if 'matches' were at all in question, *which they are not*."[2] The same diffidence that drove her to ask Mrs. Gaskell to correspond only if she had nothing better to do now made all speculations about a romance with George Smith exceedingly painful.

Longing for what she did not have, she rejected what she had: the love of James Taylor. The little man had burst the bonds of the *Athenaeum*, had grown ardent and vehement in the mails: she had repulsed him. Typically, now that he had grown cooler, she warmed. "He still sends his little newspaper," she wrote Brookroyd, "—and the other day there came a letter of a bulk, volume, pith, judgment and knowledge, worthy to have been the product of a giant. You may laugh as much and as wickedly as you please—but the fact is there is a quiet constancy about this, my diminutive and red-haired friend, which adds a foot to his stature—turns his sandy locks dark, and altogether dignifies him a good deal in my estimation."[3] Charlotte, who had pleaded the cause of plainness so eloquently in *Jane Eyre* and suffered so acutely from lack of beauty herself, was inconsistently prejudiced against the unprepossessing appearance of "the little man."

Now that she had subdued Mr. Taylor's ardor, she could enjoy his devotion comfortably: it was a security, an absurd but cocky feather in her plain cap. She was jolted, therefore, to open a letter from George Smith and find an announcement of Mr. Taylor's imminent departure for India. A letter from Taylor arrived on the heels of Smith's. His decision to quit England was the result of "a crisis" he had undergone. Could he see her at Haworth before his ship sailed? She sent a conventional reply: she and her father would be pleased to see him; she hoped Providence would guide him so far away in India, a stranger in a strange land. Puzzled and apprehensive, she awaited his visit.

He came in April, as abrupt, harsh, and red-haired as ever. Charlotte had put aside her spectacles for the occasion, perhaps from vanity, perhaps in hopes the red hair might be flatteringly dimmed. She could scarcely see from sofa to chair, but she put up her eyeglass once—and was not pleased. He looked older and thinner; the lines that seamed his face were hard. He seemed nervous, very excited. She was struck with his resemblance to Branwell. Was he ugly? No, but very peculiar. He gave her only vague hints about the reason for his departure. The Indian undertaking was "necessary to the continued prosperity" of the firm; only he could carve out the new territory; duty obliged him, etc. If there was a hint that his abrupt business tactics had impossibly grated on the more refined sensibilities of Smith and Williams, it remained unconfirmed. He was going with great personal reluctance. He would be gone five years.

At parting he drew close to her, his eyes on an unfortunate level with her own, and she was able to see him clearly. "As he stood near me, as he looked at me in his keen way, it was all I could do to stand my ground tranquilly and steadily, and not to recoil as before. It is no use saying anything if I am not candid—I avow then, that on this occasion, predisposed as I was to regard him very favourably—his manner and his personal presence scarcely pleased me more than at the first interview."[4] It was an uncomfortable scene. The little man awkwardly thrust a book into her hand, requesting briefly that she keep it for his sake, adding hastily, "I shall hope to hear from you in India—your letters *have* been, and *will* be a greater refreshment than you can think or I can tell." Only Mr. Brontë seemed oblivious to the delicacy of the situation: he bid Taylor a hearty good-by in his formal, old-fashioned manner, exhorting him to be true to himself, to his country, and his God. Then James Taylor was gone and the clock on the landing ticked through the still house louder than before.

Charlotte fretted, vexed and unsatisfied. Nothing had been decided, nothing changed. She could not return Taylor's feelings, yet his absence left "a painful blank": she had not been aware of the prop until it was withdrawn. Ellen had wished her pleasure of the visit, but it had not been pleasure, it had been pain: ". . . something at my heart aches and gnaws drearily," she confessed to her friend, "but I must cultivate fortitude."

Endlessly hypochondriacal, Papa chose Taylor's departure as a fitting occasion for a relapse.

Certainly I shall not soon forget last Friday [Charlotte wrote Ellen drearily on April 9, 1851]—and *never*, I think, the evening and night

succeeding that morning and afternoon—evils seldom come singly—
and soon after Mr T—— was gone—papa who had been better grew
much worse, he went to bed early and was very sick and ill for an
hour and when at last he began to doze and I left him—I came down
to the dining room with a sense of weight, fear and desolation hard
to express and harder to endure. . . .

An absence of five years—a dividing expanse of three oceans—the
wide difference between a man's active career and a woman's passive
existence—these things are almost equivalent to an eternal separation
—But there is another thing which forms a barrier more difficult to
pass than any of these. Would Mr T—— and I ever suit? could I
ever feel for him enough love to accept of him as a husband? Friendship—gratitude—esteem I have—but each moment he came near me—and
that I could see his eyes fastened on me—my veins ran ice. Now that
he is away I feel far more gently towards him—it is only close by that
I grow rigid—stiffening with a strange mixture of apprehension and
anger—which nothing softens but his retreat and a perfect subduing
of his manner. I did not want to be proud nor intend to be proud—
but I was forced to be so.[5]

A week later Papa had not recovered from inflammation and still
took breakfast upstairs in his room, but she was glad of the distraction,
for it kept her mind off Mr. Taylor's departure, which had become
"complete bitterness and ashes. . . . I do assure you—dear Nell—not
to deceive either you or myself, a more entire crumbling away of a
seeming foundation of support and prospect of hope . . . can scarcely
be realised."[6] Guilt haunted her: she had been unjust, unkind. In the
midst of these unhappy speculations, April 21 approached and passed:
she was thirty-five. Two days after her birthday "a quiet little note"
and a parcel of books arrived from Taylor. He had heard she was contemplating a London visit; he was leaving May 20; could he see her in
London before that date?

Her visit was fixed for June; they would not see each other again.
"There is still a want of plain, mutual understanding in this business,"
she wrote Ellen. But she had come to a conclusion:

. . . I looked for something of the gentleman—something I mean of
the *natural* gentleman [she defended herself to Ellen]; you know I
can dispense with acquired polish, and for looks, I know myself too
well to think that I have any right to be exacting on that point. I
could not find one gleam, I could not see one passing glimpse, of true
good-breeding; it is hard to say, but it is true. In mind too; though
clever, he is second-rate; thoroughly second-rate. One does not like to
say these things, but one had better be honest. Were I to marry him,
my heart would bleed in pain and humiliation; I could not, *could* not
look up to him. No—if Mr Taylor be the only husband fate offers to

me, single I must always remain. But yet, at times I grieve for him, and perhaps it is superfluous, for I cannot think he will suffer much; a hard nature, occupation and change of scene will befriend him. . . . Papa continues much better.—With kind regards to all, I am, dear Nell, your middle aged friend, C. Brontë.[7]

Having firmly dismissed James Taylor as well lost, she was thrown into doubt again by a long letter from Williams in which he spoke of the little man with great respect. Mr. Taylor had an even more vigorous champion, however: Charlotte was astounded at Papa's unprecedented approval of her suitor. Mr. Brontë had bid Taylor good-by warmly; now he praised him to his daughter in high terms. The man was respectable, solid, successful. When Charlotte complained that Taylor was no gentleman, Mr. Brontë dismissed the objection impatiently. The thing seemed incomprehensible, considering Papa's wrath in the past over marriage rumors. But perhaps he was encouraged by the fact that the event could not possibly take place for five long years.

Inevitably the Taylor affair was eclipsed by the anticipation of seeing George Smith again in London—an anticipation bridled by reason and pessimism, but keen nevertheless. The memory of the Scotland journey still lingered; the Rhine proposal promised—what? Then a letter came from Smith: because of the press of business matters, he must call off the trip up the Rhine that summer. Adept at squeezing the scorpion, Charlotte answered cheerfully, falsely:

> Your project, depend on it, has been quite providentially put a stop to. And do you really think I would have gone to the Rhine this summer? Do you think I would have partaken in all that unearned pleasure?
>
> Now listen to a serious word. You might *possibly* have persuaded me to go (I do not *think* that you would, but it does not become me to be very positive on that point, seeing that proofs of inflexibility do not abound), yet had I gone I should not have been truly happy; self-reproach would have gnawed at the root of enjoyment . . . Ergo, though I am sorry for your own and your sister's sake that your castle on the Rhine has turned out a castle in the air, I am not at all sorry for mine.[8]

With only the London visit now to look forward to, she prepared for it with unusual care, begging Ellen, who went over to Leeds frequently, to get a shop to send some black and white lace mantles to Haworth for her selection, and also some small-sized, plain chemisettes —"the full woman's size does not fit me." She chose a black lace mantle, then, coming to try it on with her good back silk dress, found that against the silk the lace looked rusty. She returned it, requesting a white mantle of the same price. Not having any in stock, the Leeds shop imported one from London, but, alas! it was a cheap thing, only £1 14s. Still it was pretty and light, and, as she wrote Ellen, her faithful counsel in matters of dress, "upon reasoning the matter over, I came to the conclusion, that it would be no shame for a person of my means to wear a cheaper thing; so I think I shall take it, and if you ever see it and call it 'trumpery' so much the worse."⁹

She would have liked Ellen's advice on buying a new bonnet but, not wishing to trouble her, went over to Leeds by train from Keighley herself. At Hunt and Hall's, she hesitated among the splendors of lace, tulle, ribbon, flowers, and rice straw, wishing heartily for her friend, finally choosing an affair lined in pink silk that looked "grave and quiet" amongst all the frippery. In the yard goods department, she hung over "beautiful silks of pale sweet colours" at five shillings a yard but, not having the daring or the means, settled for black silk at three shillings. Back home, she found that Papa would have willingly lent her a sovereign for the pastel silks. She tried on the bonnet before a glass in her austere room and found that the pink lining looked far, far too gay.

In the midst of this flurry, she indignantly repulsed Ellen, Mrs. Nussey, Tabby, and Martha for suspecting that she was going off to London to be married: "How I smile internally! How groundless and impossible is the idea!" Papa had the darkest forebodings, telling her flatly that should she marry and leave him he would give up the parsonage and go into lodgings, making it clear that the move would be the death of him. With such suspicion hanging in the air, she refused to send Ellen George Smith's enthusiastic letter fixing her arrival for Thursday, May 27: "[you] would see more in an impetuous expression of quite temporary satisfaction—than strict reality justifies."¹⁰

A week before her departure, nervous strain brought on one of her bilious attacks. Headache wracked her; she grew gray and sunken, and wrote Ellen grimly, "I shall go to London with nothing to boast of in looks." Her chief fear was for Papa's health, however: a recurrence of inflammation, a bronchial attack—and her journey might be postponed indefinitely. As May 27 drew near, Smith wrote again, begging her to come a day earlier so that she could attend Thackeray's lecture on Thursday. Papa agreed. Accordingly, she took the London-bound train from Leeds on Wednesday, arriving in pink-lined bonnet at Euston Station at ten o'clock in the evening to be met by handsome George Smith and his prudent mother.

The visit, planned for a fortnight but extended almost a month, was a cruel disappointment. Forbidding herself to hope, she *had* hoped, and now, day by day, she saw her hopes slowly, subtly shatter.

George Smith was all he had been—cordial, courteous, lively, sympathetic—but—the fact gradually and painfully emerged—he was no more.

It was the summer of the Crystal Palace, that great glass monument to progress, peace, and imperialism, brainchild of Prince Albert, design of Joseph Paxton, man of the hour. The Queen herself had opened the Great Exhibition before 25,000 people on May 1 in a burst of pomp, splendor, and loyal enthusiasm that drove Her Majesty to ecstasies. Such a tribute to England, the Crown, and, above all, her dear Albert. "The greatest day in our history," she rhapsodized to her uncle King Leopold of Belgium, "the most *beautiful* and *imposing* and *touching* spectacle ever seen, and the triumph of my beloved Albert. . . . It was the *happiest, proudest* day of my life, and I can think of nothing else. Albert's dearest name is immortalised with the *great* conception, *his* own, and my *own* dear country *showed* she was *worthy* of it. The triumph was *immense*."[11]

The evening of May 29, George Smith escorted Charlotte through thronging crowds from every corner of England and the Empire to Hyde Park and Paxton's wonder, "a blazing arch of lucid glass" leaping "like a fountain from the grass." Unlike her sovereign, Charlotte was not ecstatic. A child of the smoke-blackened district that produced many of the wonders on display, she did not believe with most Victorians that the good life depended on spinning jennies, newfangled cookstoves, mechanical pianos, sewing machines, bathtubs, and steam engines. The exhibition, she said, was like a great Vanity Fair. She peered about shortsightedly at the throngs of people, the flags of every nation floating high in the bright arches, the palm trees and machinery, the Amazon statue from Berlin and the locomotives, the huge elms enclosed right in the soaring glass cage, the Crystal Fountain, the crimson curtains, the aisles and aisles choked with 14,000 exhibits from the four corners of the world. Ruskin has dismissed the whole show with contempt, Burne-Jones found it cheerless and monotonous, Dickens pronounced himself bewildered and "used up" by the confusion, William Morris found the Crystal Palace itself "wonderfully ugly." Charlotte was a little more impressed, finding the exterior "strange and elegant" but insubstantial, the interior animated, gorgeous, and bewildering; but concluded that the whole show was not much in her way.

She went a second time, remained three hours, and was more enthusiastic, but chiefly for Papa's sake. "It is a wonderful place," she wrote him, "—vast, strange, new, and impossible to describe. Its grandeur does not consist in *one* thing, but in the unique assemblage of *all* things. Whatever human industry has created, you find there, from the great compartments filled with railway engines and boilers, with mill-machinery in full work, with splendid carriages of all kinds, with harness of every description—to the glass-covered and velvet-spread stands loaded with the most gorgeous work of the goldsmith and silversmith, and the carefully guarded caskets full of real diamonds and pearls worth hundreds of thousands of pounds. It may be called a bazaar or a fair, but it is such a bazaar or fair as Eastern genii might have created. It seems as if magic only could have gathered this mass of wealth from all the ends of the earth—as if none but super-natural hands could have arranged it thus, with such a blaze and contrast of colours and marvelous power of effect."[12] Like the government itself, Charlotte was impressed by the quiet and decent behavior of the masses that choked the aisles. With Chartism and frame-breaking not far in the past, there had been great fear that the exhibition might provoke riot and destruction. But the material glories of the Crystal Palace hypnotized the crowds into a reverent, patriotic trance. Many wept openly, overcome by the greatness of England. "The multitude filling the great aisles seems ruled and subdued by some invisible influence," Charlotte continued to Papa. "Amongst the thirty thousand souls that peopled it the day I was there, not one loud noise was to be heard, not one irregular movement seen—the living tide rolls on quietly, with a deep hum like the sea heard from a distance."

On her third excursion to the Crystal Palace she was escorted by the eminent scientist Sir David Brewster, and the mechanical and scientific exhibits she had merely stared at before now became meaningful with his simple, clear explanations. By the fourth and fifth visits—undertaken unwillingly—she was thoroughly sick of the place.

More to her taste were Thackeray's lectures, a series of talks on English humorists of the eighteenth century that had taken the fashionable world by storm and would make a pretty penny for the speaker. Charlotte arrived in time for the Titan's second lecture on Congreve and Addison: on Thursday afternoon she went with Mrs. Smith to Willis's Rooms in King Street, St. James's, "a large and splendid kind of saloon—that in which the great balls of Almack's are given. The walls were all painted and gilded, the benches were sofas stuffed and cushioned and covered with blue damask."[13] The audience was equally gilded, for, with his high social connections, Thackeray had drawn peeresses by the score. Into this throng of pale, summery silks Charlotte entered timidly in black. Trusting to scuttle inconspicuously to one of the blue damask sofas, she was surprised and rather dismayed when Thackeray recognized her and strode down the room to greet her. After a few words he led her up to a "fine—handsome—young-looking old lady"—Mrs. Carmichael-Smyth, the mother who had so dominated his life. "Mother," said Thackeray loudly, having gained nothing in discretion since his "cigar-fragrance" blunder, "you must allow me to introduce you to Jane Eyre." Silks rustled, heads turned, eyeglasses leveled at the tiny figure standing at the great man's elbow, and Currer Bell was furious with the Titan once more.[14]

After Thackeray began Charlotte became too absorbed to notice the stares still shot in her direction, although Mrs. Smith, always apprehensive about her guest's moods, was aware of them enough. Charlotte was amazed at Thackeray's poise before the cream of London society that included the beautiful Duchess of Sutherland, Queen Victoria's Mistress of the Robes: he "just got up and spoke with as much simplicity and ease as if he had been speaking to a few friends by his own fireside. The lecture was truly good: he has taken pains with the composition. It was finished without being in the least studied; a quiet humour and graphic force enlivened it throughout."[15] Of course, Thackeray *was* nervous, as he himself admitted, but his self-possession made him seem as urbane as a wit from his beloved eighteenth century.

Charlotte's unself-consciousness ended abruptly with the sound of enthusiastic, gloved applause: there were more gantlets to be run. Someone came up behind her, bent over the sofa, and murmured, "Will you permit me, as a Yorkshireman, to introduce myself?" It was, as Charlotte almost immediately recognized, the Earl of Carlisle. His Grace was followed by Richard Monckton Milnes, member of Parliament from Yorkshire, gentleman about town, the future Lord Houghton, and biographer of Keats. Turning from these men, prepared to exit quietly, she beheld to her horror that the audience had not left the room but, in tribute to the mysterious Currer Bell, had drawn up in two lines forming an aisle along which she had to pass before she could reach the door. Mrs. Smith took command. Seizing Miss Brontë's arm, she led her quickly past the rows of "eager and admiring" faces, dreading every step of the way that her companion might fall in her tracks, so violent was the trembling of Charlotte's small hand on her arm.

Charlotte nursed her indignation over the "Jane Eyre" episode through the night, and the next afternoon, when Thackeray came innocently to call, she lashed into him. George Smith, entering the drawing room, "found a scene in full progress. Only these two were in the room. Thackeray was standing on the hearth-rug, looking anything but happy. Charlotte Brontë stood close to him, with head

thrown back and face white with anger. The first words I heard
were, 'No Sir! If *you* had come to our part of the country in Yorkshire, what would you have thought of me if I had introduced you
to my father, before a mixed company of strangers, as "Mr. Warrington?"' Thackeray replied, 'No, you mean "Arthur Pendennis."'
'No, I *don't* mean Arthur Pendennis!' retorted Miss Brontë. 'I mean
Mr. Warrington, and Mr. Warrington would not have behaved as
you behaved to me yesterday.' The spectacle of this little woman,
hardly reaching to Thackeray's elbow, but, somehow looking
stronger and fiercer than himself, and casting her incisive words at
his head, resembled the dropping of shells into a fortress."[16]

Recovering his presence of mind, Smith hurried up with soothing
civilities, Thackeray apologized "half-humourously," and they parted
amiably. But the Titan must have shaken his white locks in dismay
as he quit the house. Accustomed to the polish and easy grace of
Londoners who considered all serious discussion on matters of controversy ill bred, he found Charlotte's humorless intensity extremely
provoking. "You see by Jane Eyre's letter dont you why we can't
be very great friends?" he wrote Mary Holmes a half year later.
"We had a correspondence—a little one; and met, very eagerly on
her part. But there's a fire and fury raging in that little woman a
rage scorching her heart w[h]. doesn't suit me. She has had a story
and a great grief that has gone badly with her."[17]

More than Charlotte ever knew, or would have believed, Thackeray
loved the easy life: "I reel from dinner party to dinner—I wallow in
the turtle and swim in Shampang," he had joked to Lady Blessington.
At his death, his cellar contained 1,080 bottles of vintage port and
claret in twenty-one bins.[18] Moreover he admired pretty, charming
ladies—Mrs. Caroline Norton, Lucy Duff-Gordon, the plump and
blooming Mrs. Gore, Lady Stanley, Mary and Agnes Berry, two ancient socialites who pearl-powdered and rouged and exclaimed "O!
Christ!" and "My God!" in Thackeray's beloved eighteenth-century
manner. He was charmed by young ladies, succulent pink buds, with
whom he became fatherly, writing verses in their albums and patting
their springy curls. He loved a weak, sentimental woman—platonically,
of course—a married woman, Jane Brookfield, who had solved her
neuroses by taking to her couch in approved Victorian manner and
courting with large, soulful eyes suitors she had no intention of gratifying.

Charlotte was not a socialite, or pretty, or charming. She was not
weak or sentimental. When it came to men, she had scarcely a platonic
bone in her body. But Thackeray did like her at a distance and pitied
her unhappiness. Mrs. Procter wrote him once that his own heart was

very much like that of Paul Emanuel, the hero of *Villette:* ". . . in its core was a place tender beyond a man's tenderness: a place that humbled him to little children, that bound him to girls and women, to whom rebel as he would, he could not disown his affinity nor quite deny that, on the whole, he was better with them than with his own sex."[19] Charlotte touched Thackeray's heart and admiration, yet his first feeling for her was a pity she would have scorned: ". . . if Currer Bell has not her cross in life to bear, I'm very much mistaken. God help her and all poor souls."[20]

That summer in London he tried to help her the way he knew best, offering to introduce her to great ladies who would receive her with open arms, for London society loved a celebrity. But Charlotte would have none of it. She found him a good deal spoiled by social success: "I cannot see that this sort of society produces so good an effect on him as to tempt me in the least to try the same experiment, so I remain obscure." She was disgusted to learn that he had postponed a Thursday lecture merely to please his duchesses and marchionesses, who were obliged that day to go down to Ascot with the Queen and her court. She heard with scorn of the elaborate preparations of lords and ladies for the Queen's fancy ball. "Their pet and their darling, Mr. Thackeray, of course sympathises with them," she wrote Papa. "He was here yesterday to dinner, and left very early in the evening in order that he might visit respectively the Duchess of Norfolk, the Marchioness of Londonderry, Ladies Chesterfield and Clanricarde, and see them all in their fancy costumes of the reign of Charles II, before they set out for the Palace!"[21]

"The aristocracy of nature making the ko-too to the aristocracy of accident," scoffed Harriet Martineau of Thackeray's love affair with London society. Martineau's opinion was seconded by most Victorian intellectuals. Objecting that polite society directed all conduct toward "low and petty objects," John Stuart Mill concluded that socializing could only satisfy "persons of a very common order in thought or feeling." The "moral desperado" Carlyle harangued and raged, condemning the elite as "Dwellers by the Dead Sea," and consigning his former protégé Thackeray to their number. Tennyson ventured among London society and retired in relief to Farringford, his estate on the Isle of Wight. Matthew Arnold labeled the aristocracy "barbarians." Literary rivalry was only one source of the rift between Thackeray and Dickens, for Dickens, paranoiacally insecure about his humble origins, detected condescension everywhere, envied Thackeray his social adroitness, and hated his world: "I declare I never go into what is called 'society', than I am aweary of it, despise it, hate it, and reject it. The more I see of its extraordinary conceit, and its stupendous ignorance of what is passing out of doors, the more certain I am that it is approaching the period when, being incapable of reforming itself, it will have to submit to being reformed by others off the face of the earth."[22] Dickens spoke historical truth: the aristocratic back was broken: the class was sinking into powerless decadence. Perhaps this fact alone inspired the sentimental Thackeray's sympathy for these last relics of eighteenth-century grandeur.

Thackeray of the sardonic eyebrows was bored with the heavy moral earnestness of Carlyle, Dickens, Macaulay, and, in her conversation, Charlotte Brontë. Charlotte had mistaken him for some kind of Old Testament avenging god. Instead he was satirical and urbane, criticizing to correct a world he essentially believed in. "God bless every one of 'em," he once wrote Mrs. Brookfield, "—the snobs as well as the swells, the dear old stoopids as well as the sparkling wits. They come tumbling into my memory next morning all fighting for places in the 'Ghouls of Gadar Grange,' or whatever may be the elegant society novel I am for the moment engaged on."

Charlotte and Thackeray agreed no better on literary matters. She who could never write a line unless the creative spirit possessed her could not understand a writer who molded his writing to a monthly deadline, procrastinating in the early days, sitting up night after night before the next installment was due. She felt he was not serious, not dedicated. He wrote to live well, she believed; he did not live to write. "The truth is," wrote George Smith, "Charlotte Brontë's heroics aroused Thackeray's antagonism. . . . He insisted on discussing his books very much as a clerk in a bank would discuss the ledgers he had to keep for a salary. But all this was, on Thackeray's part, an affectation; an affectation into which he was provoked by what he considered Charlotte Brontë's 'high-falutin.' Miss Brontë wanted to persuade him he was a great man with a 'mission'; and Thackeray, with many wicked jests, declined to recognize the 'mission.' "[23]

Thackeray himself, however, agreed with Charlotte on one occasion at least. "Currer Bell is right about that," he wrote Mary Holmes in 1852. "I don't care a straw for a 'triumph' Pooh!—nor for my art enough. It seems to me indecent and despicable to be doing the novelist business of 'On a lovely evening in January 2 cavaliers &c—and then the description of the cavaliers, their coats, horses the landscape &c—Shall one take pride out of this folly?"[24]

Certainly Thackeray was surprised at the difference between the novelist and *Jane Eyre*, which struck him as passionate rather than didactic. Much of Charlotte's "high-falutin" undoubtedly came from a misguided belief that she had to vindicate the reputation of Currer, Ellis, and Acton Bell from charges of immorality. Much of the "high-falutin" derived from a compulsion to be negative: Charlotte was consistently cool to warmth, warm to coolness, irreverent with pomposity, earnest with triflers. "An austere little Joan of Arc," Thackeray called her but, like the Dauphin, he found it uncomfortable to be saved. Charlotte went on Thursdays to Willis's Rooms; they parted friends; they corresponded briefly; but after the summer of 1851 they did not meet again.

The first weeks of Charlotte's visit thus passed pleasantly enough. Her headaches retreated, she was not utterly exhausted. The first of June, a Sunday, was a highlight, as she wrote Ellen: "a day to be marked with a white stone—through most of the day I was very happy without being tired or over-excited." Memories of Brussels haunted her that day: "—in the afternoon I went to hear D'Aubigny —the great Protestant French preacher—it was pleasant—half-sweet —half sad—and strangely suggestive to hear the French language once more."[25]

A week later she was ill. "I sit down to write you this morning in an inexpressibly flat state," she confessed to Ellen on Wednesday, June 11, "having spent the whole of yesterday and the day before in a gradually increasing headache, which at last grew rampant and violent, ended with excessive sickness, and this morning I am quite weak and washy." Was the illness triggered by a sudden or culminating understanding that Smith did not and could not love her? The next paragraph of the same letter seems to confirm it: "You seem to think me in such a happy, enviable position; pleasant moments I have, but it is usually a pleasure I am obliged to repel and check, which cannot benefit the future, but only add to its solitude, which is no more to be relied on than the sunshine of one summer's day. I pass portions of many a night in extreme sadness."[26]

The London visit, then, had become an exercise in self-control. With paradoxical vehemence, Lucy Snowe cried out for restraint in the matter of her feelings for Dr. John: ". . . let me be content with a temperate draught of this living stream: let me not run athirst, and apply passionately to its welcome waters: let me not imagine in them a sweeter taste than earth's fountains know. Oh! would to God I may be enabled to feel enough sustained by an occasional, amicable intercourse, rare, brief, unengrossing and tranquil: quite tranquil!"[27] But Charlotte was incapable of moderate feeling; she *had* run athirst; she had mistaken, again in her own metaphor, the transitory rain-pool of George Smith's friendship for the perennial spring yielding the supply of seasons. Now, hour by hour, she was forced to choke and crush the emotions that had flourished in spite of her control.

How much Charlotte blamed Mrs. Smith for her unhappiness is

uncertain. She recognized the strong bond between mother and son; she believed that under a teasing fondness Mrs. Smith gripped her son's allegiance with an iron hand. She went home to portray mother and son in her new novel under the guise of Mrs. Bretton and "my son John," reproducing Mrs. Smith's mannerisms closely and some of her conversation verbatim. On the surface the playful, affectionate matron seems innocent enough, but Charlotte's pen was dipped in vitriol: there is something cloying and unnatural in Mrs. Bretton's jealous adoration of her son. In one scene which Charlotte may well have witnessed, for example, Mrs. Bretton has just awakened from a doze before the drawing-room fire to be tenderly rallied by John Graham Bretton:

> "Hushaby, mamma! Sleep again. You look the picture of innocence in your slumbers."
> "My slumbers, John Graham! What are you talking about? You know I never *do* sleep by day: it was the slightest doze possible."
> "Exactly! a seraph's gentle lapse—a fairy's dream. Mamma, under such circumstances, you always remind me of Titania."
> "That is because you, yourself, are so like Bottom."
> "Miss Snowe—did you ever hear anything like mamma's wit? She is a most sprightly woman of her size and age."
> "Keep your compliments to yourself, sir, and do not neglect your own size: which seems to me a good deal on the increase. Lucy, has he not rather the air of an incipient John Bull? He used to be slender as an eel, and now I fancy in him a sort of heavy-dragoon bent—a beef-eater tendency. Graham, take notice! If you grow fat I disown you."
> "As if you could not sooner disown your own personality! I am indispensable to the old lady's happiness, Lucy. She would pine away in green and yellow melancholy if she had not my six feet of iniquity to scold. It keeps her lively—it maintains the wholesome ferment of her spirits."[28]

During this visit Charlotte sensed that the bond between George and his family was stronger than ever. "Things and circumstances seem here to be as usual," she told Ellen, "—but I fancy there has been some crisis in which his energy and filial affection have sustained them all—this I judge from seeing that Mother and sisters are more peculiarly bound to him than ever and that his slightest wish is an unquestioned law." Smith himself seemed changed—"a little older, darker and more careworn—his ordinary manner is graver—but in the evening his spirits flow back to him."[29]

She might well find him so, for Smith was experiencing rough weather at 65 Cornhill. Although *Jane Eyre*, the firm's first literary success, had turned the tide for the publishing part of the concern, Smith, Elder still staggered under a loss of more than £30,000. This sum, Smith discovered to his horror, had been embezzled over many years by his father's partner, Elder, a man the young Smith had worshiped, "a man of brilliant social gifts moving in the best circles, a fine talker, a clever writer." In the same year *Jane Eyre* appeared, George Smith, by dint of great skill and energy, managed to ease Elder out of the firm without scandal or bankruptcy. Then his task had been to rebuild Smith, Elder with his own hands. His mother and sisters watched the battle and would eventually witness his success, much of which he owed to Currer Bell, for her name lured other popular authors like Thackeray and Mrs. Gaskell to his firm. In the summer of 1851, however, Smith had not yet achieved financial stability. He often worked continuously for thirty-four hours, struggling to meet the Indian mails, sustained only by "mutton chops and green tea at stated intervals." Charlotte postponed leaving for the sake of spending a Wednesday with him: "I cannot now leave London till Friday," she wrote Ellen, June 24. "—To-morrow is Mr Smith's only holiday—(Mr T's departure leaves him loaded with work—more than once since I came he has been kept in the City till 3 in the morning) he wants to take us all to Richmond and I promised last week I would stay and go with him—his Mother and Sisters."[30]

Charlotte had little doubt that Smith would triumph. Benign planets had smiled on his birth: he seemed to her a favored being, one of those cheerful, elastic, confident people who could beat down adversity with smiles. Yet Smith could not emerge from his struggle in the harsh world of business without steel in his character and blunted sensibilities.

That summer he took her to see the great actress Rachel. The event stirred Charlotte violently: the crowded theater, the hush of anticipation, the pleasure-pain of Smith's presence next to her in the close darkness. At nine the famous actress rose like a star above the horizon: a star shining with pale grandeur, yet hollow, half consumed, and wasted like wax in flame. Torn by the violence of Rachel's performance, Charlotte turned eagerly to Smith and was surprised at his calm. She used the event in *Villette:* Lucy Snowe asks Dr. John his opinion of Vashti. " 'Hm-m-m,' was the first scarce articulate but expressive answer; and then such a strange smile went wandering round his lips, a smile so critical, so almost callous! I suppose that for natures of that order his sympathies *were* callous. In a few terse phrases he told me his opinion of, and feeling towards, the actress: he judged her as a woman, not an artist: it was a branding judgment." Judged too often as a woman rather than an artist herself, Charlotte

held Smith's callous reaction against him; it tempered her final estimation of his character in her novel: "Dr. John *could* think, and think
well, but he was rather a man of action than of thought; he *could*
feel, and feel vividly in his way, but his heart had no chord for enthusiasm . . . for what belonged to storm, what was wild and intense, dangerous, sudden, and flaming, he had no sympathy, and held
with it no communion."[31] Charlotte belonged to storm and what was
wild and intense. She could never enter Smith's cheerful, sociable,
comely world, but neither could he know her torments and passions—and she scorned him a little for it. Ellen Nussey always
claimed that George Smith proposed to Charlotte. Charlotte's bit-
tersweet portrait of him in *Villette* suggests he did not.

She postponed going home again and again, ostensibly because
the indefatigable Sir James Kay-Shuttleworth had discovered her
presence in London and pressed her into a round of activities. The days
fled by: breakfast with the old London literary wit, Samuel Rogers;
paintings at Somerset House; an excursion to the Strand with Smith
under the names Mr. and Miss Fraser to consult a Dr. Browne,
phrenologist, who told her, among other things, that her head revealed
remarkable intellectual powers and strong and enduring affections[32];
Thackeray's Thursday afternoon lectures; Richmond with the Smiths.
Besides Thackeray's lectures, the only event to compare with Rachel's
acting was Cardinal Wiseman's performance at the Roman Catholic
Society of St. Vincent de Paul. "The whole scene was impiously the-
atrical," she told Ellen, shuddering over the cardinal much as she had
shuddered over the actress who had impressed her finally as the Devil
incarnate. For Papa, a Catholic-hater time out of mind, she went into
more detail: "He is a big portly man something of the shape of Mr
Morgan; he has not merely a double but a treble and quadruple chin;
he has a very large mouth with oily lips, and looks as if he would relish
a good dinner with a bottle of wine after it. He came swimming into
the room smiling, simpering, and bowing like a fat old lady, and sat
down very demure in his chair, and looked the picture of a sleek hypocrite. He was dressed in black like a bishop or dean in plain clothes, but
wore scarlet gloves and a brilliant scarlet waistcoat. A bevy of inferior
priests surrounded him, many of them very dark-looking and sinister
men. The Cardinal spoke in a smooth whining manner, just like a
canting Methodist preacher. The audience seemed to look up to him
as to a god. A spirit of the hottest zeal pervaded the whole meeting. I
was told afterwards that except myself and the person who accompanied me there was not a single Protestant present."[33] This was
hardly strange. Only Charlotte, fascinated and repelled by the religion
of Monsieur Heger, would bother to view what she hated. To do her

justice, she was not alone in her anti-Catholicism in 1851: all England was gripped in a "Catholic scare" inspired by the Pope's announcement that England was to be divided up into Catholic dioceses.

She summed up the long, disturbing month for Ellen: "I cannot boast that London has agreed with me well this time—the oppression of frequent head-ache—sickness and a low tone of spirits has poisoned many moments which might otherwise have been pleasant—Sometimes I have felt this hard and been tempted to murmur at Fate which condemns me to comparative silence and solitude for eleven months in the year—and in the twelfth while offering social enjoyment takes away the vigour and cheerfulness which should turn it to account. But circumstances are ordered for us, and we must submit."[34] She had delayed leaving three times, because the Smiths had urged her to stay and because she lingered with morbid fascination at the scene of her dead hopes.

Paradoxically, Smith was as benevolent and attentive as before; now, however, she understood the limits of the benevolence. "He had still such kind looks," says Lucy Snowe in the novel Charlotte went home to write, "such a warm hand; his voice still kept so pleasant a tone for my name . . . But I learned in time that this benignity, this cordiality, this music, belonged in no shape to me: it was a part of himself; it was the honey of his temper; it was the balm of his mellow mood; he imparted it, as the ripe fruit rewards with sweetness the rifling bee; he diffused it about him, as sweet plants shed their perfume. . . .

" 'Good night, Dr. John; you are good, you are beautiful; but you are not mine. Good night, and God bless you!' "[35]

On June 27 she finally boarded the train north for Manchester where she intended to spend two days with Mrs. Gaskell. We may be sure that George Smith saw her to the station, with his mother in attendance. We can guess that as the train moved out of the station the face beneath the pink silk bonnet did not smile.

# 22

## *Villette*

Perhaps a presentiment prompted Charlotte to stay on in London, an intuition that this was to be almost her last contact with the great world. For a month her existence had expanded, impinging briefly on the lives of the famous, the clever, and the rich; now it was to contract steadily, year by year.

Letters from Cornhill dwindled perceptibly. Currer Bell was in some ways a disappointment to that firm. She could not be pressured to deadlines, her health seemed uncertain, she had no coterie, she did not shine in society, her name was not appended to journal articles, she did not crank out Christmas stories like Thackeray, Mrs. Gaskell, and Dickens, she did not subscribe to Wilkie Collins' slick formula for the successful novel—"Make 'em laugh, make 'em wait, make 'em cry." In such a prolific era—of huge families, long working hours, luxuriant whiskers, layers of petticoats, feverish production, and three-decker novels—Currer Bell's almost monastic simplicity was a crime. The frenetic energy of Dickens, who poured forth monthly novel installments, travel journals, Christmas stories, edited *Household Words* and *All the Year Round* and wrote half their material, staged semi-professional theatricals, traveled extensively, gave public readings, wrote volumes of letters, took twenty-mile walks every day, and fathered ten children, was nearer the norm.

And yet Charlotte was still to write her finest novel.

She answered a letter from Williams that July in autumnal mood:

> In reading your graphic account of a visit to Oxford after an interval of 30 years since you last went there—and of the disillusion which meanwhile had taken place—I could not help wondering whether Cornhill will ever change for me as Oxford has changed for you; I have some pleasant associations connected with it now—will these alter their character some day?

Perhaps they may—though I have faith to the contrary; because—I *think*—I do not exaggerate my partialities, I *think* I take fault along with excellencies—blemishes together with beauties. And besides—in the matter of friendship—I have observed—that disappointment here arises chiefly—*not* from liking our friends too well—or thinking of them too highly—but rather from an over-estimate of *their* liking for and opinion of *us;* and that if we guard ourselves with sufficient scrupulousness of care from error in this direction—and can be content, and even happy to give more affection than we receive . . . I *think* we may manage to get through life with consistency and constancy—unembittered by that misanthropy which springs from revulsions of feeling. All this sounds a little metaphysical—but it is good sense if you consider it.[1]

Cornhill *had* changed; she had overestimated Smith's feeling for her. Ironically, however, Smith had hardly waited till the train was out of sight before writing her. She received his letter, the first of a series of unusually cordial and frequent communications, at Mrs. Gaskell's house in Plymouth Grove. It immediately revived the painful question of his friendship. "I went to church by myself on Sunday morning (they are Unitarians)," Charlotte wrote back. "On my return shortly before the family came home from chapel the servant said there was a letter for me. . . . Of course I was not at all pleased when the small problem was solved by the letter being brought; I never care for hearing from you the least in the world."[2] Smith could not know the effect of his prompt, friendly letter. The London visit had seemed perfectly satisfactory to him. Besides, he very badly wanted another novel from Currer Bell.

Female friends proved more satisfactory. "The visit to Mrs. Gaskell on my way home let me down easily," she wrote Smith in the same letter; "though I spent only two days with her they were very pleasant. She lives in a large, cheerful, airy house, quite out of Manchester smoke; a garden surrounds it, and, as in this hot weather the windows were kept open, a whispering of leaves and perfume of flowers always pervaded the rooms. Mrs. Gaskell herself is a woman of whose conversation and company I should not soon tire. She seems to me kind, clever, animated, and unaffected; her husband is a good and kind man too."

Mrs. Gaskell was herself extremely social, a hostess who welcomed and charmed Thackeray, Dickens, Darwin, the Brownings, the Carlyles, the Froudes, Matthew Arnold, Ruskin, and Emerson over the years. Yet she had the tact to tune the two days of Charlotte's visit to her guest's temperament. She invited no one to the house; she let the charm and sympathy of her life quietly steal over the tense and

lonely Currer Bell. So potent was the charm that Charlotte, no lover
of children, actually fell quite in love with the four daughters—
Marianne, the eldest, self-possessed, musical; Meta, quite capable of
reading and appreciating, for example, Ruskin's *The Seven Lamps of
Architecture;* the nervous, anxious Florence; and Julia, "witty and
wild and clever and droll the pet of the house." The two younger
girls especially won her, combining as they did what she had been as
a child and what she would have wished to be. "Whenever I see Florence and Julia again, I shall feel like a fond but bashful suitor, who
views at a distance the fair personage to whom, in his clownish awe,
he dare not risk a near approach. Such is the clearest idea I can give
you of my feelings towards children I like, but to whom I am a
stranger. And to what children am I not a stranger?"[3]

Alone again at Haworth, where no perfume of flowers stole
through the open windows, but where on quiet, warm July and
August days she could "hear a bird or two singing on certain thorn
trees in the garden," she had the comfort of letters from Harriet
Martineau and Elizabeth Gaskell. Receiving a letter from each woman
on the same topics, the Great Exhibition and Thackeray's lectures, she
was driven to contrast the two personalities. Martineau's judgments
were severe and concise. She had called *Vanity Fair* "a raking up of
dirt and rotten eggs"; she was only a little less stringent about
Thackeray's "English Humorists" series, agreeing with Macaulay that
his knowledge of his subject was superficial: "Thackeray knows little of those times, & his audience less." Mrs. Gaskell, on the other
hand, admired the lectures, for which Charlotte congratulated her:
"You do well to set aside odious comparisons, and to wax impatient
of that trite twaddle about 'nothing-newness'—a jargon which simply
proves, in those who habitually use it, a coarse and feeble faculty of
appreciation; an inability to discern the relative value of *originality*
and *novelty* . . ." The very different minds of Martineau and Gaskell
she found "full striking"—"not the rough contrast of good and evil,
but the more subtle opposition, the more delicate diversity of different kinds of good. The excellence of one nature resembled (I
thought) that of some sovereign medicine—harsh, perhaps to the
taste, but potent to invigorate; the good of the other seemed more
akin to the nourishing efficacy of our daily bread."[4]

Except for disagreeing about Catholicism ("the system is not one
which should have such sympathy as *yours,*" Charlotte wrote re-
proachfully), she found herself in sympathy with many of Mrs.
Gaskell's views. They agreed, for example, about a remarkable anonymous article that appeared that July in the *Westminster Review.* It
began: "Most of our readers will probably learn from these pages for

the first time, that there has arisen in the United States, and in the most civilized and enlightened portion of them, an organized agitation on a new question—new, not to thinkers, nor to any one by whom the principles of free and popular government are felt as well as acknowledged, but new, and even unheard of, as a subject for public meetings and practical political action. This question is, the enfranchisement of women; their admission, in law, and in fact, to equality in all rights, political, civil, and social, with the male citizens of the community."[5] The author of the article was Harriet Taylor Mill, married April 1851 to the radical philosopher after twenty years of friendship; "The Enfranchisement of Women" sounded one of the first calls to action in England.

The women of England were shamefully behind their American sisters in agitating for equality, said Harriet, and women writers were worst of all:

> The literary class of women are ostentatious in disclaiming their desire for equality or citizenship, and proclaiming their complete satisfaction with the place which society assigns to them; exercising in this, as in many other respects, a most noxious influence over the feelings and opinions of men, who unsuspectingly accept the servilities of toadyism as concessions to the force of truth, not considering that it is the personal interest of these women to profess whatever opinions they expect will be agreeable to men. . . . They depend on men's opinion for their literary as well as for their feminine successes; and such is their bad opinion of men, that they believe there is not more than one in ten thousand who does not dislike and fear strength, sincerity or high spirits in a woman. They are therefore anxious to earn pardon and toleration for whatever of these qualities their writings may exhibit on other subjects, by a display of studied submission on this: that they may give no occasion for vulgar men to say (what nothing will prevent vulgar men from saying), that learning makes women unfeminine, and that literary ladies are likely to be bad wives.

Charlotte and Ellen both read the article, first guessing it to be written by Harriet Martineau, then by John Stuart Mill. Did Charlotte flinch at the paragraph about literary ladies, or at the news that the first step for emancipation in England had been taken in her own Yorkshire, when on February 13, 1851, a petition from Sheffield claiming franchise for women had been presented to the House of Lords by the Earl of Carlisle?

She need not have, for although she was no feminine activist, her novels vibrated with her *dis*satisfaction at women's lack of liberty. Yet she did not entirely like the article. Mrs. Gaskell wrote her about it, and Charlotte agreed: "Your words on this paper express my thoughts. Well argued it is—clear, logical—but vast is the hiatus of omission; harsh the consequent jar on every finer chord of the soul. What is this hiatus? I think I know; and knowing I will venture to say. I think the writer forgets there is such a thing as self-sacrificing love and disinterested devotion."[6] Like most Victorian women who laid down their lives at altars consecrated to Papa, Brother, and Husband, she sharply resented being told (by a man, as she thought) that her sacrifice had been foolish and vain. "I believe that J. S. Mill would make a hard, dry, dismal world of it," she continued; "yet he speaks admirable sense through a great portion of his article, especially when he says that if there be a natural unfitness in women for men's employment there is no need to make laws on the subject; leave all careers open; let them try; those who ought to succeed will succeed, or, at least, will have a fair chance; the incapable will fall back into their right place." Like most successful people, Charlotte could be rather coldly Darwinian. She also applauded the article's stance on maternity.

> It is neither necessary nor just to make imperative on women that they shall be either mothers or nothing [Harriet Mill had written]; or that if they have been mothers once, they shall be nothing else during the whole remainder of their lives. . . . There is no need to make provision by law that a woman shall not carry on the active details of a household, or of the education of children, and at the same time practise a profession or be elected to parliament. Where incompatibility is real, it will take care of itself: but there is gross injustice in making the incompatibility a pretense for the exclusion of those in whose case it does not exist. And these, if they were free to choose, would be a very large proportion. . . . There is no inherent reason or necessity that all women should voluntarily choose to devote their lives to one animal function and its consequences. Numbers of women are wives and mothers only because there is no other career open to them, no other occupation for their feelings or their activities. . . .

This logic appealed to both Charlotte the spinstress and Mrs. Gaskell the mother of four: Mill "disposes of the 'maternity' question very neatly," Charlotte told Mrs. Gaskell.

Although no more references to the article in Charlotte's correspondence survive, Mrs. Gaskell had not heard the last about Charlotte Brontë and "The Enfranchisement of Women." She printed Charlotte's remarks about the article in her *Life*, including, of course, such strictures as "the jar on every finer chord of the soul," "J. S. Mill would make a hard, dry, dismal world of it," and her concluding, "In short J. S. Mill's head is, I daresay, very good, but I feel disposed to scorn his heart." In 1859, Mrs. Gaskell received a bitter letter from John Stuart Mill: he was outraged that Mrs. Gaskell had printed a letter that could only defame the character of his wife Harriet, the author of the *Westminster Review* article. Mrs. Gaskell was outraged herself, finding Mill's letter "impertinent, unjust, and inexcusable": then she learned that Harriet Mill had died the previous November, 1858, and understood why she had given Mill "acute pain." She wrote him to apologize. Mill was not satisfied: he replied harshly, stating that "in publishing letters not written for publication you disregarded the obligation which custom founded on reason has imposed, of omitting what would be offensive to the feelings and perhaps injurious to the moral reputation of individuals."

It was Mrs. Gaskell's turn to be angry. She replied spiritedly, admitting that perhaps she should have omitted the "head and heart" portion of Charlotte's letter, but stoutly defending the biographer's right to use personal letters within reason. "I believe that you are the only person," she added pointedly, "who has made any complaint or remonstrance to me about the publication of Miss Brontë's *letters*."[7] Mill's grief for the wife he had waited twenty years to marry partially explains his unreasonable anger at Charlotte's remarks. Perhaps more significantly, Charlotte's words had struck home: Mill's *Autobiography* testifies how thoroughly the philosopher's head dominated his heart despite his efforts to right the balance, and Harriet Taylor Mill has been accused of the same imbalance.

Pag Taylor also kept faithful. If Charlotte preferred Mrs. Gaskell's milder nature to the potent but harsh Miss Martineau, Mary Taylor was a woman quite after Harriet Martineau's heart. Cheerful, stout letters kept arriving from New Zealand. Mary had gone into shopkeeping with her cousin Ellen Taylor. Ellen, at Charlotte's request, wrote a vivid account of that adventure:

> . . . Mary and I settled we would do something together and we talked for a fortnight before we decided whether we would have a school or shop, it ended in favour of the shop—Waring thought we had better be quiet, and I believe he still thinks we are doing it for amusement, but he never refuses to help us, he *is* teaching us book keeping, and he buys things for us now and then. Mary gets as fierce as a dragon and goes to all the wholesale stores and looks at things, gets patterns, samples etc. and asks prices, and then comes home and we talk it over and then she goes again and buys what we want, she says the people are always civil to her—Our keeping shop astonishes everybody here, I believe they think we do it for fun, some think we shall make nothing of it, or that we shall get tired; and all laugh at us. Before I left home I used to be afraid of being laughed at, but now it has very little effect upon me—

> Mary and I are settled together now, I cant do without Mary and she couldn't get on by herself—I built the house we live in, and we made the plan ourselves so it suits us . . .[8]

Charlotte also kept faith with her old friend, making up boxes of clothing and books with Ellen, which Mary and Ellen Taylor received many months later with delight and often amusement, for the little fineries of English gentility looked strange to these pioneer women of rough New Zealand. "Last Monday we stopped working to open a box and read letters," Mary wrote Ellen Nussey August 15, 1850. "Your pretty thing whatever is the name of it? came almost the first and fine amusement it was to open it. What veritable old maids you and Charlotte must be grown if you really use such a thing. Ellen and I pulled out all the things, one after another and disputed for them. The staylace was particularly amusing! I have not seen such a thing this 5 years. But the best was the garters. I have had almost a daily lecture from Ellen because my stockings wrinkled owning to my having been reduced to two bits of tape for the last six months, and being too stingy to buy any more and too idle to knit them. Ellen says you might have known."[9] Charlotte might have: Mary had never won the Neatness Prize at Roe Head.

The fresh breeze that blew from such letters soon died, leaving a deadly calm. The weird, Charlotte's term for those terrible aftermaths of London, came inexorably on. Having invited himself to farewell tea where he proved "good, mild, uncontentious," Arthur Nicholls, the curate who usually proved only dull, had left to visit relatives in Ireland. Not that she saw him much, or cared much to see him, but his leaving removed the only civilized face in the village besides John Greenwood's. In the monotony of days, the visit of Papa's old friend Mr. Morgan seemed a highlight: he came to nine o'clock breakfast and brought her as a present—God help her—a thick sheaf of religious tracts. By September 1, 1851, she was writing to Ellen in familiar strain: "It is useless to tell you how I live—I endure life—but whether I enjoy it or not is another question . . . in spite of regular exercise—the old head-aches—and starting wakeful nights are coming upon me again—But I *do* get on—and have neither wish nor right to complain."[10] September 20 to Mrs. Gaskell: "You charge me to write about myself. What can I say on that precious topic? . . . Nothing happens to me. I hope and expect little in this world, and am thankful that I do not despond and suffer more."[11] September 26 to Williams: "You inquire after 'Currer Bell.' It seems to me that the absence of his name from your list of announcements will leave no blank, and that he may at least spare himself the disquietude of thinking he is wanted when it is certainly not his lot to appear. Perhaps Currer Bell has his secret moan about these matters; but if so he will keep it to himself. It is an affair about which no words need be wasted, for no words can make a change; it is between him and his position, his faculties and his fate. . . ."[12]

She would not permit herself to write George Smith in this strain. "I am sure I am not low-spirited just now, but very happy," she wrote him September 22, "and in this mood I will write to you." Smith had told her that the firm had recently won several new authors to its ranks; she was pleased; the fact relieved some of her deep guilt at producing so slowly for Smith, Elder. "Can I help wishing you well," she continued, "when I owe you directly or indirectly most of the good moments I now enjoy?"

Gratitude for these good moments made it doubly hard to reject his plea that she consider serial publication. "Oh, that serial! It is of no use telling you what a storm in a teacup the mention of it stirred in Currer Bell's mind, what a fight he had with himself about it. You do not know, you *cannot* know, how strongly his nature inclines him to adopt suggestions coming from so friendly a quarter; how he would like to take them up, cherish them, give them form, conduct them to a successful issue; and how sorrowfully he turns away, feeling in his inmost heart that this work, this pleasure is not for him.

"But though Currer Bell cannot do this you are still to think him your friend, and you are still to be *his* friend. You are to keep a fraction of yourself—if it be only the end of your little finger—for *him*, and that fraction he will neither let gentleman or lady, author or artist . . . take possession of, or so much as meddle with. He reduces his claim to a minute point, and that point he monopolises."

Although she could write him with some cheerfulness and even with carefully controlled tenderness, she could not force herself to endure another meeting. From cordiality, from business motives, Smith had proposed that she come back to London for a short visit to "break the interval between this and Christmas." "No," she replied with a sudden burst of candor; "if there were no other objection (and there are many) there is the pain of that last bidding good-bye, that hopeless shaking hands, yet undulled and unforgotten. I don't like it. I could not bear its frequent repetition. Do not recur to this plan. Going to London is a mere palliation and stimulant; reaction follows."[13]

She fought this reaction now. On her urging, Miss Wooler came to Haworth, impressed Papa with her high-Tory, and therefore sound, sense, and briefly comforted Charlotte, who found her, like good wine, improved with age. Mrs. Gaskell, Miss Martineau, and Mrs. Forster sent invitations, but she declined them all: she could not leave, Tabby had influenza, Martha caught it and then was prostrated by an attack of quinsy, Papa had a cold, she had all the housework on her hands. Somehow she got through the autumnal equinox with its gale winds and sudden turns of weather. The autumnal and vernal equinoxes always strangely afflicted her, she told Mrs. Gaskell: "Sometimes the strain falls on the mental, sometimes on the physical part of me; I am ill with neuralgic headache, or I am ground to the dust with deep dejection of spirits. . . . This weary time has, I think and trust, got over for this year. It was the anniversary of my poor brother's death, and of my sister's failing health: I need say no more."[14]

Elizabeth Gaskell shook her head over this letter. "Strange is it not," she wrote her friend Anne Shaen, "that people's lives apparently suit them so little. Here's a note from Miss Brontë oppressed by the monotony and solitude of her life. She has seen *no one* but her father since 3rd of July last."[15] But Charlotte made that statement with a novelist's sense of truth, for in fact Ellen Nussey, Miss Wooler, and a cousin from Cornwall had all visited the parsonage since July 3. Compared with George Smith, perhaps they seemed like no one.

On November 20 she wrote to Smith about the subject nearest his heart, her next novel. Winter was her best time for writing, and although Smith must expect nothing until next autumn, she had been able to work a little recently. Of course, Smith immediately jumped on this frail sign of progress and suggested a publication date. This pressure called forth vehement objection.

> It is not at all likely that my book will be ready at the time you mention [she wrote Smith, November 28]. If my health is spared I shall get on with it as fast as is consistent with its being done, if not well, yet as well as I can do it, *not one whit faster*. When the mood leaves me (as it has left me now, without vouchsafing so much as a word of a message when it will return) I put by the MS. and wait till it comes back again; and God knows I sometimes have to wait long—*very* long it seems to me.
>
> Meantime . . . Please to say nothing about my book till it is written and in your hands. You may not like it. I am not myself elated with it as far as it has gone, and authors, you need not be told, are always tenderly indulgent, even blindly partial, to their own; even if it should turn out reasonably well, still I regard it as ruin to the prosperity of an ephemeral book like a novel to be much talked about beforehand, as if it were something great. People are apt to conceive, or at least to profess, exaggerated expectations, such as no performance can realise; then ensue disappointment and the due revenge—detraction and failure. If, when I write, I were to think of the critics who, I know, are waiting for Currer Bell, ready "to break all his bones or

ever he comes to the bottom of the den," my hand would fall paralysed on my desk. However, I can but do my best, and then muffle my
head in the mantle of Patience and sit down at her feet and wait.[16]

In December strong winds and sudden fluctuations of temperature
brought on influenza: the weary time was *not* over yet. In the same
month Emily's Keeper died. Since her death he had crouched outside
her bedroom door almost nightly, whining, his massive head between
his paws. "We laid his old faithful head in the garden," Charlotte
wrote Ellen. "Flossy is dull and misses him." Another symbol of Emily
had also vanished: during Charlotte's absence in London Papa had ordered that Emily's upright cottage piano be moved out of his parlor
and stored upstairs. Charlotte was upset at the change: why didn't Papa
let it stay in his room where it looked so well? These slight though
painful changes in the house did nothing to make her more cheerful.
Her health grew worse; her first thought was of consumption: she
"knew" her lungs were affected. She finally called in a doctor; he
spoke encouragingly, but she did not get better. She lost her appetite,
she was feverish, her nights were "very bad." Dr. Ruddock returned
and diagnosed the headache, parched mouth, and loss of appetite as
"a highly sensitive and irritable condition of the liver." In December
she begged Ellen to come to Haworth and cheer her, and Ellen faithfully came, but as soon as she left for Brookroyd Charlotte relapsed
with nausea and acute headache. Mr. Ruddock prescribed mercury;
she downed it faithfully. The medicine ulcerated her tongue and mouth
so severely that she could hardly speak and could take no nourishment
but half a teacup of liquid swallowed in teaspoonfuls through the day.

Under such misery 1852 dawned blankly enough. By January 27,
however, she was able to respond to Ellen's urging that she come
and be cared for at Brookroyd. Ellen was not to make any fuss; she
could eat only the simplest fare: no butter, no tea—only milk and water
with a little sugar and dry bread, and an occasional mutton chop.
Shortly after arriving at Brookroyd, she was surprised with a note from
George Smith proposing that he come to see her at Haworth. "I *do*
now wish I had delayed my departure from home a few days longer,"
she answered him, "that I might have shared with my father the true
pleasure of receiving you at Haworth Parsonage. And pleasure your
visit would have been, as I have sometimes dimly imagined but never
ventured to realise." She asked him instead to come to Brookroyd
where he would be warmly welcomed and find her "not exactly ill
now." "I and my friend would do our best to amuse you; it is only 6
miles distant from Leeds; you would have to stay all night. . . . Send
me a line to say whether we shall see you."[17]

But Smith did not choose to come to Brookroyd. He had wanted to see for himself the state of Charlotte's health and manuscript. The fact of her being from home and her "not exactly ill now" confirmed his suspicion that there would be no book from Currer Bell for Smith, Elder's spring list.

By February 6, Charlotte had gathered enough energy to lament to Mrs. Gaskell, "Certainly the past winter has been to me a strange time; had I the prospect before me of living it over again, my prayer must necessarily be, 'Let this cup pass from me.'"[18] Through the black winter months she had managed to write a little, although constriction in her chest pained her every time she stooped over her desk. But more often "blank and heavy intervals" numbed her powers, forcing her to put aside her work, to sit down at the feet of Patience, as she told Smith, and wait.

Concerning the Indian mail, she must also struggle for patience. Last November, 1851, letters had arrived from Taylor in Bombay, letters, as she told him, she had almost ceased to expect after so many months of silence: she had concluded that his promise to write had been a mere form of polite speech. The whole vexing question of the little man was raised again. Papa approved of him; Williams, replying to her queries in January, declared him to be a man of principle, good disposition, and character. "Good," she replied, "invaluable"—"but one would be thankful for a *little* feeling, a *little* indulgence in addition." George Smith, she believed, had disliked Taylor's harsh manner, and his opinion weighed heavily with her. Yet perhaps Taylor's harshness was mere Scots taciturnity rather than a flaw in character. Certainly at a distance the little man's hair looked decidedly auburn, his beard bristled less aggressively, and he grew a foot in stature. Marriage with Taylor became a distinct possibility, yet his letters did not mention it. She wrote Ellen that she was in "a state of absolute uncertainty about a somewhat momentous matter." She could not honestly decide whether "lasting estrangement and unbroken silence" might not be better than marriage to a man she had to coax herself to admire. Yet if she rejected him, her future was a blank. She could not bear to wipe it clean with her own hand: let fate decide.

On February 7 an echo of London came with Volume I in manuscript of Thackeray's new novel *Henry Esmond*: the Titan wanted the opinion of Currer Bell. Thanks to her influence, Smith had lured Thackeray to his firm. Grateful for Thackeray's compliment, Charlotte was still constrained to be frank: she felt on reading the novel "as much ire and sorrow as gratitude and admiration." Thackeray had captured the style and spirit of the eighteenth century masterfully: "No second-rate imitator can write in that way; no coarse scene-painter can charm us with allusion so delicate and perfect." In other respects, however, Mephistopheles had again guided his pen: "But what bitter satire, what relentless dissection of diseased subjects! Well, and this, too is right, or would be right, if the savage surgeon did not seem so fiercely pleased with his work . . . he has pleasure in putting his cruel knife or probe into quivering living flesh."[19]

This was a strange criticism coming from Charlotte, for she herself was writing a dark novel, an almost unbearably painful novel that probed the suffering mind of a heroine who, in her own words, was often both morbid and weak. "It is an excellently written book— but a very disagreeable one," Mrs. Procter would write Thackeray of *Villette*. "She turns every one 'The seamy side out.' "[20] It is our own faults we dislike most in others: Charlotte was reading much of her own relentlessness into Thackeray. Her next objection to *Henry Esmond* also applied more to her new work than to Thackeray's. "As usual, he is unjust to women, quite unjust. There is hardly any punishment he does not deserve for making Lady Castlewood peep through a keyhole, listen at a door, and be jealous of a boy and a milkmaid." At the moment, Charlotte was creating Madame Beck, a brilliant portrait of a jealous woman who peeps through keyholes and listens at doors. Her cast of female characters also included Paulina, a beautiful girl who, however, reminds the narrator of a spaniel bitch; Ginevra Fanshawe, a vain, scatterbrained minx; and Zélie St. Pierre, a hard, jealous, degenerate Parisian. Yet Thackeray is "unjust to women, quite unjust."

She concluded her evaluation of *Esmond* with the judgment that, although Thackeray was commonly ranked second to Dickens, he need not be. "God made him second to no man," she told George Smith. "If I were he, I would show myself as I am, not as critics report me; at any rate I would do my best. Mr. Thackeray is easy and indolent, and seldom cares to do his best." All her own aggressiveness and high sense of mission she missed in her hero, and could not quite forgive him for not being what she desired. Thackeray received her comments, forwarded by Smith, with a calm that would have infuriated her. "My dearest Mammy," he wrote February 26, 1852, "I don't think I have much good news or much otherwise to tell you since I wrote last. But my book has got into a more cheerful vein, that's a comfort, and I'm relieved from the lugubrious doubts I had about it. Miss Brontë has seen the first volume and pronounces it admirable and odious—will I think it is very well done and very melancholy too—but the melancholy ends pretty well with Vol. I. and everybody begins to move and be cheerful."[21]

In March when cold bitter winds afflicted her with headache, a swollen face, and "tic in the cheekbone," she opened a letter from New Zealand "which wrung my heart so, in its strong truthful emotion, I have only ventured to read it once." Ellen Taylor had died of consumption on December 27, 1851. Charlotte's heart ached for Mary, so far from home, alone now in the house they had built, the shop they had managed together. If there were any prospect of happiness or prosperity in England, she would beg her to come home again. But there was none, and Mary stayed on: "I am sitting all alone in my own house, or rather what is to be mine when I've paid for it," she wrote Charlotte in April 1852, four months after Ellen's death. "I bought it of Henry when Ellen died, shop and all, and carry on by myself. . . . I have begun to keep the house very tidy; it makes it less desolate. I take great interest in my trade—as much as I could do in anything that was not *all* pleasure. But the best part of my life is the excitement of arrivals from England. Reading all the news, written and printed, is like living another life quite separate from this one. The old letters are strange, very, when I *begin* to read them but quite familiar notwithstanding. So are all the books and newspapers, tho I never see a human being to whom it wd ever occur to me to mention anything I read in them. I see your nom de guerre in them sometimes. . . . O for one hour's talk! You are getting too far off and beginning to look strange to me. Do you look as you used to do I wonder?"

She beguiled lonely hours with writing a novel: "I have written about 1 vol. and a half. Its full of music, poverty, disputing, politics, and original views of life. I can't for the life of me bring the lover into it nor tell what he's to do when he comes"—and tending her shop: "No one can prize activity more than I do little interest [though] there is in it. I never long am without it but a gloom comes over me. The cloud seems to be always there behind me and never quite out of sight but when I keep on at a good rate. Fortunately the more I work the better I like it—I shall take to scrubbing the floor before its dirty and polishing pans on the outside in my old age.—It is the only thing that gives me an appetite for dinner."[22]

In her last surviving letter to Charlotte, Mary thus clung to her doctrine of work as the only cure for that insidious feminine liability, dependence. Many Victorian liberals agreed that a single woman needed employment. Mary, however, believed that women of all classes needed to work: it was the only cure for the boredom, vapors, pettiness, insipidity, and selfishness of the English young lady, for example, or the wealthy matron. Work was an end in itself. Was Mary Taylor happy? The question is impossible to answer. She followed her inspiration courageously, apparently without regrets. Even her grief for Ellen

Taylor and her solitude did not daunt her: she had suffered, but as she told Ellen, "there is sweet in the orange yet." Her pity was for Charlotte: ". . . your late letters to Mrs. J. Taylor talk of low spirits and illness. 'What's the matter with you *now*' as my mother used to say, as if it were the twentieth time in a fortnight. It is really melancholy that now, in the prime of life in the flush of your hard earned prosperity you can't be well!"

In March Charlotte refused an invitation from Miss Wooler because "for nearly four months now (i.e. since I became ill) I have not put pen to paper. My work has been lying untouched . . . my faculties have been rusting for want of exercise."[23] Since she would not leave home, she had undoubtedly begun to write now with more speed. *Villette*, however, was wrung out with many hesitations and revisions and agitations of the soul. She had taken up the subject of *The Professor* again but, with more than ten years to cool her passion, she could view her love for Monsieur Heger with some objectivity, as the more impersonal title *Villette* suggests. Her re-creation of Monsieur as Paul Emanuel, the fiery professor of French literature, was masterful. She drew him with assurance, humor, and understanding as a flagrantly contradictory man, a man great in his flaws.[24]

The little man (James Taylor inspired one facet of the portrait) is, for example, a male chauvinist. He cannot bear feminine rivalry. Faced with aggressive competition from a certain teacher, Madame Panache, "he honoured her with his earnest fury; he pursued her vindictively and implacably, refusing to rest peaceably in his bed, to derive due benefit from his meals, or even serenely to relish his cigar, till she was fairly rooted out of the establishment." "He would have exiled fifty Madame de Staëls," Lucy Snowe assures us, "if they had annoyed, offended, outrivalled, or opposed him."[25] Therefore he is most pleased with Lucy when she is reduced to tears by his bullying, or when she commits some gaucherie like dropping and breaking his glasses. When she struggles in humiliation over a difficult French passage, his own eyes fill with tears of sympathy. When Monsieur knits his brow or protrudes his lip over one of her compositions, however, Lucy knows that she has not committed enough faults to please him. As she grows more competent in her studies "his kindness became sternness; the light changed in his eyes from a beam to a spark; he fretted, he opposed, he curbed me imperiously; the more I did, the harder I worked, the less he seemed content."

A timid woman would have been totally crushed by such a tyrant, but under her seeming docility Lucy Snowe is the aggressive and courageous spirit Monsieur Paul Emanuel darkly suspects her to be. His tyranny only warms the blood in her veins. "Whatever my powers

—feminine or the contrary," Lucy announces, "—God has given them, and I felt resolute to be ashamed of no faculty of his bestowal." As Jane Eyre knew how to handle Rochester, Lucy knows how to handle Monsieur Paul. One day when the conflict between his ego and her aptitude reaches a crescendo, she leaves the room, returns with all her books, and pours them at his feet. " 'Take them away, M. Paul,' I said, 'and teach me no more. I never asked to be made learned, and you compel me to feel very profoundly that learning is not happiness.' "26

His bluff called, Monsieur can only be ashamed of himself. Like almost all of Charlotte's characters, Monsieur Paul's nature is founded on paradox and contradiction. His bullying ferocity protects a heart that is peculiarly tender, intuitive, and idealistic. His impossibly exacting nature compensates for a generosity that is almost too self-sacrificing. Lucy understands and thrives on these contradictions and in turn (oh, that it might have been so) Monsieur Paul recognizes in Lucy a kindred soul, in turn compounded of ferocity and timidity, humility and pride.

Lucy's triumph, however, is moderate. At the end of the book she is not given "the little man," as Charlotte calls Monsieur Paul inexorably throughout, but her own schoolroom and independence. Although Charlotte does not rate this a mean fate, *Villette* is not a happy novel. It tells in language of torture, starvation, and thirst the story of her solitary life at Brussels, her unrequited affection for George Smith, her longing for a world of health and happiness she can never attain. As a powerful record of the mental and emotional conflicts of a tortured yet strong woman, however,*Villette* is a masterpiece.

Another birthday came and went with scarcely a mention. "I have forgotten whether the 22nd is your birthday or mine," Charlotte wrote Ellen; "whichever it be, I wish you many happy returns."27 Restlessness came on with spring, an irresistible urge to leave silent house, black village, and barren moor. On the excuse of seeing to Anne's grave, she therefore left quietly and alone at the end of May for the east coast of Yorkshire, taking rooms at the Cliff House, Filey, where she and Ellen stayed after Anne's death. The resort was virtually deserted; the weather "dark, stormy, and excessively, bitterly cold"; headache, chest pains, and pain in her right side tormented her daily. She went out, however, wrapped in shawls against the keen salt wind, to walk alone on the sands and the wild rocky coast. On June 2 she wrote her father one of the kind, detailed letters she never failed to send him in her absence:

". . . The sea is very grand. Yesterday it was a somewhat unusually high tide, and I stood about an hour on the cliffs yesterday afternoon

W. S. Williams. PHOTOGRAPH FROM
THE BRONTE PARSONAGE MUSEUM

Mary Taylor. PHOTOGRAPH FROM
THE BRONTE PARSONAGE MUSEUM

The Reverend Arthur Bell Nicholls. PHOTOGRAPH FROM THE BRONTE PARSONAGE MUSEUM

Ellen Nussey in later life. PHOTOGRAPH FROM THE BRONTE PARSONAGE MUSEUM

George Smith—engraved portrait. PHOTOGRAPH FROM THE BRONTE PARSONAGE MUSEUM

Harriet Martineau—chalk drawing by George Richmond, 1849. BY COURTESY OF NA-
TIONAL PORTRAIT GALLERY, LONDON

William Makepeace Thackeray—chalk sketch by Samuel Laurence, 1852. Smith presented a copy of this picture to Charlotte. BY COURTESY OF NATIONAL PORTRAIT GALLERY, LONDON

Elizabeth Cleghorn Gaskell—portrait by George Richmond, 1851. BY COURTESY OF
NATIONAL PORTRAIT GALLERY, LONDON

The dining room, Haworth Parsonage, as it looks today. Portraits of Charlotte and Thackeray hang on the walls. The sofa is the one on which Emily died. BY COURTESY OF THE BRONTE SOCIETY

Haworth today, looking east from the top of the steep main street.
PHOTOGRAPH BY MARGOT PETERS

watching the tumbling in of great tawny turbid waves, that made the whole shore white with foam and filled the air with a sound hollower and deeper than thunder. There are so very few visitors at Filey yet that I and a few sea-birds and fishing-boats have often the whole expanse of sea, shore, and cliff to ourselves. When the tide is out the sands are wide, long, and smooth, and very pleasant to walk on. When the high tides are in, not a vestige of sand remains. I saw a great dog rush into the sea yesterday, and swim and bear up against the waves like a seal. I wonder what Flossy would say to that."

In this letter Mr. Nicholls' name, usually relegated along with Martha's and Tabby's to a concluding "please remember me to," crept into the text for the first time. She had been to a church, old and green with mold, that she would have liked Nicholls to see. He would certainly have laughed (as she struggled not to) to see the choir rise and turn their backs to the congregation to sing, while the congregation on their part wheeled around to turn their backs on pulpit and preacher—a most mystifying innovation. She did not neglect him either in the closing paragraph: "Give my kind regards, dear papa, to Mr. Nicholls, Tabby, and Martha. Charge Martha to beware of draughts, and to get such help in her cleaning as she shall need."[28]

She made the sad pilgrimage to Scarborough, to the churchyard on the Castle Hill overlooking the bay. Anne's stone, she found, had five errors; it would have to be refaced and relettered. She gave the directions and felt *that* painful duty done. If she found it mournful that Anne lay so far from home and Emily, she did not say so.

The weather moderated; she bathed from one of the queer, supposedly discreet bathing-machine contraptions; she walked on the sands and white cliffs for hours till she looked "almost as sunburnt and weather-beaten as a fisherman or a bathing-woman." Yet her writing progressed very little—"no spirit moves me." At the end of June she came home again after a month of solitude, tanned, stronger, but still waiting in vain for "the flow of power of composition," as she called it, to carry her swiftly to the conclusion of her novel. It was not to come yet and, if it had, she must have dammed it back again, for Papa was suddenly stricken with a surge of blood to the brain and acute inflammation of the eye; and though he recovered from the stroke, Charlotte was obliged to nurse him through the end of July and the first weeks of August.

To add to her frustration, letters from Bombay had stopped. In the last months, since she was under no pressure to love or marry him, Charlotte had seriously considered James Taylor. Had he returned and poked his "determined, dreadful nose" into her face again, she undoubtedly would have recoiled with her old antipathy; his silence, however, made him seem quite desirable. "You ask about India," she wrote Ellen, July 1. "Let us dismiss the subject in a few words and not recur to it. All is silent as the grave. Cornhill is silent too. There has been bitter disappointment there at my having no work ready for this season. We must not rely upon our fellow-creatures, only on ourselves, and on Him who is above both us and them. My labours as you call them stand in abeyance, and I cannot hurry them. I must take my own time, however long that time may be."[29]

She did not hear from Mr. Taylor again. Perhaps the impersonal tone of her letters discouraged him, although he had cherished them before when they were equally impersonal. Perhaps, under his harshness, he was sensitive enough to know she could not love him. Perhaps he trusted to time to win her, planning to claim her when he came back. When he did return to England in 1856, she was dead.

She was determined that nothing should interrupt her until *Villette* was finished, but in October she *had* to see Ellen: "I thought I would persist in denying myself till I had done my work, but I find it won't do, the matter refuses to progress, and this excessive solitude presses too heavily, so let me see your dear face, Nell, just for one reviving week." Ellen came, soothed Charlotte for "one little week," and left. "I do miss my dear bed-fellow," Charlotte wrote her October 26. "No more of that calm sleep."[30] At the same time she apologized for the brief scrawl: a few days before the mood had come on, she had fallen to business, and was still writing so hard and long that she could hardly see to scribble a note to Brookroyd. By the end of October 1852 she sent the bulk of two volumes to George Smith.

Although a seasoned writer, she was more anxious about this novel than about her previous books, even proposing that *Villette* be brought out under "the sheltering shadow of an incognito" if sales would not be hurt. "I seem to dread the advertisements—the large-lettered 'Currer Bell's New Novel,' or 'New Work by the Author of "Jane Eyre."' These, however, I feel well enough, are the transcendentalisms of a retired wretch; so you must speak frankly." More than with *Shirley*, she agonized over Smith, Elder's verdict: "I can hardly tell you how I hunger to hear some opinion beside my own, and how I have sometimes desponded, and almost despaired, because there was no one to whom to read a line, or of whom to ask a counsel. 'Jane Eyre' was not written under such circumstances, nor were two-thirds of 'Shirley.'" She was diffident too about the subject matter: she was not an artist engagé; she could not, like Gaskell, Dickens, or Kingsley, make unemployment, illegitimacy, poor laws, free trade, religious revival, protectionism, penal reform, corn laws, or sanitation her subject. She

had written about Luddites in *Shirley* and that novel had felt like
an ill-fitting glove. "You will see that 'Villette' touches on no matter
of public interest," she continued to Smith. "I cannot write books
handling the topics of the day; it is of no use trying. Nor can I write
a book for its moral. Nor can I take up a philanthropic scheme, though
I honour philanthropy; and voluntarily and sincerely veil my face before such a mighty subject as that handled in Mrs. Beecher Stowe's
work, 'Uncle Tom's Cabin.'" Still, there were strict limits to her
diffidence. "Remember to be an honest critic of 'Villette,'" she closes,
"and tell Mr. Williams to be unsparing: not that I am likely to alter
anything, but I want to know his impressions and yours."[31]

With what emotions Charlotte sent George Smith a fictionalized version of her thwarted love for him can only be imagined, but a spirit
of revenge cannot be discounted. Smith instantly recognized Mrs.
Bretton as his mother; his comment, "I myself, as I discovered, stood
for Dr. John," was carefully non-committal. Whether flattered or displeased or simply astounded at Charlotte's interpretation of their relationship, his criticisms of the novel focused upon the development
of Dr. John's character: he felt a discontinuity between his youth and
manhood; he felt the sudden switch of his affections from Ginevra Fanshawe to Paulina de Bassompierre insufficiently prepared for. Besides,
after such emphasis on Lucy's and Dr. John's relationship in Volumes
I and II, what would happen in Volume III when they went their
separate ways? Charlotte replied that she was devoting most of the
third volume to the development of "the crabbed Professor's character." She defended this shift from the Lucy-Dr. John to the Lucy-
Monsieur Paul interest with melancholy significance: "Lucy must
not marry Dr. John; he is far too youthful, handsome, bright-spirited,
and sweet-tempered; he is a 'curled darling' of Nature and Fortune,
and must draw a prize in life's lottery. His wife must be young, rich,
pretty; he must be made very happy indeed. If Lucy marries anybody
it must be the Professor—a man in whom there is much to forgive,
much to 'put up with.'"[32]

In the interest of fitness and truth, therefore, Charlotte created a
feminine "curled darling of Nature and Fortune" as Dr. John's mate.
In doing so, of course, she made the point that actually Dr. John
is not quite good enough for poor, plain, shadowy Lucy. "Dr. John
*could* think, he *could* feel—in his way"; but he could not think well
enough or feel strongly enough to finally be worthy of Lucy Frost
or, as she finally became, Lucy Snowe. True, Lucy exists forlornly
outside the bright-spirited world of friends, family, lovers, and prosperity. Occasionally the barrier lifts and she is allowed a brief taste
of that happy world; then profounder isolation follows. Ultimately,

however, Lucy rejects the world of Dr. John and Mrs. Bretton, of Paulina and Ginevra. Its inmates do not know the stern, elevating discipline of poverty and solitude, sorrow and labor. They do not know the great pain of unrequited love, or the profound contentment of real love, love "furnace-tried by pain, stamped by constancy." In mind and heart Lucy Snowe is superior to the other characters of *Villette*, even to the Professor, whom she patronizes rather shamelessly as "the little man."

On November 3, *Henry Esmond* arrived, looking "very antique and distinguished in his Queen Anne's garb; the periwig, sword, lace, and ruffles"—inscribed to "Miss Brontë with W. M. Thackeray's grateful regards. October 28, 1852." The third volume redeemed the overemphasis (in Charlotte's opinion) on history at the expense of story in Volume II: she found it full of "sparkle, impetus, and interest." It raised some doubts about her own third volume, almost finished. "I do not think the interest culminates anywhere to the degree you would wish," she wrote November 6 to Williams, who had commented long and candidly on the novel. "What climax there is does not come on till near the conclusion; and even then I doubt whether the regular novel-reader will consider the 'agony piled sufficiently high' (as the Americans say) or the colours dashed on to the canvas with the proper amount of daring. Still, I fear, they must be satisfied with what is offered . . ."[33]

Williams had doubts about the heroine: would she be considered weak and morbid? Charlotte answered decisively: "I consider that she *is* both morbid and weak at times; her character sets up no pretensions to unmixed strength, and anybody living her life would necessarily become morbid. It was no impetus of healthy feeling which urged her to the confessional, for instance; it was the semi-delirium of solitary grief and sickness. If, however, the book does not express all this, there must be a great fault somewhere."[34] *Villette* did express all this; there was no fault. With terrible fidelity Charlotte had recorded the ambivalences of a neurotic mind. As psychological realism the novel has no equal in Victorian fiction. What Dickens knew about the darkness of the mind, but had to cloak in strident humor and mnemonic eccentricity, Charlotte told plainly. Williams had reason to be uneasy about the heroine: she was no model of gentle Victorian womanhood.

In the same letter to Williams, Charlotte decided finally on the name Snowe instead of Frost: "If not too late I should like the alteration to be made now throughout the MS. A *cold* name she must have; partly, perhaps, on the '*lucus a non lucendo*' principle—partly on that of the 'fitness of things,' for she has about her an external coldness." Cornhill fidgeted with impatience. Williams wrote to say they wanted to set type on Volumes I and II without seeing Volume III. On November 10, Charlotte replied that the book would be finished in three weeks; she also gave permission for another edition of *Shirley*. Three years had passed since Currer Bell's last novel— enough to make any publisher despair. On Saturday, November 20, she laid down her pen with intense relief, packaged and sent the parcel to Cornhill. "I said my prayers when I had done it," she wrote Ellen. "Whether it is well or ill done, I don't know. D. V. I will now try to wait the issue quietly. The book, I think, will not be considered pretentious, nor is it of a character to excite hostility."[35]

No business woman, she had not contracted a definite sum for *Villette*. Instead, according to her custom, she had asked George Smith to invest the cash for the copyright "in the funds with the rest—except 20£—for which I have a present use and which perhaps you will be kind enough to send me in a Bank bill."[36] Papa looked forward to £700; she herself did not expect less. Then she left for Brookroyd, where she did not await the issue quietly but fretted for Smith's reaction to the last volume. On Saturday, December 4, she received a receipt from Cornhill for £500 and no accompanying letter. This was a cruel disappointment; it was the sum Smith had paid for *Jane Eyre* and *Shirley;* as a popular, established author, she deserved more.

Smith's stinginess with Charlotte was indeed unfair and hardly comprehensible. He was extremely generous with other authors: in 1859 he offered Thackeray £4,200 for a novel in twelve installments; he offered Tennyson £5,000 for a poem the length of *The Idylls of the King*, Trollope £1,000 for the copyright of a clerical novel, George Eliot £10,000 in 1862 for the rights to issue her *Romola* serially, Mrs. Gaskell £2,000 for *Wives and Daughters*, and he paid the later nineteenth-century writer Mrs. Humphrey Ward "larger sums than any other novelist received from him" and "made princely terms for her with publishers in America."[37] George Gissing was among those, over the years, who deplored Smith, Elder's treatment of Charlotte, sympathizing in his semi-autobiographical work, *The Private Papers of Henry Ryecroft*. "Yes, yes," wrote Gissing, himself a victim of life-long poverty; "I know as well as any man that reforms were needed in the relations between author and publisher. . . . A big, blusterous, genial brute of a Trollope could very fairly hold his own, and exact at all events an acceptable share in the profits of his work. A shrewd and vigorous man of business such as Dickens, aided by a lawyer who was his devoted friend, could do even better . . . But pray, what of Charlotte Brontë? Think of that grey, pinched life, the latter years of which would have been so brightened had Charlotte Brontë received but, let us say, one-third of what in the same space of time, the publisher gained by her books. I know all about this; alas! no man better."[38]

Charlotte tried to put a decent face on this shabby treatment, telling Miss Wooler that the sum "perhaps is not quite equitable—but when an author finds that his work is cordially approved—he can pardon the rest"; concluding that "£500 is not to be despised."[39] Her worry over Smith's silence was so acute that she had made up her mind to go up to London Monday when a letter came on Sunday morning, thus sparing Smith "the visitation of the unannounced and unsummoned apparition of Currer Bell in Cornhill." Contrary to what she told Miss Wooler, Smith did not cordially approve *Villette*. He did not, for example, think Paulina de Bassompierre real. Charlotte agreed that Paulina was the weakest character in the book: she had tried to make her the most beautiful, but since she was purely imaginary she "wanted the germ of the real." Most of all, Smith objected to the shift of interest from one set of characters to another. Charlotte confessed that his complaint was legitimate but, tight in the grip of her inspiration, stubbornly refused to alter a line. The new emphasis on Paul Emanuel was not pleasant, she agreed, and would probably be found "as unwelcome to the reader as it was, in a sense, compulsory upon the writer. The spirit of romance would have indicated another course, far more flowery and inviting; it would have fashioned a paramount hero, kept faithfully with him, and made him supremely worshipful; he should have an idol, and not a mute, unresponding idol either; but this would have been unlike real life—inconsistent with truth—at variance with probability."[40] Smith fidgeted at the propriety, if not the aesthetics, of Charlotte's heroine loving two men in rapid succession; Charlotte only knew she wrote truth. It was truth, furthermore, that a woman might love two men at once, for Lucy Snowe never quite renounces Dr. John. "I kept a room for him," Charlotte wrote in the most bitter-sweet passage in that very moving novel, ". . . a place of which I never took the measure, either by rule or compass: I think it was like the tent of Peri-Banou. All my life long I carried it folded in the hollow of my hand—yet, released from that hold and constriction, I know not but its innate capacity for expanse might have magnified it into a tabernacle for a host."[41]

*Villette* thus subtly withered the special relationship between Charlotte and her publisher. He did not like the novel very well, although he continued to make a mystery of his reason, writing Charlotte only that "something in the third volume sticks confoundedly in my throat." As for Paulina, Dr. John's mate, "she is an odd, fascinating little puss," but he is "not in love with her." He refused emphatically to answer more questions about the novel by mail, suggesting that Charlotte come up to London to correct proofs at Gloucester Terrace. To this purpose, he had his mother send her an invitation. Mrs. Smith's note was very kind, but the magic had gone out of her friendliness since the previous summer when—who knows to what extent through her influence?—Charlotte had been made to understand that more than friendship with George Smith was impossible. ". . . I almost wish I could still look on that kindness just as I used to do," Charlotte wrote Ellen: "it was very pleasant to me once."[42] If Mrs. Smith had detected the fact that beneath the genial, blooming matron Charlotte depicted in Mrs. Bretton lurked a cloyingly possessive mother, her heart cannot have warmed to Currer Bell. The novel would confirm another enemy. Across the Channel in Brussels, Madame Heger's darkest suspicions about Charlotte Brontë were confirmed by the French translation of *Villette* in 1855, a translation Charlotte was anxious to prevent. So furious was she at her portrait as Madame Beck that, when Mrs. Gaskell crossed the Channel to interview her for the biography, she shut the door in her face.

But animosities, objections, disappointments—as well as the personal pain that dictated much of the novel—were transitory shadows in the light of the permanent creation. George Eliot read *Villette* and felt its powerful truth. "Villette, Villette,—have you read it?" she wrote the Brays in an ecstasy. And: "I am only just returned to a sense of the real world about me, for I have been reading 'Villette,' a still more wonderful book than 'Jane Eyre.' There is something preternatural in its power." Except for George Sand, G. H. Lewes proclaimed, there was no author of their day who had "the glory and the power which light up the writings of Currer Bell." Readers would take up the cry: Currer Bell had written her greatest novel.

# 23

## The Curate

Arthur Bell Nicholls had now served Haworth church and Mr. Brontë for seven and a half years, living quietly at the sexton's house in Church Lane, conferring with Mr. Brontë every Monday evening about church and school matters, taking tea occasionally with the family, and, since Emily's death and Papa's increasing infirmity, walking the dogs out on the moors. He was an Irishman of Scots parentage; a heavy man with coal-black hair, heavy eyebrows crouching over small eyes, luxuriant beard, thick short hands, and heavy thighs. His voice was sonorous and very deep. His bearing was stiff. His convictions were deep and narrow.

When he came to Haworth in May 1845 he was only twenty-seven. A certain dignity in the young man as he read the Sunday lesson in his sonorous voice prevented Charlotte from jeering at him as she jeered at the other curates. After a month's observation, however, she did not rank him much above the others, replying shortly to Ellen's enthusiasms about a new Birstall man, "I have no desire at all to see your medical-clerical curate—I think he must be like all the other curates I have seen—and they seem to me a self-seeking, vain, empty race. At this blessed moment we have no less than three of them in Haworth Parish—and God knows there is not one to mend another."[1]

Writing *Shirley* three years later, she was somehow moved to spare Nicholls the ridicule she lavished upon the other curates, however; in fact, she compared "Mr. Macarthey" favorably to the foolish Irishman, Malone:

> I am happy to be able to inform you, *with truth*, that this gentleman did as much credit to his country as Malone had done it discredit; he proved himself as decent, decorous, and conscientious, as Peter was rampant, boisterous, and—(this last epithet I choose to suppress,

because it would let the cat out of the bag). He laboured faithfully in the parish: the schools, both Sunday and day-schools, flourished under his sway like green bay-trees. Being human, of course he had his faults; these, however, were proper, steady-going, clerical faults; what many would call virtues: the circumstance of finding himself invited to tea with a dissenter would unhinge him for a week; the spectacle of a Quaker wearing his hat in the church, the thought of an unbaptised fellow-creature being interred with Christian rites—these things could make strange havoc in Mr. Macarthey's physical and mental economy; otherwise he was sane and rational, diligent and charitable.[2]

Privately, she deplored his narrow, conventional mind while admitting at the same time that he was steady and respectable. A further cry from that lovely, amiable youth William Weightman could not be imagined, however, and she was not attracted to him. In the summer of 1846 she had indignantly squelched hints from Ellen about a clerical romance: "Who gravely asked you whether Miss Brontë was not going to be married to her Papa's Curate? I scarcely need say that never was rumour more unfounded. It puzzles me to think how it could possibly have originated. A cold far-away sort of civility are the only terms on which I have ever been with Mr Nicholls. I could by no means think of mentioning such a rumour to him even as a joke. It would make me the laughing-stock of himself and his fellow curates for half a year to come. They regard me as an old maid, and I regard them, one and all, as highly uninteresting, narrow and unattractive specimens of the coarser sex."[3]

If Charlotte found Nicholls uninteresting and conventional, what must Nicholls have thought of the strange family to which destiny had linked him when it brought him to Haworth? Within a month of his arrival he learned that the eldest daughter at least was not a person to be trifled with. One day in June 1845, a baking day at the parsonage, Nicholls, Grant, Bradley, and Smith, now curate at Keighley, had the temerity to rush in to tea on the spur of the moment. "It was Monday," Charlotte complained to Ellen, "and I was hot and tired—still if they had behaved quietly and decently—I would have served them out their tea in peace—but they began glorifying themselves and abusing dissenters in such a manner—that my temper lost its balance and I pronounced a few sentences sharply and rapidly which struck them all dumb—Papa was greatly horrified also—I don't regret it."[4] (The curates' virulent opposition to Dissenters was, of course, a measure of how deeply dissent and evangelicalism had eroded loyalty to the Anglican Church.) That same summer Branwell staggered home, dismissed from Thorp Green Hall, and plunged into a course of reckless dissipation that was apparent to everyone in the village, certainly to Nicholls. Then there was the strange, tall, shy daughter who could be observed leaving the house, whistling to the dogs, climbing over the stile, and disappearing for hours over the moors; the daughter whose burial service he had performed while the old man and the remaining daughters sat bowed and inconsolable in the family pew. Finally, it appeared that all three of these fanatically reserved young women were world-famous authors. Perhaps only Mr. Brontë's platitudinous dignity and Charlotte's simplicity and strict observance of church duty encouraged the heavy, methodical Mr. Nicholls to dream of joining his fortune to theirs. Even then it is uncertain why he would want a genius for a wife.

Dream he did and, finding Charlotte unchanged by fame, dared to believe that Currer Bell might become simply Mrs. Nicholls. Certainly of all human creatures she seemed the unhappiest and at the same time the most deserving of happiness. Nicholls remembered her at Emily's funeral, her face swollen with weeping. He had restrained Flossy from leaping after his mistress while she helped the dying Anne into the carriage the day they left for Scarborough. He had guessed her loneliness on her return. He waited for fame and success to raise her to a sphere of grandeur from which he was excluded. But her life had not changed. She still walked alone into the village in sober bonnet and shawl to buy paper and medicine. She appeared quietly and regularly in the family pew. With the exception of new crimson curtains in the dining room, the parsonage under her hand remained as simple, spotless, and orderly as before. Her loyalty to the eccentric and difficult old man seemed to him beautiful. She was often ill. She was no longer young. She might be his wife. His eyes under the heavy brows began to gaze at her with heavy meaning.

Charlotte was not blind to the changed aura about her father's curate. She could not help feeling his gaze upon her in church or recognizing the significance of their more frequent encounters in the lane. On Monday evening, December 13, he paid his weekly visit to consult with Mr. Brontë about the clerical duties he had gradually assumed over the years. The atmosphere was charged with tension. The three took tea in Papa's parlor. Nicholls' eyes, over his teacup, were constantly fixed on her face. He spoke with "strange, feverish restraint."

After tea I withdrew to the dining-room as usual. As usual, Mr Nicholls sat with papa till between eight and nine o'clock, I then heard him open the parlour door as if going. I expected the clash of the front-door. He stopped in the passage: he tapped: like lightning it flashed on me what was coming. He entered—he stood before me.

What his words were you can guess; his manner—you can hardly realise—never can I forget it. Shaking from head to foot, looking deadly
pale, speaking low, vehemently yet with difficulty—he made me for
the first time feel what it costs a man to declare affection where he
doubts response.

The spectacle of one ordinarily so statue-like, thus trembling,
stirred, and overcome, gave me a kind of strange shock. He spoke of
sufferings he had borne for months, of sufferings he could endure no
longer, and craved leave for some hope. I could only entreat him to
leave me then and promise a reply on the morrow. I asked him if he
had spoken to papa. He said, he dared not. I think I half led, half put
him out of the room. When he was gone I immediately went to papa,
and told him what had taken place. Agitation and anger dispropor-
tionate to the occasion ensued; if I had *loved* Mr Nicholls and had
heard such epithets applied to him as were used, it would have transported me past my patience; as it was, my blood boiled with a sense
of injustice, but papa worked himself into a state not to be trifled
with, the veins on his temples started up like whipcord, and his eyes
became suddenly bloodshot. I made haste to promise that Mr Nicholls
should on the morrow have a distinct refusal.

I wrote yesterday and got his note. There is no need to add to this
statement any comment. Papa's vehement antipathy to the bare
thought of any one thinking of me as a wife, and Mr Nicholls's distress, both give me pain. Attachment to Mr Nicholls you are aware I
never entertained, but the poignant pity inspired by his state on
Monday evening, by the hurried revelation of his sufferings for many
months, is something galling and irksome. That he cared something
for me, and wanted me to care for him, I have long suspected, but I
did not know the degree or strength of his feelings. Dear Nell, good-
bye.[5]

When a father has martyred a daughter and enjoyed her sacrifices
so long, he does not willingly give her up to another master. Mr.
Brontë's rage against Nicholls was deep and relentless. That penniless
opportunist who dared to better himself by plotting an alliance with
his famous daughter! That wolf, masquerading for years as a sheep
to invade the fold and steal the prize ewe! In his youth Mr. Brontë
had been an ambitious man: he had struggled up from Irish poverty
to distinguish himself at Cambridge; he had imagined himself a man
of letters until failure and consciousness of mediocrity had warped
him into misanthropy and alienation.[6] For the last five years he had
lived his own thwarted ambition through Charlotte's fame, goading
her to contacts with the rich and famous, fretting when her writing
did not progress. Was Currer Bell's glory to be wasted on a mere curate? The match would be a degradation; his daughter would be
throwing herself away. If he did permit her to marry, he had someone

far different in mind. James Taylor, by God, had at least been a man of the world. So the old, white-haired man raged, spitting out the unlucky curate's name with contempt, refusing him his home, maintaining a bitter, proud silence.

The master's anger communicated itself to the rest of the household: in the kitchen the servants felt equally insulted. Tabby thought it a terrible business; Martha was "bitter against him." The curate's landlord was outraged: John Brown vowed "he should like to shoot him." Mrs. Brown felt she had been harboring a viper in her bosom although, being a motherly person, she was horrified because since Monday evening Nicholls had stayed holed up in his room, rejecting all food.

On the Wednesday following that harrowing Monday evening, Mr. Brontë wrote Mr. Nicholls "a pitiless dispatch" which he showed to his daughter. Dismayed at Papa's cruelty, Charlotte hastily added a note of her own, explaining that, while Nicholls must *never* expect her to return his feelings, she wished "to disclaim participation in sentiments calculated to give him pain." She closed by exhorting him to courage and fortitude. Papa's letter asked for his curate's immediate resignation. Surprisingly Nicholls sent it to him. He had evidently calculated events well in advance, anticipating rejection and anger, even making vague plans to exile himself as a missionary in Australia if his suit failed. Meanwhile he remained locked in his room, ill and restless, sending a substitute to take his duty at Sunday service.

Then another note arrived at the parsonage from the invisible curate. He wished to withdraw his resignation. Mr. Brontë answered at once: he would accept the withdrawal on the condition that Mr. Nicholls never mention the subject of marriage to him or his daughter again.

Silence from Nicholls. So the matter hung, undecided, as Charlotte made plans to go up to London at Smith's urging to correct the proofs for *Villette*. For once Papa was eager to have her go, glad to get the tinder away from the match. She herself wanted to escape an oppressive situation. The stormy explosion of passion from such a stolid man, the fierce vibrations flying from the sexton's house to the parsonage seemed to Charlotte like a dream, as though a solid mountain had suddenly begun to rock and crumble on its base. On the other hand, she understood violence and passion very well; only shallow insipidity baffled her. "They don't understand the nature of his feelings," she wrote Ellen to whom she reported almost day by day the victories and defeats of the combatants, "—but I see now what they are. Mr N[icholls] is one of those who attach themselves to very few, whose sensations are close and deep—like an underground stream, running strong but in a narrow channel." Moreover, she always sympathized with the outsider, and no one could be more alone, more cast out of the graces of the parish, than the offending curate. "Dear Nell—without loving him—I don't like to think of him, suffering in solitude, and wish him anywhere so that he were happier."[7] Nor could she respect Papa's selfish and materialistic motives for rejecting the alliance. *Hers* were sound: they arose, she told Ellen, "from a sense of incongruity and uncongeniality in feelings, tastes, principles." All in all she was inclined to echo Mercutio's "a plague o' both your houses." "Yours," she concluded a letter of December 18 to Ellen, "wishing devoutly that papa would resume his tranquillity, and Mr N. his beef and pudding."

In such a state of mingled anxiety and exasperation the anniversary of Emily's death passed, and Christmas and New Year's Day. On Wednesday, January 6, 1853, she left for London. It was a winter journey in more than one sense. There were no pink silk-lined bonnets, no gala excursions planned, no suppressed hopes, no violent fears. She was met at Euston Station with kindness, but not a kindness that could stir her as of old. She looked at George Smith with some pity. He had written of his furious efforts to return Smith, Elder to solvency; she had thought he exaggerated, but his worn, hardened face testified that he had minimized matters. Miraculously his manner had not hardened: if anything he was more cordial and more deferent than before. Mrs. Smith and her daughters were looking well. Mr. Taylor was "said to be getting on well in India."

The ever attentive Sir James had urged her to let him know when she should be in London, but she "so much dreaded his excited fuss" that she put off informing him of her plans. Neither time nor custom had softened her toward this aggressive patron of the arts. Instead she stayed quietly at Gloucester Terrace, correcting proofs and battling over Smith's last-minute objections to the ending of *Villette*. Papa too had objected strongly to the death of Monsieur Paul: it was too terrible; her readers would not like it. Unlike Dickens, who gave *Great Expectations* a happy ending at the urging of Bulwer-Lytton, Charlotte relented only so far as to make the ending ambiguous. "Trouble no quiet, kind heart; leave sunny imaginations hope," she added after describing the storm that left the Atlantic strewn with wrecks. "Let them picture union and a happy succeeding life." *She* had no illusions about Lucy Snowe's destiny; the public might cherish them if they wished.

At the last minute publication of *Villette* was delayed to the end of January so it might not overwhelm *Ruth*, Mrs. Gaskell's story, daring enough for the times, of a woman who bears an illegitimate

child. Currer Bell's influence had lured Mrs. Gaskell to Smith's firm
as it had lured Thackeray. Mrs. Gaskell had sent Charlotte an outline
of the novel the previous April. Charlotte found its aim noble and
guessed that it might "restore hope and energy to many who thought
they had forfeited the right to both . . . Yet—hear my protest! Why
should she die? Why are we to shut up the book weeping?"[8] Charlotte had touched on the book's central weakness: while treating an
unwed mother with compassion, Gaskell was forced to punish the
crime with death. G. H. Lewes, reviewing both *Ruth* and *Villette*
in the *Leader* in February, took just the opposite tack: he accused
Mrs. Gaskell of evading the issue of personal guilt by making Ruth
"so innocent, so completely the victim of circumstances," that she
cannot be held responsible for her sin. This, of course, was exactly
Mrs. Gaskell's intent. Always generous, Charlotte now agreed that
*Ruth* should be given a head start with the reviewers, particularly
because she believed the book had a moral and philanthropic purpose
*Villette* lacked. She anticipated, however, that there would be in-
vidious comparisons between the novels no matter what the timing:
". . . but we need not care: we can set them at defiance; they *shall*
not make us foes, they *shall* not mingle with our mutual feelings one
taint of jealousy: there is my hand on that: I know you will give
clasp for clasp."[9]

She wrote Harriet Martineau from London expressing a strong desire that she review *Villette*. Particularly she wished to know if Harriet detected any coarseness, any indelicacy in the novel. Although
she found it characteristic of Currer Bell's impetuous honesty, Harriet
must have smiled over the note. "I know that you will give me your
thoughts upon my book," Charlotte had written, "as frankly as if you
spoke to some near relative whose good you preferred to her gratification. I wince under the pain of condemnation, like any other weak
structure of flesh and blood; but I love, I honour, I kneel to truth. Let
her smite me on the one cheek—good! the tears may spring to the
eyes; but courage! there is the other side; hit again, right sharply."[10]
Charlotte could turn the most passive of Christian doctrines to violence.

The humility of this note to Martineau flagrantly contradicted
Charlotte's mood of two years before after reading Martineau's and
Atkinson's *Letters on the Nature and Development of Man*. She had
listened to Harriet's discourse on atheism before the fire at Ambleside
with respect, if not agreement. She had actually encouraged Harriet
to publish the correspondence with Atkinson, or so Harriet later
claimed.[11] When the book actually appeared, however, she found it
extremely difficult to suppress an instinctive horror at this "unequivo-

cal declaration of disbelief in the existence of a God or a Future Life."
"The strangest thing," she had written James Taylor, "is that we are
called on to rejoice over this hopeless blank, to receive this bitter bereavement as great gain, to welcome this unutterable desolation as a
state of pleasant freedom. Who could do this if he would? Who
would do it if he could?" Taylor heartily agreed and, thus encouraged, Charlotte grew openly hostile to the book and its author. "I
deeply regret its publication for the lady's sake," she wrote back to
Taylor; "it gives a death-blow to her future usefulness. Who can
trust the word, or rely on the judgment, of an avowed atheist?"[12]
This was mean; but over the months Charlotte had evidently recon-
sidered her words. Now at least she was soliciting the judgment of the
atheist and evidently preparing to trust her word.

A few days after writing Harriet Martineau, she defended her to
Miss Wooler, who had written her old pupil warning her that to as-
sociate with an avowed atheist was to put her soul in danger:

> . . . I should grieve to neglect or oppose your advice, and yet I do
> not feel that it would be right to give Miss Martineau up entirely.
> There is, in her nature, much that is very noble; hundreds have for-
> saken her—more—I fear—in the apprehension that their fair names may
> suffer if seen in connection with hers—than from any pure convictions
> such as you suggest—of harm consequent on her fatal tenets. With
> these fair-weather friends I cannot bear to rank . . . and for her sin
> —is it not one of those which God and not man must judge?
> To speak the truth—my dear Miss Wooler—I believe if you were in
> my place, and knew Miss Martineau as I do—if you had shared with
> me the proofs of her rough but genuine kindliness, and had seen how
> she secretly suffers from abandonment, you would be the last to give
> her up; you would separate the sinner from the sin, and feel as if the
> right lay rather in quietly adhering to her in her strait—while that ad-
> herence is unfashionable and unpopular—than in turning on her your
> back when the world sets the example—I believe she is one of those
> whom opposition and desertion make obstinate in error; while pa-
> tience and tolerance touch her deeply and keenly, and incline her to
> ask of her own heart whether the course she has been pursuing may
> not possibly be a faulty course—However—I have time to think of this
> subject—and I shall think of it seriously.[13]

This patronizing but earnest tribute to her radical friend proved to
be the last kind words Charlotte would have for Harriet Martineau.
Understandably, when Harriet came upon the letter to Miss Wooler
in Mrs. Gaskell's *Life*, she did not find it kind. Usually calm and
good-tempered, she exploded at Charlotte's avowal that "hundreds
have forsaken her" or that she "secretly suffers from abandonment,"

penciling "Hallucination!" and "Fie!" in the margins of her copy. Charlotte's plea that she could not turn her back on the atheist when "the world sets the example" elicited Harriet's disgusted "Libel on the world" and "H.M. did not lose a single friend."[14] The quarrel that separated them, however, was not about atheism but about "love."

In answer to Charlotte's plea to smite her on the cheek right hard, Harriet administered, she thought, a relatively light tap. Charlotte had asked about "coarseness"; Harriet replied about "love": both women, of course, meant "sexuality." Harriet found the new novel permeated with it, from the first chapters where sixteen-year-old Graham Bretton takes the adoring child Polly into his arms and kisses "her hot little face and burning lips," to the last chapters when Lucy Snowe takes and presses and kisses Monsieur Paul's hand as it gently strokes her hair and touches her lips. After praising *Villette*, therefore, she turned to the problem she called love. "As for the other side of the question," she wrote, "which you so desire to know, I have but one thing to say; but it is not a small one. I do not like the love, either the kind or the degree of it; and its prevalence in the book, and effect on the action of it, help to explain the passages in the reviews which you consulted me about, and seem to afford *some* foundation for the criticisms they offered."[15]

Charlotte's response was a cry of rage and pain. Harriet had found her Achilles' heel. She did not stop to reason that Harriet's criticism partly reflected her own neurotic deficiency of sexual passion. She couldn't reason: the wound was too deep. She wrote about sexual love more frankly and persistently than any of her contemporaries, but so thoroughly had her strong, Victorian sense of propriety hidden this truth from her that she could not tolerate criticism on the matter. Had Harriet merely expressed regret that love should dominate her characters to the exclusion of other interests, Charlotte might have been less hurt. She might have replied quietly, pointing out that Lucy Snowe's delight in her own school almost equals her joy in Monsieur Paul's love, that Lucy scarcely pines away during the three years of Monsieur's absence ("Reader, they were the three happiest years of my life"), and that her heroine ends, tranquilly enough, a single schoolmistress. But Harriet had resurrected the old immorality charge. This Charlotte could not forgive:

> My Dear Miss Martineau,—I think I best show my sense of the tone and feeling of your last, by immediate compliance with the wish you express that I should send your letter. I enclose it, and have marked with red ink the passage which struck me dumb. All the rest is fair, right, worthy of you, but I protest against this passage; and were I

brought up before the bar of all the critics in England to such a charge I should respond, "Not guilty."

I know what *love* is as I understand it; and if man or woman should be ashamed of feeling such love, then is there nothing right, noble, faithful, truthful, unselfish in this earth, as I comprehend rectitude, nobleness, fidelity, truth, and disinterestedness.—Yours sincerely,

C. B.

To differ from you gives me keen pain.[16]

Charlotte's violent reaction to Martineau's criticism was typical of the curious double-thinking of her age. While many writers challenged convention on one or two fronts, virulent Victorian piety and prudery forced them at the same time to shore up their defenses higher on others. Thus Mrs. Gaskell found nothing wrong in writing about an unwed mother in *Ruth*—a novel that was greeted with cries of outrage—but believed in her heart that Charlotte wrote coarse novels. Charlotte could see nothing indelicate in her own novels but was repelled by Harriet Martineau's atheism. Harriet Martineau took her atheism as a matter of course but was disgusted by the love emphasis in Charlotte's novels and, later, unreasonably vicious over George Eliot's liaison with George Henry Lewes. Elizabeth Barrett Browning cried out against woman's role in *Aurora Leigh* yet condemned *Jane Eyre* as savage and free-thinking. Thackeray denounced prudery but found George Sand and Balzac obscene.

Since she had taken Charlotte's plea for the truth at face value, Harriet was understandably annoyed at her anger. She went ahead with her review for the *Daily News*, repeating substantially what she had said in her letter, no doubt supposing Currer Bell more resilient to criticism than her angry reply suggested.[17] But she had delivered a mortal wound. Robust herself, Harriet was unaware of the damage her words had caused, even when Charlotte wrote, calling off her promised visit to Ambleside. "There was never any quarrel or even misunderstanding between us," she claimed in her *Autobiography*. Currer Bell was, in fact, one of the few novelists Harriet could tolerate: she deplored Dickens, Thackeray, and particularly George Eliot —whom she never respected or *liked*—because she found in their books not moral inspiration but moral squalor. Paradoxically, the writer who claimed her works had no moral or philanthropic or social purpose escaped her antipathy: she praised Currer Bell because "her moral strength fell not a whit behind the intellectual force manifested in her works. Though passion occupies too prominent place in her pictures of Life . . . it is a true social blessing that we have had a female writer who has discountenanced sentimentalism and feeble egotism with such practical force. . . . Her heroines love too readily, too vehemently, and sometimes after a fashion which their female readers may resent; but they do their duty through everything, and are healthy in action, however morbid [that is, sexual] in passion."[18]

This was as much justice from a sternly rational woman with an antipathy toward sex as Charlotte could expect. She did Harriet less justice. When Harriet read in the *Life* Mrs. Gaskell's comment, "In spite of their short, sorrowful misunderstanding, there were a pair of noble women and faithful friends," she felt constrained to underline the word *friends* and pencil in the margin of her copy: "That word was never attained."

Charlotte's behavior in the affair almost suggested she was looking for a quarrel. Her dislike of Harriet's atheism was undoubtedly deeper than she knew, her anger half created by criticism from a woman with deeply flawed principles of her own. Miss Wooler's letter too had done its subtle damage. Charlotte's last words about Harriet Martineau were written to Ellen from Haworth, April 18, 1853: "Two or three weeks since Miss Martineau wrote to ask why she did not hear from me—and to press me to go to Ambleside. Explanations ensued—the notes on each side were quite civil—but having deliberately formed my resolution on substantial grounds—I adhered to it. I have declined being her visitor—and bid her good-bye. Of course some bitterness remains in her heart. It is best so, however; the antagonism of our natures and principles was too serious a thing to be trifled with."[19]

*Villette* was published January 28, 1853. Charlotte stayed on with the Smiths until February 3, without headache, without nausea, without elation. Lacking the time, or—after so many disasters—the heart, to make social engagements for Currer Bell, Smith let her choose her own diversions on this visit. They were wintry enough: she wished to see things instead of people, "the *real* rather than the *decorative* side of life." Smith escorted her to Newgate and Pentonville prisons, the Bank, the Exchange, the Foundling Hospital; Dr. Forbes, a London physician she had consulted the last months of Anne's illness, took her to tour Bethlehem Hospital. At Newgate Charlotte caught sight of a young female prisoner with an appealing face, immediately walked up to her, took her hand, and began to question her until a prison guard strode up with the warning, "Visitors are not allowed to speak to prisoners." It was a Victorian gesture, but for Charlotte, untrained in sentimentality and hypocrisy, undoubtedly a sincere one. "Mrs S[mith] and her daughters," Charlotte confided to Ellen, "are—I believe—a little amazed at my gloomy tastes, but I take no notice."

George Smith was cordial but distant and very busy. "Dr. John" had slipped like a cold shadow between them. Smith's open, pragmatic, cheerful soul had perhaps recoiled too at the naked pain of Charlotte's narrative, a narrative he knew to be largely autobiographical, not only because of his own and his mother's portraits and the many incidents taken directly from Charlotte's experiences with him in London, but because Charlotte had strenuously urged that a French translation be avoided. He did not care to contemplate the dark mind and violent emotion that evidently raged beneath Currer Bell's Quaker-plain exterior: he turned away: something about the woman and her book decidedly "stuck in his throat." On her part, Charlotte felt that the visit had passed well enough, but "with some sorrowful impressions." There was nothing now to keep her in London, yet she was not anxious to go home to Papa's raging, or to the sight of Nicholls himself skulking moodily about the village with downcast eyes and resentful shoulders. Papa's anger had followed her to London via the mails: one of his diatribes against the curate had been written over Flossy's signature, a mean stab, since for many months Nicholls had obligingly walked the dog in wind, rain, and snow. Knowing that Papa would not demean himself by raging in front of Ellen, Charlotte prepared for the ordeal of Haworth by asking her friend to meet her at Keighley "at 44 m. past 3 o'clock, afternoon . . . and then we can go home together." She wrote Martha instructions: they would arrive at four-thirty, all must be in readiness, tablecloths on the dining-room tables, a nice piece of cold boiled ham for supper since it could also "come in for breakfast in the morning."

She said good-by for the last time to Gloucester Terrace and its gracious drawing room of "blue damask, amber lamplight and vermillion fire-flush"; to her gracious hostess, who had always been kind, very kind; to the daughters, who were also charming and polite; to George Smith, whose sunny benevolence had once promised to warm her lonely existence. She rode for the last time down Marylebone Road past Regent's Park to Euston Station, boarded the northbound train for the last time in the icy, echoing, steam-filled vault, watched for the last time the wooded hills and hedgerow fields give way to the flatter outlines of the Midlands, then to the smoking ugliness of Leeds, then to the straggling stone fences and blue swelling outlines of the moors. As the carriage clattered round the corner after its torturous climb up the main street, Charlotte and Ellen must have been acutely aware that a pair of sad clerical eyes probably followed their progress from the sexton's upper window.

Reviews of *Villette* came in swiftly. ". . . the import of all the notices is such as to make my heart swell with thankfulness to Him who takes note both of suffering and work and motives," she wrote Ellen, February 15. "—Papa is pleased too."[20]

Her first champion carried her banner again. *Villette* "is a work of astonishing power and passion," wrote G. H. Lewes. "From its pages there issues an influence of truth as healthful as a mountain breeze. Contempt of conventions in all things, in style, in thought, even in the art of story-telling, here visibly springs from the independent originality of a strong mind nurtured in solitude." He did not spare criticism, but his objections were just and free from sex bias. He objected, for example, to extraneous incidents like the Miss March-mont episode and Lucy's visit to London (although they are so wonderfully imagined, he admitted, that one would hate to forfeit them); he objected to Charlotte's fondness for allegorical expression and her tendency to run metaphors to death. But his praise was great. "In this world, as Goethe tells us," Lewes continued, " 'there are so few voices, and so many echoes'; there are so few books, and so many volumes—so few persons thinking and speaking for themselves, so many reverberating the vague noises of others. Among the few stands *Villette*. In it we read the actual thoughts and feelings of a strong, struggling soul; we hear the cry of pain from one who has loved passionately, and who has sorrowed sorely. Indeed, no more distinct characteristic of Currer Bell's genius can be named, than the depth of her capacity for all passionate emotions. . . ."[21] Fortunately, Harriet Martineau believed and said in the review that would anger Charlotte that Currer Bell possessed great moral strength and intellectual force as well.

Buoyed by such notices and, though she did not want it, the de-votion of her father's curate, she passed the cold winter months not unhappily. "I have taken long walks on the crackling snow, and felt the frosty air bracing," she told Mrs. Gaskell, who had written pane-gyrically about *Villette*. "This winter has, for me, not been like last winter. December, January, February '51–2 passed like a long stormy night, conscious of one painful dream, all solitary grief and sickness. The corresponding months in '52–3 have gone over my head quietly and not uncheerfully. Thank God for the change and the repose! How welcome it has been He only knows! My father, too, has borne the season well; and my book and its reception thus far have pleased and cheered him."[22]

Inevitably there was adverse criticism. Martineau was appalled at Currer Bell's anti-Catholicism, an attitude Charlotte found unaccount-able in an atheist but was not unaccountable, since Harriet's inquiries into religion and philosophy had broadened rather than narrowed her views. Understandably, high-church, Puseyite journals now flirting with Rome cried out in anger. But the most slashing attack came, as it had with *Jane Eyre*, from a woman writing from Charlotte's own

Tory camp. "We want a woman at our hearth," sneered Anne Mozley anonymously in the *Christian Remembrancer;* "and her impersonations are without the feminine element, infringers of modest restraints, despisers of bashful fears, self-reliant, contemptuous of prescriptive decorum; their own unaided reason, their individual opinion of right and wrong, discreet or imprudent, sole guides of conduct and rules of manners,—the whole hedge of immemorial scruple and habit broken down and trampled upon. We will sympathise with Lucy Snowe as being fatherless and penniless . . . but we cannot offer ever the affections of our fancy (the right and due of every legitimate heroine) to her unscrupulous and self-dependent intellect. . . ."

No better tribute to Currer Bell's radical and courageous conception of womanliness can be found, but of course Charlotte sickened over the review, which clawed its way to a brutal conclusion, protesting Currer Bell's "outrages on decorum, the moral perversity, the toleration of, nay, indifference to vice which must leave a permanent distrust of the author on all thoughtful and scrupulous minds." (Did she hear a bitter echo of her injustice to Harriet—"Who can trust the word, or rely on the judgment of an avowed atheist?"—in Miss Mozley's virulent words?) The review prompted Charlotte to defend herself to the *Christian Remembrancer* in a letter that concluded, "Will you kindly show this note to my reviewer? Perhaps he cannot now find an antidote for the posion into which he dipped the shaft he shot at 'Currer Bell,' but when again tempted to take aim at other prey, let him refrain his hand a moment till he has considered consequences to the wounded, and recalled 'the golden rule.' "[23] Ironically, Charlotte's bitterest enemies were women. Male critics were often severe with Currer Bell, but only a woman, unsheathing her claws to defend traditional femininity, slashed with such fury.

Some severities were circulated privately. Matthew Arnold did not like the novel. "Why is *Villette* disagreeable?" he apostrophized Mrs. Forster. "Because the writer's mind contains nothing but hunger, rebellion, and rage, and therefore that is all she can, in fact, put into her book. No fine writing can hide this thoroughly, and it will be fatal to her in the long run."[24] It is uncertain what Arnold meant by "the long run," but the hunger, rage, and rebellion of *Villette* certainly carried the novel triumphantly out of the Victorian age into the present. Platonic lover of an interesting invalid, Thackeray exposed the prudery beneath his mask of sophistication in a letter to "dearest Mammy": ". . . Villette is rather vulgar—I don't make my *good women* ready to fall in love with two men at once. . . ." Added to this silliness, a profound insight: "Miss Brontë would be the first to be angry and cry fie on me if I did."[25]

Thackeray expanded on the subject to Lucy Baxter, a seventeen-year-old girl from New York he had met on his American tour and now regarded, Victorian style, "almost as a daughter."

So you are all reading Villette to one another—a pretty amusement to be sure—I wish I was a hearing of you and a smoking of a cigar the while. The good of Villette in my opinion Miss is a very fine style; and a remarkable happy way (which few female authors possess) of carrying a metaphor logically through to its conclusion. And it amuses me to read the author's naïve confession of being in love with 2 men at the same time; and her readiness to fall in love at any time. The poor little woman of genius! the fiery little eager brave tremulous homely-faced creature! I can. read a great deal of her life as I fancy in her books, and see that rather than have fame, rather than any other earthly good or mayhap heavenly one she wants some Tomkins or another to love her and be in love with. But you see she is a little bit of a creature without a penny worth of good looks, thirty years old I should think, buried in the country, and eating up her own heart there, and no Tomkins will come. You girls with pretty faces and red boots (and what not?) will get dozens of young fellows fluttering about you—whereas here is one a genius, a noble heart longing to mate itself and destined to wither away into old maidenhood with no chance to fulfil the burning desire.[26]

Thackeray did not know, of course, that several Tomkins *had* come —Nussey, Bryce, Taylor, even Smith—and had been rejected. Nor did he know that there was currently a Tomkins and that Charlotte was withstanding the longing to mate herself with the handsome curate rather well.

Charlotte passed some judgments of her own on Thackeray that winter as she hung his portrait, courtesy of George Smith, on the dining-room wall along with the Duke of Wellington's and her portrait by Richmond. "Thackeray looks away from the latter character with a grand scorn, edifying to witness," she told Smith, and went on to shrewdly analyze the Titan's character. "To me the broad brow seems to express intellect. Certain lines about the nose and cheek betray the satirist and the cynic; the mouth indicates a childlike simplicity—perhaps even a degree of irresoluteness, inconsistency—weakness, in short, but a weakness not unamiable." What she missed was a certain "expression of *spite*, most vividly marked in the original"; some of the man's power had been lost in the omission: "Did it strike you thus?"[27] The gift of Thackeray's portrait was one of George Smith's last gestures of gratitude and good will toward Currer Bell.

The question of Nicholls, deflected by Papa's interest in the reception of *Villette*, still vibrated dangerously in the air. The old and the young man circled each other warily: Mr. Brontë did not speak to Mr. Nicholls and Mr. Nicholls did not speak to Mr. Brontë. It was rumored about the village that the unhappy cleric had got another curacy and was only biding his time to depart. Certain church occasions, however, forced the parson, his daughter, and his curate into each other's orbits for an uneasy time. One of these was the visit of the Bishop of Ripon. For this event the parsonage was turned upside down in a fever of preparation. Extra help was procured for Martha in the kitchen, and the parish curates of Oxenhope, Oakworth, and Stanbury were invited to supper as well as to tea. "It is very well to talk of receiving a Bishop without trouble," Charlotte chided Ellen, "but you *must* prepare for him." Afternoon tea alone must be an elaborate affair: half a dozen plates of white, bran, and brown breads, thinly sliced and thickly buttered; a glass of orange marmalade in the center of the table; an assortment of cheese cakes and jam tarts; a plate laden with thin scrolls of pink ham and garnished with sprigs of green parsley.

The bishop came in March, "certainly a most charming little Bishop; the most benignant little gentleman that ever put on lawn sleeves; yet stately too." He stayed the afternoon and evening, pronounced himself most gratified with all he had seen, but left in some bewilderment at the behavior of the dark, bearded Haworth curate who had fluctuated unaccountably between dark gloom and irritability over the teacups and the supper table. Charlotte was very angry at Nicholls' conduct, which, with the strain of entertaining the bishop, had left her with violent headache and nausea. He had exhibited his dejection conspicuously, he had actually flared into temper once or twice in addressing Mr. Brontë. Moreover he had dogged her up the lane after the evening service in no pleasant manner, and then, lingering in the hall after the bishop and the other curates had stepped into Papa's parlor, had attempted to draw her aside. When she pulled away and ran quickly up the stairs, he had sent after her, according to Martha, such "flaysome" looks that the servant was struck with horror. "The fact is," Charlotte told Ellen, "I shall be most thankful when he is well away; I pity him, but I don't like that dark gloom of his. . . . If Mr Nicholls be a good man at bottom, it is a sad thing that nature has not given him the faculty to put goodness into a more attractive form." When the Inspector of Schools paid a visit shortly after, Nicholls again behaved badly: "he managed to get up a most pertinacious and needless dispute with the Inspector, in listening to which all my old unfavourable impressions revived so strongly, I fear my countenance could not but show them."[28] In fact, Nicholls was behaving with some of the abrupt rudeness of her own heroes. Escaped from the pages of her novels, it failed to charm her.

A month later, discovering that Nicholls possessed some stoicism after all, she permitted herself a small measure of admiration.

> You ask about Mr Nicholls [she wrote Ellen April 6, 1853]. . . . He and papa never speak. He seems to pass a desolate life. He has allowed late circumstances so to act on him as to freeze up his manner and overcast his countenance not only to those immediately concerned but to every one. He sits drearily in his rooms. If Mr Croxton or Mr Grant, or any other clergyman calls to see, and as they think, to cheer him, he scarcely speaks. I find he tells them nothing, seeks no confidant, rebuffs all attempts to penetrate his mind. I own I respect him for this. He still lets Flossy go to his rooms and takes him to walk. He still goes over to see Mr Sowden sometimes, and, poor fellow, that is all. He looks ill and miserable. I think and trust in Heaven that he will be better as soon as he gets away from Haworth. I pity him inexpressibly. We never meet nor speak, nor dare I look at him, silent pity is just all I can give him, and as he knows nothing about that, it does not comfort. He is now grown so gloomy and reserved, that nobody seems to like him, his fellow-curates shun trouble in that shape, the lower orders dislike it. Papa has a perfect antipathy to him, and he, I fear, to papa. Martha hates him. I think he might almost be *dying* and they would not speak a friendly word to or of him. How much of all this he deserves I can't tell, certainly he never was agreeable or amiable, and is less so now than ever, and alas! I do not know him well enough to be sure there is truth and true affection, or only rancour and corroding disappointment at the bottom of his chagrin. In this state of things I must be, and I am, *entirely passive*. I may be losing the purest gem, and to me far the most precious life can give—genuine attachment—or I may be escaping the yoke of a morose temper. In this doubt conscience will not suffer me to take one step in opposition to papa's will, blended as that will is with the most bitter and unreasonable prejudices. So I just leave the matter where we must leave all important matters.[29]

Yet any reader of Currer Bell's novels could have told her how restless she was under tyranny, how impossible it was, ultimately, for her to remain passive. Papa, Martha, Tabby, John Brown, his wife—all had taken a fatal tack in hating Mr. Nicholls. It was the sure stance destined to make Charlotte eventually accept him.

# 24

*Persuasion*

In April 1853 the metamorphosis from pity to acceptance had not taken place, however, and Charlotte left the day after her thirty-seventh birthday for the Gaskells' home in Plymouth Grove—relieved to escape Papa's inflexible anger and Nicholls' hangdog brooding. Unconsciously, she must have looked upon the Gaskell union—a famous authoress and a clergyman—with sharper interest than before.

William Gaskell, minister of Cross Street Unitarian Chapel, possessed the great energy peculiar to men who believe in their age and their role in shaping it. Preacher, lecturer to Mechanics' Institutes, college professor of history, literature, and logic, private tutor, Home Mission Board member, Portico Library chairman, social worker for improved sanitation, fewer beerhouses, more public amusements—the list goes on and on. Thoroughly involved in such commitments, he was often away from home: "William is at a ministers' meeting tonight,—and tomorrow dines with a world of professors and college people at Mark Phillips," runs a constant theme of his wife's letters. When he favored his home with his presence, he necessarily shut himself up to work long hours in his study. When he felt he needed a holiday, he "bachelorised off" by himself. Robust, self-confident, self-sufficient, he had little time or sympathy for the day-to-day trials that fret a wife and mother, or for the endless vicissitudes in the lives of four growing daughters. "Wm I dare say kindly won't allow me ever to talk to him about anxieties," Mrs. Gaskell confided to her sister-in-law in a crisis over her eldest daughter's health, "while it would be SUCH A RELIEF often." Nor did he have ready sympathy on many occasions when Mrs. Gaskell felt need of support, during the hue and cry that followed the publication of her biography of Charlotte, for example, when she "never needed kind words so much,—and no one gives me them." He controlled her entire income from her novels and stories, works she wrote at the dining-room table because from that vantage point she could keep an eye on running the house. He had every right to do so: the Married Woman's Property Act would not be passed until 1872. In short, William Gaskell was in many ways a typical Victorian male: a man who paid lip service to the sanctity of his home yet gave the best of himself—his friendship, his intellect, his energy, his emotions, his sympathy, his time—to the world.

On the other hand, he was unusual in that he granted some of the freedom he took as his natural right to his wife. Although the money and power were his and the care of the household and children strictly hers, he did not stand in the way of her writing or her life as a literary celebrity. Mrs. Gaskell traveled, visited, and entertained much as she wished, as a letter to her daughter Marianne written from London in May 1853 eloquently testifies: "Mrs. James Booth has written notes & called & I don't-know-whated to beg I will go there if only for a day or two . . . & meanwhile & previously I had promised Mrs. James to go to *her* on Wednesday—oh! *she* is a charming person . . . & Ly Coleman is vexed (in her pretty way) that I don't stay *there*, and I have so many calls to pay: & shall *utterly* offend the Carlyles, if I don't give them a day, they have said so much about it. I really think if you don't want me at home, darling I must stay on to Tuesday or Wednesday week . . ."[1]

"I don't believe William would ever have *commanded*," Mrs. Gaskell told her good friend Tottie Fox; and not surprisingly, Charlotte received the distinct impression during her brief visits to Plymouth Grove of an affectionate friendship between Mrs. Gaskell, writer, and Mr. Gaskell, clergyman. In fact, if comparisons were in question, her father's curate suffered rather badly in comparison with William Gaskell, who was liberal, broad-minded, and intellectual.

On this visit the very sociable Mrs. Gaskell was struck again with Charlotte's shrinking timidity that neither fame nor wider experience had the power to dispel. When she arrived another guest was in the room, a young woman so gentle and sensitive that Mrs. Gaskell could not imagine any objection on Charlotte's part. Yet Charlotte shrank back at the sight of the unexpected, unfamiliar face, relapsed into silence, and Mrs. Gaskell was astonished to observe from time to time a little shiver running over her body. A small evening party began with equal suffering on Charlotte's part until Mrs. Gaskell begged two of the guests, Catherine and Susannah Winkworth, to sing some Scottish ballads. "Miss Brontë had been sitting quiet and constrained till they began 'The Bonnie House of Airlie,' but the effect of that and 'Carlisle Yetts,' which followed, was as irresistible as the playing of the Piper of Hamelin. The beautiful clear light came into her eyes; her lips quivered with emotion; she forgot herself, rose, and crossed the room to the piano, where she asked eagerly for song after song."[2]

The Winkworth sisters begged her to visit them the next day when they would sing as much as she wished. Charlotte promised, but the next day her excruciating timidity overcame her longing for the music. With Mrs. Gaskell she paced up and down in front of the Winkworth home, "upbraiding herself for her folly," struggling to gather enough courage to enter the house. She could not do it, particularly since there was a third sister, Emily, to undergo meeting inside. Mrs. Gaskell was forced to knock and make her excuses while Charlotte hovered miserably out of sight.

She suffered again at a dinner party to which Mrs. Gaskell had invited two men she thought would prove congenial. Charlotte sat in stiff silence until the two began to dispute the excellence of Thackeray's lectures. Then her eyes brightened and glowed, she bent toward them eagerly, and unable finally to resist a favorite topic, she "threw herself into the discussion; the ice of her reserve was broken," and she conversed with animation the rest of the evening.

This combination in her friend of explosive feelings and pathological repression appalled and fascinated Mrs. Gaskell, but Charlotte's deep integrity won her respect and affection. "She is so true," she wrote John Forster after Charlotte's departure, "she wins respect, deep respect, from the very first,—and then comes hearty liking,—and last of all comes love. I thoroughly loved her before she left,—and I was so sorry for her! She has had so little kindness & affection shown to her; she said that she was afraid of loving me as much as she could, because she had never been able to inspire the kind of love she felt."

In the midst of pity, Mrs. Gaskell also recognized Charlotte's strength. "She gave Mr. Thackeray the benefit of some of her piercingly keen observation," she continued to Forster. "My word! he had reason when he said he was afraid of her. But she was very angry indeed with that part of The Examiner review of Esmond (I had forgotten it) which said his works would not live; and asked me if I knew if you had written it." Forster, as Dickens' friend, was prone to attack his rival. "I wish you could have heard how I back away from the veiled prophet, and how vehemently I disclaimed ever even having conjectured anything about any article in the Examiner. . . . She seems to have a great idea of Thackeray as a worshipper of 'Dutchesses & Countesses,' and to have disliked the tone of some of his lectures (that on Steele) exceedingly. She is not going to write again for some time.

She is thoroughly good; only made bitter by some deep mortification, —and feeling her plainness as 'something almost repulsive'. I am going to see her at Haworth, at her father's particular desire."[3]

Charlotte was not too morbid to recognize the good done her by such balanced souls as Mrs. Gaskell. Like a patient to a good and healing physician, she thanked her: "The week I spent in Manchester impressed me as the very brightest and healthiest I have known for these five years past."

Nicholls' departure was fixed for the end of May, but before that day of relief the ceremonies of Pentecost had to be got through. Entering the church to take communion on Whitsunday, Charlotte found herself the instigator of strange rites. Mr. Nicholls himself was distributing the wafer and the wine. The sudden vision of the woman he loved on her knees before him at the communion rail robbed him of all composure. "He struggled, faltered, then lost command over himself, stood before my eyes and in the sight of all the communicants, white, shaking, voiceless. Papa was not there, thank God! Joseph Redman spoke some words to him. He made a great effort, but could only with difficulty whisper and falter through the service. I suppose he thought this would be the last time; he goes either this week or the next. I heard the women sobbing round, and I could not quite check my own tears."[4]

That Sunday of the sacrament marked a change in Charlotte's feelings. She no longer divided her disgust between her father and Nicholls: her sympathy shifted toward the curate; her heart hardened toward her father. Someone, probably John Brown, who loathed the man, immediately carried the tale of Nicholls' behavior in church up to Mr. Brontë at the parsonage; the old man flared up in anger and pronounced the curate an "unmanly driveller." Charlotte objected: "I never saw a battle more sternly fought with the feelings than Mr. Nicholls fights with his, and when he yields momentarily, you are almost sickened by the sense of the strain upon him. However he is to go, and I cannot speak to him or look at him or comfort him a whit, and I must submit. Providence is over all, that is the only consolation."[5]

Whitmonday followed, the day all Sunday scholars, church and chapel—in rival bands—were led out in new straw hats and clean pinafores for a long walk in green fields sprinkled with king's-cups and daisies, regaled with an address by schoolmaster or preacher, and led back again for a feast of beer and cake or tea and buns. It was inevitable that on such a day Mr. Brontë and Mr. Nicholls should come face to face. To Charlotte's dismay, Nicholls was the offender on this occasion: "Papa addressed him at the school tea-drinking, with *constrained* civility, but still with *civility*. He did not reply civilly;

he cut short further words. This sort of treatment offered in public is what papa will never forget or forgive; it inspires him with a silent bitterness not to be expressed. I am afraid both are unchristian in their mutual feelings. Nor do I know which of them is least accessible to reason or least likely to forgive. It is a dismal state of things."[6]

Yet her sympathy was fixing itself firmly upon Nicholls. She could not help being pleased, she told Ellen, that the villagers were getting up a testimonial to be presented at his departure; nor did she fail to note that many parishioners had begun to express "commiseration" and "esteem" for him. It seemed too that Nicholls could be generous with his antagonist. "The Churchwardens recently put the question to him plainly. Why was he going? Was it Mr. Brontë's fault or his own? 'His own,' he answered. Did he blame Mr. Brontë? 'No! he did not: if anybody was wrong it was himself.' Was he willing to go? 'No! it gave him great pain.'" Yet in justice, she was forced to admit that the old faults still stained the new white virtues: he was "a curious mixture of honour and obstinacy; feeling and sullenness."[7]

The public presentation of a gold watch to Nicholls by the teachers, scholars, and congregation of St. Michael's was marked by Mr. Brontë's absence. On May 26, Nicholls preached his last Sunday service, "a cruel struggle." That same evening he walked up the lane to the parsonage to turn over church and school records to Mr. Brontë and bid him good-by. From the upstairs window, Charlotte saw the stolid, dark-bearded figure approach. She heard his knock at the door, his footsteps in the passage. She knew he looked for her in the dining room, felt his shock of disappointment when he found the room empty and dismantled for heavy spring cleaning. She knew he expected her momently to appear in Papa's parlor, but she did not go down.

"He went out thinking he was not to see me, and indeed, till the very last moment, I thought it best not. But perceiving that he stayed long before going out the gate, and remembering his long grief, I took courage and went out trembling and miserable. I found him leaning against the garden gate in a paroxysm of anguish, sobbing as women never sob. Of course I went straight to him. Very few words were interchanged, those few barely articulate. Several things I should have liked to ask him were swept entirely from my memory. Poor fellow! But he wanted such hope and such encouragement as I *could* not give him. Still I trust he must know now that I am not cruelly blind and indifferent to his constancy and grief. . . ."[8]

At six o'clock the next morning, Monday, May 27, Nicholls left Haworth, and Charlotte, who had waited impatiently for that dark, gloomy figure to stop haunting the church, the lane, and the moors, now sensed a loss. She had leisure now to reflect upon the ironies of life. Like her own Jane Eyre, she would willingly have submitted to have the bone of her arm broken, or a bull toss her, or a horse dash its hoof at her chest—to win affection. Now she was rejecting affection. She had once haunted the classrooms and gardens of a pensionnat to catch a glimpse of a little, choleric professor. Now she could give no hope to a man who hungered for her as she had hungered for Monsieur. Cruel that she, with a deep, pure well of love waiting to be drawn, could not love the man who loved her. Or was this her fate? To scorn what was given, unasked; to pant after what was withheld? So it almost seemed, except that, in effect, Papa was withholding Mr. Nicholls from her. There lay a certain challenge in the fact.

She wrote Ellen with an apparent sense of finality. "Papa has been far from strong lately. I dare not mention Mr Nicholls's name to him. He speaks of him quietly and without opprobrium to others, but to me he is implacable on the matter. However, he is gone—gone—and there's an end of it. I see no chance of hearing a word about him in the future, unless some stray shred of intelligence comes through Mr Sowden or some other second-hand source."[9]

Obstinate and single-minded, Arthur Nicholls had no intention of giving up the battle, however: he had merely beat a prudent retreat. In July Charlotte had a letter. He was not in Australia but in Yorkshire. He would take the post of curate in Kirk Smeaton in August. Would she authorize a correspondence? She received five letters, read them behind a closed door, and thrust them out of sight, unanswered. The sixth she replied to, briefly: she advised him to submit heroically to his lot. Made crafty by desperation, Nicholls seized this opening: her letter, he told her, was such a comfort—he must have a little more.

What was to be done? On long summer evenings after Papa and Tabby and Martha had gone up to bed and the clock on the stairs ticked on toward midnight, Charlotte pondered her loyalties as she paced up and down the quiet room. Much as she cherished her father as the last of the family that had been all in all to her, much as she disciplined herself to obey his wishes, she was forced to admit his injustices. Her poor frail mother, six children in almost as many years, his aloofness to them all, the Clergy Daughters' School, her dead sisters—none of it his fault, exactly, yet inextricably linked with him nevertheless. His unfairness to her: his obliviousness to her needs because she was plain and a girl; his unimaginative exhortations to "womanly duties"; the hours of writing time she had sacrificed to please him; his eternal restraints on her freedom. The time, when she was nineteen and would have been thankful for an allowance of a penny a week, and she asked him for a tiny sum, and he said, "What does a woman want with money?" How Aunt's money, not his, had paid for

Brussels, and the school prospectuses, and the paper and ink for their writing, and the publishing of the poems and of *Wuthering Heights* and *Agnes Grey*. His greed for her fame, his fret when her writing would not come, his snobbery, his misanthropy, his selfishness, his silence. *Her* endless sacrifices . . .

She answered Nicholls' letter, and when he replied, ecstatic, she answered him again. There had always been secrets at the parsonage— tiny manuscripts, private games in the nursery, scribbled papers, whispered confidences, smothered laughter, hidden letters and caches of laudanum, rustling proof sheets, stifled sobbing, restless pacing. The old man had sat like a rock in his parlor while tides of misery, pain, hope, and despair flowed past him. But no secret came to weigh upon Charlotte more than this forbidden correspondence with the man Papa hated and she did not yet love.

Elizabeth Gaskell paid her promised visit in September, arriving on Monday the nineteenth, stepping into an atmosphere of cold, sup- pressed hostility between father and daughter. As she reported all her activities minutely in her breathless, vivid style, she reported her four days at Haworth to John Forster:

> We turned up a narrow bye-lane near the church—past the curate's, the schools and skirting the pestiferous churchyard we arrived at the door into the Parsonage yard. In I went,—half blown back by the wild vehemence of the wind which swept along the narrow gravel walk— round the corner of the house into a small plot of grass enclosed within a low stone wall, over which the more ambitious grave-stones towered all round. There are two windows on each side the door and steps up to it . . . in at the door into an exquisitely clean passage, to the left into a square parlour looking out on the grass plot, the tall headstones beyond, the tower end of the church, the village houses and the brown moors.
>
> Miss Brontë gave me the kindest welcome, and the room looked the perfection of warmth, snugness and comfort, crimson predominat- ing in the furniture, which did well with the bleak cold colours with- out. . . . She is so neat herself I got quite ashamed of any touches of untidiness—a chair out of its place,—work left on the table were all of them, I could see, annoyances to her habitual sense of order; not an- noyances to her temper in the least; you understand the difference. . . .
> My room was above this parlour, and looking on the same view, which was really beautiful in certain lights, moon-light especially. Mr. Brontë lives almost entirely in the room opposite (right-hand side) of the front door; behind his room is the kitchen, behind the parlour a store room kind of pantry. Mr Brontë's bedroom is over his sitting- room, Miss Brontë's over the kitchen. The servants over the pantry. Where the rest of the household slept when they were all one large family, I can't imagine. The wind goes piping and wailing and sob-

bing round the square unsheltered house in a very strange unearthly way.

We dined—she and I together—Mr Brontë having his dinner sent to him in his sitting-room according to his invariable custom, (fancy it! and only they two left). . . .

In the evening Mr Brontë went to his room and smoked a pipe,—a regular clay,—and we sat over the fire and talked—talked of long ago when that very same room was full of children and how one by one they had dropped off into the churchyard close to the windows. At ½ past 8 we went into prayers,—soon after nine everyone was in bed but we two;—in general there she sits quite alone thinking over the past; for her eyesight prevents her reading or writing by candle-light, and knitting is but very mechanical and does not keep the thoughts from wandering. Each day—I was 4 there—was the same in outward arrangement—breakfast at 9, in Mr Brontë's room—which we left immediately after. What he does with himself through the day I cannot imagine! He is a tall fine looking old man, with silver bristles all over his head; nearly blind; speaking with a strong Scotch accent. . . . There was not a sign of engraving, map, writing materials, beyond a desk, &c. no books but those contained on two hanging shelves between the windows—his pipes, &c. a spittoon, if you know what that is. He was very polite and agreeable to me, paying rather elaborate old-fashioned compliments, but I was sadly afraid of him in my inmost soul; for I caught a glare of his stern eyes over his spectacles at Miss Brontë once or twice which made me know my man; and he talked at her sometimes; he is very fearless. . . . Moreover to account for my fear—rather an admiring fear after all—of Mr Brontë, please to take into account that though I like the beautiful glittering of bright flashing steel I don't fancy firearms at all, at all—and Miss Brontë never remembers her father dressing himself in the morning without putting a loaded pistol in his pocket, just as regularly as he puts on his watch. There was this little deadly pistol sitting down to breakfast with us, kneeling down to prayers at night to say nothing of a loaded gun hanging up on high, ready to pop off on the slightest emergency. . . . But all this time I wander from the course of our day, which is the course of her usual days. Breakfast over, the letters come; not many, sometimes for days none at all. About 12 we went out to walk. At 2 we dined, about 4 we went out again; at 6 we had tea; by nine everyone was in bed but ourselves. . . . And on enquiring I found that after Miss Brontë had seen me to my room she did come down every night, and begin that slow monotonous incessant walk in which I am sure I should fancy I heard the steps of the dead following me. She says she could not sleep without it . . .[10]

Comparatively free herself, Mrs. Gaskell was shocked at Charlotte's subjection to her father. On long walks over the brown hills, during intimate confidences by the fireside, she urged Charlotte to escape.

She gave her the address of a respectable lodging house in London, since Charlotte no longer wanted to intrude upon the Smiths; lodgings where Nicholls could call on her if she wished. She sympathized with the clandestine correspondence. Charlotte took temporary encouragement: she engaged the rooms in November, was on the verge of leaving for London, then called off the trip. She continued to write to Nicholls. The torture of deception, however, soon became too sharp to bear. On one of her evenings of pacing, she determined to tell her father: "sheer pain made me gather courage to break it."

She entered his sitting room in great fear and stood before her old father, whose face had grown hard and cold with enraged pride. She spoke very quietly.

"Father, I am not a young girl, not a young woman even—I never was pretty. I now am ugly. At your death I shall have £300 besides the little I have earned myself—do you think there are many men who would serve seven years for me?"

In scorn and impatience he cried out, would she marry a *curate?*

"Yes, I must marry a curate if I marry at all; not merely a curate but *your* curate; not merely *your* curate but he must live in the house with you, for I cannot leave you."

The old man pulled himself to his feet, trembling with rage, his silver hair bristling.

"Never," he shouted. "I will never have another man in this house!"

He did not speak to her for a week.

Then Tabby left her chair by the kitchen fireplace and, hobbling into his sitting room, asked the old man indignantly, did he wish to kill his daughter? and sought out Charlotte "and abused Mr. Nicholls for not having 'more brass.'"[11] The result was that Mr. Brontë relented and grudgingly, coldly, granted her leave to send an occasional letter.

Encouraged by this chink in the armor of Mr. Brontë's hatred, Nicholls made plans to come into the neighborhood in January and Charlotte again approached her father, this time with the request that she be allowed to become further acquainted with the curate during his visit. This too was grudgingly granted. As a result, Nicholls came to Oxenhope in the first month of the new year, 1854, to stay with his curate friend Joseph Brett Grant. A flagged field path runs over the moor between Oxenhope and Haworth. On this wind-flailed path on biting cold winter days Charlotte met the dark, bearded curate and heard his protestations of love and devotion.

Apart from her father's objection to the match, Charlotte's dilemma was this: should she marry a man she did not love and—

should she marry at all? For most Victorian women, the first objection was trivial, the second unimaginable. For Charlotte both objections were life and death. The only man who stirred her imagination was the man superior to her in intellect, achievement, and experience. She believed Nicholls to be superior in none of these. How could she kneel at his knee? What crowns could he offer? A wife was obliged to obey and honor her lord and master. How could she obey and honor such a husband without violating her integrity?

Should she marry at all? What would become of Currer Bell? "You had better do all your writing before you are married," Mrs. Gaskell had warned: "you will do none after." "If two ride together," went the old saying, "one must ride behind." Who would ride behind—the obscure clergyman or the famous author? She was not wild to be married. She did not live for some Tomkins, as Thackeray supposed. "The evils that now and then wring a groan from my heart—lie in position," she had written Ellen, "—not that I am a *single* woman and likely to remain a *single* woman but because I am a *lonely* woman and likely to be *lonely*." If Emily, Anne, or Branwell were alive, if the three sisters were still writing and planning, reading and sewing together in the firelit, crimson-curtained room, Nicholls might have pleaded and wept in vain.

In the first chapters of *Villette*, Charlotte had depicted brilliantly the pathetic subjection of female to male in the story of little Polly Home, her father, and John Graham Bretton, a handsome youth of sixteen. Little Polly is brought by her father to Mrs. Bretton's house to stay while Papa goes away on business. Polly is shattered: she loves no one but Papa: "Papa, Papa!" is her moan and her plea as long as he is gone. When he returns Polly rushes to meet him, hectic and feverish with joy. During tea she presses to his side; no one can pour his tea or hand him the sugar but herself. "Kiss Polly," she demands fiercely, and he kisses her tense little upturned face. But Papa must leave Polly again for the great world of masculine affairs. Polly is prostrated with grief at this second abandonment until Mrs. Bretton's son begins to exert some fascination. Soon she is as slavishly devoted to the careless young Graham as she was to Papa.

" 'Ma'am,' she would whisper to Mrs. Bretton, '—perhaps your son would like a little cake—sweet cake, you know—there is some there . . . One little piece—only for him—as he goes to school: girls—such as me and Miss Snowe—don't need treats, but *he* would like it.' " When Graham has time he plays with Polly and teases her and tosses her into the air. But he is absorbed in his masculine school world, and for the most part forgets her existence. Polly never forgets Graham for a minute: she half dies, crouching forgotten outside his door, waiting to be noticed. Eventually Polly must leave the Bretton home. She does so in anguish, for Graham does not love her. She raises her burning face for a kiss, then blurts out, " 'I *do* care for you, but you care nothing for me.' "

Lucy Snowe, Charlotte's alter ego, watches Polly's enslavement with distaste, judging her a monomaniacal personality, totally dependent on men who are by and large indifferent to her. " 'Paulina,' " Lucy warns, " 'you should not grieve that Graham does not care for you so much as you care for him. It must be so.' Her lifted and questioning eyes asked why. 'Because he is a boy and you are a girl,' " Lucy answers. It was the unanswerable answer, the heart of the problem.

And now her father's curate was asking her to submerge her identity in his, to make his interests hers, her time his own: in short, to be his wife. If she was not to serve Papa she was to serve a husband. What would become of Currer Bell?

Besides, her health and her body were frail. She did not love children and she did not know how to prevent them. Her mother had borne six children, one after the other, and had died. She was not as strong or as young as her mother. What would become of Currer Bell?

If she survived childbirth, would maternity inevitably put an end to her writing? Woman's "grand function," as everyone knew and said, was not art but childbearing. A single woman might write, but only because accident had barred her from "that sweet domestic and maternal sphere to which her whole being spontaneously moves."[12] Literary and biological creativity were rivals: it was unnatural for the first to prevail in a married woman. And once fulfilled in motherhood and domesticity, proclaimed the sages, a woman's nature must be half lamed for art. What would become of Currer Bell?

Nicholls argued and pleaded. He recognized her superior intellect, her genius; but he did not really know her. This very ignorance gave him the courage to proceed and overwhelm her doubts about the great differences between them. He was sure he could make her happy. Fifteen years ago she had dismissed Henry Nussey because she was not willing to die for him and it "must be in that light of adoration that I will regard my husband." But that dream lived long ago, when she "walked in life's morning march, when her spirit was young." She was disillusioned now, and lonely: surely it was madness for one so lonely to throw away such great devotion. Stolidity, dependability—these were not the qualities she had thought to admire in a husband, but they were good qualities, she respected them, and respect might turn to love. There was the promise of sexual knowledge, perhaps even enjoyment.

" 'Will you,' " Madame Beck had demanded of Lucy Snowe, " 'go backward or forward?' indicating with her hand, first, the small door of communication with the dwelling-house, and then the great double portals of the classes or schoolrooms."[13] It was a moment of great decision for Lucy Snowe. Should she retreat to the easy, passive life of nursery governess and live forever, safely but half alive, feeding on "the strange necromantic joys of fancy"? Or should she accept Madame's challenge to enter the world, to assert herself, to adopt a profession—even though the step meant struggle, hard work, and possible failure?

Charlotte now faced a similar challenge. Even the symbolism of Lucy's dilemma was apt. How much easier to retreat back through the small door—to be Papa's daughter, to live singly and safely, feeding on the "strange necromantic joys of fancy"—than to go forward, through the great double portals to marriage, and struggle and loss of identity and possible failure. Lucy had gone forward. Charlotte went forward now, fearful, doubtful, but embracing life and reality.

She agreed to marry Nicholls. Encouraged by the daughter, Nicholls attempted a visit to the parsonage. He found no welcome there, however: Mr. Brontë was "very, very hostile, bitterly unjust."

After ten days Nicholls returned to Kirk Smeaton and Charlotte was left to win over her father. Despite all appearances to the contrary, Mr. Brontë was not totally unreasonable. He loved his daughter; he feared his Maker. He recognized the stubbornness of Charlotte's will. Moreover, he had acquired an incurable antipathy for his new curate, Mr. de Renzi. After so many years, he was used to Nicholls, the parish was used to Nicholls. The new fellow got damnably on his nerves. If Nicholls would come back to St. Michael's, if Charlotte would promise not to leave him . . . Brooding on these considerations as the dark winter days lengthened into spring, Mr. Brontë relented, slowly, painfully, like a great old oak toppling finally to the ax. In April, Nicholls returned to the neighborhood.

> I told Mr Nicholls the great obstacles that lay in his way [Charlotte wrote Ellen, April 11, 1854]. He has persevered. The result of this, his last visit, is, that Papa's consent is gained—that his respect, I believe, is won, for Mr Nicholls has in all things proved himself disinterested and forbearing. He has shown, too, that while his feelings are exquisitely keen—he can freely forgive. Certainly I must respect him, nor can I withhold from him more than mere cool respect. In fact, dear Ellen, I am engaged.

Mr Nicholls, in the course of a few months, will return to the curacy of Haworth. I stipulated that I would not leave Papa, and to Papa himself I proposed a plan of residence which should maintain his seclusion and convenience uninvaded and in a pecuniary sense bring him gain instead of loss. What seemed at one time impossible is now arranged, and papa begins really to take a pleasure in the prospect. For myself, dear Ellen, while thankful to One who seems to have guided me through much difficulty, much and deep distress and perplexity of mind, I am still very calm, very inexpectant. What I taste of happiness is of the soberest order. I trust to love my husband —I am grateful for his tender love to me. I believe him to be an affectionate, a conscientious, a high-principled man; and if, with all this, I should yield to regrets, that fine talents, congenial tastes and thoughts are not added, it seems to me I should be most presumptuous and thankless.

Providence offers me this destiny. Doubtless then it is best for me. Nor do I shrink from wishing those dear to me one not less happy.

It is possible that our marriage may take place in the course of the Summer. Mr Nicholls wishes it to be in July. He spoke of you with great kindness, and said he hoped you would be at our wedding. I said I thought of having no other bridesmaid. Did I say rightly? I mean the marriage to be literally *as quiet as possible*.

Do not mention these things just yet. I mean to write to Miss Wooler shortly. Good-bye. There is a strange half-sad feeling in making these announcements. The whole thing is something other than imagination paints it beforehand; cares, fears, come mixed inextricably with hopes. I trust yet to talk these matters over with you. Often last week I wished for your presence, and said so to Mr Nicholls, Arthur as I now call him, but he said it was the only time and place when he could not have wished to see you. Good-bye.—Yours affectionately,

C. Brontë.[14]

# 25

*A Solemn, Strange,
and Perilous Thing*

Like Mr. Brontë, Ellen believed that Nicholls was not good enough
for Charlotte. Inevitably, too, she felt some of the jealousy of an old,
faithful friend, and some bitterness at her own bleak future.[1] Thus
she had written Mary Taylor in the summer of 1853 deploring Charlotte's interest in Nicholls' suit. Receiving the letter many months
later, Mary blazed back in high indignation in February 1854:

> You talk wonderful nonsense abt C. Brontë in yr letter. What do
> you mean about "bearing her position so long and enduring to the
> end"? and still better—"bearing our lot whatever it is". If its C's lot
> to be married shd n't she bear that too? Or does your strange moral-
> ity mean that she shd refuse to ameliorate her lot when it lies in her
> power. How wd she be inconsistent with herself in marrying? Be-
> cause she considers her own pleasure? If this is so new for her to do, it
> is high time she began to make it more common. It is an outrageous
> exaction to expect her to give up her choice in a matter so important,
> and I think her to blame in having been hitherto so yielding that her
> friends can think of making such an impudent demand.[2]

When Ellen read Charlotte's announcement of her engagement, she
had not been edified by Mary's anger; she greeted the news with less
than enthusiasm. But the real pathos lay in Charlotte's own doubts
about marriage to Arthur Bell Nicholls. A week after breaking the
news to Ellen she wrote Mrs. Gaskell, confessing her uncertainties:
"I cannot deny that I had a battle to fight with myself; I am not sure
that I have even yet conquered certain inward combatants. . . . It is
of no use going into detail. After various visits and as the result of

perseverance in one quarter and a gradual change of feeling in others, I find myself what people call 'engaged.' "

"I find myself what people call 'engaged' "—the pale, lifeless words mocked Jane Eyre's electrifying cry for Rochester: "Reader, I married him!"

"I could almost cry sometimes that in this important action in my life I cannot better satisfy papa's perhaps natural pride," she continued. "My destiny will not be brilliant, certainly, but Mr Nicholls is conscientious, affectionate, pure in heart and life. He offers a most constant and tried attachment—I am very grateful to him. I mean to try to make him happy, and papa too. . . ."[3]

The triumph of being able to announce her engagement to George Smith was as brief as it was small: he wrote back congratulating her and informing her of his own marriage on February 11, two and a half months before, to Elizabeth Blakeway, daughter of a London wine merchant. Coincidentally, he had chosen a wife very like the fictional Paulina Charlotte had bestowed upon Dr. John in *Villette*. When Mrs. Gaskell met Smith in 1856 she found a man "too stout to be handsome" with "a very pretty, Paulina-like little wife." Charlotte returned congratulations, then assessed her own situation with her chronic mixture of honesty and pessimism: "What *I* have to say is soon told. The step in contemplation is no hasty one; on the gentleman's side, at least, it has been meditated for many years, and I hope that, in at last acceding to it, I am acting right . . . There has been heavy anxiety—but I begin to hope all will end for the best. My expectations however are very subdued—very different, I dare say, to what *yours* were before you were married."[4]

It was the last of Cornhill. The previous winter Charlotte had written Williams about the packages of books that ever since the triumph of *Jane Eyre* had arrived faithfully at the parsonage: packages that in her cultural and geographical isolation had "something of the magic charm of a fairy gift about them, as well as of the less poetical but more substantial pleasure of a box from home received at school." Now she deliberately cut this tie: "Do not trouble yourself to select or send any more books. These courtesies must cease some day, and I would rather give them up than wear them out." Her letter to George Smith also ended on an autumnal note: "I sometimes wonder how Mr Williams is, and hope he is well. In the course of the year that is gone, Cornhill and London have receded a long way from me; the links of communication have waxed very frail and few. It must be so in this world. All things considered, I don't wish it otherwise."

Charlotte also had lingering doubts about her father. She *trusted* that his illusions of ambition were quite dissipated, she wrote Ellen;

she *hoped* affection would resume some power. She coaxed him, she assured him she would never leave him. She read him passages from Nicholls' letters in which the curate promised to prove his gratitude to Mr. Brontë by supporting him and consoling him in his old age. He would resume his care of church and school: to the credit of the old incumbent, Haworth church would again flourish like a green bay tree. Mr. Brontë heard, and weighed the advantages alone in his parlor over the clay pipe. He seemed to approve. His health grew better, his spirits lifted, and he went down to the church to preach two sermons one Sunday and one again on Wednesday. Yet watching his proud face, searching for a tender glance from the glinting spectacles, Charlotte could only *hope* and *trust*.

On the first of May 1854, Charlotte left for a last round of visits before the wedding. Nicholls had stipulated for July, although she felt July was very soon; then June was settled upon. She went first to the Gaskells in Plymouth Grove, hardly comforted by the thought that, although the Unitarian Gaskells were ready to receive Mr. Nicholls, Nicholls' high-church bigotry against Dissenters might put an end to this cherished friendship. Immersed in the strong sea of her doubts and fears, Charlotte clung anxiously to the reassurances of Mrs. Gaskell and two frequent callers, Catherine and Emily Winkworth. Her shyness with the girl who had sung "The Bonnie House of Airlie" so enchantingly had disappeared, as Catherine's exhaustive report of her conversation with Charlotte to her sister-in-law, Emma Shaen, testifies:

> . . . So I went in on Wednesday. Lily drew me directly to the room, whispering: "Say something about her marriage." . . . When she was summoned away I began:
> "I was very glad to hear something Mrs Gaskell told me about you."
> "What was it?"
> "That you are not going to be alone any more."
> She leant her head on her hand and said very quickly: "Yes, I am going to be married in June."
> "It will be a great happiness for you to have some one to care for, and make happy."
> "Yes; and it is a great thing to be the first object with any one."
> "And you must be very sure of that with Mr Nicholls; he has known you and wished for this so long, I hear. . . ."
> "But, Katie, it has cost me a good deal to come to this."
> "You will have to care for his things, instead of his caring for yours, is that it?"
> "Yes, I can see that beforehand."
> "But you have been together so long already that you know what

his things are, very well. He is very devoted to his duties, is he not?—and you can and would like to help him in those?"

"I have always been used to those, and it is one great pleasure to me that he is so much beloved by all the people in the parish; there is quite a rejoicing over his return. But those are not everything, and I cannot conceal from myself that he is *not* intellectual; there are many places into which he could not follow me intellectually."

"Well; of course every one has their own tastes. For myself, if a man had a firm, constant, affectionate, reliable nature, with tolerable practical sense, I should be much better satisfied with him than if he had an intellect far beyond mine, and brilliant gifts without that trustworthiness. I care most for a calm, equable atmosphere at home."

"I do believe Mr Nicholls is as reliable as you say, or I wouldn't marry him."

"And you have had time to prove it; you are not acting in a hurry."

"That is true; and, indeed, I am quite satisfied with my decision; still—" here Lily came in, and Miss Brontë repeated what I had been saying, ending with—"still such a character would be far less amusing and interesting than a more impulsive and fickle one; it might be dull!"

"Yes, indeed," said Lily.

"For a day's companion, yes," I said, "but not for a life's: one's home ought to be the one fixed point, the one untroubled region in one's lot; at home one wants peace and settled love and trust, not storm and change and excitement; besides such a character would have the advantage that one might do the fickleness required one's self, which would be a relief sometimes."

"Oh, Katie, if *I* had ever said such a wicked thing," cried Lily; and then Miss Brontë:

"Oh, Katie, I never thought to hear such a speech from *you!*"

"You don't agree with it?"

"Oh, there is truth in it; so much that I don't think *I* could ever have been so candid," Miss Brontë said; "And there is danger, too, one might be led on to go too far."

"I think not," I said; "the steadiness and generosity on the other side would always keep one in check."

But they made a great deal of fun and laughing about this, and then Lily was called away again, and Miss Brontë went on:

"He is a Puseyite and very stiff; I fear it will stand in the way of my intercourse with some of my friends. But I shall always be the same in my heart towards them. I shall never let him make me a bigot. I don't think differences of opinion ought to interfere with friendship, do you?"

"No." And we talked about this a little, and then I said: "Perhaps, too, you may do something to introduce him to goodness in sects where he thought it could not be."

"That is what I hope; he has a most sincere love of goodness wherever he sees it. I think if he could come to know Mr Gaskell it would change his feeling. . . ."

Summing up the situation, Catherine continued:

He thinks her intellectually superior to himself, and admires her gifts, and likes her the better, which sounds as though he were generous. And he has very good family connections, and he gets on with her father, and all the parishioners adore him; but they will be very poor, for the living is only £250 a year. If only he is not altogether far too narrow for her, one can fancy her much more really happy with such a man than with one who might have made her more in love, and I am sure she will be really good to him. But I *guess* the true love was Paul Emanuel after all, and is dead; but I don't know, and don't think that Lily knows. . . .[5]

Mrs. Gaskell suppressed the same doubts, reassuring Charlotte that the long duration and vehemence of Nicholls' devotion outweighed his lack of a liberal and intellectual mind. Thus Charlotte said good-by to her Manchester friends, somewhat saddened, somewhat reassured, and went on to Hunsworth to Joe and Amelia Taylor, her closest link to Mary, where Amelia told her graciously that she was not looking well—rather ugly as usual, and then to Brookroyd, where she stepped over that threshold for the last time and embraced her oldest friend once more. Did gray threads silver Ellen's smooth brown hair, lines etch the plump cheeks and wide-set brown eyes? Miss Nussey of Brookroyd had kept her own decorous, unhurried pace through the years—pouring tea, gracing church bazaars, netting bags; harassed by ladylike coughs and indispositions; saddened by deaths and illnesses into gentle melancholy. Yet many mornings, like the heroine of that depressing Victorian testimonial *Passages in the Life of a Daughter at Home,* Ellen must have woken up to the bitter, familiar knowledge of the purposelessness of her life. Many times, like the young Florence Nightingale (who escaped her fate), she had sat in the evenings, idly leafing a book or a tract, watching the drawing-room clock, wondering whether it would ever strike ten. Her last attempt to escape the monotony and dependence of Brookroyd as a companion to an elderly clergyman and his wife had failed when the invalid couple offered insultingly low wages to be paid after their deaths.[6] Yet for Charlotte, wracked all her life by ambivalent and violent impulses, Ellen would always be a symbol of repose, as tranquil as when she had tried to call up her calm image to sooth her tortured nights at Roe Head so many years ago. For the last time they curled their hair before the fire, exchanging confidences. Then Charlotte left for Leeds to buy bonnets and materials for bride and bridesmaid, not pink silk bonnets or pearly shimmering silks, but something decently plain that could be turned to use after the wedding.

After missing a train and twirling her thumbs at Leeds for four hours, she got home at seven o'clock on May 13 to be immediately plunged into the kind of prenuptial flurry she had heard about but never expected to experience herself. Papa had given Mr. de Renzi notice, Nicholls was to leave Kirk Smeaton June 11, the end of June was the latest possible date for the wedding since Nicholls demanded a month's honeymoon and Mr. de Renzi was reluctant to stay for many weeks after his dismissal. Alterations in the house had to be supervised: the peat house, a small room that had once housed the pet geese Adelaide and Victoria, was being refurbished with fresh paper and curtains in green and white as a study for Mr. Nicholls. Charlotte found herself sewing chemises, chemisettes, gowns "against time." Her wedding clothes must be ordered and made at Halifax. Invitations must be sent—*her* list was not long, but Nicholls turned out to have "no end to his string of parson-friends."[7] The envelopes were not right: she wanted them perfectly plain with a silver initial. A tablecloth must be bordered for the wedding breakfast. Then Nicholls declared he must come for a visit. He was suffering from acute rheumatic pains. He feared chronic rheumatism; indeed his tendency that way had been one of Mr. Brontë's objections to the marriage. Charlotte awaited his visit with impatience and anxiety.

He came, suffering, and Charlotte sympathized until she discovered that his affliction lodged more in his mind than in his joints. "I soon discovered that my business was—instead of sympathizing—to rate him soundly," she wrote Ellen. "He had wholesome treatment while he was at Haworth—and went away singularly better. Perfectly unreasonable however on some points—as his fallible sex are not ashamed to be—groaning over the prospect of a few more weeks of bachelorhood—as much as if it were an age of banishment or prison." Branwell's weaknesses had always roused in her similar disbelief, but not amusement. "There is not a female child above the age of eight but might rebuke him for the spoilt petulance of his wilful nonsense," she concluded.[8] Or was this last-minute bravado, for in a few weeks this member of the "fallible sex" would be master of her person, her income, her time, her bed?

Papa contributed to the flurry by a sudden attack of deafness during a spell of "sultry and electric" weather, then bewildered Charlotte by suddenly recovering and going down to the church to preach two sermons in a day, as hearty as ever. His only concern now was to get the wedding over and done with. De Renzi was absolutely leaving the twenty-fifth of July, Nicholls would have to find substitutes for every day thereafter. Charlotte was thus coerced into agreeing to the end of June although she "sadly wished to defer it till the 2nd week in July." By June 16 she was making final arrangements with Ellen for her arrival with Miss Wooler: "Would it not be better, dear Nell, if you and she could arrange to come to Haworth on the same day, arrive at Keighley by the same train, then I could order the cab to meet you at the station and bring you on with your luggage. In this hot weather, walking would be quite out of the question . . . Mr Nicholls is a kind considerate fellow, with all his masculine faults in some points; he enters into my wishes about having the thing done quietly . . . He and Mr Sowden will come to Mr Grant's the evening before . . . Precisely at 8 in the morning they will be in the Church, and there we are to meet them. Mr and Mrs Grant are asked to the breakfast, not the ceremony."[9]

The wedding day was set at last for Thursday, June 29. Monsieur Heger's letters to Charlotte do not survive: perhaps she destroyed them now. On Wednesday Miss Wooler and Ellen stepped out of the cab at the parsonage gate and pressed Charlotte's tiny, fragile hands in their own. She had, they noted, a cold. There was much business still to attend to that summer day: gowns to be smoothed and pinned, the last details of silver and china and boiled ham for the wedding breakfast to be gone into with Martha, consultations about Papa's comfort in Charlotte's absence, the going-away trunk to be packed. At eight-thirty the household knelt for prayers in Mr. Brontë's parlor, Miss Wooler, now in her early sixties, stouter and more dignified than ever, Ellen quiet and unfaded, Charlotte like a frail child beside them. Closing up his Bible, Mr. Brontë then greeted the company with the news that he intended to stop at home tomorrow morning: he felt too unwell to give his daughter away in church. Here was a bitter caprice, a last assertion of will! Perhaps Charlotte guessed at something less selfish: a stubborn refusal to cement a marriage he now approved of in fact but dreaded in his bones. Tall and stiff, the old man bid them good night in his distant, courteous way and took his way to bed, stopping to wind the clock on the stairs. The three friends bent their heads over the prayer book. A friend, it seemed, could give the bride away; there was no stipulation as to sex. Besides the bride, groom, bridesmaid, and officiating minister, there was to be only one guest. Miss Wooler gallantly offered to deliver her old pupil to her groom.

Who can believe Charlotte's sleep that night was untroubled? Very early Thursday, a dim, quiet morning, she rose and washed her face and hands in the basin, and with Miss Wooler's and Ellen's help donned the white muslin dress carefully laid out the night before and a white bonnet trimmed with green leaves, and laid a white lace mantle over her shoulders, and walked with her two friends down the churchyard past the mute slabs of stone to the church. Years ago in one of her strange, prescient dreams she had a dreamed of a wedding at Haworth church and seen the faces of the bride and groom and even the guests crowded around the door with brilliant clarity: six months later the identical wedding had taken place. The oracles had been silent about her own fate. If she ever dreamed her own wedding, she had not seen the face of the man who now waited for her in the dim church.

They were married by Nicholls' friend, Sutcliffe Sowden. He wrote "Clerk" after Nicholls' name in the space provided on the marriage certificate for profession. After Charlotte's name in the same column he drew a canceling line.

She had sent invitations to George Smith, to Mrs. and the Misses Smith, to Williams, and to the Gaskells among others, but instead it was village people who caught word of the event and gathered at the church door to see her come out on the arm of her husband: faces she had known all her life—sexton, postmaster, stationer, Sunday scholar. If some smiled to see t'Parson's daughter looking "like a snowdrop" in her white, and green leaves, others must have sighed at the marked contrast between the delicate, birdlike bride and the sturdy groom almost two years younger. By the time the little party stepped into the dining room for the wedding breakfast, Mr. Brontë had recovered his spirits: Martha Brown remembered that he was "the life and soul of the party." Then Charlotte left and reappeared in her new mauve shot-silk traveling dress, hands were pressed, good-bys exchanged, admonitions given—she must take care of her cold, not take a chill—and she stepped out the door, through the gate, and into the cab on her husband's arm, and waved as the cab clattered down the lane and disappeared around the sexton's house at the corner.

That same evening, to Ellen:

> I scribble one hasty line just to say that after a pleasant enough journey—we have got safely to Conway—the evening is wet and wild, though the day was fair chiefly with some gleams of sunshine. However, we are sheltered in a comfortable inn. My cold is not worse. If you get this scrawl tomorrow and write by return—direct to me at the Post-Office, Bangor, and I may get it on Monday. Say how you and

Miss Wooler got home. Give my kindest and most grateful love to Miss Wooler whenever you write. On Monday, I think, we cross the Channel. No more at present.—Yours faithfully and lovingly,

C.B.N.[10]

After eight years at Haworth, Arthur Nicholls was thoroughly acquainted with the fortunes of the Brontës, but Charlotte knew hardly anything of her husband's family and origins. She had the English prejudice against the Irish and Ireland: it was a country her father had struggled free of to become a respectable Anglican clergyman. She had pilloried a "typical" Irishman in *Shirley* as boisterous, vain, and mean; pressed, she would also admit to believing the Irish shiftless and dirty. Fully acquainted with his wife's antipathy as well as his father-in-law's dark suspicions about the respectability of his family, Nicholls had planned the honeymoon as a vindication. The chief interest of the journey began, therefore, after they left Wales at Holyhead for Ireland and arrived in Dublin on Tuesday, July 4, 1854.

"Three of Mr Nicholls' relatives met us in Dublin—his brother and 2 cousins. The 1st (brother) is manager of the Grand Canal from Dublin to Banagher—a sagacious well-informed and courteous man— his cousin is a student of the University and has just gained 3 premiums. The other cousin was a pretty lady-like girl with gentle English manners."[11] Arthur Bell Nicholls' vindication had begun. What Nicholls' brother Alan, his cousin Joseph Bell, and his favorite cousin, dark-eyed Mary Anne Bell, a young woman of twenty-four, thought of the famous author who had so predictively chosen their family name for her nom de plume is unrecorded. Certainly they felt it unfortunate that the bride should be suffering from such a bad cold and cough on her honeymoon. After touring the main sights of Dublin, in particular Nicholls' university, Trinity College, its library, museum, and chapel ("and should have seen much more—had not my bad cold been a restraint upon us"), the party of Nichollses and Bells set off by train west for Banagher and Cuba House, the home of Nicholls' uncle, Dr. Alan Bell, now dead, who had raised his two nephews from childhood.

Banagher itself proved to be a double row of houses fronting a narrow street that crawled uphill to a church. Cuba House lay a quarter of a mile beyond, and with the passing of the carriage through wrought-iron gates and down an avenue of limes, Nicholls' vindication was complete. The estate was a peculiar combination of private dwelling and institution. Seventeenth-century Cuba House stood like a great mausoleum topped by high thin stacks of chimneys;

beyond ranged the dormitories and classrooms of the Royal School to which Dr. Bell had been headmaster. Lacking grace, Cuba House had history and solidity to recommend it, and Charlotte was interested, impressed, and enlightened. "I cannot help feeling singularly interested in all about the place," she wrote Miss Wooler. "In this house Mr Nicholls was brought up by his uncle Dr Bell. It is very large and looks externally like a gentleman's country-seat—within most of the rooms are lofty and spacious and some—the drawing-room—dining-room &c. handsomely and commodiously furnished.— The passages look desolate and bare—our bedroom, a great room on the ground-floor would have looked gloomy when we were shewn into it but for the turf-fire that was burning in the wide old chimney."[12]

A clan of cousins had assembled to meet her—James, Alan, Arthur, William, and Harriet Bell, as well as Joseph and the dark-eyed Mary Anne, who had come along from Dublin. Dominating the group was the late uncle's widow, Harriet Lucinda Adamson Bell, a gracious, stately lady of fifty-three. This kindly woman took Charlotte firmly in hand, for Arthur's poor bride was in a sad state. The fatigue of travel and meeting new faces, of being constantly with another person instead of constantly alone, had shattered Charlotte's nerves, and her cough was very bad. Under the older woman's motherly care, Charlotte gradually stopped trembling and coughing and began to revive.

All in all, she was very pleased with Cuba House. Having firm opinions about "Irish negligence," she had expected washy tea, ashes in the grate, and tardy meals. But her scrupulous sense of precision was satisfied: the household had "an English order and repose." She found her new relations equally satisfying. Particularly she leaned toward the regal widow, who, far from being an Irish barbarian, read widely, played the piano, and, according to her granddaughter, was such a lady that she "never struck a match in her life, and never put coals on the fire." "She is like an English or Scotch matron," Charlotte told Miss Wooler, paying one of her highest compliments. Finally she discovered that Currer Bell's novels were read and revered at Cuba House. Altogether she was forced to look at the curate with new eyes: the dull, statue-stiff man became gilded. "My dear husband too appears in a new light here in his own country," she confessed to Miss Wooler, betraying how deep her dissatisfaction had been. "More than once I have had deep pleasure in hearing his praises on all sides. Some of the old servants and followers of the family tell me I am a most fortunate person for that I have got one of the best gentlemen in the country. His Aunt too speaks of him with a mixture of affection and respect most gratifying to hear."[13]

From Cuba House they journeyed west again along the Shannon to Limerick and then to Kilkee in County Clare where they lodged at the West End Hotel, an inn where there was a good deal of Irish negligence to carp at, Charlotte observed, had they been in carping humor. Instead they spent their days out of doors: "Such a wild, iron-bound coast—with such an ocean-view as I had not yet seen and such battling of waves with rocks as I had never imagined." At the sight of the sea her old enthusiasm rose up to grip her as it had at Bridlington so long ago. The unpoetical Ellen had tactfully withdrawn down the beach to allow her romantic friend to wrestle with her emotions in solitude. Could the equally unpoetic Nicholls be as discreet? He could and was, as she reported to Catherine Winkworth: "The first morning we went out on to the cliffs and saw the Atlantic coming in all white foam, I did not know whether I should get leave or time to take the matter in my own way. I did not want to talk—but I *did* want to look and be silent. Having hinted a petition, licence was not refused—covered with a rug to keep off the spray I was allowed to sit where I chose—and he only interrupted me when he thought I crept too near the edge of the cliff. So far he is always good in this way—and this protection which does not interfere or pretend is I believe a thousand times better than any half sort of pseudo sympathy. I will try with God's help to be as indulgent to him whenever indulgence is needed."[14]

From Kilkee they wended their way through western Ireland from Tarbert to Tralee to Killarney. At Killarney Charlotte had a brush with death. "We saw and went through the Gap of Dunloe," she wrote, again to Catherine Winkworth. "A sudden glimpse of a very grim phantom came on us in the Gap. The guide had warned me to alight from my horse as the path was now very broken and dangerous—I did not feel afraid and declined—we passed the dangerous part—the horse trembled in every limb and slipped once but did not fall—soon after she (it was a mare) started and was unruly for a minute—however I kept my seat—my husband went to her head and led her—suddenly without any apparent cause—she seemed to go mad—reared, plunged—I was thrown on the stones right under her—my husband did not see that I had fallen—he still held her—I saw and felt her kick, plunge, trample round me. I had my thoughts about the moment—its consequences—my husband—my father—When my plight was seen, the struggling creature was let loose—she sprung over me. I was lifted off the stones neither bruised by the fall nor touched by the mare's hoofs. Of course the only feeling left was gratitude for more sakes than my own."[15]

From Killarney they proceeded south to Glengarriff, then turned eastward to Cork and finally returned to Dublin. The journey had suited Nicholls immensely: haggard before the wedding with the uncertainties of courtship, he had gained twelve pounds and was looking hale and strong. By then, July 28, Charlotte was chafing to be home, however. Papa, deciding that the honeymoon had lasted long enough, had reminded her again that he was ill. It was enough to rouse all Charlotte's daughterly compulsions, suppressed with difficulty for a whole month. ". . . I have been longing, *longing intensely* sometimes, to be at home," she wrote Ellen from Dublin. "Indeed, I could enjoy and rest no more, and so home we are going."[16]

She sent Martha instructions for their arrival at about seven o'clock the evening of August 1. "I feel very anxious about Papa—the idea of his illness has followed me all through my journey and made me miserable sometimes when otherwise I should have been happy enough. I longed to come home a fortnight since . . . Have things ready for tea on Tuesday Evening—and you had better have a little cold meat or ham as well—as we shall probably get no dinner—and Mr Nicholls will want something."[17] She came home to the parsonage she longed for when away and loathed when there—and would never leave it again.

In London that same July 1854, a Mary Ann Evans scribbled a hurried note to Charles and Cara Bray and Sara Hennell—"Dear Friends—all three—I have only time to say good bye and God bless you. Poste Restante, Weimar for the next six weeks, and afterwards Berlin. . . ."[18] Then she fled to Germany with Charlotte's keenest critic, George Henry Lewes (stopping three days in Brussels to wander the streets and gaze at the scenes Charlotte had brought so vividly to life in *Villette*). Their twenty-four-year liaison would close many doors to her—not Lewes (Thackeray's swells were also prudes)—but it opened many more, for, stimulated by Lewes' intelligence, experience, and encouragement, Mary Ann Evans metamorphized into George Eliot and took the throne as England's greatest woman writer. Just as surely as Mary Ann Evans' union with Lewes expanded her powers, Charlotte's marriage to Nicholls blighted the great powers of Currer Bell, quite apart from the question of whether the marriage was a happy one or Nicholls a good husband (for by his lights he certainly was).

On the honeymoon, Charlotte had taught Nicholls what it was to cater to the existence of a hypersensitive, ailing, intellectual wife. Inevitably, the honeymoon over, Nicholls now taught Charlotte what it was to cater to the demands of a conventional husband. She found the experience both gratifying and disturbing. Breakfast with Papa, morning in the dining room with writing or letters, a walk, a solitary dinner, tea alone at four, the long evenings—these were no more. Instead, she was busy from morning to night, always called for, desired for something, full of small business. This change was "a marvellously good thing," as she told Ellen, adding naïvely, "As yet I don't quite understand how some wives grow so selfish." Surely, her whole existence was now submerged in her husband's.

"Dear Nell," she continued, "—during the last 6 weeks—the colour of my thoughts is a good deal changed: I know more of the realities of life than I once did. I think many false ideas are propagated perhaps unintentionally. I think those married women who indiscriminately urge their acquaintance to marry—much to blame. For my part— I can only say with deeper sincerity and fuller significance—what I always said in theory—Wait God's will. Indeed—indeed—Nell—it is a solemn and strange and perilous thing for a woman to become a wife. Man's lot is far—far different."[19]

With wonder she found her preferences and opinions put aside for his, although in the event—again wonderfully—his seemed best. ". . . My time is not my own now," she told Miss Wooler, with pride, with regret; "Somebody else wants a good portion of it—and says we must do so and so. We *do* 'so and so' accordingly . . ."[20] Voices broke the quiet of the parsonage as Nicholls' "endless string of parson friends" came for tea. Projects were undertaken: "We have been busy lately giving a Supper and tea-drinking to the Singers, ringers, Sunday-School Teachers and all the Scholars of the Sunday and National Schools—amounting in all to some 500 souls. It gave satisfaction and went off well."[21] The gala was a gesture of thanks for the hearty welcome given Nicholls on his return to the parish. The villagers and parishioners, taking their cue from Mr. Brontë perhaps, had reversed their opinion of the curate, and Charlotte heard his health proposed— in tea—as a "consistent Christian and a kind gentleman" with pride. She was more gratified to see his stolid figure in cassock and surplice appear behind the three-decker pulpit on a Sunday morning, to know that he was fulfilling his promise to relieve and comfort the old man. Her anger with her father had dissolved with the triumph of her will. The tyrant had vanished: she saw only an old man with silver stubble on his chin, and faded, half-blind eyes, as stubborn as the old thorn trees in the garden that bent against the blast of the moor winds, and as familiar. His hold over her was broken. As a result, she cared more than ever to cherish his life in the years to come. And the truce that had been called between her father and her husband seemed unbroken.

Time, time—I have no time. It was her half-complaining, half-gratified theme that autumn. "Women never have a half-hour in all their lives (excepting before or after anybody is up in the house) that they can call their own, without fear of offending or of hurting some-one," Florence Nightingale, a fellow sufferer, cried in her essay "Cassandra." "Women have no means given them whereby they can resist the 'claims of social life'. They are taught from their infancy upwards that it is a wrong, ill-tempered action and a misunderstanding of 'women's mission' (with a great M) if they do not allow them-selves *willingly* to be interrupted at all hours."[22]

Charlotte now felt the pressure that caused many Victorian women to take to their couches and feign illness, to exaggerate the sick, in-fectious aspect of the menstrual mystique, to wish aloud that they could break an arm or leg so that they could have a moment to themselves. If Elizabeth Barrett Browning had not been an invalid, she might not have been a poet. "Take warning, Ellen, the married woman can call but a very small portion of each day her own. Not that I complain of this sort of monopoly as yet, and I hope I never shall incline to regard it as a misfortune, but it certainly exists."[23] To Miss Wooler: "My own life is more occupied than it used to be: I have not so much time for thinking: I am obliged to be more practical, for my dear Arthur is a very practical as well as a very punctual, methodical man. Every morning he is in the National School by nine o'clock; he gives the children religious instruction till ½ past 10. Almost every afternoon he pays visits amongst the poor parishioners. Of course he often finds a little work for his wife to do, and I hope she is not sorry to help him. I believe it is not bad for me that his bent should be so wholly towards matters of real life and active usefulness—so little inclined to the literary and contemplative. As to his continued affection and kind attentions—it does not become me to say much of them but as yet they neither change nor diminish."[24] Yet there were 500,000 women who would have made good clergymen's wives; and only one Currer Bell.

Still, Currer Bell could not die. Her life was different—"May God make me thankful for it!" (but not, "I *am* thankful"); her husband good and devoted; every day, she told Mrs. Gaskell, she felt her attachment to him stronger. But there were rooms in her soul he could not enter: rooms hung with the rich, red velvet of imagination; dark, black-webbed rooms of melancholy and hypochondria; empty, high-vaulted rooms echoing with longing and memory, and Branwell's curses and Emily's rattling breath; a small, iron-doored room wherein dwelt pride. "In showing my treasure, I may withhold a gem or two," she had written in *Shirley*, "—a curious unbought, graven stone—an amulet, of whose mystic glitter I rarely permit even myself a glimpse."

Love, devotion might one day persuade Charlotte to reveal this mystic amulet, but not yet, not yet. Meanwhile, in the few moments left to herself, she began to write again.

The moors were glorious that September, glowing in rich purple bloom as if in last salute. She was impatient for Ellen's visit, planned for days when the heather reached its height, but, alas, deferred until October when the moors were brown and sere. The visit posed the delicate problem of adjustment between new husband and old friend. One could not linger at the fireside exchanging confidences while a husband tapped his foot upstairs in the bedroom; nor could Ellen any longer share her bed. Perhaps to atone for such matters, Charlotte gently rebuked her husband on one of their walks over the moors, for he wished to walk between them. "Even you should not come between us," she said, and motioned Ellen to her side. Charlotte must have complained half laughingly to Ellen that visit about trying to find time to get on with her new novel, for Ellen believed to the day of her death that Nicholls tried to prevent Charlotte from writing, declaring flatly: "I did not marry Currer Bell, the novelist, but Charlotte Brontë, the clergyman's daughter. Currer Bell may fly to heaven tomorrow for anything I care."[25] Meanwhile, a plan was set afoot to further the interest Nicholls' friend Sutcliffe Sowden had shown in Ellen at the wedding: Nicholls said often to his wife that he wished Miss Nussey were well settled in life. But Mr. Sowden's interest waxed and waned most annoyingly, perhaps because he was only a poor curate while Ellen was Miss Nussey of Brookroyd.

Sowden's poverty came near being mended. On November 11 the indefatigable Sir James Kay-Shuttleworth descended upon the parsonage with his urbane manner and white-toothed smile to announce that he had come to see what kind of a fellow his authoress had got for a husband. This was Saturday; he intended to stay only a day, but liked Nicholls so well that he hung on till Monday. As a result, Sir James offered the curate the living of Padiham near Gawthorpe, with a fine church and new parsonage. Having given his promise to Mr. Brontë, Nicholls of course declined, but recommended Sowden in his stead. Sowden, with a fixed income of only £80 a year, was immediately interested, and walked over to Haworth from Oxenhope "on a wild rainy day" to talk it over. But Sir James was a patron of literary celebrities, not the friends of husbands of literary celebrities. The living fell through and with it Charlotte's hopes for Ellen and the curate.

Ellen's inquiries after Sowden in letters to Charlotte proved he was not a matter of indifference to her; it was an autumn of disappointment.

And shock, for, opening a letter from Charlotte in October, she found herself confronted with instructions to burn it.

> Arthur has just been glancing over this note. He thinks I have writ-ten too freely about Amelia, &c. Men don't seem to understand making letters a vehicle of communication, they always seem to think us in-cautious. I'm sure I don't think I have said anything rash; however, you must BURN it when read. Arthur says such letters as mine never ought to be kept, they are dangerous as lucifer matches, so be sure to follow a recommendation he has just given, "fire them" or "there will be no more," such is his resolve. I can't help laughing, this seems to me so funny. Arthur, however, says he is quite "serious" and looks it, I assure you; he is bent over the desk with his eyes full of concern. I am now desired "to have done with it," so with his kind regards and mine, good-bye, dear Ellen.[26]

However lightly Charlotte took Nicholls' orders, he persisted in his demand.

> Dear Ellen,—Arthur complains that you do not distinctly promise to burn my letters as you receive them. He says you must give him a plain pledge to that effect, or he will read every line I write and elect himself censor of our correspondence. He says women are most rash in letter-writing, they think only of the trustworthiness of their im-mediate friend, and do not look to contingencies; a letter may fall into any hand. You must give the promise, I believe, at least he says so, with his best regards, or else you will get such notes as he writes to Mr Sowden, plain, brief statements of facts without the adornment of a single flourish, with no comment on the character or peculiari-ties of any human being, and if a phrase of sensibility or affection steals in, it seems to come on tiptoe, looking ashamed of itself, blushing "pea-green" as he says, and holding both its shy hands before its face. Write him a promise on a separate slip of paper, in a legible hand, and send it in your next.[27]

Ellen did not write out a promise, and Nicholls, coming in and catch-ing his wife writing to Brookroyd in the same confidential strain, again insisted. This time Charlotte stipulated terms: if Ellen would burn her letters, might they write anything they pleased without his censorship? They might. So Ellen sent the following guarantee:

> To the Revd. The Magister: My Dear Mr Nicholls,—As you seem to hold in great horror the ardentia verba of feminine epistles, I pledge myself to the destruction of Charlotte's epistles, henceforth, if you pledge yourself to *no* authorship in the matter communicated.— Yours very truly,
>
> E. Nussey.

But since Nicholls continued to peer over his wife's shoulder and complain about her confidences, Ellen considered the pledge void. She did not burn Charlotte's letters, and Charlotte, when she could escape Nicholls' sharp eye, continued to write much as before.

Charlotte had always cherished her genius. "I am thankful to God who gave me this faculty," she had written to Williams, "and it is for me a part of my religion to defend this gift and profit by its possession." One dark autumn night as she sat with her husband before the fire, Charlotte said, "If you were not with me, I would be writing now," and rising from her chair, went upstairs and came down with ten pages of manuscript written in the finest pencil in her hands. It was the beginning of a new novel, *Emma*.[28] She read it to Nicholls, holding the pages up to her face in her nearsighted way. Because she used all personal and immediate experience, the narrator of this tale was a married woman whose calm, almost Austen-like objectivity seemed to reflect a new tranquillity. But the married woman is not telling her own story, and after a few pages the narrative plunged back into the old restless style, the old theme of alienation and unhappiness. A thin, homely, but well-dressed child is left at a boarding school like Roe Head by a flashy, seemingly wealthy man; presumably she is his daughter. The mercenary headmistress fawns over her; the other pupils resent and avoid her. The child herself seems miserable under the headmistress' attentions, as though haunted by the knowledge that she does not deserve them. When the first quarter's tuition fails to arrive, the child's uneasiness is explained; on inquiry, her "father" has vanished. The headmistress disowns the child, but a protector comes forth, a bluff, eccentric bachelor, who undertakes to discover the unhappy child's past. At that point Charlotte laid down the manuscript, for she had got no further.

"I fear critics will accuse you of repetition," her husband objected. *Villette* had begun with an eccentric and unhappy child whose Papa has left her with friends and gone away, and Jane Eyre, of course, was an unhappy orphan at Lowood institution.

"Oh, I shall change all that," Charlotte replied.

Tantalizing words, for in the event she did not have the chance. If she had lived, would there have been more novels? Would Nicholls have permitted her to write? Since she *was* writing and even reading her work to him, it seems he would, and that even his inadvertent demands on her time and energies still permitted her some hours alone with pen and paper. But Charlotte was an intensely personal writer who would not write a line she had not experienced or felt as truth. She would now turn to the subject of marriage. Free to express herself, she might have given the world one of the frankest, truest pictures of the conflicts and fulfillments of marriage ever written. But would Nicholls have allowed this? He had laughed over her acrimonious portraits of the other curates. Would he laugh at a frank portrait of himself as a husband? Devoted, true, and kind, he was also parochial, rigidly private, capable of deep resentments, jealous. The fact that Charlotte shifted the narrative interest of *Emma* from the married woman to the child so quickly is suggestive, as though she could already foresee her husband's censorship and was rapidly skating away from thin ice.

A further question. Like many Romantic writers, Charlotte's creative impulse was fed by her alienation from society and the ceaseless tensions between her conscious and unconscious mind. Would marriage socialize her? reconcile her? release the torrents churning and foaming behind the dam into a broad, placid stream? Or would marriage generate new and creative tensions to be shaped into art?

She had an artist's own bent to the course—inborn, decided, resistless. Surely nothing could thwart it. Or was her death to be in a sense voluntary—an unconscious solution to an unsolvable conflict—as she felt it—between her art and her marriage?

# 26

*Frost at Midsummer*

One day toward the end of November, Nicholls called his wife from the dining room where she was writing a letter to Ellen to take a walk. "We set off not intending to go far, but though wild and cloudy it was fair in the morning. When we had got about half a mile on the moors, Arthur suggested the idea of the waterfall—after the melted snow he said it would be fine. I had often wanted to see it in its winter power, so we walked on. It was fine indeed—a perfect torrent raving over the rocks white and bountiful. It began to rain while we were watching it, and we returned home under a streaming sky. However I enjoyed the walk inexpressibly, and would not have missed the spectacle on any account."[1]

As a result of this thorough soaking, Charlotte took a cold. This, and the fact that Ellen's sister Mercy was recovering from typhoid fever, prevented a much-longed-for but often postponed visit to Brookroyd, as did the circumstance, not admitted to Ellen, that she was pregnant.

No joyful words survive about this pregnancy that Charlotte had been taught to dread, but the dream that Jane Eyre relates to Rochester on the eve of their wedding conveys some of the terrors it held for her.

> During all my first sleep [Jane tells her prospective bridegroom], I was following the windings of an unknown road; total obscurity environed me; rain pelted me; I was burdened with the charge of a little child: a very small creature, too young and feeble to walk, and which shivered in my cold arms, and wailed piteously in my ear. I thought, sir, that you were on the road a long way before me; and I strained every nerve to overtake you, and made effort on effort to utter your name and entreat you to stop—but my movements were fet-

tered; and my voice still died away inarticulate; while you, I felt, withdrew farther and farther every moment.[2]

Besides the fear of death conveyed in the "total obscurity," the "cold arms," the "fettered movements," and the "voice dying away," there is Jane's terror of being left alone with a burden almost too great to bear. Once free to stride beside Rochester, she is now fettered emotionally and physically by responsibility for the child and can only watch her unburdened husband disappear on the rim of her rapidly shrinking horizon. Significantly, Charlotte had used a similar metaphor to express her frustration as a woman writer, burdened with woman's duties, competing with men: "They are always for walking so fast and taking such long steps," she had complained to Williams, "one cannot keep up with them." Now there would be "the charge of a little child," feeble, small, wailing piteously in her ear, diverting her energies. Yet with her growing affection for her husband, perhaps her gratification was almost as potent as her fears.

On December 7 the visit to Ellen was still unrealized:

> I shall not get leave to go to Brookroyd before Christmas now, so do not expect me. For my own part I really should have no fear, and if it just depended on me, I should come; but these matters are not quite in my power now, another must be consulted, and where his wish and judgment have a decided bias to a particular course, I make no stir, but just adopt it. Arthur is sorry to disappoint both you and me, but it is his fixed wish that a few weeks should be allowed yet to elapse before we meet. Probably he is confirmed in this desire by my having a cold at present. I did not achieve the walk to the waterfall with impunity, though I changed my wet things immediately upon returning home, yet I felt a chill afterwards, and the same night had sore throat and cold; however, I am better now, but not quite well. . . . I am writing this in haste. It is almost inexplicable to me that I seem so often hurried now, but the fact is, whenever Arthur is in, I must have occupations in which he can share, or which will not at least divert my attention from him; thus a multitude of little matters get put off till he goes out, and then I am quite busy. Good-bye, dear Ellen, I hope we shall meet soon.[3]

Prevented from going to Brookroyd where Ellen's tranquillity had always done her good, Charlotte and Nicholls accepted, however, Sir James Kay-Shuttleworth's invitation to Gawthorpe Hall in the first week of January 1855, ostensibly to rediscuss the Padiham living. Sir James had not been impressed with Sutcliffe Sowden, he was determined to oblige Nicholls, he pressed Nicholls again to accept the living, and Nicholls again refused. There was another motive for the in-

vitation, however: the one-tenth artist Charlotte had found in Sir
James's soul surfaced on this occasion: coincidentally he produced a
novel he was writing, read it to the captive Currer Bell, and strongly
hinted that she could do him a good turn by mentioning the manuscript to Smith, Elder. Perhaps to escape these attentions Charlotte
went out for walks in her thin shoes in the icy January rain. By the
time she reached home she was very ill.

Writing to Ellen, January 19, she strongly hinted that her illness was
connected less with a cold than with pregnancy, however:

> I very much wish to come to Brookroyd—and I hope to be able to
> write with certainty and fix Wednesday the 31st Jany as the day—
> but the fact is I am not sure whether I shall be well enough to leave
> home. At present I should be a most tedious visitor. My health has
> been really very good ever since my return from Ireland till about
> ten days ago, when the stomach seemed quite suddenly to lose its tone
> —indigestion and continual faint sickness have been my portion ever
> since. Don't conjecture—dear Nell—for it is too soon yet though I cer-
> tainly never before felt as I have done lately. But keep the matter
> wholly to yourself—for I can come to no decided opinion at present.
> I am rather mortified to lose my good looks and grow thin as I am do-
> ing—just when I thought of going to Brookroyd. . . . Dear Ellen I
> want to see you and I hope I shall see you well.[4]

Nausea, like nothing she had ever experienced before, tortured her.
Weakness drove her to her chair before the fire or to the sofa. Resolved to bear up quietly, she did not complain, and would not see a
doctor, until on his own initiative Nicholls called in Dr. MacTurk
from Bradford, not content to rely upon a Haworth opinion. MacTurk
came on the thirtieth of January, examined the frail, tormented body,
told Nicholls that the illness would be "of some duration," but that it
was not dangerous since it was due to natural causes. Hardly comforted, she took to her bed. Food nauseated her. She began to vomit
constantly. Soon she could not look at the little bowls of broth and tea
that Martha carried upstairs and tried to persuade her to drink. Her
brown hair lay in lank loops on the pillow; her hands on the coverlet
shrank to tiny claws. Think of the baby, Martha would say, trying to
cheer her, but she would toss her head restlessly. "I dare say I shall
be glad someday," she whispered, "but I am so ill—so weary—"

Then Tabby, cherished Tabby, fell ill, and on February 13, Charlotte roused herself to scrawl a note to Dr. Ingham in the village requesting that he send medicine for the old servant. The next day she
was too weak to answer Ellen's anxious note from Brookroyd.

> Dear Miss Nussey [Nicholls wrote in her stead],—It is difficult to
> write to friends about my wife's illness, as its cause is yet uncertain—

at present she is completely prostrated with weakness and sickness and frequent fever—all may turn out well in the end, and I hope it will; if you saw her you would perceive that she can maintain no correspondence at present. She thinks of you . . . and longed much to hear from you.[5]

A few days later Charlotte managed to write Amelia Taylor to comfort her in Joe's severe illness and to seek some aid in her own behalf:

Dear Amelia,—Let me speak the plain truth—my sufferings are very great—my nights indescribable—sickness with scarce a reprieve—I strain until what I vomit is mixed with blood. Medicine I have quite discontinued. If you can send me anything that will do good—*do*. As to my husband—my heart is knit to him—he is so tender, so good, helpful, patient.[6]

On February 17, Tabitha Ackroyd died. She was eighty-four and too old and tired now to serve the master's daughter in her greatest crisis. On the same day Charlotte made her will: "In case I die without issue I give and bequeath my husband all my property to him absolutely and entirely, but, In case I leave issue I bequeath to my husband the interest of my property during his lifetime, and at his death I desire that the principal should go to my surviving child or children; should there be more than one child, share and share alike. . . ."[7]

On the twenty-first she penciled a feeble scrawl to Ellen:

. . . I want to give you an assurance which I know will comfort you— and that is that I find my husband the tenderest nurse, the kindest support—the best earthly comfort that ever woman had. His patience never fails, and it is tried by sad days and broken nights. . . . Papa, thank God! is better. Our poor old Tabby is *dead* and *buried*. Give my truest love to Miss Wooler. May God comfort and help you.

C. B. Nicholls.[8]

Had she been able to raise herself from her pillow that day, she would have seen her husband in cassock and surplice lead a little band of mourners from the church to the foot of the low parsonage wall just below her bedroom window, and there perform the last rites as Tabby's coffin was lowered into its grave.

In early March the nausea receded, she rallied, and craved food and ate eagerly. But this recovery was as false as a warm day in January. The spring equinox came on. One day she heard the wind suddenly veer to the northeast where, gathering force, it thundered "strong and horizontal" across the bare moors to sweep screaming and wailing around the unsheltered stone house. The winds of the spring and fall equinox had always tormented her with strange mental and physical distress. Her condition changed now. A "low, wandering delirium came on"; she begged incoherently for food and stimulants, but she was too exhausted to swallow, and fell back on her pillow, away from life. Did memories flicker through her half-consciousness? A child's fingers numb with cold, Branwell's flaming hair, schoolrooms, church bells, Anne's downcast eyes, Emily's weight against her shoulder as they paced a foreign garden, the fragrance of a cigar, pens scratching in a quiet room, Papa's bandaged eyes, Ellen's face by firelight, London postmarks, "Currer Bell" in gilt letters, a warm London night, a clergyman weeping by the gate. Love, hate, pain, triumph—and now peace. Waking suddenly from stupor, she saw her husband at her side, his face worn with grief, and heard murmured words of prayer. "Oh," she whispered faintly, "I am not going to die, am I? He will not separate us, we have been so happy." Early on Saturday night, March 31, 1855, she ceased to breathe.

The coffin maker came, measured, and went away to fashion a resting place for a tiny figure, four feet nine inches tall. Dr. Dugdale, just beginning his long career as the Haworth obstetrician, recorded "Phthisis" as the immediate cause and did not mention pregnancy. A more modern diagnosis of Charlotte's mortal illness is "hyperemesis gravidarum"—severe, pernicious morning sickness in pregnancy. This disorder only seems to become excessive in neurotic or "high-strung" women with serious personal or family worries, say the doctors, "and they require firm kind treatment to get them better." Some doctors believe that hyperemesis gravidarum is caused by the mother's unconscious rejection of the baby.[9]

"Our dear Charlotte is no more," Arthur Nicholls wrote Ellen. "She died last night of exhaustion. For the last two or three weeks we had become very uneasy about her, but it was not until Sunday evening that it became apparent that her sojourn with us was likely to be short. We intend to bury her on Wednesday morning.—"[10]

"I always told you, Martha," said Mr. Brontë to the servant, "that there was no sense in Charlotte marrying at all, for she was not strong enough for marriage." With Nicholls the old man grimly held his peace.

. . .

Having heard nothing from Haworth for many months, Mrs. Gaskell was shocked at the news sent by John Greenwood, Charlotte's closest friend in the village. "I cannot tell you how VERY sad your note has made me," she wrote back April 4. "My dear friend that I shall never see again on earth! I did not even know she was ill. . . . strangers might know her by her great fame, but we loved her dearly for her goodness, truth, and kindness & those lovely qualities she carried with her where she is gone. . . . I loved her dearly, more than I think she knew. I shall never cease to be thankful that I knew her: or to mourn her loss."[11]

Dead, Charlotte exercised a strange and potent influence over Elizabeth Gaskell. She regretted that John Greenwood had not dared to write her of Charlotte's illness for fear of meddling. She became confident that she could have saved Charlotte's life had she come to Haworth "even though they had all felt angry with me at first"; confident that her positive spirit could have counteracted Charlotte's fatalistic view of marriage, illness, and childbirth.[12] She became obsessed to learn every detail about her unusual friend, intending to write it down so that "the time may come when her wild sad life, and the beautiful character that grew out of it may be made public."

It was almost like a mystic call, then, when Mr. Brontë, urged on by Ellen Nussey, contacted her in June 1855, against Nicholls' wishes, to write the story of his daughter's life. The old man was more than ever jealous for his daughter's fame. She took the train from Manchester to Keighley, a conveyance from Keighley to Haworth, and stepped across the threshold into a house now quiet with the sense of final loss. Her interview with the two men during which both Mr. Brontë and Mr. Nicholls broke down and "cried sadly," her acceptance of the task—"No quailing, Mrs. Gaskell," Mr. Brontë admonished her as she prepared to leave; "no drawing back!"—*The Life of Charlotte Brontë* she wrote and Smith, Elder published in 1857 is literary history.

Harriet Martineau had one more brush with the parsonage which confirmed her already dark opinion of its male occupants. She wrote asking for particular letters of hers to be returned, was ignored, and wrote again threatening legal action. Her letters were speedily returned and Harriet considered that she had roundly beaten the uncooperative Mr. Brontë and Mr. Nicholls. "I fancy these gentlemen (who are *not* gentlemen, however) have never before been opposed or called to account," she wrote a friend. "In their own parish they reign by fears: and I hope it may be good for them to find they can get wrong." Age had not softened Harriet Martineau's tongue or opinions. "Poor C.B. was lost upon them," she concluded flatly.

Mary Taylor's shop in New Zealand throve but, never quite adjusting to the cultural barrenness of that new land, she returned to settle in Yorkshire in 1860 when she was forty-six. Fitting into polite Yorkshire society like a square peg, she isolated herself in her own newly built house, High Royd, in Gomersal, dropping almost all her old friends, including Ellen Nussey. There she wrote, publishing essays and finally her novel *Miss Miles*, which preached the doctrine she clung to till her death: "a woman who works is by that alone better than one who does not." Legends grew up about the strange, emancipated woman returned from New Zealand: did she really keep a loaded pistol at her side ready to blast off at any sign of danger? Whatever peculiarities assigned her by the neighborhood, her chief oddity lay in the fact that she fought conventional opinion courageously all her life.

Ellen Nussey lived on quietly among her teacups and lace collars and dark-clad clerics, never marrying, defending Charlotte's memory till the end of her days. She possessed some five hundred of Currer Bell's letters, a distinction that made her almost a public figure; and she co-operated with Mrs. Gaskell and the scholars who eventually came to her door, only destroying the angriest and most interesting of Charlotte's communications. She could not understand Mary Taylor, who refused to feed public curiosity by burning all of Charlotte's letters but one: "Mary Taylor the 'Rose York' in *Shirley* is living," she replied to T. J. Wise's query in 1892, "but has always proved herself *dead* to any approach on the Brontë subject, and it is understood that she long ago destroyed her letters. She is so peculiar that she might prove otherwise than helpful."[13] Ellen lived until 1897, giving interviews, writing reminiscences, staunchly loyal to Charlotte and the friendship that had been her life's one great event.

Mr. Brontë lived on six years after his daughter, proud of her memory, secretly snipping her letters into little scraps to satisfy autograph collectors—for Nicholls guarded his wife's memory jealously, once causing the old memorial tablet to Charlotte to be broken up and buried so that souvenir collectors could not lay hands on it. The old man still went down to the church to preach an occasional sermon extempore in his strong voice almost to the day of his death, although his step when he approached the pulpit was very slow.

Arthur Nicholls fulfilled his promise to Charlotte, staying on at the parsonage and taking church duty until his father-in-law's death in June 1861. "Aye," John Brown the sexton told Mrs. Gaskell darkly on one of her pilgrimages to Haworth, "aye, Mester Brontë and Mester Nicholls live together still *ever near* but *ever separate*." But no villager had ever quite guessed what passed in that silent, tormented house. Perhaps peace reigned between the two adversaries at last. Mr. Brontë's will, after allotting certain sums to his brother and sisters, and thirty pounds to Martha Brown "for long and faithful services," bequeathed the residue of his estate to "my beloved and esteemed son-in-law, the Rev. Arthur Bell Nicholls, B.A."

On Mr. Brontë's death, Nicholls expected to inherit the incumbency of Haworth, but one vote defeated him. He returned to Ireland where he married his dark-eyed cousin Mary Anne and prospered the rest of his long life.

· · ·

So few voices, so many echoes. A wonderfully urgent voice was silenced. "Currer Bell is dead!" exclaimed Harriet Martineau, and everywhere there was shock that such original, potent energy could be stilled.

It is a commonplace to observe that as a novelist Charlotte Brontë does not belong to the tradition of the social novel with its wide scope, objectivity, and often corrective purpose—the novel as Fielding, Scott, Thackeray, George Eliot, and Henry James wrote it. Her physical isolation in Yorkshire and her intellectual, moral, and economic alienation from the middle-class society she knew—the Sidgwicks, Smiths, and Robinsons, for example, or even the Taylors and the Nusseys—prevented her from observing society on a large scale and from identifying with what she did observe. Intelligent, proud, passionate, innately gifted, she found all these great assets balked rather than encouraged by society. As a result she was driven to write about the outsider in revolt against her destiny: she is a novelist of alienation. Isolated by poverty, lack of beauty, depth of feeling, and merit, characters like Jane Eyre, Louis Moore, Crimsworth, and Lucy Snowe look upon the secure but shallow world of the middle classes and for the most part dislike its occupants heartily.

As a subjective novelist whose chief business is to convince the reader of one individual's capacity for love, hate, suffering, pride, self-discipline, and triumph, she is hardly equaled, if indeed she is equaled, by any other English writer. Had she lived to write one or two more novels like *Jane Eyre* and *Villette*, she must have occupied a separate but equal niche across from Thackeray and George Eliot, for it is because of her slender output, not the quality of her work, that she suffers in comparison with the prolific Victorians. *Villette* promised much. In objectivity—the ability of Lucy Snowe to laugh wryly at her own faults and hopes, for example—in the more subtle observation and analysis of character, particularly in its psychological truth, the novel is considerably more mature and realistic than its more glamorous predecessor, *Jane Eyre*.

If Charlotte Brontë's isolation from society and the literature that depicted it was thus a liability since it excluded her from "the main stream" of British fiction, it was also an asset, for she escapes many of the faults of the Great Victorians. She is not sentimental. She does not shamelessly finagle the windings of the plot to keep serial readers amused. She does not create white heroines and black villains to avoid confusing popular notions of morality. She is quite innocent of conventional manners so that her characters behave with refreshing originality. She did not know that a writer was supposed to sublimate and objectify his experience, so she filled her novels with the tensions of her own ambivalent desires. She was too naïve to know when she was being "coarse" and as a result avoided both prudery and unreality. She did not know that a prose writer was supposed to stick to prose, so her fiction is colored by the language, rhythms, themes, and emotion of poetry.

Most significantly, she fully understood but did not often agree with conventional notions of womanhood. Women feel just as men feel, she had the audacity to say. Women need the same scope for their talents and energies as men need. It is cruel to deprive them of it, or to laugh at their efforts to improve their lot. Her life was a frustrating yet productive struggle between living dutifully and yet, as a woman of genius, unconventionally. The tensions generated by this struggle electrify her fiction. They also give her novels their realism, because for most intelligent and talented Victorian women life could not be other than a battle between conformity and rebellion. This is why Charlotte Brontë's novels still speak to us so persuasively of what it was to suffer and triumph as a Victorian woman and—since the issue of women's equality has still not been resolved—as a woman today.

# Acknowledgments

Among the recent works of Brontë scholarship I consulted, I would like to acknowledge particular debt to Winifred Gérin's *Charlotte Brontë: the Evolution of Genius*, Margaret Lane's *The Brontë Story*, Inga-Stina Ewbank's *Their Proper Sphere*, Charles Burkhart's *Charlotte Brontë: A Psychosexual Study of Her Novels*, and Joan Stevens' *Mary Taylor: Friend of Charlotte Brontë*. I would also like to express my thanks to Karl Kroeber, Columbia University, for help and encouragement with Brontë studies over the years; to Amy G. Foster, archivist of the Brontë Society, Haworth, for her prompt, informative replies to my many queries; to Ruth Abbott Schauer, English Department, University of Wisconsin-Whitewater, for her acute criticism of portions of the manuscript; to the Rev. Paul Hoornstra, Rector of Grace Church, Madison, Wisconsin, for his lively and learned explanations of some of the intricacies of Anglicanism; to Robin Bernacchi, the University Library, Whitewater, for help in securing hard-to-find materials; to Donna Lewis, English Department secretary, for hours of typing and duplicating; to Elsie Merkel McCullough and Barbara Dutrey Malin, for invaluable help in proofreading; and to my husband Arthur L. Peters, for his generous encouragement and unfailing wisdom.

# Notes

The Shakespeare Head Brontë edited by T. J. Wise and J. A. Symington, 19 vols. (Oxford: 1931–38), is generally considered the standard text for the letters and novels of the Brontës. The Brontë letters are collected in the first four volumes of the *Shakespeare Head* under the title *The Brontës: Their Lives, Friendships, and Correspondence*, and I have used this edition of Charlotte's letters, occasionally supplementing from Clement Shorter's *The Brontës: Life and Letters*, 2 vols. (New York: Scribner's, 1908; reprinted New York: Haskell House Publishers, 1969). A definitive edition of the Brontë novels is in preparation and the first volume of the Clarendon Edition edited by Ian and Jane Jack has appeared: *Jane Eyre*, edited by Jane Jack and Margaret Smith (Oxford: 1969). For this biography, however, I have used texts of Charlotte's novels more readily available to most readers:

*The Professor*. London: J. M. Dent & Sons, 1965.

*Jane Eyre*. Edited by Mark Schorer. Boston: Houghton Mifflin (Riverside Editions), 1959.

*Shirley*. London: J. M. Dent & Sons, 1965.

*Villette*. Edited by Geoffrey Tillotson and Donald Hawes. Boston: Houghton Mifflin (Riverside Editions), 1971.

The following abbreviations stand for texts frequently cited in the notes:

*Autobiography:* Harriet Martineau. *Autobiography.* 3 vols.

*BST: The Brontë Society Transactions.* Vol. 1 (1895) to Vol. 16 (1973).

*Letters: The Letters of Mrs. Gaskell*, edited by J. A. V. Chapple and Arthur Pollard.

*Life:* Elizabeth Gaskell. *The Life of Charlotte Brontë.*

*Memoir:* Sidney Lee. *George Smith: A Memoir*, with "Some Pages of Autobiography" by George Murray Smith.

*Miscellaneous: The Miscellaneous and Unpublished Writings of Charlotte and Patrick Branwell Brontë*, edited by T. J. Wise and J. A. Symington. 2 vols.

*Poems: The Poems of Charlotte and Patrick Branwell Brontë*, edited by T. J. Wise and J. A. Symington.

Shorter: Clement Shorter. *The Brontës: Life and Letters.* 2 vols.

Stevens: *Mary Taylor: Friend of Charlotte Brontë,* letters edited with narrative by Joan Stevens.

W & S: *The Brontës: Their Lives, Friendships, and Correspondence,* edited by T. J. Wise and J. A. Symington. 4 vols.

CHAPTER 1

1. Patrick Brontë was born on St. Patrick's Day, 1777, in the parish of Drumballyroney, County Down, Ireland, one of ten children of Hugh Brunty, Protestant and farmer, and Eleanor M'Clory, converted Roman Catholic. An ambitious young man, Brontë became a schoolteacher, first at a Presbyterian, then at an Episcopalian school. Finally, encouraged by his vicar, Mr. Tighe, he left Ireland at the age of twenty-five with £7 in his pocket, the only Brunty child to do so. He entered St. John's College, Cambridge, took Anglican orders in 1806, and accepted a curacy at Wethersfield in Essex. Before coming to Haworth, he held curacies in Wellington, Shropshire, and Dewsbury, Hartshead, and Thornton, Yorkshire. During this time his name is variously recorded as Brunty, Branty, Bruntee, Bronte, Bronty, Bronté, and finally Brontë. On December 29, 1812, he married Maria Branwell of Penzance, Cornwall, one of eleven children of Thomas Branwell, town councilman, recently deceased. Daughters Maria and Elizabeth were born in 1813 and 1815 at Hartshead. The other four children were born at Thornton: Charlotte, April 21, 1816; Patrick Branwell, June 26, 1817; Emily Jane, July 30, 1818; Anne, January 17, 1820.

2. Maria Branwell to the Rev. Patrick Brontë, A.B., Hartshead; Woodhouse Grove, October 21, 1812. W & S 8, I, 18–20.

3. Maria Branwell to the Rev. Patrick Brontë, A.B., Hartshead; Woodhouse Grove, October 3rd, 1812. W & S 7, I, 17–18.

4. *Jane Eyre,* 260.

5. CB to Ellen Nussey, February 16th, 1850. W & S 527 (418), III, 77–79.

6. Patrick Brontë to the Rev. John Buckworth. [Haworth] near K[eighley], Yorkshire, November 27th, 1821. W & S 11, I, 58–60.

7. Patrick Brontë to Miss Burder, Finchingfield Park, Near Braintree. Haworth, Keighley, July 28th, 1823. W & S 14, I, 62–64.

8. Mary Burder to the Rev. Patrick Brontë, Haworth, Near Keighley. Finchingfield Park, August 8th, 1823. W & S 14, I, 64–66.

9. *Life,* 35–36.

10. [Prospectus B] School for Clergymen's Daughters, reprinted in *BST,* 12, Pt. 63.

11. Register, Clergy Daughters' School, Cowan Bridge, 1824, printed in Ernest Raymond, *In the Steps of the Brontës* (London: Rich and Cowan, 1948).

12. *Jane Eyre,* 44–45, 51, 58–59.

13. *Life,* 45.

14. *Jane Eyre,* 56.

15. *The Children's Friend*, Kirkby Lonsdale, 1826. Printed in Winifred Gérin, *Charlotte Brontë: The Evolution of Genius* (London: Oxford University Press, 1967), 13–14. Here and throughout this book I have taken the liberty of paragraphing dialogue not paragraphed in the original text.

16. *Jane Eyre*, 74–75.

17. Ibid., 75.

18. PBB, "Caroline," *Poems*, 318–28.

19. [Prospectus A] Cowan Bridge College, printed in *BST*, 11, Pt. 56.

20. CB to WSW, November 5th, 1849. W & S 488 (388), III, 33–34.

CHAPTER 2

1. Ellen Nussey's reminiscences of Charlotte's early life at Haworth, W & S, I, 110–16.

2. CB, "History of the Year," *Miscellaneous*, I, 78–79.

3. June the 31st, 1829, *Life*, 53–54.

4. PB, "The History of the Young Men," *Miscellaneous*, I, 78–79.

5. *Life*, 56–57.

6. Mary Taylor's narrative, written from New Zealand, January 18, 1856, W & S, I, 89–92.

7. Ellen Nussey's narrative originally published as "Reminiscences of Charlotte Brontë" by "E." in *Scribner's Magazine*, Vol. 2 (1871); reprinted in W & S, I, 92–100.

8. Ibid., 97.

9. Mary Taylor's narrative, W & S, I, 91.

10. *Villette*, 137.

11. Mary Taylor's narrative, W & S, I, 90.

12. Ellen Nussey's narrative, W & S, I, 96.

13. Ibid., 96.

14. CB to PBB, Roe Head, May 17th, 1831, W & S 19 (3), I, 87–88. Mr. Brontë defended his support of the Reform Bill to Elizabeth Firth Franks in a letter of April 28, 1831: "I am in all respects *now* what I *was* when I lived in Thornton—in regard to all political considerations." Evidently old Thornton friends had heard rumors of his turning progressive. The letter is reprinted in John Lock and W. T. Dixon, *A Man of Sorrow* (London: Thomas Nelson, 1965), 286–87.

15. Charlotte re-created the Taylor family and the Red House as the Yorkes and Briarmains in her second published novel, *Shirley*. "I have not seen the matted hall and painted parlour windows so plain these 5 years," Mary Taylor wrote from New Zealand, August 13, 1850. "But my Father is not like. He hates well enough and perhaps loves too but he is not honest enough. It was from my father I learnt not to marry for money nor to tolerate any one who did . . ."

16. CB to WSW, Jany 3rd, 1850. W & S 412 (405), III, 63–64.

17. But Charlotte did not forget Mary's opinion of her looks. Mary Dixon, a cousin of Mary Taylor's, offered to do her portrait and send it to

Mary Taylor as a gift; Charlotte vetoed the suggestion: "You are mistaken however in your benevolent idea that my portrait will yield pleasure to Mary Taylor—do not give it to her, or if you do—do not expect thanks in return—she likes me well enough—but my face she can dispense with—and would tell you so in her own sincere and truthful language if you asked her." Letter undated, but probably written between January 30 and June 1843. Reprinted in part in Stevens, 42; full letter reprinted but with several errors of transcription in Winifred Gérin, *Charlotte Brontë: The Evolution of Genius* (London: Oxford University Press, 1967), 219.

18. Ellen Nussey's narrative, W & S, I, 100.

## CHAPTER 3

1. Edward Baines, *History, Directory and Gazetteer of the County of York*, 2 vols., printed and published by Edward Baines at the *Leeds Mercury* Office: 1822. Reprinted as *Baines' Yorkshire* (New York: Augustus M. Kelley, 1969). "Haworth, in the parish of Bradford, wap. of Morley, and honour of Pontefract; 4 miles S of Keighley. Population, 4668." "Bronte Rev. Patrick, curate," is the first citizen listed by Baines, who gives the clergy and principal tradespeople of each Yorkshire town and village, as well as the local gentlemen (John Belfield is the only one listed for Haworth), carriers, historical landmarks, coach schedules, and mail deliveries.

2. Mrs. Gaskell to ?John Forster [September 1853]. *Letters*, No. 166, 242–47.

3. CB, "Corner Dishes" (May 28–June 16, 1834), in Fannie E. Ratchford, *The Brontës' Web of Childhood* (New York: Russell and Russell, 1964), 93–94.

4. CB, fragmentary journal, in Fannie E. Ratchford and William Clyde DeVane, *Legends of Angria* (New Haven: Yale University Press, 1933), xxviii.

5. CB, "The Green Dwarf" (September 2, 1833), *Legends of Angria*, 41.

6. Writing to T. J. Wise, November 18, 1892, Ellen Nussey claimed she had once had more than 500 letters from Charlotte. This same number is mentioned in a letter from Monsieur Heger to Ellen in 1863. Wise and Symington print about 370 of these; if Ellen's statement is correct, then about 130 are missing. Ellen said that the request for Charlotte's letters for Gaskell's *Life* caused her to destroy a large number immediately, but since 500 are mentioned in 1863, six years after the *Life* appeared, she cannot have destroyed many. Ellen edited Charlotte's letters freely before turning them over to Mrs. Gaskell and later scholars, suppressing some passages, striking out words, and otherwise altering the texts. The dating of the letters in Wise and Symington is also frequently unreliable. For a discussion of the textual problems and missing manuscripts that plague Brontë scholars, see Tom Winnifrith, *The Brontës and Their Background* (London: The Macmillan Press, Ltd., 1973), Chapters 1 and 2.

7. CB to EN. Haworth, March 13, 1835. W & S 35 (17), I, 126–27.

8. CB to EN. [Roe Head, 1836]. W & S 52 (24), I, 146.

9. CB to EN. Haworth, July 4th, —34. W & S 32 (14), I, 121–22.

10. For a discussion of early Victorian prudery and its causes, see Maurice J. Quinlan, *Victorian Prelude* (Hamden, Conn.: Archon Books, 1965).

11. CB to EN. Haworth, July 21st, 1832. W & S 23 (5), I, 103–4.

12. CB to EN. Haworth, September 5th, 1832. W & S 24 (6), I, 104–5.

13. Ellen Nussey's narrative, W & S, I, 110–16.

14. CB, "Angria and My Angrians," *Miscellaneous*, II, 11–12.

15. Ellen Nussey's narrative.

16. Mrs. Gaskell to George Smith. Plymouth Grove, Friday [? July 25, 1856]. *Letters*, No. 297, 398–99. "Mr. Gaskell says they would make more than 50 vols of print," Mrs. Gaskell adds. She read through the tiny manuscripts as hastily as the fine printing allowed and did not use many of them in her *Life:* they were too strange.

17. CB to EN. July 2nd, —35. W & S 38 (19), I, 129–30.

CHAPTER 4

1. "Memoir of Ellis Bell," prefixing 1850 edition of her poems.

2. Mary Taylor to Mrs. Gaskell. W & S, I, 136–37.

3. CB, fragmentary journal, in *Legends of Angria*, xxx–xxxi.

4. CB, "Zamorna's Exile" (January 9, 1837), in *Legends of Angria*, 133–47.

5. CB to EN. Roe Head, May 10th, —36. W & S 44 (20), I, 139–40.

6. CB to EN. Roe Head, [1836]. W & S 45 (21), I, 139–40.

7. CB to EN. Roe Head, [1836]. W & S 46 (22), I, 141.

8. CB to EN. [Roe Head] Sep^br. 26th, —36. W & S 52 (24), I, 146.

9. CB, autobiographical fragment, in *Miscellaneous*, II, 255–56.

10. PBB, "Charles Wentworth's Visit to Verdopolis," *The History of Angria*, V (May 1836), in *Miscellaneous*, II, 182–85.

11. PBB to the editor of *Blackwood's Magazine*. Haworth near Bradford, Yorks, December [7], 1835. W & S 41 (32), I, 133–34.

12. PBB to the editor of *Blackwood's Magazine*. Haworth, near Bradford, Yorks, April 8th, 1836. W & S 42 (33), I, 135.

13. PBB to the editor of *Blackwood's Magazine*. 9th January 1837. W & S 56 (34), I, 150–51.

14. PBB to William Wordsworth. Haworth, near Bradford, Yorkshire, January 19th, 1837. W & S 57 (35), I, 151–52.

15. Robert Southey to CB. Keswick, March 1837. W & S 59 (28), I, 154–56.

16. CB to Robert Southey. Roe Head, March 16th, 1837. W & S 60 (29), I, 157–58.

17. Robert Southey to Caroline Bowles. W & S, I, 156–57.

CHAPTER 5

1. CB to EN. [Roe Head, December 14, 1836?]. W & S 54 (39), I, 148–49.

2. CB to EN, Batheaston, Bath. Dewsbury Moor, August 24th [1837]. W & S 64 (42), I, 161–62.

3. CB to EN. Roe Head [1836]. W & S 46 (22), I, 141.

4. CB to EN, Brookryod [sic]. Roe Head [December 6, 1836]. W & S 53 (40 and 27), I, 147–48.

5. CB to EN. [Roe Head, 1836]. W & S 48 (41), I, 142–43.

6. CB to EN. [January 4, 1838]. W & S 66 (44), I, 163–64.

7. CB to EN. Haworth, June 9th, 1838. W & S 68 (46), I, 166–67.

8. CB to the Rev. Henry Nussey. Haworth, March 5th, 1839. W & S 72 (48), I, 172–73.

9. CB to EN. Haworth, March 12th, 1839. W & S 73 (49), I, 173–75.

10. CB to EN. Haworth, April 15th, 1839. W & S 74 (50), I, 175–76; W & S 73 (49), I, 174. The housemaid, however, was the hardest worked and lowest paid of any employed Victorian female.

11. AB, *Agnes Grey* (Oxford: The Shakespeare Head Press, 1931).

12. CB to EN. W & S 74 (50), I, 175.

13. CB, "Captain Henry Hastings," *Five Novelettes*, transcribed and edited by Winifred Gérin (London: The Folio Press, 1971), 178–270.

14. CB to EJB. Stonegappe, June 8th, 1839. W & S 75 (51), I, 178–79.

15. CB to EN. [Swarcliffe, June 30, 1839]. W & S 76 (52), I, 180–81.

16. CB to EJB. July –, 1839. W & S 77 (53), I, 181.

17. CB to EJB. W & S 75 (51), I, 179.

CHAPTER 6

1. CB to EN. Decr. 21st, –39. W & S 85 (60), I, 193–94.

2. CB to EN. Aug. 4, –39. W & S 79 (55), I, 183–85. Mr. Bryce—"a strong, athletic-looking man"—died suddenly less than six months later of a ruptured blood vessel.

3. CB to EN. W & S 78 (54), 79 (55), 80 (56), 81 (57), I, 182–86.

4. CB to the Rev. Henry Nussey. Haworth, October 28th, 1839. W & S 84 (59), I, 191–93.

5. Ibid., 193.

6. CB to EN. Ap. 7, –40. W & S 92 (64), I, 202–3.

7. Ibid., 203.

8. Ibid., 203.

9. CB to EN. September 29th, 1840. W & S 104 (76), I, 215–18.

10. CB to EN. [July 14, 1840]. W & S 101 (73), I, 212–13.

11. CB to EN. W & S 104 (76), I, 217.

12. Ibid., (72), 217.

13. CB to EN. March 3rd, 1841. W & S 109 (82), I, 225–27.

14. CB to EN. Rawdon, March 21st, 1841. W & S 110 (83), I, 227–28.

15. CB to EN. Nov. 20th, –40. W & S 106 (78), I, 219–22. The closing lines ("Ellen, Helen," etc.) are from the version in Shorter (78), I, 195–98: W & S do not print them.

16. CB to EN. Haworth, June 9th, 1838. W & S 68 (46), I, 166–67.

17. CB to EN. January 3rd, 1841. W & S 107 (79), I, 222–23.

18. CB to the Rev. Henry Nussey, Earnley Rectory, Chichester, Sussex. Jan. 11th, 1841. W & S 108 (81), I, 223–24.

19. CB, "The Last of Angria" in *Miscellaneous*, II, 403–4.

20. CB to William Wordsworth. [1840]. W & S 100 (68), I, 211–12.

21. CB to EN. [December 28, 1839]. W & S 86, I, 194–95.

22. PBB to John Brown. March 13, 1840. W & S 90 (65), I, 198–200.

23. This is the most frequently repeated version of what occurred in Lancashire. Very little factual evidence exists about Branwell's reasons for returning home.

CHAPTER 7

1. CB to EN. September 29th, 1840. W & S 104 (76), I, 215–18.

2. "I thought you would wonder how we were getting on when you heard of the Railway Panic," Charlotte wrote Miss Wooler, January 30, 1846, "and you may be sure I am very glad to be able to answer your kind inquiries by an assurance that our small capital is as yet undiminished. The 'York and Midland' is, as you say, a very good line, yet . . . I cannot think that even the very best lines will continue for many years at their present premiums, and I have been most anxious for us to sell our shares. . . ." But Emily would not yield: "therefore, I will let her manage still, and take the consequences. Disinterested and energetic she certainly is, and if she be not quite so tractable or open to conviction as I could wish, I must remember perfection is not the lot of humanity." Shorter, No. 174, I, 314–15.

3. CB to EN. March 3rd. 1841. W & S 109 (82), I, 225–27.

4. Mr. Strickland in the *Westminster Gazette* (May 1901), quoted in Shorter, I, 203.

5. CB to EN. [Upperwood House, April 1, 1841]. W & S 111 (84), I, 228–29.

6. EJB, Diary Paper. W & S I, 238.

7. CB to EN, Earnley Rectory, Chichester, Sussex. Upperwood House, Augst. 7th, –41. W & S 119 (91), I, 240–41.

8. AB, Diary Paper. W & S, I, 239.

9. CB to EN. W & S 119 (91), I, 240–41.

10. CB to Elizabeth Branwell, Haworth. Upperwood House, Rawdon, September 29th, 1841. W & S 121 (92), I, 240–43.

11. CB to EN, Earnley Rectory, Chichester, Sussex. [Rawdon, November 2, 1841]. W & S 123 (94), I, 244–46.

12. CB to EN. [January 20, 1842]. W & S 129 (101), I, 249–50.

CHAPTER 8

1. *Villette*, 41.

2. *The Professor*, 46.

3. In *Villette* Charlotte described the Pensionnat Heger minutely and accurately as Mrs. Gaskell and Clement Shorter, for example, discovered when they visited Brussels in 1856 and 1908. Winifred Gérin gives a de-

tailed history of the buildings and neighborhood in *Charlotte Brontë: The Evolution of Genius.*

4. CB to EN. [Brussels, May 1842]. W & S 131 (103), I, 259–61.

5. *Villette*, 62.

6. CB to EN. [Brussels, July 1842]. W & S 137 (104), I, 266–67.

7. CB to EN. W & S 131 (103), I, 260.

8. Quoted in Mrs. Ellis H. Chadwick, *In the Footsteps of the Brontës* (London: Sir Isaac Pitman and Sons, 1914), 303.

9. A composite letter from Mary and Martha Taylor and Charlotte Brontë to Ellen Nussey. March–April 1842. Stevens, No. 2, 28–32.

10. As we know from *Villette*, Charlotte did attend at least one art exhibit at the Brussels Salon, and two or three concerts, et cetera, either with teachers from the Pensionnat or with the Wheelwrights. But her letters and *Villette* also make it clear that her overwhelming impression of Brussels was of the solitude she suffered there.

11. Mary Taylor to Mrs. Gaskell. New Zealand, January 18, 1856. W & S, I, 215–16.

12. CB to EN. [Brussels, July 1842]. W & S 137 (104), I, 266–67.

13. Mary Taylor to Ellen Nussey. Undated, but annotated, probably by EN, "24 Sep 1842." Stevens, No. 8, 37–38.

14. Patrick Brontë had Weightman's funeral sermon printed afterward in Halifax, price 6d, "the profits, if any, to go in aid of the Sunday School." Text printed in part in *A Man of Sorrow*, 308–10. The profits—if any—are unknown.

15. Martha Taylor to Ellen Nussey. Hunsworth Mills, Friday, August 19, 1842. W & S 141 (105), I, 271.

16. Mrs. Gaskell said Martha died of "low fever"; Charlotte said that she died of the same disease as William Weightman. The circumstances of Martha's death, however, are very obscure: the fact that no doctor signed the certificate, that no cause of death was recorded, that she was buried hastily, for example. It has been suggested that Martha died in childbirth.

17. CB to EN. Haworth, November 10th 1842. W & S 147 (110), I, 282.

18. Charlotte describes the Protestant cemetery minutely in Chapter 19 of *The Professor* and the death of Martha, as Jessy Yorke, in *Shirley*, Chapter 9.

19. Mary Taylor to Ellen Nussey. 11 Rue de la Régence, Brussels, October 30th, 1842. W & S 145 (109), I, 274–75.

20. PBB to Francis H. Grundy. October 25th, 1842, and 29th October 1842. W & S 143 (107) and 144 (108), I, 272–73. The official cause of Elizabeth Branwell's death was "exhaustion from constipation."

CHAPTER 9

1. Extracted from the District Probate Registry at York attached to Her Majesty's High Court of Justice. W & S, I, 277–78.

2. PBB's notebook, in Winifred Gérin, *Branwell Brontë* (London: Thomas Nelson and Sons, 1961), 202.

3. Monsieur Heger au Révérend Monsieur Brontë, Pasteur Évangélique, et cetera. Samedi, 5 Obre. [1842]. Shorter, (112), I, 248–50.

4. CB to EN. Haworth [January 15, 1843]. W & S 151 (117), I, 285.

5. *Villette*, 42–43, and *Life*, 168.

6. *Villette*, 68–69.

7. CB to EN. Brussels, March 6th, 1843. W & S 154 (120), I, 293–94.

8. CB to EN. [Brussels, April 1, 1843]. W & S 155 (121), I, 294–96.

9. CB to PBB. Brussels, May 1st, 1843. W & S 156 (123), I, 296–98.

10. CB to EJB. Brussels, May 29th, 1843. W & S 158 (124), I, 298–300.

11. CB to EN. Brussels, Agust 6th, 1843. W & S 161 (125), I, 301–2.

12. CB to EJB. Bruxelles, September 2nd, 1843. W & S 162 (126), I, 303–4.

13. CB to EJB. Oct. 1, 1843. W & S 163, I, 304–5.

14. *Villette*, 100.

15. CB to EJB. W & S 163, I, 304–5.

16. EJB to EN. [May 22, 1843]. W & S 157, I, 298.

17. CB to EN. Brussels, Octr. 13th, 1843. W & S 165 (127), I, 306–7.

18. CB to EN. Brussels, Nov. 15th, 1843. W & S 166 (128), I, 308–9.

19. CB to EN, Earnley Rectory, Chichester. Haworth, January 23rd, 1844. W & S 169 (131), II, 2–3.

20. Quoted from Gérin's translation of the letter in the Brontë Parsonage Museum, *Charlotte Brontë: The Evolution of Genius*, 253.

21. *Villette*, 404–5.

22. CB to EN. W & S 169 (131), II, 2–3.

## CHAPTER 10

1. CB to EN. W & S 169 (131), II, 2–3.

2. CB to EN. March 25th, 1844. W & S 172 (132), II, 5.

3. CB to EN. [June 23, 1844]. W & S 176 (138), II, 6.

4. CB to EN. [July 16, 1844]. W & S 177 (133), II, 7–8.

5. CB to EN. [July 20, 1844]. W & S 178 (137), II, 8–9; Sept 16th, 1844. W & S 183 (141), II, 16–17.

6. CB to EN. Novb. 14th, –44. W & S 186 (143), II, 19–21.

7. CB to EN. July 29th, 1844. W & S 181 (139), II, 15.

8. CB to EN. [October 2, 1844]. W & S 184 (142), II, 17.

9. CB to EN. Novb. 14th, –44. W & S 186 (143), II, 19–21.

10. Monsieur Heger's letters to Charlotte do not survive. Perhaps there were five of them, since that is the number of Lucy Snowe's "precious letters" in *Villette*. Charlotte probably destroyed them before her marriage. In *Villette*, however, she describes in great detail Lucy wrapping the letters in oiled silk, binding them up with twine, and putting them into a jar which she takes to a druggist to be hermetically sealed. She then buries them at the roots of an old tree. The incident seems so factual that it is tempting to wonder whether it is autobiographical like so much else in the novel.

11. CB to Monsieur Heger. July 24th, 1844. W & S 179, II, 11–14.

12. CB to Monsieur Heger, No. 32 Rue d'Isabelle, Bruxelles. October 24th, 1844. W & S 185, II, 17–19.

13. CB to Monsieur Heger, No. 32 Rue d'Isabelle, Bruxelles, Belgique. Jany. 8th, 1845. W & S 188, II, 21–24.

14. Mary Taylor to Mrs. Gaskell. W & S, II, 26. Stevens comments on Mary's letters to Mrs. Gaskell: "Mrs. Gaskell applied to Mary Taylor for help with her *Life* of Charlotte Brontë, and received, it seems, two letters. The first, dated 18 January 1856, supplied material which was used in the first edition of the *Life*, published in February 1857. The second, to which Mrs. Gaskell referred in her own letter of 3 June 1857 (*Letters*, No. 348) as recently received, provided some details which were incorporated in the third edition. The MS. of these letters has not been located . . ."

15. Mary Taylor to Ellen Nussey. 19 April to 10 May 1856. Stevens, No. 28, 126–29.

16. CB to EN. Feb. 20th, 1845. W & S 190 (148), II, 25–26.

CHAPTER 11

1. CB to EN. March 24th –35 [sic]. W & S 192 (151), II, 27–29.

2. See, for example, John Miller, *Early Victorian New Zealand* (London: Oxford University Press, 1958); Marjorie Appleton, *They Came to New Zealand* (London: Methuen, 1958).

3. CB to EN. April 2nd [1845]. W & S 194 (152), II, 29–31.

4. CB to EN. W & S 192 (151), II, 28.

5. *Villette*, 229.

6. CB to EN. W & S 194 (152), II, 30.

7. CB, "Reason," *Poems*, 239–40.

8. EJB to EN. Haworth, Friday [July 11, 1845]. W & S 205, II, 41.

9. CB to EN. July 31st, '45. W & S 207 (162), II, 42–43.

10. CB to EN. [January 6, 1845]. W & S 187 (147), II, 21.

11. CB to EN. November 4th, 1845. W & S 217 (169), II, 65–66.

12. EJB, Diary Paper, Haworth, Thursday, July 30th, 1845. W & S II, 49–51.

13. AB, Diary Paper, Thursday, July the 31st, 1845. W & S, II, 52–53.

14. CB to EN. Augst. 18th [1845]. W & S 209 (164), II, 57–58.

15. CB to Monsieur Heger. Haworth, Bradford, Yorkshire, November 18th, 1845. W & S II, 69.

16. *Villette*, 271.

17. According to Charlotte's Brussels friend Laetitia Wheelwright, Charlotte stopped writing to Constantin Heger when he suggested that she address her letters to the Athénée Royale because the correspondence disturbed his wife: she refused to stoop to such subterfuge. But Charlotte's letters to Heger make it clear that Monsieur's cold silence finally forced her to give up writing him.

18. *Poems*, untitled, undated, 240–41.

CHAPTER 12

1. PBB to Francis H. Grundy. October 1845. W & S 216 (154), II, 64–65.

2. Quoted from Gérin, *Branwell Brontë*, 240.

3. CB to Miss Wooler. Jany. 30th, '46. W & S 224 (174), II, 76–77.

4. AB, *The Tenant of Wildfell Hall* (Oxford: The Shakespeare Head Press, 1931), 56–57.

5. CB to Messrs Aylott & Jones. Jany. 28th, '46. W & S 227 (177), II, 81.

6. CB, "Biographical Notice of Ellis and Acton Bell," written for the second edition of *Wuthering Heights* and *Agnes Grey*, 1850.

7. Ibid.

8. The Brontës borrowed most of their books from the Keighley Mechanics' Institute, although Mary Taylor lent Charlotte books, many of them French, from the Red House library. For a list of volumes available to the Brontës, see "Where the Brontës Borrowed Books: a catalogue of books available at the Keighley Mechanics' Institute, 1841," *BST*, 11, Pt. 60.

9. CB to Messrs. Aylott & Jones. W & S 228 (178), 229 (179), 231 (180), 232 (181), II, 81–83.

10. CB to Messrs. Aylott & Jones. March 11th, '46. W & S 234 (183), II, 84–85.

11. *Poems*, 29–41.

12. Ibid., 16–20.

13. CB to EN. June 17th, '46. W & S 251 (198), II, 96–97.

14. PBB to J. B. Leyland. [circa June or July 1846]. W & S 253, II, 98–99.

15. CB to Messrs. Aylott & Jones. April 6th, '46. W & S 238 (186), II, 87.

16. CB to Messrs. Aylott & Jones. April 11th, '46. W & S 239 (187), II, 87–88.

17. *The Professor*, 193–96, 199.

18. *Athenaeum* (July 1846), 46.

19. W & S, II, 102.

20. CB, "Biographical Notice of Ellis and Acton Bell."

CHAPTER 13

1. On Manchester as the cradle of the Industrial Revolution and the "new England" see Asa Briggs, *Victorian Cities* (New York: Harper and Row, 1963). Carlyle viewed Manchester with mixed awe and repulsion— "sooty Manchester" built upon "the infinite abyss"; Dickens portrayed it as the red and black inferno of Coketown in *Hard Times;* Mrs. Gaskell, who lived there, looked upon the impoverished working classes with lively curiosity and sympathy.

2. CB to EN. W & S 264 (202), II, 106–7.

3. CB to EN. [September 22, 1846]. W & S 268 (206), II, 110–11.

4. CB, "*La Chute des Feuilles* [The Fall of the Leaves]," dated "*le 30 mars 1843.*" Reprinted with translation in *BST*, Vol. 12, Pt. 65, 376–83.

5. CB to EN. Aug. 9, –46. W & S 263 (201), II, 105–6.

6. CB to EN. Augst. 26 [1846]. W & S 265 (203), II, 107–9.

7. CB to EN. Octr. 14th, '46. W & S 273 (208), II, 114–15.

8. CB to EN. July 10th, '46. W & S 257 (199), II, 100–1.

9. *Jane Eyre*, 105–6.

10. CB to EN. Dec. 13th, '46. W & S 276 (211), II, 117–18.

11. PBB to J. B. Leyland. [January 24, 1847]. W & S 280, II, 123–25.

12. CB to EN. Feb. 14th, –47. W & S 282 (215), II, 126–27; [March 24, 1847] 284 (217), II, 129–30.

13. CB to EN. Haworth, March 1st, '47. W & S 283 (216), II, 128–29.

14. CB to EN. April 21st, '47. W & S 286 (219), II, 131–32.

15. CB to EN. May 14th, 1847. W & S 288 (221), II, 133.

16. CB to EN. May 20th [1847]. W & S 290 (223), II, 134.

17. CB to Messrs Smith, Elder and Co. July 15th, 1847. W & S 287 (232), II, 139.

18. CB to Messrs Smith, Elder and Co. August 24th, 1847. W & S 300 (234), II, 141.

19. George Smith, *Memoir*, 87–88.

20. CB to Messrs Smith, Elder and Co. October 19th, 1847. W & S 311 (237), II, 149.

21. William Makepeace Thackeray to W. S. Williams. Oct. 23rd, 1847. W& S, II, 49.

CHAPTER 14

1. Carol Ohmann discusses how the tone of reviewers changed from admiration to shock and disgust when Ellis Bell was found to be a woman in "Emily Brontë in the Hands of Male Critics," *College English*, 32 (1971), 906–13.

2. Miss Anne Mozley, an anonymous review, *Christian Remembrancer* (June 1848), 32.

3. *The Morning Call, a Table Book of Literature and Art*, 4 vols. (London, 1850–52). Mrs. Ellis' review quoted in *BST*, 72 (1962), 20–22.

4. CB to Messrs Smith, Elder and Co. December 1st, 1847. W & S 323 (247), II, 158.

5. George Henry Lewes (1817–78). When he came into Charlotte's orbit, Lewes was living at 26 Bedford Place, London, with his wife Agnes Jervis Lewes and their four sons. "The perfect pair of love-birds," as Jane Carlyle called them, began to go separate ways after Agnes bore a second child to family friend Thornton Hunt. Lewes had accepted Hunt's and Agnes' first child as his own but, when the offense was repeated a second, third, and fourth time, ceased to regard Agnes as his wife, although by law he could not divorce her. Charlotte evidently knew nothing about Lewes' marriage or his eventual liaison with George Eliot; at least she never publicly referred to the subject.

6. CB to G. H. Lewes. November 6th, 1847. W & S 315 (241), II, 152–53.

7. CB to G. H. Lewes. November 22, 1847. W & S 319 (244), II, 156.

8. William Makepeace Thackeray to W. S. Williams. Oct. 23rd, 1847. W & S II, 149.

9. CB to WSW. December 11th, 1847. W & S 325 (252), II, 159–60.

10. CB to WSW. Haworth, January 28th, 1848. W & S 343 (266), II, 183–84.

11. CB to WSW. February 15, 1848. Shorter, No. 271, I, 395–97.

12. AB to EN. Haworth, January 4th, '48. W & S 337 (261), II, 175.

13. We do not know Branwell's opium dreams, of course, but opium-induced dreams evidently often have these characteristics. See, for example, Aletha Hayter, *Opium and the Romantic Imagination* (Berkeley: The University of California Press, 1968), and Thomas de Quincey's *Confessions of an English Opium Eater* (Middlesex, England: Penguin Books, 1973). I borrowed this dream from De Quincey.

14. CB to WSW. Jany 4th, 1848. W & S 336 (260), II, 173–74.

15. From *The Letters and Journals of Queen Victoria*, edited by G. E. Buckle and A. C. Benson, quoted in *BST*, 11 (1949), 247; and Theodore Martin, *Queen Victoria as I Knew Her* (1908), quoted in Lytton Strachey, *Queen Victoria* (New York: Harcourt, Brace & World, 1949), 287–88.

16. CB to WSW. W & S 343 (266), II, 184.

### CHAPTER 15

1. CB to WSW. April 20th, 1848. W & S 361, II, 203–4.

2. CB to EN. April 28th, '48. W & S 365 (285), II, 207.

3. *Life,* 230.

4. Mary Taylor to CB. June to 24 July 1848. Stevens, No. 16, 73–79.

5. *Jane Eyre,* 240.

6. CB to Mary Taylor. Haworth, September 4th, 1848. W & S 390 (297), II, 250–54. All quoted portions of Charlotte's account of the London visit are from this letter.

7. *Memoir,* 89–91. All quoted portions of Smith's comments on meeting Currer Bell are from these pages.

8. CB to WSW. Haworth, July 31st, 1848. W & S 384 (301), II, 240–43.

### CHAPTER 16

1. CB to EN. July 28th, 1848. W & S 383 (300), II, 239–40.

2. Gérin, *Branwell Brontë,* 280; originally, Searle G. Phillips, "Branwell Brontë," *The Mirror* (December 28, 1872).

3. PBB to John Brown, sexton, Haworth. Sunday, Noon. W & S 377, II, 224.

4. CB to EN. W & S 383 (300), II, 239–40.

5. CB to EN. August 18th, 1848. W & S 387 (303), II, 246–47.

6. Francis Grundy. W & S II, 258–59. W & S ends with "nothing else." The rest is from Gérin, *Branwell Brontë,* 292, quoting from Francis Grundy's *Pictures of the Past* (London: Griffith and Farrar, 1879).

7. CB to WSW. October 2nd, 1848. W & S 394 (306), II, 261–62.

8. CB to WSW. Octb. 6th, 1848. W & S 395 (307), II, 262–63.

9. CB to WSW. W & S 394 (306), II, 261.

10. CB to WSW. October 18th, 1848. W & S 398 (310), II, 266–67.

11. CB to WSW. November 2nd, 1848. W & S 400 (312), II, 268–70.

12. CB to EN. November 23rd, '48. W & S 404, (315), II, 288.

13. CB to EN. [November 27, 1848]. W & S 405 (316), II, 289.

14. CB to WSW. December 7th, 1848. W & S 406 (317), II, 289–91.

15. CB to WSW. December 9th, 1848. W & S 408 (318), II, 291–92.

16. CB to Dr. Epps. December 9th, 1848. W & S II, 292. Charlotte dated this letter the 29th mistakenly.

17. CB to EN. December 10th, 1848. W & S 409 (319), II, 292–93.

18. CB to EN. [December 19, 1848]. W & S 410 (320), II, 293.

19. CB to WSW. December 25th, 1848. W & S 412 (322), II, 294–95.

20. Charlotte also found a scrap of letter in Emily's desk dated February 15, 1848, evidently from a publisher, with the words "shall have great pleasure in making arrangements for your next novel." This would seem to prove conclusively that Emily was writing a second novel, although the fragment might have been addressed to Anne.

21. CB to WSW. November 16th, 1848. W & S 402 (313), II, 271–72.

22. John Gibson Lockhart (1794–1854), Scottish lawyer and literary critic, son-in-law of Sir Walter Scott and his biographer (7 vols., 1837–38), editor of the *Quarterly*, 1825–53. Elizabeth Rigby [Lady Eastlake], "*Vanity Fair*—and *Jane Eyre*," *Quarterly Review* (December 1848), 162–76.

23. CB to WSW. Jany 18th, '49. W & S 416 (326), II, 300–1.

24. AB to EN. April 5th, 1849. W & S 434 (342), II, 320–21.

25. CB to EN. March 29th, '49. W & S 432 (340), II, 318–19.

26. CB to WSW. May 8th, 1849. W & S 440 (349), II, 328–30.

27. Ellen Nussey wrote an account for Mrs. Gaskell in 1855 of Anne's last days from notes made at the time. *Life*, 271–72.

28. CB to WSW. No. 2 Cliff, Scarbro, May 27th, 1849. W & S 444 (353), II, 332–33.

29. CB to WSW. 2, Cliff, Scarbro', June 4th, 1849. W & S 446, II, 337–38.

30. CB to EN. [June 23, 1849]. W & S 450 (357), II, 347–48.

31. Mr. Brontë had the well cleaned on one occasion by two men with a pump-sucker. Entry in his notebook: "the water was tinged yellow—by eight tin cans in a state of decomposition. It had not been cleaned for twenty years before."

32. "Haworth of the Brontës: An Unromantic View," in Ian Dewhirst, *Gleanings from Victorian Yorkshire* (Yorkshire: The Ridings Publishing Co., 1972), 36–38.

CHAPTER 17

1. CB to WSW. Feby 4th, '49. W & S 421 (329), II, 306–7.

2. CB to James Taylor, Cornhill. March 1st, 1849. W & S 425 (332), II, 312–13.

3. CB to WSW. March 2nd, 1849. W & S 426 (333), II, 313–14.

4. CB to WSW. April 2nd, 1849. W & S 433 (341), II, 319–20.

5. CB to WSW. August 31st, 1849. W & S 463 (369), III, 15–16.

6. CB to EN. Haworth, July 14th, '49. W & S 454 (360), III, 7–8.

7. CB to EN. August 23rd, 1849. W & S 460 (366), III, 13.

8. CB to WSW. August 29th, 1849. W & S 462 (368), III, 15.

9. CB to WSW. Augst 24th, '49. W & S 461 (367), III, 13–14.

10. CB to WSW. September 13th, 1849. W & S 469 (374), III, 19–20.

11. CB to WSW. September 21st, 1849. W & S 474 (378), III, 23–24.

12. Ibid.

13. CB to WSW. August 16th, 1849. W & S 458 (364), III, 11–12.

14. CB to WSW. Sept. 17th, '49 and September 29th, 1849. W & S 471 (376) and 477 (381), III, 21, 25.

15. Mrs. Gaskell to George Smith. Plymouth Grove, Manchester, June 4 [1855]. *Letters*, No. 242, 345–48. Mrs. Gaskell quotes part of a letter from John Greenwood ("for he seems to have adopted me as his correspondent since Miss Brontë's death").

16. CB to G. H. Lewes. November 1st, 1849. W & S 485 (386), III, 31.

17. CB to WSW. November 1st, 1849. W & S 483 (384), III, 29–30.

18. Jane Carlyle to John Forster, November 7, 1849. Quoted from the original in Lawrence and Elisabeth Hanson, *Necessary Evil: The Life of Jane Welsh Carlyle* (New York: Macmillan, 1952), 393.

19. CB to WSW. April 16th, 1849. W & S 438 (346), II, 325–27.

20. Sara Coleridge to Mrs. H. M. Jones in E. M. Delafield, *The Brontës: Their Lives Recorded by Their Contemporaries* (London: The Hogarth Press, 1935), 184.

21. Catherine Winkworth to Eliza Patterson. 5 December 1849. W & S III, 55.

22. CB to WSW. Novr 15th, '49. W & S 490 (390), III, 35–36.

23. CB to WSW. November 19th, 1849. W & S 494 (392), III, 38–39.

24. CB to WSW. [November 20, 1849]. W & S 495 (393), III, 40.

25. *Autobiography*, II, 323–28.

26. CB to EN. Westbourne Place, Bishop's Road, London [December 4, 1849]. W & S 501 (398), III, 52–53.

27. From *The House of Smith and Elder*, privately printed (1923); reprinted in E. M. Delafield, *The Brontës: Their Lives Recorded by Their Contemporaries*.

28. Ibid.

29. "The Last Sketch," *Cornhill Magazine* (April 1860).

30. CB to Margaret Wooler. Haworth, Feby 14th '50. W & S 526 (419), III, 74–77. Elizabeth Barrett Browning is quoted along with other commentators on the Brontës' "coarseness" in *BST*, 72 (1962), 20–25.

31. CB to Laetitia Wheelwright. Haworth, Keighley, December 17th, 1849. W & S 508 (400), III, 59.

32. *Autobiography*, II, 324–27.

33. Mrs. Gaskell to Anne Shaen. [? December 20, 1849]. *Letters*, No. 60, 96–97.

34. CB to WSW. December 19th, 1849. W & S 510 (401), III, 61–62.

CHAPTER 18

1. William Margetson Heald to EN, Birstall, near Leeds. January 8th, 1850. W & S 513 (406), III, 64–65.

2. Mary Taylor to EN. 11 March 1851. Stevens, No. 23, 103–5.

3. CB to WSW. March 19th, 1850. W & S 537 (424), III, 88–90.

4. Shorter, II, 57.

5. *Memoir*, 101–2. Mary Taylor to Mrs. Gaskell. Circa June 3, 1857. Stevens, 163.

6. CB to EN. January 28th, 1850. W & S 522 (413), III, 71.

7. CB to EN. February 4th, 1850. W & S 524 (416), III, 73.

8. *Edinburgh Review* (January 1850), 153–61.

9. CB to G. H. Lewes. [January 1850]. W & S 516 (408), III, 67.

10. CB to G. H. Lewes. January 19th, 1850. W & S 518 (409), III, 68.

11. Mary Taylor to CB. April 1850. Stevens, No. 20, 93–94.

12. CB to WSW. May 12th, 1848. W & S 368 (288), II, 212–16.

13. CB to WSW. Haworth, June 15th, 1848. W & S 373 (292), II, 219–22.

14. Queen's College for Women, founded in 1848 by Frederick Maurice and fellow Christian Socialists to improve the education, and therefore the wages, of governesses. Persuaded by one of her ladies in waiting, Queen Victoria consented to bestow her title on the college as a protection against charges of conservatives who considered a woman's college subversive and unladylike.

15. CB to WSW. July 3rd, 1849. W & S 452 (358), III, 4–6.

16. I am indebted in this discussion of *Shirley* as a feminist novel to Charles Burkhart's *Charlotte Brontë: A Psychosexual Study of Her Novels* (London: Victor Gollancz, 1973).

17. CB to Miss Wooler. Jany. 30th, '46. W & S 224 (174), II, 76–77.

18. Mary Taylor to CB. June to 24 July 1848. Stevens, No. 16, 73–79.

19. Mary Taylor to EN. 9 Feb. 1849. Stevens, No. 17, 80–81.

20. Letter (May 24, 1854) and statistics quoted from John Miller, *Early Victorian New Zealand*, 161ff.

21. Mary Taylor to CB. Stevens, No. 20, 95–96.

22. CB to EN. March 5th, 1850. W & S 529 (420), III, 81.

23. CB to EN. Haworth, March 19th, 1850. W & S 536 (423), III, 86–88.

24. Ibid.

25. CB to EN. February 16th, 1850. W & S 527 (418), III, 77–79. The visitor *was* the Rev. John Barber, vicar of Bierley.

26. CB to EN. [February 5, 1850]. W & S 525 (417), III, 74–75.

27. CB to EN. February 16th, 1850. W & S 527 (418), III, 77–79.

28. CB to WSW. April 12th, 1850. W & S 544 (428), III, 98–99.

29. CB to G. H. Lewes in Tom Winnifrith, *The Brontës and Their Background*, 23.

30. CB to EN. May 11th, 1850. W & S 554 (436), III, 108–9.

31. CB to James Taylor. May 22nd, 1850. W & S 558 (439), III, 111–12.

CHAPTER 19

1. CB to the Rev. P. Brontë. 76 Gloucester Terrace, Hyde Park Gardens, June 4th, 1850. W & S 564 (444), III, 116–17.

2. *Memoir*, 92.

3. CB to EN. June 12th, '50. W & S 565 (445), III, 117–19.

4. Ibid.

5. CB to WSW. January 10th, 1850. W & S 515 (407), III, 66–67.

6. CB to EN. W & S 565 (445), III, 117–19.

7. Anne Thackeray Ritchie, *Chapters from Some Memoirs* (London: Macmillan, 1894), 60–65.

8. CB to EN. January–, '47. W & S 279 (213), II, 121–22.

9. Adelaide Procter, a minor poetess, wrote the words for that famous inspirational Victorian song, "The Lost Chord."

10. *Shirley*, 81–82.

11. CB to EN. 76 Gloucester Terrace, Hyde Park Gardens, June 21st, 1850. W & S 568 (447), III, 120–21.

12. CB to George Smith. Brookroyd, June 27th, 1850. W & S 569, III, 121–22.

13. CB to EN. Augt 7th, '50. W & S 582 (455), III, 132–33.

14. CB to George Smith. Haworth, August 1st, 1850. W & S 579 (453), III, 130.

15. CB to EN. August 16th, 1850. W & S 586 (455 in part), III, 138–39.

CHAPTER 20

1. Mrs. Gaskell to Lady Kay-Shuttleworth. Knutsford, May 14 [1850]. *Letters*, No. 72, 115–18.

2. Mrs. Gaskell to Catherine Winkworth. Plymouth Grove, Sunday Evng [August 25, 1850]. *Letters*, No. 75, 123–26.

3. Ibid., 124.

4. Ibid., 124.

5. CB to WSW. Sept 5th, 1850. W & S 597 (467), III, 155–56.

6. Mrs. Gaskell to Eliza Fox. Tuesday [27] Aug: 1850. *Letters*, No. 126–27. Sir James was a physician with a strong interest in public reform. Two of his books can still be found in libraries: *The Moral and Physical Condition of the Working Classes Employed in Cotton Manufacture in Manchester* (1832) and *Memorandum on Popular Education* (1868).

7. CB to EN. Haworth, Augst 26th, 1850. Shorter, No. 462, II, 162–63.

8. Mrs. Gaskell to unknown. [circa August 25, 1850]. *Letters*, No. 76, 126–27.

9. CB to Mrs. Gaskell. August 27, 1850. W & S 592 (463), III, 149–50.

10. Mrs. Gaskell to Eliza Fox. Tuesday, a week ago [circa February 1850]. *Letters*, No. 68, 106–7.

11. "Woman's Mission." *Westminster Review* (January 1850), 181–96.

12. This is the dichotomy in the case of Robert Moore and Caroline Helstone in *Shirley:* "When a man has been brought up only to make money, and lives to make it, and for nothing else, and scarcely breathes any other air than that of mills and markets," Moore says to Caroline, "it seems odd to utter his name in a prayer, or to mix his idea with anything divine; and very strange it seems, that a good, pure heart should take him in and harbour him, as if he had any claim to that sort of nest," 97.

13. CB to EN. September 14th, 1850. W & S 599 (469), III, 157–58.

14. Sydney Dobell, "Currer Bell," *Palladium*, 1 (September 1850), 162ff.

15. CB to James Taylor. September 5th, 1850. W & S 596 (466), III, 153–55.

16. Mary Visick discusses Anne Brontë's last poem, finished January 28, 1849, and Charlotte's alteration of it in "Anne Brontë's Last Poem," *BST*, 13 (1959), 352–56. Charlotte substantially rewrote this and other of Anne's poems, seldom improving them.

17. *Memoir of Ellis and Acton Bell* prefixed to the posthumous edition of their *Poems*, 1850.

18. CB to WSW. Sept 5th, 1850. W & S 597 (467), III, 155–56.

19. CB to EN. September, 1850, and Haworth, Octb. 23rd, 1850. W & S 607 (475) and 614 (475), III, 166, 173–74.

20. CB to EN. W & S 614 (475), III, 173–74.

21. Elizabeth Parkes to Elizabeth Gaskell. October 3rd, 1850. W & S III, 167–69. Elizabeth (Bessie) Parkes, later Belloc, was a minor writer, convert to Roman Catholicism, and mother of Hilaire Belloc (1870–1953), poet, essayist, and Roman Catholic apologist.

22. See Harriet Martineau, *Autobiography*, 3 vols.; Vera Wheatley, *The Life and Work of Harriet Martineau* (Fairlawn, N.J.: Essential Books, Inc., 1957); R. K. Webb, *Harriet Martineau: A Victorian Radical* (London: William Heinemann, 1960).

23. *Autobiography*, II, 235.

24. CB to EN. The Knoll, Ambleside, December 21st, 1850. W & S 627 (483), III, 189.

25. CB to the Rev. P. Brontë. Ambleside, December 21st, 1850. W & S 629 (485), III, 190–91.

26. CB to James Taylor. November 6th, 1850. W & S 617 (478), III, 177–79.

27. CB to James Taylor, Cornhill. January 15th, 1851. W & S 637 (492), III, 199–201.

28. *Letters of Matthew Arnold*, collected and arranged by George W. E. Russell, 2 vols. (New York and London: Macmillan, 1895), I, 15–16.

29. Written April 1855. First published in *Fraser's Magazine* (May 1855). "There will be some lines of mine in the next *Fraser* (without name) on poor Charlotte Brontë," Arnold wrote his mother April 25, 1855. "Harriet Martineau is alluded to in them, and if she is well enough you must forward the copy of the magazine. . . . I am glad to have the opportunity to speak of her with respect at this time, and for merits which she undoubtedly has." *Letters*, I, 50. Harriet Martineau ("Lies expecting from Death/in mortal weakness, a last/Summons") had been advised by a specialist that she had a bad heart; she gave herself up, and friends and the public expected her to die any day. Actually she lived twenty-one more years until 1876, vital and productive to the end.

30. CB to WSW. January 3rd, 1851. W & S 632 (489), III, 193–94.

31. *Autobiography*, II, 327–28.

CHAPTER 21

1. CB to EN. [January 20, 1851]. W & S 638 (493), III, 201–2.
2. CB to EN. January 30th, 1851. W & S 641 (494), III, 204–5.
3. Ibid.
4. CB to EN. April 5th, 1851. W & S 654 (501), III, 220–21.
5. CB to EN. April 9th, 1851. W & S 655 (502), III, 222.
6. CB to EN. April 12th, 1851. W & S 657 (503), III, 223–24.
7. CB to EN. April 23rd, 1851. W & S 666 (504), III, 228–29.
8. CB to George Smith. April 19th, 1851. W & S 660, III, 227–28.
9. CB to EN. W & S 666 (504), III, 228–29.
10. CB to EN. [May 26, 1851]. W & S 670 (508), III, 237.
11. *The Letters of Queen Victoria*, 3 vols. 1908. II, 317–18.
12. CB to the Rev. P. Brontë. 112 Gloucester Terrace, Hyde Park, June 7th [1851]. W & S 674 (514), III, 242–43.
13. CB to the Rev. P. Brontë. 76 Gloucester Terrace, Hyde Park, London, May 31st, 1851. W & S 672 (512), III, 239–40.
14. *Memoir*, 99.
15. CB to the Rev. P. Brontë. W & S 672 (512), III, 239–40.
16. *Memoir*, 99–100.
17. *The Letters and Private Papers of William Makepeace Thackeray*, collected and edited by Gordon N. Ray, 4 vols. (Cambridge, Mass: Harvard University Press, 1945–46), III, 12–14. February 25, 1852.
18. I am indebted to Gordon N. Ray's *Thackeray: The Age of Wisdom* (*1847–1863*) (New York: McGraw-Hill, 1958) for this and other details of Thackeray's life.
19. Mrs. Procter to Thackeray, 8 March, 1853. *Letters*, III, 230–31.
20. Thackeray to Mary Holmes. 1 March 1852. *Letters*, III, 19.
21. CB to the Rev. P. Brontë. 112 Gloucester Terrace, Hyde Park, June 14th, 1851. W & S 678 (516), III, 246–47.
22. *Letters of Charles Dickens*, edited by Madeline House and Graham Storey. 2 vols. (London: Oxford University Press: 1965, 1969).
23. *Memoir*, 100.
24. Thackeray to Mary Holmes. 25 February 1852. *Letters*, III, 12–14.
25. CB to EN. 112 Gloucester Terrace, Hyde Park, June 2nd, [1851]. W & S 673 (513), III, 240–41.
26. CB to EN. 112 Gloucester Terrace, Hyde Park, June 11th, 1851. W & S 677 (515), III, 245–46.
27. *Villette*, 153.
28. Ibid., 160.
29. CB to EN. W & S 673 (513), III, 240–41.
30. CB to EN. 112 Gloucester Terrace, June 24th, 1851. W & S 683 (519), III, 250–52.
31. *Villette*, 220–23. Charlotte describes the theater evening in the chapter "Vashti" (Rachel). She evidently saw Rachel twice during this visit at the St. James Theatre. The French actress' performance of Camille in Corneille's

*Les Trois Horaces* powerfully affected Charlotte. "I shall never forget her—She will come to me in sleepless nights again and again," she wrote Sydney Dobell, June 28, 1851 (W & S III, 252). For more details on Rachel's performance in London, 1851, see Gérin, 481–82.

32. *Memoir*, 93–95. Dr. J. P. Browne's "A Phrenological Estimate of the Talents and Dispositions of a Lady" (367 Strand, June 29, 1851) is remarkably insightful, particularly in his judgment that CB was both poetic and idealistic; critical and intellectual. He overestimates her musical tendencies, however. The estimate is printed in full in the *Memoir* and in Gérin, Appendix B, 576–78. A famed phrenologist who read George Eliot's head, on the other hand, did very poorly with her character.

33. CB to the Rev. P. Brontë. 112 Gloucester Terrace, Hyde Park, London, June 17th, 1851. W & S 680 (517), III, 248–49.

34. CB to EN. June 19th, '51. W & S 681 (518), III, 249–50.

35. *Villette*, 307.

CHAPTER 22

1. CB to WSW. July 21st, 1851. W & S 629 (523), III, 262–63.

2. CB to George Smith. July 1st, 1851. W & S 688, III, 255–56.

3. CB to Mrs. Gaskell [Undated]. W & S 700 (526), II, 271.

4. CB to Mrs. Gaskell. Haworth, August 6th, 1851. W & S 697 (525), III, 267–69.

5. Harriet Taylor Mill, "The Enfranchisement of Women," *Westminster Review* (July 1851), 149–61.

6. CB to Mrs. Gaskell. September 20th, 1851. W & S 708 (533), III, 277–79.

7. Mrs. Gaskell to John Stuart Mill. July 14, 1859. *Letters*, No. 435, 563–64; 42 Plymouth Grove, Manchester August 11th, 1859. No. 567, 567–69.

8. Mary and Ellen Taylor to CB. 13 August 1850. Stevens, No. 21, 96–100.

9. Mary Taylor to EN. 15 August 1850. Stevens, No. 22, 100–3.

10. CB to EN. September 1st, '51. W & S 702 (528), III, 273–74.

11. CB to Mrs. Gaskell. September 20th, 1851. W & S 708 (533), III, 277–79.

12. CB to WSW. September 26th, 1851. W & S 711 (535), III, 281–82.

13. CB to George Smith. September 22, 1851. W & S 709, III, 279–80.

14. CB to Mrs. Gaskell. November 6th, 1851. W & S 718 (540), III, 286–87.

15. Mrs. Gaskell to Anne Shaen. [? early November 1851]. *Letters*, No. 106, 168–69.

16. CB to George Smith. Haworth, November 28th, 1851. W & S 726, III, 294–96.

17. CB to George Smith. Brookroyd, Birstall, Leeds, January 29th, 1852. W & S 744, III, 310–11.

18. CB to Mrs. Gaskell. February 6th, 1852. W & S 746 (554), III, 312–13.

19. CB to George Smith. February 14th, 1852. W & S 749 (555), III, 314–15.

20. Mrs. Procter to Thackeray. 8 March 1853. *Letters*, III, 230–32.

21. Thackeray to Mrs. Carmichael-Smyth. 26 February 1852. *Letters,* III, 15–16.

22. Mary Taylor to CB. 1852. Stevens, No. 24, 107–10.

23. CB to Margaret Wooler. March 12, 1852. W & S 758 (565), III, 323–24.

24. Frederika Macdonald, in *The Secret of Charlotte Brontë* (London: T. C. and E. C. Jack, 1914), sharply contradicts Charlotte's assessment of Monsieur Heger. She was a pupil at the Pensionnat Heger from 1859 to 1861 when she was fourteen to sixteen. Admitting that Monsieur Heger was an inspired teacher, she disagreed with Charlotte's portrait of him as Paul Emanuel: ". . . I never found nor saw in the real Monsieur Heger the lovableness under the outward harshness,–the depths of tenderness under the very apparent severity and irritability–the concealed consideration for the feelings of others, under the outer indifference to the feelings of anyone who ruffled his temper; nor yet did I ever discover the meekness and modesty in him, under the dogmatic and imperious manner that swept aside all opposition. In fact, I never found out that M. Heger wore a mask . . . *just as he seemed to be, so in reality, in my opinion, M. Heger actually was*" (159–60). On the other hand, Frederika Macdonald revered Madame Heger, remembering her for her "*Tranquillité, Douceur, Bonté.*"

25. *Villette,* 295–96.

26. Ibid., 298–99.

27. CB to EN. Apr. 22, 1852. W & S 765 (571), III, 331.

28. CB to the Rev. P. Brontë. Cliff House, Filey, June 2nd, 1852. W & S 772 (574), III, 335.

29. CB to EN. Haworth, July 1st, 1852. W & S 777 (579), III, 340–41.

30. CB to EN. Haworth, July 1st, 1852, and Haw. Oct. 9, 1852. W & S 788 (590) and 791 (591 and 527), IV, 10, 12–13.

31. CB to George Smith. Oct. 30th 1852. W & S 792 (592), IV, 13–14.

32. CB to George Smith. Nov. 3rd. 1852. W & S 795 (593), IV, 16–17.

33. CB to WSW. November 6, 1852. W & S 797 (596), IV, 17–18.

34. Ibid.

35. CB to EN. Nov. 22nd. 1852, Monday evening. W & S 800 (598), IV, 20–21.

36. CB to George Smith. Nov. 23rd 1852. W & S 801, IV, 21.

37. *Memoir,* 4–67.

38. (London: J. M. Dent and Sons, 1964) 166–67.

39. CB to Margaret Wooler. Brookroyd, Decbr 7th, 1852. W & S 804 (600), IV, 23–24.

40. CB to George Smith. December 6th, 1852. W & S 803 (599), IV, 22–23.

41. *Villette,* 386.

42. CB to EN. Dec. 9th, 1852, Thursday Morning. W & S 805 (601), IV, 24–25.

CHAPTER 23

1. CB to EN. June 18th, –45. W & S 202 (159), II, 39–40.

2. *Shirley,* 501.

3. CB to EN. July 10th, '46. W & S 257 (199), II, 100–1.

4. CB to EN. W & S 202 (159), II, 39–40.

5. CB to EN. December 15th, 1852. W & S 807 (602), IV, 28–30.

6. Patrick Brontë published in all two sermons, three pamphlets, and four books (two in verse, two in prose): *Cottage Poems* (1811), *The Rural Minstrel* (1813), *The Cottage in the Wood* (1815), and *The Maid of Killarney* (1818). Less than mediocre in style and content and heavily moralistic (*The Maid of Killarney*, for example, contains diatribes against dancing and card playing), the books brought him little profit. He published no more books after his wife's death.

7. CB to EN. Jany 2nd, 1853, and Haworth, December 18th, '52. W & S 811 (604) and 808 (603), IV, 32–33, 30–31.

8. CB to Mrs. Gaskell. April 26th, 1852. W & S 766 (570), III, 332.

9. CB to Mrs. Gaskell. London, January 12th, 1853. W & S 813 (606), IV, 34–35.

10. CB to Harriet Martineau. January 21st, 1853. W & S 815 (609), IV, 38.

11. Harriet Martineau to the Rev. R. P. Graves. Thursday [November 27, 1857]. "I must explain, wh. I do with sorrow, that I have long ceased to consider C. Brontë truthful. . . . On all hands, her want of sincerity and good faith is coming out. E.g. her stimulating and encouraging me to the utmost to bring out the Atkinson Letters, while, at that very time, and from my house, she was writing to a stranger, prepossessing him against the unpublished book, is the sort of thing I mean." This severe letter, written during the storm of protest Mrs. Gaskell's *Life* excited in some quarters, is reprinted in *BST*, 16 (1973), 200–1. Nothing is known of the letter Martineau alleges Charlotte wrote from her house, December 1850: only letters to Ellen and her father have survived. This letter closes with Martineau's explanation of her reference to Mr. Brontë in a previous letter to Graves: "Mr. Brontë's 'heartlessness' I infer from his conduct to his children, and especially to C.B. I don't think he had the slightest affection for her,— or perhaps for any of them. He made a mere convenience of her."

12. CB to James Taylor, Cornhill. February 11th, 1851, and March 24th, 1851. W & S 644 (496) and 649 (500), III, 208, 214.

13. CB to Margaret Wooler. 112, Gloucester Terrace, Jany 27th, 1853. W & S 816 (608), IV, 38–40.

14. Wheatley, 328–31. Martineau's copy of Gaskell's *Life* has been preserved.

15. Harriet Martineau to CB. W & S 819 (610), IV, 41.

16. CB to Harriet Martineau. W & S 820 (611), IV, 42.

17. *Daily News* (February 3, 1853). "Everything written by Currer Bell is remarkable," Harriet began, putting her finger aptly on the chief quality of Charlotte's fiction. But she protested the novel's pervasive pain and torment, its anti-Catholicism, and, of course, the "love."

18. Obituary notice, "Death of Currer Bell," *Daily News* (April 6, 1855).

19. CB to EN. W & S 842 (629), IV, 60.

20. CB to EN. Haworth, Feby 15th, 1853. W & S 824 (615), IV, 45–46.

21. *Leader* (February 2, 1853).

22. CB to Mrs. Gaskell. February 24th, 1853. W & S 829 (620), IV, 48.

23. CB to the editor of the *Christian Remembrancer*. Haworth, July 18th, 1853. W & S 861 (643), IV, 79.

24. Matthew Arnold to Mrs. Forster. London, April 14, 1853. *Letters*, I, 33–34.

25. Thackeray to Mrs. Carmichael-Smyth. 25–28 March 1853. *Letters*, III, 247–49.

26. Thackeray to Lucy Baxter. 11 March 1853. *Letters*, III, 232–34.

27. CB to George Smith. Haworth, February 26th, 1853. W & S 828 (619), IV, 47–48.

28. CB to EN. March 4th, 1853. W & S 831 (621), IV, 49–50.

29. CB to EN. Haworth, April 6th, 1853. W & S 838 (623), IV, 56–57.

CHAPTER 24

1. Elizabeth Gaskell to Marianne Gaskell. Crix–Sunday Eveng [May 29, 1853], *Letters*, No. 158, 232–33.

2. The events of Charlotte's visit are taken from Gaskell's *Life*, 379–80.

3. Elizabeth Gaskell to John Forster [?late April 1853]. *Letters*, No. 155, 230–31.

4. CB to EN. May 16th, 1853. W & S 847 (632), IV, 65–66.

5. Ibid.

6. CB to EN. Haworth, May 19th, 1853. W & S 848 (633), IV, 67.

7. Ibid.

8. CB to EN. Haworth, May 27th, 1853. W & S 849 (635), IV, 68–69.

9. Ibid.

10. Elizabeth Gaskell to John Forster [September 1853]. *Letters*, No. 166, 242–47; to (unknown) [end of September 1853], No. 167, 247–50.

11. Ibid. To John Forster, Wednesday night [May 17, 1854], No. 195, 286–91.

12. The words are George Henry Lewes' in his essay "The Lady Novelists," *Westminster Review* (1852). Victorian critic Gerald Massey, among many others, echoed Lewes' view: "Women who are happy in all home-ties, and who amply fill the sphere of their love and life, must in the very nature of things, very seldom become writers." Unlike many male critics, however, Lewes took women writers seriously. Elizabeth Barrett Browning advanced a counterthesis in *Aurora Leigh:* "No perfect artist is developed here/From any imperfect woman"—that is, unmarried or childless women cannot produce major works of art because their natures are incomplete. *Women's Liberation and Literature*, edited by Elaine Showalter (New York: Harcourt, Brace, Jovanovich, 1971), includes several essays on Victorian feminist theory and women writers.

13. *Villette*, 65–66.

14. CB to EN. Haworth, April 11th, 1854. W & S 886 (661), IV, 112–13.

CHAPTER 25

1. In the Wise and Symington edition of Charlotte's letters there is a gap in her correspondence with Ellen from June 20, 1853, to March 1, 1854. Only one letter to Ellen exists during this period of Nicholls' courtship, his visiting in the district, and Charlotte's acceptance of his proposal. Two explanations seem to offer: one, that Charlotte may have written bitterly or detractingly about Nicholls and/or her father, and that Ellen destroyed the letters after Charlotte's death or before, either out of discretion or fear that they might eventually fall into Nicholls' hands; or that Ellen and Charlotte quarreled over Nicholls and that Charlotte actually stopped writing during these months. Mary Taylor's angry letter to Ellen indicates how deeply the latter disapproved of the idea of Charlotte marrying Nicholls.

2. MT to EN. 24 Feb. to 3 March, 1854. Stevens, No. 26, 119–22.

3. CB to Mrs. Gaskell. April 18th, 1854. W & S 889, IV, 116.

4. CB to George Smith. April 25th, 1854. W & S 892, IV 118–19.

5. Catherine Winkworth to Emma Shaen. Alderly Edge, May 8th, 1854. W & S 896, IV, 121–25.

6. The Rev. Francis Upjohn, vicar of Gorleston near Great Yarmouth, Norfolk, and his wife. They proposed that Ellen should live with them and care for them on an experimental basis, and that, if the results were mutually satisfactory, they would "adopt" Ellen with the prospect of willing her an indefinite sum. Mary Taylor was highly indignant at this news and suggested that Ellen write this reply: "My Dear Mr Clergyman and Mrs Clergyman [—] I have received your letter expressing a wish to have my services as companion. Your terms are so indefinite and so low that I had rather have nothing to do with you. As I understand your proposal you offer me board and lodging but no clothes or means of getting any. . . ." May to July 21, 1853, Stevens, No. 25, 116.

7. Elizabeth Gaskell to John Forster. Wednesday night [May 17, 1854], *Letters*, No. 195, 286–91: "To make up for my dull letter I enclose you Miss Brontë's Announcement of her marriage-to-be—It is quiet, quaint, & a little formal; but like herself, & meaning the full force of every word she uses."

8. CB to EN. Haworth, May 27th, 1854. W & S 899 (668), IV, 127–28.

9. CB to EN. June 16th, '54. W & S 902 (671), IV, 130–31.

10. CB to EN. Thursday Evening. W & S 904 (672), IV, 133–34.

11. CB to Margaret Wooler. Banagher, July 10th, '54. W & S 905 (673), IV, 134–35.

12. Ibid.

13. Ibid.

14. CB to Catherine Winkworth. Cork, July 27th, 1854. W & S 907, IV, 137–38.

15. Ibid.

16. CB to EN. Dublin, July 28th, 1854. W & S 909, IV, 143.

17. CB to Martha Brown. Dublin, July 28th, 1854. W & S 908, IV, 143.

18. Quoted in Gordon Haight's *George Eliot: A Biography* (New York: Oxford University Press, 1968), 147.

19. CB to EN. Haworth, Augt 9th, 1854. W & S 910 (674), IV, 145–46.

20. CB to Margaret Wooler. Haworth, August 22nd, 1854. W & S 913 (676), IV, 148–49.

21. CB to EN. Haworth, Augt 29th [1854]. W & S 914 (675), IV, 150.

22. "Cassandra," a part of her book *Suggestions for Thought to Searchers after Religious Truth,* quoted in Duncan Crow, *The Victorian Woman* (New York: Stein and Day, 1972), 43.

23. CB to EN. Haworth, September 7th, 1854. W & S 915 (679), IV, 150–51.

24. CB to Margaret Wooler. Haworth, Septbr 19th, 1854. W & S 917 (681), IV, 152–53.

25. Quoted from Sir Wemyss Reid's *Memoirs* (London: Cassell, 1905), 239–40. Sir Wemyss visited Ellen Nussey and quoted her directly. "I do not vouch for the absolute truth of this story, but I give it as I heard it from Miss Nussey, and I am quite sure that when she told it to me, she believed it to be true." Against Ellen's statement must be compared Nicholls' disavowal to Mrs. Humphrey Ward, November 28, 1899: "I must say that I fail to see any confirmation in them [Charlotte's letters written after her marriage and published in Mrs. Gaskell's *Life*] of the statement that 'I encouraged her to give up novel writing . . .' I never interfered in the slightest degree with her liberty of action." Gérin, who quotes this letter on p. 554, believes that Nicholls' statement clears up the entire matter of his interference. But the reader must judge. Charlotte's letters do show that she suffered for lack of writing time, but by the very nature of Victorian marriages, Nicholls was perhaps unaware of this.

26. CB to EN. [October 20, 1854], Friday Morning. W & S 920 (684), IV, 155–56.

27. CB to EN. Haworth, October 31st, 1854. W & S 921 (685), IV, 156–57.

28. After Charlotte's death Mrs. Gaskell went to Haworth to try to persuade Nicholls to give up some of Charlotte's manuscripts. To this purpose, she took along Sir James Kay-Shuttleworth, for both Mr. Brontë and Mr. Nicholls stood in some awe of the baronet. Sir James "coolly took actual possession of many things while Mr Nicholls was saying he could not possibly part with them. I came away with the 'Professor' [and] the beginning of her new tale 'Emma'—about 10 pages written in the finest pencil writing . . ." To George Smith, *Letters*, No. 297, 398. *Emma* was published in George Smith's *Cornhill Magazine*, I (1860), 485–98. *Cornhill's* editor, William Makepeace Thackeray, wrote an accompanying introduction, "The Last Sketch." *Emma* has been reprinted in *BST*, 2, Pt. 10, 87.

CHAPTER 26

1. CB to EN. Haworth, November 29th, 1854. W & S 927 (689), IV, 161–62.

2. *Jane Eyre*, 267.

3. CB to EN. Haworth, December 7th, 1854. W & S 930 (690), IV, 164–65.

4. CB to EN. Haworth, Jany 19th, 1855. W & S 936 (693), IV, 170–71.

5. CB to EN. Haworth, Feb. 14th, 1855. W & S 942 (697), IV, 174.

6. CB to Amelia Taylor [February 1855]. W & S 946, IV, 176.

7. Extracted from District Probate Registry at York attached to Her Majesty's High Court of Justice. Reprinted in Shorter, II, 392.

8. CB to EN. Haworth [February 21, 1855]. W & S 944 (699), IV, 175.

9. Phillip Rhodes, "A Medical Appraisal of the Brontës," *BST*, 16 (1972), 101–9. Dr. Rhodes (a professor of obstetrics and gynecology, University of London, St. Thomas's Hospital Medical School) states that it is "quite clear" that Charlotte died of hyperemesis gravidarum; that Mrs. Gaskell's report of her illness is a classic description of the disease. Modern pregnancy manuals describe the disease, and recommend, blandly, that the expectant mother "talk to her doctor if anything is troubling her" (*Prenatal Care* [New York: Child Care Publishers, 1970]).

10. Arthur Nicholls to EN. Haworth, March 31st, 1855. W & S 950 (702), IV, 177–78.

11. Elizabeth Gaskell to John Greenwood. 17 Cumberland Terrace, Regent's Park, London, Wednesday, April 4 [1855]. *Letters*, No. 232, 335.

12. Ibid., to John Greenwood. 11 Princes Terrace, Hyde Park, London, Thursday [April 12, 1855]. No. 233, 336–37.

13. Quoted in Stevens, 146–47.

# Bibliography

VICTORIAN ENGLAND

Appleton, Marjorie. *They Came to New Zealand*. London: Methuen, 1958.

Avery, Gillian. *Victorian People in Life and Literature*. New York: Holt, Rinehart and Winston, 1970.

Baines, Edward. *History, Directory and Gazetteer of the County of York*. 2 vols. 1822. Reprinted New York: Augustus M. Kelley, 1969.

Bentley, Nicholas. *The Victorian Scene: A Picture Book of the Period 1837–1901*. London: Weidenfeld and Nicholson, 1968.

Best, Geoffrey. *Mid-Victorian Britain 1851–1875*. New York: Schocken Books, 1971.

Black, Adam and Charles. *Black's Guide to Yorkshire*. 12th ed. Edinburgh: Black, 1885.

Briggs, Asa. *Victorian Cities*. New York: Harper and Row, 1963.

Bulwer-Lytton, Edward. *England and the English*. Edited by Standish Meachum. Chicago: University of Chicago Press, 1970.

Craven, A. B. *Victorian and Edwardian Yorkshire from Old Photographs*. London: B. T. Batsford, 1971.

Cunnington, C. Willett and Philiss. *A Handbook of English Costume in the Nineteenth Century*. London: Faber, 1966.

Dewhirst, Ian. *Gleanings from Victorian Yorkshire*. Driffield, Yorkshire: The Ridings Publishing Company, 1972.

Herbert, Christopher. *London: The Biography of a City*. New York: William Morrow, 1970.

Houghton, Walter E. *The Victorian Frame of Mind*. New Haven: Yale University Press, 1966.

Korg, Jacob. *London in Dickens' Day*. Englewood Cliffs, N.J.: Prentice-Hall, 1964.

Miller, John. *Early Victorian New Zealand*. London: Oxford University Press, 1958.

Pike, E. Royston. *Golden Times: Human Documents of the Victorian Age*. New York: Schocken Books, 1972.

Quinlan, Maurice J. *Victorian Prelude*. Hamden, Conn.: Archon Books, 1965.

Reader, W. J. *Life in Victorian England*. Edited by Peter Quennell. New York: Capricorn Books, 1967.

Strachey, Lytton. *Queen Victoria*. New York: Harcourt, Brace and World, 1949.

Tate, W. E., and Singleton, F. B. *A History of Yorkshire*. London: Darwen Finlayson, 1960.

Wingfield-Stratford, Esmé. *Those Earnest Victorians*. New York: William Morrow, 1930.

Young, G. M. *Victorian England: Portrait of An Age*. London: Oxford University Press, 1937.


LITERARY VICTORIAN ENGLAND

Arnold, Matthew. *Letters of Matthew Arnold*. Collected and arranged by George W. E. Russell. 2 vols. New York and London: Macmillan, 1895.

—— *Poetical Works*. London: Macmillan, 1907.

Buckley, Jerome Hamilton. *The Victorian Temper: A Study in Literary Culture*. New York: Random House, 1951.

Carlyle, Jane Welsh. *Letters to Her Family 1839–1863*. Edited by Leonard Huxley. Garden City, N.Y.: Doubleday, Page and Company, 1924.

Cecil, David. *Victorian Novelists*. Chicago: University of Chicago Press, 1958.

Chesteron, G. K. *The Victorian Age in Literature*. London: Oxford University Press, 1966. First pub. 1913.

De Quincey, Thomas. *Confessions of an English Opium Eater*. Middlesex, England: Penguin Books, 1973.

Dickens, Charles. *The Letters of Charles Dickens*. Edited by Madeline House and Graham Storey. 2 vols. London: Oxford University Press, 1965, 1969.

Eliot, George. *The Letters of George Eliot*. Edited by Gordon Haight. 6 vols. London: Oxford University Press, 1954.

Gaskell, Elizabeth Cleghorn. *The Letters of Mrs. Gaskell*. Edited by J. A. V. Chapple and Arthur Pollard. Cambridge, Mass.: Harvard University Press, 1967.

——. *Mary Barton: A Tale of Manchester Life*. Middlesex, England: Penguin Books, 1970.

——. *Ruth*. London: Smith, Elder and Company, 1853.

Haight, Gordon. *George Eliot: A Biography*. New York: Oxford University Press, 1968.

Hayter, Alethea. *Opium and the Romantic Imagination*. Berkeley, Calif.: University of California Press, 1968.

Hirshberg, Edgar W. *George Henry Lewes*. New York: Twayne Publishers, 1970.

Kettle, Arnold. *An Introduction to the English Novel.* 2 vols. New York: Harper and Row, 1960.

Lee, Sidney. *George Smith: A Memoir,* with "Some Pages of Autobiography" by George Murray Smith. London: privately printed, 1902.

Martineau, Harriet. *Autobiography.* 3 vols. London: Smith, Elder and Company, 1877.

———. *Deerbrook.* London: Smith, Elder and Company, 1817.

Pollard, Arthur. *Mrs. Gaskell: Novelist and Biographer.* Cambridge, Mass.: Harvard University Press, 1967.

Ray, Gordon N. *Thackeray: The Age of Wisdom (1847–1863).* New York: McGraw-Hill, 1958.

Ritchie, Anne Thackeray. *Chapters from Some Memoirs.* London: Macmillan, 1894.

Ritchie, Hester, ed. *The Letters of Anne Thackeray Ritchie.* London: John Murray, 1924.

Thackeray, William Makepeace. *The Letters and Private Papers of William Makepeace Thackeray.* 4 vols. Collected and edited by Gordon N. Ray. Cambridge, Mass.: Harvard University Press, 1945–46.

———. *Works.* 21 vols. New York: Scribner, 1923.

Tillotson, Kathleen. *Novels of the Eighteen-Forties.* Oxford: Clarendon Press, 1954.

Webb, R. K. *Harriet Martineau: A Victorian Radical.* London: William Heinemann, 1960.

Wheatley, Vera. *The Life and Work of Harriet Martineau.* Fairlawn, N.J.: Essential Books, 1957.

### THE "WOMAN QUESTION"

Andrews, Sir W. L. "Charlotte Brontë: The Woman and the Feminist," *BST* 12 (1965), 351–60.

Banks, Joseph and Olive. *Feminism and Family Planning in Victorian England.* New York: Schocken Books, 1964.

Blom, M. A. "Charlotte Brontë, Feminist *Manquée,*" *Bucknell Review* (Spring 1973), 87–102.

Browning, Elizabeth Barrett. *Aurora Leigh.* London: Smith, Elder and Company, 1900.

Burkhart, Charles. *Charlotte Brontë: A Psychosexual Study of Her Novels.* London: Victor Gollancz, 1973.

Crow, Duncan. *The Victorian Woman.* New York: Stein and Day, 1972.

Cunnington, C. Willett. *Feminine Attitudes in the Nineteenth Century.* London: William Heinemann, 1935.

Deming, Barbara. "Two Perspectives on Women's Struggle," *Liberation* (June 1973), 30–37.

Eliot, George. "Silly Novels by Lady Novelists," *Westminster Review* 66 (1856), 442–61.

Ellis, Sarah Stickney. *The Family Monitor* including *The Women of Eng-*

*land* (1839), *The Wives of England* (1843), *The Mothers of England* (1843), *The Daughters of England* (1845). New York: 1848.

Ewbank, Inga-Stina. *Their Proper Sphere: A Study of the Brontë Sisters as Early Victorian Female Novelists.* London: Edward Arnold, 1966.

Fuller, Margaret. *Woman in the Nineteenth Century.* New York: Norton and Company, 1971. First pub. 1845.

Hays, H. R. *The Dangerous Sex: The Myth of Feminine Evil.* New York: Pocket Books, 1965.

Lewes, George Henry. "Currer Bell's 'Shirley,'" *Edinburgh Review* 183 (1850), 153-73.

——. "The Lady Novelists," *Westminster Review* 113 (1852), 70-77.

Martin, Hazel T. *Petticoat Rebels: A Study of the Novels of Social Protest of George Eliot, Elizabeth Gaskell, and Charlotte Brontë.* New York: Helios, 1968.

Martineau, Harriet. "Criticism on Women," *Westminster Review* 63 (1838-39), 241-52.

——. "The Woman Question," in *Autobiography*, Vol. I. London: Smith, Elder and Company, 1877.

Mill, Harriet Taylor. "Enfranchisement of Women," *Westminster Review* 109 (1851), 149-61.

Mill, John Stuart and Harriet Taylor. *Essays on Sex Equality.* Edited by Alice S. Rossi. Chicago: University of Chicago Press, 1970.

Millett, Kate. *Sexual Politics.* New York: Avon, 1971.

Neff, Wanda. *Victorian Working Women: An Historical and Literary Study of Women in British Industries and Professions, 1832-1850.* London: Cass, 1966.

Ohmann, Carol. "Emily Brontë in the Hands of Male Critics," *College English* 32 (1971), 906-13.

Parker, John. "Woman's Mission," *Westminster Review* 103 (1850), 181-96.

Rigby, Elizabeth [Lady Eastlake]. "*Vanity Fair, Jane Eyre,* and the Governesses' Benevolent Institution," *Quarterly Review* 84 (1848), 153-85.

Rover, Constance. *The Punch Book of Women's Rights.* New York: A. S. Barnes, 1970.

Ruskin, John. "Of Queen's Gardens" in *Sesame and Lilies.* London: Smith, Elder and Company, 1865.

Sharma, P. P. "Charlotte Brontë: Champion of Women's Economic Independence," *BST* 14 (1965), 38-40.

Showalter, Elaine, ed. *Women's Liberation and Literature.* New York: Harcourt, Brace, Jovanovich, 1971.

——. "Women Writers and the Double Standard" in *Woman in Sexist Society.* Edited by Vivian Gornick and Barbara K. Moran. New York: New American Library, 1972.

Tennyson, Alfred Lord. *The Princess.* 2nd ed. London: Moxon, 1848.

Thomson, Patricia. *The Victorian Heroine: A Changing Ideal, 1837-1873.* London: Oxford University Press, 1956.

Vincinus, Martha, ed. *Suffer and Be Still: Women in the Victorian Age.* Bloomington, Ind.: Indiana University Press, 1972.

WORKS ABOUT THE BRONTËS

Benson, E. F. *Charlotte Brontë.* New York: Benjamin Blom, 1971. First pub. 1932.

Bentley, Phyllis. *The Brontës.* London: Barker, 1947.

——. *The Brontës and Their World.* New York: Viking Press, 1969.

——. *The Brontë Sisters.* London: Longmans, Green, 1950.

*Brontë Society Transactions.* Keighley, Yorkshire: Keighley Printers. Vol. 1 (January 1895) to Vol. 16 (1972).

Burkhart, Charles. *Charlotte Brontë: A Psychosexual Study of Her Novels.* London: Victor Gollancz, 1973.

Chadwick, Mrs. Ellis H. *In the Footsteps of the Brontës.* London: Sir Isaac Pitman and Sons, 1914.

Christian, Mildred G. "The Brontës" in *Victorian Fiction: A Guide to Research.* Edited by Lionel Stevenson. Cambridge, Mass.: Harvard University Press, 1964, 1–14.

Craik, W. A. *The Brontë Novels.* London: Methuen, 1968.

Delafield, E. M. *The Brontës: Their Lives Recorded by Their Contemporaries.* London: The Hogarth Press, 1935.

Dooley, Lucile. "Psychoanalysis of Charlotte Brontë as a Type of Woman of Genius," *American Journal of Psychology* 31 (July 1920), 221–72.

Ewbank, Inga-Stina. *Their Proper Sphere: A Study of the Brontë Sisters as Early Victorian Female Novelists.* London: Edward Arnold, 1966.

Gary, Franklin. "Charlotte Brontë and George Henry Lewes," *Publications of the Modern Language Association* 51 (June 1936), 518–42.

Gaskell, Elizabeth Cleghorn. *The Life of Charlotte Brontë.* London: J. M. Dent, 1960. First published 1857.

Gérin, Winifred. *Branwell Brontë.* London: Thomas Nelson and Sons, 1961.

—— *Charlotte Brontë: The Evolution of Genius.* London: Oxford University Press, 1967.

Gregor, Ian, ed. *The Brontës: A Collection of Critical Essays.* Englewood Cliffs, N.J.: Prentice-Hall, 1970.

Hanson, Lawrence and E. M. *The Four Brontës.* London: Oxford University Press, 1949.

Hinkley, Laura J. *The Brontës, Charlotte and Emily.* New York: Hastings House, 1945.

Kroeber, Karl. *Styles in Fictional Structure: The Art of Jane Austen, Charlotte Brontë, and George Eliot.* Princeton, N.J.: Princeton University Press, 1971.

Lane, Margaret. *The Brontë Story: A Reconsideration of Mrs. Gaskell's "Life of Charlotte Brontë."* London: William Heinemann, 1953.

Lock, John, and Dixon, Canon W. T. *A Man of Sorrow: The Life, Let-*

*ters, and Times of the Reverend Patrick Brontë, 1777–1861.* London: Thomas Nelson and Sons, 1965.

Macdonald, Frederika. *The Secret of Charlotte Brontë.* London: T. C. and E. C. Jack, 1914.

Martin, Robert. *The Accents of Persuasion: Charlotte Brontë's Novels.* London: Farber and Farber, 1966.

Maurat, Charlotte. *The Brontës' Secret.* Translated by Margaret Meldrum. New York: Barnes and Noble, 1970.

Peters, Margot. *Charlotte Brontë: Style in the Novel.* Madison, Wisc.: University of Wisconsin Press, 1973.

Pollard, Arthur. *Charlotte Brontë.* London: Routledge, 1968.

Ratchford, Fannie E. *The Brontës' Web of Childhood.* New York: Russell and Russell, 1964.

Reid, Sir Wemyss. *Memoirs.* London: Cassell and Company, 1905.

Sinclair, May. *The Three Brontës.* Port Washington, N.Y.: Kennikat Press, 1967. First published 1912.

Stevens, Joan. *Mary Taylor: Friend of Charlotte Brontë.* New Zealand: Auckland University Press, 1972.

Winnifrith, Tom. *The Brontës and Their Background: Romance and Reality.* London: Macmillan, 1973.

Wroot, Herbert E. *The Persons and Places of the Brontë Novels.* New York: Burt Franklin, 1970. First published 1906.

### WORKS BY THE BRONTËS

The most complete edition of the Brontë works is *The Shakespeare Head Brontë,* edited by T. J. Wise and J. A. Symington, 19 vols. Oxford: 1931–38. *Jane Eyre* and *Wuthering Heights* are available in many paperback editions. With the exception of Anne Brontë's novels, I have cited texts more readily available to readers than the Shakespeare Head edition.

Brontë, Anne. *Agnes Grey.* Oxford: Shakespeare Head Press, 1931.

——. *The Tenant of Wildfell Hall.* Oxford: Shakespeare Head Press, 1931.

Brontë, Charlotte. *Emma: A Fragment* by Currer Bell with "The Last Sketch," an introduction by William Makepeace Thackeray in *Cornhill Magazine* 1 (1860), 485–98. Reprinted in *BST* 2 (1899), 84–101.

——. *Five Novelettes.* Transcribed and edited by Winifred Gérin. London: The Folio Press, 1971.

——. *Jane Eyre.* Boston: Houghton Mifflin, 1959.

——. *Legends of Angria.* Compiled by Fannie E. Ratchford and William Clyde DeVane. New Haven: Yale University Press, 1933.

——. *Shirley.* London: J. M. Dent, 1965.

——. *The Professor.* London: J. M. Dent, 1965.

——. *Villette.* Edited by Geoffrey Tillotson and Donald Hawes. Boston: Houghton Mifflin, 1971.

—— and Patrick Branwell. *The Miscellaneous and Unpublished Writings of Charlotte and Patrick Branwell Brontë.* 2 vols. Oxford: Shakespeare Head Press, 1934.

—— and Patrick Branwell. *The Poems of Charlotte and Patrick Branwell Brontë.* Oxford: Shakespeare Head Press, 1934.

Brontë, Emily. *Wuthering Heights.* With Currer Bell's "Autobiographical Notice of Ellis and Acton Bell." Edited by William Sale, Jr. New York: W. W. Norton, 1963.

—— and Anne. *The Poems of Emily Jane and Anne Brontë.* Oxford: Shakespeare Head Press, 1934.

Shorter, Clement. *The Brontës: Life and Letters.* 2 vols. New York: Haskell House, 1969. First published 1908.

Wise, T. J. and Symington, J. A., eds. *The Brontës: Their Lives, Friendships, and Correspondence.* 4 vols. Oxford: Shakespeare Head Press, 1932.

# Index